Y0-CDM-322

BREAKING INDIA
Western Interventions in
Dravidian and Dalit Faultlines

BREAKING INDIA
Western Interventions in
Dravidian and Dalit Faultlines

Rajiv Malhotra
Aravindan Neelakandan

AMARYLLIS

AMARYLLIS

Copyright © Infinity Foundation 2011

All rights reserved. No part of this book may be used or reproduced, stored in or introduced into a retrieval system, or transmitted, in any form, or by any means (electronic, mechanical, photocopying, recording or otherwise) without the prior written permission of the Publisher. Any person who does any unauthorized act in relation to this publication may be liable to criminal prosecution and civil claims for damages.

Rajiv Malhotra and Aravindan Neelakandan
assert the moral right to be identified
as the authors of this work

This edition first published in 2011
Seventeenth impression 2017

AMARYLLIS

An imprint of **Manjul Publishing House**
7/32, Ansari Road, Daryaganj, New Delhi 110 002
Website: www.manjulindia.com

Registered Office:
10, Nishat Colony, Bhopal 462 003 - India

Distribution Centres:
Ahmedabad, Bengaluru, Bhopal, Kolkata, Chennai,
Hyderabad, Mumbai, New Delhi, Pune

ISBN: 978-81-910673-7-8

Printed and Bound in India by
Thomson Press (India) Ltd.

Contents

Introduction

This book has emerged as a result of several experiences that have deeply influenced my research and scholarship over the past decade. In the 1990s, an African-American scholar at Princeton University casually told me that he had returned from a trip to India, where he was working with the 'Afro-Dalit Project'. I learnt that this US-operated and -financed project frames inter-jati/varna interactions and the Dalit movement using American cultural and historical lenses. The Afro-Dalit project purports to paint Dalits as the 'Blacks' of India and non-Dalits as India's 'Whites'. The history of American racism, slavery and Black/White relations is thus superimposed onto Indian society. While modern caste structures and inter-relationships have included long periods of prejudice toward Dalits, the Dalit experience bears little resemblance to the African slave experience of America. But taking its cue from the American experience, the Afro-Dalit project attempts to empower Dalits by casting them as victims at the hands of a different race.

Separately, I had been studying and writing about the 'Aryans', as to who they were, and whether the origin of Sanskrit and Vedas was an import by 'invaders' or indigenous to India. In this context, I sponsored numerous archeological, linguistic and historical conferences and book projects, in order to get deeper into the discourse. This led me to research the colonial-era construction of the Dravidian identity, which did not exist prior to the nineteenth century and was fabricated as an identity in opposition to the Aryans. Its survival depends upon belief in the theory of foreign Aryans and their misdeeds.

I had also been researching the US Church's funding of activities in India, such as the popularly advertised campaigns to 'save' poor children by feeding, clothing and educating them. In fact, when I was in my twenties living in the US, I sponsored one such child in South India. However, during trips to India, I often felt that the funds collected were being used not so much for the purposes indicated to sponsors, but for indoctrination and conversion activities.

Additionally, I have been involved in numerous debates in the US with think-tanks, independent scholars, human rights groups and academics, specifically on their treatment of Indian society as a sort of scourge that the west had to 'civilize'. I coined the phrase 'caste, cows and curry' to represent the exotic and sensational portrayals of India's social and economic problems and their interpretation these as 'human rights' issues.

I decided to track the major organizations involved in promulgating these various theories, as well as those spearheading political pressure, and eventually the prosecution of India on the grounds of human rights violations. My research included following the money trail by using the provisions of financial disclosure in the US, studying the promotional materials given out by most such organizations, and monitoring their conferences, workshops and publications. I investigated the individuals behind such activities and their institutional affiliations.

What I found out should sound the alarm bell for every Indian concerned about our national integrity. India is the prime target of a huge enterprise—a 'network' of organizations, individuals and churches—that seems intensely devoted to the task of creating a separatist identity, history and even religion for the vulnerable sections of India. This nexus of players includes not only church groups, government bodies and related organizations, but also private think-tanks and academics. On the surface they appear to be separate and isolated from one another, but in fact, as I found, their activities are well coordinated and well funded from the US and Europe. I was impressed by the degree of interlocking and cooperation among these entities. Their resolutions, position papers and strategies are well articulated, and beneath the veneer of helping the downtrodden, there seem to be objectives that would be inimical to India's unity and sovereignty.

A few Indians from the communities being 'empowered' were in top positions in these Western organizations, and the whole enterprise was initially conceived, funded and strategically managed by Westerners. However, there are now a growing number of Indian individuals and NGOs who have become co-opted by them, and receive funding and mentorship from the West. The south Asian studies in the US and European universities invite many such 'activists' regularly and give them prominence. The same organizations had also been inviting and giving intellectual support to Khalistanis, Kashmir militants, Maoists, and other subversive elements in India. So I began to wonder whether the campaigns to mobilize Dalits, Dravidians and other minorities in India were somehow part of the foreign policy of certain Western countries, if not openly then at least as an option kept in reserve. I am unaware of any other major country in which such large-scale processes prevail without monitoring or concern by the local authorities. No wonder so much has to be spent in India *after* such a separatist identity gets weaponized into all out militancy or political fragmentation.

The link between academic manipulations and subsequent violence is also evident in Sri Lanka, where manufactured divisiveness caused one of the bloodiest civil wars. The same also happened in Africa where foreign-engineered identity conflicts led to one of the worst ethnic genocides ever in the world.

About three years ago, my research and data had become considerable. Moreover, many Indians are simply unaware of the subversive forces at work against their country, and I felt that it ought to be organized for wider dissemination and debate. I started working with Aravindan Neelakandan, based in Tamil Nadu, to complement my foreign data with his access to the ground reality in India's backwaters.

This book looks at the historical origins of both the Dravidian movement and Dalit identity, as well as the current players involved in shaping these separatist identities. It includes an analysis of the individuals and institutions involved and their motivations, activities, and desired endgame. While many are located in the US and the European Union, there are an increasing number in India too, the latter often functioning like the local branch offices of these foreign entities.

The goal of this book is not to sensationalize or predict any outcomes. Rather, it is to expand the debate about India and its future. Much is being written about India's rise in economic terms and its implications to India's overall clout. But not enough is written on what can go wrong given the rapidly expanding programs exposed in this book and the stress they put on India's faultlines. My hope is that this book fills this gap to some extent.

Rajiv Malhotra
Princeton, USA
January 2011

1

Superpower or Balkanized War Zone?

Acivilization provides a shared identity composed of the images that we have of ourselves, as a people, with a collective sense of history and a shared destiny. It gives a definite sense of who 'we' are, and ensures a deep psychological bond among ourselves, along with the feeling that the nation is worth defending. Without this bond, who is the 'we' to be defended and what are the sacrifices for? Breaking a civilization is, therefore, like breaking the spine of a person. A broken civilization can splinter, and the balkanized regions can undergo a dark metamorphosis to become rogue states – transforming an entire region into a cataclysm of gigantic proportions.

Is the spine of Indian civilization vulnerable to such a rupture? And what forces, if any, are attempting to do this? Are they external or internal, or both? Where do they originate? How do they evolve? How are they managed? This book addresses these questions, with specific reference to the Dravidian and Dalit identities, and the role of the West in exploiting them.

India's centripetal forces—economic growth, corporate and infrastructure development, and improved national democratic governance—bring the nation together. Much is being written about these positive forces. Less often discussed and seldom studied in detail, are the centrifugal forces, both internal and external. The internal ones include communalism and socio-economic disparities of various kinds.

The external forces that bring divisiveness among Indians, are more complex, and these have linked up with India's internal cleavages. This shows how various global nexuses with their own agendas now control these internal forces to an unprecedented degree. Yet, this book is not screaming a doomsday scenario, but rather, an original analysis of the danger the nation is facing.

It is not just Pakistan stirring up disruptive forces in India, or China linking up with Indian Maoists, or the evangelical churches of Europe and North America fostering separatism. It is all of these, and more. These centrifugal forces are deep, subtle, complexly interlinked, and operate as loosely coupled multinational networks.

The nexus this book uncovers might seem far removed from the visions of violence and chaos conjured up by the notions of 'secessionism', 'insurgency', and 'rebellion'. Yet, it establishes that certain academic centers of the West control, or at least heavily influence, the socio-political discourse on India. These are coupled with political think-tanks, Church activism, and social organizations that feed the centrifugal forces in India. They invent new fault lines and nurture existing ones. Surprisingly, there is little counter-discourse on the side of India's unity.

India's Built-in Tendencies to Fragment

While it is tempting to blame all problems on outside forces, one must come to terms with India's own weaknesses and centuries-old tendencies to fragment. This troubling side has not received enough attention by those enjoying the successes of the newly vibrant economy. Some of the hard realities are as follows:

* India has the largest number of poor citizens in the world, the largest number of children without schooling, a serious and growing shortage of water that is required to sustain life in the hinterlands, and conflicts across its many groups.
* There are social injustices that are partly historical and partly modern. Some have originated within the Indian society, while others are bred and fed by foreign influences to gain leverage in India.

- The trickle-down effect of economic success has not adequately filtered to the lowest strata, where it is needed with the greatest urgency. While millions of Indians enjoy careers based on a technical education subsidized by the Indian public, a much larger number have not received even a basic education. The middle class, aspiring to modernize or Americanize, boasts of the new automobile infrastructure, yet the investments made towards farming and water infrastructure are dismal. India's public health system is atrocious.[1]

- Separatist movements threaten everyday life in Kashmir, parts of India's northeast, and in numerous Indian states afflicted with rural Maoist terrorism. There are sporadic Islamist terror-attacks in various parts of India, and there have been eruptions of Hindu-Muslim violence. Separatist movements by the Dravidians and Dalits create violence across the South, and these are the topics of this book.

- Even cyberspace, which was seen as an Indian haven, has become India's vulnerability. A recent, highly publicized study on cyber espionage terms India as the 'most victimized state', whose sensitive defense networks, embassy communications, in India and around the world, have been highly compromised by Chinese espionage agents.[2] Vital information thus obtained by the Chinese can then be passed on to the Maoist insurgency raging at the mineral-rich heart of India, where a vicious cycle of state apathy, foreign interventions and Maoist terrorism is bleeding India.

- India is surrounded by unstable and radicalized nations, including those that are becoming failed states; cross-border violence is being exported into India, tying up crucial economic and military resources.[3] The Indian experience of democracy has led to a very large number of political parties, thereby fragmenting vote banks and voices in the social mosaic. This has brought opportunism and shortsightedness, with long-term policy compromises and vacillations. One wonders if India has too much democracy – or, at least, too little governance.

Yet, India's resilience is also remarkable. For example:

- While the US has become highly militarized to protect its homeland against terrorism, India has not done so to the same extent, despite having been attacked by terrorists far more frequently and for many more years. There is no 'Fortress India' mindset. After the terror-attacks killed one hundred and sixty-six people in Mumbai in 2008, trains started to run, shops reopened, and normal life resumed within a few days.

- India has the second-largest Muslim population in the world, and a vast majority of its Muslims remain well grounded in local, native cultures, and are integrated into Indian society with their Hindu neighbors. Insofar as it has resisted attempts to be co-opted into international pan-Islamist programs, Indian Islam offers a model for inspiring Muslims worldwide into cultural syncretism and harmonious co-existence with other religions.

- India's resilience is partly based on its civilization's strength of accommodation and flexibility, but also on hard policy-choices implemented by its leaders since independence from British rule in 1947. Thus, India's version of affirmative action—known as 'reservations', and implemented by successive governments for over sixty years—has brought remarkable advancement in the plight of the impoverished Dalits (the former 'untouchables') and other disadvantaged groups. But given the scope of the problem, this is too little and too late. Many worthy Indian NGOs (non-governmental organizations) have filled the vacuum left by the government and provided assistance successfully.

External Forces

India's internal performance must be judged on how it benefits its least-privileged citizens, and it certainly deserves harsh criticism. Yet if the nation-state were severely undermined in its *external* capacity to deal with other forces, the result could invite invasions, re-colonization, cultural and psychological imperialism, and other unwanted interventions. This has happened numerous times in India's history; for instance, when the British used human-rights cases as pretexts to act against many Indian rulers.

Ironically, the British themselves committed many horrible acts while justifying them by compiling what is known as atrocity literature[4] to depict the savagery of Indians. They claimed that their own acts were designed to help bring about 'civilization' for Indians. For example:

- The Criminal Tribes Act was passed in 1871 and made it lawful to perform genocide against a list of Indian tribes who were deemed to be 'criminals', including every member of these tribes right from birth. Many tribes were condemned not because they were 'criminal' (even if there is such a thing as a whole tribe being criminal), but because they were fighting against the British destruction of their jungles and other habitats. The Thugs were one such group that got so badly maligned via atrocity literature that their name has entered the English language as being synonymous with criminals.

- Atrocity literature played its part in downgrading women's rights, too. Veena Oldenburg's seminal book, *Dowry Murder*, gives details on how the British encouraged the Indians to dish out cases of atrocities that could then be blamed on the native culture.[5] They systematically compiled these anecdotes, mostly unsubstantiated and often exaggerated and one-sided. This became a justification to enact laws that downgraded the rights of common citizens. The book shows how the dowry extortions that have become so common in middle-class India today, were actually started when women's traditional property rights were taken away by the British through convoluted logic.

- Nicholas Dirks is one of many scholars to have shown how the British used atrocity literature in order to exacerbate conflicts between the jatis in order to 'solve' their problems by intervening. This helped the British to gain further power and extort Indian wealth.[6]

- Claims of atrocities against workers were used to outlaw various Indian industries, including textiles and steelmaking, in which India had a lead over Britain. Meanwhile, the British started their own Industrial Revolution to supply these goods to India as a captive market, turning Indians from world-class producers and exporters into importers and paupers. According to British author William Digby, between 1757 and 1812, the inflow of profits from India into Britain was estimated at between 500 million pounds and 1 billion pounds.[7] The value of this sum in today's purchasing power would be over a trillion dollars. A more recent study by economist Amiya Bagchi establishes that the British imposed a drain on India, equivalent to five-six[8] percent of 'current GDP' (1984). The British were very diligent in documenting alleged cases of atrocities against workers, by the Indian manufacturers who were their competitors, and then outlawed many Indian industries on the charge of violating workers' rights. The massive poverty and unemployment that resulted, only made the workers' plight worse.

In his landmark monograph written over a century ago, *Hind Swaraj*, Gandhi discusses how the Indians working for the British Empire were unwittingly helping to sustain it. They imagined themselves as being patriotic Indians because they were unaware of the larger picture and of the British aims that they were serving. A hundred years after Gandhi wrote his famous diagnosis of the colonized Indians, we need to introspect:

- Whether the West has become even more sophisticated in its nurturing and deployment of Indian sepoys than its British predecessor. It co-opts Indian intellectuals at various levels, ranging from lowly data-gatherers, to identity-engineering programs in the murky backwaters of NGOs, to mid-level scholars in India, all the way to Indian Ivy League professors and award-winning globetrotters.
- What the civic society's and government's relationship is to the Western churches.
- The role of the human rights industry as a 'fifth column' to selectively target and undermine political opponents.

- In what ways the leading private foundations—Ford Foundation, Carnegie Foundation, Rockefeller Foundation, Luce Foundation, Pew Trust, Templeton Foundation, to name just a few—serve as vehicles for the US government and billionaires to collaborate on fulfilling what many Americans have seen as their manifest destiny.

This book shows that Indian centrifugal forces have not only up-linked with the international influences, but have also strategically interlinked among themselves for greater synergy. What, then, should be the proper definition of a 'minority' when such a group now functions as part and parcel of a global majority? Specifically, this book exposes the formation of Dravidian and Dalit identities over nearly two hundred years, and the role played by Western nexuses.

2

Overview of European Invention of Races

Western Academic Constructions Lead to Violence

In the past five centuries, the European nations colonized many regions of Asia, Africa, and the Americas. These Western powers variously imposed a Eurocentric worldview on the colonized cultures. The histories of the local cultures, as well as a global historic narrative, were constructed to justify colonization. Today, even though many of these biases have been exposed, they still wield power in the academic and socio-political discourses. In the next several chapters, we will see the forces that led to these colonial constructs, and explore the reasons for their continued existence. With reference to Fig 2.1, a brief outline of each of the components is given next.

Europe

In the eighteenth century, when the traditional religious edifice of Europe was threatened by the Enlightenment, Europeans looked for a golden past. Many hoped they could find it in India, which had been the source of much of Europe's imports for centuries. In this search for identity, they began to hypothesize and construct an idealized 'Aryan race' through a distorted reading of Indian scriptures. Fed by virulent German nationalism, anti-Semitism and Race Science, this manipulation ultimately led to the rise of Nazism and the Holocaust.

India

In the late eighteenth century, the Indologist Max Müller proposed the Aryan category strictly as a linguistic group, but it soon got transformed into the Aryan race by colonial administrators who used Race Science to make a taxonomical division of traditional Indian communities. The castes designated as 'non-Aryan' were marginalized or excluded in depictions of Hindu society. In parallel, the Church evangelists working in South India constructed a Dravidian race identity. They de-linked Tamil culture from its pan-Indian cultural matrix, and claimed that its spirituality was closer to Christianity than to the Aryan North Indian culture.

Sri Lanka

In Sri Lanka, the Buddhist revival spurred by the Theosophical Society also spread ideas of the Aryan race theory. Bishop Robert Caldwell and Max Müller categorized the Tamils as Dravidians and the Sinhalese as Aryans. This division was encouraged by colonial administrators. Gradually, many south Indians who had assumed a Dravidian identity adopted this division and turned it into antagonism toward the so-called Aryans. The result has been the deadly ethnic civil war that continued in Sri Lanka for a few decades.

Africa

The Hamitic myth of the Bible, in which the descendants of Noah's son Ham were cursed, was used by slave traders and slave owners to justify slavery. Hamitic linguistic groups were identified and separated from the rest of Africans. African civilization's contributions were explained as the work of an imaginary sub-race of Whites invading and civilizing

Africa. Western classification of traditional African communities into races led to bitter rivalries, including genocide, as in Rwanda.

The following six chapters will go into details of how the present Dravidian identity came about in a period of less than two centuries.

Fig 2.1 How Eurocentric Constructs Lead to Violent Conflicts throughout the World

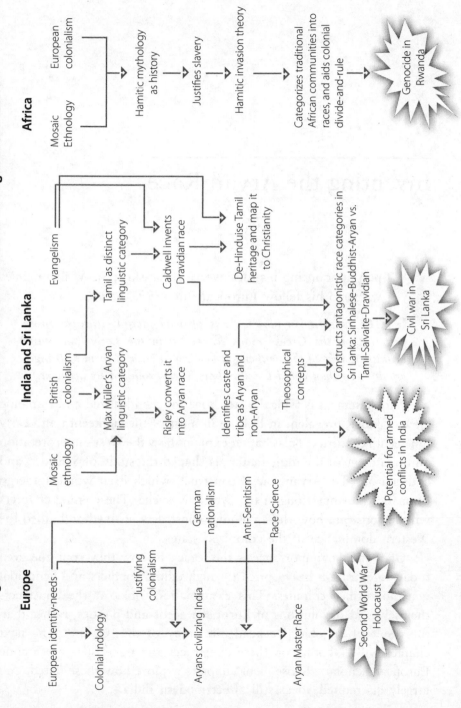

3

Inventing the Aryan Race

Upon announcing his 'discovery' of Sanskrit, Sir William Jones wrote to his fellow Europeans in 1799, that:

> The Sanskrit language . . . is of a wonderful structure; more perfect than the Greek, more copious than the Latin, and more exquisitely refined than either, yet bearing to both of them a stronger affinity . . . than could possibly have been produced by accident.[1]

This statement is typical of the tone for the idealized and romantic view of India, prevalent in Europe in most of the eighteenth and early nineteenth centuries. This chapter explains how the West's interpretation and treatment of the Indic materials shaped the study of Sanskrit, and churned out the 'Aryan' racial construct, which itself would undergo dramatic transmutations in the Western psyche. The coming chapters will demonstrate how these colonial constructs justified and aided the Western dominance of the colonized states.

Of particular importance is the legacy of how they continue even today to extract a heavy price through ethnic conflicts and genocidal wars in former colonies. This examination looks at the constructs themselves as devolutions of European needs and politics, rather than the result of an objective academic study of the 'Orient'. The next chapter will elaborate on these constructs and trace their use among European scholars. Subsequent chapters explore how these dated, and largely discredited, ideas still affect modern India.

Fig 3.1 presents the 'Study of India' as influenced by European romanticists and colonial Indologists. It encapsulates the following stages of European intellectual history concerning India, and how these ideas shaped European superiority:

- **European Romanticists** needed a historical basis to escape the rigid framework of Judeo-Christian monotheism that was already in crisis as a result of new challenges from the modern period. There was a fierce search for a spirituality that could be made to fit their own history, so they could trace their romanticist view in their own past. India was discovered, and quickly became the premier vehicle for this search for their own golden origin.
- **Indologists** historicized classical India in a way that served colonial needs as well as the needs of the emerging nation-states in Europe. They created the notion of Aryans as harbingers of civilization to all humanity. A glorified European ancestry was traced to these idealized Aryans. The European Aryans were seen as racially pure and blessed with the spiritually superior Christianity, whereas the North Indian Aryans were of mixed breed resulting from European Aryans mixing with inferior natives, resulting in idolatry, polytheism and racial impurity.
- A **Master Aryan Race** was then constructed out of the broad Aryan category, largely by German nationalist thinkers. Nascent Race Science was invoked to lend credibility to this fabrication. European anti-Semitism used the Aryan construct to separate Europeans from Jews. The notion of 'Aryan Christ' became popular in Europe.

The nationalistic pride created by the Aryan master-race theory in Germany played a significant role in the rise of Nazism and the Holocaust. After the Second World War, European academic and social institutions made a great effort to exorcize the Aryan race theory from the European psyche, but they still continue to apply these ideas to the study of India.

This chapter traces how the Aryan race theory was molded by deep-rooted European needs, and how it eventually brought disaster on Europe. Subsequent chapters will examine the impact these racial stereotypes are still having on the colonized societies.

Fig 3.1 Aryan Race Creation for European Identity Politics and its Consequences

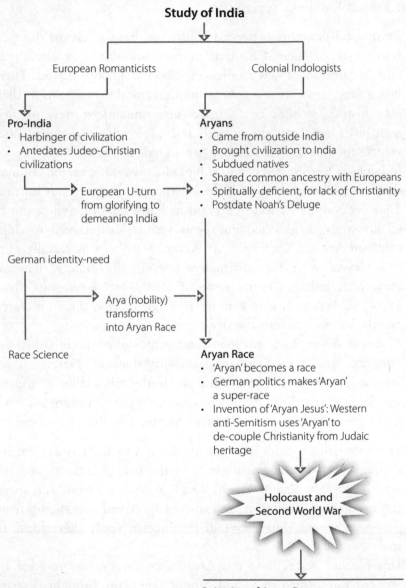

Overview of Indian Impact on Europe: From Renaissance to Racism

Raymond Schwab's seminal book, *The Oriental Renaissance* (1984), discusses many key Asian influences that impacted Europe during the Renaissance and the Enlightenment, that directly preceded and coincided with eighteenth-century colonialism. Schwab explains that in the late 1700s, the widespread arrival of the translations of the *Zend Avesta*, the Zoroastrian seminal text, and the *Bhagavad Gita* provided 'the first approach to an Asian text totally independent of the Biblical and classical traditions [i.e. Greco-Roman traditions]'.[2] India became popular among academics with the publication of John Holwell's *Interesting Historical Events Relating to Bengal* in 1765.[3] Hinduism became the source for important arguments in theological debates among Christian theologians. The 1789 English translation of Kalidasa's *Shakuntala* by William Jones was retranslated into German in 1791, and influenced many prominent intellectuals such as Herder, Goethe, and Schiller.

There were two phases in the evolution of European racism, both driven by similar factors: first, the growth and evolution of German national identity which was competing with other nascent European ethnic and nation-state identities; and second, European colonialism, particularly the British, with an overlay of missionary agendas.

The first phase lasted until the middle of the nineteenth century. European scholars were obsessed with the use of Sanskrit in the construction of a linguistic origin for the European culture. Philology, a new academic discipline, was born, and essentially owed its beginnings to Sanskrit studies. It provided a great impetus to the European quest for the origins of peoples.[4] Europeans from different countries quarreled over their newly discovered philological ancestry, whose progenitors they named variedly as Aryans, Indo-Germans, Indo-Europeans, and Caucasians. They used the terms loosely, referring variously to a people, a race, or a nation, and sometimes to a family of languages. Franz Bopp (1791–1867), a prominent Sanskrit scholar and founder of Comparative Linguistics, advocated against referring to the Sanskrit-related language family as 'Indo-Germanic' because that could cause a schism between Germanic and non-Germanic Europeans. He preferred the term 'Indo-European' because it unified Europeans.

The first phase of this era of India-inspired European academic activity culminated with the publication of Max Müller's series of *Sacred Books of the East* in 1875. The preceding century had reshaped Christian images of geography, because the discovery of Sanskrit had liberated Europeans from their exclusive focus on the Mediterranean area as the source of their cultural heritage. Sanskrit studies provided alternatives to Cartesian absolutism, and led to inquiries into the unlimited, the unconscious, and the philosophical role of negation. This Indological churning also generated internal ethnic-political strife within Europe, culminating in French and German radicalism. Meanwhile, British scholars emphasized the 'mystical' character of Indian society, usually framed within a Christian context, as being romantically primitive and otherworldly. This enabled them to claim Western superiority over worldly affairs and validate the spread of their own civilization.

The second phase, which lasted at least through the Second World War, was characterized by an intellectual obsession for an Aryan race theory, a theory which justified and enflamed anti-Semitism. There was an explosion of speculative philosophy and historiography that focused on the Aryans and the Hebrews, the imagined speakers of the Aryan and Semitic language-groups. The identities of these two ancient (but partly imaginary) civilized peoples set in motion several intellectual and political tidal waves, whose ultimate impact shaped Europe and beyond. The study of the mythical Aryans and Hebrews went well beyond philology as scholars began building ethnographic profiles.

For instance, philosopher Ernest Renan (1823–92) claimed that the Hebrews brought the gift of monotheism to the world, and that Jews were self-centered, troublesome and static. The Aryans had noble virtues like imagination, reason, science, arts and politics, and were therefore dynamic, and these qualities became linked to polytheism and pantheism.[5] Aryan polytheism was dynamic and contrasted with the monotheistic stagnation of the Semites. This sort of profiling led to tension between pro-Aryan scholars and the Christian establishment.

Despite their serious differences with each other, most of the nineteenth-century scholars were bound by the dogma of providential or revealed Biblical history, which assumed that European Christians were inevitably superior to other civilizations because of God's invisible hand. This underlying belief retained its power even after European thinkers had adopted methods from positivism, natural sciences, and comparative studies.[6] Europeans wanted to think of themselves as evolved from the best aspects of both the Semites and Aryans. Re-imagining their ethnic ancestry as Aryan went along with the contemporary intellectual explorations into the historical relations between the Old and the New Testament, and the linguistic relations between Hebrew, Greek, and Latin. At stake was control of history as being driven by the hand of God in favor of certain people. Renan attempted to utilize both Aryan and Semitic heritage as the two parents of Europeans, with a view to getting the best features of both as Europe's heritage.

The study of Sanskrit revolutionized the social sciences, from history to mythology to comparative religion to 'Race Sciences', European identity politics was transformed forever, in ways far removed from what could have been imagined at that time. Almost a century after William Jones, Friedrich Max Müller (1823–1900), one of the most influential European scholars of his time, wrote:

> Thanks to the discovery of the ancient language of India, Sanskrit as it is called . . . and thanks to the discovery of the close kinship between this language and the idioms of the principal races of Europe . . . a complete revolution has taken place in the method of studying the world's primitive history.[7]

Once the Indian texts had been mined for their treasures, and these had been processed through translations, mistranslations, plagiarism, rejections, and extrapolations, and Indian knowledge had been securely relocated as 'Western', the Indian source lost its earlier glamour. Now the motifs, including poetic and philosophic elements which had been adopted from India, came to be used similar to the way clip-art elements are used by a modern computer-based graphics artist. They could be cut-and-pasted to give color and exotic appeal to what was being constructed as European civilization's history. Indian culture became a collection of decorations, souvenirs and memorabilia belonging to the Europeans. In effect, India entered the museums of Europe as the 'romantic but primitive past'. Its 'spell' on the Europeans was over because it was their past. In the process, Indian civilization lost its own integrity and unity, becoming a collection of parts that could be separated from one another, de-contextualized from their native soil and milieu, and then re-contextualized into European circumstances.[8] All along, rival European national interests—principally England, France and Germany—revamped their respective ethnic worldviews.

Herder's Romanticism

One of the early voices of Indology in Germany was Johann Gottfried Herder (1744–1803), a forerunner of German Romanticism and prolific writer on many subjects. He shifted between idealizing groups such as Jews, Egyptians, and Brahmins, and then demonizing them. His writings vacillated between racism and pluralism. For Herder, India represented humanity's innocent childhood – a primitive religion in the midst of nature. Such stereotyped images of India later became well accepted by the Romantics,[9] including Indologists like Schlegel (discussed below) and philosophers like Schelling. These Romantics treated India as a source for literary and cultural 'regeneration' to buttress their own European identities through appropriation and misappropriation.

Herder valued the contributions of Sanskrit to human thought. He claimed that Sanskrit belonged to *his* Indo-European ('Aryan') past. Europe's 'discovery' of India was a 're-discovery' of Europe's own foundation it had forgotten. Using this trajectory, the East was not the 'other' of the West, but its origin. In this line of reasoning, Herder seriously disagreed with G.W.F. Hegel (1770–1831). Hegel saw history as going forward, away from the past, and thus was critical of those who advocated primitiveness as a glorified origin of humanity. Despite Hegel's enormous influence, Herder's philosophy of glorifying antiquity persisted for half a century after his death, and was later picked up by thinkers like Ernest Renan and Max Müller.

Karl Wilhelm Friedrich Schlegel (1772–1829)

Friedrich Schlegel's career in Indology ushered in a new chapter in the West's intellectual history, because it later led to claims of 'rediscovering' the West's Aryan origins. The romanticizing of India in the Germanic imagination served to create a fabled origin of the European nations in a poetic dawning of humanity.

Schlegel lived at a time when Germany and France were bitter enemies, not only militarily and politically, but also culturally. France had the advantage of being seen as a Renaissance nation and successor to the great ancient civilizations of Greece and Rome. Spain and Portugal had their own glorified identities as the colonizers of the Americas. Britain had India, the jewel in its crown, and the prosperous Empire built around it. But Germany had none of these. Rather, Germans were described in French and other textbooks as barbarian tribes who had violently attacked and destroyed the great Roman civilization.

Schlegel played a pioneering role in developing the theory of racial hierarchy, both internally (among Europeans) and externally (with respect to non-Europeans). He was familiar with William Jones's writings on Indian religions. Jones had proposed a racial classification of all humanity, but did not claim that the Indo-European family had originated in India.[10] After his initial romantic embrace of India, Schlegel rejected Indian spirituality, which in his Christian doctrine, was branded as pantheism.

Although he rejected Jones's specific ideas on race, Schlegel nevertheless picked up some of the assumptions about Indian racial identity, which became mixed with the Sanskrit he studied in Paris starting in 1802.[11] After his romance for India had soured into his bitter rejection of Indian religions, Schlegel's India studies were mainly driven by his interest in the Germanic past and the origins of feudalism. His obsession with Indology was now as a vehicle to show that the Germanic culture and the structure of its social groups were more legitimate and advanced than those of ancient Greece, with which the French culture and French Republicanism were proudly linked. Indology enabled him to claim that German culture and feudal social structures had originated in ancient India, giving them a very respectable antiquity to counteract Renaissance-based French supremacy.

Imagining the German Past Using Schlegel's Fabrication of India

Despite his rejection of India's religions and his conversion to Catholicism, Schlegel's Indian studies remained a critical way to blend German nationalism, medievalism, and Catholicism into his newly minted myth of Germany.

India was no longer a source of religious inspiration, but it supplied an honorable historical ancestor to the Germans and their Medieval feudalism. The older version of the myth of India's influence in German Romanticism included Herder's belief in the ultimate antiquity of India and its role as the cradle of civilization. While the previous myth of India was aesthetic and religious, the new myth was driven by German political chauvinism. The main objective in both was to find an alternative to the Greek origin of the European culture. While the romantic myth of India was directed against Neo-Classicism[12], the new myth was meant to lift the status of the German culture against the French culture. The new myth was also opposed to the political configurations associated with the French and Greco-Roman antiquity.

Schlegel's first myth was built on India's historical role as the source of German greatness. He claimed that the ancestors of the modern Germans had migrated from India. He described India as 'the happiest and most fertile land of earth', compared to the remote and inhospitable north of Europe. He noted the Indian veneration for legendary northern mountains, and concluded that material motives alone couldn't have been the cause for this migration led by pious people.[13] On their way north, they were supposedly joined by many smaller tribes, which led to the ethnic diversity of the Northern Europeans.

A second wave of Indian migration went westward and founded the civilizations of Greece and Rome. These were heretic sects that worshiped nature and supposedly had to leave India due to fierce religious struggles.[14] It was important for Schlegel to see the ancient Germans as a highly civilized nation, superior to the ancient Greeks and Romans. This, then, was precisely the service his myth of the origin of the Germans from India could give him. While most historians identified the ancient Germans as the barbarian destroyers of classical Greco-Roman civilizations, Schlegel's myth proposed that the Germanic tribes were actually 'noble savages' who lived in a state of natural innocence in the wilderness of Europe, defending their freedom against the decadent Romans. The nobility of their ancestral character came from their Indian Aryan roots. This played well in Schlegel's nationalistic call to fight against injustices of Napoleonic France.

Fig 3.2 shows the stages of Schlegel's revised theory of the origins of civilizations.

Fig 3.2: The Origins of Civilizations According to Schlegel's Revised Theory

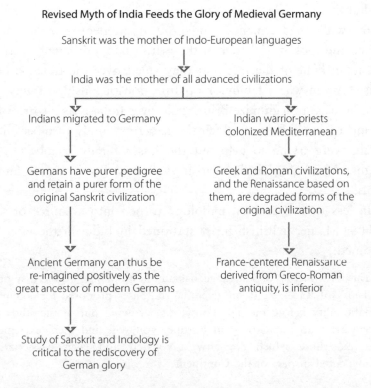

Revised Myth of India Feeds the Glory of Medieval Germany

Sanskrit was the mother of Indo-European languages

India was the mother of all advanced civilizations

Indians migrated to Germany

Indian warrior-priests colonized Mediterranean

Germans have purer pedigree and retain a purer form of the original Sanskrit civilization

Greek and Roman civilizations, and the Renaissance based on them, are degraded forms of the original civilization

Ancient Germany can thus be re-imagined positively as the great ancestor of modern Germans

France-centered Renaissance derived from Greco-Roman antiquity, is inferior

Study of Sanskrit and Indology is critical to the rediscovery of German glory

'Arya' Becomes a Race in Europe

While the word 'Arya' was known in Sanskrit literature, it was Max Müller who first applied it as the name of a family of languages and of the peoples who spoke them. The Aryan race concept quickly took a life of its own and became the basis for twentieth-century Nazism. Max Müller did try to propose an amicable divorce between philology and ethnology, but only *after* his work had found its way into Race Sciences; even then, he distanced himself only partially from its implications, which he had set in motion. The role of scholars of high repute in preparing the ground for racism (and eventually Nazism) for well over a century, is an important chapter in the history of Indology, and/or south Asian studies, where the term 'Aryan' has now largely been replaced by the term 'Indo-European'. However, as we shall see in Chapter Six, the Dravidian opposite that was constructed relative to the Aryan construct remains well-entrenched and is the focus of this book.

But while the Germans adopted the Aryan identity as their national essence and took it to extremes, the British had a different relationship with it, in light of the fact that they ruled over the Indians. For the British, Aryan was a family or organization of kinship groups, which could be used to legitimize British rule over Indians as a sort of family reunion or love affair in which the superior family members, i.e. the British, were trying to help out the lesser family members, i.e. the Indians. At no time in the British view was this seen as a family of equals.

In less than a century, philology turned into a source of racism. Sir H.S. Maine, a British jurist stationed in India in the late 1800s, explained:

> The new theory of Language has unquestionably produced a new theory of Race . . . If you examine the bases proposed for common nationality before the new knowledge growing out of the study of Sanskrit had popularized in Europe, you will find them extremely unlike those which are now advocated and even passionately advocated in part of the Continent.[15]

Ernest Renan and the Aryan Christ[16]

Ernest Renan started his career as a Hebrew scholar, at a time when Hebrew was out of fashion and Indo-European studies were in vogue. Once he became an established authority on Semitic languages, he turned this knowledge into a powerful weapon to compare the two civilizations through their respective languages. The Semitic languages conveyed harsh monotheism, he said, because their verb was incapable of being conjugated for tense and mood. They were unable to formulate multiplicity; hence, the Semites never conceived of diversity or plurality, and were unable to articulate the many facets of nature. In other words, according to Renan, their simplistic language had limited the Semites' capability of rational abstraction, metaphysics and creative intellectual activity. By contrast, Aryans, thanks to their rich grammar and syntax, understood the dynamism and multiplicity inherent in nature. Citing Max Müller, Renan pointed at the plurality of natural phenomena represented in the names of the Aryan gods. Behind each word's root there lurked 'a hidden god'. The difference between the Semitic and the Indo-European peoples is striking not only in language but also in religion: Aryan religion turns out to be 'an echo of nature' and hence multiple specialized divinities are worshiped, unlike in the Semite's monotheism.

Renan hypothesized that the Aryans were more creative because of their mythology and the proliferation of gods, and this creativity turned into an advantage as it later led them to discover metaphysics and science. Semitic monotheism, which had been a great asset initially, thus turned into 'an obstacle to human progress'. The early glory of the Semitic race ultimately worked against it. While they were the first to recognize a unique, solitary and perfect divinity, their destiny became capped in early childhood. They had 'less fertile natures who, after a blessed childhood, achieve only a mediocre virility'. Their religion, like their languages, was monotonous and hence static, causing them to remain stuck at an infantile stage of human development. Semites thus deserved credit for their initial service to humanity, but were eventually decidedly inferior to the Indo-European 'substratum' of all civilizations.[17]

In other words, the initial Semitic contributions to civilization were superseded by the Aryan contributions. Even Semitic monotheism could be seen reflected in an Aryan mirror. Semites were thus incorporated into Aryan history. Renan separated Jesus from Judaism and made him the 'Aryanized' Christ, which he conceptualized as follows:

- Aryans began as polytheists but were later transformed into Christian monotheists.
- As a product of the same Aryan/Christian encounter, Christianity assimilated the spirit of the diverse Aryan peoples it had converted. Renan wrote that the new Christianity 'completely transcended the limits of the Semitic spirit'.
- Renan thought that this had caused Christianity to break away from Judaism, thereby making Christianity 'less purely Semitic' than Judaism or Islam, and 'the least monotheistic' of the three Abrahamic religions.

In his inaugural lecture at the College de France, Renan said, 'The victory of Christianity was not secure until it completely broke out of its Jewish shell and again became what it had been in the exalted consciousness of its founder, a creation free from the narrow bonds of the Semitic spirit.' He also wrote: 'Originally Jewish to the core, Christianity over time rid itself of nearly everything it took from that race, so that those who consider Christianity to be the Aryan religion par excellence are in many respects correct'. He felt that Christianity actually contradicted the Jewish religion: 'Christianity improved itself by moving farther and farther away from Judaism, and seeing to it that the genius of the Indo-European race triumphed within its bosom'.[18]

Renan's view of the development of various civilizations is depicted in Fig 3.3.

Fig 3.3 The Development of Various Civilizations According to Renan

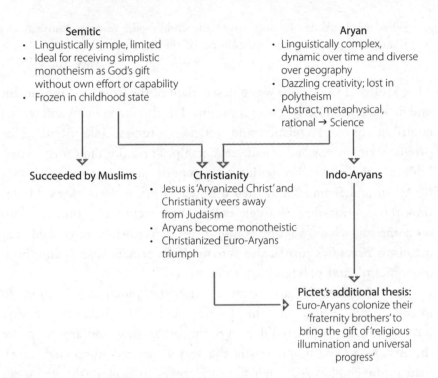

Renan's history of humanity is, thus, the march of civilization consisting of two strands, Aryan and Semitic. For this Aryan-Semitic genealogical drama, he and his contemporaries were seeking a Christian victory in which the Aryans were the linguistic and cultural ancestors, and the Semites the childlike founders of monotheism.

The religion of Jesus had to be Aryanized, freed from its congenital Semitic shortcomings, in order to progress. And along the way, it became possible to venerate Jesus Christ while overlooking his Jewish birth. Renan, thus, used philology to put Christianity on a scientific footing, by discarding superstition and integrating it with the Enlightenment.

Friedrich Max Müller

> While in the Veda we may study the childhood, we may study in
> Kant's *Critique* the perfect manhood of the Aryan mind.
>   – Max Müller[19]

Max Müller (1823–1900) was a descendant of the Romantic movement
and its longings for civilization's origins. He also made many influential
contributions to linguistics and religious studies. Like Renan, his
prolific writings reached a wide readership. For more than forty years,
both the scholars worked with the concept of race, using the categories
of Aryan and Semite.[20] But they differed in major ways. Max Müller
took the position that no single culture had exclusively come up with
monotheism, which was the common property of humanity, and that
linguistic structures turned this into multiple religions, including both
monotheistic and polytheistic forms.

Max Müller did not want to use the Indian civilization to
introduce polytheism into the development of Christianity the way
Renan wanted to. Nor did he go the other way and try to make
the Aryans appear monotheistic the way Pictet did (discussed later).
Instead, he emphasized linguistic differences to explain the divergent
religious views. Müller wanted a science of religions to reveal the
divine in all things. The use of comparative methods, the new
discipline, like other natural sciences, should strive to reveal the
providential unity underlying the variegated world of appearances.
This providential order had been inscribed in nature at the beginning
of time, and it was the task of comparative philology and mythology
to find its traces in myths and religions, among which Christianity
of course occupied a unique position.[21]

Max Müller served as a functionary for the colonialists and for
Christian evangelists, while being deeply interested in ancient Indian
texts. This orientation is reflected in one of his letters addressed to
the duke of Orgoil, who was the British secretary of state for India.
Müller wrote on 16 December 1868: 'The ancient religion of India is
totally doomed and if Christianity doesn't step in whose fault will it

be?' In a letter addressed to his wife in 1868, Müller also wrote: 'I hope I shall finish that work and feel convinced that though I shall not live to see it, yet this edition of mine and translation of Vedas will hereafter tell to a great extent on the fate of India and on the growth of millions of the souls in this country'. In the same letter, he further observed: '[The Veda] is the root of their religion and to show them what the root is, I feel sure, [is] the only way of uprooting all that has been sprung from it during the last three thousand years'.[22] In other words, he saw contemporary Indian civilization, especially its multiple gods, as a corrupt form of ancient glory.

Adolphe Pictet

Adolphe Pictet (1799–1875), a Swiss linguist, was another ethnographer determined to praise the Aryan heritage in Christian Europe. He was fully committed to the notion of European Aryan origins and superiority. According to him, as a favored race, blessed with 'innate beauty' and 'gifts of intelligence', the Aryans were destined to conquer the world. His particular emphasis, even obsession, concerned the notion that the normative religious orientation of the Aryans was monotheism, which was only fully realized among the Aryans when Christianity ruled. He further contended that originally Indians did have a sense of monotheism, but it was underdeveloped and later lapsed into polytheism. Pictet determined that the proper religious orientation of the Aryan mind was monotheism, this providing the justification for the Christian European Aryans to colonize the Indian Aryans who had lapsed from monotheism.

His goal, like that of Renan and Müller, was to deploy philology to bring to Europeans the appreciation of the 'birthplace of the world's most powerful race, the very race to which we belong'.[23] He wanted to interpret the Aryans so that they seemed as monotheistic as possible, claiming that despite having 'poetic polytheism' they also had a 'primitive monotheism'. Applying linguistic analysis to Sanskrit, he claimed that ancient Indians had primitive monotheism that lacked rigor, so they fell into polytheism as a way to 'explain the multiplicity of natural phenomena'. Christianity should perform the critical role of reviving the seed of monotheism first planted by the Aryans.

According to Pictet, the Indo-European heritage had unity-in-diversity inherently built into it: there was a diversity of Aryan dialects from the outset, and there was a prehistoric political solidarity of Indo-European peoples. The historian's task, he felt, was to reveal the role assigned by God to each race in the world. Like Renan, he felt that the Hebrews and Aryans each had their qualities.[24] Given their love for freedom and liberty (as contrasted with the Semites), the Aryans had lost their way in polytheism at first, but after they had mastered the material realm of nature, they marched confidently toward Christian monotheism. Christianity was the synthesis of the best of all, and hence designated as the future of humanity. Christians were destined to rule the entire globe.

In this process, people in India who were the descendants of the 'early Aryans', and who represented the original homeland, had now become colonized by the Euro-Aryans to receive the 'beneficent influence' of modern civilization. The Euro-Aryans were fraternity brothers of the Indo-Aryans, and were bringing them 'religious illumination and universal progress'. Pictet glorifies European colonization of India, remarking 'Is it not curious, moreover, to see the Aryas of Europe, after a separation of four to five thousand years, finding their way back, via a vast, circuitous route, to their unknown Indian brothers [so as] to dominate them and bring them the elements of a higher civilization and to discover among them the ancient proof of a common origin?'[25] Therefore, colonization of India is ethical because it is decreed by providence. Civilization has to spread through Christian colonization.

Rudolph Friedrich Grau

With R.F. Grau (1835–93), the emphasis shifted almost entirely to presenting a unified Biblical tradition that duly acknowledges the Semitic inheritance of Christianity in order to minimize dissent within its own camp. By doing so, he reasoned, the task of converting non-Christians, especially Indians, would be greatly facilitated.

Grau was a German minister and Lutheran apologist who wanted to counteract the prodigious praising of the Aryans (whom he called Indo-Germans) because the danger of favoring Aryans was that Christ would be forgotten. So he gave the Semites importance as being the sole link between God and his new-chosen people, the Christian faithful. Separating Indo-Germans from the Semitic underpinnings of the Church would threaten the equilibrium of the modern world. Like many Europeans of his time, he embraced Semitic monotheism but separated it from the Jews, whom he hated. The best strategy was to blend the monotheism of the Semites with the dynamism of the Indo-Germans (Aryans) within a Christian context.

Grau declared: 'The marriage between Semitic spirit and Indo-Germanic nature is sealed in heaven'.[26] Separately, neither had the backbone supposedly provided by Christianity, but thanks to this wedding, they were destined to rule the world. The extraordinary dynamism of the Indo-Germans, embodied in the arts and sciences, took on meaning only within the Christian Church. Without Christianity, they would sink into barbarism. To illustrate this point, he explained that Indians had so much uncontrolled creativity that only 'the Semitic savor' through Christian domination could save them from chaos. The cross had to be planted firmly at the center of any venture of cultural understanding. Several of Grau's books were translated into English and used by missionaries in their efforts to embed Vedic thought within Christian symbols to apply in the conversion of Hindus and other Dharmic peoples in India.

Gobineau and Race Science

Joseph Arthur Comte de Gobineau (1816–82), a French diplomat, philosopher, historian, and novelist, claimed that European Aryans, after invading India, had become debased by mixing with the darker native races. The importance of India to him was that it served as a case-study confirming his racial theories.

In 1853, the same year in which Karl Marx explained that India has no history of its own apart from foreign invasions, Gobineau began publishing his racist theories in the four-volume book, *Essay on the Inequality of Human Races*. His work was translated into several European languages, and later it became the seminal source in feeding Race Sciences. India played a paradigmatic role in Gobineau's theories because he could cite the Aryan invasion to explain the caste system. He was well-read in Indological literature. He rejected linguistic classifications of races, insisting instead that all of the civilizations of the world had emerged from the White race, but that all geographical areas except for northern Europe had declined because of intermarriages.[27]

Gobineau worked within the Biblical framework, starting with the assumption that 'Adam is the originator of our white species' ('Adam soit l'auteur de notre espèce blanche'). He wrote of the 'superiority of the white type and, within that type, of the Aryan family'. As per his ideology there were three races – white, yellow and black. At the top he placed the whites because they had the ability to create and spread culture. However, this cultural expansion into areas inhabited by inferior races caused interbreeding and brought about the decline of the purity of the supposedly superior race.

The example of India was the cornerstone that Gobineau used to prove his thesis. Halbfass summarizes Gobineau's thesis: 'The Aryans, representing the highest potential of the "white race", invaded the Indian subcontinent and began to merge with the native population. Realizing the danger, the Aryan lawgivers implemented the caste-system as a means of self-preservation. Accordingly, the processes of bastardization and degeneration have been much slower in India than in other civilizations'.[28]

In other words, caste was made by pure whites to slow down the intermixing of their race with inferior peoples. Gobineau explained that the Indian Brahmins were degraded Aryans due to this intermixing. However, he agrued, this degradation would have been worse in the absence of caste separation. Gobineau invoked the India example to argue against the ideas behind the French Revolution as well as the emerging ideas of Marxist class-struggles.

Wilhelm Halbfass explains how the Aryan construct thus shifted over time:

> During Gobineau's lifetime, the old theory of the Asian origin of the European languages and traditions, and of cultural movements from the East to the West, increasingly gave way to speculations on primeval movements from the West to the East, and on Aryan migrations from Europe, specifically Northern Europe, or even the North Pole, to India. According to these speculations, the European or Northern invaders gave their superior culture to the Indians and then lost their superiority through mixing with the local inhabitants and perished in a climate for which they were not suited. In 1903, E. de Michelis summarized this view by stating that Asia, and India in particular, was not the 'cradle', but the 'grave of the Aryans'.[29]

Aryan Theorists and Eugenics

Gobineau's race theory was not an isolated phenomenon. During the 1870s, the Oxford lecturer John Ruskin instilled in his students like Cecil Rhodes, the concept that Europeans were 'the best northern blood' and should rule the world. Rhodes later used his immense wealth from the plunder of Africa to fund his famous Rhodes scholarship, which was initially meant to promote the White youth only. Such racist ideas were riding on a wave of eugenics that was gathering within Ivory Towers and capital cities of colonial Europe. In the nineteenth century, theories such as eugenics were flooding the halls of academia.

The term 'eugenics' was first used in 1883 by Francis Galton, a half-cousin of Charles Darwin. Darwin had written that 'The civilized races of man will almost certainly exterminate, and replace, the savage races throughout the world'.[30] Eugenics refers to selective breeding by preventing birth among 'inferior' races and encouraging birth among 'superior' races in order to improve the quality of human race. Galton used the British upper-class as the criterion for measuring how 'civilized' a race was. Departure from that criterion determined the 'savagery' of any given race.

This schema was turned into a more 'scientific' taxonomy for classifying human races by Georges Vacher de Lapouge (1854–1936), a theorist of eugenics. In 1899, de Lapouge published *L'Aryen et son rôle social* (The Aryan and His Social Role). His hierarchy placed the 'Aryan White race' at the pinnacle of humankind. He later became one of the leading inspirations of Nazi racist ideology. The Harvard professor William Z. Ripley used de Lapouge's classifications in his 1899 book, *The Races of Europe*, which had a large influence on white supremacists in America. The Aryan doctrine propounded by Madame Blavatsky, the charismatic founder of Theosophical Society and the foremost occultist of the West at that time, spread throughout Germany and Austria.[31]

Chamberlain: Aryan-Christian Racism

Houston Stewart Chamberlain (1855–1927) was a British author who wrote books on philosophy, history and culture. He took Gobineau's ideas further, in an effort to give the theories a more 'scientific' and philosophical basis. In so doing, he became an authoritative influence on the Nazi leadership. His magnum opus was *The Foundations of the Nineteenth Century* (1899). Though he was English, Chamberlain wrote the book in German in order to emphasize his Aryan-Teutonic heritage.[32] The book became an instant bestseller in Europe, and by 1942 had gone through twenty-eight editions. *Die Christliche Welt,* a magazine for Protestant liberal theology, described *The Foundations* as a book for which 'our Christian world will have much to thank'.[33]

The Foundations of the Nineteenth Century linked Indian caste with race, and projected Teutonic heritage as the most evolved among Aryan races:

> . . . wherever the Aryans went they became master. The Greek, the Latin, the Kelt, the Teuton, the Slav – all these were Aryans: of the aborigines of the countries which they overran scarcely a trace remains. So too in India, it was 'varna' colour which distinguished the white conquering Arya from the defeated black man, the Dasyu, and so laid the foundation of caste. It is to the Teuton branch of the

Aryan family that the first place in the world belongs, and the story of the Nineteenth Century is the story of the Teuton's triumph.[34]

Chamberlain saw India as an example of a nation where the 'stock of the strength' of the Aryans had decayed.[35] To him, this had also happened in the spiritual realm of India. The concept of Brahman had become so 'sublimated that nothing remained from which to create new living form'.[36] Buddhism represented 'the senile decay of a culture which has reached the limits of its possibilities'.[37] Against this picture of the East as a spiritually and racially spent force, *The Foundations* presented Jesus as 'the Birth of a new day, of a new civilisation dawning under the sign of the Cross, raised upon the ruins of the old world, a civilisation at which we must work for many a long day before it may be worthy to be called by His name.'[38] Chamberlain starts his chapter on Jesus with a quotation from the *Mahabharata*, presented in such a way so as to suggest that ancient Indian sacred literature somehow expected the arrival of Christianity.[39] This tactic would later become a favorite evangelical tool employed in India by missionary scholarship.

Chamberlain saw Christianity as a pan-European and essentially Teutonic phenomenon. He admired the Roman Catholic religion as a bulwark against liberalism, that was seen as a Jewish conspiracy. He looked to Lutheranism for the doctrinal basis of a German national Church. He appreciated St Paul for the rejection of Judasim.[40] But unlike Gobineau, Chamberlain was aware of the limitations of the Biblical basis of the Aryan myth, and even had a premonition that one day the notion of a historical Aryan race might be fully disproved. Yet he felt that such a notion was important for Europe, and wrote:

> Though it were proved that there never was an Aryan race in the past, yet we desire that in the future there may be one. That is the decisive standpoint for men of action.[41]

Chamberlain introduced 'scientific', 'philosophical' and Christian elements into the Aryan narrative. He explained the benefits Christianity would derive by projecting itself as a pan-European phenomenon that supported German racial supremacy. This approach made the blatant Aryan racism of Gobineau acceptable among the influential circles throughout Europe. Anthropologist Kenneth A.R. Kennedy concludes:

> [B]oth Gobineau and Chamberlain transformed the Aryan concept, which had its humble origins in philological research conducted by Jones in Calcutta at the end of the eighteenth century, into the political and racial doctrines of Adolf Hitler's Third Reich.[42]

Nazi Germany posthumously honored Chamberlain, declaring him 'the seer of Third Reich'.[43]

Nazis and After

Such theories continued to develop further throughout the nineteenth and early twentieth centuries, and were very influential in political and intellectual fringe-movements around 1900. They selectively took information from Indology to build histories of civilizations and races in a manner that fit European supremacy.

All this influenced Hitler. G. Lanz-Liebenfels (1874–1954) started a journal called *Ostara*, in which he developed his racist theory about dark-skinned chandala ('tschandlas', as recorded in his writings) and blond Aryans. In 1908, two issues of the journal were dedicated to *Manusmriti* and race cultivation among the ancient 'Indo-Aryan'.[44] Hitler was a regular reader of this journal. Numerous such works ended up serving as veritable textbooks for the Third Reich. Halbfass explains, 'India is invoked in order to articulate and justify ideas and programs of unparalleled arrogance and destruction'.[45]

When the racist ideas from Germany entered fascist Italy, they got further complicated. Kate Cohen explains the Jewish condition in fascist Italy:

> The word ariane, Aryan, had taken on an equally bizarre meaning when applied to Fascist Italy: a swarthy Southern Catholic was Aryan whereas a blond and blue-eyed Milanese Jew was not. . . . Fascist words certainly pushed [the] ridiculous to the limit: one could become Aryan, which would seem to be biologically impossible. Children

of mixed marriages who had been baptized by a certain time were officially Aryan . . . But trying to be Aryan or discriminated had a price . . . The idea of an Italian Aryan race, already laughable was rendered more absurd by the possibility of being Aryanized. All one had to do was prove that one's father was not Jewish but Aryan and one did that by claiming that one was born as a result of one's mother's adultery.[46]

Giulio Cogni, an Italian professor, was highly instrumental in bringing Nazi Aryan ideas into Italy. Though he later fell out of favor with Mussolini, he was highly influencial in shaping the thoughts of the fascist dictator. He combined Catholic theological stands on Jews with German Nazism. As historian Aaron Gillette explains:

[Cogni] claimed that 'if [a] Jew loved Christ . . . he would be ipso facto outside Judaism; he would be transfigured, in his veins would begin to flow Aryan blood.' This conception of Jew was essentially that of the Catholic Church . . .[47]

After the Second World War, revulsion against Hitler and the Holocaust brought an end to Race Science and eugenics in the European mainstream, and special efforts were made to remove the notion of the Aryan race, not just from the academic vocabulary but also from the public psyche of Europe.

Blaming the Indian Civilization

Despite the fact that it was European scholarship which had misappropriated, distorted, and abused Indian traditions for the benefit of European identity politics, there is still a tendency among certain western scholars to put the blame for European racism and Nazism at India's door. Sheldon Pollock, professor of Sanskrit at Coloumbia University, promotes this view. According to Pollock, 'high Brahminism' as represented by the Mimamsa school, contributed to the 'ideological formations of precolonial India', and Nazism tried implementing this 'at home' in Germany.[48] Pollock argues that it was this that ultimately led to the 'legitimation of genocide'.[49] However, the truth is entirely different. The historian Raul Hilberg, in his seminal three-volume work, *The Destruction of European Jews*, had presented what the historian William Nicholls calls:

> . . . a remarkable table of comparison between canonical laws of the Church in the medieval period and the later measures of the Nazis, showing beyond doubt that the latter were not original but followed a known precedent.[50]

(In 2010, Pollock was honored by the Government of India with the Padma Shri award.)

Wilhelm Halbfass takes Pollock's thesis to fabricate far-reaching speculations:

> Would it not be equally permissible to identify this underlying structure as 'deep Nazism' or 'deep Mimamsa'? And what will prevent us from calling Kumarila and William Jones 'deep Nazis' and Adolf Hitler a 'deep Mimamsaka'?[51]

We can see the implications of Western Indologists continuing to use the idea of the Aryan in the Indian context, with references to 'Aryan invasions' and so forth. As will be shown in subsequent chapters, European racial ideas conveniently made their way into India, where they were reframed in terms of light-skinned 'Aryans' and dark-skinned 'Dravidians'. These distinctions were first promoted in colonial times, but remain powerful to this day in the various studies of India.

4

Imperial Evangelism Shapes Indian Ethnology

This chapter discusses how Biblical stories were imposed as historical facts on colonized communities, and were used to justify colonial dominance. Later chapters will show how a false history continues to impose cultural and theological dominance on India. Fig 4.1 shows this development. Its major components are as follows:

Mosaic Ethnology

European scholars and explorers explained Asian and African societies through the Biblical myths of Noah's deluge, the curse on Ham, and the Tower of Babel. This resulted in what Trautmann has called the 'Mosaic Ethnology', which then became the standard interpretation regarding the histories and cultures of various kinds of colonized people. Dissenting voices existed, but were ignored or suppressed.

Myth of Ham and African Colonizers

Africa witnessed armed expeditions as well as slave raids from Europe, transferring large numbers of captured African peoples to distant lands.

The institution of slavery became a major constituent of European and American economies. The Bible's Hamitic myth, in which the descendants of Ham were cursed by Noah into perpetual slavery, was used by the Europeans as the established truth to interpret the skin-color of Blacks and justify the institution of slavery. This Hamitic myth was merged with Aryan invasion theories, and then became the dominant explanation for ethnic diversity in India. Appendix C traces the centrality of the Hamitic myth in the narrative that led to the recent African genocides.

Babel Myth and Indologists

The leading Indologist of the late 1700s, Sir William Jones, explained the relationship between Sanskrit and European languages through the Biblical story of the Tower of Babel. Hindu mythologies and scriptures were classified as corruptions of 'Christian Truth', and the original peoples of India were described as descendants of Ham who went to India after Noah's deluge. This Biblical myth became the blueprint from which later racial stereotypes and racist interpretations of Indian society were constructed. It also justified the British rule in India as a civilizing mission to rescue the Indians, who had corrupted the 'original Biblical truth'.

Institutional Mechanisms

Many of the academic institutions that study Indian culture today were created during the colonial period. Some of the main axioms of Biblical ethnology continue to be extant and influential in this study to this day.

Fig 4.1 Biblical Mythology Shapes Colonial Ethnology

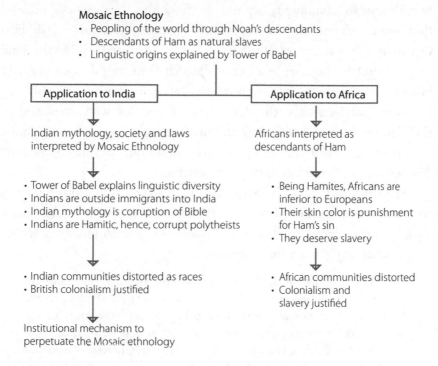

Mosaic Ethnology
- Peopling of the world through Noah's descendants
- Descendants of Ham as natural slaves
- Linguistic origins explained by Tower of Babel

| Application to India | Application to Africa |

Indian mythology, society and laws interpreted by Mosaic Ethnology

Africans interpreted as descendants of Ham

- Tower of Babel explains linguistic diversity
- Indians are outside immigrants into India
- Indian mythology is corruption of Bible
- Indians are Hamitic, hence, corrupt polytheists

- Being Hamites, Africans are inferior to Europeans
- Their skin color is punishment for Ham's sin
- They deserve slavery

- Indian communities distorted as races
- British colonialism justified

- African communities distorted
- Colonialism and slavery justified

Institutional mechanism to perpetuate the Mosaic ethnology

Biblical Theory of Race and the Myth of Ham

According to the Bible, there was a great flood in ancient times, after which the descendants of Noah repopulated the earth. Noah's three sons were Ham, Shem and Japheth. On one occasion, Ham laughed at Noah's nudity, who felt insulted and cursed the descendants of Ham that they must forever live in servitude to the descendants of the other two sons.[1] This Biblical account of how the world was populated by the three descendants of Noah, was accepted as veritable history in Europe.

When European colonialists captured various parts of the world, their missionaries and merchants encountered unfamiliar non-Western cultures. Very soon, European accounts were constructed to fit all the populations of other cultures into the Biblical framework as descendants of one of the three sons of Noah. There was considerable debate amongst rival European intellectuals as to how each given non-European community should fit into this framework, because that would determine the community's status in terms of Biblical hierarchy. The narratives of natives were dismissed as 'myths' and 'superstitions'. The Europeans considered it their moral authority, and indeed, responsibility, to compose the 'true history' of all cultures. In most such accounts, the dark-skinned peoples were identified as the descendants of Ham. Any culture that got branded as Hamitic was classified as barbaric, uncivilized, immoral, at times cunningly intelligent, and therefore deserving servitude.

Stephen R. Haynes, a Biblical historian, explains that this tendency to associate skin-color with the character of a people—particularly their ability to accept Christianity—had been institutionalized within Christianity right from the beginning:

> For over two millennia, Bible readers have blamed Ham and his progeny for everything from existence of slavery to serfdom to the perpetuation of sexual license and perversion, to the introduction of magical arts, astrology, idolatry, witchcraft and heathen religion. They have associated Hamites with tyranny, theft, heresy, blasphemy, rebellion, war and even deicide.[2]

The founder of the Protestant movement, Martin Luther, besides being a virulent anti-Semite,[3] believed categorically that Ham and his descendants were possessed by 'Satanic and bitter hatred'. The Bible, thus, supplied the theological legitimacy for using the physical attributes of the body as the basis for moral degeneration and justification for servitude.

Origen of Alexandria (185–254 CE), one of the founding fathers and prominent theologians of the early Christian Church, wrote that the Egyptians went into bondage because 'Egyptians are prone to degenerate life' and indulge in vices. He wrote:

> Look at the origin of the race and you will discover that their father Ham, who had laughed at his father's nakedness deserved a judgment of this kind that his son Chanaan should be servant to his brothers,

in which case the condition of bondage would precede the wickedness of his conduct. Not without merit, therefore, does the *discolored* posterity imitate the ignobility of the race.[4]

Goldenberg explains the use of the term 'discolored' by analyzing Origen's approach to skin color:

One must ask why Origen chose to mention the Egyptians' skin color while describing their bondage. . . . The answer, I think, can be deduced from Origen's extensive exegetical treatment of dark skin elsewhere in the Bible. He explains the dark color of the maiden of Son 1:5 saying darkness is due to prior sinful condition . . . 'black because of the ignobility of birth.'[5]

Between 1517 and 1840, it is estimated that twenty-million Africans were captured, transported to the Americas, and enslaved in a manner that can only be considered a holocaust.[6] By the eighteenth century, as slavery became a core institution supporting Europe's economy, the Hamitic myth dominated the discourse on race relations by providing justification for slavery. Haynes writes that the advocates of slavery included 'respected professionals such as doctors, lawyers, politicians, clergymen and professors', who regarded the 'Curse of Ham' as historical fact.[7]

More importantly, even the Africans who converted to Christianity themselves accepted this version of their history, as taught to them by the European masters. Thus, the slave and Black poetess, Phyllis Wheatley, wrote in 1773: 'Remember Christians, Negroes black as Cain may be refined and join the angelic train'.[8] In 1843, a book titled *Slavery as it Relates to the Negro or the African Race* appeared in America. Its writer, Josiah Priest, justified black slavery by dramatizing how Noah had cursed Ham:

Oh Ham, my son, it is not for this one deed alone which you have just committed that I have, by God's command, thus condemned you and your race; but the Lord has shown me that all your descendants will, more or less, be like you their father, on which account, it is determined by the Creator that you and your people are to occupy the lowest condition of all the families among mankind and even be enslaved as brute beasts going down in the scale of human society, beyond and below the ordinary exigencies of mortal existence . . . and must be both in times of peace and war, a despised, degraded and oppressed race.[9]

The book immediately became a bestseller in America: during 1843–5, it was reprinted three times in New York, and in 1852–64 it had six editions in Kentucky alone.[10] The book was later called *Bible Defense of Slavery*, and the author, Josiah Priest, became a celebrity.

In 1895, Troup Taylor, another devout Christian, wrote a pamphlet that became very popular and saw many reprints. It was titled *The Prophetic Families or The Negro – His Origin, Destiny and Status*. It explained how the curse on Ham was passed on through Cannan to the entire 'Negro' race:

Cannan, who is certainly the father of the negro family, was adapted to a destiny suited only to an inferior people. The prophecy begins by saying, 'Cursed be Cannan; a servant of servants shall he be unto his brethren' . . . Let us see how literally the prophetic law embraced in this verse has been fulfilled by the negro and negro alone.[11]

William Jones Maps Indians onto Biblical Ethnology

The idea of a hierarchal 'family tree' structure for the races has a long history in the Western mind. Moses is traditionally considered to be the author of the Book of Genesis, which describes nations and races that originated from the descendants of Noah. Trautmann refers to this idea as 'Mosaic Ethnology'.[12]

Aristotle's 'scale of civilizations', when combined with Mosaic Ethnology, prepared the West to embrace a hierarchy with the white man naturally placed at the apex. This became the normative European paradigm from about 1780 to approximately 1850 CE, as successive colonial Indologists theorized and debated how best to map the Indians onto the Biblical framework. These luminaries included William Jones, Max Müller, Brian Houghton Hodgson, and Bishop Robert Caldwell, among others. As will be demonstrated, their imprint has left modern Indian identities divided and fragmented.

William Jones adopted this framework as the template onto which he mapped the languages of the world.[13] Thus, Indian linguistics was mapped onto Biblical ethnology. Jones is famous for praising Sanskrit, and arguing that the European renaissance was brought about in part by the study of ancient Indian texts. But he is less well-known for his project of racial profiling of Indians, which as Trautmann explains, formed 'a rational defense of the Bible out of materials collected by Orientalist scholarship . . .'[14] Noah's three sons, Ham, Shem, and Japheth, were, within the Biblical framework, considered to be the ancestors of all civilized peoples. Jones mapped Indians as the offspring of Ham, Arabs as the offspring of Shem, and Tartars as the offspring of Japheth.[15] Jones used his newly discovered Sanskrit materials to claim that the Hindus had the character of Ham, and that Sanskrit literature was linked to Biblical events.

Through the extrapolation of coincidental syllabic similarities, Jones related the Hindu deity Ram to the Biblical Raamah, and Ram's son Kusa to the Biblical Cusa the grandson of Ham, and so forth. Using similar-sounding names and other accidental homophones, Jones attempted to extrapolate their Biblical origins. His theory was that soon after Noah's flood, Rama reconstituted Indian society. India was therefore one of the oldest Biblical civilizations. His project extracted Biblical correlations to verify Hindu concepts and terms. He intended to prove that the Sanskrit texts confirmed the truth of Moses' narrative in the Bible.

In doing so, Jones mapped Manu as Adam and located Vishnu's first three avatars within the story of Noah's flood. Jones then created a different Manu, whom he claimed, was Noah. In this fantastic version, the Biblical legend of eight humans aboard the Ark is really also about Manu plus the seven rishis sailing in the ship.[16] The fourth Vishnu avatar, Narasimha, is translated as Nimrod, a descendant of Ham who is associated with the Tower of Babel. In other words, the legitimacy and relevance of Sanskrit literature was measured and based on where and how much it fit incidentally into the Biblical master-narrative.[17]

Those Indian elements that did not naturally fit into the Bible were either distorted to force them to fit, or simply rejected. For example, Jones used the Biblical time-scales established by the earlier British Protestants, such as Archbishop Usher's seventeenth-century proclamation that God had created the world in 4004 BCE, and the flood of Noah had taken place in 2349 BCE. This meant that the Indian *yugas* had to be rejected because they involved huge time-spans running into millions and billions of years (which, incidentally, are very close to contemporary scientific estimates regarding the age of the universe). If something was mentioned in Sanskrit texts that somehow did not fit into the Bible, it was labeled as mythology. Whatever could be made to 'fit', became *the* history of the Indian peoples according to Jones. In this manner, the Vedic and Puranic texts were digested into Biblical chronology. This Bible-centric framework of timescales is what led Max Müller many decades later to establish his dates for the so-called Aryan invasion of India, which influences scholars to this day.

European scholars also saw ancient Greece and Rome as the source of western civilization. Jones endeavored to make his translations of Sanskrit fit into the Greco-Roman frameworks. He formulated a series of parallels between the Hindu deities and the pagan gods of Greco-Roman times. He perceived that all these civilizations were descendants of Ham who had fallen into idolatry. Ultimately, the Greco-Romans were saved by European Christianity, but the Hindus remained pagan. Jones's correlation of Hindu deities to Greco-Roman gods has endured till today, and is assumed true by both Hindus and non-Hindus.

Jones's mapping of ancient India onto the Mosaic framework also served as evidence against the atheists who opposed Christianity. He used Hinduism as an independent corroboration of Biblical history following the Great Flood. He exaggerated areas of similarity between Hinduism and Christianity to serve this agenda. Indeed, Hindu texts were used by him to argue logically in support of Christianity. Because of this overarching agenda, Jones thus positioned Hinduism from being a threat to a passive reinforcement of Christianity.

Rasiah S. Sugirtharajah, a scholar of Indian Christianity, has remarked how William Jones's philology became a theological project to fit Hindu texts into a Biblical mythology. Sugirtharajah writes:

With a concern to reinforce Christianity, Jones' hermeneutical tactic was to redraw the chronological map of the world. He summarily dismissed outright the cumbersome and long-drawn-out Indian history, which did not fit in with his timeframe. [. . .] The history recorded in Genesis became the benchmark for discerning other histories, and those which did not fit in had to be squeezed in, erased or dismissed as wild allegorical imaginings.[18]

There was no doubt in Jones's mind that Christianity was the only true religion. He mapped the Hindu trinity of Brahma, Vishnu and Siva as the *degraded* version of the Christian Trinity, caused by the pagans' fall from grace into polytheism. Europeans, he believed, had superior reasoning skills and were far ahead of Asians in civilization. Asians were 'mere children' in the area of science. The interest in studying Indian astronomy and science was to understand history, and not because they could possibly make significant mathematical and scientific contributions relevant for the present or future.[19] Regardless of all his scholarly study of Sanskrit, Jones expressed a strong dislike for the Indians, whom he described as:

. . . deluded and besotted . . . who would receive liberty as a curse instead of a blessing, if it were possible to give it to them, and would reject as a vase of poison . . .[20]

Trautmann shows the compromises Jones made to fit Indian society into the Biblical ethnology. For instance, he was very familiar with the *Manusmriti*, having translated it in 1794. However, his description of the *jati* (caste) structure was a distortion of the way it is described in the *Manusmriti*, thus enabling Jones to fit Indians into Biblical ethnology. After his death, the East India Company in England erected a statue of him in St Paul's Cathedral, showing him carrying the books of Manu. Sanskrit texts were now positioned as a boost to Biblical history, and not as a heathen threat. Jones served as an early appropriator of Hinduism in order to enhance the credibility of Christianity. The conservative Protestant establishment recognized him for this complex if convoluted role.[21]

Another reason for early Indologists' infatuation with India was the work of Lord Monboddo (1714–99), who linked ancient India to

Egypt. However, the eventual decipherment of Egyptian hieroglyphics disproved his theory of the unity of Egyptian and Sanskrit. It was an academic fashion at that time to map Puranic descriptions of Indian places onto Biblical geography and European topography.[22] Ancient Ireland's history was 'proven' by evidence from Sanskrit texts, with Mosaic Ethnology serving as the governing paradigm.[23] In other words, the integral unity of Indian civilization was compromised, as its various components were separated from each other and from the Indian context, and selectively used as devices to boost Biblical and European supremacy.

In summary, Jones's work brought together three implicit principles:

1. He used Moses' account in the Bible of the origin of all the peoples of the world as his ethnology to classify everyone.
2. The chronology of events found in non-Western texts had to fit the time-periods mandated by the Christian officials. What did not fit was either distorted to make it fit, or rejected as myth, or simply ignored.
3. The ancient wisdom found in Sanskrit texts was given great respect in the context of humanity's shared heritage, and selectively appropriated and used as evidence to argue in favor of Christianity.

Following Jones's work, German and British strands of Indology shaped the Victorian era's ideas and policies on India. Unlike the British, the Germans were not obsessed with colonialism, but were interested in mining Indian knowledge to build a Germanic identity. Some Germans plagiarized Indian thought while others argued against it, and both these camps shaped what became known as the German thought.

Some British evangelists, such as those in the Pritchard School, co-opted Jones's works into their own notions of the racial inferiority of Indians. Other evangelists, like Robert Caldwell, sought to separate north Indians from south Indians and foster an anti-north Dravidian identity (This is examined in Chapter Six). British Sanskritists have had an enduring effect on the British conception of India and influenced subsequent Eurocentric constructions of Indian history and ethonography. Trautmann describes how they shaped the 'principles of classification and interpretation at the highest level of generalization, which gave a degree of overall organization and intelligibility to the vast masses of ethnographic materials the personnel of the British Indian administration generated'.[24] This process can be seen as an Indological legacy, which established overarching categories and presumptions about India, that have been passed down through generations of scholars.

Yale linguist Joseph Errington's recent book, *Linguistics in a Colonial World*,[25] explains the role of William Jones to pave the way for the claim that the earliest speakers of Sanskrit belonged to the Aryan 'race'. This view was denounced by some European scientists at that time, but managed to become mainstream due to the rhetorical power of the early colonial Indologists who worked unchallenged and were exalted by colonial authorities. Gradually, in certain circles the idea of an Aryan race was seen as inappropriate and consequently, the terms 'Indo-European' or 'Proto-Indo-European' slowly became acceptable euphemisms for the imagined race. Errington writes about the immense power of colonial linguistics in these fabrications:

> One influential approach to colonialism as a world historical phenomenon, then, is to read complex, scattered events of four centuries into patterns of more and stronger flows of people, goods, capital, and technology around the globe . . . From this angle, linguists can be regarded as a small, rather special group of colonial agents who . . . devised necessary conduits for communication across lines of colonial power. However different the methods they used or objects they described, they transformed familiar alphabets into images of strange speech: their writing systems, or orthographies, were the common beginning point for the work of writing grammars, dictionaries, instructional texts, and so on . . .[26]

Colonial Indologists developed the discourse that even though the initial Aryan invasion from Europe to the Indian subcontinent had brought an infusion of civilization, the Indians had later degenerated.

Colonialism was, therefore, seen as a good thing since it was a continuation of the previous infusion of the civilized Aryan-European culture into the corrupted Asian milieu. Europeans were needed to lift the degraded Indian brothers to their past glory. By the early twentieth century, it became seen as a matter of fact that the British colonizers were simply following in the footsteps of the earlier, superior Euro-Aryans entering India. The *Oxford History of India*, a standard textbook for candidates in the Indian Civil Service and higher education, made the idea of race explicit:

> [F]rom the Vedic hymns it has been possible to piece together a reasonably coherent picture of the Aryan invaders on their first impact with the black, noseless [flat-nosed] dasyus who comprised their native opponents and subjects.[27]

One Hundred Years of British Indological Institutions

The newfound Indological knowledge became recognized as an efficient tool for undermining Indian civilization and establishing British supremacy. A vast educational infrastructure was set up both in India and Britain to deal specifically with the production and dissemination of information about India from a colonial perspective. These institutions employed native Indians as collaborators to gain their knowledge, in an effort to map Indian texts and Sanskrit terms onto European frameworks. Also, the colonists wanted to use the Indian informants to influence other Indian scholars, using them as intermediaries to alter the dynamics of native scholarship in the long run.

Protestant evangelists and colonialists of the East India Company set up separate Indological institutions.[28] Many of these institutions were constituted with mandates to weaken the Indian civilization and strenghen the British side. Some of the primary institutions established by Britain in the early years of Indology are shown in Fig 4.2.

Fig 4.2 : Colonial Centers for Evangelical-Indological Nexus

Year	Institution	Purpose
1784	Asiatic Society, Calcutta	Promoting Orientalism as represented by William Jones. Among its major accomplishments was the decipherment of the Brahmi inscriptions of Ashoka. But only in 1829 did it start to admit Indians as members; until then, Indians were used as helpers/native informants, without a voice.
1800	College of Fort Williams, Calcutta	Three-year education for all 'writers' of East India Company before being assigned to different posts across India.
1806	East India College, England (Charles Grant had key role)	To prevent the risk of the young English lads 'going native' and compromising their English ways, the goal was to innoculate young Englishmen against Indian culture prior to sending them to India-based colleges and posts.[88]
1814	College of Fort St George, Madras	Founded by colonial administrator Francis Whyte Ellis, an important figure in identifying Tamil as belonging to a distinct linguistic family. It gathered and translated Tamil and Telugu manuscripts.
1818	Serampore Seminary, Calcutta	Founded by missionaries to train Indians for evangelism.
1823	Royal Asiatic Society, London with branches in Madras and Bombay	Founded as British counterpart to William Jones's Asiatic Society of Calcutta.
1827	Boden Chair, Oxford, England	In order to rule over Indians, officials of East India Company were trained here in Indian languages and culture. Sanskrit developed as a field of academic study. There were professorships of Sanskrit at University College, London (1852), Edinburgh (1862) and Cambridge (1867).
1862	Haileybury and Imperialist Service College	Many pioneers of the social sciences got their education at this college, which was set up explicitly to educate the East India Company's civil servants about the people of India. These pioneers included Malthus and Bentham.
1888	Indian Institute, Oxford	Set up by Monier Williams.

The role of such institutions in producing skewed knowledge about India is further illustrated by a remark in the preface to the famous *Sanskrit–English Dictionary* by Sir Monier Williams (1819–99). As the professor occupying the prestigious Boden Chair for Sanskrit Studies at Oxford, Monier Williams explained the objective of Col Joseph Boden, who endowed that prestigious Chair.[30] Monier Williams wrote:

> Col Boden stated most explicitly in his will (dated Aug. 15, 1811) that the special object of his munificent bequest was to promote the translation of the scriptures into Sanskrit; so as to enable his countrymen to proceed in the conversion of the natives of India to the Christian religion.[31]

Monier Williams also famously wrote:

> When the walls of the mighty fortress of Brahmanism are encircled, undermined, and finally stormed by the soldiers of the cross, the victory of Christianity must be signal and complete.[32]

Colonial Indology was based on collaborations between Western academics and Indian scholars.[33] This approach can be compared to similar arrangements in today's south Asian studies, which involve collaborations between the US government, corporations, private foundations, universities, and human rights groups. These linkages, and their ability to control Indian institutions, will be explored later in the book.

5

Lord Risley Morphs Jati-Varna into Race

Once the eighteenth-century European scholars had invented 'Race Science', colonial administrators were quick to recognize the potential of this emerging field and utilized it as an effective governing tool. Employing imaginary racial categories based on vague Biblical reference points, they imposed these racist categories like signposts on top of the many distinctive regional and linguistic communities in India. These imported classifications led to greater fragmentation and conflicts within the country. Max Müller's interpretation of Vedic literature in terms of a clash between two racial groups, led him to search for physical features in the Vedas that would identify the groups physically. And so, Müller tentatively interpreted nose-length as one such differentiating feature.

Sir Herbert Hope Risley (1851–1911) was a powerful colonial bureaucrat at the Royal Anthropological Institute, and developed the Nasal Index based on Max Müller's speculation. This Nasal Index, much like Phrenology, became a tool of Race Science in an effort to classify the traits of Indian communities. During the four decades of his stay in India, Risley made an extensive study of Indian communities, based on the Nasal Index. His goal was to separate the Aryan communities from the non-Aryan communities.

His taxonomical classification and massive documentation of Indian jatis froze the dynamic quality and mobility found in the jati system within the varna matrix.[1] Various colonially inspired studies transformed jatis into racial categories rather than identities based on occupation. The Nasal Index not only separated the jatis into Aryan and non-Aryan, it also classified those considered non-Aryan as distinct from mainstream Hindu society. Risley compared the black plantation-workers in America with the so-called non-Aryan communities in India. This foreshadows the Afro-Dalit-Dravidian projects of today, which are essentially the expansion of Risley's project of ethnic fragmentation of India.

Building on Max Müller's Work

Prior to colonialism, the jati-varna system in India had little, if anything, to do with race, ethnicity, or genetics. It was better understood as a set of distinctions based on traditional or inherited social status derived from work roles. Jati is a highly localized and intricately organized social structure. One of the important aspects of jati, which was conspicuously overlooked by western Indologists, is its dynamic nature – allowing social mobility as well as occupational diversification.[2] These rural social structures were more horizontally organized than vertically stratified. It was this inherent feature of the jati-varna system that led Gandhi to postulate the model of 'oceanic circle' for the ideal Indian village society, rather than the Western pyramidal model.[3]

Nevertheless, the colonial imposition of the hierarchical view, coupled with distortions of jati in order to fit it into a racial framework, grossly distorted the characteristics of jati and greatly amplified its negative features. Max Müller, who was largely responsible for entrenching the racial framework for studying jati, had his own evangelical motive. In his view, caste:

> . . . which has hitherto proved an impediment to conversion of the Hindus, may in future became one of the most powerful engines for the conversion not merely of the individuals, but of whole classes of Indian society.[4]

Max Müller's interpretation of the *Rig Veda* claimed that only the first three varnas are Aryan, while the fourth, shudra, is not Aryan. However, he explicitly admitted that there was no evidence of physical differences between Aryans and non-Aryans in Sanskrit texts. He made only one incidental reference to physical differences – that noses were described differently for different tribes in the *Rig Veda*. He based this notion on a single Sanskrit word, *anasa* (*Rig Veda*: V.29.10), that was used infrequently. Müller himself drew no important conclusions from this casual observation. But his prejudice was passed on through others who were more eager to do the dirty work openly. One of the common threads throughout the West's study of India has been the manner in which subsequent scholars pick and choose from someone else's work, often out of context, and with their own arbitrary assignment of priorities. This is what happened between Max Müller's writing and its manipulative use by Risley years later.

The younger Risley was greatly influenced by the senior and legendary figure of Max Müller. The development of racist theories between these two men was an important step in shaping the future identities of people across India. Publicly, Müller was cautious and wanted to protect his image, so he criticized the use of linguistics for racial profiling. But indirectly and privately, he encouraged it in various ways. For instance, Müller gave the following input in a private letter to Risley, prior to Risley's census of 1901:

> It may be that in time the classification of skulls, hair, eyes, and skin may be brought into harmony with the classification of language. We may even go so far as to admit, as a postulate, that the two must have run parallel, at least in the beginning of all things.[5]

In the same letter, he encouraged Risley by saying that students of ethnology have regarded 'the skull, as the shell of the brain' to be an indicator of 'the spiritual essence' of the person.[6] In other words, Max Müller spoke from both sides of his mouth when it came to racial implications of cultural and linguistic factors. This ambiguity was often deliberately nuanced in codified terms, which enabled more blatantly racist men like Risley to proceed further.

Ronald Inden has pointed out that Max Müller's caution against conflating language with race was an act of hypocrisy:

> We should not be misled by this into thinking that these scholars were anti-racist. They did not have to rely on a theory of race as such, for they had their own global theory that was fully able to inferiorize the languages (and by implication the cultures) of the other purely on linguistic grounds. Max Müller's linguistic taxonomy was a Hegelian hierarchy in which . . . cultural geography [becomes] the same as world history.[7]

Risley's Race Science

Risley took the casual Vedic nose-reference in Müller's writings, and turned it into the centerpiece of his racist ethnology of India. He further distorted Müller's interpretations of the *Rig Veda*. Without having any Sanskrit knowledge and relying solely upon Müller's works, he falsely stated that the Vedas had '*frequent* references to the noses of the people whom the Aryans found in possession of the plains'. He commented that nobody who glanced at the Vedas could miss such accounts. He wrote that the Aryans '*often* spoke' of the noses of the aborigines. This was simply not the case.

Risley became the leading authority on Indian ethnology. His long and powerful tenure in the British civil service in India lent strength to his ideas. His work became institutionalized within the workings of the British Empire. He was appointed the commissioner for India's censuses, from where he imposed his taxonomy and racial framework for Indian people. He created mutually exclusive ethnic categories and using the census assigned them legal signifcance. In 1910, Risley became president of the Royal Anthropological Institute.[8] To this day, Indian society's legal framework is Risley's creation, and his taxonomy of India's communities dominates today's caste wars and shapes Indian politics.

Risley wrote that he wanted his 'scientific' research to 'detach considerable masses of non-Aryans from the general body of Hindus'.[9] He adopted the popular Race Science measurement methods used by

French experts, according to which physical traits, such as the size of the nose, were a more reliable measure than skin color. Risley was an enthusiastic champion of the newly fashionable science called anthropometry, which measured various parts of the head to characterize different peoples. He used his measurements of people in India to conclude that there was a remarkable correspondence between two kinds of data, namely, (i) the 'gradations of type' as brought out by certain indices of head measurements, and (ii) the 'gradations of social preference'. This, he wrote, 'enables us to conclude that the community of races, and not, as has frequently been argued, the community of function, is the real determining principle . . . of the caste system'.[10] His 1891 ethnographic study of Bengal became the model for similar studies across India. His program measured Bengali heads and noses with calipers in order to establish hierarchies based on physical body dimensions.

Risley's Nasal Index became the standard in the science of anthropometry for British classification of Indians, with data pouring in to compare Dravidians, Santhals, and other communities, based on nose dimensions. Risley used his clinical data to pronounce far-reaching conclusions. Besides claiming to validate his two-race theory of Aryan and non-Aryan populations in India, he graded various castes according to the Nasal Index. He wrote: 'The social position of a caste varies inversely to its Nasal Index'.[11] Using his Nasal Index data, he went even further and classified jatis as Hindu, and tribes as non-Hindu. This is how the category of 'tribes' became officially institutionalized, the definition of which is still used for legal purposes in India. Risley was particularly interested in measuring what he called the 'wild tribes' of India. He claimed that different castes were biologically separate races. These classifications were *enforced* through the British censuses of India that were carried out every ten years and required every jati to submit its data based on the official classification system of the British.

The Vedas were interpreted to show clear and emphatic racial distinctions between Aryans and aborigines. A major reference work in 1912 translated Vedic Dasas and Dasyus as 'dark-skinned savages', whereas classical Indian interpreters like Sayana had explained their differences as being one of faith and language only.[12] Colonial Indologists also stretched and distorted Max Müller's interpretation of varna and used it to mean white/black races, citing the histories of the south of the United States as well as South Africa to claim that the same kind of racial north/south divide existed in India as well. The mapping of Aryan/non-Aryan Indians to white/black in the sense of Western racism was made explicit and decisive. Trautmann criticizes this 'over-reading' and 'text-torturing' of Vedic literature to fit into Western racism. He concludes:

> The racial theory of Indian civilization alludes to racial attitudes of whites towards blacks, found in the segregated southern United States after the Civil War and in South Africa, as a constant of history, or rather as a transcendent fact immune to historical changes that is as operative in the Vedic period as it is now.[13]

Risley Freezes the Castes

Risley took Max Müller's linguistic hierarchies and turned them into a solid link between language and race. He reasoned: 'That some races produce sounds which other races can only imitate imperfectly is a matter of common observation, and may reasonably be ascribed to differences of vocal machinery'.[14] His Aryan/non-Aryan divide was very concrete and based on anthropometrical evidence rather than philology.[15] The British colonial administration claimed that science was being used for partitioning Indians into divergent camps.

Based on his research, Indians were classified into seven major races located on a linear scale, with Aryans and Dravidians as the two opposite poles. He also organized 'social types' into seven groups. To protect himself, he wrote numerous disclaimers against blatant racism, and against taking things too far. Yet that was precisely what he did and wanted others to do. He claimed that according to his data, 'the correspondence between the two sets of groupings', namely, the seven races and the seven social types, was sufficiently close.

He thereby concluded that Indian tribes had turned into castes. He described the various tribal types in the order of their primitiveness, positioning the Dravidians as the lowest, assigning manual labor as their 'birthright', along with human sacrifices to a goddess.[16] Those tribes that had developed professional specialization became castes, while those that had remained in a limited geographic territory were still classified as tribes.

Scholars such as Risley claimed that the European society had evolved quite differently. He wrote that: 'In Europe, indeed, the movement has been all in the opposite direction. The tribes consolidated into nations; they did not sink into the political impotence of caste'.[17] Fig 5.1 shows Risley's theory of how races ended up forming nations in Europe, while India lacked any sense of nationhood due to caste as the form.

Fig 5.1 Divergent Evolution of Race in India and Europe According to Risley

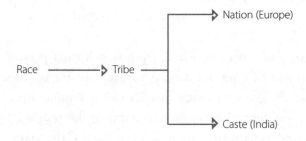

In India, the once-glorious Aryans had become contaminated by intermixing with the inferior Dravidians, leading to the caste system. Risley wrote: 'In India alone were the Aryans brought into close contact with an unequivocally black race'.[18] The conquering 'men of the dominant race' have 'intercourse with the women whom they have captured'. But it is 'out of the question' that the 'men whom they have conquered' should be allowed 'equal rights in the matter of marriage'. So, it is white men having sex with women of color that produces the various inferior offspring races of half-breeds.[19] The motive, in Risley's perception, was, 'the antipathy of the higher race for the lower, of the fair-skinned Aryan for the black Dravidian', which he claimed was actually based verbatim on the Vedas.[20] According to him, this is how caste came about in India. He was knighted by Britain soon after he published his caste theories. His thesis on India resembled Social Darwinism, in that the superior racial groups were quite naturally and properly at the top of society, where they had arrived through a process of natural selection.[21] He argued that 'the caste, tribe or race to which he belongs' is the most reliable form of identity that an Indian could be expected to know.

As the commissioner of the 1901 census of India, Risley wrote the section on caste, which was published in the highly influential *Imperial Gazetteer of India*,[22] and became the template for academicians and colonial administrators to do their studies. He decided that Indians consisted of 2,378 main castes and tribes (with sub-castes), and 43 races. To implement his hierarchy of castes, he decided not to list them in alphabetical order in the census forms, but rather in order of what he considered 'social preference' based on his evaluation of 'native public opinion'.[23] Thus, a hierarchy was constructed and made official.

The bewildering array of castes he listed, from which each person was required to choose when filling out official government forms, ran into so many pages that it 'gives so much trouble to the enumerating and testing staff and to the central offices which compile the results'.[24] He acknowledged the administrative sources of error in the data-gathering, because the caste identities selected by people would:

> . . . undergo a series of transformations at the hands of the more or less illiterate enumerator who writes them down in his own vernacular, and of the abstractor in the central process of sorting, referencing, cross-referencing, and corresponding with local authorities, which ultimately result in the compilation of a table . . . .[25]

Once his structures got established in the colonial bureaucracy, Risley wanted to distance himself from the racial implications he had set in motion, and to blame the whole thing on the peculiarities of the Indian mind. Having created a ridiculously complex and administratively unworkable system, he blamed the Indians for lacking the intellect to apply it. For example, he claimed that India's negative condition had been:

> ... promoted and stimulated by certain characteristic peculiarities of the Indian intellect – its lax hold of facts, its indifference to action, its absorption in dreams, its exaggerated reverence for tradition, its passion for endless division and subdivision, its acute sense of minute technical distinction, its pedantic tendency to press a principle to its farthest logical conclusion, and its remarkable capacity for imitating and adapting social ideas and usages of whatever origin.[26]

Risley translated the dharma of various jatis as 'race sentiments', and made it his ambition to scientifically prove that a comparatively pure 'Aryan type' existed in North India.[27] His obsession with noses caught on with other colonial administrators. For example, noses of Indians became the subject of scientific inquiry for Edgar Thurston, author of the voluminous *Castes and Tribes of Southern India* (1909). Thurston even used his 'Lovibond Tintometer' (originally an instrument for quality-testing in breweries) to measure the racial features of Indian villagers.[28]

Risley's views that 'caste is race' and that 'social position of caste varies inversely as Nasal Index' were opposed by a few scholars, based on scientific arguments and data. But such critics were marginalized and ignored, and even felt the personal animosity of the powerful Risley.[29] There was also Indian criticism of Risley's work, which he simply ignored.[30]

It is interesting to note that Risley used American slavery as his frame to project the interaction of Aryan invaders with the native Dravidians, calling it 'the same way as some planters in America behaved to the African slaves, whom they imported'.[31] He explained that this racial interaction 'formed the ultimate basis of caste'.[32] As we shall see later in Chapter Twelve, these false racial categories paved the way for the subsequent Afro-Dalit-Dravidian movements. It also fanned the flames of anti-Brahmin movements.

Ambedkar Demolishes Nasal Index Racism

Dr Ambedkar (1891–1956), a Dalit leader who was also the architect of the Indian constitution, was a historian and scholar of ancient Indian society. After studying the voluminous Nasal Index data of various castes across India that had been published by anthropologists, he came to a striking conclusion using Risely's own data to disprove his thesis:

> The measurements establish that the Brahmin and the Untouchables belong to the same race. From this it follows that if the Brahmins are Aryans, the Untouchables are also Aryans. If the Brahmins are Dravidians the Untouchables are also Dravidians. If the Brahmins are Nagas, the Untouchables are also Nagas. Such being the facts, the theory . . . must be said to be based on a false foundation. [33]

Appendix A offers additional details of Risley's Nasal Index and Ambedkar's debunking of it. It matters little whether such ideas have any basis in fact. Once an idea becomes entrenched in the institutional machinery and eventually in the collective imagination of the public, it can be used for all sorts of exploitation.

6

Inventing the 'Dravidian' Race

Colonial administrators and evangelists were able to divide and rule the peoples of the Indian subcontinent, based on imaginary histories and racial myths – to the extent of inventing an entire race called 'Dravidians'. This application of Race Science to India included many conflicting concepts and contradictions that are too numerous and preposterous to explore in great detail here. Instead, this chapter traces how evangelical and colonial interests worked in tandem with ethno-linguistic scholarship to fabricate the Dravidian identity.

British Colonial administrators, such as Francis Whyte Ellis and Alexander D. Campbell, studied the grammar of Tamil and Telugu and proposed that these languages might belong to a different language-family from other Indian languages. Another British administrator, Brian Houghton Hodgson, invented the term 'Tamulian' to refer to what he considered to be the non-Aryan indigenous population of India. While Ellis and Campbell proposed a linguistic theory, Hodgson had a race-based perspective.

But the catalyst who is credited with the construction of the 'Dravidian race' was a missionary-scholar from the Anglican Church. His name was Bishop Robert Caldwell (1814–91), an evangelist for the Society for the Propagation of the Gospel, who combined the linguistic theory of Ellis with a strong racial narrative. He proposed the existence of the Dravidian race in his *Comparative Grammar of the Dravidian Race,* which enjoys extreme popularity with Dravidianists to this day. Bishop Caldwell proposed that the Dravidians were in India before the Aryans, but got cheated by the Brahmins, who were the cunning agents of the Aryan. He argued that the simple-minded Dravidians were kept in shackles by Aryans through the exploitation of religion. Thus, the Dravidians needed to be liberated by Europeans like him. He proposed the complete removal of Sanskrit words from Tamil. Once the Dravidian mind would be free of the superstitions imposed by Aryans, Christian evangelization would reap the souls of Dravidians.

Fig 6.1 summarizes the role played by colonial administrators and the Anglican Church in this racist enterprise.

Fig 6.1 British Colonial Evangelical Construction of Encouraged Dravidian Identity

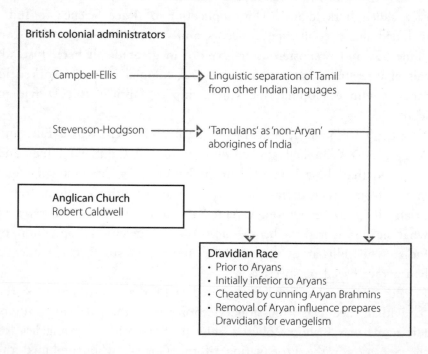

Hodgson Invents 'Tamulian'

In 1801, H.T. Colebrooke (1765–1837) published an important article which claimed that all Indian languages originated from Sanskrit. But by 1816, when Franz Bopp (1791–1867) was establishing the foundations of comparative philology, a critical role was played by Alexander D. Campbell and Francis Whyte Ellis, collector of Madras, who claimed that the south Indian family of languages was not derived from Sanskrit. Ellis had influential friends at College of Fort St George in Madras, which was an active center for producing colonial knowledge about India and teaching new officers arriving in India. Trautmann refers to this as the 'Madras School of Orientalism'.[1] There was rivalry between the Calcutta and Madras schools of colonial Orientalists. Ellis explicitly broke ranks with the thesis supported by William Carey, a missionary-scholar in Calcutta's College of Fort Williams, that Sanskrit unified all the Indian languages. The Campbell-Ellis book, *Grammar of the Teloogoo Language* (1816), opened the door for later intervention in India's internal sociopolitical structures. It argued that Tamil and Telugu had a common, non-Sanskrit ancestor. No Indian thinker had made such a claim before.

Because the assumption of Mosaic ethnology was well established, it was important to secure both families of languages within that framework. Ellis claimed that Tamil is connected with Hebrew and also with ancient Arabic. Their logic was that since William Jones considered Sanskrit to be the language of Ham, and other scholars claimed that Sanskrit descended from Noah's oldest son, Japheth, by the process of elimination the remaining son of Noah, Shem, must be the ancestor of the Dravidian people. This made Dravidians a branch of the Scythians or in the same family as Jews.[2]

The next major milestone came in the 1840s, when Reverend John Stevenson (1798–1858), who was sent by the Scottish Missionary Society,[3] and Brian Houghton Hodgson (1800–94), proposed a category of 'aboriginal' languages. Into this category they lumped all the languages that are today classified in the Dravidian and Munda families that allegedly predated the arrival of Sanskrit from outside of India. In 1848–9, Hodgson came out with a very clear theory of Tamilians as the aborigines of India whose many languages were spread across the nation prior to the Aryan invasion.

In 1856, the aboriginal thesis received a major boost among scholars with the publication of *Comparative Grammar of Dravidian Languages* by Bishop Caldwell.[4] This work claimed that Dravidian was one of the major language-groups of the world.[5] Caldwell coined the term 'Dravidian' from the Sanskrit *dravida*, which was used in a seventh-century text to refer to the languages of south of India.[6]

Caldwell: Transforming Linguistics into Ethnology

Bishop Caldwell became one of the pioneering missionaries in South India who shaped what now flourishes as the Dravidian identity.[7] At the age of twenty-four, he arrived in Madras with the London Missionary Society, and later joined the Society for the Propagation of the Gospel. He divided Indians linguistically and religiously, and mapped some of these religions on to Biblical frameworks. He became the Bishop of Tirunelveli, and his extensive research resulted in one of the most influential books on south Indian identity: *A Political and General History of the District of Tinnevely* (1881), published by the East India Company's Madras Presidency.

His work had far-reaching consequences. It established the theological foundation for Dravidian separatism from Hinduism, backed by the Church. It was accompanied by Christian usurpation of many of the classical art-forms of South India. The concept of dissociating Tamils from mainstream Hindu spirituality provided Caldwell an ethical rationale for Christian proselytization.[8] Eighty years after his death, a statue of Caldwell was erected in Chennai's Marina Beach alongside the statue of another missionary scholar, G.U. Pope. It is a major landmark in that city today.

Timothy Brook and Andre Schmid, in their work on the creation of identities in Asia, explain Caldwell's importance as the founder of today's Dravidian identity:

It was through his *Comparative Grammar* (1856) that he systematically laid the foundation of Dravidian ideology . . . It was not so much the philological findings in the work that had such a profound impact, as the way Caldwell interpreted and expressed them in the lengthy introduction and appendix. He not only managed to erect a racial, linguistic, and religio-cultural divide between the minority Brahmin and majority non-Brahmin (Dravidian) population of South India, but also provided a systematic project for reclaiming and recovering an ancient and 'pure' Dravidian language and culture.[9]

The missionaries' strategy was two-pronged: First, they intensely studied the devotional Tamil literature and praised it in glowing terms to Tamil scholars. Second, they projected the Tamil culture as being very different and totally independent from the rest of India. Their work provided the ideological underpinnings of later Tamil racist politics. Chandra Mallampalli, a Christian scholar, explains:

> South Indian political culture of non-Brahminism drew its inspiration from Dravidian ideology: this ideology posited a distinct linguistic and racial identity for south Indians. Non-Brahmin agitators pitted Dravidian culture, which most often championed the Tamil language, against Hindu, Aryan or Sanskritic cultures from the North. Champions of Dravidianism and non-Brahminism drew upon the cultural and linguistic resources provided by missionaries such as Robert Caldwell and G.U. Pope.[10]

Missionary scholarship stimulated a new local ethnic identity, which was instructed to reject its Hindu nature. It became strategic to show that Tamil religion had strong ethical underpinnings, on par with 'civilized' religions, and that 'civilized' meant monotheistic. These positive features were isolated and claimed to be indigenous to the Tamils, and shown to be in opposition to the 'foreign' traits that were attributed to the Aryans. Historical and philological works were produced to 'discover' that quasi-Christianity had already existed in the earliest Tamil literature. Among these discoveries emerged the myth that St Thomas had preached Christianity in South India shortly after the death of Christ, an idea promoted mainly by the Catholic Church to bolster its standing.

To achieve this new Christian-friendly identity, two kinds of Tamil religious literature became privileged. One kind was a universal, 'non-sectarian' humanism, that was best embodied in the *Kural* belonging to the post-Sangam Age. The other was the Saiva Siddhanta corpus of scriptures, seen as representing a native monotheistic counterpart to Christianity. Brook and Schmid identify two key steps in the way these Tamil classics were used: first, separating Brahmins and non-Brahmins using the *Kural*; and second, linking Dravidian ideology with Saiva Siddhanta as an interim step towards further linking it with Christianity:

> Caldwell's central argument was that Dravidian languages, peoples and cultures had a genealogy independent of those of Brahmans. This independence and difference followed, he argued, from the fact that the Dravidians were of a completely different racial stalk, what he called a Scythian stalk . . . This radical distinction underpinned Caldwell's celebration of Dravidian 'identity'.[11]

Caldwell essentialized the Dravidians by constructing their racial 'others' as Brahmins. He claimed that Sanskrit was read in the South only by 'the descendents of those Brahminical colonialists'.[12]

Through this manipulation, the Brahmins were made into the colonizers while the actual colonizers like Caldwell were projected as saviors of the Tamil people!

A Conspiracy Theory is Born: Cunning Aryan Brahmins Exploited Innocent Dravidians

On the one hand, Caldwell emphasized Dravidian identity for the purpose of dividing them from the pan-Indian body of Hindus, and on the other, he considered Dravidians as inferior to the Aryans because the Aryans were seen as racially derived from the Europeans. According to him, Dravidians had derived their 'mental culture' and 'higher civilization' from the superior Aryans. But they did not achieve parity with Aryans, because the gifts of the Aryans were 'more than counterbalanced by the fossilizing caste rules, the impractical pantheistic philosophy, and the cumbersome routine of inane ceremonies, which were introduced amongst them by the guides of their new social state'.[13] So Dravidians were inferior, but they could be civilized. However, the cunning Brahmins, in the guise of civilizing them, had actually subdued them by making them unaware prisoners in the 'new social state'.

Caldwell's recommended solution was that south Indians should disown Sanskrit influences and rediscover their original culture through Biblical categories. Those elements in the south Indian religious life which could thus be seen as similar to Christianity were the 'real' Tamil religion, while those that did not fit such mapping were blamed as Brahminical influences that ought to be removed. For instance, he claimed that Tamil did not have its own word for 'idol', and that such words had been brought from Sanskrit, and ought to be removed:

> Tamil can readily dispense with the greater part or the whole of its Sanskrit, and by dispensing with it, rise to a purer and more refined style . . . Of the entire number of words which are contained in this formula there is only one which could not be expressed with faultless propriety . . . in equivalent of pure Dravidian origin: that word is 'graven image' or 'idol'. Both word and thing are foreign to primitive Tamil usages and habits of thought; and were introduced into Tamil country by Brahmins, [along] with the Puranic system of religion and worship of idols.[14]

De-Indianizing the Tamil Traditions

Since colonial days, there has been an ongoing attempt to construct an ethnic-religious Tamil identity separate from the rest of India, and to find Christian roots for this so-called 'Tamil religion'. Once the Tamil language was mapped on to a non-Sanskrit framework, particularly an anti-Sanskrit framework, the same process began with the Tamil literature. This entailed manipulating the interpretations of the literary core of Tamil tradition, which consists of three main elements: (i) *Thirukural*, a classical Tamil text containing ethical literature that is very much a part of the Indian Smriti tradition; (ii) Saiva Siddhantha, a Vedanta branch of Saiva philosophy; and (iii) a huge body of classical devotional literature. These are briefly discussed below, followed by a more in-depth treatment.

Fig 6.2 shows the processes used by Caldwell and Pope to create the Christian Dravidian identity. The main Tamil classics mentioned are introduced next.

Thirukural

From Robert Caldwell's point of view, nothing ethical could emerge from the Dravidian mind, either by itself or under the influence of Vedic religion. Consequently, he attributed the *Thirukural* to Jain influences. G.U. Pope, another evangelist, maintained that it was Christian influence on Thiruvalluvar that produced this literary work. Christian scholars at his time, and for decades later, rejected this theory. However, it is being revived today by evangelical movements in Tamil Nadu.

Saiva Siddhantha

Dravidianist scholars have tried to position Saiva Siddhantha as something unique to Tamil spirituality and not linked to Hinduism. Although the traditional works on Saiva Siddhantha cite the Vedas as their authority, this is circumvented by conjuring up a separate Tamil spirituality from a distant past. For G.U. Pope and other evangelists, Saiva Siddhantha is seen as an approximation to, but not an equal of, Christianity. Thus, it is to be used as an indirect and diluted form of Christianity that works as a stepping stone towards direct, pure Christianity. Once people are convinced that for many centuries they have practiced a corrupted version of Christianity, it would be easy to upgrade them to the accepted or contemporary Christianity.

Tamil Devotional Literature

A great body of Tamil devotional and mystical literature composed by devotees and mystics over a period of centuries, forms the basis of Tamil spirituality. Though written in Tamil, this literature has a pan-Indian nature. Thus, all Saivaite hymns written in Tamil speak of Siva as living in the Himalayas and even address him as 'Arya'. Evangelists and Dravidianists fabricated the origins, and distorted the interpretation of their contents to suit their agendas.

Fig 6.2 De-Indianizing and Christianizing Tamil Spiritual Traditions

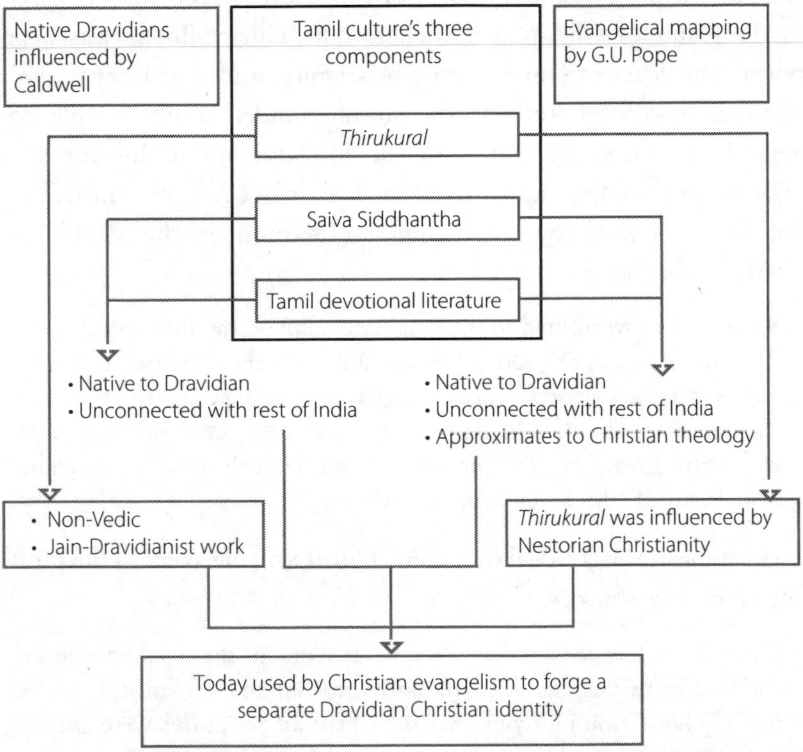

Christianizing the *Thirukural*

George Uglow Pope (1820–1908) was another legendary missionary Indologist[15] who played the lead role in claiming Tamil classical literature to be un-Indian, un-Hindu, and linked to Christianity. Pope's first translation was of the Tamil classic *Thirukural* (often simply called *Kural*), which is a Tamil treatise on ethics and conduct, written by the great sage Thiruvalluvar. Through the ages, this has been one of the most cherished works of Tamil literature, as explained in the closing remark of the entry for *Thirukural* in *The Encyclopedia of Indian Literature*: 'If a Tamil is asked to name one work in Tamil literature of 2,000 years, *Thirukural* would be the immediate response. *Kural* that encapsulates a whole universe in an atom, this tribute is more than a millennium old'.[16]

Once this decoupling of *Kural* from Hinduism had been achieved, Pope pushed the missionary case further. He declared that *Thirukural* was the result of Christian influence, that Thiruvalluvar was a great pioneer who learned ethics from Christianity, and that he was sharing it through his poem so that the simple-minded Tamil people could benefit from Christian ethics. In the introduction to his translation of *Thirukural*, Pope constructed a scenario of how Thiruvalluvar composed this work by borrowing the 'Sermon on the Mount' from Christian preachers:

> We are quite warranted in imaging Tiruvalluvar, the thoughtful poet, the eclectic . . . pacing along the seashore with the Christian teachers, and imbibing Christian ideas, tinged with the peculiarities of the Alexandrian school, and day by day working them into his own wonderful *Kurral* . . . the one Oriental book much of whose teaching is an echo of 'the Sermon on the Mount'.[17]

He unhesitatingly declared that *Thirukural* derived its inspiration from Christian sources:

> Christian influences were at the time at work in the neighbourhood, and that many passages are strikingly Christian in their spirit. I cannot feel any hesitation in saying that the Christian Scriptures were among the sources from which the poet derived his inspiration.[18]

Evangelists in the nineteenth-century India encouraged such ideas.[19] Their basic premise claimed that St Thomas, a direct disciple of Jesus Christ, preached in India starting in 52 CE. This will be explored in more detail in Chapter Eight and Chapter Nine. But these ideas had been rejected centuries earlier by mainstream Christianity, and even sometimes labeled as heresies. Even many pro-missionary Dravidianist scholars found it hard to accept such spurious claims.[20]

Many of those who rejected the theory of Christian influence claimed *Thirukural* as a Jain work[21] because Jainism was not a threat to be overcome, whereas Hinduism was. In fact, this trend can be traced to Bishop Caldwell himself, who surmised that a treatise on ethics with such lofty ideals could not have originated from within the indigenous Tamil tradition. Attributing *Thirukural* to Jain origins fit with his conviction of the ethnic inferiority of Tamils. This also compelled him to ascribe very late dates to classical Tamil literature.[22]

Caldwell was convinced that in the absence of Brahminical influence, the chief obstacle to the evangelization of Dravidians was the 'density of their ignorance'.[23] Therefore, attributing *Thirukural* to Jain missionaries, who had been in South India since ancient times, would provide a code of ethics relatively higher than aboriginal/Dravidian ethics, but still inferior to Christianity. It should be noted that Caldwell himself had no respect for Jainsim as such, considering it a form of atheism. However, mapping Tamil ideas on to the Jains was a useful tool. Brook and Schmid point this evangelical strategy through Caldwell's own words:

> . . . it may be expected that the Dravidian mind will ere long be roused from its lethargy, and stimulated to enter upon a brighter career. If the national mind and heart were stirred to so great a degree a thousand years ago by the diffusion of Jainism . . . it is reasonable to expect still more important results from the propagation of the grand and soul-stirring truths of Christianity.[24]

Thus, the claim of Jain origins of *Kural* was an interim vehicle to counteract Hinduism, in anticipation of a full-fledged Christian takeover that was hovering on the horizon. Pope's Christian-origin theory gradually became a cottage industry of evangelists and academicians repeating the fiction until it became the 'established fact'. Over time, the dissenting scholarship faded away, leaving the playing field to the divisive ideologues.

Erasing the Hindu Nature of *Kural*

One has to understand the unmistakable Hindu ethos of *Thirukural* in order to appreciate the damaging effect of this distortion on the subsequent generations of scholars. For example, the Hindu dharma recognizes pleasure or 'kama' as an integral part of life. This is reflected in the 250 couplets of *Thirukural's* third book, that are devoted to Kama Purushartha, and stands diametrically opposed to the Protestant puritanism professed by missionaries like Pope. Kamil Zvelebil explains that it was 'the nineteenth-Century Christian-oriented morality' which made early missionary translators declare the third book of *Kural* (the Kama Purushartha) as untranslatable 'without exposing the translator to infamy'. Pope admitted that his own Christian prejudice had 'kept him from reading the third part of the *Kural* for some years'.[25] Even after Pope eventually overcame his Christian narrow-mindedness and translated the third book of *Kural*, he apologized for it in the hope that, 'I shall be regarded as having done good service in doing so.'[26]

Also, there are many couplets in *Thirukural* that go directly against the cardinal concept of Jain *ahimsa* (non-harming). For instance, there is a Jain injunction against ploughing fields because it brings harm to the organisms in the soil.[27] The *Kural* violates this. It also opposes the Jain doctrine of *ahimsa* by advising that the king should execute murderers just like weeds are removed from the crop field.[28]

Additionally, *Kural* refers to the Puranas and other Hindu texts in many of its couplets, including frequent references to Hindu gods. Indra is mentioned in several couplets.[29] There is an obvious reference to the measuring of the world by Vamana, an incarnation of Vishnu.[30] *Kural* states that the goddess of wealth resides in the houses of men who show hospitality.[31] It warns against sloth as something disrespectful to Lakshmi.[32] In tune with the Hindu shastras, it links the prosperity and spirituality of the land to the rule of a just king.[33] It further states that the power of the king forms the mainstay of the scriptures of Brahmins and dharma.[34]

Christian theologians used *Kural* as a weapon to mobilize the Dravidians against Hinduism, by claiming that it was originally egalitarian and got later contaminated by Hinduism. But *Kural's* statements on egalitarianism are mixed. It explicitly condones the social norms of Indian society prevalent at that time. It says that even if a Brahmin forgets the Vedas he can learn them back, but that he must not lapse from the morality with which he is born.[35] It also states that those whom a king employs as ambassadors should be from a noble family.[36]

However, *Kural* does not mention the fourth purushartha of Hindu dharma, concerning *moksha* (liberation). Pope used this as evidence that Tamil society was morally degraded and uncultured, and hence Thiruvalluvar had left out *moksha* because he 'thought his people were not prepared for the higher teaching'.[37] Today's Dravidian scholarship has a different strategy, and interprets the absence of *moksha* to claim that the *Kural* rejected the other-worldly metaphysics of the Vedic Aryans.[38] But there is a simple non-convoluted explanation for this. Economist Ratan Lal Bose points out that many other Indian texts such as *Arthashastra,* discuss only three basic motivations (*purusharthas*) and that this is in tune with 'the traditional Indian view that there should be a perfect balance of the *trivarga* (three pursuits) – i.e. *dharma* (ethics), *artha* (material resources) and *kama* (fulfillment of sexual and other desires)'.[39] Justice Rama Jois points out that the popular Hindu law book *Manusmriti* also speaks of Trivarga.[40] Thus, there is nothing unique about Thiruvalluvar mentioning only the three *purusharthas* and leaving out the fourth; this has been a pan-Indian practice in works of ethics.

Mapping Saivism on to Christianity

The attempts to co-opt Saivism into Christianity were neither spontaneous nor the natural responses of missionaries who had discovered the beauty of a local spiritual tradition. It was a strategy used by colonial scholars only after the Saivite theologians effectively rebutted the initial attacks on Saivism.

In their very first encounter with Saivism, the protestant missionary scholars condemned Saivism in the strongest words possible. For example, the American Missionary Seminary (in Batticotta, Sri Lanka), a fundamentalist Protestant group working among Tamils, used its Tamil-English journal, *Morning Star* (1841), to attack Saivites and Tamils as living in darkness:

There is nothing in the peculiar doctrines and precepts of the Siva religion that is adapted to improve a man's moral character or fit him to be useful to his fellow men . . . If the world were to be converted to the Siva faith, no one would expect any improvement in the morals or the happiness of men. Every one might be as great a liar or cheat – as great an adulterer – as oppressive of the poor – as covetous – as proud, as he was before – without sullying the purity of his faith.[41]

The missionaries further claimed that Saivism was merely a creation of the Brahmins, that it contains nothing of value, and that it shares nothing with Christianity. This attack on Saivism proved to be counterproductive because it was too disrespectful towards such a cherished tradition, and was effectively countered by Sri Lankan Tamil Saivite scholars, such as Arumuga Navalar.[42]

Therefore, the strategy was changed into one of appropriation rather than denigration. Because Saiva Siddhantha is closely related to devotional music and dance, G.U. Pope considered it the most attractive target for Christian appropriation. In 1900, he brought out his translation of one of the most popular texts of the Saiva Siddhanta, called *Thiruvasakam*. He explained that its importance to missionaries was that Saivism could be respectfully projected as an earlier form of Tamil religion that shared common features with Christianity. For example, both taught that there is one supreme personal God and not a mere metaphysical abstraction of unity, as in Buddhism and Jainism. The Saiva text gave importance to the notion of guru, which Pope equated with Christ. He wrote that the author of the text:

> . . . also taught that it was the gracious will of Siva to assume humanity, to come to earth as a Guru [. . .] He announced that this way of salvation was open to all classes of the community. He also taught very emphatically the immortality of the released soul [. . .] It will be seen how very near in some not unimportant respects the Saiva system approximates to Christianity . . .[43]

Pope is remembered with gratitude by many Tamils for translating into English the devotional hymns of Manichavasagar, a great Saivaite saint of the ninth century CE, whose devotional songs are sung in every Siva temple in Tamil Nadu.[44] However, Pope's introductory note clearly reveals his elaborate evangelical intentions to map Saivism on to Hebrew psalms and Christian poetry:

> The fifty poems which are here edited, translated, and annotated are recited daily in all the great Caiva[45] temples of South India, are on every one's lips, and are as dear to the hearts of vast multitudes of excellent people there as the Psalms of David are to Jews and Christians . . . It should be earnestly desired that *the transfusion of much great European and sacred poetry into popular, easy, rhythmic Tamil verse resembling that of Manikka-Vacagar should be attempted.* If a foreigner has bestowed infinite pains (would that it had been with greater results!) on the study of the Thiruvasagam, perhaps some of the native scholars of South India, versed in English and Tamil, may be induced to inquire whether they cannot find fitting material for study, imitation and translation in that inexhaustible mine of beauty and profound thought which is opened up on English sacred verse, from the Hebrew psalms down to Christian poetry of the present day.[46]

Whenever Pope finds something positive about the Tamil poetry he wants to show it as resembling Christianity. Whatever he finds 'corrupt' is blamed on Hindu superstitions:

> It will be seen how very near in some not unimportant respects the Saiva system approximates to Christianity; and yet some of the corruption to which it has been led by what almost seems a necessity, are amongst the most deplorable superstitions anywhere to be found.[47]

Later Christian theologians taking their cue from Pope started portraying Saiva Siddhanta as closer to Christianity, and yet falling short of it. For example, a London-based Christian publication claimed in 1942:

> [Saiva Siddhanta] believes fully in a God of love. It also believes that this God of love, out of His boundless compassion, comes to the world to help His devotees. But it does not go further. The Christian belief is that Love goes further. God identified himself with man. He was born as Christ.[48]

Pope was ruthless when it came to eliminating every trace of Hinduism that contradicted Christian theology. In 1853, when a

Christian Tamil convert, Vedanayakam Sastri, composed Tamil hymns for church liturgy, Bishop Pope vehemently opposed him on the grounds that the composition contained a traditional Tamil poetic signature element, which Pope rejected as un-Christian. Stuart Blackburn, a scholar on Indian literary history, writes:

> Sastri defended, to no avail, the signature verses in his hymns as part of an ancient Tamil tradition of sacred poetry, intended to express and celebrate the devotee's devotion to his God with no connotations of self-aggrandizement . . . In 1853 the very year of Pope's appointment to Tanjore, the American missionary E. Webb published *Christian Lyrics for Private and Social Worship*, the first major published collection of Protestant hymns by Tamils, Webb noted in the title page that Vedanayaka Sastri was the author of most of the hymns in the collection, but he did not include the signature verses from the poems in this or in the edition that followed in 1859.[49]

This missionary success in selectively appropriating and spreading confusion has permeated academic Tamil studies ever since.

Revisionist History of Classical Tamil Literature

M.S. Purnalingam Pillai's book, *A Primer of Tamil Literature* (1904), took the missionary thesis as its basis and framed Tamil literary history in terms of the Aryan/Dravidian struggle. The *Kural* and Saiva Siddhanta were recontextualized as part of this framing. Pillai assigned the *Kural* to the *Sangam* period up to 100 CE, which he claimed was the most influential Tamil period and free from the influence of Aryans and Sanskrit. He echoed Pope's praise for *Kural* as the greatest masterpiece of the ancient Tamil paradise describing highly developed forms of religion and philosophy. He felt that the treatise contained a universal code of morals, that could be appreciated by the whole civilized world.[50]

According to Pillai's history of Tamil literature, the Sangam period was followed, between 100 CE and 600 CE, by the age of the Buddhists and the Jains. He emphasized that Buddhists and Jains (both as peoples and their religions) were non-Tamil outsiders. During this period, the Tamil nation was populated by three different ethnic groups: Tamils, Aryans and Buddhist/Jains. According to Pillai, while the Buddhists and Jains also came from North India, they, unlike the Aryans, 'lived peaceably with their neighbours', 'never attacked the ancient, unadulterated Saivaism', and were not caste-oriented.[51] Dravidianist-Evangelist narratives portray this period as conducive to the growth of Tamil literature, though ironically it subverted the native Tamil religion.

Pillai calls the next period 'The Age of Religious Revival', from 700 CE to 900 CE. He claimed that this was when the ancient Tamil religion began to reassert itself after several centuries of darkness, though it underwent several shameful compromises with 'Aryanism' in order to do so. He explains:

> In the course of centuries the Tamil Saivas, who were vegetarians and who had looked upon the Aryas as *mlecchas* for their [habits of] meat-eating and drinking intoxicants and as untouchables came, by the force of juxtaposition, of aryan adaptability, and of political contingencies, to be reconciled to the ways and habits of their neighbours and to accept the authority of the Vedas, [. . .] Saivaism, accepting the Vedic rule, became metamorphosed into Vedic or Vaidika Saivaism.'[52]

Pillai appealed to Tamils to purge the Saiva Siddhanta of all its Aryan and Puranic influences, and to return it to the pristine condition it had enjoyed in antiquity. He wrote:

> The Saiva Siddhanta is the indigenous philosophy of South India and the choicest product of the Tamilian intellect. [. . .] This high and noble system, based on the Agamas or Saiva scriptures, was corrupted by the puranic writers, whose sole object was to reconcile the Vedas and the Agamas [. . .] The Tamilar, overbourne by the political ascendancy of the Aryans, accepted the system, [. . .] Bhakti or loving piety, the root idea of the Saiva system, ennobled the persons, whatever their caste, colour or creed [. . .] Such a widely tolerant, ennobling, rationalistic faith has been made to assume the garb of a thoroughly intolerant, fictitious, and meanly selfish system. The Tamilar, therefore, are in duty, bound to throw off the puranic veil which dims their vision and to realise the old conception of

Him as enshrined in the ancient Tamil poems based on the Tamilian Agamas.[53]

A Primer of Tamil Literature was written specifically to fulfill university examination needs, and even included an appendix with sample questions for students. Through its widespread usage, it became what Ronald Inden has called the 'hegemonic text', and hence the prevailing consensus on the true, original 'Tamil religion' before it was allegedly corrupted by Hinduism.

Thus, we see how Tamil nationalism emerged in the search for a glorious past to counteract the inferiority complexes instilled by colonialism. It accomplished this by positioning itself against the 'Aryan religion'. This construction of a Tamil religion played to subaltern aspirations by claiming caste-free ethics based upon egalitarian bhakti.[54] Still, Pillai warned that the contemporary Saiva Siddhanta could not be called truly egalitarian as it sanctioned the social divide between high-caste and low-caste non-Brahmins. He called for the return to a purer Saiva Siddhanta of an imagined ancient pristine past.

'Tamil Religion' Becomes 'Early Indian Christianity'

The subsequent theories constructed by the missionaries were attempted to show that the *Kural* and Saiva Siddhanta were anti-Aryan and similar to Christianity. Recently, the highly endorsed evangelist propaganda book *India is a Christian Nation,*[55] builds upon the foundations started by Caldwell and Pope to reinterpret Tamil spirituality as a part of Christianity. It discusses 'the great possibilities to discern the hidden truths of Saivism and Vaishnavism as nothing but "Early Indian Christianity"'.[56]

The institutional and transnational support given to this thesis shall be discussed further in Chapter 9. Presently, suffice it to say that the colonial racial categorization of the Indian population, and the deconstruction of India's religions and spirituality, have become a deadly mixture leading towards a disastrous future.

Dravidian Racism and Sri Lanka

We have seen how the academic study of languages played a role in European Race Science, and how colonial administrators and evangelicals adapted this scholarship for a divide-and-conquer strategy. In Sri Lanka, pure fantasy was added to deepen the divisions of the racial identities. These are so strong today that people shed blood over them.

The present chapter traces this development, using the following key constructs:

Sinhalese-Aryan-Buddhist Identity

The Theosophical Society, founded in the US, used its South India base to trigger Buddhist revivalism in Sri Lanka by fashioning a Buddhist-Aryan-Sinhalese identity. This was meant to be a way to oppose aggressive colonial evangelism. The Sri Lankan Sinhalese began to see themselves as Aryans who had discovered Sri Lanka and brought civilization to it. In the process, they stigmatized Tamils as an inferior race. Things got out of control over time.

Sri Lankan Dravidian Identity

Meanwhile, the Theosophists propagated the idea of the lost continent of Lemuria, and this became popular in Tamil Nadu. From there it became integrated into the Dravidian grand-narrative and generated Dravidian racism, and finally started to spread to Sri Lankan Tamils. Already alienated by Sinhalese nationalism, the Sri Lankan Tamils embraced this form of Dravidianism to boost their own claims to a great antiquity. The Dravidian myth of the Lemurian origins allowed Tamils to claim that they were the indigenous population of Sri Lanka, and to describe the Sinhalese as alien Aryan intruders.

The Clash of Identities

Thus, two racial identities crystallized on the small island. The seeds sown by evangelical ethnography and nurtured by colonial administration created a harvest of human disaster that left about a hundred thousand dead in a long civil war.

Fig 7.1 summarizes the process.

Fig 7.1 Clash of Colonial-Evangelical Constructs in Sri Lanka

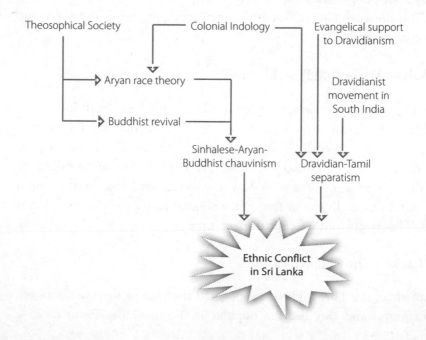

Outdated Geology Mixes with Theosophical Fantasy

As a reaction to Robert Caldwell's early depiction of Tamil inferiority, native Tamil scholars began to construct a positive and chauvinistic Tamil identity. They attempted to remove the racially inferior position given to Dravidians in Caldwell's narrative. Toward this end, they incorporated the theory of the lost continent of Lemuria, which had been formulated in 1864 by the British zoologist Philip Lutley Sclater (1829–1913).[1] According to this theory, a massive continent called Lemuria once spread across the vast Indian Ocean region from present-day Madagascar to India and Sumatra, and then it became submerged beneath the Indian Ocean. This was Sclater's explanation for similarities between the plants and animals of the two continents of Africa and India. This was yet another instance in which an idea from the natural sciences was used to support racist notions. In 1876, Frederick Engels added a Marxist twist to these fancy geological theories and helped to spread the Lemuria fantasy further.[2]

In the 1880s, Madam Helena Petrovna Blavatsky (1831–91), co-founder of the Theosophical Society, took this idea of Lemuria and popularized it among the occult circles. She claimed that Lemurians had 'built large cities, cultivated arts and sciences and knew astronomy, architecture, and mathematics to perfection'.[3] Blavatsky arrived in India in 1879, settled in Adayar, Madras, where she relocated the headquarters of the Theosophical Society.[4] She combined the fashionable Indo-Aryan ethnology with her spin on 'karmic evolution', to construct a mystical form of racism. She said that all races had originated 'from one single progenitor . . . who is said to have lived over 18,000,000 years ago, and also 850,000 years ago – at the time of the sinking of the last remnants of the great continent of Atlantis'.[5] Blavatsky believed that the Aryans were superior to others. Thus, in Theosophical fantasy, Atlantis (home of the white Europeans) came first, and then Lemuria, but the details varied depending on where the story was being told. Before the south Asian audiences, Atlantis was never mentioned, and Lemuria was discussed mixed with ancient Tamil memory of the sea devouring their old civilization.

Hindu image-worship was a gross superstition, according to Blavatsky, and this proved that Hindus were a race which had degenerated from the pristine Aryan religion. She wrote:

> Esoteric history teaches that idols and their worship died out with the Fourth Race, until the survivors of the hybrid races of the latter (Chinamen, African Negroes, etc.) gradually brought the worship back. The Vedas countenance no idols; all the modern Hindu writings do.[6]

Thus, the Vedas belonged to the foreign Aryans, who were pure, while the modern Hindus were degenerate bastard offsprings of these White Aryans mating with the inferior Dravidian natives. However, the Dravidians were now being given their own glorious past with their origins in Lemuria. Once brought into prominence by the Theosophists, this 'history' made its entry into the official manuals of British colonial administrators in India. Charles D. Maclean of the Indian Civil Service introduced Lemuria as the likely origin of the Tamils.[7] The Lemurian theory of Dravidian origins was also cited by Lord Risley, albeit with mild skepticism. Risley was the administrator, as we saw earlier, who classified all Indians by the sizes of their noses.[8]

Native Tamil scholars felt proud of this mythic sunken continent of their ancestors, and linked it to the ancient deluge mentioned in Tamil literature, that was said to have destroyed many Tamil cities. M.S. Poornalingam Pillai's book, *A Primer of Tamil Literature* (1904), explained the origin of Tamils thus: 'The Tamils or Tamilar were *certainly* the natives of the ancient Tamilaham or Lemuria, a continent in the Indian Ocean about the equator, submerged a hundred centuries ago'.[9] European racist histories were thus accepted and internalized by native Tamil scholars, who added their own ethno-supremacist spins to the narratives. T.R. Sesha Iyengar's book, *Dravidian India,* published in 1925, is hailed even today by anti-Hindu ideologues as 'one of the major pioneering books of Dravidology'.[10] The book weaves a picture of the Lemurian origins of the Tamils:

> Who then are these Dravidians? They are distinguished, says H. Risley, by their low stature, black skin, long heads, broad noses and long fore-arm, from the rest of the inhabitants of India.

They form the original type of the population of India . . . The Hebrew scriptures have preserved a distinct account of an appalling deluge . . . Geological research has shown that the Indian Ocean was once a continent and that this submerged continent, sometimes called Lemuria, originally extended from Madagascar to Malay Archipelago connecting South India with Africa and Australia . . . There are unmistakable indications in the Tamil traditions that the land affected by the deluge was contiguous with Tamilakam and that after the subsidence the Tamils naturally took themselves to their northern provinces . . .[11]

Thus, Risley's racist classification of Indians by different body-types became gradually projected into the common psyche of Tamil people as a scientifically proven fact. The Lemurian fantasy was mixed with the Biblical story of the Deluge and the sons of Noah. Now the Tamils had a new history and a new racial identity – all constructed using European notions.

Lemurian Origins Linkup with Bishop Caldwell

Devaneya Pavanar (1902–81), an Indian Christian Tamil scholar, combined the Lemurian theory with Caldwell's conspiracy theory of the 'cunning alien Brahmin keeping the Tamil subservient'. In the preface to his 1966 work, he wrote:

Westerners do not know as yet, that Tamil is a highly developed classical language of Lemurian origin, and has been, and is being still, suppressed by a systematic and coordinated effort by the Sanskritists both in the public and private sectors, ever since the Vedic mendicants migrated to the South, and taking utmost advantage of their superior complexion and the primitive credulity of the ancient Tamil kings, posed themselves as earthly gods (Bhu-suras) and deluded the Tamilians into the belief that their ancestral language or literary dialect was divine or celestial in origin.[12]

Pavanar's view continues to enjoy axiomatic status in Tamil studies. Even the Tamil Nadu state government's museum at Kanyakumari has an exhibit showing Lemuria (also known as Kumari Kandam). Many university textbooks as well as academic papers speak of Lemuria as a *proven fact,* even though for more than a century the idea of a sunken continent has been discarded by geologists. In 1970, for example, the education minister announced on the floor of Tamil Nadu legislative assembly that a Jesuit scholar had proven the Lemurian origin of Dravidians. He proclaimed that:

> Father Heras has shown how [Dravidian] civilization moved from Lemuria to southern India, and then reached Harappa and Mohenjodaro and from there latter went to the Tigris and Euphrates and Rome and so on . . . This also I learnt when I was studying at Annamalai University.[13]

The stranglehold of the Lemurian theory on the academic establishments of Tamil Nadu can be gauged by the following passage, excerpted from a research paper that was read at a seminar organized by Pondicherry Institute of Linguistics and Culture with Tamil Nadu government sponsorship in 2003:

> Speaking about Lemurian Tamils, Paavaanar will trace the development of Tamil between 100,000 and 50,000 BC. Spencer Wells and his team of scientists have now found out that the first man originated before 60,000 years. We Tamils somehow have become addicted to the use of the phrase 'two-thousand years old' to claim a hoary past for our culture. Christian calendar alone cannot be the period of inception of the Dravidian culture. Millions of years ago what happened, we have to indulge in a quest, and not be satisfied with the accidental unearthing of the Indus Valley Civilization.[14]

K.P. Aravaanan, former vice chancellor of a south Indian university, uses the thesis of Lemuria to assert an ethnic kinship between Dravidians and Africans:

> The Dravidians and black Africans might have belonged to one stalk of race . . . once there must have been some kind of land bridging both the African and Dravidian continents in the Indian Ocean . . . They called this lost continent 'Kumari'. Modern geography confirms the legendary theory of 'Lost Lemuria' (Kumari).[15]

The modern Afro-Dravidian movement sprang up by drawing on both the Hamitic myth and the Lemurian myth.

Theosophy – Buddhism Uses Aryans to Counter Evangelism

In parallel with the creation of a Dravidian separatist identity in South India, another similar mischief was going on in Sri Lanka. A new identity was in the process of being created by fusing Buddhism as the religion, Sinhalese as the language, and Aryan as the race. In 1856, Robert Caldwell, in his comparative grammar, argued that there was no direct affinity between the Sinhalese and the Tamil languages. In 1866, another scholar, James D'Alwiss, seized upon the idea that Sinhalese belonged to 'the Aryan or Northern family, as contradistinguished from Dravidian or the Southern class of languages'.[16] However, D'Alwiss, who could be considered as the first Sinhala language nationalist of British Sri Lanka, rejected the thesis that Sinhalese language was a Sanskrit derivative; rather, both came from a common ancient race. He also rejected any kinship of Sinhalese with the mainland Indian populations.[17] The British also imposed racial categories on the inhabitants of Sri Lanka by requiring the people to identify their races in the 1871 census.[18]

There was also the opposing view by scholars like Christian Lassen and James Emerson Tennent, who grouped Sinhalese and Tamil into one language family. Then there was the distinguished Sinhalese scholar W.F. Gunawardhana, who pronounced as early as 1918 that there were affinities between Sinhalese and Tamil languages.[19] But the Max Müller–Caldwell camp won in shaping the consensus that Sinhalese and Tamil are two separate linguistic and racial categories. This became decisive in bifurcating the island and its future destiny.[20]

Dharmapala was a Sri Lankan Buddhist monk who was highly influenced by Theosophy and became instrumental in popularizing the Sinhalese-Buddhist-Aryan identity among the Sri Lankan public. In 1886, when Theosophists C.W. Leadbeater and Henry Steel Olcott visited Sri Lanka, Dharmapala accompanied them.[21] An important figure in this process was a Dutch convert to Buddhism, Alfred Ernst Buultjens, who travelled around Sri Lanka, lecturing on Buddhism. Sri Lankan Buddhists began to take Buultjens seriously, feeling proud that an educated white man had endorsed them. According to one report from that time:

> At such a time while the Europeans are in Sri Lanka stating Christianity is the whole truth and Buddhism completely untrue, the Buddhist people gathered to hear Buultjens [and were] surprised that such educated people would embrace Buddhism. [22]

Thus, when a magazine run by Buultjens in Sri Lanka, *The Buddhist*, published an article in 1897, titled 'The Aryan Singhalese', it exerted considerable influence among the national intelligentsia.[23] Another Theosophist, Dr Daly, encouraged the Sinhalese public to emulate Buultjens. Criticizing western misinterpretations of Buddhism, Buultjens argued that Buddhism was more rational than Christianity. Using his own translations of Pali Sutras, he depicted his version of Buddhism as a Western ideal.[24]

Clash of Colonial Constructs: Aryan-Buddhist-Sinhalese vs. Dravidian-Saivite-Tamil

In its fight against the proselytizing activities of Christian missionaries, Sri Lankan Buddhism started re-inventing itself as a respectable rational faith. Gananath Obeysekere explains:

> Sri Lankan monks and educated laypersons found the Western interpretation of Buddhism especially appealing in their fight against the Protestant and Catholic missions. Soon the indigenous scholarship, strongly influenced by Western critical methods, carried on into the present day a rational view of Buddhism, treating the mythic, cultic, devotional elements as inessential to the religion, as accretions or interpolations superadded to a pristine, pure form of Buddhism. Concomitantly, the folk beliefs of ordinary peasants were viewed as animism, or superstitions, unworthy of the rational theosophy of old religion.[25]

This newly constructed, 'pure' Buddhism was designed to be respectable in front of Westerners, and it also identified some enemies, chief among which were the Tamils, now described as inferior non-

Aryans. Dharmapala, the chief protagonist of this movement, started referring to Tamils as *hadi demalu* (filthy Tamils).[26] In the 1880s, Madame Blavatsky had started to classify Sri Lankan Tamils and Africans as essentially inferior to Aryans: 'No amount of culture, nor generations of training amid civilization, could raise such human specimens . . . to the same intellectual level as the Aryans, the Semites, and the Turanians so called'.[27]

From these beginnings, the cultivation of racial animosities turned Sri Lanka into the scene of a thirty-year civil war that has killed over 80,000 people,[28] displaced more than 900,000,[29] and boosted global weapons' trade.[30] In 2008, Sri Lanka was one of the 20 nation states listed by Carnegie Endowment for International Peace, as failing states that were closest to collapse.[31] The ethnic conflict peaked in the summer of 2009, when 20,000 civilians were killed.[32] Even though violence has ended after the death of the Tamil separatist leader, the deep wounds of suspicion that became ingrained by manipulated histories, identities and linguistics, are yet another horrible legacy of Indology.

Sri Lanka is certainly not alone in acting out extreme violence along racial lines established by the Europeans. Appendix C traces a similar process that contributed to the Rwandan genocide.

The preceding chapters have shown how invented histories, identities, and racial categories were formed and nurtured by colonial powers. Even with the end of colonialism, such categories survive because they serve vested interests. Control of narrative offers the colonizing civilization not only cultural superiority but also economic advantages and political dominance over the controlled civilization. Once the native peoples have passively accepted the imposed narrative, civil wars can be triggered. This has been true of both Rwanda and Sri Lanka, where the internal fragments were nurtured to the point of genocidal conflicts. Such conflicts then give the controlling powers a reason to interfere once again, now under the cloak of humanitarian concerns.

In India, such internal fragmentations have also been nurtured and groomed by vested interests. These fragments have now networked with international forces. This will be taken up toward the end of the book.

8

Digesting Hinduism into 'Dravidian' Christianity

A series of processes in South India has started to assimilate Hinduism into Christian history and dogma. It uses a version of Dravidian history according to which St Thomas came to India and that the Tamil classics were composed under his Christian influence. The allegation is that these classics are not Hindu, but rather, a form of Christianity that is distinctly south Indian. The Tamil classics, it is asserted, should actually be called Dravidian Christianity. In this manner, the Dravidian movement and Christian evangelism collaborate to undermine a common enemy. As we shall demonstrate, it is the Christian side that is co-opting the Dravidian side, because of the former's superior funding-capacity, its globally positioned nexuses, and its long-term experience in strategic thinking – all of which the former lacks. The discourse further claims that Tamil spirituality got infiltrated by ulterior Aryan influences, which contaminated the purer Dravidian spirituality, and that this earlier Dravidian spirituality was similar to Christianity. Various institutional mechanisms have been involved in these large-scale programs of fabrication. Some of the leading institutions that are involved will be discussed in this chapter.

Referring to Fig 8.1, each of its building blocks of this process mentioned will be introduced next and elaborated later in the chapter.

The Myth of St Thomas

The story that places the Apostle St Thomas in India in 53 CE is a lingering medieval myth.[1] It implicitly includes colonial and racial narratives; for instance, that the peaceful apostle ministered to the dark-skinned Indians, who turned on him and killed him. This myth, however, has no historical basis at all. Nevertheless, it has been shaped by various Christian churches into a powerful tool for the appropriation of Hindu culture in Tamil Nadu, by giving credit to 'Thomas Christianity' for everything positive in the south Indian culture, while blaming Hinduism for whatever is to be denigrated. It further serves as a tool to carve out Tamils from the common body of Indian culture and spirituality.

Rejection by Indian Christian scholars

When first proposed, the myth of St Thomas was rejected by Christian scholars. This included Father Henry Heras (1888–1955), the famed Jesuit Indologist, who hotly contested the claim that Thomas's grave had been found in Madras. The attempt of early missionary scholars like G.U. Pope to appropriate Tamil culture through this myth was aborted after Christian scholars failed to find any trace of Christian influence on ancient Tamil literature.

Revival of the St Thomas Myth

However, in the 1970s, a zealot named M. Deivanayagam began twisting the Tamil classical texts by superimposing on them a Christian meaning. At that time, the ground politics was such that the powerful Catholic clergy started to promote his thesis in academic circles. Though repeatedly rejected by the well-established Tamil scholars, Deivanayagam's work was promoted by academic bodies that were controlled by Dravidian identity politics. This included the International Institute of Tamil Studies and the specially created Christian Studies Chair at Madras University. Thus, a St Thomas Dravidian Christianity took shape in a well-planned segment of the academy.

Fabrication of Archeological Evidence

Some enterprising churchmen went on to fabricate archeological evidence with heavy financial support from the Vatican. Suddenly, startling 'discoveries' were announced of St Thomas crosses being found near famous Hindu pilgrim centers. Naturally, this provocation created social tension, which provided fodder for international Christian propaganda claiming that the Hindus were attacking Christianity. One such hoax concerning the St Thomas myth involved the archbishop of the Madras diocese, and this was publicly exposed in the Madras high court in 1975.

Institute of Asian Studies

In parallel, the Christian-controlled Institute of Asian Studies in Tamil Nadu embarked on a project to divide the Tamil culture and spirituality into two parts: Aryan and Dravidian. The 'good' components of Tamil spirituality were thus classified as Dravidian Christianity and the 'bad' portions condemned as Aryan Brahminism. The stage was set to digest Tamil Hindus into Christianity in a manner that feeds their Dravidian pride. This is depicted in Fig 8.1.

Fig 8.1 Preparing the Stage for Digestion of Hinduism into 'Dravidian' Christianity

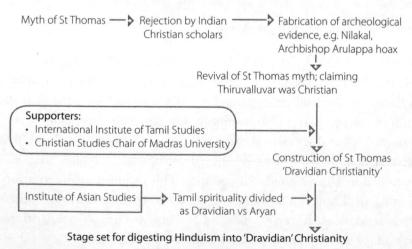

Evangelism and the Dravidian Movement

In Chapter Six, we saw that missionary scholars such as Robert Caldwell spearheaded the idea that Brahmins were Aryan invaders who had used the varna system to subjugate the Dravidians under a sacred pretext. The crystallization of this anti-Brahmin discourse into a political ideology was led by non-Brahmin Tamils, with the support of British administrators. The Justice Party, founded by Tamil natives in 1916 and encouraged by the British, became the first political vehicle of this ideology. It labeled Brahmins as destructive alien intruders of a different race.[2] This later evolved into the Dravidian movement, which rapidly became virulently anti-Brahmin in a very explicitly racist sense. It allied with Mohammad Ali Jinnah's separatist demands. By 1944, the movement was demanding the establishment of an independent nation-state, to be called Dravidasthan. The movement was subservient to British colonialism. It went to the extent of proclaiming India's Independence Day, 15 August 1947, as a 'black day'.[3] Soon, this movement evolved to become a very powerful political party of the present times, called Dravida Munnetra Kazhagam, or DMK, which means Dravidian Upliftment Association.

The earlier conception of Robert Caldwell became the basis for the Dravidian movement's construction of anti-Brahmin discourse in racial rather than socio-economic terms. A scholar of South Asia, Peter van der Veer, explains:

> The general conviction underlying much Dravidian radicalism—that the subjection of non-Brahman Dravidian peoples and cultures was based on the Aryan conquest of the Dravidian south—was in large part an invention of Robert Caldwell. Caldwell, who labored for fifty years in the Tinnevelly Mission . . . like most other missonaries who had to justify the fact that they could only report conversions of the very lowest caste groups, was especially resentful of the Brahmans, who frustrated his effort to proselytize. . . . Caldwell's antipathy toward Brahmans . . . has secured a hallowed place in the citational structures and justificatory rhetorics of anti-Brahminism up to the present day. [4]

According to Peter van der Veer, Dravidianists have dropped one of Caldwell's main points from their discourse, which concerned conversion to Christianity. 'Caldwell's dislike for Brahmans was directly connected to his concern over Brahmans' resistance against conversion to Christianity and their considerable influence over lower social strata, who resisted as well'.[5] This removal of Caldwell's agenda has enabled Dravidianists to make Caldwell seem secular enough. Another Caldwell point that did not suit the Dravidian movement was his strategic demand that 'until caste was abolished there would be no hope for Christian conversion'.[6] This too was dropped, because the DMK movement was built on non-Brahminical caste identities.

The evangelical strategy planted at the heart of the entire Dravidian movement was camouflaged by the rhetoric of social emancipation. Today, the Catholic as well as Protestant evangelical movements are aggressively reviving the Christian–Dravidian nexus at different levels.

Evangelical Pseudo-scholarship

Until the late 1960s, the Dravidian movement was multi-religious and unified across various religions, its identity being defined entirely by language and ethnicity.

This started to change subtly in 1969, when M. Deivanayagam, a young Hindu convert to Christianity, published a Tamil book titled *Was Thiruvalluvar a Christian?* The central thesis was that St Thomas had converted Thiruvalluvar, the most important classical Tamil writer, to Christianity. This would make *Thirukural* a Christian text written to oppose Brahmins and Aryans.[7] His Christianized interpretation of *Thirukural*, for example, claims that verses praising the glory of rain are actually praising Christianity's Holy Ghost. Verses praising the glory of those who renounced the world became interpreted as praising Jesus the sacrificed son of God. The first three chapters of *Thirukural*, according to this reinterpretation, were meant to be a tribute to the Christian trinity of the Father, Son and Holy Ghost. Encouraged by political support, Deivanayagam produced further works that distorted and mapped the explicitly Hindu concepts of Thiruvalluvar into Christian concepts.[8] He borrowed the discredited speculation of G.U. Pope that Thiruvalluvar was influenced by Christianity, and added the further claim that Thiruvalluvar had, in fact, met St Thomas.

What catapulted the book from being crackpot speculation to a political weapon, was the backing it received by politicians. At that time, Tamil Nadu was being run by the pro-Dravidian DMK party, whose chief minister gave a laudatory preface to the book, while the same party's state minister released it. The book received another boost in 1972 when the director of Christian Arts and Communication Center in Madras organized a symposium to promote it under the leadership of well-known Christian Dravidian supremacists.[9] These sudden developments shocked the Tamil Hindus, who had adopted what they naively felt was Dravidian ideology without suspecting it to be a preparation to sneak in Christianity.

Initial Rejections and Eventual Church Acceptance

These works of Deivanayagam were at first widely attacked by Tamil Christian theologians as well as academic scholars. For example, S. Rasa Manikkam, a Tamil Jesuit and department head of Tamil Studies at Venkateshwara University in Thirupathi, rejected the claim that Thiruvalluvar was a Christian. He wrote:

> Now let me analyse the work of Deivanayagam, who has been recently propagating the idea that Thiruvalluvar was a Christian. He is giving new interpretations to many non-Christian ideas present in *Thirukural*. Further, he has published many books under titles like *Is Thiruvalluvar Christian?*, *Who is the Renounced?*, *Seven Births*, *Who Are the Three?* etc. Despite reading his works deeply, **we cannot accept the interpretations he is giving.** He says that Thiruvalluvar did not accept the concept of rebirth and that it was Jesus whom Thiruvalluvar means when he talks about one who has overcome the five senses, that the glory of rain is actually praising Holy Ghost, and by noble person Thiruvalluvar meant Christianity, etc. Neither these interpretations nor the methods he uses to put forward these ideas are satisfactory. **Thirukural *does not show any of the specific***

Christian ideas. Even the name of Jesus does not figure in it. Rather, Thiruvalluvar explicitly uses many Hindu Gods like Indra (25), Vishnu (610, 8, 103), Lakshmi (167, 84, 617), Kama (1197), celestial Devas (906, 1073, 18, 346), etc.[10]

In 1975, yet another Tamil scholar, Kamatchi Srinivasan, who had converted to Christianity and was specially appointed by the Tamil Nadu government for *Thirukural* research, wrote: 'When one reads the books written by Deivanayagam, doubts rise in the mind as to whether this man has really understood *Thirukural*, and also it is doubtful if this man has properly studied the history of the origin and development of Christian religion'.[11]

A 1979 PhD dissertation at Madras University, titled 'The Developments in *Thirukural* Research in the Twentieth Century,' reached the following conclusions about Deivanayagam:

> He has designed his research in such a manner to prove that his Christian religion's Biblical concepts form the inner core of *Thirukural*. Thus, the research contention that began in the start of this century asserting *Thirukural* as a Saiva Siddhanta text has ended in modern times with the claims that Bible provided the concepts of *Thirukural*.[12]

However, no amount of scholarly criticisms stopped Deivanayagam from using the Dravidian identity politically. This was a way to alienate the Tamil speakers from Hinduism, and subsequently encourage them on to Christianity.[13] He not only survived a decade of attacks by Christians against his theory of the Christian origins of Dravidian culture, but published yet another Tamil book in 1980, titled *Thirukural and Bible*. He was on a roll. In 1983, his PhD dissertation, titled *Bible, Thirukural and Saiva Siddhanta,* was accepted by the Madras University. The prestigious International Institute of Tamil Studies published Deivanayagam's dissertation as a book.

Leading exponents of the Saiva Siddhanta exposed the dissertation's numerous flaws, misinterpretations and distortions. Dharampuram Atheenam, a traditional Saiva monastery and seat of Saivite learning, organized an elaborate two-day symposium in 1986 on the matter. Subsequently, the late Saiva Siddhanta scholar, Arunai Vadivel Muthaliar, wrote a 300-page rebuttal, which was published by the International Saiva Siddhanta Association in 1991.[14] Rather than face his critics and debate to offer evidence in support of his thesis, Deivanayagam organized Dravidianists and leaders of lower castes to issue a declaration that the 300-page rejoinder to his work was an attempt by Aryan Brahmins to enslave the Dravidian race.[15]

Deivanayagam publishes a Tamil magazine from Chennai, called *Dravidian Religion*. His preposterous claims have expanded to include a certain sect of Jainism as well as Mahayana Buddhism as movements arising out of Thomas Christianity.[16]

Hoaxes: Archeological and Literary

While Deivanayagam was busy fabricating textual interpretations, the archbishop of Mylapore was manufacturing archeological evidence to prove the myth of St Thomas. In 1975, he hired a Christian convert from Hinduism to fabricate epigraphic evidence proving the visit of St Thomas to South India. When this hired gun failed, the archbishop sued him in court. The *Illustrated Weekly of India* raised questions alleging corruption in this case.[17]

Meanwhile, in a very famous Hindu pilgrimage center in the forests of Kerala, a Catholic priest proclaimed that his parish had unearthed a stone cross established by Thomas in 57 CE. The location was close to the ancient Mahadeva temple at Nilakkal, in the sacred eighteen hills of the deity of Sabarimala.[18] Soon, a church with a five-foot granite cross was erected and consecrated by top Catholic clergy, and daily prayers were started.[19]

Many eminent citizens were suspicious of the newly discovered cross, including prominent Christians such as Dr C.P. Mathew, who published the following letter in a prominent newspaper:

> A piece of granite in the shape of a cross [that is] said to have been recovered from the site is going to strike at the very root of communal harmony in the state. If at all it has any significance, it is for the

Department of Archeology [to decide]. *Some narrow-minded, selfish Christian fanatics (both priests and laymen) are behind this. The Christian community in general is not interested in this episode.*[20]

The Hindus saw this as an invasion of one of their most popular pilgrimage sites, and Hindu temples throughout Kerala hoisted black flags and priests wore black pendants in protest. A Hindu swami challenged the church to prove that any such cross had been installed by St Thomas, and questioned the right to build a church near the sacred temple on Hindu lands. The Bishop's subcommittee announced that it would shift the church to another location. The mysterious cross suddenly disappeared when Hindus insisted that under the law, any ancient archeological piece would be subject to the scrutiny and independent research of the Archaeological Survey of India, a government body which controls all archaeological sites and findings. Being afraid of the independent scrutiny of the Archaeological Survey of India, the perpetrators of the fraud preferred to retreat.[21]

A historian of Kerala, Dr C.I. Isaac, explained that the first Christian communities in Kerala were merchant centers located only at the seacoast. He wrote:

> The church hierarchy claims that there was one more Christian hinterland settlement called Chayal near Sabrimala pilgrim centre; but it was not a Christian settlement because the place was not an abode of human beings and is still not a habitable one. Scholars have not so far identified whether the place Chayal is near Sabari hills or not, beyond doubt. Therefore, this argument of the church has no locus standi.[22]

Fabricating the History of St Thomas

The central claims of Deivanayagam and his associates may be listed as follows:

- St Thomas visited India around 52 CE, which resulted in the emergence of Sanskrit as a tool for propagating Christianity in North India, though the language was later appropriated by evil Brahmins.

- Vedas were written after Jesus, as late as second century CE.
- Saivism, Vaishnavism and all sculptural, iconographic, and devotional developments in Hinduism are traceable to the influence of Thomas Christianity.
- Brahmins, Sanskrit, and Vedanta are evil forces that need to be eradicated in order to re-purify Tamil society.

The Church has now forged an intimate strategic alliance with Deivanayagam in order to produce evidence for the visit of St Thomas to India, and to highlight Christian goodness contrasted with Hindu intolerance. As a result of this alliance, the St Thomas Museum was formed by the Roman Catholic Church in 2006.[23] It houses many stone sculptures and inscriptions which are claimed to be originals from the time of St Thomas. One such sculpture shows two figures, under one of which is the following explanation:

> The double-figured pedestal was found near the tomb of St Thomas. One figure is said to be of St Thomas holding a book in his left hand, with the right hand in the 'blessing' or 'teaching' pose.

Under the other figure, the explanation reads:

> This figure is identified as that of Kandappa Raja (Gondophares) the supposed king of Mylapore whom St Thomas converted.

However, Gondophares was not the king of Mylapore, but the first Indo-Parthian king who ruled over Kabul valley located over a thousand miles away. The museum website dates the sculpture as belonging to the seventh century, but Gondophares ruled in the first century BCE. The website also makes yet another strange claim about the sculpture:

> The left hand seems to hold a book or some instrument. If it is a book, the figure may represent an apostle too! Perhaps St Bartholomew who is said to have brought to India St Mathew's Gospel . . . Two Apostles of India! Though the Apostolate of St Bartholomew in India is not yet as much proved as that of St Thomas. It is rather significant that the new Divine Office (after Vatican II) has this note on 24 August: '. . . after the Lord's ascension, tradition has it that he preached the gospel in India and there suffered martyrdom'.[24]

However, since the New Testament was compiled in the fourth century CE and Bibles in bound-book form became popular only after the printing press was invented in 1455, St Thomas could not have been carrying a pocket-sized Bible when he came to India. Even the earliest Biblical papyrus belongs to a century later than St Thomas. Nonetheless, in combination with St Thomas, the inclusion of St Bartholomew into the south Indian Christian pantheon prepares for yet another movement in Dravidian India, in which St Bartholomew brings about further changes to Hinduism!

The altar at the Mount Church of St Thomas displays a painting of Jesus with Mary, clearly belonging to the Italian renaissance period. Yet, the Church declares it to have been brought by Thomas himself and painted by none other than St Luke. A recent western visitor, Martin Goodman, while being sympathetic to the Thomas myth, writes facetiously about this fabrication:

> Beneath the altar is a portrait of the Madonna and child brought to India by Saint Thomas and attributed to Saint Luke. In its prefiguring of skills acquired in the Italian Renaissance, it is almost as much of a miracle as a bleeding cross.[25]

At the mount there is a stone cross, which is said to have been carved by St Thomas himself.[26] A board placed inside the altar states:

> It was on this sacred spot that St Thomas the apostle was pierced with a lance and killed. There is recorded evidence that the stone cross on the altar was carved by St Thomas himself.

The picture placed inside the altar shows a dark-skinned Hindu with a typical Brahmin hairstyle piercing the apostle from behind while St Thomas is solemnly engaged in prayer before the cross. Official Catholic publications have described the death of St Thomas as an assassination by Brahmins:

> On 3 July 72 AD, the apostle on the way to the Mount encountered some Chennambranar Brahmins proceeding to the temple for a sacrifice. They wanted St Thomas to take part in the worship; he of course refused to oblige and on the contrary destroyed the place of

worship with a sign of Cross. The Brahmins in their fury pierced St Thomas with a lance.[27]

But centuries of testimonies contradict these claims. In the thirteenth century, Marco Polo described the legend of Thomas in India, but he made no mention of any Brahmin killers or martyrdom. In tales associated with St Thomas, his death was always described as an accidental killing by a tribal who was trying to shoot an arrow at a peacock. According to Marco Polo's story:

> Thomas was outside his hermitage in the woods, raising his prayers to the Lord his God. All around were many peacocks . . . As St Thomas was saying his prayers, a certain idolater belonging to the race and lineage of Gavi, shot an arrow from his bow, in order to kill one of the peacocks that were gathered round the Saint.[28]

W.W. Hunter details how this simple story, which had been in vogue in Christendom, collected an overlay of fraudulent fabrications over time:

> Patristic literature clearly declares that St Thomas had suffered martyrdom at Calamina . . . The tradition of the Church is equally distinct that in 394 AD the remains of the Apostle were transferred to Edessa in Mesopotamia. The attempt to localize the death of St Thomas on the south-western coast of India started therefore, under disadvantages. A suitable site was however, found at the Mount near Madras, one of the many hill shrines of ancient India which have formed a joint resort of religious persons of diverse faiths – Buddhist, Muhammadan and Hindu . . . Portuguese zeal, in its first fervours of Indian evangelization felt keenly the want of a sustaining local hagiology. [. . .] A mission from Goa dispatched to the Coromandel coast in 1522 proved itself ignorant of or superior to the well-established legend of the translation of the Saint's remains to Edessa in 394 AD and found his relics at the ancient hill shrine near Madras, side by side those of a king whom he had converted to faith. They were brought with pomp to Goa, the Portuguese capital of India, and there they lie in the Church of St Thomas to this day. The finding of the Pehlvi cross . . . at St Thomas's Mount in 1547 gave a fresh coloring to the legend. So far as its inscription goes, it points to a Persian, and probably

to a Manichaean origin. But at the time it was dug up, no one in Madras could decipher its Pehlvi characters. A Brahman impostor, knowing that there was a local demand for martyrs, accordingly came forward with a fictitious interpretation. The simple story of Thomas's accidental death from a stray arrow had, before this grown into a cruel martyrdom by stoning and lance thrust, with each spot in the tragedy fixed at the Greater and Lesser Mount near Madras.[29]

The history of the Indian Church is replete with examples of its keen ability and sense of timing regarding the miraculous unearthing of relics strategically discovered near Hindu sacred sites that it wants to appropriate or occupy. Certainly, it is nothing new for missionary scholarship to blame those 'wily Hindu heathens' for any fraudulent fabrications that may be brought to light, such as the unnamed Brahmin impostor who was blamed for the fraudulent translation of the inscription on the crucifix.[30]

Archeological Evidence Concerning San Thome Church

The identification of the tomb discovered by the Portuguese as that of St Thomas has been thoroughly repudiated even by those scholars who are sympathetic to the Thomas legend. For example, Jesuit archeologist Fr H. Heras writes: 'Some early Portuguese writers have kept the details of the original account, and these details are quite enough for disclosing the untruthfulness of the discovery'.[31] Another Christian scholar, T.K. Joseph, states with regard to the burial place of Thomas: 'I am fully convinced that it has never been in Mylapore. I have stated that many times'.[32]

There is also evidence to show that the present San Thome was built on the remains of a Hindu temple, which was originally the Kapaleeswara Temple. For example, a PhD dissertation done years before the recent re-surfacing of these controversies, states:

From the artifacts discovered by archeologists at San Thome, one can infer that the temple should have existed elsewhere and most probably it existed at San Thome beach . . . because remnants of the old temple were discovered at San Thome beach. In 1923 when archeologists conducted excavations at San Thome cathedral they discovered inscriptions and statues. The inscriptions indicated a temple. [. . .] Saint Arunagiri Nathar also mentions that Kapaleeswara temple existed by the side of the beach. . . . Hence, in conclusion, one can state that the old Kapaleeswara temple was destroyed by Portuguese in the fifteenth century and was built in its present place by Nattu Nayiniappa Muthaliar and son in the sixteenth century.[33]

Archeological studies by the Government of India confirm that the Portuguese built the church on the ruins of a Hindu temple. They have recovered an inscription of Rajendra Chola, the Imperial Chola who was devoted to the Vedic religion. A 1967 report of the Archaeological Survey of India on the recovery of the eleventh-century inscription of Rajendra Chola from San Thome Church in Madras states that the inscription mentions the Chola king as favored by Lakshmi, 'who grants him victory and prosperity'.[34]

Nevertheless, these independent reports are downplayed and suppressed. For example, in the sixth-standard social science textbook taught across Tamil Nadu, it is blatantly stated as a matter of fact that St Thomas 'stayed at St Thomas Mount and preached Christianity. He was murdered due to religious strife. His body was buried at Santome Church'.[35] None of this is substantiated by empirical evidence. (See Appendix D on the same hoax played against the natives of America by the missionaries interested in conquering them and taking their land.)

The Silver Screen

Recently, a mega-budget film on St Thomas has been planned by the Catholic Church to propagate this myth. A newspaper reports:

> With Hollywood epics such as *Ben-Hur* and the *Ten Commandments* in mind, and with a budget to match, the Archdiocese of Madras-Mylapore will produce a rupees thirty-crore silver screen version of the life and ministry of St Thomas, one of the twelve apostles who is believed to have spread the message of Christ in India. Work on the 70 mm, two-and-a-half-hour feature film with Hollywood collaboration and the bigwigs of the Indian film industry [. . .] The

film has special significance for Kerala and Tamil Nadu, where St Thomas spent a major portion of his time in India. He is believed to have established seven churches in Kerala, before being martyred in 72 AD at Mylapore. Films such as *Arunachalam of Thiruvannamalai* and *Annai Velanganni* have had the effect of people receiving spiritual consolation, said the Archbishop. He felt [that] a film on the life of St Thomas would have a similar effect, as it evolved around the theme of equality and dignity for all people.[36]

Rumors that Thiruvalluvar would be shown as a disciple of St Thomas in the film led to protests that it was a false claim. The film's scriptwriter, Paulraj Lourdhu Sami, defended the script by stating that Deivanayagam's PhD dissertation accepted by Madras University had provided the evidence for Thiruvalluvar meeting St Thomas.[37] This is how crackpot speculation has traveled, via academic legitimization, into mainstream discourse and popular culture.

Hinduism Declared as Aryan-British Conspiracy

These St Thomas fabrications merged with earlier ideas about conquering Aryans and caricatures of 'evil' Brahmins. In 2000, Deivanayagam published a book titled *India in Third Millennium,* a grand attempt to usurp Hindu spirituality and reduce it to a subset of Christianity. Predictably, the Aryans are portrayed as the quintessential villains:

> Aryans do not have a religion of their own. In reality, Aryans are a people without any religion. They do not have any knowledge on the concepts of monotheism, heaven, hell, rebirth and so forth. They used to bake the meat of cattle and sheep in fire and eat it with drinks called soma and sura. They were a gay people enjoying nature – worship, dancing and singing folk songs. In course of time, these folk songs were known as the 'Vedic Hymns' . . . The term 'Aryan' is a common collective name given to the Persians, Greeks, Romans, Sakas, Kushanas and Huns, all of whom were foreigners who entered India without any religion of their own.[38]

He elaborates his conspiracy theory that Hinduism started as an 'evil' joint venture between foreign Brahmins and British colonialists:

The color of Britishers is white. The Britishers noted that already in the Hindu law (Manu Dharma) the non-white Dravidian Indians (Avarnas) are condemned as inferior and white coloured foreigners (Savarnas) are treated as superior. . . . Hindu religion is born out of joint conspiracy. *Aryan Brahmins and Britishers, both of whom are foreigners, joined together and conspired against the Indian people.* They jointly created and started spreading a concept that the English word 'Hinduism' (which originally meant Hindu Law) also can mean 'Hindu Religion', i.e., Indian Religion.[39]

He further claims that Sankara, Ramanuja and Madhva were Aryan Brahmins who distorted the earlier writings of Vedavyasa, who he claims was a Dravidian.[40] In other words, those aspects of Hinduism that can be accommodated with Christianity are credited to Christian influences, whereas those that contradict it are denigrated as the distortions of foreign Brahmins. While he was originally seen as a crackpot, Deivanayagam's tenacity and persistence gradually made him important among mainstream churches. By 2004, evangelical missionaries were attending his formal courses that are up to six months of duration (as of 2010).

Institute of Asian Studies

The Institute of Asian Studies was founded jointly by a Japanese Buddhist scholar and an Indian Christian named John Samuel. It has brought out a large number of books and a periodical called *Journal of the Institute of Asian Studies.* While the Institute had benign beginnings, Samuel took it over from the Japanese partner and shifted its research and education agenda towards decoupling Tamil identity and culture from Hinduism. To appeal to local sentiments, it started out by glorifying the Tamil culture as the origin for everything positive, while downplaying pan-Indian identity and cultural history. Hindu traditions were positioned as separate, alien and fragmented, while Christianity and Buddhism were presented as coherent religions. The website of the Institute shows that it teaches religions that are classified as: Buddhism, Christianity, Kaumaram, Panniruthirumarai, and Folk studies.[41] There is no such thing as Hinduism at all. The Institute has gained importance by establishing research connections with University of California, Berkeley, and through that with the Institute for Indology and Tamil Studies, University of Cologne and other worldwide projects.[42]

Siva and Nataraja Declared 'Dravidian'

A typical example of the Institute's scholarship is found in a book it published in 1985, titled *Ananda-tandava of Siva Sadanrttamurti.* The author, a noted Czech Dravidianist named Kamil V. Zvelebil, declares emphatically that the concept of Siva as the divine dancer, and in particular, as performing the *ananda tandava,* is 'no doubt an Indo-Dravidian invention'.[43] He emphasizes that, 'we must distinguish between the North and the South of India'.[44] Then he flippantly dismisses all evidence of Siva in North India as being insignificant:

> Although there exist a few pre-Chalukya, pre-Vakataka and pre-Pallava representations of Siva as a dancing deity found in the North of India, there can hardly be considered anything but early precursors of the Siva Nataraja theme.[45]

Zvelebil acknowledges the archeological evidence of the fifth-century dancing Siva in North India from the Gupta period, but is quickly dismissive that 'in Gupta sculpture, the Nataraja theme was not too important', and that, 'in fact the few representations of Siva as dancing deity occurring in the late Gupta period were created under the impact and inspiration of the concept of Nataraja originated and evolved in the South'.[46] This brief analysis allows him to conclude with confidence that Nataraja is a Dravidian from South India. He ignores the massive evidence of Siva's organic association with the North that has developed over the millennia into the collective spiritual psyche of India, such as:

• The artifacts of Siva found in the Indus Valley civilization
• Siva's abode of Mount Kailash lies in Tibet
• The Himalayas are regarded as his sacred geography

- Siva's Ganga flows in the North
- The famous cave in Amarnath attracts pilgrims specifically because of its Sivalinga
- Archeological findings of Saivite sites in central Asia

In his effort to further decouple South India's culture from the rest of India, Zvelebil cites early post-Sangham literature mentioning Siva's dances, and concludes:

> It is clear that the Tamil South had an important independent tradition of a dancing god which began to fully flourish and develop during the Pallavas of Kanci.[47]

Even scholars who work within the Aryan/Dravidian divisive paradigm, have pointed out that in *Rig Veda* itself there is mention of Rudra's (i.e. Siva's) dance and music.[48] An image of Siva bearing a musical instrument belonging to the north Indian Sunga dynasty of second century BCE has been pointed out by C. Sivaramamurthi, who is considered an expert in Nataraja iconography.[49] Though Zvelebil extensively cites the other work of C. Sivaramamurthi, he ignores this data.

South India has made a vast contribution to Indic spirituality, specifically in evolving and perfecting the divine icon of Siva as Nataraja. However, some Dravidianists aim to establish that *South Indian traditions are entirely independent traditions which are only artificially linked to pan-Indian or Vedic traditions*. This de-contextualizing of South India's spiritual traditions from Indian culture then becomes an interim step for re-contextualizing these traditions as Christian.

Appropriating Skanda-Muruga

In 1991, the Institute of Asian Studies published another book authored by Zvelebil, titled *Tamil Traditions on Subrahmanya-Murugan*. It further illustrates the agenda of propagating the Aryan/Dravidian divisiveness. The book repeatedly equates Brahmins with Aryans, and describes Hinduism as their mechanism to annihilate

Buddhism and Jainism. It explains that the 'strategy' of the cunning Brahmins has 'always been to adopt the most prestigious features of their opponents'. Hinduism is thus, 'a product of a particular mind in a particular environment, a special kind of religion which must be met in its own terms'.[50]

To position himself as a balanced scholar, Zvelebil first cautions against 'the pitfall of the simplistic view of Indian cultural development, which reduces everything to the tension between autochthonous features (primarily Dravidian) and imported Indo-Aryan traits'.[51] But merely two pages later, he falls into the same pitfall he warned against, by accusing Brahmins-Aryans of appropriating Dravidian spirituality into Sanskrit models. He claims that the indigenous Tamil framework, 'was invaded, partly violated and raped, partly adopted and adapted, by the attempts of later commentators to force Tamil ideology into the procrustean mould of the Brahminic-Sanskritic models'.[52]

He then downgrades the great bhakti (devotional) literary renaissance of Tamils as a downfall brought about by Sanskrit influence. According to him, the wicked Aryans brought the social evils, including the 'overpowering growth of epic, puranic, Aryan mythology; Sanskritization of language; rigidization of ritual purity; pollution paradigm; rigid casteism; the god-king idea used in feudal structures; rigid and elaborate ritualism'. As a result of the oppression, Tamil people resorted to 'bhakti as an emotional deluge drowning rational attempts to solve the problems of life; an irrational and anti-rational approach to life and its problems'.[53] With typical European supremacy, Zvelebil asserts that 'Tamilnadu has known no "real" [R]enaissance-like development . . . there was no development comparable to the European rinascimento of the fifteenth–sixteenth centuries, to European rationalism of the seventeen–eighteenth centuries or to European empiricism and positivism of the nineteenth century'.[54] But while being inferior to the Europeans, the Tamils were better off prior to the Hindu bhakti movement corrupting them, because they were secular, optimistic and heroically eating meat and drinking wine. Zvelebil writes:

However, until before the bhakti trend set in, before the so-called 'dark ages', in the Tamil classical age, in the age of Murugan, the Tamil man seems to have had a clear, optimistic, rather simple, very secular view of life, in a heroic age of meat-eating and wine-drinking pre-feudal society, with relatively simple but meaningful religious conceptions.[55]

Thus, Zvelebil rehashes Caldwell's thesis that before Brahmins cheated and enslaved Tamil spiritually, it was a primitive, pre-feudal culture that was ready for proper Christianity. The intervention by Brahmins caused harm, whereas the 'upgrade' by Christianity is what the Tamil people really needed in order to have a valid religion. Caldwell had proposed that once the deceit of Brahmins was removed, the simple-minded Dravidians would be ready for the evangelical harvest.

John Samuel's mission at the Institute of Asian Studies was to continue where Caldwell had left off. He is helped by Patrick Harrigan, a Western scholar working with a variety of NGOs in South India and Sri Lanka.[56] Harrigan has established himself as a major researcher of Hindu mysticism and folk traditions of South India and Sri Lanka, through which he has produced an impressive database and forty websites on Tamil spirituality and prominent Hindu temples.[57] He used his contacts with the custodians of the immensely popular Murugan worship tradition[58] to help Samuel to Christianize that tradition, which had been resistant to Church appropriation. Murugan is a very popular deity in Tamil Nadu. Samuel has conducted several International Murugan conferences in which Murugan is explained outside the Hindu context. This would pave the way for the claim that the deity is a corrupt form of the Christian deity or a misidentified Christian saint. *Hinduism Today* interviewed Samuel and Harrigan at their 1999 conference and reported the subtle anti-Hindu bias of Samuel to reduce the divinity of Murugan, a charge that Harrigan helped dilute by restating what had been reported.[59]

Samuel has endorsed Deivanayagam, asserting that the major Hindu spiritual traditions arose under the influence of St Thomas Christianity. Even the well-known Somaskanda sculpture, showing the

child-form of Skanda-Murugan sculpture called Somaskanda, flanked
by his parents Siva and Parvathi, is now supposedly derived from the
Christian Trinity. John Samuel writes:

> It is crystal clear that the Somaskantha figures and the concept
> of ammai-appan-magan are nothing but the revelation of the
> Christian Trinitarian teaching. It is to be noted here that there
> was no father to Lord Murugan in the beginning. The honour
> of taking up detailed research on the influence of the Trinitarian
> teaching of Saivism belongs entirely to Dr M. Deivanayagam and
> Dr D. Devakala.[60]

Thus, erstwhile academic institutions have supported an obvious
fabrication by a religious zealot. After creating the aura of academic
legitimacy, the next step is to integrate 'Thomas Dravidian Christianity'
into the popular anti-Brahminical Dravidian polity. The result is a
divisive ethnic-religious identity for Tamils.

Fabricating the 'Fifth Veda'

Robert de Nobili (1577–1656), the notorious Jesuit who masqueraded
as a Brahmin, committed a fraud by claiming to have discovered what
he termed as Fifth Veda, which would show the entire Indian tradition
to be a corrupted subset of Christianity. It was presented as the Jesus
Veda and made popular by European Indologists. In France it was
supported by famous intellectuals including Voltaire, who wrote in
praise of it:

> This manuscript undoubtedly belongs to the time when the ancient
> religion of the gymnosophists had begun to be corrupted; except for
> our own sacred books, it is the most respectable monument of belief
> in a single God. It is called Ezour Veidam: as if one were to say the
> true Veidam, the Veidam explained, the pure Veidam.[61]

In 1774, a French naturalist and explorer named Pierre Sonnerat
visited India with a copy of this *Ezour Vedam*. He studied with
Brahmins to understand the real Vedas, so as to be able to authenticate
this Fifth Veda. He concluded that this document was a fake and a

fraudulent mapping of Vedic spiritual elements on to Christian theology. Adjustments were made to disguise the Christian theology so that one would not be able to recognize the missionary under the disguise of the Brahmin. In 1782, the Frenchman published his accounts of his journey to India and revealed the fraud of *Ezour Vedam*:

> One ought to guard oneself against including among the canonical books of the Indians the *Ezour Vedam*, of which there is a so-called translation in the Royal Library, and which has been published in 1778. It is definitely not one of four Vedams, not withstanding its name. It is a book of controversy, written by a missionary at Masulipatam. *It contains a refutation of a number of Pouranons devoted to Vichenou, which are several centuries later than the Vedams. One sees that the author tries to reduce everything to the Christian religion; he did introduce a few errors, though, so that one would not be able to recognize the missionary under the disguise of the Brahmin.* Anyhow, Mr Voltaire and a few others were wrong when they gave this book an importance which it does not deserve, and when they regard it as canonical.[62]

The discredited document was made obscure to save embarrassment, and is archived under the nondescript name of 'Exhibit No 452' of the Nouvelles Acquisitions Francaises. Even after this project had failed, the nineteenth-century Indologists like Max Müller made fervent efforts to absolve de Nobili of the forgery, or at least tried to minimize his contribution to the fraud by blaming the whole episode on some Indian servant of Nobili. As late as 1861, nearly a century after the hoax had been exposed, Max Müller expressed admiration for de Nobili's attempt:

> . . . the very idea that he came, as he said, to preach a new or a fifth Veda, which had been lost, shows how well he knew the strong and weak points of the theological system he came to conquer.[63]

Despite this failure, the missionaries started to call Christianity the true and original Vedic religion. The success of this propaganda is evident by the fact that today in the three southern districts of Tamil Nadu (Thirunelveli, Tuticorin and Kanyakumari), the term Vetham (Vedic religion) is used by even common Hindus to refer to Christianity, the term Vetha-koil (Vedic temple) refers to a church, and Vetha-puthakam (Vedic text) refers to the Bible. Missionary gatherings and conventions are termed 'Vedagama preaching meets' and its theological colleges are called 'Vedagama schools'. This Christian usurpation of Vedas continues unchallenged.

In continuation of Robert de Nobili's legacy, many Vedic terms are becoming Christianized to create confusion among Hindus. For instance, *Dharma Deepika* is a missionary research journal published by Mylapore Institute of Indigenous Studies, an evangelical institution. In 2000, it published an article which presented an evangelical strategy of projecting the Prajapati in the Purusha Hymn of the *Rig Veda* as 'a prophetic revelation about the atoning sacrifice of Jesus Christ'. It examined the possibilities of showing Prajapati as a Vedic prophecy of Jesus Christ, and thus, 'Jesus is the real Prajapati'.[64] This was followed by a major evangelical propaganda campaign in South India. In the same year, another evangelical group in Chennai, with recent converts, launched a dance-drama titled 'Prajapathi'.[65] The drama has become an aggressive proselytizing device being performed near important Hindu pilgrim centers such as Rameshwaram and Kanchipuram. In areas of potential Hindu/Christian conflict, the performances of the drama have been presided by the state government's minister of tourism, among other politicians – all belonging to the Dravidian movement.[66]

The idea that Vedas are the prophecy of Jesus' arrival, and hence, that Christianity is the fulfillment of the Vedas, was also advanced by some very prominent theologians, such as Raimundo Pannikar, a Jesuit. One popular Chennai-based evangelist, Chellapa, describes himself as a sadhu and runs an evangelical organization called Agni Ministries, named after the Vedic deity. He claims that because Prajapati in the Vedas is the anticipation of the coming of Jesus, therefore the Vedic quest is incomplete without Jesus. His prime target is the vulnerable community of Sri Lankan Tamil Hindus who are scattered as refugees throughout the world.[67] In 2009, he put up large posters announcing a Christian-Brahmin association. This led to angry Hindus in the area to point out that the term Christian-Brahmin was deceptive, and the Chennai police removed his posters.[68]

Christianizing Hindu Popular Culture

Navratri is a festival worshipping the divine Mother Goddess for nine continuous nights. The tenth day marks an important south Indian Hindu tradition known as Vijayadasami (called Dussehra in North India). This is an auspicious day for Hindus in South India to initiate their children into literacy. Christians have also started initiating their children into literacy on this day. In 2008 a parallel function was organized to imitate the Hindu rituals within the Christian context:

> While the Hindu children wrote '*Hari Sree Ganapathaye Namaha*', Christians wrote words in the praise of Jesus Christ . . . There was a good turnout for the ceremony. Children wrote words like 'Yeshu Daivam' (Jesus God) in a plate of rice grains [69]

This success encouraged the clergy of St Baselieus Church at Kottayam, a prominent Kerala town, to go even further. In 2009 they claimed that Vijayadasami festival had a Christian historical background, because that is when Jehovah enlightened Jesus with Knowledge. In this Christianized version, Saraswati and Lakshmi, the goddesses of wisdom and wealth, respectively, have been replaced by the Christian saints Paul and Sebastian. The clergy further claimed that the festival Maha Sivaratri (the great night of Siva) was the corrupted version of the Messiah Night, which was the day when Jesus wanted his disciples to keep eternal vigil.[70] These are examples of the manner in which Hindu festivals are being steadily Christianized in South India as the St Thomas mythology becomes entrenched.

Christianizing Hindu Art

> Actually, dance forms an intrinsic part of worship in the temples. . . . India alone has a concept of a God who dances. Siva is Nataraja, Lord of dancers, who dances in the Hall of Consciousness and weaves into it the rhythm of the Universe. Within His Cosmic Dance are included the Divine prerogatives of Creation, Preservation, Regeneration, Veiling and Benediction . . . Dance in India has been

so closely linked with religion, that today it is impossible to think of it divorced from this essential background.

– Rukmini Devi Arundale[71]

Hindu art-forms and other aspects of the Vedic traditions are being targeted by missionary-scholars for Christian infiltration and appropriation. Bharata Natyam is a popular Hindu spiritual dance-form whose origin is traced to the references of dance in the Vedas. It had been formalized even before Bharat Rishi wrote *Natya Sastra,* the seminal text on performing arts and aesthetics in the second century BCE. The Tamil epic *Chilapathikaram* gives a detailed description of classical dance performances in ancient urban centers. The performing arts were positioned as spiritual practices for the general public, including those who lacked the qualifications and aptitudes to directly access the scriptures.

Dance has always had a sacred dimension, and among those who maintained, cultivated and propagated its techniques were Pâshupata (Shaiva) ascetics who used it as a method of inducing ecstasy.[72] Bharata Natyam is based on Hindu cosmology's cycles of birth-sustenance-dissolution, which is also seen as the Dance of Siva. In the words of Dr Ananda Coomaraswamy:

> In the night of Brahma, Nature is inert, and cannot dance till Shiva wills it: He rises from His rapture, and dancing sends through inert matter pulsing waves of awakening sound, and lo! matter also dances appearing as a glory round about Him. Dancing, He sustains its manifold phenomena. In the fullness of time, still dancing, he destroys all forms and names by fire and gives new rest. This is poetry; but none the less, science.[73]

This dance-form that unites the spiritual, artistic and philosophical realms, has inspired many modern Westerners, such as the physicist and philosopher Fritjof Capra, who wrote: 'For the modern physicists, then, Shiva's dance is the dance of subatomic matter'.[74] The late astrophysicist Carl Sagan saw in the image of Siva 'a kind of premonition of modern astronomical ideas'.[75] Rukmini Arundale explains the philosophy of Indian dance thus:

It is the spirit of Purusha and Prakriti, an expression of evolution of movement, a truly creative force that is handed down the ages. This embodiment of sound and rhythm creating spiritual poetry is called dance or Natya. . . . The first glimpse of the dance comes to us from Siva Himself, a Yogi of Yogis. He shows us the Cosmic Dance and portrays to us he unity of Being. . . . The Cosmic Rhythm of His dance draws around Him ensouled matter, which manifests itself into the variety of this infinite and beautiful universe.[76]

Buddhists, Jains and later, the Sufi Muslims, held the aesthetics of these performing arts in high esteem, especially dance, poetry and music. They adopted these for their own religious as well as secular performances.

Christian Denigration of Indian Spiritual Dance

From the seventeenth century onwards, Christian missionaries made scathing attacks on the Indian classical dance-forms, seeing them as a heathen practice. This was often expressed by attacking the *devadasi* system on the grounds of human rights. The devadasis were temple dancers, dedicated in childhood to a particular deity. The system was at its peak in the tenth and eleventh centuries, but a few hundred years later, the traditional system of temples protected by powerful kings had faded away under Mughal rule, especially since the Mughals turned it into popular entertainment, devoid of spirituality. The devadasi system degenerated in some cases into temple dancers used for prostitution, although the extent of this was exaggerated by the colonialists.

Many of the English-educated elites of India accepted the colonial condemnation of their heritage and apologized for its 'primitiveness'. Some of them turned into Hindu reformers, and found the devadasi system detestable for moral and even social-hygienic reasons.[77] However, the devadasis saw their very existence threatened and sent handwritten pleas to the colonial government, explaining the spiritual foundation of Bharata Natyam. They quoted Siva from the Saiva Agamas, saying, 'To please me during my puja, arrangements must be made daily for *shudda nritta* (dance). This should be danced by females born of such families and the five acharyas should form the accompaniments'. Since these Agamas are revered by every Hindu, the devadasis asked, 'What reason can there be for our community not to thrive and exist as necessary adjuncts of temple service?' They opposed the proposed draconian punishment for performing their tradition, calling the legislation 'unparalleled in the civilized world'.[78]

Instead of abolition of their traditional profession, they demanded better education to restore their historical status. They wanted the religious, literary and artistic education as in the past, saying, 'Instill into us the *Gita* and the beauty of the *Ramayana* and explain to us the Agamas and the rites of worship'. This would inspire devadasi girls to model themselves after female saints like Maitreyi, Gargi and Manimekalai, and the women singers of the Vedas, such that:

> . . . we might once again become the preachers of morality and religion.
> . . . You who boast of your tender love for small communities, we
> pray that you may allow us to live and work out our salvation and
> manifest ourselves in *jnana* and *bhakti* and keep alight the torch of
> India's religion amidst the fogs and storms of increasing materialism
> and interpret the message of India to the world.[79]

Despite such attempts, the missionary influence continued to dominate Bharata Natyam, which came to be seen as immoral and faced almost-certain extinction. For example, a Dravidianist supported by missionary scholarship called the dance 'the lifeline that encourages the growth of prostitution'.[80]

However, Hindu savants worked tirelessly to remove the Christian slurs cast on this art form. Chief among them was Rukmini Devi Arundale (1904–86), who protected and revived this dance by founding the Kalakshetra Academy of Dance and Music in 1936. She made it an acceptable norm for girls (and even boys) from middle-class households to learn Bharata Natyam. Though operated like a modern institution, it functioned as a traditional *gurukula*, focusing on prayers to the deity Ganapati, vegetarianism, and a *guru-shishya* relationship. Throughout Tamil Nadu, the guru-shishya form of decentralized, one-on-one learning spread in various ways as part of this revival. Thus, far from being dead as intended by missionaries, colonialists and their Indian cronies, Bharata Natyam again became well established as a spiritual art-form in South India, and started to achieve acclaim throughout India and abroad. Kalakshetra grew into a university with a large campus in Chennai.

Strategic Shift: Subtle Christian Appropriation of Hindu Dance

In recent years, missionaries are again targeting Bharata Natyam. But this time, as a takeover candidate for digestion into Christianity. This reversal of strategy is in response to the growing enthusiasm for Bharata Natyam, including among many Western feminists who see Indian dance as a valorization of feminine sexuality.[81] Westerners took up this dance initially showing respect for Hindu practices and symbols, and studied under Hindu gurus, who naively welcomed the Christian disciples. Each of the individuals who are at the forefront of Christianizing the Bharata Natyam today, was initially taught by Hindu gurus.[82] In India there are many unsuspecting, or perhaps opportunistic, Hindu gurus who take this genre of Christian students under their wings. These Christian disciples worked very hard and many became exemplars, dancing to Hindu themes and enthralling the media and audiences.

However, they ran into conflicts between traditional Hindu art and Christian aesthetics and dogma. Father Francis Barboza, a prominent Roman Catholic priest and dancer of Hindu art forms, confesses that 'the main difficulty I faced in the area of technique' concerned what is Indian classical dance's unique feature, namely, the hand gestures (*hasta*) and postures. He confesses:

> I could use all of them in the original form except for the Deva
> Hasta [hand gestures], because the nature and significance of the
> Bible personalities are totally different and unique. Hence, when I
> wanted to depict Christ, the Christian Trinity (Father, Son and the
> Holy Spirit), I drew a blank. I realised that I had to invent new
> Deva Hasta to suit the Divine personalities and concepts of the
> Christian religion. This was a challenge to my creative, intellectual

and theological background. Armed with my knowledge of Christian theology and in-depth studies of ancient dance treatises, I then introduced a number of Deva Hasta to suit the personalities of the Bible. These innovations succeeded in making my presentation both genuinely Indian and Christian in content and form.[83]

Dr Barboza has Christianized the Bharata Natyam by inventing the following Christian *mudras*: God the Father; Son of God; The Holy Spirit; The Risen Christ; Mother Mary; The Cross; Madonna; The Church; and The Word of God; as well as two postures: Crucifixion, and The Risen Christ.[84] This strategy is strikingly similar to the development of Christian Yoga and Jewish Yoga by western practitioners who take what they want from yoga but reject or replace any symbols or concepts that are too explicitly Hindu.

Another example is the Kalai Kaveri College of Fine Arts, founded by a Catholic priest in 1977 as a cultural mission. He received patronage from various sources and sent out priests and nuns to learn from the unsuspecting Hindu gurus. The college claims to offer 'the world's first, off-campus degree program in Bharathanatyam', with another program in south Indian classical music (both vocal and instrumental). Its website's home page shows Dr Barboza's 'Christian mudras' using the Christian 'Father Deity' as the Bharata Natyam mudra replacing thousands of years of Hindu mudras.[85] Kalai Kaveri is backed and funded as a major Church campaign. The Tamil Nadu government is also actively funding and promoting it.[86]

Kalai Kaveri also has overseas branches. Its UK branch, with Lord Navnit Dholakia as its patron, 'administers performances and educational workshops in the UK by the dancers and movement instructors from Kàlai Kàveri College in south India'.[87] Its website contains a passage from its twenty-fifth anniversary handbook, *Resurgence*, which reveals the time-tested Christian technique of first praising Indian spirituality and then mapping it to Christian equivalents, such as the subtle the use of the phrase 'holy communion', which has specific religious importance to Christians that might not be noticed by others. It starts out with respect for the Vedic tradition:

Music and dance, when viewed in Indian tradition, are fundamentally one spiritual art, an integral yoga and a science of harmony. . . . According to the Vedas, the Divine Mother Vak (Vag Devi) sang the whole creation into being. God's eternal life-force, Para Sakthi, entered, or rather, assumed the perennial causal sound Nada through the monosyllabic seed-sound Om (Pranava). Thereby, the phenomenal world with its multiple forms evolved. This process of physical, vital, mental and soul contact or holy communion with God aims at complete harmony, perfect integration, and absolute identification with God, in all His manifested as well as unmanifested Lila (divine play and dance) at the individual, cosmic and supra-cosmic levels of existence.[88]

But as the article continues, the mapping turns more explicitly Christian:

Therefore, it is possible to trace each human sound or word back to its source by retracing step-by-step to the positive source, until the body of Brahman, called Sabda Brahman, is reached: 'In the beginning was Prajapathi, the Brahman (Prajapath vai idam agtre aseet) With whom was the word (Tasya vag dvitiya aseet) And the word was verily the supreme Brahman' (Vag vai paraman Brahman). This Vedic verse finds parallel in the fourth Gospel of the Christian New Testament: 'In the beginning was the word and the word was with God and the word was God.' (John 1.1) The 'Word' referred to here is the primal sound or Nama. It cannot be the spoken word, and hence it is the creative power of God. The mis-named Odes of Solomon, which are probably from second-century Christian Palestine or Syria convey the same truth metaphorically: 'There is nothing that is apart from the Lord, because He was before anything came into being. And the worlds came in to being by His word.' (Ode XVI:18-19)[89]

Father Saju George, a Jesuit priest from Kerala, is a Kalai Kaveri celebrity who learned from various Bharata Natyam gurus. He performs both Christian and Hindu themes. Kalai Kaveri boasts that:

. . . having also danced before Pope John Paul II in New Delhi, he has thus raised Bharathanatyam to the realm of Christian prayer and worship. . . . Here is a rare opportunity to experience a new flowering of an ancient vine. In the concerts, imageries of Radha Krishna share a platform with the crucifixion and resurrection of Jesus Christ.[90]

Blatantly Rejecting Hinduism while Christianizing the Bharata Natyam

Rani David, the founder of Kalairani Natya Saalai in Maryland, USA, (strategically located right next to a prominent Hindu temple) is even more blatant about Christianizing the Bharata Natyam. Her website does not hesitate to reveal her disdain of Hindu symbols that are a part of Bharata Natyam, and her vow to remove them from the dance. She wants to make Bharata Natyam non-Hindu:

> At one of the elaborate 'Salangai poojai', in spite of her conviction, she was embarrassed because her Christian values would not permit her to bow down before a statue, whether one of Nataraja, Mary or even Jesus Christ. It was then that she vowed to herself that one day she would fashion this beautiful art into one that could not be exclusively claimed by any one religion. That vow began its fulfillment at Edwina Bhaskaran's arangetram in '92 when a patham on Christ, 'Yesuvaiyae thoothi sei', was included.[91]

But her initial posture of pluralism leads to an exclusively Christian dance as an 'innovation', of which she is proud:

> Edwina's grandfather, Elder Edwin, congratulated Rani and inquired, 'Can you stage a full program with *only Christian items*?' . . . Consequently, 'Yesu-Yesu-Yesu', a two hour program on Christ was innovated and staged first in Maryland and then taken on tour to many parts of USA.[92]

Rani David is also proud of her collaborations with Father Barboza and other Indian Christians. In a tellingly titled article: 'The Concept of Christianizing', she begins by comparing the problems of Bharata Natyam with similar problems supposedly found in the Bible, making her assessment seem even-handed:

> History of Bharathanatyam reveals that it was misused by religious people and became a social stigma. Likewise, the word 'dance' itself in the Bible has had two bad 'sinful' references: once with the Israelites and the golden calf, and the other by Salome, who danced before Herod. [93]

In the next sentences, this façade of equal treatment is replaced by focusing on the positive aspects of dance *only* in the Bible. Citing particular verses that mention dance, she concludes:

> . . . dance is strongly implied to be present in God's Kingdom. But is there an unquestionable support? Yes, in Psalms 149:3 and 150:4 there are definite commands to include dances in the praising of God! One can hardly get any more definite than that![94]

In other words, when dance is condemned in the Bible, it maps onto the Hindu nature of Bharata Natyam, and both share the problem equally; but when dance is positively depicted in the Bible, it is solely a Christian phenomenon, without any Hindu parallels.

What is neatly glossed over is the obvious fact that Bharata Natyam was developed, institutionally nourished and theologically refined within Hinduism precisely because it is a tradition of embodied spirituality that valorizes the body—both male and female, and even animal—whereas the Abrahamic tradition, precisely because of its obsession with sin and fears of idolatry, has stifled the possibility of such bodily representation as a divine medium.[95]

Rani David then explains the challenges in trying to make Hinduism and Christianity co-exist in the dance. She states that there are:

> . . . two major differences that we cannot overlook. Hinduism is liberal and will accept anything 'good' as sacred. Christianity, on the other hand, is based on a 'zealous' God who commands you cannot worship any other gods. Christian form of worship is simplicity; that is why you see Christians dressed in white when they go to church. But a Hindu devotee believes in elaboration in worship. The more you beautify, the more acceptable! So where does one bring in Bharathanatyam? It is not an easy task to merge the two worlds. . . . it was the Catholic Priest Father Barboza who laid down some definite mudras, which you see displayed on this page. With the idea of making a universal adaptation, I have used some of these mudras in my choreography.[96]

Anita Ratnam, a prominent dancer, goes even further and claims in her 2007 event in Maryland: 'Rani David laid down facts and demonstrated that Christianity existed along with Bharathanatyam and Sanga Thamizh, but history lost in time has given Christianity a western outlook'.[97]

It is interesting to note how self-conscious and strategic the various Christians are when engaged in this cross-religious activity. Their Christianity is very explicitly present in their minds and they are deliberate in making their strategic choices. On the other hand, Hindus engaged in such cross-religious activities are easily lost in ideas of 'everything is the same' and 'there is no us and them'. One side (i.e. Christian) has a strategy and is constantly reworking and perfecting it in order to expand itself. The other side (i.e. Hindu) is naively unconcerned, and unwilling to see this is a competitive arena.

The Leela Samson Scandal

Rukmini Arundale, a guru who rescued the dance form from the era of colonial evangelism, speaks of dance as 'Sadhana which requires total devotion'.[98] Kalakshetra, the institution she founded to specifically stress the Hindu spiritual roots of Bharata Natyam, was recently captured by Christian evangelists led by Leela Samson. Samson started her connection to Kalakshetra as a high-school student and went on to a career as a dancer and teacher. According to a contemporary guru who knew her, Rukmini had reservations about admitting Leela Samson:

> Leela Samson, a senior artist today, came to Kalakshetra as a young girl. Because of her Judeo Christian background she had not had much exposure to traditional Indian culture. [Rukmani] was therefore hesitant about including her as a student. However, on examining her on various related aspects we found that she had the attributes of a good dancer. I then persuaded [Rukmani] to give her a chance and she did so, but with some reluctance.[99]

In 2005, Samson was appointed as the new director of Kalakshetra. In 2006, she provoked a media storm by justifying the elimination of the spiritual roots of Bharata Natyam. Trouble started in 2006, when Sri Sri Ravi Shankar, the head of Art of Living foundation, expressed his concern over the attempt of Leela Sampson to thwart the participation of Kalakshetra students in the inaugural function of a 'Health and Bliss' religious course being conducted by him in Chennai. According to *Ananda Vikatan,* a popular Tamil weekly, the most disturbing aspect was the reason cited by Leela Samson. She explained: 'This function is concerned with Hindu religion. So Kalakshetra students need not participate in it'.[100]

This was soon followed by an article that appeared in *Hindu Voice,* a magazine run by Hindu nationalists, which claimed that under the Samson tutelage at Kalakshetra, most of the Vinayaka images for which regular pujas had been historically conducted by the students, were removed. Only after a lot of criticism did she replace one image but not all. Samson ordered all prayers to the deity to be stopped, and the clothes adorning the deities were removed.[101] As this progressed into a major controversy, Samson was forced to react but denied all the charges. She made the claim that 'Kalakshetra never had idols that were worshipped. A lamp was all that was lit in every place we worshipped, according to Theosophical principles and the highest philosophical principles upheld by our elders'.[102]

Whereas Siva's Nataraja form represents the Cosmic Dancer, the dancing form of Ganesha has customarily been invoked by Indian dancer and worshipped before a performance. The suppression of these 'idols' by Leela Samson was an attempt to detach Bharata Natyam from its traditional roots, under the guise of secularization, and then remapping it within Christian theology and symbolism. Her response against 'idol worship' contradicts her mentor and the institution's founder, Rukmini Arundale, who had defended the Hindu worship of various deities' images:

> All the songs we dance to are of Gods and Goddesses. You may ask, why so many Gods and Goddesses? The only reply I can give is, *Why not so many Gods and Goddess?*[103]

Rukmini did not support the vague notion of a 'universal religion' and in fact, specifically critiqued this sort of generic spirituality, saying:

> Some people say, 'I believe in universal religion', but when I ask them whether they know anything about Hinduism, they answer in

negative. They know nothing about Christianity, nor about Buddhism or about any other religion either. In other words, universality is, knowing nothing of anything. . . . Real internationalism is truly the emergence of the best in each. . . . But, in India, when I say India, I mean the India of the sages and saints who gave the country its keynote, there arose the ideal of one life, and of the divinity that lives in all creatures; not merely in humanity.[104]

In the morning assembly, Samson allegedly told the students and teachers that idol worship is superstition and should be discouraged at Kalakshetra. There were complaints that her hand-picked teachers explained the *Gita Govinda* in denigrating tones. The certificate that was designed by Rukmini Arundale with Narthana Vinayakar, had the emblem of Siva on it. The present certificate has been changed and is without any Hindu symbols.[105]

Samson has been criticized for undervaluing the Hindu stories and symbols to the point of ridicule, comparing them with Walt Disney's characters, Batman and 'the strange characters in Star Wars'.[106] In contrast, Rukmini explains the deep meaning of symbolism in the ballad *Kumarasambhava*:

> Why does the story of *Kumarasambhava* please me? It is because of the symbolism. Finally what Parvati wins is not passion but the devotion and sublimation of herself. Parvati wins Siva and she becomes united with Him, because she has discovered the greater, indeed the only way of discovering God. This is very beautiful symbology. Siva burnt to ashes all that is physical. So must a dancer or musician burn to ashes all thought which is dross and bring out the gold which is within.[107]

She speaks of the *Ramayana* and *Mahabharata* as the 'essential expressions of Indian dance'.[108] Far from being man-made stories, as Leela Samson considers Indian narratives to be, Rukmini Arundale speaks of Sri Rama, Sri Krishna and Buddha in the following manner:

> Why was India a world power? Because Sri Krishna had lived in this country, Sri Rama had lived here and so had Lord Buddha. It was their Teaching that made India a great world power.[109]

Where Leela Samson sees the equivalents of Batman and Mickey Mouse characters, the founder of Kalakshetra sees great world teachers and symbolism of the most sublime kind. In Samson's appropriation, Bharata Natyam was denied its vital spiritual, devotional, aesthetic and pedagogical dimensions, and dragged down to the fantastic, garish level of cartoons. Thus, in Leela Samson's own words, the process of usurpation can be seen in its crucial stages: initially de-Hinduizing and secularizing the art form, and then Christianizing it.

Christianizing the Tamil Folk-Arts

Missionary scholarship tirelessly continues to establish a mutually exclusive divide between folk-art and Hinduism. The conceptual framework for this is derived from the works of Risley, Hodgson and Caldwell from a century ago. 'High' art is shown as oppression by Brahmins, and folk-art as revolt from the Dravidians.

Art that is considered as the 'high' tradition and art that is seen as beloning to the folk-level or 'little' traditions, actually constitute the two symbiotic poles of a single continuum across India. The high tradition typically provides the ritual and theological framework at the folk level, where practices are less formal and meant to serve popular interests. The cultural image of Nataraja is an example of a bridge between these two poles: the Pashupata ascetic of 'high' culture is shown in a state of ecstatic trance representing the 'folk' culture.

A Jesuit college, with a folklore department funded by the Ford Foundation, released a textbook on folklore, which employs exclusively western tools from colonial Indology and Marxism.[110] One of its scholars, S.D. Lourdu, claimed that his study of folklore would help to re-formulate the identity of Tamil folk-gods. According to Lourdu, most Tamil folk-gods and goddesses came from Jainism or Buddhism, and were later transformed by Saivism. He substitutes a Christianized version of a Hindu folk-song as an example of equally authentic folk-literature. The original folk-song describes how Valli, the bride of the Tamil god Murugan, ran and hid herself near a mountain. (A variant speaks of Valli hiding beyond the Milky ocean.) Lord Muruga, who could not bear the separation from the Divine face of Valli, searched for her.[111] Lourdu equates this with a Christian song: 'Jesus ran and hid himself in the bush. Mary searched for Jesus across the ocean of Milk'.[112] While a folk-song evolves organically within a community through generations, here a scholar re-formulates the existing Hindu folk-traditions into Christian ones, and in the process, confuses the erotic relationship of Valli and Muragan with the mother–child relationship of Mary and Jesus.

It is not surprising that in a book published by the Jesuit college to commemorate the fiftieth anniversary of India's independence, Lourdu makes obscene puns on India's much-beloved national song, 'Vande Mataram', such as 'Vande Mataram! I want to urinate (Muthram). Bring a vessel and drink'.[113]

9

Propagation of 'Dravidian' Christianity

S ince 2000, the St Thomas Dravidian Christianity hoax has been taken to the public square of Tamil Nadu and has received support from international forces that are tangibly hostile to India. This chapter traces this development through a series of conferences that served to forge close collaborations between India-based and foreign-based interests. Fig 9.1 shows the major milestones these collaborations have achieved thus far, which are as follows:

- All caste problems in Tamil Nadu were blamed on a Brahmin-Aryan conspiracy, and Dravidian Christianity was offered as the solution.
- Once caste was explicitly conflated with race, proponents of Dravidian Christianity wrote to the Durban anti-racism conference that India was the mother of international racism.
- Propaganda materials were published, declaring India as a Dravidian Christian nation.
- American evangelicals began to exploit the opportunity to evangelize the Tamil diaspora by establishing a positive association between the Dravidian identity and Christianity.
- Conferences in 2007 and 2008 went several steps further by claiming that Dravidian mysticism, literature, sculpture, and dance

were really manifestations of Christianity and were rooted in the work of St Thomas.

These developments will be elaborated in this chapter.

Fig 9.1 Dravidian Christianity Enters the Public Square

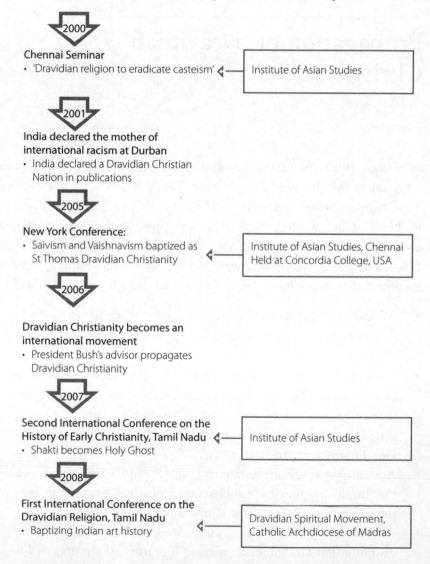

2000

Chennai Seminar
- 'Dravidian religion to eradicate casteism' ← Institute of Asian Studies

2001

India declared the mother of international racism at Durban
- India declared a Dravidian Christian Nation in publications

2005

New York Conference:
- Saivism and Vaishnavism baptized as St Thomas Dravidian Christianity ← Institute of Asian Studies, Chennai Held at Concordia College, USA

2006

Dravidian Christianity becomes an international movement
- President Bush's advisor propagates Dravidian Christianity

2007

Second International Conference on the History of Early Christianity, Tamil Nadu ← Institute of Asian Studies
- Shakti becomes Holy Ghost

2008

First International Conference on the Dravidian Religion, Tamil Nadu ← Dravidian Spiritual Movement, Catholic Archdiocese of Madras
- Baptizing Indian art history

2000: Seminar on 'Dravidian Religion to Eradicate Casteism'

The Institute of Asian Studies under John Samuel has transformed itself into a nodal point for promoting Deivanayagam's thesis. In 2000, Deivanayagam and the institute organized a seminar in Chennai, with an innocent-sounding goal: How to eradicate caste and religious clashes in India, and restore India's peace and social harmony. It was heavily attended by Dravidianist political leaders and served as a watershed event to cement the relationship between Dravidianism and Christianity. The seminar ended with a declaration that may be summarized as follows:

1. Dravidians should realize their historical greatness if they want to free themselves from the ongoing Aryan oppression. They should shed off their inferiority complex by realizing their universal spiritual excellence, which can be traced through historic evidence.
2. When Dravidians are called upon to declare their religion, they should opt to declare it as 'Dravidian Religion' or by some other acceptable term, which has a historic basis. They should shun Hinduism, which has been harmful for the great Dravidian identity.[1]

2001: India Declared the Mother of International Racism

At the United Nations World Conference against 'Racism, Racial Discrimination, Xenophobia and Intolerance', held in Durban, South Africa, activists continued to develop the theme that a conspiracy by Hinduism, Brahmins, and Aryans was responsible for virtually every social problem worldwide. Deivanayagam and his daughter Devakala distributed their book, *International Racism is the Child of India's Casteism*.[2] They explained their conclusions as follows:

- Sanskrit came after Christianity, and it was created by Dravidians (p. 9). William Jones was fooled by the similarity between Sanskrit and Greek/Latin into thinking that it was ancient. (p. 10)

- Thomas brought early Christianity to India, but the crafty Brahmins, particularly Adi Shankara, perverted it by introducing casteism into it. (p. 15)
- Racism was originated by the Aryan Brahmins of India, and it penetrated Christianity, which was already under the control of White Europeans. This happened because the Europeans were made to believe that they were also Aryans by race. (p. 14)

The conflation of Aryans and/or Brahmins with the Whites, and of Dravidians with the Blacks, has deepened and merged with the Afro-Dalit movement that conflates Dalits with Africans. The mission of this movement is to bring together Dravidians and Dalits, representing them as the oppressed 'Blacks' of India. This will be explained further in Chapter Twelve.

Deivanayagam's book called on the UN to put an end to racism everywhere in the world. Though it is an altruistic demand, his methods primarily consist of a vicious attack on a core Hindu institution: the Shankara Mutts. These are monastries established in the ninth century CE by the legendary Shankara, a south Indian saint. Although these four Matts, or religious institutions, are located geographically in the four corners of India and are heralded as a symbol of India's cultural unity, Deivanayagam attacked them as the historical source of all racism 'throughout the world', demanding their closure:

> To eradicate racism from the world, casteism should be removed from India. As casteism is linked with manipulated religious beliefs, hereditary privileges and rights given to religious heads, i.e., Shankara Mutts should be removed. When hereditary privileges given to religious heads will be removed, India's casteism will be abolished. When casteism will be abolished from India, racism will be eradicated from the world. If this does not happen . . . it will not only maintain racism throughout the world, but also it will spread the cancer of casteism all over the world by manipulated religious beliefs, and will destroy world peace.[3]

In another pamphlet, Deivanayagam explains that:

> Aryan Brahmins captured the religions of the Dravidians, namely, Buddhism, Jainism and Vaishnavism. They took the monotheistic

concept of Saivism and Vaishnavism from the Bhakthi movement of Tamil Nadu and twisted it into monism (I am God); thereby claiming that Brahmin is God. . . . The Brahmins established Shankara Mutts in the nineth century AD all over India to maintain racism and casteism . . .[4]

2004: 'India is a Dravidian Christian Nation, and Christians Made Sanskrit'

In 2004, Devakala published a four-hundred-page guidebook for field missionaries and evangelical institutions, titled *India is a Thomas-Dravidian Christian Nation . . . How?* [5] The book is filled with hatred such as:

> Dravidian rulers were cunningly cheated by Aryans through women, diabolic schemes, drugs, and denial of education. The idea of 'Aham Brahmasmi' was another evil atheist idea brought by Aryans. Originally, Aham Brahmasmi meant 'God is in me' but Shankara cunningly twisted it as 'I am God'.[6]

The book makes some ridiculously misinformed claims in the question-answer section meant for training missionaries, such as:

> Question: What is the period of Sanskrit?
> Answer: Sanskrit belongs to 150 CE. It originated after Jesus.
> Question: What seven languages form Sanskrit?
> Answer: Tamil, Pali, Hebrew, Greek, Latin, Persian and Aramaic.
> Question: Who created Sanskrit language?
> Answer: Thomas Christians created Sanskrit language. The purpose of Sanskrit was to help spread Christianity to other parts of India where Tamil was not spoken.[7]

2005: New York Conference on Re-imagining Hinduism as St Thomas Dravidian Christianity

In 2005, three organizations came together to hold the 'First International Conference on the History of Early Christianity in India from the advent of St Thomas to Vasco da Gama'. These were: the Institute of Asian Studies, the Dravidian Spiritual Movement that was founded by

Deivanayagam, and New York Christian Tamil Temple. An information piece about the event boasted its evangelical orientation:

> May this great project enthuse our evangelists to work with a deep sense of pride and commitment with rich and fascinating material for the expansion of the kingdom of our Lord on this earth, and thus to shower peace and prosperity on humanity at large and Indian nation in particular.[8]

The official announcement of the New York conference unhesitatingly claimed that India's classical traditions, including Tamil literature, Saivism, Vaishnavism, and Mahayana Buddhism, had been shaped out of Christianity:

> Christianity in Tamil Nadu . . . was a very potential force and its ethics and other theological codes find powerful expression even in secular Tamil Classics like *Thirukural* and *Naladiyar*. Its impact is felt in the native worship and especially in the local religions like Saivism and Vaishnavism. It is obvious that India received a number of missionaries, many of whom belonged to Asia and other parts of the world. The Yavanar, probably people from Greece and Rome, spread the message of Christianity in the length and breadth of Indian soil. Anyhow, we are able to understand that Christianity was deeply rooted in the Indian milieu, thanks to the works of proselytism by men of eminence, starting from St Thomas. But most of the records have been lost or destroyed and Christianity might have underwent lot of sea-changes owing to many a time of adversity faced by it. It has left its strong impact on the other religions of India; it was instrumental for the emergence of many Indian religions. Its presence is felt in all religions of India in various forms. Its impact on the emergence of Mahayana Buddhism, especially in the conception of the Bodhisatva as well as the second coming of the Maitreya Buddha, is indeed marvelous.[9]

The conference souvenir contained color images of a scene of Thiruvalluvar listening in rapt attention to St Thomas, implying that classical Tamil literature originated from St Thomas. Another image shows a semi-clad person with a Kudumi hairstyle (marker of a Brahmin)[10] killing the saffron-clad Thomas, who is shown absorbed in prayer.[11]

This was a high-profile game plan to appropriate not only Hinduism but the entire spectrum of Indian and Asian spiritual traditions, including Buddhism and Jainism. It received support from several American authorities, including Senator Hillary Clinton, who wrote:

> The first International Conference on the History of Early Christianity in India will successfully combine different and diverse resources to fully explore the presence of early Christianity in India. *I am confident that the breadth of resources presented during the conference will shed light on the impact of Christianity on medieval and classical Indian and its effect on the cultural and political climate of India and throughout the world.*[12]

Many papers presented the impact of St Thomas on Tamil culture, as a matter of established fact. All Tamil spiritual cardinal values were traced back to an imagined Thomas Christianity. Colonial-era evangelical views of Indian 'myths' and history, despite being widely discredited, were recycled to support the claims. For example, in a paper titled 'History of Early Christianity in India – a survey', the authors asserted that there are 'scholars who believe that . . . the Krishna cycle of stories have borrowed extensively from Christian sources'. Among the scholars cited is Sir William Jones, who 'held that the four gospels which abounded in the first years of Christianity found their way to India and were known to the Hindus'. The authors listed every similarity between Krishna and Christ, not in a spirit of ecumenicism, but to prove the primacy of the Christian version. All this was built on the idea that Krishna worship was a late development in India, starting only after the time of Christ.[13]

These ideas are all rooted in the nineteenth-century colonial-evangelical historiographies, which have long been rejected by scholars, but are strangely now in vogue once again. Established scholars are clear on the history of Krishna, as illustrated by Edwin Bryant, who wrote: 'The worship of Krishna as a divine figure can be traced to well before the Common Era'. He then offers numerous detailed references to Krishna in various writings that go back to the fourth century BCE.[14] Bryant is just one of the sources that cite references to Krishna made by ancient Greeks several centuries before Christ:

The earliest archeological evidence of Krishna as a divine being is the Besnagar or Heliodorus column . . . dated to around 100 BCE. The inscription is particularly noteworthy because it reveals that a foreigner has been converted to the Krishna religion by this period – Heliodorus was a Greek.[15]

But such evidence is ignored by the Christian Dravidianists, who quote and re-quote one another as authorities. Of the twenty-six publications listed in the 'select bibliography' included in one article, at least eighteen belong to evangelists.[16]

John Samuel was pleased by the reception given to his Institute of Asian Studies by American Churchmen and the Tamil diaspora:

Scholars from all sections of Indian society, including the Indologists of various countries, congratulated this center for having dared to undertake pioneering and bold studies . . . The Indian media and political circle appreciated the efforts of the Institute of Asian Studies in glowing terms when it embarked on further new projects connected with Saivite and Vaishnavite studies . . .[17]

However, ironically, once his Christian game plan became clear among the indigenous Tamil population and things were no longer going so smoothly, Samuel explains that he had to change his evangelical strategies and reshuffle the basic organization of his institution. He wrote:

But we faced unforeseen opposition when we declared about our programmes pertaining to Christian studies, which is a vital part of the Asian sensibilities and heritage. Although this forms the basic agenda of this center and a significant component of its constitution, we found it very difficult to execute the projects connected with early Christianity till we made a thorough reshuffling of the basic structure of this organization.[18]

The synopses of key papers presented at the conference are given in Appendix E.

'Christian Essence' in Tamil Literature

Taken together, these papers claimed a Christian origin for every significant achievement of Tamil society throughout the ages. One presenter, Professor Hepzibah Jesudan, got swept up by this fever and the official synopsis of her paper described it as follows:

> This paper focuses on the influence of Christianity in Tamil literature. *Thirukural* embodies the concepts of Christianity in its verses. *Cilapathikaram*, a Jain literature, mentions a 'Son of God' who attained heavenly body at the age of thirty three – commandments which are like Ten Commandments are found in the later portion of *Cilapathikaram*. Krishnapillai declares Kampan's Iramavatharam to be Christian in outlook. The Bhakti movement literature abounds with expression Christian values [sic]. Civavakkiar, an eminent Siddha, talks of 'the one who died and then lived' – there are many indirect references to Jesus Christ in Siddha Literature; which makes them Christian in essence.[19]

This shocked many secular-minded Tamil intellectuals such as Jeyamohan, a prominent Tamil Marxist and Gandhian writer of modern Tamil literature. Referring first to Hepzibah Jesudan's husband, also a well-known scholar, Jeyamohan traces the Christian biases:

> Prof Jesudasan is one of the important starting points of this thought process. . . . In his old age he along with the help of his wife, Prof. Hepzibah Jesudasan wrote the literary history of Tamil elaborately in three volumes. This was named *Count down from Solomon*. Explaining his title, Professor stated that the most ancient reference to Tamil literature comes from the Songs of Solomon in Old Testament. Here he mentions the belief that Thomas came to South India in one place. . . . In her last days Prof Hepzibah Jesudasan started arguing that such values as love, righteousness, integrity of character, etc., came into existence in Tamil literature only through Christianity, as heathen ancient Tamil minds could not have had such lofty conceptions.[20]

Christian Roots of Tamil Bridal Mysticism

The rich tradition of bridal mysticism is important in Tamil devotional literature. The mystic poet Andal considered herself the bride of Vishnu; and many Alwars and Nayanmars relate to Siva or Vishnu through the feelings of bridal mysticism. These ideas have shaped the inner terrain of the Tamil spiritual psyche and the larger public devotional culture. For example, during the Tamil month of Markhazhi, Hindus collectively sing the hymns of Andal.

Though there are clear Vedic roots to bridal mysticism,[21] Christian scholars trace the roots of Tamil bridal mysticism to Solomon's Song of Songs in the Bible. This idea can be put to use by evangelists, as in an article that appeared in the *Institute of Asian Studies Journal*:

> The Tamil tradition and the Hebrew tradition, as depicted in The Song of Songs, move on parallel lines. But at the same time, there is one important difference – between these two traditions, the Hebrew tradition is based on religion while the tradition of Tamils is purely secular.[22]

In other words, while the Tamils had similar sentiments as the Semitic people of the Bible, they lacked the true religion of the Bible. Even while conflating Tamil classics with Judeo-Christian origins, there is always the explicit or implicit superiority of the Bible as the 'original' and 'pure' version, and the Tamil culture as an incomplete version that needs to return to its pure source. The article then explains the history of Christian missionaries who brought the 'true religion' that turned earlier Tamil songs into Bhakti mysticism:

> The middle ages is a period of Devotional Literature as far as Tamil literature is concerned . . . During this period, which begins from the first century AD, a number of Christian saints like St Thomas and scholars like G.U. Pope, Ellis and Fr Beschi emerged in the scenario . . . Tamil literature, which had been hitherto free from any religious or sectarian influence began to come under the spell of various sects. . . . Though the prime object of the Christian missionaries was to propagate Christianity, their service to Tamil literature is really invaluable. Because of their deep-rooted love of Tamil literature and because of their poetic talent and erudition, they contributed a lot for the advancement of Tamil literature. The above saints and scholars did not directly contribute anything to the bridal mysticism. The Hebrew tradition, enshrined in the Old Testament, began to slowly find its place in Tamil literature also! . . . This took place during the medieval period. Countless Bhakti literature sprang up in the form of devotional songs. These are comparable with the Song of Songs of Solomon.[23]

The author goes on to list the great Bhakti poets of Tamil literature whose poetry exhibits bridal mysticism. He concludes:

> The technique of Bridal Mysticism has taken a deep root in Tamil Literature and has added luster to it. It is a great contribution of Christianity and we are highly indebted to that tradition.[24]

The chronological sequence being implied is a glaring falsification. Every Christian mentioned herein, except for St Thomas, actually lived many centuries *after* the great bridal mystic devotional poets of Tamil tradition. G.U. Pope (1820–1908), Beschi (1680–1747) and Ellis (1779–1819) came long after the Tamil poets named in the article, such as Gnana Sambandar (seventh century), Kulasekhara Alwar (eighth century), and Andal (ninth century). Yet the scholar ignores the chronology in order to claim that Tamil Bhakti was a great contribution of Christianity and they are highly indebted to that tradition. The same scholar presented a paper at the 2005 New York conference with the following synopsis in the program brochure:

> The present paper aims at studying the generic relationship that exists among the songs of bridal mysticism in the Christian tradition and devotional corpus of the Tamil tradition. . . . The study reveals the fact that the Christian tradition has exerted deep impact on the Tamil devotional poetry.[25]

2006: Dravidian Christianity Becomes an International Movement

Immediately after the New York conference, Deivanayagam's supporters in the US formed a World Tamil Spiritual Awareness Movement. In 2006, a Dravidianist organization called Periyar Tamil Peravai, headed by a man described as 'a firebrand separatist, pro-LTTE leader, hardcore Tamil nationalist',[26] honored Deivanayagam with the 'Spiritual Champion of People's Development Award'.[27] Indeed, Deivanayagam has evolved from a small-time, discredited crackpot to a powerful catalyst who is bringing together Christian evangelists and Dravidian separatists.

Among the well-placed Christian fundamentalists who have been influenced by Deivanayagam, one example is Prof M.M. Ninan, a retired college principal and brother of a former governor of Nagaland. In the brief about his e-book *Hinduism: What Really Happened*, Ninan defines Hinduism as: 'heresy of the Thomas Christianity in India'.[28]

President Bush's Advisor Propagates Dravidian Christianity

Marvin Olasky, an advisor to President George W. Bush, also chief editor of the *World Magazine*, writes for his huge American readership about global Christianity. His article titled 'How Did Jesus Change Hinduism?' introduces the history of Hinduism to American readers, saying that:

> the two major denominations of Hinduism today—Vishnu-followers and Shiva-followers—arose not from early Hinduism but from early Christian churches probably planted by the apostle Thomas in India from AD 52 to 68.[29]

He goes on to explain that prior to the arrival of Christianity, the Indian religions were either based on animal sacrifices or were atheistic (by which he means Buddhism and Jainism). It was St Thomas who gave Indians the religion of salvation by faith, without any need for animal sacrifices. This was part of Christianity's gift of 'a Trinitarian faith that proclaimed God's willingness to come to earth as an avatar (incarnation)'.[30]

Deivanayagam bonded with Olasky by taking him to a famous temple at Kanchipuram. He interpreted the Hindu temple for Olasky through his Christian lens, which the latter uncritically accepted. Later, Olasky gave the following examples of Christian influences in the Hindu temple:[31]

- Since the shape of the temple was not square, Olasky felt it must be 'loosely modeled on the Temple in Jerusalem'.
- The priest gave coconut water and some solid pieces of a medicinal leaf, while chanting, and Olasky saw this as 'a Hindu imitation of communion'.

- Another image reminded Olasky of Christians being persecuted in India. He described 'a figure of a man undergoing punishment by being impaled on a sharp stake. Both of his arms were thrust out so the portrayal looked like a man on a cross. Next to that icon was the figure of another man, hung upside down as (by tradition) Peter was in Rome'. Having made these observations, Olasky asked, 'Is this what happened to the early Christians of India?'

- Hindus could not explain to his satisfaction why the number three repeats so often as a motif in Hinduism. Olasky, therefore, felt that it was referring to the Christian Trinity, which Hindus did not understand.

Further Expansion into India

One of the attendees of the 2005 New York Conference was Dr J. David Baskara Doss, whose PhD dissertation was titled 'Six Darshanas and the Religion of Tamils in the Light of the Bible'. He conducts seminars on disguising Christian evangelism, and is the curriculum director of an evangelical institution with a secular name: National Institute of Leadership Training (NILT).[32] It describes its aim of 'leadership training' as leading 'heathens' to Jesus:

> Lead Heathens to look upon God to beseech, 'Draw me, we will run after thee.' (Song 1:4) If they do so, certainly Father will draw them near to Jesus (Jer. 31:3). Jesus proclaimed that they come to Him, because the Father had drawn them to Himself (John 6:44). Jesus will lift up these folks to be with Him one day (John 12:32).[33]

An article by Doss, titled 'Contribution of St Thomas to the Development of Indian Religion and Philosophy', states:

> The atheistic religions of Buddhism and Jainism were well rooted in India as early as sixth century BC. The minor-god-worship, King-worship, Hero-worship, nature, worship, polytheism, henotheism, sacrificial worship of the Dravidians and such worship of the Aryans, etc., were prevalent in India at the time of the advent of St Thomas. . . . The interrelationship between 'karma' and 'dharma' is thus misinterpreted as religious sanctions by the Aryans to subjugate the

Dravidians using their own philosophies. . . . The sacrifice of the 'historical avatarin', Isa (Isan > Iswaran = Jesus) for the remission of sin was the message that St Thomas had propagated in India and it had permeated into the Indian religion and Indian philosophy and had developed as doctrines.[34]

Another article by Doss's institute asserts that Vyasa was a Thomas-Christian, which then explains the similarities between the Gita and the Gospels:

Almost every Indian philosophy and religion agrees that the soul had fallen into bondage. But they do not explain how this bondage came into being. . . . Vedanta plays an important role in the history of religion and philosophy of India. The contribution of Vyasa school of thought in the Indian cultural background needs a thorough investigation, for it is harmonious with the doctrine of Christianity.[35]

Many Hindus, including gurus, are duped into thinking that this kind of thesis showing Hindu-Christian similarities is a genuine way to promote harmony or to show the equal validity of both faiths. In fact, many Hindu leaders actively promote this kind of cross-mapping of Hinduism on to Christian reference-points and frameworks. They are unaware that they play into the hands of a carefully formulated strategy for not only conversions, but also for the manufacture of a distinct non-Hindu and non-Indian ethnic identity for Tamils, run by a well-managed machinery.

The Pope Confuses the Issue

In 2006, Pope Benedict XVI gave a speech in which he said that St Thomas came to India through Persia and evangelized in western India, which would really mean modern-day Pakistan. This passing reference so upset the powerful Thomas lobby in India that the story was amended in its published version. The controversy led to an article in *The Times of India*, headlined 'Thomas's Visit Under Doubt'.[36] This incident suggests that **the Thomas story, so essential to Dravidianists and evangelists, is at best vague even in Rome.** Importantly, this very contemporary example of revisionist storytelling shows how the Thomas tale can be adjusted as local politics may require.

2007: Second International Conference on the History of Early Christianity in India

The success of the New York Conference of 2005 led to the second conference on 'early' Indian Christianity, in 2007 in Chennai. The proponents of Thomas Dravidian Christianity basically re-quoted each other's old papers as authoritative references to substantiate their preposterous claims. Indian audiences and readers were fed this as scholarship that had been accepted in the USA, and this boosted its credibility. For example, Ezra Sargunam, founder of Evangelical Church of India, wrote an article in the conference souvenir, titled 'Impact of Christianity on the Belief Systems, Cultural Heritage of India'. It said:

> It is a well accepted scholarship that it was Vednatha Vyasar, a Dravidian scholar, who reduced into writing the oral traditions of the Vedas, Upanishads. According to Dr Deivanayagam and other Oriental scholars, Vedantha Vyasar (or his school) was responsible for spreading the Dravidian form of Christianity in India. Vyasar approved of the rituals like offering incense, sacrifice and prayers found in the core of the Semitic-Dravidian religions.[37]

While most articles recycled the papers presented at the first conference, there were some significant expansions. For example, Hephzibah Jesudason's paper claimed to show that Kampan's and Tulsi's Ramayans have 'the influence of Christianity on them'.[38] Baskara Doss discussed the influence of the Old Testament on *Purva Mimamsa* and the influence of the New Testament on *Uttara Mimamsa*.[39]

Other scholars became bolder in their claims. For example, Moses Michael Faraday's 2005 paper in New York had made the more modest claim that 'the cryptic connotations ensconced in Siddha poems have to be deciphered with the tools of Christian concepts and teachings, which will also reveal the influence of Christianity in Siddha literature'. But now his claim was more emphatic:

> The aim of this paper is to bring out the influence and impact of Christianity and teachings of Christ on these [Siddhas'] strange voices of the religious world. . . . The paper tries to prove that the reasons behind the boldness of Tamil Siddhas could be understood only when we indentify the influence of Christian teachings in them.[40]

Other notable papers included: 'Christianity and *Mahabharatha*', 'Christian Thoughts in Tribal Lore', and 'Adaptation of Indigenous Telugu Folk Art Forms for Evangelism'.[41]

Shakti Becomes the Holy Ghost

In order to facilitate the Christianization of Tamil culture, it is essential to co-opt the philosophy and worship of Shakti into Christianity, due to the importance given to Shakti by Hindus everywhere, and because a similar feminine divinity is missing in Abrahamic religions. The ploys used, once again run across the spectrum: from blatant and crude attempts to sophisticated theological conjectures. An approximate template of the process is as follows:

- The first goal is to decouple Tantra and related feminine empowerment away from Hinduism and identify it with Dravidian 'tribalism'.
- This break up of Hinduism then makes it vulnerable to further manipulation.
- The next project is to transform and assimilate components of Hinduism, like Tantra and Shakti, into Christianity.

Alf Hiltebeitel, who has extensively studied Mother Goddess worship in south Indian rural areas, admits that among his western peers, 'One suspects a motivation to find Dravidian epic roots for the cult of the allegedly "northern Aryan" Draupadi'.[42] The following account is typical of the manner in which western academicia attempts to make Tantra distinctly 'Dravidian' and anti-Aryan. A novel feature in this rendering is the assertion that Kali came from the European Alps – presupposing that in antiquity, some dark-skinned people lived there. Kali's iconography is meant to signify her fight against light-skinned Aryans. This is yet another version of the patronizing methodology designed to export divisiveness within India by appealing to Tamil people as victims of Aryan hegemony:

> In the beginning was the original Tantric-Dravidian Kali, who was eventually superseded by the 'official' one. If you want to fully

grasp her secret Dravidian significance, you must notice that all the heads, all the corpses are male and have either a white or swarthy complexion: no women, no dark skinned people. . . . The Alpino-Mediterraneans were of mixed indigenous origin, lived in the hot Indian tropical climate and had dark skin like Dravidians today. But their northern enemies were 'pale faces'. . . . Kali is therefore, an emanation of the Good Mother, a manifestation of her ire toward her enemies. Now who were the Dravidians' enemies if not the fearful Aryans? Kali thus incarnates hatred for the Aryans and in order to better fight and crush them she is heavily armed with the Dravidians' favorite weapons except for the trident, which is Shiva's prerogative.[43]

There are even Hindu thinkers who have supported such claims that locate Hindu deities in the European past. They are oblivious to the larger game or how such mappings play out in the long run. Father Bede Griffiths, a Catholic priest who spent his career in South India and often dressed and behaved like a Hindu monk, employed similar ideas to Christianize Hinduism. He made Hindus feel proud that their faith resembled Christianity and it could thus be seen as universal. But his work had a different effect upon Dravidians, and he fed evangelical strategies. He proposed separating Tantra from Hinduism, saying that, 'This movement of Tantra came into Hinduism and Buddhism. It was a movement from below and must have come from pre-Aryan people. It's not Aryan which is patriarchal, but pre-Aryan'.[44] After his death, Hiltebeitel's thesis has been propagated by the Bede Griffiths Trust, whose newsletter wrote:

> Bede marvelously traces how historically the Tantric texts, which first begin to appear in the third century CE, rise up out of the indigenous Dravidian Shaivism of South India, where devotion to God as mother is very strong, so the tendency is to assert the values of nature and of the body, of the senses and of sex. Many things which tended to be suppressed in the Aryan Vishnu tradition came to be reverenced by Tantra.[45]

Father Thomas Berry is a well-known 'liberal' Catholic theologian who studied Hinduism much of his career and wrote extensively about it in the West. Most scholars of religion think of him as someone very sympathetic towards Hinduism, having borrowed so much from it in order to reformulate his own ideas of liberal Christianity. He acknowledges that Sri Aurobindo treated Tantra as integral to unified Indic traditions. But he asserts that recent 'research' has shown that Tantra was Dravidian and separate from Aryan, and that Sri Aurobindo was unaware of these 'facts'. Berry states that it is the Dravidian Tantra that is truly 'Indian', unlike the Aryan Sanskrit traditions. He 'regrets' this 'deficiency' in Sri Aurobindo's understanding that Tantra 'was derived more from these pre-Aryan and non-Aryan traditions than from the Aryan, Sanskrit tradition'.[46] He uses patronizing language to praise Sri Aurobindo for introducing Dravidian Shakti into the Aryan Vedas, 'and so enabling India to rise up again gloriously in the sight of the nations'.[47]

Once this decoupling of Tantra from Hinduism has been achieved, and Dravidian Tamil Tantra has been placed in tension against Aryan Sanskrit Vedas, the stage is set to co-opt Tantra and Shakti into Christianity. Devakala can then claim Christian origins for Tantra and Shakti:

> There was no theistic religion in pre-Christ era in India . . . History of religions reveals that the doctrine of divinity, and the doctrine of Avatar, Fulfillment of Sacrifice and the doctrine of salvation by surrendering oneself by faith, are the basic doctrines of Christianity. Christianity that developed in India from the early centuries of Christian era (say from first century AD) in the Indian soil Indian culture and Indian language, is Early Christianity or St Thomas Christianity or St Thomas Tamil/Dravidian Christianity . . . When the Trinity was explained as Father, Holy Spirit and Son, some envisioned the Holy Spirit in a female form.[48]

2008: First International Conference on the Religion of Tamils

In 2008, the Catholic diocese of Chennai and Deivanayagam's World Tamils Spiritual Awareness Movement jointly announced their First World Conference on Tamil Religion. While this title implied all Tamil religions, in fact there was not a single Hindu

among the coordinators. The coordinators included Archbishop
Malayappan Chinnappa, Auxiliary Bishop Lawrence Pius Dorairaj,
D. Deivanayagam, and his daughter Devakala. The introductory note
to the conference lists the subjects to be discussed:

> Lemurian theory of human origin; Tamils establishing Sumerian
> civilization; Tamil as the universal language before the Babel event; . . .
> Memorial stone worship in Indus civilization and worship of stone
> in Bethel as described in Bible . . . Siva's dance in relation to
> resurrected Jesus – the living stone. . . . Enslaving of Tamil language,
> culture and religion; Brahmins – aliens-aryans . . . Sanskrit evolved
> only after second century AD. The reason why Sanskrit authors
> like Veda Vyasa, Kalidasa and Vanmiki (Valmiki) were Dravidians;
> the reason why Asoka's edicts do not have Sanskrit; who created
> Sanskrit.[49]

The conference began with the inaugural address of Cardinal
Vithayathil, president of the Catholic Bishops' Conference of India,
in which he emphasized that the conference was the result of the
Second Vatican Council, and that Dravidian spirituality should find
its fulfillment in Jesus.[50]

With just a little bit of investigation, it can be seen that the scholar-
evangelist Christian nexus is securely shielded in Western academic
environs, from where certain lenience is shown to Dravidians, claiming
the Tamil origin of world civilizations and other chauvinistic claims.
The grand strategy is to allow, and seemingly even encourage, such
chauvinism if it serves to undermine the unity of India by encouraging
a clash between Dravidians and other Indians. The Lemurian origins
theory is the climax of Dravidian chauvinism and the Lemurian card
gets played from time to time to win hearts.

Return of the Lemurian-Tamil Origins Thesis

The conference sessions repeated the same themes encountered in the
previous two conferences held by the Institute of Asian Studies.[51] On
the opening day, it was claimed that humanity originated in Lemuria
or Kumari Kandam. Victor's paper claimed to derive various non-

Indian words from Tamil to show that Tamil had been the fount of civilization. He then claimed that the Bible's Genesis speaks about Kumari Kandam and that Tamils were dispersed during the deluge. Migration myths narrated in the Bible were linked with Tamil places and Indus Valley Civilization.[52] Another scholar claimed that the Egyptian, Native American and Australian people originated from Tamil Nadu and that Sanskrit was a language that was created in the post-Christian era. He also showed that the Egyptian terms such as Pharaoh, Akanaten, Tutankhamun, and Mesopotamia, were actually derived from Tamil. During the question-answer session he claimed that the Aryans were a branch of Tamils who migrated to the western deserts outside India and came back in a degenerate yet cunning manner to enslave Tamils.[53]

Deivanayagam provided a handout titled 'World's first language – Tamil: World's first human – Tamil: World's first race – Tamil race: Common name of world's religions – Tamil religion. How?' Thirty points were enumerated in his pamphlet, including the following:

> . . . Sanskrit had no existence prior to second century AD. There is no epigraphic or numismatic evidence for Sanskrit. The first Sanskrit inscription is dated as 150 AD. But Tamil inscriptions are dated to third century BC. . . . Indus valley civilization has been proved to be the civilization of Tamils. Before Indus valley civilization, Tamil antiquity is spoken of by the Kumari Kandam, which was destroyed in the Deluge. Old Testament, which gives an account of the origin of man, is written in Hebrew. Victor has written a book that derives Hebrew from Tamil. M.K.G. Maulana has stated that the Sethu bridge in Rameshwaram is named after third son of world's first man Adam, whose name was Seth. . . . The verses of the Bible (Genesis 11:1 and 2) explain that World's first language was Tamil and these verses link Sumerian civilization with Indus valley civilization. In Chennai at the Tamil Nadu government tourism exhibition, at stall number 31A these developments of Tamil religion are explained and we request Tamil people to visit the stall. Tamils and Tamil religion today are enslaved. To know how and who will liberate Tamil religion, visit our stall . . .[54]

Demonizing Sanskrit, Darwin and Vedanta

The attempts of the Christian-Dravidianist missions to portray Sanskrit as post-Christian builds on some colonial Indologists' preposterous position that Sanskrit was the result of Alexander's invasion. The leading proponent of this view was the Scottish philosopher Dugald Stewart (1753–1828). Thomas Trautmann explains:

> Stewart's conjunction, briefly put, was that the Brahmins coming into contact with the Greek language through the conquest of Alexander, who reached into the Panjab, invented a new language in which the words of their native dialect were joined with terminations and syntax taken from Greek . . . In brief, the reason Sanskrit resembles Greek is not because the two are historically related through a common ancestral language . . . but because Sanskrit is Greek in Indian dress.[55]

Trautmann goes on to show how 'The whole argument is carried out under the distinctly Protestant trope of priest craft, applied alike to Catholic clergy and the Brahmins'.[56] In this current metamorphosis, the familiar thesis has been resurrected once again, except that in this incarnation, the age of Sanskrit is further reduced to the post-Christian era rather than the colonial version of the thesis that showed it as originating in the post-Greek era. The invasion of Alexander is now replaced by the coming of St Thomas, to explain how Sanskrit entered India. The demonizing of Sanskrit and campaigns to destroy it have been adopted by the present Dravidianists from colonial Indology. According to Trautmann, ending the 'tyranny of Sanskrit' was the goal of Race Science during its formative period in the nineteenth century. However, the resulting race-based political trajectories are still very operative within the Indian society.[57]

Deivanayagam's paper claimed that Tamil grammar itself reflected what he called the 'soul science', because it showed proximity to Christian theology. The session chair, a veteran Tamil scholar, Auvai Natarajan, expressed that Deivanayagam was wrong and that his thesis was influenced by his religion. Deivanayagam ignored these criticisms and proceeded, by using creationist arguments, to attack Darwinian evolution.[58] Furthermore, he attacked the idea of reincarnation as atheistic. His severest attack was reserved for Advaita: He stated that Islamic and Christian theologies consider Advaita to be Satanic.[59]

Baptizing Indian Art History

Devakala, Deivanayagam's daughter, was an active participant in numerous sessions, where she repeated that Christianity brought by St Thomas had degenerated into forms which became known as Saivism, Vaishnavism, Mahayana Buddhism and Svethamabara Jainism. In her slide show, which was also published in the conference souvenir, almost all major Hindu-Buddhist sculptures were claimed to represent either Christian or Christian-influenced doctrines. Fig 9.2 summarizes the father-daughter duo's re-imagination of Indian art history.

Fig. 9.2: Christianizing the Hindu/Buddhist Art History

	Hindu/Buddhist Art	Devakala-Deivanayagam Claim
1	Statue of Buddha with round marks on feet and palms found in Udayagiri caves, Orissa	'Buddha with nail pierced palms and feet … reminds of nail pierced Son of God'
2	Pre-Christian era Buddhist stupa lacks figure of Buddha, as against post-Christian era where Buddha statues can be found.	'Because of the concept of "Avatar"' (God became Man/Guru)
3	Sivalinga with Siva face	Sivalinga with faces can be found only in the Post-Christian era.
4	Buddha statue	'God who took a form of a man is visualized as a Guru'
5	Arthanareeswara statue: androgynous form of Siva with Shakthi	'Supreme God with spirit of God in Male and Female form'
6	Sankara Narayana form	'Supreme God with spirit of God in both male forms'
7	Elephanta cave Mahadeva	'Triune God – Expression of three persons in one essence: concept of "Homoousious"'
8	Siva as Nataraja: Cosmic dance	'Reminds of resurrection concept'

Source: (Devakala, D, 2008)

Social Inequalities seen as Exclusively Hindu

At this conference, issues concerning both Dravidians and Dalits were interwoven, with a new emphasis on caste appearing in Dravidian writings. The Dalit issue will be discussed extensively in later chapters. The two issues come together around the idea that caste equals race – a demonstrably false idea that has been recently resurrected from colonial roots and is now being worked to empower several divisive trends.

At the conference, the session on the caste system started with a paper read by Prof Samson.[60] The copious references to socially stratified hierarchical society that Tamil Sangam literature shows, were explained away through hair-splitting rhetoric that played on the emotions of Tamils. The strategy is to portray caste as a 'foreign evil imposed on Tamils', in order to win their sympathies. While ancient Tamil literature did not identity Brahmins as alien to Tamil society, now they were repeatedly attacked in the name of Tamil purity. It was also alleged repeatedly that caste-like stratifications were unique to Indian society and that no other religion except Hinduism sanctioned inequalities based on birth. Traditional Tamil terms for Brahmins, and references to caste were blamed on foreign influences injected into Tamil by the cunning Brahmins, as impurities into the pristine Tamil society. Brahmins were accused of winning over Tamil kings by enticing them with women. When someone raised the issue of the ill-treatment of Samarians in Biblical times, the response was that this ill-treatment was merely political and not religious, whereas the Indian caste system was rooted in Hindu religion.

Deivanayagam said that Jews had destroyed Israeli temples and tyrannized Samaritans, and because of those sins, Jews had to suffer for two thousand years. He described the Holocaust as a judgment by God, because Jews did not accept absolution of their sin through the fulfillment of sacrifice (implying that they suffered the Holocaust because they did not accept Jesus).[61] A thread of such anti-Semitism runs throughout this Dravidian Christian theorizing. Deivanayagam also stated that prior to Jesus the concept of after-life in heaven/hell was not present in any theistic religion. According to him the only religions prior to Christianity in India were Jainism and Buddhism, which were atheistic religions. Thus, a fully formed theistic religion was Christianity's gift to India.

Christian-Dravidianism vs Modern Archeology

Most modern propagandists of Thomas Dravidian Christianity base their arguments on premises formulated by the father-daughter team, Deivanayagam-Devakala. Fig 9.3 highlights these premises, most of which have their origins in the colonial period, and have already been falsified by several decades of archeological discoveries.

Fig 9.3: Modern Archeology Falsifies Dravidian Christianity

	Dravidian Christianity	Modern Archeology
1	The concept of tri-faced God is post-Christian.	'Siva "tri-murti" form is recognizable in the three-headed horned god familiar to the Indus people and to modern Hindu's. (Woolley, 1958, 82)
2	Earliest Sanskrit inscriptions are dated second century CE, making Sanskrit a post-Christian development to propagate Christianity to North India.	'Earliest Sanskrit inscriptions appear in epigraphic use in the first century BCE at Ayodhya, Ghosundi and the Hathibada stone inscription's. (Solomon, 1998, 86)
3	The Sivalinga with Siva's face is a post-Christian development.	Sivalingas with multiple faces have been unearthed belonging to eras as early as second century BCE. (Kramrisch, 1994, 179)
4	Avatar concept (God coming in human form) is post-Christian.	Idea of Krishna as divine incarnation of Vishnu is pre Christian. (Bryant 2007, 4-7)
5	Before Christian influence in India there was no theistic religion that spoke of the after-life, or the moral conduct in this life for the sake of after-life, etc.	Indic religion, that antedates Christian era is not only theistic but also speaks of liberation after death and offers a code of conduct to live by, as clearly stated by the inscription in the Garuda standard erected by the Indo-Greek ambassador to the Sunga king in 110 BCE.
6	Prior to Christianity, all worships necessitated blood sacrifice.	Sacrificial as well as non-sacrificial worships have co-existed in Hinduism since antiquity, and sacrifice did not necessarily require blood.
7	Concept of heaven and hell/after-life first propounded by Jesus, and is not part of any theistic theology prior to Jesus.	Christian notions of hell, like those of angels and of the Devil, may derive more from ancient Zoroastrian traditions than from scant Biblical references. (Bennett, 2001, 95)

Assessing the Robustness of the Thomas Myth

Given all the evidence to the contrary, one wonders why there is such a persistent myth among missionaries associating St Thomas with India. One of the factors is the Gospel of Thomas, discovered in a Coptic papyrus manuscript discovered in 1945 at Nag Hammadi, Egypt. According to Richard Valantasis, the scholarly consensus for the date of the Gospel of Thomas is between 60 to 120 CE.[62] This makes the work one of the oldest Gospels. Elaine Pagels of Princeton University puts forth the possibility that, contrary to the evangelists' claim of Thomas bringing Christianity to India, the exact reverse was the case, namely, that Thomas was the one who represented Indian religions (especially Buddhism) in influencing early Christianity. She wrote:

> Yet the gnostic Gospel of Thomas relates that as soon as Thomas recognizes him, Jesus says to Thomas that they have both received their being from the same source . . . Does not such teaching—the identity of the divine and human, the concern with illusion and enlightenment, the founder who is presented not as Lord, but as spiritual guide—sound more Eastern than Western? Some scholars have suggested that if the names were changed, the 'living Buddha' appropriately could say what the Gospel of Thomas attributes to the living Jesus. Could Hindu or Buddhist tradition have influenced gnosticism? The British scholar of Buddhism, Edward Conze, suggests that it had. Trade routes between the Greco-Roman world and the Far East were opening up at the time when gnosticism flourished (AD 80–200); for generations, Buddhist missionaries had been proselytizing in Alexandria. We note, too, that Hippolytus, who was a Greek-speaking Christian in Rome (c. 225), knows of the Indian Brahmins, and includes their tradition among the sources of heresy: 'There is . . . among the Indians a heresy of those who philosophize among the Brahmins, who live a self-sufficient life, abstaining from (eating) living creatures and all cooked food . . . They say that God is light, not like the light one sees, nor like the sun nor fire, but to them God is discourse, not that which finds expression in articulate sounds, but that of knowledge (gnosis) through which the secret mysteries of nature are perceived by the wise.' Could the title of the Gospel of Thomas—named after the disciple who, tradition tells us,

went to India—suggest the influence of Indian tradition? These hints indicate the possibility, yet our evidence is not conclusive.[63]

While Dravidian Christian politics claim Thomas to be the intermediary bringing Biblical influence to India, the exact opposite is found in the writings of Western scholars such as Pagels, who are not associated with church evangelism in India. They show that the Gospel of Thomas is in many ways contradicting and undermining the foundations of what is today known as Christianity. The Church was threatened by these Indian gnostic ideas, because they undermined the authority of the institutionalized church as intermediary between man and God, thereby empowering every individual seeker's direct *sadhana*. The early Church ruthlessly destroyed the gnostic dimensions. It replaced Gnosticism with the Thomas myth, in order to justify destroying the Indian sources of gnosticism as heresies. It is plausible that the Indian Thomas was morphed into the Christian Thomas, and then deployed to reverse the direction of the historical flow of influence.

Even as such academic debunking of Dravidian Christianity happens, the real danger is that the massive institutional mechanism that the Church has built in south India is leading to its infiltration of Dravidian politics and to an ethnic-religious identity that can be controlled by powerful global forces. Many south Indian Hindus have swallowed the bait of Aryans Dravidian antagonism. Even though prominent Saiva Siddhanta scholars have refuted the anti-Vedic Dravidian identity, this corruption of history and religion has entered the mainstream and has become a major player in the Christianization of south Indian spirituality.

Dravidian Spirituality as Interim Stage for Christianizing

In the nineteenth century, most Tamil scholars and Saiva Siddhanta experts condemned the European scholars' idea of a Dravidian separatist identity built in opposition to Vedas. Even those Tamil scholars who regarded Tamil literature and civilization to be superior to Sanskrit did not demonize Sanskrit. A good example was 'Manonmaniam' Sundaram Pillai (1855–97). He claimed that Tamil was superior to Sanskrit because Tamil was still used in his day as a popular language. A Tamil song by him has been recognized as the official song of Tamil Nadu. However, he never denigrated or rejected Sanskrit, and visualized Tamil and Sanskrit as two eyes of the Goddess of learning, though for him Tamil was the right eye. When Bishop Caldwell dated the seventh-century Saiva saint Thirugnana Sambandar at the end of the thirteenth century, Sundaram Pillai refuted this dating and emphatically established that Sambandar could not be dated later than seventh century CE.[64]

Another Saiva Siddhanta scholar, Sabaratna Mudaliar (1858–1922) examining the research of Caldwell on Saivite saints, said:

> Dr Caldwell was a Christian missionary and although he has rendered some service to Tamil literature, still he cannot be said to be free from his Christian prejudice.[65]

J. M. Nallaswami Pillai (1864–1920) was another great scholar who toiled to popularize Saiva Siddhanta, and he closely corresponded with G.U. Pope. Though initially he trusted Pope to be a genuine admirer of Saiva Siddhanta, Pilllai was later horrified that Pope slandered Saiva saints in his work and attributed these attacks to his 'pure ignorance'.[66] Pillai vehemently rejected the idea that Saiva Siddhanta was not related to Vedas and Sanskrit. He stated emphatically:

> All the terms and forms we use are derived from Sanskrit: and the bulk of literature in Tamil dwindles to insignificance when compared with the vast 'Agama' Literatre in Sanskrit. Our Tamil acharyas were also great Sanskritists . . . Our author states expressly . . . how this precious religion and philosophy is based on the Vedas and Agamas.[67]

Thirumuruga Kirupananda Vaariyar (1906–93) was both a great Saivite scholar and an authority on classic Tamil literature and spirituality. When asked whether Saivites should use Sanskrit mantras, he responded:

Sanskrit being the common language of all people (in India) the
Mantras are in Sanskrit . . . From time immemorial Saivites have
recited the Mantras from Samhitas as a tradition. To analyse this
with hatred, is not beneficial.[68]

Despite this background, today there is a growing movement
of Tamil-based non-Vedic rituals, being spearheaded by a section
of Dravidianists. One such popular movement is run by Sathyavel
Murugan, an electrical engineer turned self-styled Saiva Siddhanta
theologian and Tamil ritualist. He popularizes the concept of 'Tamil
marriages' where Vedic rituals are rejected and replaced by Tamil
hymns. He states that:

> . . . the Sanskrit word 'vivaha' means to abduct, i.e. abducting a girl
> for purpose of marriage, which act, needless to say, is barbarian. . . .
> Moreover, in Sanskrit-marriage, the mantrams chanted are neither
> understandable to us nor to those chanting them, for Sanskrit is a
> dead language. There are many rituals in Sanskrit-marriage which are
> insipid, irrational, immoral, obscene and objectionable . . .[69]

When the DMK government in Tamil Nadu changed the traditional
Tamil new year from Chitrai to Thai, he welcomed it with accolades,
saying that every Tamil should worship the direction in which the chief
minister was sitting.[70] He propagates a theology of Saiva Siddhanta
designed to dissociate its salient features from the rest of Indian
spirituality, and explicitly mapping it to Christianity. Fig 9.4 illustrates
this.

Fig 9.4 Genuine Saiva Siddhanta vs Claims of Bogus Dravidian Christianity

Traditional Saivite principle	Claim of Dravidian religion	Pathway towards Christianity
Pasu-Pathi-Pasam: The term is explained as Pathi (Lord of sacrifice), Pasu (individual atman, the sacrificial animal), Pasam (the rope that ties it). When the rope Pasam is burnt, the atman is set free to identify itself, with Pathi (God). (Sivaratnam,C., 1978, 21). The term Pathi is explained traditionally as the most satisfying explanation of Vedic and Upanishadic texts. (Mudaliar, 1968, 28)	Pathi, Pasu and Pasam mean the Shepherd, Sheep and the Shackle. (Murugan, 2009)	Saiva Siddhanta's traditional reinforcement of Vedas gets removed and replaced by the imagery of Jesus as the unique and universal shepherd.
The Saiva Siddhanta text *Thirumantra* explains Sivalinga at various levels: at the macro level it represents the entire Cosmos; at the micro level it represents the physical body; and at the inner level it symbolises the consciousness whose sound symbol is Pranava.	'Finding so many criterions [sic] in common between the Lord, the light and flame, Dravidians started off worshipping the Lord through flame … Finding them infeasible with flame, they resorted to image of stone, resembling the flame, erect in position. Never-the-ess, anointing the image required them to form a base around it for collection of water and cleaning thereof with channel-like end for way out. This is how the image of Lingam had come into existence.' (Murugan 2009)	Reduces Linga to worship of deity as light in the Abrahamic sense.
'Social harmony' as envisioned in Saiva Siddhanta, is based on Vedic dictum of *Ekam Sath Vibra Bahuthavathanthi*. (N. Pillai, 1911:2009, 274)	Completely ignores this, and states: 'Lord Siva will be harsh towards a Christian who is not true to it, towards a Muslim who is not true to it and in just the same way towards all other 'religionists who are not true to their respective religion'. (Murugan, 2009)	This conveys a punishing deity similar to the Abrahamic deity, and positions Christians and Muslims as victims.
In traditional Saiva Siddhanta schools, antiquity of Siva is traced to Vedas. (N. Pillai; 1911:2009, 274)	Argues the antiquity of Siva by 'talking Christianity as the first instance' and restates a nineteenth century missionary claim that, 'the earl est mention of this God' is in the books of Amos (Chapter V, 25-26). (Murugan, 2009)	This falsely distances Siva worship from its Vedic roots, and gives the appearance of Siva being mentioned in Bible.

10

Dravidian Academic-Activist Network Outside India

What started out as a linguistic speculation among Western academicians about classical India has been turned into a mechanism for intervention and domination through a divide-and-rule methodology. Herbert Risley's Race Science of the nineteenth century is gone, but in its place there is now an implicitly racial interpretation of classical India and its literature. Owing to the persistent 'scholarship' of Western Indologists, this has eventually superseded centuries of harmonious and pluralistic native interpretations. These powerful constructs have percolated into India's polity, combining with pre-existing fault lines.

Political activists build organizations that morph into secessionist movements. There is a loose web with one end in the academic centers of Western institutions, and the other in conflict in places like South India.

After the Second World War, the academic center of gravity for ethno-linguistic research shifted from England to the United States, especially Harvard, Yale, and the University of California at Berkeley. Their distinct roles of these three universities' programs can be summarized as follows:

Yale

Yale University's project of a Dravidian Etymological Dictionary served as a geopolitical tool to boost Dravidian identity politics, which had been nascent and smoldering within Tamil Nadu, and to legitimize its tendencies for secession from India. Yale academicians fostered what can be termed to as linguistic secessionism.

Harvard

Western scholars later launched projects to identity numerous linguistic fragments within India, giving the communities the status of separate ethnicities that had been subjugated by foreign Aryans. At first, these ideas were used to support only Dravidian secessionism. More recently, the focus has shifted from Dravidian to Munda as the 'original natives', and many Western scholars are reclassifying even the Dravidians as 'outsiders'. The creation of ever smaller group-identities increases fragmentation and conflict. This has been one of the persistent consequences of Western academia, i.e., to bring about linguistic fragmentation. The present Maoist militancy regions in central Indian states are precisely where this work has focused for the past twenty years.

Berkeley

The study of the classical literatures of Indian languages provides opportunities for creating divisiveness. We can see the example of the Berkeley Tamil Chair, where scholars have created tension between Tamil literature and the rest of Indian literature. Every tiny local distinction available to them is exaggerated, but elements that are common with the rest of India and that unify all Indians are claimed to be the result of Brahmin manipulation.

Once a linguistically separate Tamil identity has been created, the ground is set to promote a Tamil transnational movement. Activists are nurtured to exacerbate the centrifugal forces in India. Western money flows in, and scholars from the West have strategic links in the conflict zones, where they covertly or openly support secessionist movements. Proselytizers support these movements and utilize Tamil studies in the West to link evangelical Christian institutions and Tamil identity, as we will see in detail in this chapter.

Fig 10.1 Roles of Western Academic Networks in Tamil Identity Politics

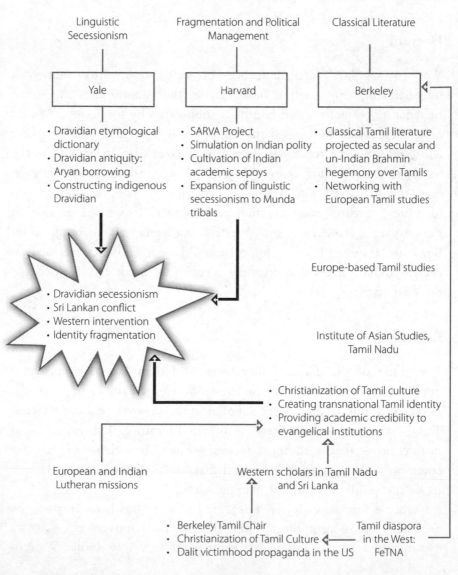

Linguistic Secessionism

Fragmentation and Political Management

Classical Literature

Yale

Harvard

Berkeley

- Dravidian etymological dictionary
- Dravidian antiquity: Aryan borrowing
- Constructing indigenous Dravidian

- SARVA Project
- Simulation on Indian polity
- Cultivation of Indian academic sepoys
- Expansion of linguistic secessionism to Munda tribals

- Classical Tamil literature projected as secular and un-Indian Brahmin hegemony over Tamils
- Networking with European Tamil studies

- Dravidian secessionism
- Sri Lankan conflict
- Western intervention
- Identity fragmentation

Europe-based Tamil studies

Institute of Asian Studies, Tamil Nadu

- Christianization of Tamil culture
- Creating transnational Tamil identity
- Providing academic credibility to evangelical institutions

European and Indian Lutheran missions

Western scholars in Tamil Nadu and Sri Lanka

- Berkeley Tamil Chair
- Christianization of Tamil Culture
- Dalit victimhood propaganda in the US

Tamil diaspora in the West: FeTNA

Several organizations have sprung up to promote these complex linkages. For example, FeTNA is a US-based Tamil Diaspora organization that finances the Tamil Chair in Berkeley and acted as a vehicle for ethno-political separatism, with links to the Tamil Tigers. It supports the Christianizing of Tamil culture and offers a doorway into Indian politics for right-wing evangelical American politicians and Western geo-political strategists.

Fig 10.1 presents a visual flowchart of the role played by some prominent institutions in providing intellectual fodder, credibility, political clout and in some cases, funding, to various ethnic conflicts in Tamil Nadu.

Oxford-Yale Origins of the Dravidian Linguistic Canon

The Dravidian Etymological Dictionary, compiled by Murray Barnson Emeneau (1904–2005) of Yale University,[1] and Thomas Burrow (1909–86) of Oxford University, was a scholarly landmark in the development of separatist Dravidian ideology. It can also be seen as the starting point of a major relocation of Western Indological studies from Europe to the United States.

Emeneau was a Yale University scholar who came to India in 1943 for three years, and undertook the 'historical study [of] the minority languages as seriously as those with literary traditions'.[2] These languages were Badaga, Kolami and Toda. His work was seen as very important in the West and in 1949, he was made the president of the Linguistic Society of the United States. In a paper published in 1956, he famously declared India as 'a Linguistic Area'.[3] This implied that India was a geography co-inhabited by unconnected language-groups reflecting a long history of conflicts and conquest without any history of kinship, an idea which became a powerful tool for further anthropological and linguistic fragmentation of communities in India. It helped the construction of sub-national identities based on claiming linguistic disconnectedness among various groups of Indians.

Thomas Burrow was a British Indologist who had the very prestigious title of Boden Professor of Sanskrit at Oxford from 1944 to 1976. He collaborated with Emeneau and in 1961 they published on the subject of 'loanwords' in Dravidian languages from Indo-Aryan. In 1966 they published *A Dravidian Etymological Dictionary*, followed by a supplement in 1968.[4] With a revised 1984 second edition, it has become the 'indispensable guide, tool, and authority for every Dravidianist'.[5]

The basic premise they claimed was that Dravidian languages were older than Sanskrit and that Sanskrit appropriated the Dravidian vocabulary. The political analogy could now be made, and the idea took root that the Aryans had conquered and oppressed the Dravidians, who now must reassert their identity.

Belated Doubts

Initially, Emeneau was very confident of the Dravidian origin of the non-Sanskrit substratum in Vedic languages. However, later he publicly acknowledged that the Dravidian origins which he and Barrow had ascribed to most of the Rig Vedic substratum words were, in reality, largely conjectures and not empirical facts. In 1980, he stated that the words loaned from Dravidian into Indo-Aryan are 'in fact all merely suggestions'; 'all etymologies are in the last analysis unprovable'; and that such theories are 'acts of faith'.[6] Emeneau conceded, 'It is clear that not all of Burrow's suggested borrowing from Dravidian will stand the test of his own principles.'[7]

But such belated backtracking was too mild and too late, because by then the academic speculation about a Dravidian substratum had already become entrenched and assumed a life of its own. Dravidian discourse was now very political, and had become hardened in the hands of separatist ideologues. For instance, Devaneya Pavanar, inspired by such examples of Western Indology, had already based his Tamil chauvinism theories on substratum claims. His 1966 book, *The Primary Classical Language of the World*, extended the analysis of Burrow and Emeneau and concluded that the 'old or Lemurian Tamil was not only the parent of the Dravidian family of languages, but also the progenitor of the Indo-European form of Speech'.[8]

The Emeneau–Burrow thesis had very quickly travelled far from linguistics into the grassroots politics of separatism, and the retraction by Emeneau was simply ignored. Scholars who didn't accept the Aryan/Dravidian colonial framework were sidelined in the academy as well as in popular Tamil circles. Over time, such interpretations were abandoned in favor of the theory generated by Western academics that Aryan peoples had colonized South India and subjugated its original inhabitants.

An example of a different interpretation of the common words shared by Tamil and Sanskrit is the refreshing 1979 observation of Franklin Southworth, a linguist from the University of Pennsylvania. According to his analysis: 'these two lists [Dravidian and Indo-Aryan] both seem to suggest a rather wide range of cultural contacts, and that they do not show the typical (or stereotypical) one-sided borrowing relationship expected in a colonial situation'. Southworth continued, 'No picture of technological, cultural or military dominance by either side emerges from an examination of these words'.[9] But Burrow, who was situated in a more politically powerful position than was Southworth, insisted that there was some linguistic evidence for the Indo-Aryan invasion, even while acknowledging that there was no archeological evidence for this.[10] Southworth eventually acquiesced to the academic politics, and has joined a project to extend the etymological constructions commenced by Burrow and Emeneau.

B.A. Sharada and M. Chetana, of the Central Institute of Indian Languages in Mysore, made an exhaustive analysis of citation statistics in the Emeneau–Burrow dictionary. They show that the dictionary was cited with increasing frequency throughout the 1960s and 1970s, the period that also witnessed frenzied ascendancy of Dravidian politics in Tamil Nadu.[11] This raises the important question: Were academic Dravidianists encouraging politics of separatism on the ground? Or was the ground politics in India demanding academic credibility from abroad? The answer is both: The local and the global were often parallel developments that reinforced each other.

Today, Burrow and Emeneau have become iconic figures in shaping the Dravidian discourse. Their etymological dictionary has become a canonic authority in south Asian linguistics, particularly Tamil studies. Their importance in support of a separate Dravidian identity is only overshadowed by the colonial evangelist Robert Caldwell.

The idea of a Dravidian substratum for Vedic languages has also become popular among Afro-Dravidianists, who claim a common root for Dravidians and Africans, based on questionable legends and archeology. This is discussed in Chapter Twelve. In one example of this political confluence, a leader from Senegal, who later became its prime minister, quoted Burrow and Emeneau as his sources in a lecture titled 'Negritude and Dravidian Culture', delivered in Madras under the auspices of the International Institute of Tamil Studies in 1974.[12]

Once the Dravidian identity was successfully separated and put in tension with other Indians, it became co-opted by numerous geopolitical forces, such as African nationalism, fostering a racial bond with Dravidians, Christians penetrating the Dravidian identity politics to Christianize the populace, Dalit caste mobilization seeking to assimilate Dravidians within the Dalit identity, and various permutations and combinations of these.

Academic Discourse Drives Indian Politics: Annadurai

This new Dravidian identity was not simply a matter of ethnic pride. Rather, the same period that saw the publication of the *Dravidian Etymological Dictionary* gave rise to separatist political movements. Yale University continued to play a role by nurturing the career of a prominent Dravidianist politician, C.N. Annadurai (1909–69), who was the chief minister of Tamil Nadu from 1967 to 1969.

Annadurai emerged as the main ideologue and mass leader of Dravidianism. Crawford Young explains that his vocal separatism was drawing together 'the anti-Brahmin, Dravidian heritage and the Tamil cultural themes in a belligerent challenge to the Indian government'.[13] In 1949, he helped found the Dravida Munnetra Kazhagam (DMK), a political party with separatist views. This party continues to dominate politics in Tamil Nadu today. His position on the fragmentation of

India is clear in the following well-publicized speech delivered during Mahatma Gandhi's independence struggle:

> India is a continent; it should be divided into a number of countries.
> . . . Aryan influence increases within a single country called India.
> Welfare of the other races is crushed under Aryan rule. Uniting different races under a single country leads to rebellions and troubles. In order to prevent such troubles and bloodshed in India, we should divide India according to racial lines now. . . . The reason one race has not choked another race to death in India so far is the British guns. When the British leave, India will become a killing field.[14]

There were forces in the United States which covertly supported Annadurai's separatist ideology during the Cold War, as a ploy to counteract Nehru, who was tilting towards the Soviets, and thereby undermine what US policymakers regarded as the Nehruvian threat from the Third World. The 1962 Chinese invasion of India created a strong wave of Indian nationalism and led to a constitutional amendment that made separatism illegal. That is when DMK dropped the secessionist part of its official ideology. In 1965, however, DMK launched a massive violent agitation against Hindi becoming the official language of India. The movement became militant, and exposed for the world to see the potential faultlines for balkanization of the nascent Indian state.

Moves by the American CIA and other intelligence agencies are always difficult to document. However, the biography of T.N. Seshan, the former chief election commissioner of India, attempted to expose such an alleged link:

> There was clearly a foreign hand behind [Dravidian] agitation
> . . . Some Dravida leaders had been influenced with American money routed through Sri Lanka and they became, if unsuspectingly, ready instruments of destabilizations. *Annadurai perhaps did not know it but he was becoming an effective plaything of America's intelligence machinery.*[15]

The Seshan biography, published in 1994, soon became controversial, and there were even attempts at physical violence against him. The book remains unofficially banned in Tamil Nadu, instead of triggering an open discussion and inquiry into the matter.[16]

Yale's long-term involvement can be seen in Annadurai's invitation by the US State Department[17] to participate in the prestigious Chubb Fellowship program at Yale in 1968, making him the first non-American to be so honored. A recent book, titled *Life and Times of Anna*, by R. Kannan, argues that Annadurai was using anti-nationalism for political posturing within India only, but that he was not anti-India at heart.[18] However, the legacy that he left behind, albeit inadvertently, did not follow his heart and rather followed his politics.

SARVA Project and Identity Politics

After the *Dravidian Etymological Dictionary*, the next major activity in Western Indology with implications for sub-national identity politics is now being carried out by the Department of Sanskrit and Indian Studies at Harvard University. The South Asia Residual Vocabulary Assemblage (SARVA) project is led by the following scholars:

- Michael Witzel, Wales Professor of Sanskrit at Harvard University.
- Franklin C. Southworth, University of Pennsylvania, who as we noted earlier, was opposed to interpreting the Tamil-Sanskrit relationship as a one-way asymmetric one, until he got involved with SARVA.
- Steve Farmer, who worked for the American National Security Administration (NSA) in the 1960s, and claims to be 'independent' of any particular institution.[19]

The overarching strategy of this project is in three steps:

1. Establish the separate identities among various Indian tribes, by showing their linguistic separation from Sanskrit.
2. Reinterpret their oral narratives in a manner that maximizes the difference from or opposition to Sanskrit culture.

3. Develop a history that shows these tribes' ancestors to be the inhabitants of the Indus-Sarasvati civilization, prior to 'foreign Aryans' colonizing them, overrunning them, pushing them into the South, and oppressing them.

Archeological artifacts of the ancient Indus Valley Civilization have been appropriated to support the claim that the Dravidians were the original peoples of the subcontinent. In this manner Dravidians, and subsequently smaller tribal and/or social groups, have been handed politicized identities that position them as hypothetical historical victims in their relationships to the population of the rest of India. However, this manipulated Dravidian identity served as an interim stage, and is now being superseded by the creation of even smaller fragments. This systematic balkanization of India will continue until India is ultimately represented at the level of tiny, independent, unconnected communities as the social unit. This is important when seen in the context of recent Maoist separatist violence in the same tribal areas in which these scholars have been present and where they provide intellectual fodder for NGO's claims of separatist histories and identities.

SARVA uses the prestige and power of American universities and, in turn, enhances their position as important players in building identity politics in India.[20] At the same time, these scholars politicize and brutally caricature almost all opposing academic points of view. Edwin Bryant of Columbia University explains this atmosphere in Western Indology:

> One must beware of falling into a kind of uncritical Indological McCarthyism towards those open to reconsidering the established contours of ancient Indian history, irrespective of their motives and backgrounds, and of lumping all challenges into a simplistic, convenient and easily-demonized 'Hindu Nationalist' category.[21]

SARVA's goal is to produce a speculative etymological dictionary much on the lines of the *Dravidian Etymological Dictionary* done by Burrow and Emeneau in the 1960s.[22] This goes beyond mere philological reconstruction. Southworth explains how this project can be used to drive the reconstruction of tribal communities' histories:

> Our ultimate concern is the discovery of patterns of linguistic interaction that will lead to reconstructions of the times, places, and cultural circumstances under which prehistoric language contact took place in the subcontinent.[23]

However, this seemingly benign 'concern' has often been used as a pretext for shifting the argument from linguistics to politics, so that 'language contact' is rephrased in terms of 'victimhood' and 'oppression'.[24]

Just as in the 1960s when the *Dravidian Etymological Dictionary* was correlated with heightened Dravidian separatism on the ground, one can now see different tribal identity politics intensifying with the intellectual support of this project. Once these tribal groups are identified and alienated from their shared Indian heritage, they are easy targets for conversion efforts of every kind. For example, the militant Maoist organizations operating in tribal areas claim that 'tribals are not Hindu. They are nature worshippers'.[25] As if nature worship is alien to Hinduism! Under the banner of providing 'leadership training' and 'youth empowerment', various NGO programs have been established with the purpose of instilling this divisive history of separatism into young people. It is interesting to note that the same tribal groups have been subjected to new conversion efforts by evangelical Christians,[26] who consider the Munda to be at the front lines of global evangelism because as a community they are still relatively unconverted.

There are many parties interested in SARVA's work. When one of Witzel's colleagues pointed out that a Pakistani webpage's reconstruction of the Harappan past was ideologically motivated and historically inaccurate, Witzel brushed aside the concern, calling it 'nothing new under the sun'. He referred to 'nationalistic views of history by Indians, Pakistanis, Bangladeshis, Dravidians, Mundas, Kashmiris, Kalasha, Nepalis, Bhutanese, Manipuris, etc., etc.' as the political theater in which such scholarship operates.[27] Thus, sovereign nation-states get lumped together with separatists in one category as 'nationalists'.

This scholarship on India has crossed the boundary of pure academics. It gathers data from the fringes of India, processes it with ideological motives, and supplies it to the US policymakers dealing with India. Witzel and Farmer lead a project team on 'Simulating the Evolution of Political-Religious Extremism: Implication for International Policy Decisions'. One of the team members, Richard Sproat, has worked on projects funded by the Central Intelligence Agency as well as the National Security Agency.[28] The project studies the effect of new communication technologies (such as the Internet) in the hands of extremist groups, using Hindu nationalist movements as the target of research. According to the project description:

> Evidence supporting this thesis is suggested in our research on the global expansion in the last decade of extreme Hindu nationalist ('Hinduthva') movements [9-11], which provide useful models for study of the growth of other extremist groups. . . . Second-generation simulations are planned that will extend the same methods to analyzing data from real-world extremist groups, using input from Internet and other quasi-real-time information sources. One idea we plan to test in our early simulations is the hypothesis that attempts to isolate members of potential extremist groups implementing a real world policy decision, may paradoxically help sustain violent tendencies by limiting opportunities for the negotiated changes known on long time-scales to weaken such tendencies.[29]

The project 'Simulating the Evolution of Political-Religious Extremism' is not a mere academic exercise. Steve Farmer explains on his webpage that its goal is to 'allow policy analysts and historians to build cultural simulations without any formal programming'.[30] The term 'cultural simulations' means the ability to simulate 'what if' the USA were to collaborate with group X against group Y, and various permutations and combinations of scenarios for such 'cultural interventions' in India. One can see similar theoretical interventions actually being implemented in Afghanistan, Pakistan, Iraq and Yemen.

The recent controversy over the Indian epigraphist Iravatham Mahadevan illustrates how the Western Indologists *use* selected scholars from India to do some of their 'dirty work', but once the Indian scholars have served the purpose, they are discarded and slandered in the academic circles. Mahadevan, a recognized expert in his field, was used by Harvard Indologists to defame N.S. Rajaram, a persistent academic opponent. Witzel and Farmer, with approving inputs from Mahadevan, inflated an error by Rajaram into an intentional hoax, which became a major scandal against Rajaram. But later, when Witzel and Farmer charged Mahadevan with distortions in his own Indus sign concordance, a saddened Mahadevan wrote:

> 'As they say, garbage in, garbage out,' says Michael Witzel of the Harvard University. These quotations from an online news item (*New Scientist*, 23 April 2009) are representative of what passes for academic debate in sections of the Western media over a serious research paper by Indian scientists published recently in the USA (*Science*, 24 April 2009). . . . The provocative comments by Farmer and Witzel will surprise only those not familiar with the consistently aggressive style adopted by them on this question, especially by Farmer.[31]

A detailed analysis of how the Western Indologists have used Mahadevan for their agenda and then slandered him is given in Appendix D.

Academic Support for Tamil Separatist Conferences

'Tamil Eelam' is the name given by Tamil separatists to the state they hoped to create in Sri Lanka. This idea, which helped inspire the Tamil Tigers in the Sri Lankan civil war, was promoted and given legitimacy by American academics such as Bryan Pfaffenberger at the University of California at Berkeley. From 1973 to 1975, Pfaffenberger studied Sri Lankan Tamil castes and became a strong supporter of the Tamil separatist movement in Sri Lanka. The Institute for International Studies and the Department of Anthropology at the University of California, Berkeley, supported his work. He also received funding from the Foreign Area Fellowship of the Social Science Research Council and the American Council of Learned Societies. His fellowship from the National Endowment for the Humanities, a US government body, helped him to situate his 'Sri Lanka evidence in the wider context of the literature on Tamil India'.[32]

In 1991, an International Tamil Eelam Research Conference was organized by Switzerland-based International Federation of Tamils and by the Department of Government, California State University, Sacramento. The conference was titled 'Tamil Eelam – A Nation without a State'.[33] Here Pfaffenberger presented a thesis, also to be included in the *Encyclopedia of World Cultures,* that promotes the separate nation of the people of Tamil Eelam.[34] The conference saw a mixture of academic papers that boosted the historical pride of Tamils, making them seem separate from the rest of Indian culture.[35] Political observations were made that compared the Sri Lankan Tamil conflict to the Kashmir conflict.[36] The concept of 'a Tamil nation without a state' has now been extended to the Tamils of India and not just Sri Lanka.[37]

Another scholar who attended this conference was George L. Hart, a professor of Tamil at the University of Wisconsin. Hart gave a scholarly veneer to some rather crude histories that are often popularised in the public rhetoric of the Dravidianist movement. For example, Hart presented Dravidianist propaganda exemplying the 'cunning Brahmin responsible for all social evils'.[38]

Hart emphasized selective aspects of Tamil literature in order to show that it was ethnically different from the Vedic traditions and the remainder of Indian literature. Appendix B shows how George Hart and Hank Keifetz wrongly portray the Sangham classic *Purananuru* in their translation, *The Four Hundred Songs of War and Wisdom: An Anthology of Poems from Classical Tamil,* as being 'composed before Aryan influence had penetrated the south'. They claim that it has 'universal appeal' because it makes 'no basic assumptions about karma and the afterlife'.[39] Hart has regularly associated himself with Tamil politics and uses his academic credentials to reinforce Dravidianism.

The Berkeley Tamil Chair

In 1996, the University of California at Berkeley launched a Tamil Chair, calling it 'the first of its kind . . . in an American University'. The person hired for the chair was not a native Tamili speaker, but Professor George L. Hart, whose pro-Dravidian politics were mentioned above.

One of the major campaigners and fund raisers for the Berkeley chair was the Federation of Tamil Sangams of North America (FeTNA),[40] whose links with militant Tamil nationalist movements are explained later in this chapter.

The first visiting professor invited to Berkeley as part of the work done by the Chair was Professor Ilakkuvanar Maraimalai from Chennai. Ilakkuvanar had previously visited the United States in 1987 to attend a linguistic conference. At that conference, he expressed his delight to have learned 'many things about the Mormon religion and the Church of the Latter Day Saints'. The Mormon Bible reminded him 'of a prominent religious literature in Tamil, *Tiruvachagam*'.[41] Like a true Dravidianist, Ilakkunavar believes that the Government of India discriminates against its Tamil citizens and that 'India remains north',[42] and that present-day India is 'a torture camp for religious minorities'.[43] His writings feature topics like 'sexual assault on Christian nuns' in India, and 'I love America'. He praised the 'nobility and greatness of George Hart',[44] and in turn, Hart wrote to the Government of India, supporting Ilakkuvanar's Dravidianist positions, including his opinions on the status of Tamil studies in India.[45]

Hart has used the Berkeley Tamil Studies Chair to boost those scholars who emphasize the separateness of Tamil from Indian traditions. He accomplishes this by organizing forums where such scholars come together to reinforce Dravidian separatist identity politics in India. For instance, he organized a meeting of Western Tamil educators featuring Thomas Malten, whose Tamil Studies department at Cologne University was closely associated with Germany's Lutheran Church (whose activities in India are discussed in Chapter 17 and also Appendix H). Another guest was Norman Cutler of the University of Chicago, who studied Tamil under an American National Defense Foreign Language fellowship and whose work is considered to have opened up for US policymakers 'an India that does not speak Hindi and looks back to nearly two-thousand years of tradition outside of Sanskrit'.[46]

Tamil conferences organized by the Berkeley Tamil Chair often feature papers that deconstruct traditional Tamil images of devotion, in the same manner as is found in modern Dravidian politics. For example, a paper by Hart interprets *Ramayana* as 'a strange work' filled with contradictions between 'Brahminical thought' and 'martial valor'. He sees *Ramayana* primarily and yet 'subtly' as a way to oppress the Dravidians. Hart claims that this was later reflected in the way that the 'great military and imperial power of the Cholas was leavened by the Brahmanical system that they supported'. This nuanced anti-Brahminism is camouflaged in academic language. Hart stresses that his interpretation 'brings to mind some modern political themes'.[47] In this manner, India's classics are deconstructed as a method to tease out the oppression inherent in Indian civilization.

Berkeley has also established a lecturer post for Telugu in its Department of South and Southeast Asian Studies, which is funded by the US Telugu community. The post was awarded to Hephzibah (Hepsi) Sunkari, a Christian evangelist.[48] In its 2008 brochure, the right-wing fundamentalist group Christian Family Conference, praised her:

> Obeying to the Great commission of the Lord along with her husband, she has been actively involving in the ministry among the Indians and international students on the US campuses. She has been a translator for Family Radio, a Christian Radio Station and some other Christian ministries in the US. She also worked as honorary editor for the newsletter of Telugu Christian Fellowship, San Francisco Bay Area.[49]

FeTNA

The Federation of Tamil Sangams of North America (FeTNA) is an umbrella organization of Tamil associations within the United States. While it calls itself 'a literary, educational, cultural, charitable, secular, and nonpartisan organization',[50] FeTNA has been accused of supporting LTTE (which sponsors the Tamil Tigers terrorist movement), and one of its former directors[51] was arrested by the FBI for trying to bribe US officials in order to get the ban on LTTE lifted.[52]

FeTNA uses its US academic links to spread demonic images of Indian society, with the help of Tamil Nadu-based Dalit activists.[53]

FeTNA often presents one-sided sensationalist events.[54] FeTNA also honored Jagat Gasper, a Catholic propagandist, who has used his proximity to Dravidian power centers for Christianizing the Tamil culture.

In 2005, according to the *Chicago Tribune*, Illinois Congressman Danny K. Davis went on a FeTNA-sponsored trip to the Sri Lankan Tamil regions. Referring to FeTNA, the Congressman acknowledged that he 'knew that they were associated with the Tamil Tigers'.[55] Later, he told the Associated Press that as far as he knew, his trip had been paid for by FeTNA.[56]

FeTNA has also aligned itself with pro-Dravidian Indologists in a California controversy involving the portrayal of ancient Indian history and religion in sixth-grade Social Studies school textbooks.[57] FeTNA's testimony at the California Curriculum Commission made the blatantly erroneous claim that 'the early Tamil texts clearly distinguish between Tamils and Aryans'.[58] Appendix B offers evidence that shows this perspective to be patently false.

Europe-based Tamil Studies

European evangelical missions to India have also forged a network of academic-activist-evangelical institutional ties in Europe, as well as maintaining ties with departments of Tamil Studies in the United States. The field of Tamil Studies has become a respectable device for supporting a worldwide network of considerable intellectual and political influence.

Tamil Studies was introduced in Germany in 1711 by Bartholomäus Ziegenbalg (1682–1719), possibly the first Protestant missionary in India. He was a Lutheran, associated with what is now known as the Martin Luther University in Halle. However, the field did not get any serious attention for the next century, though there were isolated European missionary scholars translating Tamil literature. Despite the lack of institutional frameworks to study Tamil, Germany became a repository of a large number of palm-leaf manuscripts of Tamil works that were brought there by missionaries returning from India.[59]

With the rise of the Dravidianist movement in South India in the 1960s, Tamil Studies found a renewed interest in Germany.[60] In 1998, the Institute of Indology at the University of Cologne was renamed as the 'Institute of Indology and Tamil Studies', as though Tamil is separate from Indian civilization. Expanding the link between modern Tamil Studies and India-based missionary projects, the Institute has developed close relations with the Gurukul Lutheran Seminary in Chennai, the De Nobili Research Institute at Loyola College,[61] and the Institute of Asian Studies.[62] Habil Michael Bergunder, a theologian from Halle University, is another Tamil scholar who does research on separatist identity formation in South India as well as Christian movements in India.[63] In a dictionary of consultants on South Asian Christianity, he is listed as one of the consultants for evangelicals.[64]

The Free University of Amsterdam also has missionary connections with India. The university was started as the first Protestant university in the Netherlands in 1880. It has links with the Gurukul Lutheran Theological College and Research Institute in Chennai, through various theology programs.

Peter Schalk, a professor at the Department of Theology at Uppsala University, Sweden, is another prominent European scholar associated with controversial socio-political movements in Sri Lanka, and to some extent, in South India. In one of his papers, he equates the violent terror campaign of LTTE with Gandhi's non-violent Quit India campaign, and with the Indian independence struggle of Subhash Chandra Bose.[65] Schalk was the convener of the Tamil panel at the eighteenth European conference on Modern South Asian Studies at Lund, Sweden, in 2004.[66] A Tamil scholar, well-known for his strong, pro-LTTE views, he criticized the curtailing of LTTE activities by the European Union in 2006. He wrote that LTTE has 'strong support of Tamil-speaking people – not only in [Sri] Lanka and in exile but also in Tamil Nadu'.[67] His 2007 paper on the 'Religion Among Tamil Speaking Refugees from Sri Lanka', claimed that the Saivism of Sri Lankan Tamils is turning into a 'theology of liberation', where the term 'liberation' was used as political separatism.[68] His political clout is evident from the fact that he accompanied a European Parliamentary Delegation that visited Sri Lanka as a diplomatic representative.[69]

Uppsala University offers a research course with the innocent-sounding title of 'Mission Archives and Approaches to the Study of the Christian Churches in India'. The course is coordinated by Peter B. Andersen, professor of cross-cultural and regional studies at Copenhagen University, whose evangelical focus came out in a lecture titled 'Tamil Evangelical Lutheran Church among Catholics, Pentacostals and Hindus'.[70] At the twentieth European conference on Modern South Asian Studies, Andersen presented a paper explaining the rationale. The panel gained academic respectability because it was convened by the Princeton Theological Seminary and by Butler University.[71] Uppsala University conferences have featured topics such as 'Hindutva as a Political Religion'. Basically, the goal is to educate the Western policymakers, academics, missionaries, and related parties about the opponents of proselytization and the strategies that must be developed and implemented in order to establish Christianity across India.

It is obvious that the colonial constructs of previous centuries have transformed themselves subtly, yet persistently, today. They have become more radical, and hence, more dangerous than before. The institutional mechanisms and networks that keep these constructs alive do so for various political, economic, and theological vested interests. In general, such academicians have become tools in facilitating strategic Western interventions.

11

Western Discourse on India's Fragments

Many international nexuses are at work in India, with connections in the UK, continental Europe, and the US. In the remaining chapters of this book, we will examine their connections, agendas and functioning. Simultaneously, we also examine how the subsidiaries and affiliates of these western forces work on different levels in India. Thus, a paradoxical mixture of academics and activists are lifted across continents to give testimonies against India. Left-wing academicians of India collaborate with right-wing forces of the West, typically via intermediaries. Pro-India perceptions are ignored and the Indian legacy of supporting the rights of down-trodden are dismissed derisively. Worldviews that emphasize conflicts are encouraged. Ideologues give open call to racial civil wars, which are published by prestigious academic publishing houses of the West. US governmental monitoring mechanisms focus on India with distorting lenses and quote and requote their own reports to project a savage imagery of India as a dark frontier region ripe for Western intervention.

In both Europe and the US, powerful political and religious forces use academic studies to support their own agendas. These include Christian churches, left-wing and right-wing foundations and think-tanks, NGOs claiming to help the oppressed, and Western governments looking for leverage. While they have different intentions, taken together, they have the effect of dividing, destabilizing and weakening India, while at the same time demonizing, distorting and/or co-opting its culture. All this creates some very strange linkages. Right-wing American politicians support NGO service projects run by liberals they would scorn at home, and left-liberal academics share the stage with right-wing fundamentalist Christians in the service of some 'oppressed' people in India that neither group understands adequately.

Fig 11.1 shows many of the institutions that shape the western discourse on India in the social sciences and humanities.

Fig 11.1 Western Institutional Control of Social Discourse in India

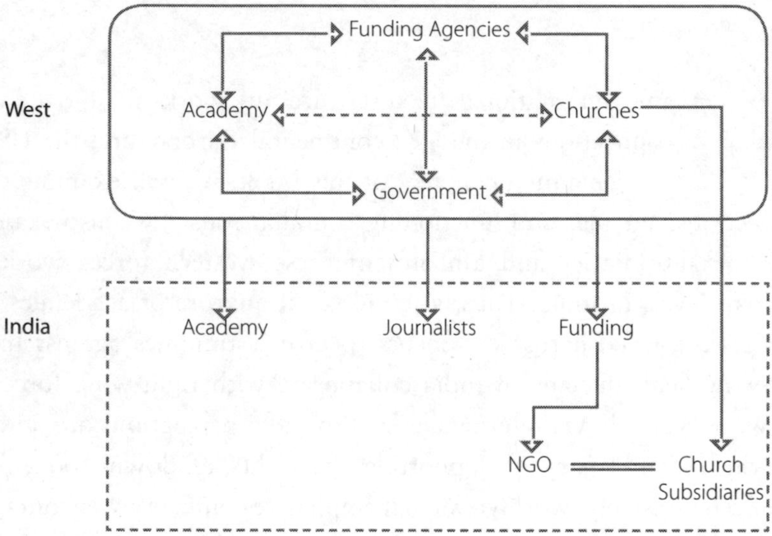

The Western institutions at the top of the chart drive funds and influence 'downwards' into Indian institutions and opinion leaders. This is a complex phenomenon made murky by the lack of transparency and disclosure. Western funding agencies work closely with their respective governments, academic institutions and churches. The overall mission is to influence Indian intellectuals in the academy, media and NGOs. This occurs both directly and indirectly. Each institutional component shown has its own function, as summarized below.

Government

Western governments have within them strong elements that harbor stereotypes of civilization superiority and geopolitical ambitions. Unfortunately, academic and other think-tanks often go along with this and reinforce these stereotypes of India. Government officials also associate with evangelical religious organizations operating in India, which are seen as carrying their civilization's flag into the non-Western world. The government role can vary, and can include moral, political and financial support as ways of lending credibility to Christianity. For example, the US government uses USAID to channel funds through transnational evangelical organizations such as World Vision.

Funding Agencies

These agencies provide financial assistance for specific types of research to be carried out in India, and they cull out and propagate the elements of data that suit Western political and strategic needs. For example, Infemit, a transnational network of evangelicals targeting India, is funded by Crowell Trust, a US-based Christian fundamentalist funding agency. Infemit sponsors seminars on Indian politics in US right-wing policy institutes like the Ethics and Public Policy Center. Similarly, Cadburys sponsored a disputed and controversial study by a Christian organization on caste discrimination among the Indian diaspora in the UK.

Academy

Academic studies of India in the West sometimes discover/create new fault lines or intensify the existing ones. Many academicians tend to treat the Indian nation-state as an artificial construct which is inherently oppressive. Often, the academic study of India overlaps with a type of activism that encourages centrifugal forces in India. The direction of academic studies is influenced by the funding agencies, and in turn, the academic studies influence international policies on India.

Churches

Western churches and evangelical organizations have close links with private funding agencies and government organizations. Western governments see their nations' evangelical missions operating in India as flag-bearers of an altruistic civilization and also as creating special interest-groups in India that are loyal to them. Special institutional collaborations are well-established between various Western institutions and their respective subsidiaries in India, with the official support of Western governments.

This powerful inter-organizational efficiency enhances the leverage of their Indian subsidiaries. For example, US-based evangelical movements have launched the Dalit Freedom Network, which in turn has an Indian associate called All India Christian Council (AICC). AICC sponsors intellectuals and academics who present a very one-sided Christian view of Dalits, and they supply their US sponsors with large quantities of atrocity literature.[1] This discourse is manufactured in India for US sponsors. It has positioned itself as a global voice of Dalits, offering those who tow their lines with routine access to US governmental hearings and influential think-tanks. Similarly, Church-backed institutional networks in India have considerable influence and support of Western governmental organizations. The impact of such networks on India's strategic positioning, security and eventually its sovereignty, will be discussed in detail.

Media

The transnational forces discussed above have also built a media infrastructure in India, which aims to create Indian writers who are emotionally bonded to Western forces and financially dependent on them. There is an extensive evangelical media network in India that is allied with certain 'secular' media. For example, two Europe-based media-missionary networks, Gegrapha and BosNewsLife, work with Indian Christian journalists to produce news specifically about 'Christian victims' of Indian civilization.

Fig 11.1 was also intended to show the enormous interactions among the various Western parties. On the Indian side, there are very few players and little overall strategy. Indians are not well coordinated in their study of these Western institutional interventions. On the contrary, most Indians in positions of influence are happily complacent, and some even support such interventions quite openly. Interestingly, while the Chinese government, industrialists, and intellectuals are very influential in the academic studies of China from a nationalistic position, there is no significant role by the Indian government or any other Indian institution acting squarely on behalf of India's interest in the global study of India.

Deconstructing India Systematically

Fig 11.2 shows the way India is deconstructed in many academic and think-tank projects in the West. The left side of the diagram shows the secular lenses being applied in a Eurocentric manner, while the right side shows the Biblical lenses. In between are shown the topics of study.

Fig 11.2 Western Perception of India Through Two Powerful Lenses

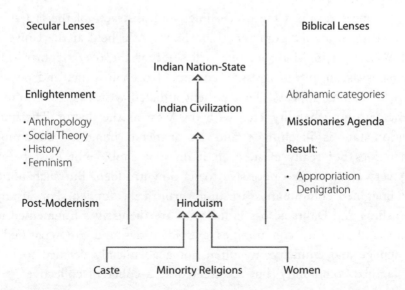

Starting at the bottom, Fig 11.2 shows that the primary categories of academic study are castes, minorities and women. The overall methodology is designed to show that these groups are oppressed as the result of Indian civilization's flaws. These results are the building blocks that feed the approach to studying Hinduism, which in turn, feeds a negative attitude towards Indian civilization in general. At the top of the pyramid are scholars who explore whether India is a dysfunctional nation-state defined by its human rights crises and other problems.

This is a simplified view of the template used explicitly or implicitly for discussions of India in South Asian Studies departments in the Western academic world. As an example, academic Dalit studies encourage Dalit writing only from a separatist and divisive perspective, and not as an important contribution to mainstream Indian literature. It deliberately ignores the significant cooperation between the Dalits and the *savarnas* when important texts of Indian literature are translated, edited and published, and also ignores that many of the sacred texts, including the *Ramayana, Mahabharata*, and much of bhakti literature, were written by Dalits. There are studies being done on how, for instance, Raja Rao is prejudiced against his Muslim characters, or how there are very few Muslim characters in texts by Hindu writers such as Tagore.

If one scrutinizes the proceedings and abstracts of the last thirty-five years of annual conferences on South Asia held at the University of Wisconsin in Madison, one will see that the overall portrayal of India is as an anti-progressive country, frozen in time, and poverty-stricken. India appears like a patient afflicted with caste, sati, dowry, feticide, untouchability, etc., with the West as the doctor. The Indian nation-state is illegitimate and an artificial 'imagined community' that does not really exist, or if it does, it should not exist because its very existence is oppressive to its downtrodden. But such notions of imagined communities are quite arbitrarily applied. For instance, Muslims and Dalits across India, who are themselves fragmented into thousands of tiny communities and identities and are separated by language and ethnicity, are often not academically deemed to be an 'imagined community' but are treated as a coherent collective.

It is ironic that while the sense of national identity in the West is getting stronger, in the less developed countries scholarship is encouraged toward self-deconstruction. The national identities of the USA, China and Japan are becoming stronger, and the European Union is becoming a strong super-nation. They are not deconstructing themselves with comparable force or feeding their own centrifugal forces. But somehow the intellectual fashion being exported to Indian intellectuals and other third-world intellectuals is to 'deconstruct your and its civilization'. While the power of the West enables it to demand the deconstruction of India, the Indian intellectuals lack the power to do the same in reverse to the Western states.

One hears that there is a lot of postmodern thinking on American campuses that deconstructs their own civilization as well. However, what is not noted is that this kind of deconstruction is mostly from the fringes of power, and that such scholars do not have political clout. Nobody in positions of authority takes them seriously, and the media rarely notices them, except as radicals. They are certainly not advising the policymakers, and they do not influence think-tanks and major funding. They just are cocooned in the academy. The powers that govern and dominate the discourse are very nationalistic and the nation-state is as strong as ever.

But the situation concerning the discourse on India is quite different. Postmodernism has provided academic respectability to a whole generation of bright Indians to deconstruct their own nationality and civilization. This self-flagellation is made fashionable by association with West-based, 'successful' Indian scholars, and is encouraged through funding and career paths. India is to be replaced by a large number of 'sub-nations' according to this trendy theory. Homi Bhabha, a co-director for Harvard's South Asia Program, is regarded as the pioneer in developing the theory of 'hybridity' of cultures and identities. An implication of this is that because Indians have lost their native identity to colonialism, they should stop trying to reclaim it because doing so is futile. On the contrary, they should celebrate their hybrid 'whitened Indian' identities as a form of protest against the colonizers. While this is not the place to analyze such theories, it is easy to point out the strange contradictions they land us in. If the very same theory were applied to Dalits, then the conclusion would be to discourage them from revolting against the upper caste, more powerful groups in India, and instead to hybridize with the mainstream Hindus. Add to this the fact that these theories are written in such utterly incomprehensible and convoluted language that they have been criticized as a form of 'Brahmin-like' hegemony, based on linguistic exclusivity and perceived superiority. While trying to champion the subaltern strata, these theories are largely inaccessible and meaningless to the subaltern people themselves.

Fig 11.3 shows some of the academic disciplines, especially pertaining to the Tamil culture, that have served to create separatist identities among Indians. This process continues to this day, and has become entrenched beyond the intellectual forums and entered into the psyche of the general public. These projects might have initially started out as strictly academic, but they fed one another and eventually entered the public discourse.

Fig 11.3 Academic Disciplines and Dravidian Identity Implications

Academic Discipline	Framing Used	Identity Implications
Tamil Linguistics	Separate Aryan/Dravidian grammars	Separate the origin of languages of South India
Tamil Classical Literature	Distinct originality of subaltern literature	Separate worldview and intellectual history of South India
Art and Cultural Studies of South India	Tensions against India as a Nation	Separate ethnicity suggesting incompatibility with other Indians
History	History of each given group shown as independent and isolated from rest of India, except as victims of India.	Separate ethnic/ racial identity
Anthropology of Caste	Equated with jati and varna. Uniquely Hindu problem, ignoring other Indian religions and other countries. Abusive only, not also social capital. Blamed for all social abuses.	Dalit separatist identity combined with Dravidianism, becomes 'Aryan Brahmins enslaved Dravidian shudras'.

Each of the disciplines shown in the table will be briefly explained next. Linguistics became an important new discipline in Europe largely due to the influence of Indology. Later, it became integrated with Race Science of the nineteenth century. Its overarching agenda was set by European missionary scholars as well as colonial administrators, the goal being to reinforce separate ethnic identities among various Indian groups. First they maximized the linguistic differences by constructing separate grammars, and then showed that Tamil classical literature was a narrative of conflicting ethnic identities throughout Indian history.

The European approach to Indian literature was superimposed on top of the divisive approach to Indian linguistics. In a linguistically plural nation like India, the scope for studying the classical literature in each language is abundant. Indian experience has been the essential unity in diversity expressed in classical literature of all her languages. However, the Western study of classical literature of different languages in India is premised on a different view. Studies in the voluminous Tamil classical literature were undertaken to identify crucial ethnic elements, isolating it from the rest of Indian literature. Often these features would be highlighted as 'this-worldly' or 'secular' Tamil poetry, to contrast it from the supposed 'other-worldliness' of Sanskrit literature.[2]

The local forms of art and culture are now being studied by foreign-funded scholars as well as Indian scholars with affiliations to Western institutions. The common trend is to identify local differences and play them up as the essence of the culture. Sometimes even the art is associated with imagined Christian influences.

In the case of history, any common Indian narrative is dismissed as artificial or a conspiracy of oppressive Brahmins or later nationalists. The 'spread' of any common cultural element is depicted as the strategy of cunning kings and Brahmins who want to subordinate the independent ethnic groups. While in the West there are armies of scholars publishing the positive elements in every aspect of their own culture, Indian scholars are encouraged by Western agencies to deconstruct every aspect of Indian culture. This is being done as a gift to the subalterns, the 'real' Indians, by giving them their true history freed from that of India as a nation.

The exhaustive work on caste anthropological studies done by colonial administrators, Herbert Risley and Edgar Thurston, was done within the framework of nineteenth-century Race Science. It transformed Indian community units that were distinguished by their occupational roles into ethnic/racial groups. Since then, the racial nature of caste has dominated in most of the studies in India and abroad. This colonial legacy continues largely unchallenged to this day. Each caste group is encouraged to identify itself with a racial identity that it considers as indigenous, and blames all its perceived and actual problems on a conspiracy of other castes and on India as a whole.

As we have seen in the previous chapters, linguistics, caste anthropology, and mythology became powerful instruments in the hands of colonial powers, serving to create new intellectual frameworks with the potential to deepen existing divisions. In the post-colonial period, scholars have continued, sometimes inadvertently, to build upon the same frameworks and to serve the same agendas. We also see imported ideas about race getting grafted on to Indian movements in the name of social justice. Dravidian identity politics gets mixed with movements for Dalit rights, although most Dravidians are not Dalits and most Dalits are not Dravidians. Even so, the idea that 'caste equals race' is now projected onto the world stage, with India and Hinduism painted as the villains.

Such multi-dimensioned, conflict-oriented identity construction at micro-levels can coalesce into major, violent ethnic conflicts, as we will see in the concluding chapter of this book.

Atrocity Literature as a Genre

The control over discourse by supplying meta-narratives serves as a part of political control. In support of colonialism, there developed a genre of literature in the West that became known as 'atrocity literature'. Over the past four centuries, a corpus of academic and fictional writings that have been adapted into Broadway plays and Hollywood movies have portrayed Western encounters with other cultures—Indians, Native Americans, Blacks, Mexicans, Filipinos, Japanese, Chinese, Haitians, Cubans, Vietnamese, and Arabs—reinforcing the idea that the rest of the world is inferior to European/American culture and must be won over for their own good. Only then can John Wayne fade peaceably into the sunset on his horse.

Atrocity literature was integral to portraying other cultures' strangeness and exotica by emphasizing the dangers they posed. One way to understand the power of atrocity literature is to examine it in the context of American history since the early 1600s, where it played a role in every episode of prejudice, territorial acquisition, and economic expansion.[3] The process may be briefly stated as follows:

- As European settlers in America expanded westward across the American continent, they pushed the natives ahead of them along an ever-shfting frontier, which was understood as a demarcation line between civilization and savagery.
- The myth-making consisted of painting a vivid picture of the native American as being 'dangerously savage' – a people who were a threat to the innocent, God-fearing Christian folks. The imagery sometimes suggested that America was the Biblical Eden, now belonging to European colonialists, and it was being violated and threatened by evil savages from the frontier. This notion of the 'frontier' came to represent the collective rest of the non-Christian, hence, 'uncivilized' world.
- The natives were typically depicted in scenes of 'idol worshipping', replete with grotesque divinities, as opposed to the one true God of Western Christendom. These 'others' were packaged to appear primitive: lacking in morals and ethics, and prone to violence. This trio—lack of aesthetics, lack of morality, and lack of rationality—is found over and over again in atrocity literature.
- When conflicts erupted, the Whites, as civilizing people, were depicted as responding legitimately and dutifully to the actions of savages. Thus, the brutalities by the colonizers were depicted as justified and reasonable measures.

- The savage cultures were also shown to victimize their own women and children. Therefore, the violent civilizing mission of the Whites seemed to be in the best interests of the savage societies at large.

- This kind of atrocity literature gave intellectual sustenance to imperialist doctrines like Manifest Destiny, White Man's Burden, etc.

- It also offered an emotional hook. The exciting adventures of frontiersmen, including explorers, soldiers, and cowboys generated even more such literature.

- This genre of literature thrived on half-truths, selecting items from here and there, and stitching themes together into a narrative that played on the reader's psyche with pre-conceived stereotypes.[4] It sought to create a sense of heightened urgency in dealing with savagery.

- The non-Western cultures portrayed in this way may or may not have committed the alleged atrocities attributed to them. The truth, in all probability, was not as one-sided as depicted. Typically, conflicts were exaggerated and sensationalized in order to make an ideological point.

- In contrast to the approach towards non-Western civilization, the social ills and atrocities in Western societies are characterised as aberrations: racism, colonial genocide, the two World Wars, the Holocaust, sexual abuse, etc., are considered as isolated acts that deviate from the true Western character.

- As Western colonization expanded worldwide, the myth of the frontier proved successful in subduing the natives of America, Africa and Asia. It was compatible with other forms of European expansionism. Now the frontier could be anywhere outside of western civilization.

- Once established in the popular mind, atrocity literature was often used to justify the harsh subjugation of the people on the frontier. The same myth that excused genocide of Native Americans later excused large-scale violence such as the Vietnam War and the Iraq War.

In every era of Western expansion, many scholars naively participated in producing such atrocity literature without taking into consideration how the material would eventually be used. Once a target culture is branded and marked in this way, it becomes the recipient of all sorts of untoward allegations. It becomes impossible for the leaders of any such branded culture to defend themselves against the bombardment of false charges and depictions. In order to defend oneself, one has to first acknowledge the false allegations, which legitimize them and make a victory for the other side. Anyone effectively criticizing the Western powers is quickly put on the list of suspected dangerous savages and stigmatized. One thing that atrocity literature insists is that savages almost always lie. Therefore, normal rules of evidence and fair representation no longer apply, and another 'savage culture' is neutered.[5]

Atrocity Literature Feeds India's Fragmentation

Guided by myths, many westerners have long viewed India at the extreme end of the exotic scale – filled with images of polytheism, weird 'gods', caste system, human rights atrocities, moribund and grotesque aesthetics, irrational thinking, and an overall image of chaos. All of this correlates in the Judeo-Christian mind with evil or lack of civilization. Starting in the early 1800s, European and American Christian missionaries depicted the people of India as savages who were in need of being saved from darkness. Similar ideas in more recent times about India also feed into images of Indian culture being inferior to the West in dealing with the human condition.

The British claimed to be colonizing India to improve its human rights – the so-called civilizing mission. This created a trend among Indian leaders to go to the British with complaints against one another, and they were encouraged to blame Indian culture as the cause of their problems. The same kind of civilizing role is presently being played by America. Thus, American right-wing politicians, who are not enthusiastic about affirmative action policies in their own United States, call for active interventionist policy by the US to combat Indian caste-based discriminations.[6]

India: Frontier for Western Intervention

As we mentioned earlier, Western institutions which study India, do so through two different lenses. The evangelical organizations working under the Dalit banner and the right-wing think-tanks and policy centers see India through a Biblical lens. They utilize church subsidiaries in India to provide testimonies against India in Western media, government hearings and international bodies. They build up a steady mass of atrocity literature against India.

There are tens of thousands of new churches of various denominations being planted across India's hinterland. They use a variety of campaigns and tactics to enrich their 'soul' harvests and vote banks. The contrast between evangelism in the United States and India shows that Indian churches promote a hard-line Christianity, and often cause tensions and conflicts into previously well-integrated communities. At times, communities of the same caste and clan background become split due to conversions.

These intolerant varieties of Christianity escape the criticisms that such groups attract within the US. It is ironic that while the left-wing in America thrives on attacking evangelist Christian agendas, the left-wing in South Asian Studies not only ignores similar behavior in India, but in fact, lends intellectual support to what is being classified as 'religious freedom' and 'progress'.[7]

Scholars in South Asian Studies departments and liberal think-tanks see India through a secular lens based on Western ideas of human rights. They deploy subaltern studies and postmodern theories to deconstruct the Indian state as a catastrophe constructed artificially by colonialism, and to show its very nature as oppressive, undemocratic, inherently anti-minority, anti-women and anti-Dalit. They export these models to their Indian counterparts, forming a self-sustaining system. They also feed these visions into media and government hearings.

Thus, these two supposedly opposing intellectual streams converge to provide an image of India as a frontier necessitating Western intervention.

Western Intervention in Human Rights

While it is certainly true that India's complexity brings with it a heavy burden of social problems, and that criticism is important to bring reform, we must consider what happens when the West intervenes in India's domestic affairs. For example:

- One must ask whether Indian activists who take domestic matters to international forums are undermining India's own legal, political and human rights structures. Would it not be better to focus on improving India's domestic mechanisms so that the rights of citizens can be secured in the long run? Have the activists adequately made every effort to enhance India's own mechanisms for resolving matters in a given case?
- Could the internationalizing of an issue distract from the problems on the ground, and turn cases into high-profile media events that bring fame to a few 'champions of human rights', but do nothing to resolve the actual problem?
- Does such foreign-sponsored, interventionist activity lead to increased alienation among India's youth, and a sense of dependence on outsiders, rather than encouraging them to sort out their own future?
- Does it facilitate foreign missionaries who, in their misguided actions to alter the identities of Indian communities, create more conflicts?
- Can international appeals, disguised as human rights activism, eventually be used by Western nations against India in the same manner as has happened against so many other nations whose scholars ingest and regurgitate Western atrocity literature?
- Does atrocity literature feed the xenophobic fantasies of some American reactionaries?
- Does the overall effect add fuel to the centrifugal forces that threaten India's integrity?

Fig 11.4 shows the chain reaction.

Fig 11.4 Vicious Cycle of Atrocity Literature

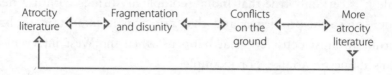

Furthermore, the entire global human rights industry must be asked some additional questions:

- Are Western institutions qualified to 'cure' Indian society?
- What is the track-record of Western powers intervening in third-world domestic issues in the past?
- Who are they accountable to, as the self-appointed 'doctors'?
- Does the West have a superior human rights record compared to the rest of the world?
- Are Western agendas constructed for their own benefit to justify meddling?
- Are human rights definitions and the case selections biased?
- Do globetrotting Indian activists have personal vested interests?

While such questions go unexamined, many human rights mobilizations create a centrifugal force, putting pressure to break up India. In some cases, the forces have acquired a life of their own and are seen as normal and even desirable. For instance, there are serious cases of abuse by evangelist groups who see the problem not as economic or historical, but in terms of a flawed civilization that must be replaced by a better imported one. These serve to alienate the sections of India's poor from their cultural moorings, and ultimately, from India as a nation-state. This process is most advanced in India's northeast, where the rejection of native and tribal religions, engineered by evangelical activity, has been accompanied by a rejection of fellow Indians and a violent war against the Indian state.

Later chapters of this book show that Tamil Nadu could well slide in a similar direction. Many Indian intellectuals and activists have fallen into such vortices, while they imagine themselves to be helping improve human rights on the ground. Alignments that seem advantageous and noble in the short run may have huge negative consequences in the long run. One of the aims of this book is to explain the larger geopolitics at work, in order to enable human rights activists to assess their alignments in a broader context. The goal is to expose the darker side to the activities of some academics and NGOs.

Indian Minorities Serving the Global Majorities

In the free market for identity competition, groups that are Hindu, Muslim, Christian, and Maoist openly compete with inducements, propaganda, political bloc voting, and even litigation to gain market share. However, many of these groups operate as local subsidiaries of global enterprises, some more tightly coupled to their foreign parents than others. This means that the funding, appointment of leaders, strategic planning, operational-tactical support, as well as international media, public relations and political lobbying, are often being done from the foreign headquarters. Yet this aspect of globalization has not been subject to the same kind of reporting rigor and monitoring as is normal for commercial multinational corporations. The human rights and religion industries have been exempt from scrutiny and thus not held to the same standards of transparency.

The net result has been to exacerbate the centrifugal forces that challenge India by co-opting its most deprived and vulnerable. Violent conflicts have followed. Even when it may not be immediately traced to any foreign nexus, a growing portion of the violence may be seen as a delayed and secondary effect of the shift in identities brought about by the intellectual meddling.

Today, there is no isolated local context possible anywhere in the world. Every so-called 'local' Indian issue has been co-opted by one or more global multinational religious or human rights organizations and/or NGOs operating for some foreign interest. This is one of the lesser noticed strands of globalization. South Asian Studies research has failed to recognize the parallel globalizations being spread by Western churches, human rights groups, and Saudi and Iranian madrasas. Indian authorities, unlike their Chinese counterparts, do not pay attention to what this represents – global expansionism in the name of religious freedom or human rights.

America and China are two major world powers who see India as a potential competitor, and it is to their benefit to champion subaltern and minority causes that fragment India. While this is widely accepted in the case of China, the case of America is not commonly discussed. The specific forces in America that treat India as an incoherent 'frontier' of fragments are discussed in detail in later chapters. Thus, foreign funding, which comes with guidance, research, activism and publicity for certain causes, must bear the burden of doubt in demonstrating that it is not furthering imperialism.

One must wonder if the vulnerable third-world 'minorities' could end up as unwitting agents for imperialism and as the new global 'coolies' and 'sepoys'. Where a foreign nexus exerts strong influence, should the 'minorities' perhaps be reclassified as branch offices of a multinational enterprise? It is appropriate to ponder over the definition of a minority. If someone in India goes to a local McDonald's restaurant that may be run by a few natives from the lower strata of Indian society, one does not conclude that it is a 'minority' or 'subaltern' establishment just because the local employees are minorities. One clearly recognizes that it is the local presence of a global giant.

The same criterion should also be applied to local churches, local madrasas, local NGOs, and by the same token, local Hindu temples and schools that are operated by foreign-based enterprises, regardless of the particular religion or the stated goals of that enterprise. The rules that one would apply to a branch office of a multinational enterprise should also be applied to the Southern Baptist Church, which is a huge multinational with a big network of churches in Nagaland and Tamil Nadu, and has a business plan for establishing tens of thousands of churches in South India. Rather than classifying their members as minorities, we should call them branch offices or subsidiaries of global multinationals. Why is it that if the product being sold is 'God's love', then the rules designed for multinationals do not apply? Apparently, 'God's love' is exempt from scrutiny and transparency; since it is dispensed by fallible and ambitious humans, this attitude is naive.

There is a need to redefine the notion of minority, keeping the following factors in mind: If a minority is working for, funded by, appointed by, or trained by a foreign global nexus, then it is not really a minority. It is part of a bigger enterprise. This global enterprise is what should be studied; yet, too often we see academics focusing on some so-called minority group in some isolated village.

An Example: The Afro-Dalit Project

Even in cases where the faultlines have existed historically, the global nexuses have taken oversight in various capacities to promote their respective agendas. A good example is the Afro-Dalit Project (discussed in detail in a later chapter), which exploits India's class inequalities and recasts them in a different light. It is a Western project that promotes the thesis that India's two hundred million Dalits are racially related to Africans, and that the upper-strata Indians are 'white' Aryan immigrants/invaders. Thus, the history of American slavery and exploitation provides the framework in which Dalit youths are to be re-educated as victims of other Indians. There is an impressive level of cooperation between the Western-based intellectual leadership and grassroots Dalit groups in India.

Their activities have included 'youth empowerment' programs as ways to inculcate a hostile, separatist identity that works against India's sovereignty. The Dalit youth-leaders created by such programs are turned into trainers of more such youth re-engineering. There are conferences held to instill the notion that they belong to a pan-African solidarity movement. Many such groups then become takeover targets by either Christian evangelists using African-American missionaries to plant the seeds, or by pan-Islamic groups who position Islam as the true religion of Blacks worldwide. Afro-Dalitism is thus, an interim preparation stage to de-couple the target communities from Indian roots and to soften them for further conversion.

Thus, what was once a deep, historical African-American connection with core elements of Indian civilization—such as Gandhian

non-violent protest and consensus-building adopted by Rev Martin
Luther, Jr—has been turned on its head. Indian civilization, rather
than being a source of inspiration, is seen as the cause of suffering of
Indian groups such as Dalits, who are mythically linked to African-
Americans. Such stances are made possible and lent credibility by
academic theory-making, a process over which India has exercised
little influence.

The Afro-Dalit myth of a shared oppression is based on the view
of history that claims a racial clash of civilizations between Aryans and
Dravidians, which supposedly occurred thousands of years ago and is
shaping community relations in India and Africa today. Ironically, the
intellectual support for this thesis comes from the very same academic
scholars who condemn Samuel Huntington's proposition that the
modern world is afflicted by various clashes of civilizations, of which
the one between Islam and the West is presently on centerstage. They
condemn such a thesis, arguing that it triggers tensions and is politically
dangerous and socially divisive. Yet the same kind of internal clash in
India is actively promoted under the excuse of championing human
rights![8]

Afro-Dalitism is just one of many such projects to alienate India's
subalterns from India. Such movements are based on a wild assortment
of identity politics, often backed by their respective foreign nexuses,
and the intellectual ammunition is borrowed from the works of
specialized scholars.

Separatist movements in India have often originated in the world
of scholars; or if they pre-existed, it was scholarship that gave them
explosive sustenance. This is summarized below:

- Intellectual separatism has been an implicit meta-narrative for
  Indian social sciences and humanities scholars ever since subaltern
  studies applied Marxist class-struggle theories to India. This has
  fed the development of alternative histories 'from below', which
  typically drift toward showing that the poor and the underdogs
  are victims of India's statehood.

- New communal tensions are created and old ones are exacerbated
  when these theories are disseminated by activists, resulting in re-

engineered 'youth identity' and 'empowerment' programs that are sometimes masked as human rights activities.

- These eventually become separatist or/and totalitarian movements, similar to what led to the creation of the Nagaland movement in India and East Timor independence from Indonesia.

- They nurture hostile youth leaders to see the Indian nation-state as their main enemy and the oppressor. The process is in many respects similar to the genesis of the Taliban in Afghanistan, and similar movements among Islamic youth.

- This is the intellectual pipeline supplying ideology to future militants downstream. Until there is a physical manifestation of violence on the ground, much of this activity remains off the radar of security analysis. In fact, many of the scholars who directly or indirectly champion such separatist identities are the very same ones (or their students) who interpret the resulting violence years later. By then, both the separatists and the Indian military/police have committed excesses and atrocities, which then become the target of inquiry.

- A new and subtle form of atrocity literature has become a genre of South Asia Studies, and various funding sources support the scholars for foreign trips, jobs, books, rewards, human rights conferences, and testimonies before the US government. Numerous examples will be provided in the chapters that follow.

Identity Faultlines for Western Intervention

The academic theories that are formed in the Western establishment have political motives as well as ramifications on the ground. Disciplines such as linguistics and classical Tamil literature invent further fragments in India or deepen the existing ones. The approach to linguistics creates an ethno-linguistic narrative which reinforces South India's secessionist politics, using racial categories formed in the colonial era. Secessionist politics can evolve into a major ethnic war of genocidal proportions, as seen in the case of Sinhalese-Tamil conflict in Sri Lanka. Institutions as well as individuals in India, cross the boundaries of pure academic work to become involved in ethno-political activism. The diaspora is encouraged to form a transnational identity based on its particular language, and this is used to abet identity dissonance in India. International institutional networks work in synergy with transnational evangelical institutions that have Indian subsidiaries.

Recolonizing India

In Europe, where a residual colonial imagery of India already lurks deep inside its psyche, Christian groups have established Dalit front organizations with support networks in the UK and continental Europe. They cultivate top government bureaucrats, members and officials of United Nations and European Union bodies, as well as radical politicians at the extreme ends of the political spectrum. They constantly supply them with atrocity literature and controversial studies that undermine diasporic Indians and reinforce negative stereotypes. They are also active in the academy, projecting themselves as the vehicles for studying India. Thus, they facilitate an activist-academic anti-India nexus. Together, all these form a strong anti-India advocacy in UN bodies, at strategic events like the Durban Conference in 2001, and in bodies like the parliament of the European Union.

A 'Christian Umma'

Transnational evangelical organizations, using the support of Western government and media agencies, have been creating a large network of institutions in India, giving them huge financial investment. Apart from institutions that mould and control activists, a zealous media infrastructure has also been built, which is connected to the evangelical right-wing media of the West, particularly the United States. The result is what a Christian researcher calls a 'Christian Umma' emotionally and financially bonded to the West.[9]

Fig 11.5 shows the various forces at work, which will be examined individually in the rest of this book.

Fig 11.5 India Getting Prepared for the Second Coming of the Western Empire

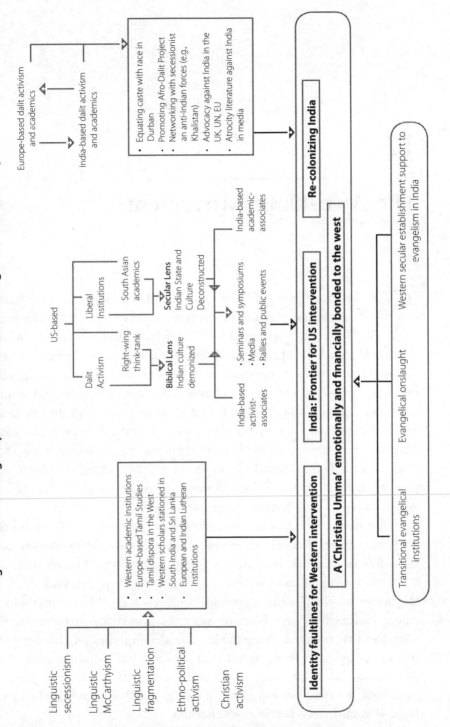

12

The Afro-Dalit Movement

We have already seen that academic studies, evangelical ambitions and administrative projects have worked together to create strong racial identities and divisions, which developed into Dravidian separatism. We find similar elements in the parallel Dalit empowerment movement. The word 'Dalit', originally meaning 'broken' and 'untouchable', denotes a traditional socio-economic status. Dalits can be found all over India, and do not share a common ethnic or religious heritage. Recently, however, the caste structure has been conflated with ideas of 'race', which owe their origins to the Hamitic myth in the Western Bible. Thus, the continuing poverty among Dalits can be blamed on racism tied to the tale of Aryan invasion and Brahmin exploitation.

This model of identity creation led to genocide in Rwanda and civil war in Sri Lanka. A recent academic book, *Christianity and Genocide in Rwanda*, by Timothy Longman, is based on research into the church-related causes for the genocide in that country.[1] Appendix C elaborates on the Rwanda genocide to show how Biblical mythology, colonial necessities and Western anxieties joined forces to create the narrative that resulted in genocide. The striking parallels between the socio-political narratives developed by colonial administrators and the evangelical institutions in Rwanda and South India will now be examined, as they offer a stark warning of what may lie ahead for India if such forces continue unchecked.

Aryan/Dravidian and Hutu/Tutsi Parallels

In both South India and Rwanda, relations between two local groups were reinterpreted in a racial framework with conspiracy theories and negative stereotyping of one group as cunning and scheming, and the other as a pure and innocent victim. In India, this type of discourse is becoming more elaborate and institutionalized, developing into a hate narrative. Fig 12.1 shows how the Rwandan model is reflected in similar developments in South India.

Fig 12.1 Importing the Rwanda Genocide Model

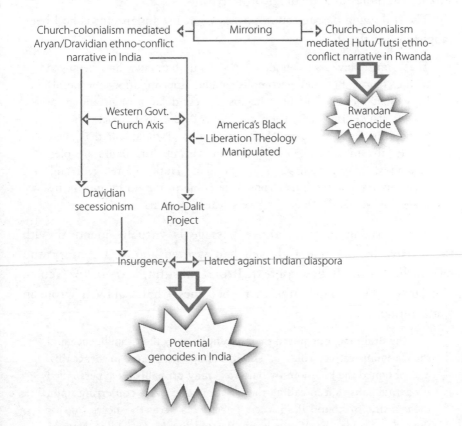

We saw that the Dravidian polity has been nurtured for almost a century by the Aryan/Dravidian race theory and the imagery of evil

Brahmins. This, in turn, has generated hatred in Tamil society, which receives explicit support from various Western agencies.

There is a collaboration of academics and activists that seeks parallels between Dalits in India and Blacks in the United States, and also claims a common racial origin for Dalits and Blacks. It is an inverted version of nineteenth-century racism mixed with Black liberation movements. The Dalit activism based on this ideology finds support from Western evangelists, left-liberal NGOs, and government bodies. The proponents of the Afro-Dalit project claim Hinduism to be a racist structure. This is often supported by academic ethnic studies, subaltern studies and theological activism.

The following passage summarizes what Rwandan Hutus had been taught about the Tutsi:

> The 'Tuutsi' invaders conquered the land that once had belonged to the 'Hutu'. But they accomplished this appropriation not simply by violent means. And here begins a second layer of meanings of the 'Tuutsi'/'Hutu' pair: They, the 'Tuutsi', did so by trickery: . . . Before the Tutsi came, the Hutu were not Hutu at all; they were simply abantu which . . . signifies in Kirundi 'the Bantu peoples' or simply, 'human beings'. . . . The name Hutu, the refugees said, was imported by the Tutsi from their home in the north and means 'slave' or 'servant'. Thus . . . 'we became their slaves'.[2]

It is amazing that the above passage is virtually identical with the divisive history that Caldwell had written almost a century and half earlier in the Indian context. If one substitutes Aryan for Tuutsi, and Dravidian for Hutu, the myth becomes what Caldwell wrote in south India:

> . . . the Brahmanas acquired their ascendancy by their intelligence and their administrative skill. . . . The Brahmans who came in 'peaceably, and obtained the kingdom by flatteries' may probably have persuaded the Dravidians that in calling them Sudras they were conferring upon them a title of honor. If so, their policy was perfectly successful; for the title of Sudra has never been resented by the Dravidian castes;[3]

Caldwell's thesis of south Indian Dravidians as victims of north Indian Aryans was converted into a social movement by E.V. Ramasamy (popularly known as EVR).[4] EVR further developed the racial strains that Caldwell had planted and turned them into explicit racial hatred, and issued a call for Dravidians to rise against north Indians:

> Comrades, we are the original inhabitants and descendants of the race that ruled this land. We are second to no other race in pride, valor, intelligence, force and civilization. Yet a small group of barbaric, nomadic, non-working race of usurpers has enslaved us for thousands of years. This minority race had no weapons like swords. Yet they have reduced us to the level of beasts while they have acquired for themselves economics, politics and theology.[5]

EVR even advocated extreme violence against the Brahmins, hinting of ethnic cleansing. Jacob Pandian explains:

> His main thesis was that Brahmins had debased Dravidian culture, which in turn had demoralized non-Brahmin youth; and that in order to salvage Dravidian culture from its impure state, Brahminical priesthood and Sanskritic scriptural tradition must be destroyed and Brahminical religious practitioners expelled from Dravidian-Tamil society. [6]

Lloyd Rudolph, a well-respected Western anthropologist of India, explains the violence being generated by this movement:

> On occasion, DK Leader E.V. Ramaswami Naicker has called for Brahmin killings and burning of agraharams (Brahmin quarters of cities and towns) . . . These various elements of Dravidian movement's populism have been linked together and given overall coherence by the conspiratorial and demonological theme of anti-Brahminism. . . . The movement also expresses itself in direct action. In recent years EVR and DK have carried on campaigns to erase Hindi lettering from railroad signs, to burn effigies of Rama and smash 'idols' of Hindu deities, to burn the Indian flag, or remove or erase the term Brahmin displayed at 'Hotels' (cafes or restaurants) to burn the Indian Constitution and destroy statues of Gandhi and to burn the maps of India.[7]

The construction of the Brahmin as the racial enemy is found unabashedly in the history textbooks of Tamil Nadu, especially by Christian authors. For example, *History of Tamil Nadu up to 2000*

AD is a prescribed text for undergraduates and postgraduates at many colleges of Tamil Nadu. Written by the head of the history department at N.M. Christian College, it teaches as a matter of hard fact that Brahmins came from outside Tamil Nadu and set themselves in superior positions through their religion and proximity to Tamil kings:

> The Sangam rulers gave much importance to Aryanisation. The highly educated Brahmins influenced the rulers and gradually dominated politics and religions. It improved the position of the Brahmins. When activities of temples and politics increased, the demands for Brahmins also increased. Hence, more and more Brahmins were invited to Tamil Nadu from its northern parts. The Brahmins possessed separate culture and language. They considered the people of Tamil Nadu as their enemies. . . . They never mingled with local population and led a separate life. . . . The Brahmins who worked in temples imposed the Agama principles of the Aryans in the religious worship. Within a short period the system of worship was also Aryanised. . . . Thus, the Brahmins acted as landlords and enjoyed all political and religious privileges. They suppressed the common people and treated them as slaves.[8]

This stereotyping of the Brahmin and the repeated assertion that Hinduism is nothing but a construct to enslave Tamils, are being carried out at all levels of Tamil politics, academics and media.

American History Defines the Afro-Dravidian Movement

When African-Americans wanted to reclaim their African heritage after being emancipated from slavery, they did it largely through the institutions of Black churches by appropriating the Biblical narratives as their own. George Wells Parker (1882–1931), an African-American political activist, wanted to 'inspire the Negro with new hopes; to make him openly proud of his race and of its great contributions to the religious development and civilization of mankind'.[9] He founded an organization for this purpose in 1917, and named it 'Hamitic League of the World'. Its purpose was to create a positive global history of the descendants of Ham, using the Biblical framework.

Black ideologues started seeking parallels in India. The myth of the White-Aryan-barbaric-Brahmin-cunning-invader versus the native-innocent-cultured-Black-Dravidian was given a boost. Drusilla Dunjee Houston (1876–1941), daughter of a Black Baptist minister, was one of the earliest popularizers of this pan-Africanism. She identified the Dravidians as having the 'familiar traits and customs of Cushite Ethiopians':

> The Brahmins were probably a much later and intermixed branch of the inhabitants of Hindu-Kush. That they were intermixed we can tell by their cruelty. Full-blooded Cushites are very gentle. . . . These Dravidians . . . represent the unmixed Cushite type. . . . They were a part of that advancing wave of the Old Race that swept eastward and westward, peopling primitive Arabia, Egypt and Chaldea.[10]

This Pan-African mythology claims how the 'original' Africans were superior in various respects, but were conquered by the trickery of wily Aryan-Brahmins. This myth of subjugation of black-skinned Dravidians by white-skinned Aryan-Brahmins spread over the years, beyond the academy, into American foreign policy. For example, in 1968, when a former US assistant secretary of state in charge of security was queried about the Indian caste system, he equated the Dravidian with the negro as examples of dark-skinned peoples under the heel of a caste system.[11]

The Biblical myth of Ham has become appropriated by the pan-African movement as a framework to project Black supremacy to counteract White supremacy. An example is provided by the *Afrikan History* theme diary for 2002, published by Nottingham-based Afrikan Caribbean Cultural Education Services (ACCES). The diary is essentially a propaganda tool for the pan-African movement operating within the Abrahamic framework. This theology, known as Ma'at, claims that Christianity is Black, that Africa is the source of the Ten Commandments, and that 'the foundation of Judaism, Christianity, Islam and Buddhism can be traced back to ancient Kemet (Egypt)'.[12]

The diary has a section on Egyptian Yoga based on a book by Muaa Ashby.[13] Citing this book, Caroline Shola Arewa writes:

The originators of yoga are people known as the Dravidians. These Afrikan people migrated from Egypt carrying with them many spiritual practices. These ancient spiritual practices were integrated with Indian spirituality practices and further developed into the yoga we know today which has become popular the world over.[14]

Under the title 'The Buddha's Teaching', it says:

The earliest people of India were black Africans, they are believed to be from Ethiopia, often called Dravidians. They brought with them many spiritual sciences originated in Africa: Yoga, Kundalini, Reflectology. Buddha, Krishia, etc., were Black sages who rose from successive Cushite civilization, including king Asoka.

The passage further states that Buddha forbade idol worship.[15] The diary insists that the Bible originated in Africa.[16] It also claims that Africans built the Indus Valley Civilization and that Ganges is named after an Ethiopian king who conquered India.[17] Ironically, even though the Hamitic myth has been used to oppress Africans, many Africans appropriate it for their own empowerment.

The Afrocentric *Institut Fondamental d'Afrique Noire/ Institut Français d'Afrique Noire* (IFAN), founded in colonial French Africa, publishes papers supporting the Afro-Dravidian thesis.[18] These research papers are in turn quoted as evidence by Afrocentric ideologues, such as Clyde Ahmed Winters, in papers with titles such as, 'The genetic unity of Dravidian and African languages and culture',[19] 'Are Dravidians of African Origin?'[20] etc. During the 1980s, his works found their way into the academic journals of India, receiving high degrees of acceptance in the academic establishment of South India. His work 'The Harappan Writing of the Copper Tablets', was published in the *Journal of Indian History*.[21] 'The Proto-Culture of the Dravidians, Manding and Sumerians',[22] was published in an academic journal, *Tamil Civilization*. 'The Indus Valley Writing and Related Scripts of the 3rd Millennium BC',[23] was published in *India Past and Present*. 'The Far Eastern Origin of the Tamils' was in the *Journal of Tamil Studies*.[24] Winters weaves a picture of the ancient world in which Dravidians are racially and linguistically identical with various African peoples as well as with ancient Sumerians and Elamites. His theories have been deemed 'crackpot' by many academicians, yet they have been influential among Tamilians.[25]

America's Black Liberation Theology

Because of the role being played by American Black evangelism in India, it is useful to briefly explore the hybrid Marxist-Christian ideology, which is prominent among the upper-strata, educated Blacks in America.

During the period of slavery in America, Whites were initially vehemently opposed to converting slaves to Christianity, because:

1. It was feared that they could use religious organizations as cover to plot against slavery;
2. Some Christians claimed that Christians could not enslave other Christians and thus Christianity could undermine slavery; and
3. Many Whites were repulsed at the suggestion that Blacks could go to heaven and become their neighbors, especially in light of the Christian belief that people live in heaven in the same physical bodies which they had on earth. Some Whites even tried to argue that Blacks were less than human.

But by the early 1700s, evangelism was in full swing by American slave owners, because Christianity was now reinterpreted to justify slavery on the following basis:

1. The curse of slavery had been placed on the 'sons of Ham', who were interpreted to be Black;
2. Slavery was considered a religious good, because it transported unsaved heathens from Africa to Christian America, where they could convert and be saved in Heaven after death; and
3. Freedom from slavery was unimportant because life on earth was insignificant compared to the reward waiting in Heaven.

By the mid-1700s, American slaves started meeting privately to worship, because they felt intimidated in White churches in front of their masters. They reinterpreted God as a loving Father, and believed that praying to Him would free them from slavery just as he had freed Israel from Egyptian bondage. Heaven came to refer to a state of liberation in the *present* body, and the slaves used various coded messages in song to confuse their masters, so as not to arouse suspicion.

The early 1900s saw new stirrings among educated African Americans, such as the founding of the National Association for the Advancement of Colored People, a key player in the civil rights movement that eventually bore fruit in the 1960s. The pioneers of Black liberation theology claimed that the Bible is not infallible, and is not meant to be taken literally and that Christ's person is the only true revelation. This enabled them to reconcile many racist statements in the Bible, including the Hamitic narrative, and yet be able to adopt Christianity as exemplified by Jesus' life.[26] They started to teach that the Bible should be used as a 'pointer' to the meaning in Jesus' life, and not literally.

The American Black Power movement that arose in the mid-1960s triggered interest in formulating a new theology among the educated, middle-class Black clergy. It responded to the challenge from Islam, and its spokesman, Malcolm X, argued that Christianity was a 'slave religion'. Black liberation theology emerged as the Christian way to implement Marxism within the Biblical framework. In this theology, 'black' and 'white' related *not* to skin pigmentation but correspond to Marxist classes: the oppressed and the oppressors, respectively. These categories also classify attitudes. Whiteness symbolizes sickness and oppression, not a skin color, and a white-skinned person could be black if he ideologically opposes oppression. Black liberation theology looks for evidence for Yahweh's concern for social, economic, and political injustice. This same God is now working for the deliverance of oppressed Blacks, and because God is helping oppressed Blacks he is considered 'black'. Jesus is also explained as Black, and therefore symbolizes the universal freedom for all who are oppressed.

God-as-activist inspires liberation not as a heavenly state but as social, economic and political freedom rights here on earth – an idea closer to Marxism than to Christianity. Blacks have to become active to liberate themselves, including through the use of 'some' violence when it becomes unavoidable. This emphasizes human activism, and not dependence on divine help. Marxism was married to Christianity, based on the theological claim that the Biblical God and Jesus always helped the oppressed. Black liberation theology can be divisive, as illustrated in the following core message from the foremost Black liberation theologian, James Cone:

> Black theology refuses to accept a God who is not identified totally with the goals of the Black community. If God is not for us and against White people, then he is a murderer, and we had better kill him. The task of Black theology is to kill Gods who do not belong to the Black community . . . Black theology will accept only the love of God which participates in the destruction of the White enemy. What we need is the divine love as expressed in Black Power, which is the power of Black people to destroy their oppressors here and now by any means at their disposal. Unless God is participating in this holy activity, we must reject his love.[27]

Misuses of Black Liberation Theology in India

Black theology has a historical reason that serves the needs of oppressed black Americans. Decoupling Christianity from the literal interpretations of the Bible was a great accomplishment. But in some ways, it merely inverts the race hierarchy in the Bible and makes the Blacks as God's 'truly' chosen people. The export of these ideas to India is problematic, especially since it was carried out by organizations with a chauvinistic, expansionist agenda.

For example, many proponents of this theology in India include White evangelists, who operate with a double standard: they fear Black theology at home in America as a threat to their White supremacy, and yet they use it in India to fight the bigger threat of Hindu 'paganism'. This is the divide-and-conquer policy to create clashes among the non-Western peoples. This deployment of Christianity is insincere and a divisive ploy. Other Western advocates of this theology in India are leftists who oppose Christian evangelism and fundamentalism in their own countries, but still wish to export it.

While Dalits certainly have legitimate grievances that need to be addressed, the true application of the spirit of Black theology would be for oppressed Indians to find similar resources in their *own* classical narratives, such as Puranas, *Kural*, Saiva Siddhanta, etc., and thereby do what black theologians have done, i.e. to use internal spiritual resources for their own sociopolitical empowerment.

Hinduism has a long tradition of such internally generated revolts, uprisings and 'new theologies'. From Sri Ramanuja (traditionally 1017–1137 CE) through Ayya Vaikundar (1808–51 CE) to Sri Narayana Guru (1855–1928 CE), such Hindu liberation movements are singularly marked by the absence of race theories and tendencies to segregate human beings. Of these, the last two spiritual leaders, venerated as Avatars, were born among the marginalized Dalit sections of the society. Within a few generations, these groups transformed themselves into economically and politically empowered Indians, showing that in fact Dalits can work for their own agendas within Indian frameworks instead of relying on the international Dalit movements run by transnational Christian groups.

Afro-Dalit and the Racist Gods of Hindus

The Afro-Dalit idea has started percolating among American Blacks and in the African Diaspora, as well as the mainstream media. For example, in an article published in a Denver newspaper, a Kenyan surgeon views his newly arrived Indian colleagues in Colorado through the prism of the Afro-Dalit framework. His article, 'A History of Racial Tension', speaks of a 'natural chill' between Blacks and Indians working in medical establishments, which he attributes to the alleged Hindu mindset of treating Blacks 'a rung below the untouchables':

> Hindus can't help themselves. Humanity exists in a rigid chamber in Hinduism; one's caste never changes. Brahmins are empowered; lower castes enslaved. Blacks fit nicely within this group.[28]

He blames Hindu gods, 'who consign a large number of its children to slavery and bondage' and finds them 'suspect and odious'. Simultaneously, he sees Christianity as a liberating influence that 'releases the Hindu mind from its rigid shackles, unraveling the tight coils of dogma'. To him, the 1972 expulsion of the Indian community by Ugandan dictator Idi Amin was a legitimate expression of 'the frustration, anger and envy that many Ugandans felt'.[29]

In a rebuttal, another Colorado resident, Mohan Ashtakala, pointed out that the prejudice against Indians was the result of a colonial social experiment in which Indians were imported into British African colonies as administrators, so that 'the Indians became the face of colonial administrations around the world and, in some ways, bore the brunt of anger against the oppressors, where the real perpetrators of injustice—the European colonialists—escaped with little blame'.[30]

Western Government-Church Axis influences Afro-Dravidian-Dalit

Christian missionary literature in India is filled with racial hatred based on the Biblical myth of Ham, which serves as the framework for Dravidian race theory. For example, a popular Christian evangelical book endorsed by mainstream church authorities across the denominations, has a complicated version of the Aryan invasion story:

> Indus Valley Civilization is one of the most ancient, most advanced and amazingly developed urban civilizations of the Dravidians. . . . Between sixth century BC and fourth century AD white skinned foreigners namely Persians (sixth century BC), Greeks (fourth century BC), Kushans (first century AD) and Huns (fourth century AD) invaded India. During this period, white-skinned Romans also came to India for trade. The dark-skinned native Dravidian Indians called these six groups of foreigners together as 'Aryans' to mean that they were the invading aliens. . . .[31]

After explaining how the Aryans took over everything positive in Dravidian life, religion, and culture, including all the major world religions that the Dravidians supposedly had founded, it asserts:

. . . the civilization of Dravidians and Sumerians is almost identical. Thus Abraham whose civilization is Dravidian can be called a Dravidian. Jesus Christ, who is a descendant of Abraham, is also thus a Dravidian. In Tamil literature, Noah is called 'Dravidapathi'. Fr Heras considers Indus Valley Dravidians as the descendants of Ham, the son of Noah.[32]

Such a portrayal of Jesus as belonging to a specific race is not new to Christian political history. For the Nazis, Jesus was an Aryan hero crucified by the Jews.

At a conference on Dravidian Spiritual Awakening in Chennai in 2001, it was declared that: 'Hinduism is not a religion but it is only a way of life of the Aryans and hence the Dravidian Indians should hereafter declare their religion as Dravidian religion'. Among those who made the declaration was Rajshekar, editor of a magazine called *Dalit Voice*.[33] In 2005, Rajshekar told a Kerala church: 'Hinduism is our enemy. We are its victims. But Christianity is a liberating religion'.[34]

Dalit Voice promotes the church's stand that Dravidians and Dalits are a Black race related to Africans, and it gets support from radical black supremacists.[35] *Dalit Voice* promotes anti-Semitism and Brahminical-Zionist conspiracy theories for world domination and persecution of Blacks in Africa and India. It claims that the 9/11 tragedy in United States was a Zionist conspiracy.[36] It cautions China that democracy is a Zionist ploy.[37] It praises Hitler and describes *Mein Kampf* as a great book of philosophy, claiming that Hitler fought against 'the international Jewry, which programmed to dominate and control the earth planet not directly but through stooges. And their wonderful strategies converted America itself as its biggest stooge.'[38] *Dalit Voice* claims that the Brahmin race was of Jewish origin.[39]

Dalit Voice represents a nexus between Afrocentrists, Indian Dalit activists, Dravidian separatists, and Christian evangelists. The Christians use the Dalit cause to gain political leverage over the Indian government. For example, at the International Dalit Human Rights Conference in London (2000), the head of Asia Team for Christian Aid presented a paper recommending that the governments which give aid to India should consult and act according to the advice provided by the missionary Dalit groups operating from the West.[40] This reminds one of the colonial era when the well-funded global missionary establishment gained a stranglehold over India on the grounds of helping India's downtrodden.

Peter Prove, convener of International Dalit Solidarity Network (IDSN) in Geneva,[41] gleefully declared: 'The Indian Government can be put to embarrassment in international fora over the prevalence of descent-based discrimination in the country, as the United Nations has recognized what it means to be a Dalit'.[42]

Vijay Prashad, a US-based academic and prominent leftist activist, has endorsed Rajshekar and the Afro-Dalit movement, thereby justifying racism as a way to fight racism. He appears to endorse the Lemurian thesis that 'India and Africa was one land mass', which leads him to make the following conclusion: 'So both the Africans and the Indian Untouchables and tribals had common ancestors'. He also points out that Dalits 'resemble Africans in physical features'.[43] Prashad is not alone among academicians who have adopted these views.[44] Besides academic and political support from Western capitals, this movement also has media support.[45]

Ramayana *interpreted as a Racist Epic*

Meanwhile, colonial-era representations of Hinduism are being used by Afro-Dalits to spread a hate-based ideology against other Indians. Several threads come together in the way *Ramayana* has been distorted through racial interpretations that perpetuate ethnic conflicts in South India and Sri Lanka.

While the West has been quick to repudiate the race-oriented discourse within European populations, it still holds on to the distorted racist interpretations concerning African and Asian countries, especially India. For example, the discredited Aryan invasion model is still being used to interpret Hindu scriptures and epics. Western educators do not hesitate to use such interpretations as pedagogic tools. For example, www.historyforkids.org, an educational website, suggests the following *Ramayana*-based activity for children:

The *Ramayana* is partly a metaphor for the Aryans trying to invade the people of southern India. It's an Aryan story, and they show the people of southern India as bad monkeys – not even human. How should we feel about this? Should we not perform the play? Should we try to show that Hanuman and the monkeys are people too? How could we rewrite the play from the point of view of the southern Indians?[46]

When Indian scholars pointed out to Dr Karen Carr, Associate Professor of History, Portland State University, who maintains the website, that such interpretation of *Ramayana* was wrong, she responded by saying that though she was not an expert on Indian history, and would rely on Western scholars interpreting Indian history and culture, rather than the perception of Indians themselves on Indian epics.[47] This idea of identifying the monkeys of *Ramayana* with south Indians had been used by British colonial administrators to justify their presence in India as being morally and ethically superior. For example, in his 1886 address to graduates of the University of Madras, Governor Mountstuart Elphinstone Grant-Duff made a reference to *Ramayana* as follows:

> The constant putting forward of Sanskrit literature as if it were pre-eminently Indian should stir the national pride of some of you Tamil, Telugu, Cannarese. You have less to do with Sanskrit that we English have. Ruffianly Europeans have sometimes been known to speak of natives of India as 'Niggers', but they did not, like the proud speakers or writers of Sanskrit, speak of the people of the South as legions of monkeys.[48]

Westerners continue to ignore that Tamils themselves have a rich tradition of *Ramayana* rendered in their own language by their great poet Kambar. The aforementioned website's (www.historyforkids. org) interpretation of *Ramayana* itself is a throwback to the colonial period's anti-Brahminical zealotry and racism. This interpretation has been rebuked by many Western scholars, including several who otherwise subscribe to Dravidian identity theories. For example, George Hart, a professor of Tamil language at the University of California, Berkeley, with a PhD in Sanskrit, states:

Unfortunately, for a short period it became fashionable to read this epic in cultural terms – Aryan vs. Dravidian. This, in my view, is a misreading of the fundamental premise of the epic: the opposition between two views of life, one epitomized by Rama, the other by Ravana. What makes Kamban so great is that he presents both views in extremely convincing and beautiful terms – Ravana is the greatest of all kings and symbolizes this world, Rama symbolizes another dimension. And don't forget, Ravana is a Brahmin.[49]

Historian and epigraphist S. Ramachandran, from the South Indian Social History Research Institute (SISHRI) in Chennai, points out the factual flaws in portraying Rama as belonging to an Aryan race.[50] Despite such denunciations, the nationalistic Singhalese hold Ravana as a native Singhalese king and symbol of racist pride, while eschewing Rama as an Indian intrusion which should be rejected.[51] Tamil chauvinists as well as separatists of Sri Lanka share this hatred of *Ramayana* by using their own racial mapping. The official radio of LTTE, 'The Voice of Tigers', broadcast a drama titled 'Soil of Lanka', where Rama was shown as an Aryan invader racially related to present-day Singhalese, and Ravana was portrayed as a glorious indigenous Dravidian emperor from whom Aryans cunningly usurped the throne. In his message praising the drama, the late LTTE leader Prabhakaran stated that the present-day conflict was shown as a continuation of these events.[52]

13

India: A Neo-Con Frontier[1]

This and the subsequent chapter describe how both the Christian right-wing and the liberal, secular left-wing come together to depict India as a region of darkness. Whether they use the Biblical lens or the secular humanistic lens, they converge with the images of a chaotic and oppressive savage frontier, requiring urgent US intervention. This chapter describes organizations using the Biblical lens, while their liberal secular counterparts will be described in the next chapter.

Fig 13.1 shows a network of right-wing think-tanks in the US, which are influential at the policy-level. They monitor India to gather atrocity literature in order to reinforce the negative view of Indian society, conduct media briefings and promote anti-India advocacy. They also advocate US intervention in India's affairs from a Judeo-Christian interest. Under the guise of human rights, Dalit activism in the US is really a front for Christian right-wing subversion. All the ills of India are explained by the evil tendencies inherent in Hinduism, and Christian evangelism is shown as bringing liberation to a humanity exploited by a dark, heathen system.

Most of the evangelical missions in developing countries are seen by the Western governments as their civilization-flag bearers, and as an investment in building third-world communities loyal to the West – in other words, a benign form of colonialism. For the evangelical organizations, India provides the richest harvesting ground for souls vulnerable to being herded and controlled. Though evangelism has been a part of the foreign policy of the West for more than a century, it expanded dramatically during the Cold War, and now in the era of globalization evangelism, operates as multinational enterprises.

Fig 13.1 Preparing the Ground for US Intervention in India

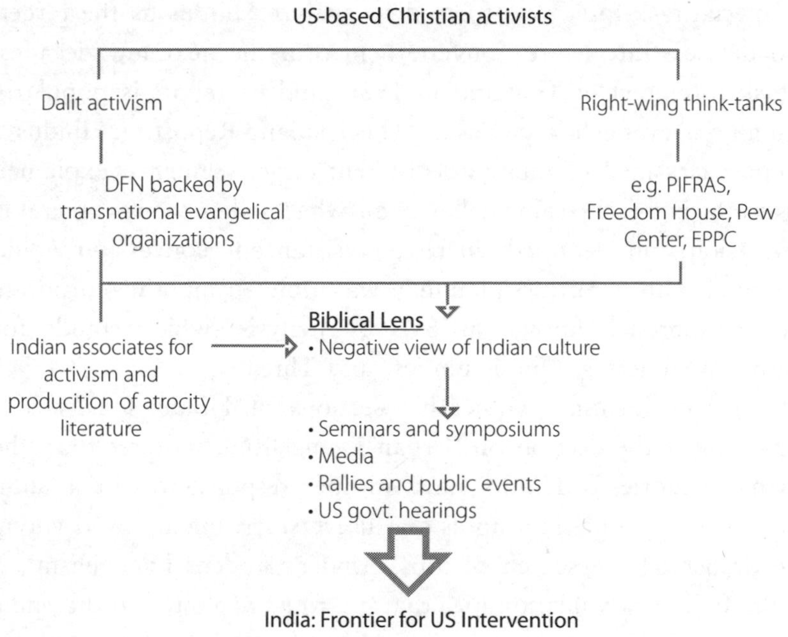

US-based Christian activists

Dalit activism

Right-wing think-tanks

DFN backed by
transnational evangelical
organizations

e.g. PIFRAS,
Freedom House, Pew
Center, EPPC

Indian associates for
activism and
production of atrocity
literature

Biblical Lens
• Negative view of Indian culture

• Seminars and symposiums
• Media
• Rallies and public events
• US govt. hearings

India: Frontier for US Intervention

Corporate Multinationals to Convert Hindus

A major event took place in 1966 when the Billy Graham Evangelistic Association, in partnership with America's *Christianity Today* magazine, sponsored the World Congress on Evangelism in Berlin. The event brought together 1,200 delegates from over 100 countries. The sequel to this was held in 1974 when some 2,700 participants from over 150 nations gathered in the Swiss Alps town of Lausanne for ten days of strategic discussions. The *TIME* magazine described the Lausanne Congress as 'a formidable forum, possibly the widest-ranging meeting of Christians ever held'.[2] The blueprint that emerged is referred to as Lausanne Occasional Papers, and is described as 'historically important documents that have emerged from global consultations involving widely recognized evangelical leaders'.[3] Subsequent mobilizations have been held in different parts of the world to create a Christian world, or what author Pradip Ninian Thomas calls the 'Christian umma'.[4]

A special task-force was formed to analyze Hindus as the target, and to devise strategies to convert them over the next few decades. This task force met in Thailand in 1980, and its report is popularly known among evangelical circles as 'The Thailand Report on Hindus'.[5] The report classified Hindus into different target segments, explained the issues facing each segment based on what makes them vulnerable to conversion, and identified where the resistance to conversion would come from. This strategic planning was done using the corporate marketing approach known as SWOT Analysis (which stands for Strengths, Weaknesses, Opportunities, and Threats).

The report identifies vulnerable sections of Hindu society. For example, under the dection on 'Urban Evangelism', it states that 'the following categories of Hindus have an open response to Christ: slum dwellers; young people in schools and universities; unemployed young people desperately in search of jobs'. Under 'Student Evangelism', it notes the following vulnerabilities that are to be exploited in the name of Jesus:

> Students from a traditional Hindu home appear open to the Christian gospel due to the breakdown of their religiosity while in the secular atmosphere of the college/university. Students coming from a rural background to study in a city are lonely, and open to Christian influence through friendship. The students from other language areas studying in linguistically strange areas are open for friendship from Christian youth (e.g. a Bengali north Indian studying in an engineering/medical/technical college in Hyderabad). International students are another group open to new influences (e.g. Malaysian, Iranian, and African students in India).[6]

The strategies for evangelization of students include such programs as:

- Train Christian students to develop close friendships with Hindu students
- Conduct special Bible studies for Hindu students
- Help them financially when the students are genuinely needy

The 'strategy for social concern' warns the missionary not to 'give room for suspicion on the part of the government or the public'. The report instructs evangelicals that whenever possible, they should relate social service to evangelism, reminding the social worker that 'long-term planning and budgeting of the local church for social service should reflect the priority of the evangelization of the non-Christian community around them.' The report was prepared by a committee chaired by the Evangelical Fellowship of India, and included World Vision officials, among other transnational church groups.[7]

India's Strengths Identified as Barriers for Evangelism

In 2000, the Theology Strategy Working Group and the Intercessory Working Group under the Lausanne Committee for World Evangelization hosted a workshop for sixty key strategists, on what they called 'spiritual conflict spiritual warfare'. The purpose was to use the Biblical framework to identify the 'enemy', how he was working, and how evangelical organizations could fight this enemy for the 'most effect in the evangelization of all peoples'.[8] One Tamil Nadu-based missionary, who participated in the seminar, went on to claim on his website that Jesus had ordered him to 'Raise Me an Army', and that he had raised 'over 16,000 zealous ministers' through seminars and camps.[9] In his paper titled 'Spiritual Conflict in the Indian Context', he identified the unity of India as a major impediment to Christianity:

> But the spirit of being Indian is the binding factor which has totally integrated the country into one. Today, displaying the 'unity in diversity', India portrays one entity. *What is considered as the merits of India, are unfortunately the deterrents for evangelization.*[10]

In exchange for the international travel, career opportunities, and prestige provided by the foreign churches, many Indians involved in such gatherings have dished out whatever the Western funding sources wanted to hear. It is not surprising that the above referenced paper by the Indian evangelist goes on to claim that 'the ancient literature of Tamil does not refer to any idols or idol worship', and that the Aryans introduced idols into India. 'Those who give themselves to idol worship are really foolish people, though they profess to be wise. The Lord said that he would give them up to vile passions. This explains how the people in India, idol worshippers, are perverted and given to every kind of vile passions'. Poverty, epidemics and natural disasters are all explained as God's curses on India because of idol worship. For example, the paper explains a major earthquake as God's anger against celebrating Ganpati Puja. Sivalinga worship, as well as Ayyapan worship prevalent in South India, are cited as examples of 'moral and sexual perversions', which 'are very many in the Hindu religion'.[11]

Development as Evangelical Tool

As it matured and gained expertise based in India, the movement appropriated the language of development for evangelization. Evangelical scholar Edgar J. Elliston explains:

> Beginning with the Berlin Congress on World Evangelization in 1963 and continuing through the countless meetings of the Lausanne Movement and AD 2000 Movement as well as the current research by Asian, African and Latin American development leaders, the focus is much more on a contextualized balance. Evangelicals no longer must choose between 'evangelism' or 'development' but rather now they look for ways these issues can be appropriately balanced in local situation.[12]

Evangelicals use the term 'development' in ways that differ from the secular meaning. The Universal Declaration on Cultural Diversity (UNESCO 2001) explains development by stating that cultural diversity is 'necessary for humankind as biodiversity is for nature' and emphasizes the importance to 'achieve a more satisfactory intellectual, emotional, moral and spiritual existence'. However, evangelistic development aims at destroying spiritual diversity by collapsing all religiosity into homogeneous monotheism. *Elliston explains the strategy: 'Development is the process by which men and women are brought into a committed relationship with the living God through the faith in Jesus Christ'.*[13]

The Lausanne Movement coordinates with groups like World Vision who have infiltrated secular developmental agencies like the United Nations Development Programme, in order to gain easy entrance without suspicion. Bryant Myers, vice president for Development and Food Resources at World Vision International, quotes another evangelical scholar to support his position that 'although Good Samaritan service sometimes has chronological priority over evangelism, the mission of the church is not fulfilled until we declare the message of reconciliation and redemption'.[14]

In an economically poor society, such evangelical development activity can play havoc, leaving enormous amount of power in the hands of the Church and Church-controlled institutions. Timothy Longman, studying the role of Christianity in the Rwandan genocide, shows how such evangelism-based development gave churches the same absolute power it had enjoyed in medieval Europe:

> The parish priest enjoyed extensive power because of his ability to hire and fire, distribute aid and determine who could be baptized, married and buried in the church . . . the church was the real center of social, economic, political and spiritual power.[15]

Evangelical Content: Pat Robertson

It is incorrectly believed by many that it was the former US President George W. Bush who initiated the evangelical expansion overseas with US governmental support. Niall Ferguson, a Harvard historian, points out how evangelical activities overseas have been something 'the British Empire and today's American empire have in common', because 'even small numbers of evangelical missionaries can achieve a good deal, furnished as they are with substantial funds from congregations at home'.[16]

The foreign policy involvement and powerful influence of organized Christianity have already existed for at least a century, and even 'liberal' presidents like Jimmy Carter and Bill Clinton were evangelical and supported foreign proselytizing by US churches. Ever since the 1600s, large percentages of Americans have felt more comfortable with their political leaders who were publicly Christian. Today, it is imperative for any mainstream US political candidate to display publicly and convincingly that he or she is a devout Judeo-Christian. Even Barack Obama had to say repeatedly that he worshipped in church, and his early campaign speeches (like those of his rival Hilary Clinton) were very often made from a church.

Pat Robertson is one of the living icons of this strain of American culture. A typical example of the images of Hinduism being fed to average Americans can be found in a video documentary featuring Pat Robertson and his son, Gordon Robertson, on a visit to India to profile Hindu weirdness. They are shown mocking the early morning prayers of Hindus, referring to the Ganga as 'Siva's sperm', and claim that the people 'were supposed to wash away their sins in the sperm of the God'. Robertson goes on to characterize Hinduism as having evil tendencies such as polytheism. He supports his son's claim that, 'Wherever you find this type of idolatry, you'll find a grinding poverty. The land has been cursed'.[17]

Americans often consider 'demonic' being explicitly or implicitly likened to Hinduism. Robertson says, 'Siva [is] the God of Destruction, and his consort, the Goddess of Death [Kali] – that black, ugly statue with all those fierce eyes'. He then suggests that the evil tendencies of death and destruction are found in those who worship Hindu deities: 'I mean, these people are out to kill other human beings in the name of their God'. By accusing Hinduism of being demonic, Robertson is merely reinforcing an age-old stereotype. Dr Gordon Melton, director of the Institute for the Study of American Religions, and author of several reference books, explains: 'In approaching Eastern religions and African religions, it has been the stance of most conservative

Christians that the deities of those religions are, in fact, personified demons'.[18]

Converting Hindus into Christianity is popularly marketed in America as an act of saving the heathens from a lifetime of fear and demonic oppression, and the target includes Hindu deities, gurus, society, rituals and any spokespersons who dare to speak up on behalf of dharma. Prof Kusumita Pedersen said that such anti-Hindu statements refer back to the 1920s when the Ku Klux Klan was on the rise, and the national belief was that all Americans must be Christians. 'What Robertson is really saying is that . . . the Hindu engineers, doctors and computer experts who are living here should go home. This is a very big statement that he has made'.[19] Such hate speech has led to genocides in the past.

As cultural identities are profiled in a xenophobic manner, killing them seems to become somewhat acceptable. Prof Peterson continues: 'It happened in Rwanda. The press and media started to build up rhetoric that so and so should be killed. After that went on for some months, so and so started getting killed. There is a line to be drawn somewhere on free speech, but we as Americans just don't know quite where yet'.[20] The seeds of hate, if unopposed, could once again mutate into the weeds of violence.

Pat Robertson has said on his widely viewed TV show: 'Of all of India's problems, one stands out from the rest. That problem is idol worship. It is said there are hundreds of millions of Hindu deities. All this has put a nation in bondage to spiritual forces that have deceived many for thousands of years'. His son elaborated further: 'The Bible talks in terms of the land being cursed on behalf of what the inhabitants have done to it. You erect all these idols under every green tree, on top of every hill, you're going to curse your land. And the oppression, we see it in evidence'.[21]

These views have become increasingly mainstream across Christian America, and are the result of a well-funded and planned long-term movement. In 1999, the Southern Baptist Convention in the USA released a guide to Hindus during Diwali, with the statement: 'Mumbai is a city of spiritual darkness. Eight out of every ten people are Hindu, slaves bound by fear and tradition to false gods'.[22] One must take note of the fact that the liberal former presidents Jimmy Carter and Bill Clinton were lifelong Southern Baptists until 2006, when both men were instrumental in forming a new and more inclusive Baptist convention. Many Indian Christian evangelists based in North America have been enlisted to echo such far-right protestant supremacist ideas, and some like Vishal Mangalwadi have become leaders of these heavily-funded Western evangelical programs in India. Some of them are now being deployed as the frontline generals in this new global civilization war.

Dalit Activism by the American Christian Right

US evangelical organizations pull the strings of US-based Dalit lobbies, with the specific goal to promote the view that all caste problems in India are caused by Hinduism, and that Hinduism is 'nothing but caste'. In short, Hinduism = caste = racism. These organizations depend on a section of academicians and activists from India who are affiliated with the Indian subsidiaries of US evangelical organizations.

American right-wing politicians and conservative think-tanks join hands and mobilize Dalit Christian evangelists to provide the view that most of the problems of India are the result of heathenism. The cure is Christianity. The work of two such groups, the Dalit Freedom Network and All India Christian Council, illustrates these complex linkages.

Dalit Freedom Network (DFN)

Dalit Freedom Network, based in Colorado, USA, is an example of a West-run organization that professes to champion Indian Dalit emancipation through policy advocacy in the power centers of the USA. It describes its mission as, 'to follow the command of Jesus Christ who called us to be "the salt of the earth" and "the light of the world"'.[23] It was founded in 2002 by Dr Joseph D'souza, head of the All India Christian Council (described later in this chapter), along with Nanci Ricks, a former missionary.[24] Its Christian agenda is explicit in the affiliations of its well-connected executives.[25] A close look at this list of directors reveals some of these links.

One of its directors is a former top staffer of right-wing US congressman, Trent Franks. Another is a vice president of the Moody Bible Institute, which the *Encyclopedia of Christianity* calls 'the flagship of interdenominational fundamentalism in the twentieth century'.[26] Two directors are from OM (Operation Mobilization), a US-based 'international Christian mission agency with over 5,400 workers in more than 110 countries and onboard two ocean-going ships'.[27] Another is the lead singer of Cademon's Call, a Christian rock group whose lyrics demonize India using Biblical imagery. For instance, its 'Mother India' song refers to the serpent in the Bible's Garden of Eden as the cause for India's suffering, and goes as follows:

> Father God, you have shed your tears for Mother India. Your Spirit falls on India and captured me in Your embrace. The Serpent spoke and the world believed its venom. . . . Father, forgive me, for I have not believed. Like Mother India, I have groaned and grieved.[28]

Among the Advisory Board Members of DFN are:[29]

- William Armstrong, a former Republican senator who is now with Colorado Christian University, which regularly sends evangelical teams to India.[30]
- Luis Bush, whose evangelical activities with strategic implications have been exposed in Tehelka's investigative report.[31]
- Thomas McCallie, representing Maclellan Foundation, which describes itself as a 'Christian education charitable trust',[32] and funds the USA's foremost institute for creationism in opposition to science.[33]
- George Miley, International President of Antioch Network, an organization rooted in 'North American Evangelical stream of Christianity', which adopted the pro-missionary Lausanne Covenant as their 'Statement of Faith'.[34]
- John Gilman, head of Dayspring International, which describes its goal in India very directly:

> The worship of a hundred million gods will disappear. Idolatry will be cast down. But what will replace it? National Dalit leaders plead to the Church in India, saying, 'Come and tell us about your Jesus. Teach us your scriptures.' They believe this is the only hope for India, a nation that could be on the brink of a bloody civil war – or on the brink of an outpouring of the Holy Spirit unlike any in history. There has never been a better soul-winning opportunity than right now in the nation of India.[35]

DFN uses a Dalit face to hide the fact that it is the hardcore operational wing of American right-wing designs on India. The Dalit label gives it the social status to intervene in Indian causes, as it did in a California textbook controversy in 2006. The *Wall Street Journal* reported how DFN gave testimony in support of the negative stereotyping of Indian culture. They positioned themselves as Hindu untouchables:

> Other Hindu groups—including members of the 'untouchables' caste—entered the fray on Mr Witzel's behalf. The Dalit Freedom Network, an advocacy group for untouchables, wrote to the education board that the proposed Vedic and Hindu Education Foundation changes reflected 'a view of Indian history that softens . . . the violent truth of caste-based discrimination in India. . . . Do not allow politically-minded revisionists to change Indian history.[36]

The textbook controversy was useful to establish DFN's credentials as a legitimate humanitarian advocacy group. This is quite typical of how lobbying groups establish credibility in the US.

Examples of DFN's Political Advocacy

Benjamin Marsh is in charge of DFN's liaison with the US State Department. He frequently speaks on behalf of DFN at churches and conferences across the US.[37] He worked closely with Western academicians in the California textbook controversy, where he was admitted into a group designated as south Asian academician while in fact he is a political evangelist. In this group, DFN was introduced as 'a real mover and shaker in Washington on behalf of the Dalit movement'.[38] Marsh accused the north American Hindus for opposing DFN's lobbying effort that wants the US congress to 'deal with caste or its modern-day effect'. He blamed these Hindus for opposing DFN's attempt 'right now to pass a resolution recognizing the ongoing presence of untouchability in India'.[39]

The moderator of an academic Indology forum asked its members to get familiar with DFN.[40] Soon thereafter, Marsh introduced into the forum a petition to promote the rights of Christian proselytizers in India. Even though the petition was signed by numerous groups known for their Christian fundamentalism—such as National Association of Evangelicals, Southern Baptist convention, Open Doors International, and www.rightmarch.com (a radical right-wing group)—the academic forum's moderator gave it a special endorsement.[41]

DFN has infiltrated the US government with the help of its widespread support-base in academia and the churches. It brings speakers and activists from India to testify before US government commissions, policy think-tanks and churches, with the explicit goal of promoting US intervention in India.[42] One such activist is Udit Raj, chairman of All India Confederation of SC/ST Organisations.[43] Raj became famous for organizing a huge Dalit rally and mass conversion of Hindus to Buddhism in India, much to the liking of evangelical Christians in the USA. But ethical issues were raised about this activity by some Indian Christians, such as Sanal Edamaruku, president of Rationalist Association of India, who pointed out the secret motive to bring large amounts of American money into Indian churches. Edamaruku explained the manipulations by these transnational organizations in India:

> The official organizer of the Delhi meeting was the All India Conference of Scheduled Castes and Tribes, an umbrella organization of government employees with a membership of more than three millions. Secret wire puller and financier of the event, however, was the All India Christian Council (AICC), an outfit of the Evangelical Church, which comprises of [sic] all kinds of neo-protestant 'born-again' and missionary organizations and is dominated by Baptists and Pentecostals.[44]

Specially honored at the rally were evangelists with foreign affiliations: Joseph D'souza and K.P. Yohannan. Edamaraku explains that these Baptists and Pentecostals were promoting a mass-conversion to Buddhism for financial resons:

> Why does the Evangelical network sponsor a mass conversion of Hindus to Buddhism? A PR-campaign, launched in June for supporters and donators in the USA and elsewhere, opened hearts and purses by giving the wrong impression that a big catch was heading straight for the Christian net. 'Gospel for Asia', the 'largest church-planting movement in the subcontinent', started focusing on the plight of the Dalits and their plan to leave Hinduism. . . . Money flew generously. But while advertising the big catch, the AICC leaders knew and appreciated very well that the Dalits would convert to Buddhism only. Their targets were not the converts of Delhi, though they used them to water their donators' mouths. Their plan was to use the Buddhist conversions as a wedge to open the gates of India for the great millennium crusade. This plan could only succeed under the condition that the missionary finger in the pie remained unseen in India.[45]

The AICC website explains Raj's role in US politics to advocate intervention in India as a part of its foreign policy:

> Dr Udit Raj, the National Chairman of the Confederation of SC/ST Organisations, has met Mr Trent Franks (a US Congressman) in Delhi two years back and explained the situation of the Dalits in India. And subsequently, Dr Udit Raj has visited the USA, especially Washington, giving a clear picture of what is happening with the Dalits in the villages and towns of India and seeking involvement of American companies that are starting businesses in India to cater to the Dalit community in India. As a follow up to his visits to Washington, the partner agency, Dalit Freedom Network, pursued the matter and got this concurrent resolution passed in the House of Representatives of the United States.[46]

Trent Franks is a US congressman from Arizona, a state with few Dalit residents. He has taken such an interest in Dalit affairs because of his alignments with the Christian right-wing. Introducing the resolution in 2007, Franks said, 'This resolution will ensure that we as a government and as a people in no way encourage or enforce caste discrimination and untouchability through our policies with India or through our foreign direct aid'. The rest of the speech offers a good example of how atrocity literature finds its way into high places of authority.[47]

Resolutions of this type are merely statements of opinion with no force of law. Many are passed as favors to special interests, and few US congressmen actually read them before voting. However, it would sound impressive in India, and would add one more piece to the paper trail for anyone pushing for US intervention. In fact, a pseudo-Dalit website trumpeted the resolution as a 'historic legislation'.[48]

Kancha Ilaiah: 'We Want to Kill Sanskrit'

Another important ideologue being globally promoted by DFN as 'the leading Dalit rights campaigner', is Kancha Ilaiah. DFN awarded him a post doctoral fellowship.[49] One of his books, *Why I am not a Hindu,* is prescribed in introductory courses on Hinduism at many American universities. Koenraad Elst, a Belgian Indologist, reviewed the book and found parallels with the anti-Jewish caricatures in Nazi literature:

> These anti-Hindu forces are exploiting the Aryan Invasion Theory to the hilt, infusing crank racism in vast doses into India's body politic. Read, e.g. Kancha Ilaiah's book *Why I Am Not a Hindu* (Calcutta, 1996), sponsored by the Rajiv Gandhi Foundation, with its anti-Brahmin cartoons: move the hairlocks of the Brahmin villains from the back of the head to just in front of their ears, and you get exact replicas of the anti-Semitic cartoons from the Nazi paper, *Der Stumer.*[50]

Equally vehement is Ilaiah's hatred for Sanskrit. *The Indian Express* reports that he made a strong presentation before India's National Conference on Human Rights, saying, 'We want to kill Sanskrit in this country'.[51] In an interview he also advocated, 'We should close down the IITs and the IIMs as they pander to the upper-caste economy of the country'.[52] Ilaiah's work illustrates how the Dalit movement has absorbed the rhetoric of the Dravidian separatists, such as demonizing Sanskrit and Hinduism as being the roots of oppression. Much of India's shared heritage is made out to be the root of Dalit grievances.

The *Christianity Today* magazine lists among Ilaiah's achievements, that 'he recently testified at a widely-reported Congressional hearing in the USA', in which he blamed Hinduism for 'the ongoing reality of violence and discrimination against Dalits'.[53] In an interview with *Christianity Today*, he equated Hinduism with Nazism, and characterized it as 'spiritual fascism'. His argument relies upon Hitler's misappropriation of Hindu symbols, for which he blames Hinduism. 'Hinduism is a kind of spiritual fascism', he explains, 'because the Hindu books say that Aryans wrote that, and Nazi Germany Hitler believed he belonged to an Aryan race'; and hence, 'the symbols that Hindus and Aryan Germans used are the same, the swastika and the concept of a few people always being superior to the other . . . So Hinduism is a very spiritually fascist system and because of that our country has suffered in many ways'.[54]

Ilaiah is routinely hosted by evangelical organizations to tour the United States, with the goal of building him up as a great leader of civil rights, and thereby upgrading his influence. For example, Texas-based organization Gospel for Asia announced:

> Gospel for Asia is pleased to host Dr Kancha Ilaiah, one of India's most influential human rights leaders. . . . What Martin Luther King, Jr. meant to the civil rights movement in this country, Dr Ilaiah means to the civil rights movement in India today. . . . In his role as consultant to the All India Christian Council, he advises leaders on the socio-economic, religious, and political conditions among India's lower castes.[55]

Ilaiah has also been a celebrated speaker at academic South Asian Studies conferences that are held annually at the University of Wisconsin, Madison.

In his latest book, titled *Post-Hindu India*,[56] Ilaiah constructs a racist ideology of hatred against Hinduism in general and Brahmins in particular. He also attempts to revive pseudo-scientific racism. Purporting to study what he terms as 'Brahmin psychology', he starts with the statement: 'No study has been conducted to understand the psychology of the Brahmins'. Then he goes on to characterize Brahmins as sub-humans, stating that Brahmin communitarianism 'acts like the communitarianism of penguins and sheep, which hardly builds the energy for individual struggle for survival'. He states that Brahmins are worse than animals because in their case, even the animal instincts are 'underdeveloped':

> The process of hunting and grazing among animals take[s] place with the individual enterprises of animals, within their broad social collectivity. But Brahmins did not allow any individual enterprise in their own social collectivity. They carried the underdeveloped animal instinct of penguins and sheep into human beings.[57]

He goes on to revive the pseudo-science of racism: 'Different racial characteristics of the human beings construct the instincts of the human beings differently'. Next, he proceeds towards a hate rhetoric couched in social Darwinism:

> All parasites suffer from a constant fear of individualism. . . . The Brahmins as a community shared the animal instinct of not being able to produce anything from the earth. This human caste differs from all the other social communities ever since human beings evolved out of the apes. . . . This unusual instinct of parasitism forced the Brahmans to construct a social process of spiritual fascism that became the fortress of this parasitism.[58]

He concludes that the Brahmin childhood formation itself has 'genetic and social characteristics of non-transformability'.[59] Based on this hate, he envisions a civil war in India, urging the Dalit-Bahujans to start a civil war at the macro and micro level.[60] Citing his distorted imagery of Hindu gods, Illaiah suggests a full-blown 'war of weapons' in India:

> Historically-upper castes have suppressed the lower-caste masses with weapons, as the Hindu gods' origin itself is rooted in the culture of weapon usage. The SC/ST/OBCs will then have to turn to a war of weapons in the process of elimination of Hindu violence from India.[61]

Predicting a 'major civil war' on the lines of the violent upheavals that happened in Europe, Illaiah sees it as a 'necessary evil'[62] and claims that 'Dalits have enormous potential to lead the civil war in India' with inputs from 'Buddhism and Christianity . . . growing into planthood'. However, Illaiah's mention of Buddhism is only lip service in order to build up a unified army against Hinduism, because elsewhere in the book he states that Indian Dalits find Jesus to be a more powerful liberator than Buddha.[63]

That such a vitriolic, hate-filled book has been published by a prestigious publishing house like Sage Publications, should be a warning sign. What is even more surprising, is that Sage took the unusual step of adding a special publisher's note up-front, appreciating the 'unique methodologies and subtleties of the argument' of the author.

Recent DFN Activities

In 2005, DFN representatives, along with Kancha Ilaiah, provided testimony to a US government subcommittee on human rights, in which they advocated US interventionist policies against India. The hearing was titled, 'Equality and Justice for 200 Million Victims of the Caste System'.[64] The chairman of the US Commission on Global Human Rights supported DFN's position, saying, 'Converts to Christianity and Christian missionaries are particularly targeted, and violence against Christians often goes unpunished'. John Dayal, who has close ties with DFN, hailed this criticism of India as a 'historic moment'.[65]

In 2006, a 'Religious Freedom Day' was organized on Capitol Hill in Washington by the right-wing Christian fundamentalist, Senator Rick Santorum. Joseph D'souza of DFN gave the keynote speech, in which he held 'Hindu extremism' responsible for all religious violence. He urged the global community to intervene in the internal conflicts of India and to protest against the legislation in Indian states that prohibits coercive means for conversion.[66] The occasion was used to announce that 100,000 Dalit Christians would participate in a 'World Religious Freedom Day' rally in India. *Christianity Today* magazine supported allegations by Christian Solidarity Worldwide, which seeks to repeal Indian laws to prevent abusive evangelical practices.[67]

In 2007, DFN and its affiliates played a dominant role in a briefing before the Congressional Human Rights Caucus, titled 'Untouchables: The Plight of Dalit Women'. The caucus heard testimonies from Nanci Ricks (DFN President), Joseph D'souza (DFN International President), Kumar Swamy (All India Christian Council). Smita Narula, a known US-based activist against India, also carried the DFN message.[68] This briefing paved the way for a concurrent resolution.

Apart from such advocacy for international intervention in India's internal problems, DFN also channels funds for what it calls 'Dalit empowerment'. One such front is Operation Mercy Charitable Company (OMCC), which aims to establish explicitly Christian 'Good Shepherd' schools.[69] It has an ambitious plan of creating '1,000 Dalit Education and Emancipation Centers'.[70] The website informs readers that the organization believes in 'the free democratic traditions given to us by Gandhi, Nehru and Ambedkar'. However, DFN president Joseph D'souza himself depreciates the value of Mahatma Gandhi's service to eradicate caste.[71] Thus, the OMCC simply serves as another front of DFN, and gives it a pro-Gandhi face in order to balance out the anti-Gandhi stance.

All India Christian Council (AICC)

Although DFN is based in the US, it is affiliated with the All India Christian Council, which is described as 'the largest alliance in India of Church bodies and Christian entities' and a 'nation-wide alliance of Christian denominations, mission agencies, institutions, federations and Christian lay leaders'.[72] It has been affiliated with Christian Solidarity Worldwide (CSW), which is led by Baroness Caroline Cox.[73] (See Chapter Sixteen for more details on CSW and the baroness.) CSW has facilitated the globalization of the Christian-Dalit axis, such as at the 2001 Durban conference, where it championed a stand against the government of India.[74] One of its heroes, John Dayal, has been delivering many testimonies on India's atrocities and calling on various Western bodies to intervene.[75]

AICC is adept at presenting Indian atrocity literature in ways that get attention. For example, US Congressman Edolphus Towns, who wanted to declare India a terrorist state in 1998,[76] used atrocity literature developed by AICC to portray India as 'a theocratic tyranny, not a real democracy', and stated that the United States 'must impose the sanctions appropriate for a violator of religious freedom'.[77]

Continuing its public relations push, AICC credited its partnering with Christian Solidarity Worldwide and DFN for resulting in the UK Foreign Office issuing 'a statement on Dalit slavery'. In 2007, AICC briefed Human Rights Commission and European Union MPs in Brussels and also participated in hearings in Scotland and Norway. When the British House of Commons debated caste oppression that year, one MP openly talked about AICC hosting his Indian visit.[78]

After AICC and DFN leaders had testified about the plight of Dalit women before the US Congressional Human Rights caucus in 2007,[79] Nickelodeon TV, a children's channel, broadcast a program titled 'Untouchable Kids of India' in an Emmy Award-winning, popular kids' news show, in which it featured AICC and Operation Mercy.[80] After developing this widespread publicity, AICC built its base for further political influence. AICC's President met with US senators and the US ambassador at large for the Prevention of Trafficking in Persons, to lobby for a resolution about Dalit exploitation, his advocacy being specifically directed against the Indian state. AICC and Christian Solidarity Worldwide actively collaborate to brief US and EU officials on 'Dalit and Christian persecution'.[81]

In 2009, Joseph D'souza of AICC was presented as the crusader for Dalit rights on a TV talk show of Canada-based Crossroads Christian Communications. He described the atrocity on Dalits as the mainstream norm across all parts of India, leading the TV host to exclaim that India's democracy was a sham. For D'souza it is not Ambedkar or Gandhi who improved the lives of Dalits, but the movie *Slumdog Millionaire,* which he misinterprets to claim that in Dalit villages, all the girl children above the age of five are sold by their parents into sexual slavery for one thousand or two thousand dollars.[82] The program was telecast by an Evangelical media group called '100 Huntley Street', which is known for its fundamentalism and slandering of non-Christian groups.[83] The American media had already gone on for several months with speculation about whether the young woman who stars in *Slumdog Millionaire* might have been sold for a large sum by her downtrodden yet money-hungry family.

AICC deftly positions itself as a representative of oppressed peoples. For example, when Ms Asma Jahangir, United Nations Special Rapporteur on Freedom of Religion or Belief, visited India, Christian Solidarity Worldwide 'had kindly introduced the Special Rapporteur's staff to AICC leaders in Secunderabad. CSW advocacy officers met Jahangir during her visit to London last year'.[84] Jahangir echoed the views of the Christian organizations in her report, and the AICC news-brief stated that her 2008 visit to India was organized by AICC as partner of CSW (UK). After visiting Orissa, her report articulated concern over state-level freedom of religion laws which restricted conversion by unethical means, and it further demanded that Christians belonging to former Dalit communities must be given a share in government affirmative programs reserved for Hindu Dalits. Both ideas are the pet themes of AICC.[85]

With its US networking, AICC has also started flexing its muscles in Indian politics. It presented the ruling party with its own list of Christian candidates for the state elections in the Indian state of Maharashtra.[86]

Examples of US Politicians and Bureaucrats Linked with Christians Lobbying Against India

Since the 1980s, many American politicians and appointed bureaucrats have had strong links with the evangelical groups that back intervention in India. We will list a few such politicians as examples of this.

US Congressman Christopher Smith, chairman of the Committee on Africa, Global Human Rights and International Operations, held a hearing in 2005 on human rights violations and discrimination faced by Dalits in India. DFN activists dominated the various events and Congressman Smith supported their line. Smith is a staunch Christian known for anti-abortionist and other fundamentalist beliefs, and has systematically blocked programs which empower Dalit women who do not comply with his Christian values: It is Christianity, not Dalit empowerment or women's rights, that he is lobbying for.[87]

Another congressman sponsoring DFN's activities is Joseph Pitts. In 2004, he went on a fact-finding mission to India, and concluded that the laws preventing abusive conversion methods were undemocratic.[88] He also attended the PIFRAS (Policy Institute for Religion and State)[89] seminar on India that year,[90] and is known for his pro-Pakistan stand.[91] (PIFRAS is described later in this chapter.) In 2001 he tried to set up a Kashmir Forum in the US Congress. In 2003 he inaugurated on Capitol Hill a pro-Pakistan conference on Kashmir. He is known to be a 'long time sympathizer of the pro-Pakistani lobby' and Indian officials boycotted his events.[92] As a Christian conservative, he received a hundred percent rating for his voting record from the American Conservative Union in 2005 and the Christian Coalition in 2004.[93] Pitts, along with the former US Senator Rick Santorum, helped sponsor a Religious Freedom Day in 2006 for DFN.[94] Pitts is known for his support for US intervention in Iraq, and also tried to sneak Christian Intelligent Design theory into the national school curriculum.[95] He is now a senior fellow with the Ethics and Public Policy Center, where he heads a new program called 'America's Enemies', which will 'focus on identifying, studying, and heightening awareness of the threats posed to America and the West from a growing array of anti-Western forces that are increasingly casting a shadow over our future and violating religious liberty around the world'.[96]

Congressman Trent Franks introduced a resolution in the US Congress, calling for interventionist measures by United States in India's caste problems. This has been hailed as a historic victory by DFN, AICC and their affiliates. He also attended the PIFRAS 2004 seminar on India.[97] He is a strong right-wing conservative who calls for

US intervention for the marginalized sections in India, and yet in the US the largest and oldest civil rights group, the National Association for the Advancement of Colored People, has given him a very low rating because of his lack of support for marginalized people in the US.[98] He also appeared on the radically evangelical GOD TV channel to ask Christians all over the world to pray for the defeat of Barack Obama.[99]

William Armstrong is a former US senator who is an active member of the advisory board of Dalit Freedom Network.[100] He serves as the president of Colorado Christian University,[101] which 'recognizes the need for an environment that fosters evangelization', by sending its students, faculty, and staff to 'places like India'.[102]

Senator Sam Brownback, who works closely with right-wing Christian groups, has served on the US Senate Foreign Relations Committee. The Methodist Church was delighted at his stance that Hindu 'extremism' was threatening peace in South Asia, and he advised that 'the United States needs to be aggressively involved diplomatically in South Asia'.[103] Brownback, along with Pitts and several other important politicians, is part of a somewhat secretive group that calls itself 'The Family', and which has influenced US foreign policy for decades.[104]

Edolphus Towns is a congressman and an ordained Baptist minister who cited AICC reports as his authority to condemn India in the US Congress, on the charge that India's Foreign Contributions Regulations Act monitors the flow of foreign funds for evangelization.[105] His persistent stand against India's sovereignty is illustrated by the following statement:

> There are steps that we can take to support the rights of all people in South Asia. It is time that we take these steps. They include cutting off our aid and trade with India and putting the US Congress on record in support of self-determination for the Sikhs of Punjab, Khalistan, the Christian people of Nagaland, the Kashmiris, and all the people of South Asia, who are seeking freedom. Only by exercising their right to self-determination, which is the essence of democracy, can the people there finally live in freedom, peace, and prosperity.[106]

Unlike most of the politicians described here, Towns is an African American, Democrat, and representative of a cosmopolitan left-leaning urban district. Clearly, AICC and DFN have been successful in appealing to multiple constituencies.

Our final example is that of Mr Susai Anthony, of the US Office of Personnel Management in Washington, DC. He submitted a document to the US Congress, claiming that it represented 'the collective thoughts of Indian American Christians' to bring them 'facts on persecution of Christians in India'. He defined Hinduism with the statement that 'most Hindu practices were brought over by Aryans', and that 'Hinduism is not a tolerant religion, as propagated'. He gave statistics of the exact number of 'cases of atrocities against untouchables and indigenous people' by year, and by state. He conveniently ignored the widespread existence of caste atrocities within Indian Muslim and Indian Christian communities as well. It is missionary education, he claimed, that enables Indians to do work 'other than the types the Hindu tradition enjoins'. He felt that India's secularism was not legitimate and criticized the law in Madhya Pradesh that banned the use of 'force, fraud, or allurement' to convert a person's religion. Data on 'anti-Christian crimes by top ten states' of India were submitted in his report, and accepted without any attempt by US authorities to independently verify the charges. The US government was told that, 'the problem of Christians in India is not an internal matter', and that international intervention was required.[107]

Right-wing Think-tanks and Policy Centers

Numerous US institutions take the atrocity literature being produced by Christian-funded entities, repackage it in a professionally compelling style, and feed it to the policy makers at the US centers of power. They churn the stories to show savage behavior through the sophisticated language of theology and right-wing politics. A few key examples of such institutions are described below.

Policy Institute for Religion and State (PIFRAS)

The Policy Institute for Religion and State is a powerful advocacy group which states its mission in an objective, neutral manner:

> To encourage a democratic basis for the interaction between religion and state, by promoting an understanding of the role of democracy, human rights and freedom of conscience in creating sustainable societies.[108]

However, it is noteworthy that every board member of PIFRAS belongs to the Abrahamic religions. In fact, many of its members also represent evangelical institutions with a direct interest conflicting with Hinduism. For example, John Prabhudoss, its executive director, represents the Federation for Indian American Christian Organizations of North America (FIACONA), as chairman of its Governmental Affairs Committee. FIACONA has intensely lobbied in Washington to spread awareness about alleged Hindu atrocities against Christians.

B. Raman, an expert on security and anti-terrorism operations, who headed India's counter-terrorism division of the Research and Analysis Wing (RAW) for six years and is presently director, institute For Topical Studies in Chennai, has made an in-depth investigation of PIFRAS and FIACONA. He found the executive director to be a man of mysterious conduct and several aliases, who:

> . . . calls himself sometimes as John Prabhudoss (when he went to Iraq after the US invasion and occupation, for example) and sometimes as P.D. John (when he visited Gujarat after the riots in 2002, for example) and that he wears two hats. It is also alleged that he uses other aliases such as J.P. Doss.[109]

Even more revealing was Raman's explanation of the bias evident in PIFRAS activity in tandem with FIACONA. Describing Prabhudoss, he says:

> FIACONA focuses on lobbying in Washington DC on the issue of the violations of the rights of the religious minorities and the restrictions on the right of the Christians to proselytize in India, the PIFRAS

largely concentrates on backing the Bush Administration's policy of promoting democracy and good governance, particularly in the Islamic world. . . . My research and enquiries also indicated that while he and his organisations have been very vocal in their criticism of the violations of the human rights of the Christians and Muslims in India, they have been mute on the violations of the human rights of the Sunni Muslims of Iraq by the US troops, the alleged brutalities committed by the US troops at the Abu Gharaib prison and the alleged massacre of the Iraqi Sunnis, particularly at Falluja, by the US troops. Nor did I find any activism by him and his organisations on the brutal violations of the human rights of the Muslim detainees at the Guantanamo Bay in Cuba.[110]

Another board member of PIFRAS is Bruce C. Roberston, Chair of South Asia Studies at Johns Hopkins University and the son of missionaries working in India. He was also chairman of South Asia Area Studies at the Foreign Service Institute, NFATC, US Department of State.[111] He is influential among Christian evangelicals, and was also instrumental in giving a controversial grant from the US National Endowment of Humanities to develop a school curriculum on *Ramayana*. The teacher training-manual that resulted, included a song portraying Rama as racist, anti-Muslim and oppressor of women, among other things.[112]

PIFRAS Conferences

There are conferences all over the world where academics gain prestige, lobbyists push agendas, and politicians curry favor. These are the forums where important networks of influence are developed. By examining a few of these conferences, we will show how a combination of evangelical, academic and governmental forces converge and provide continual inputs to create the picture of an oppressive Indian state, a failed democracy which persecutes its helpless religious minorities. The message is that saving India's oppressed peoples is in the religious and political interests of the United States.

In 2002, PIFRAS held a South Asia conference, sponsored by United Methodist Board of Church and Society and the National

Council of Churches of Christ in the USA. Other prominent think-tanks (mostly right-wing or evangelism-oriented) also joined in sponsoring, including: Ethics and Public Policy Center, the Center for Religious Freedom, Freedom House, the Institute for Religion in Public Policy, and the Apostolic Commission for Ethics and Policy.

In the conference, John Dayal contended that minorities could not count on the Indian state to protect them, or to prosecute crimes committed against them. Bruce Robertson urged faith-based non-governmental organizations (i.e. foreign Christian-sponsored groups) to provide more of the community services that governments are not providing in India. K.P. Singh, who is on the faculty of the University of Washington in Seattle, went unchallenged on his outrageous claim that 'since India's independence, about three million Dalit women have been raped and one million Dalits have been killed'.[113]

Effects Within India

On the eve of India's General Elections in 2004, PIFRAS, along with Centre for the History of Religious and Political Pluralism (University of Leicester, England), organized a panel discussion on 'India's National Elections and US Foreign Policy Interests', where Marxist historian Ram Punyani was the invited speaker along with Mr John Prabhudoss, executive director of PIFRAS. The main position presented was that India's forty million Christians are threatened by 'Hindu state governments' that have passed laws to hold evangelism accountable for coercion. With this backdrop, the purpose of the panel was advertized as analysis of the impact of India's election and recommendation of US foreign policy towards India.

Clearly, such think-tanks influence US policy towards India on internal affairs ranging from evangelism, birth control and HIV/AIDS, and other agendas set by US Christian groups. American assistance for health programs, including AIDS funding under PEPFAR (President's Emergency Plan for AIDS Relief) comes with strings attached. Many of these rules are intended to keep American money from being spent on abortions, a hot issue with the American right-wing. The result, however, is to channel funds through evangelical NGOs. The general effect is to limit, or at least fail to increase, women's access to all family planning and gynecology/obstetrics services. Until a 2008 revision, one third of PEPFAR funds were required to be spent on programs pushing 'abstinence' as the best method for AIDS prevention, because both Catholic and Evangelical groups have an aversion to birth control.

A *Tehelka* investigative report of 2004 showed that massive foreign funding claimed to be for HIV/AIDS programs was being used by Christian groups for evangelism. According to the report, even the official government slogan for AIDS prevention was changed by Christian NGOs. The government policy, ABC for 'Abstinence, Behavioral change and Condoms', was modified to replace 'Condoms' with 'Convert/Christ'.[114]

There are also direct foreign efforts to alter the Indian law. When the Indian government felt that the foreign funds of NGOs needed more transparency, John Dayal, who presides over the All India Christian Council and United Christian Forum for Human Rights, testified against the Indian government at PIFRAS-sponsored hearings and symposiums at Washington. The institute's press release stated:

> Mr Dayal has been at the forefront in addressing government allegations that the money received from foreign sources is being used for religious conversions. . . .[115]

Freedom House

Freedom House is another powerful institution which relies almost exclusively on the testimonies from Christian-sponsored Dalit activists. These testimonies are highly exaggerated, sensationalized and distorted accounts of Indian political developments.

Freedom House has a liberal-sounding entity called 'Center for Religious Freedom'. However, its report on The Rise of Hindu Extremism (2003) relied heavily on 'generous contributions' made by Rev Cedric Prakash as well as 'significant work' done by Timothy

Shah, Vinay Samuel, and the Director of PIFRAS, John Prabudoss. These persons, as the reader shall see, continue to appear across most of these think-tanks and the commissions and symposiums they conduct. Also involved were John Dayal and Joseph D'souza of the All India Christian Council, and representatives of the Dalit Freedom Network, the Indian Social Institute Human Rights Documentation Center, the United Christian Forum for Human Rights, the All India Federation of Organizations for Democratic Rights, the Catholic Bishops' Conference of India, and the National Alliance of Women.[116] There was no equivalent representation from opposing views, nor any context provided to explain the geopolitical agendas in which these individuals and groups operate. In other words, their heavy conflict of interest was simply buried, and the report's mostly American readers did not bother to demand transparency.

India's Freedom of Religion Act is designed to prevent fraudulent conversion. Freedom House's report falsely stated that under this law, 'emphasizing the spiritual benefit of a particular religion could be a cause for arrest'. There is no such provision in the law. The report goes on to emphasize that conversion-based conflicts in India are present because the upper-caste Hindus fear the emancipation of Dalits through Christianity, without hinting whatsoever at the aggressive proselytizing campaigns to demonize Hinduism. The report laments that despite George Bush's emphasis on freedom of religion, 'these fine words seldom shape the foreign-policy bureaucracy' of the USA.

The report called for US intervention in India on the grounds of US political interests, and claimed that, 'The most egregious persecuting states . . . tend to be those that act against US interests. Conversely, those with good records are likely to be good US allies'.[117] But in reality, the exact opposite has been true: Many 'good US allies' are military dictatorships with the worst human rights violations and yet have been treated with kid gloves, while democracies like India come in for heavier criticisms. *The Times of India* mentioned this bias in report:

While secular and democratic countries such as India merit a litany, a country like Saudi Arabia, one of the least free countries in the world, was turned over in thirty-two pages. The US has shown no inclination to punish allies it bankrolls, such as Egypt and Turkey, while berating countries less relevant to it.[118]

Asia Society in New York

Asia Society was funded by the Rockefeller family and included former CIA director William Colby among its founding members.[119] Until recently when it started to seek funds from Indian industrialists, it provided a consistent streaming of negative images of India into the psyche of influential Americans. The basic democratic nature of India was constantly questioned. At meeting its in 2003, the topic of hot debate was whether India was a 'fascist state'. Vishakha Desai, the current president of Asia Society, organized a seminar in New York whose stated purpose was 'to see whether there is a fundamental shift in India's secularism'. The moderator, Celia Dugger, who served as *New York Times* co-bureau chief in New Delhi from 1998 to 2002, took the stand that India was becoming a fascist state.[120] However, in the new US-India climate, Asia Society has indeed broadened its scope to focus on India as a rising economic power that offers potentials for US policy.

Sustained and Biased Perceptions

Yet another instance of biased reporting by a prestigious think-tank is the RAND Corporation's grouping of RSS (a socio-cultural organization with Hindu nationalist leanings) with al-Qaeda. It clubbed both as examples of violent 'new religious movements' that are characterized by two defining characteristics: a high degree of tension between the group and its surrounding society; and, a high degree of control exercised by leaders over their members.[121] Though the two characteristics mentioned above arguably fit the Hindu organization in question, it should be noted that it would equally fit well many of the Christian evangelical churches and born-again groups operating in

India as well as United States. It would also fit close-knit communities like Mormons.

The Ford Foundation also provides transnational monitoring of Indian policies, as illustrated by its sponsorship of an Australian conference on India that was entirely centered on the Bharatiya Janata Party. The whole program consisted of issues about BJP, with several papers on 'BJP economics', 'BJP rural governance', 'BJP and media', 'BJP and textbooks', 'BJP and the southern states', etc. Thus, India was defined entirely in terms of images of BJP, as if no other aspect of India mattered.[122]

Gujarat as Savage India

The 2002 Gujarat riots came as a great opportunity for the forces that have wanted to demonize India. For the United States, which was in dire need to show the Arab world that the aggressive Afghan and Iraq invasions were not a crusade against Islam, the Gujarat riots provided an opportunity to prove that it stands by the Muslims at the expense of the Hindus. Many advocacy groups, evangelical institutions, and related think-tanks, went into a hyperactive mode, inviting activists from India to give testimony in the US regarding gruesome violence of the Gujarat riots.[123] Hinduism thus served as fodder for US appeasement of Islam.

The violent Hindu retaliation to the Godhra carnage is unconditionally condemnable. Many credible voices have adequately shown that in 2002 it was the lack of adequate response at the highest levels of the Gujarat government that led to a Hindu-Muslim bloodbath, that both sides lost lives but that the Muslims lost more. The issue here is the manner in which the incident has been used in the US to reinforce the savage imagery of India. Gujarat has become the favorite site for generating fresh atrocity literature. Such images reinforce the deep myth of the 'fontier' that requires the identification of a savage 'other' from which the innocent natives need to be rescued by the forces of civilization.

This new frenzy served many human rights activists for whom it became more important to promote US intervention than to support the human relief efforts on the ground or the due legal process in India's own courts. The rewards included foreign travel, contacts in high places, and the chance to build a reputation as a frontiersman fighting savages in the Gujarat frontier. Fig 13.2 shows how the American frontier myth served as the template to import sensational data about Gujarat and extrapolate it for all Hindus, and thus dish out political mandates.

Fig 13.2 Reinforcing the Frontier Myth in Indian Context with Gujarat

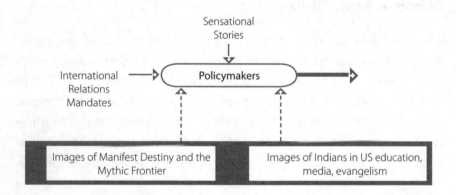

Stereotypes, sweeping statements, and images were mobilized about 'Hindu problems' such as caste, sati, dowry, weird gods, primitiveness, irrationality, etc. Unfortunately, the many voices involved in this exercise have conflated the specific episodes with all of Hinduism. For example, the EPPC (described below) sponsored a conference in which six experts on South Asia discussed the impact of increasing religious militancy. Co-sponsoring the conference was INFEMIT, a network of third-world theologians and activists led by Dr Vinay Samuel. As a result of this high-power gathering, Congressman Joseph Pitts made the following speech before the US House of Representatives:

Trained combatants in Gujarat entered villages and attacked men, women and children. Pregnant women had their wombs ripped open and unborn babies were ripped out and tossed into burning fires. Approximately three hundred women were gang-raped. Over two thousand people died. I have photos too gruesome to show, in my office . . . Mr Speaker, our government must respond to these brutal attacks and the underlying extremism. The silence of the US Government is deafening. [124]

Ethics and Public Policy Center (EPPC)

The Ethics and Public Policy Center openly and officially calls itself the 'premier institute dedicated to applying the Judeo-Christian moral tradition to critical issues of public policy' in Washington. This is a powerful group, one of whose directors was the late US Ambassador to the UN, Jeane J. Kirkpatrick, a tough right-wing Reaganite who repeatedly condemned and opposed India at the time of Indira Gandhi and notoriously helped arm Pakistan with US weapons. Michael Cromartie, the vice president of EPPC, runs its Evangelicals in Civic Life Program, whose aim is 'to expand the civic dialogue among evangelical leaders and expound an evangelical understanding of civic engagement'.[125] Cromartie has also been serving as a member of the United States Commission for International Religious Freedom (USCIRF) since 2004, including two terms as chairman. This shows the magnitude of the nexus between the policy institutes and governmental agencies. Cromartie is also a senior adviser to the Pew Forum on Religion and Public Life, and a senior fellow with the Trinity Forum. Thus, EPPC has strong links with other funding groups, evangelical organizations, and governmental agencies.

Among its activities, it has coordinated strategic visits by Father Cedric Prakash, a Jesuit priest in India operating as a human rights activist, who is also a liaison for the Local Capacities for Peace Project at Harvard University, and is the spokesperson of the United Christian Forum for Human Rights. Father Prakash was invited to testify in Washington before the US Commission for International Religious Freedom in 2002. Additionally, he was invited in the same year to Luxembourg, and then London, for interactions with the European Union and with the Foreign and Commonwealth Office of the British government, respectively.[126] His testimony was a long litany of alleged atrocities being committed by Hindus. In the climax of his speech, he made a powerful appeal for intervention: 'In the name of the thousands of victims . . . I earnestly appeal to you, to make all necessary interventions . . .'.[127]

Besides facilitating these visits, EPPC also holds its own events for lobbying political leaders in Washington, concerning alleged Hindu atrocities. Once such conference was titled 'Hindu Nationalism vs Islamic Jihad',[128] and was convened by Timothy Shah, an Indian Christian who was the Director of South Asia Affairs at EPPC. Having worked on projects that reflect on how faith influences public life in the United States and overseas, and armed with a Harvard PhD on religion and politics, Shah has received a Harvey Fellowship which 'seeks to encourage Christian graduate students to integrate their faith and vocation and pursue leadership positions in strategic fields where Christians tend to be under-represented'. He also gave testimony before USCIRF in 2004.

Dr Shah has since then moved on to bigger things at the Pew Charitable Trusts, a prominent foundation promoting the US government's Christian interventions in developing countries. His official background boasts that he served as the 'research director for an international study of Evangelical Protestantism and Democracy in the Global South, funded by The Pew Charitable Trusts, and is currently co-editing a four-volume series on this subject to be published by Oxford University Press'.[129] He is also involved at Harvard as co-director of the Religion in Global Politics research project, for which he is writing on 'the relationship between religion and democratization',[130] particularly evangelical Christianity and 'the global south'.[131] He is also writing a book on the political impact of Hindu nationalism in South Asia.

Another speaker was Stanley Kurtz, a senior fellow at EPPC at that time, and a known right-wing radical thinker also with a PhD from Harvard. He was among the strongest advocates for the US invasion of Iraq with the objective to bring democracy there, and he praised Lord Macaulay's work to convince the British to civilize Indian savages. Arguing his case in *The Wall Street Journal*, he quotes Macaulay's plan to fashion an Indian leadership class who would be 'English in taste, opinions, morals, and intellect' and recommended that now Americans must do the same in Iraq. Kurtz wrote, 'Can we do deliberately in Iraq what the British did inadvertently in India?'[132] In other words, he regards British colonialism as a good role-model and example for US foreign policy in the non-Western world.

Kurtz works as a researcher at the prestigious Hoover Institute, embedded in Stanford University – a good example of scholars who start by studying Indian religion, and later morph into political experts in powerful institutions that shape foreign policy. There are a large number of such American equivalents of the kind of role that was once played by Lord Macaulay, except that today's intellectuals such as Kurtz are far more sophisticated in their India-based field work, textual knowledge, and academic experience.

Many Tracks

Fig 13.3 summarizes the example of the three key personalities— Kurtz, Kirkpatrick and Shah—mentioned in the foregoing account, their respective institutional affiliations that give them clout, and how they came together to shape US policy towards India in order to further global Christianity. Many such collaborations exist, and this trend has been rapidly expanding in the past quarter century, with no report or analysis by anyone on the implications for India. Fig 13.3 also highlights how the government-church-academics collaborations work as one, using a network of 'autonomous' think-tanks as facilitators.

The connecting thread in all these is the message that Indian society is deficient in its humanness. The reason for this inhumanity is traced invariably to the spiritual deficiency of Hinduism. The complementary message is the need for US intervention. This intervention at this stage consists of facilitating evangelism, arm-twisting India through aid and

Fig 13.3 Working of a US Right-wing Think-tank in Shaping American Policy Towards India

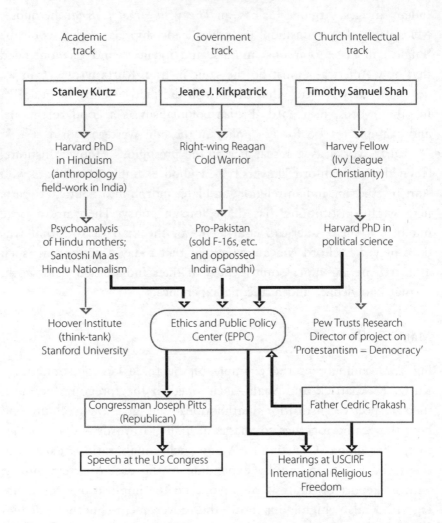

commercial restrictions, and using official US missions to interact with special-interest groups in India, thus effectively undermining India's sovereignty.

14

India: A Left-wing Frontier

We saw in the last chapter how Westerners looking through a Biblical lens perceive India. In this chapter, we shall see how the secular lens also delegitimizes India as a nation state. This is ironic because within the US, the Biblical view and the secular humanist view are at loggerheads against one another. Even so, each undermines Indian civilization for different reasons and ends up facilitating the opposite side's agendas. While the US right-wing neo-cons support the idea of a Christian India, the left-wing has a general sympathy towards Islam. Both these have Hinduism and classical Indian civilization as their common enemy. Hence, the collaboration is considered mutually fruitful. But the fact that they live in contradiction with respect to their core ideology is never discussed openly, the common outlet for anger being what they think of as 'Hindu India'.

Fig 14.1 shows the various elements involved in the secular approach to India. Its main components are discussed next.

Liberal-Left Think-tanks

Liberal and left-wing think-tanks surprisingly arrive at the same conclusions as the right-wing institutions. Indian society is examined as a collection of fragments that are victims of Indian state oppression. India is a prison for sub-national identities that are held together by brute force. Such portrayals become tools in the hands of those who demand the US-mediated balkanization of India.

Academic South Asian Studies

Another powerful voice that supports the fragmentation of India is found in academic South Asian Studies in the US universities. They depict India as a colonial construct that has no historical validity of its own. In this view, Indian culture is inherently anti-Dalit, anti-minority and anti-women. Both Indian culture and the Indian state are shown as opponents of freedom.

The Secular Lens

Both the academic and non-academic institutions that are liberal-left take up the cause of the minority groups of India. Ironically, left-

Fig 14.1 Left-wing Contribution to Making India a Frontier for the US

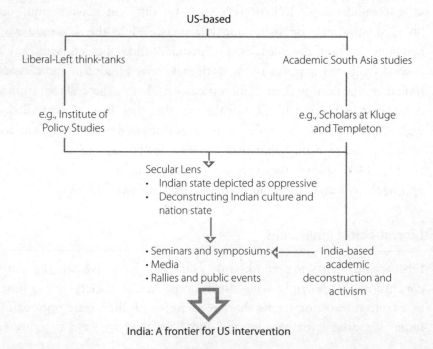

wing secularists do not hesitate to share platforms with representatives of extremist right-wing religious organizations in order to share and propagate images of Indian savagery, even though in theory there is hostility between these two ideological camps. There is also the camp of postmodernist deconstruction of India, prevalent in the academy. In studies of the United States or of other modern nation states like China, such deconstruction of the nationhood or cultural unity is typically kept at the periphery. But exactly the opposite is true when looking at India.

Example of Left-Right Collaboration in Washington

After the 2008 US election, Dalit Freedom Network decided to diversify beyond its right-wing base in order to cultivate powerful Democrats, including Senator Joseph Biden, who had just been elected as the vice president. Benjamin Marsh, DFN's head lobbyist in Washington, commented that Vice President Biden would provide the direction for South Asia policy decisions.[1] Therefore, in order to gain entry into the new administration, Marsh started to cultivate Biden's key advisor on South Asia, Jonah Blank.[2] Marsh had a meeting with Jonah Blank and found his book *Arrow of the Blue-skinned God* 'not disappointing', and endorsed the chapter on caste as 'a good introduction to the issue from a historical and anthropological view'.[3] Jonah Blank's background and attitudes offer insight into the kind of networking that goes on across partisan lines, academic disciplines and professional specialties.

Jonah Blank completed graduate studies in anthropology at Harvard, where his fellowship was funded by the US National Security Education Program, which focuses on geographic areas, languages, and fields of study deemed critical to protect US interests.[4] Blank traveled extensively across India and Pakistan, and learned Sanskrit, Hindi, Gujarati and Urdu. He developed extensive knowledge and experience of the traditions and teachings of Hinduism and Islam. His first book, *Arrow of the Blue-skinned God: Retracing the Ramayana through India,* explores the *Ramayana* and broader Indian religions and society using the Aryan/Dravidian racial binary. For example, he quotes a Dravidianist scholar to conclude that Aryan deities are immoral, whereas Dravidian deities have a 'high standard'.[5] He interprets Hanuman worship in Deccan as a sort of psychological mechanism for transforming 'contempt' into 'self-respect'. His next book, *Mullahs on the Mainframe Islam and Modernity among the Daudi Bohras* (Chicago University Press, 2001) was on how the Dawoodi Bohra Muslim community of Mumbai was very modern. He became one of the US policymaking experts on South Asia, and is a Hinduism consultant for Beliefnet, a prestigious religious portal.[6]

In 2002, he participated in a conference titled 'Hindu Nationalism vs Islamic Jihad: Religious Militancy in South Asia', sponsored by Ethics and Public Policy Center. (EPPC was discussed among the right-wing groups in the previous chapter.) The co-sponsor was INFEMIT, an evangelical network headed by Vinay Samuel[7] and supported by Cromwell Trust, which calls itself an organization 'dedicated to the teaching and active extension of the doctrines of Evangelical Christianity'.[8] Here Jonah Blank talked of the necessity to prevent L.K. Advani, then the deputy prime minister of India, from 'becoming Slobodan Milosevic'. He cautioned that the 2002 communal violence in Gujarat should not be forgotten even after the violence had ended, and spoke of 'cycles of violence' in India that would 'sooner or later harm the US national interest'. Hence, the US should be 'deeply engaged, both because it is in the US national interest and because it's the right thing to do'.[9]

To illustrate that such religious intervention in the US is part and parcel of dealing with secular issues, it is useful to note that Jonah Blank shaped the Democratic Party's 2008 report that advised for a 'dramatic strategic shift' in South Asia. He was one of the thirty-three top Pakistan specialists in Washington who formulated this new strategy which led to the proposal for the Obama administration to 'provide $7.5 billion in economic and development aid to Pakistan over the next five years'. This was introduced by Senator Joe Biden, then vice-president elect, under whom Blank worked. This report helped overcome the hard facts that most of the US aid to Pakistan was being diverted to the Pakistani army in violation of the agreements, including use against India.

Blank is now the policy advisor on South Asia/Near East policy to the Senate Committee on Foreign Relations, and is also a member of the prestigious Council on Foreign Relations. He is on the faculty of South Asia Studies at John Hopkins University, where he teaches 'The Politics of Religion in South Asia: Community and Communalism in Sociological Context'.[10]

With this background, we can appreciate the complexities of strategic confluences, such as this one between the Christian right-wing Benjamin Marsh of Dalit Freedom Network and Jonah Blank, an advisor to liberal Vice President Joe Biden.

US-based Academic Deconstruction of India

Many liberal, left-wing scholars are consciously or unconsciously feeding the right-wing designs on India by providing studies that could facilitate US intervention. Several Indian scholars have joined this enterprise because it offers prestige, funding, and a sense of being at the vanguard of saving the world's oppressed.

This section gives a glimpse into this widespread phenomenon by briefly examining a few individuals only. These will be discussed at length later in the book.

- A particularly rabid voice in this category is Martha Nussbaum, who argues that India's internal clash today is between the good guys, who are Westernized liberal Indians, versus the bad guys, who are branded as militant 'Hindu thugs'.
- Lise McKean provides an example of a western academician who harbors hatred of Indian traditions, seeing the whole guru tradition as part of the oppressive 'Hindu nationalism'. Her sensationalist book was published by the prestigious University of Chicago Press.
- Romila Thapar argues that the entire Indian civilization, and by extension the Indian state, are nothing but oppressive devices

controlled by dominant ethnic groups, and that they need to be dismantled.

- Meera Nanda was originally a bio-technologist, but then moved to the humanities with a second PhD dissertation, 'Prophets Facing Backward: Postmodern Critiques of Science and New Social Movements in India'.[11] She has been virulently denouncing Indian culture and Hinduism as being intrinsically anti-scientific, whereas she sees Protestantism (whose Templeton Foundation funds her) as scientific and progressive. She accuses India's nation builders of a neo-Nazi mindset and pseudo-science.

- Vijay Prashad has championed the Afro-Dalit collaboration to shape the identity of marginalized Indians, and leads a prominent Marxist organization that tries to recruit young Indian American students on US campuses through a variety of activities.

- Angana Chatterji is the most prominent Indian face on the faculty of California Institute of Integral Studies, a San Francisco-based private institution of higher education that was set up explicitly to promote the teachings of Sri Aurobindo in the West. Ironically, she has used this podium in the opposite direction, by lashing out against anything Hindu, seeing it as an evil conspiracy to oppress innocent people.

A closer look at these scholars will illustrate their funding, their connections, and their agendas.

Martha Nussbaum

Martha Nussbaum is professor of Law and Ethics at the University of Chicago, and is widely seen as a powerful voice of American liberalism. But when it comes to India, she is aligned against Indian civilization and embraces radical Eurocentrism. For example, she stated that a Hindu nation is not 'a benign establishment like the Lutheran Church of Finland' but something that would treat Muslims as second-class citizens.[12] (An entire section in Chapter Seventeen and also Appendix H are devoted to examining the role of the Lutheran Church in India.)

Her interest in India started while working for Amartya Sen in an intimate relationship that she has bragged about.[13]

After some foreign academics were found to be linked with secessionist movements, the Indian government wanted foreign participants to get permission to come to conferences. Nussbaum threatened, 'We'll see how bad publicity (which I intend to give them, here and elsewhere) may bring pressure to bear against them'.[14] At a Yale seminar on anti-Semitism, her focus was to link Hinduism with fascism, as reflected in the notes that she distributed to the participants:

> In India the perpetrators of violence are not Muslims (who are usually poor and downtrodden, but not involved in perpetrating violence, except in the special instance of Kashmir), but Hindus who sought their ideology in Fascist Europe and who model their stance on European anti-semitism of the 1930s.[15]

She further informed them that the Hindu political ideology was derived from 'European romantic nationalism and its darker aspirations to ethnic purity'. While her academic specialty is the philosophy of Aristotle, Nussbaum has written extensively to condemn Indian civilization. Her book, *The Clash Within: Democracy, Religious Violence, and India's Future,* is a recent example. Here she supported the divisive position that the Indus Valley Civilization was Dravidianist, before the Sanskrit-speakers moved in. She wrote:

> The people who spoke Sanskrit almost certainly migrated into the subcontinent from outside, finding indigenous people there, probably the ancestors of the Dravidian peoples of South India. Hindus are no more indigenous than Muslims.[16]

She not only presents a controversial speculation as a historical fact, but extrapolates it into the present Indian political discourse. She equates the modern Hindus with 'Sanskrit-speakers who migrated into the subcontinent' and excluded Dravidian speakers. This is very similar to the world view of Risley in colonial times, and of Dravidian separatists today. In explaining the Aryan 'invasion' scenario, she simply omits that it has been rejected by archeologists universally,[17] and while grudgingly distancing herself from the invasion scenario, she supports the 'Aryan migration' scenario, which amounts to the same thing.[18] Those Indian scholars who are outside the supervision of the Western academy and funding agencies, and who critically examine the western interpretation of ancient Indian history, are branded as part of the Hindu Right.

Nussbaum disregards that the foreign Aryan model was vehemently rejected by Ambedkar and many others unrelated to any Hindu Right. She ignores that the model had been highly popularized by the British soldier-turned-archeologist Mortimer Wheeler, who declared pompously that the Vedic deity Indra stands accused of committing massacre in Mohenjo-Daro. This was not a 'casual' mistake of hypothesis, as Nussbaum wants her readers to believe. Edmund Leach, the famous British anthropologist, notes:

> Common sense might suggest that here was a striking example of a refutable hypothesis that had in fact been refuted. Indo-European scholars should have scrapped all their historical reconstructions and started again from scratch. But that is not what happened. Vested interests and academic posts were involved. Almost without exception the scholars in question managed to persuade themselves that despite appearances the theories of the philologists and the hard evidence of archeology could be made to fit together. The trick was to think of the horse-riding Aryans as conquerors of the cities of the Indus civilization in the same way that the Spanish conquistadores were conquerors of the cities of Mexico and Peru or the Israelites of the Exodus were conquerors of Jericho. The lowly Dasa of the *Rig Veda*, who had previously been thought of as primitive savages, were now reconstructed as members of a high civilization.[19]

Without the required qualifications or training to speak with authority on the subject, Nussbaum proceeds to pontificate on the date of the Vedas, concluding that any claim of Vedic antiquity before 1200 BCE or claims of cultural continuity of the Harappan culture to the present day, brand a person as belonging to the Hindu Right. Fig 14.2 compares a few of Nussbaum's positions on Indology with those of secular scholars of various backgrounds.

Fig. 14.2: A Comparison of Claims by Martha Nussbaum and Secular Scholars Regarding Ancient India

	Claims by Nussbaum	Claims by Secular Scholars
1	'Older dates to *Rig Veda* that place it as early as 3,000 BCE are a ploy by Hindu Right to establish Vedic-Harappan idenitity.' ((Nussbaum, 2007, 219)	Upinder Singh, a historian, points out that scholars using astronomical references have dated Vedas variedly:'Dates falling within the late third millennium BCE or the early second millennium BCE (calculated on the grounds of philology and/or astronomical references) cannot be ruled out. The date of the *Rig Veda* remains a problematic issue.' (Singh, 2009, 185) Prof Nussbaum cannot label Upinder Singh as a historian of Hindu Right as Upinder Singh is the daughter of India's Prime Minister Dr Manmohan Singh and a scholarly historian by her own merit.
2	Criss-cross pattern of ploughing noticed in Harappa can be noticed in the Haryana farms today. Martha Nussbaum rejects this continuity of civilization as 'hardly remarkable.'	The veteran Indian archeologist B.K. Thapar, who headed the archeological exploration of the Harppan site at Kalibangan, stated that the pattern of pre-Harappan ploughed field showed 'remarkable similarity to modern ploughing in that area.' (Thapar B.K. and Shaffer J.G. 1999, 278)
3	Identification of red pigment by archeologists at the parting of hair seen in the terracotta figurines of Harappa is dismissed by Nussbaum with these words: 'The paint on the terracotta figure is so badly worn that it is hard to tell what was red and what wasn't...the style is not like of any Indian woman known to me.' (Nussbaum, 2007, 221)	Jonathan M. Kenoyer, archeologist from University of Wisconsin (Madison), mentions female figurines dated 2600 BCE with traces of red pigment at the parting of the hair, as a significant indicator of the continuity of traditions. (Kenoyer, 1998, 44-45)

Clearly, Nussbaum promotes her political ideology over the other alternatives that fit the hard facts of archeological excavations. Though she is a non-specialist with regard to archeology, or linguistics, or culture, and her exposure to India is limited to contemporary politics, she dismisses the entire Indian archeological academic establishment as belonging to the 'Hindu Right'. She dismisses the cultural continuity of Indian civilization from Harappan times as 'suppositions and not serious scholarly claims'. This is proven false by archeologists Jim Shaffer and Diane Lichtenstein who, in the context of the relation between the Harappan and post-Harappan in India, state that 'available data indicate that south Asian cultural history must be studied within a context of indigenous cultural continuity, not intrusion and discontinuity'.[20]

Nussbaum advances her balkanization view of India through clever uses of ancient Indian history. Her account of Indian history begins with the invasion of / migration to India by the Aryan Hindus, who are different from the Dravidian natives of India; any Indian scholarship that questions this is considered a Hindu right-wing conspiracy. Where the western bias becomes too extreme to be deniable, she considers the errors as unintentional, but Indian scholarship, regardless of its merits, is said to have political motivations.

She alleges that India has jumped on the bandwagon of fighting terrorism as a ploy to justify its own violence against religious minorities. Terror is a pretext to cover up India's 'values involved in ethnic cleansing', which she wants to be 'a definite deterrent to foreign investment'.[21] After providing extensive gruesome details and highly sensationalized and exaggerated atrocity literature of Gujarat violence (including claims that have been exposed as fabrications), she cautions the world about Indians: 'The current world atmosphere, especially the indiscriminate use of the terrorism card by the United States, has made it easier for them to use this ploy'.[22]

She accuses the Indian government of using al-Qaeda as 'a scare tactic', without providing any basis. She outright denies the existence of any India-based Islamic terror-network with Pakistani connections.[23] India is not justified in enacting any special laws to control terror cells, she insists. She laments that the United States is not monitoring India as a threat to world democracy:

> What has been happening in India is a serious threat to the future of democracy in the world. The fact that it has yet to make it onto the radar screen of so many Americans, is evidence of the way in which terrorism and the war in Iraq have distracted Americans from events and issues of fundamental significance.[24]

Many of Nussbaum's political stances are full of contradictions. For instance, in 2007 she argued against British unions that were boycotting Israeli academic institutions that were accused of political bias. But she took the opposite stand on Indian academic institutions and individuals, criticizing the world's failure to not utter 'a whisper about boycotting' the Indians.[25]

Nussbaum diluted the attempts to deal with the Mumbai terror attack of 2008, stating that 'it's important to consider Indian terrorism in a broader context. Terrorism in India is by no means peculiar to Muslims'.[26] In discussions on the Mumbai attacks of 2008, she quickly diverts the discussion away from Islamic terror by citing the 2002 violence in Gujarat and the 2008 Hindu-Christian violence in Orissa, without giving the full context of either. By manipulating the contexts, she equates local communal incidents with terrorism: 'All of this is terrorism, but most of it doesn't reach the world's front pages'.[27] In this manner, she has been effective in shifting attention away from anti-India terrorism.

Lacking her own direct scholarship on the complex issues concerning ancient Indian civilization, Nussbaum has parroted others who fit her politics. What many uninformed readers of Nussbaum do not realize, is the fascist origins of many of the ideas she spreads concerning the nature of ancient India, the so-called 'Aryans', and the origin of Vedas and Hinduism. The old Race Science ideas explained in Chapter five of this book are alive and well in a cabal of scholars, even though only some of them operate explicitly as white supremacists, while others write similar things using liberal frameworks. For instance, it is interesting to compare Nussbaum's intellectual positions on ancient India with those of notorious white supremacists such as Roger Pearson, a British anthropologist and former colonial officer in the British army in India.[28]

Lise McKean

Lise McKean is an academic anthropologist working with a Chicago non-profit group dealing with American social issues. She provides an example of how left-wing western academics can harbor bias against Indian traditions, to the point of colluding with right-wing and evangelical forces. Whenever there is unrest in India, she shows up as a commentator to educate American audiences about what is wrong in Indian culture. Her book, *Divine Enterprise: Gurus and the Hindu Nationalist Movement* was based on her research in India. In it she associates everything even remotely connected with Hindu spirituality (such as a cement advertisement featuring a yogi) to the ominous image of Hindu nationalism. A whole chapter is devoted to macabre details of child sacrifices and murky allegations appearing in the local press against Hindu 'godmen'. Some of the book's section headings are sensational for an academic work that was published by the University of Chicago Press. For example, one section-heading is about 'a world more macabre than a Stephen King horror story'.[29] When her examination of actual organizations yielded no macabre evidence, she depicted them as a *potential* threat to secularism in India. Even the well-respected Divine Life Society in Rishikesh was not spared:

> The Divine Life Society represents itself as having no murky depths; it claims to have no 'secret doctrines nor esoteric sections or inner circles. It is purely spiritual organization having no leanings towards politics.' The respectability of the Divine Life Society, no less than the sensationalization of guru scandals and human sacrifice, however, tends to obfuscate the problem this book addresses: the relation of gurus, religious organizations, and rituals to circuits of power and domination in India.[30]

She sees even Mahatma Gandhi as belonging to the 'lineage of Hindu nationalists'.[31] Nehru too is guilty because he used terminology that resonated with India's spiritual tradition:

> Nehru's discussion of the spirit of the age (yuga-dharma) accommodates the ideas of practical spirituality espoused by Vivekananda, and later institutionalized by Hindu organizations such as Ramakrishna Mission, the Divine Life Society . . .[32]

McKean participated in the 2002 symposium conducted by PIFRAS, which was described in the previous chapter as a right-wing evangelical policy institute.[33] She resonates with the Christian Right's demand that US foreign policy should be based on protecting the specific interests of non-Hindus in India.[34]

Romila Thapar

Romila Thapar, a prominent historian specializing in ancient India, has furthered a view of India that emphasizes its fragmentation. For this, she has been credited with changing the way Indian history is studied.[35] She falsely accuses Indian nationalists of using the Aryan race theory to identify themselves with the British and to justify their dominant position in caste hierarchies.[36] This became entrenched among Indian historians and other intellectuals as 'patriotism = Aryan caste conspiracy', and led many to question the concept of India itself. This grounds the very popular view today that India is founded as an oppressive upper-caste system, against which low-caste insurgencies need to be organized. Echoing Bishop Caldwell, G.U. Pope and other colonial-era Christians, Thapar speaks of identifying a 'substratum religion, doubtless associated with the rise of subaltern groups'.[37] This merges the south Indian Dravidian separatism with a much broader base of pan-Indian subaltern movements, by giving them a respectable theory backed by prestigious Western institutions.

For example, a Cambridge Jesuit theologian, Michael Barnes, has strategically positioned the Church with 'the recent phenomenon of low-caste insurgency', which he defines as an 'agitation against the hegemonic culture of Brahminically dominant elite'.[38] He advocates for the Church to support insurgents who see a unified Indian civilization as a 'narrow interpretation of Indian culture, derived from Vedic times as a creation of the Aryan people'.[39] Citing the authority of Romila Thapar, he states that 'the influence of both orientalist and Hindu-nationalist concepts of "Indian identity" are being held up to an increasingly critical scrutiny'.[40] Thus, Romila Thapar has become a powerful tool to reject the historical and cultural continuities that unite India and its civilization.

Another example of this is Robert Eric Frykenberg, a professor of South Asia Studies at the University of Wisconsin, who presented a paper titled 'Hindu Fundamentalism and the Structural Stability of India' at the American Academy of Arts and Sciences.[41] He states that the ideas of India and Hinduism are 'by-products of official policies' of the British Company's Raj, and he dismisses 'the fallacy of assuming that some sort of inclusive Hinduism existed'. He quotes Romila Thapar as his authority, especially her statement that ancient Indians should be seen as mere 'a cluster of distinctive sects and cults'.[42] This characterizes Indian civilization as an amorphous and random collection like the tribes of other third-world nations before the European conquest. Under this view, Hinduism is the result of recent 'manufactured mechanisms' and 'structures of statecraft'. It reinforces the ideologies supporting the balkanization of India, seeing India as an artificial combination of thinly bonded or disconnected communities that must be liberated through separatist movements.

Thapar analyzes many Hindu mythologies and traditions in terms of 'clan-conflicts'. Hindu spiritual experiences are devalued as even pathological.[43] She resorts to a quasi-scholarly speculation of racial hatred as existing in entire Indian traditions when she wonders, 'as to whether the references to the *rakshasa*, the *preta* and the *daitya*, demons and ghosts of various kinds, could have been a reference to the alien people of the forest. Demonizing the "other" is sometimes a technique to justify holding such people in contempt and even attacking them'.[44] This is exactly the same thesis that is being spread today by Maoist insurgents working among remote tribes in central India, namely, that demons mentioned in Hinduism are actually references to tribal people.

She accepts the myth of St Thomas and his martyrdom in South India as 'credible'.[45] Thapar does recognize the legitimacy of Jesus as the Christ and accepts the historicity for his existence while denying historicity for Rama.[46] She joined hands with western Indologists led by Michael Witzel in opposing the edits proposed by Indian parents in the California textbooks controversy, and dismissed the long list of factual errors in textbooks as a conspiracy of Hindu fundamentalists.[47]

In 2003 Thapar was appointed 'as the first holder of the Kluge Chair in Countries and Cultures of the South at the Library of Congress.'[48] The press release from the US Library of Congress stated that she had 'created a new and more pluralistic view of Indian civilization . . .'[49] In 2008 she gladly accepted the million-dollar

Kluge Prize, whereas she had twice declined the Indian government's Padma Bhushan.[50] She did so because she did not want to be seen as politically linked to any ideology. But the Kluge award is well-known for being often given to Christian evangelicals.[51] The Kluge endowment brings scholars to Washington to do research and 'interact with policy makers'.

It is this pronounced pro-Christian bias in the Kluge endowment which makes the choice of a Marxist historian[52] like Thapar really strange. The contradiction is highlighted by the fact that while Thapar received recognition for demolishing the legitimacy of ancient Hinduism, the man who shared the 2008 Kluge Award with her, Peter R.L. Brown, did the exact opposite in the case of Christianity. A historian of early Christian monasticism, Brown's work has brought out a positive picture of Christian monasticism that is equivalent to the Indian spiritual culture which Thapar condemned as life-negating escapism.[53]

Meera Nanda

Meera Nanda, originally a bio-technologist, crossed over to humanities and did her second PhD dissertation, titled 'Prophets Facing Backward: Postmodern Critiques of Science and New Social Movements in India'.[54] Since then, she has been writing articles and giving lectures denouncing Indian culture as inherently anti-scientific and accusing Indian nation builders of paving the way for pseudo-science and even of having a Nazi mindset.

Another of Nanda's article – 'Calling India's Freethinkers', accuses Swami Vivekananda and Bankim Chandra (forefathers of the Indian national resurgence) of the 'cardinal sin' of trying to appropriate modern scientific thought for Hinduism. Even Nehru, who fostered scientific rationalism, gets lumped into this charge.[55] She calls on the 'progressive scientists' of India to 'carefully but firmly un-twine the wild and uncontrolled intertwining of science and spirituality that has been going on in Hinduism since the time of Swami Vivekananda in the late nineteeth century'. All attempts to investigate Hinduism in the light of science are declared to be linked to Hindutva, including work by the 'apologists associated with the Ramakrishna Mission and Aurobindo Ashram'. She finds that any claim of Indian culture being scientific 'constitutes the central dogma of Hindutva'. Links between Indian culture and science resonate with 'deeply Hindu and Aryan supremacist overtones'.[56]

In what seems to be a blatant contradiction, she solicited and was awarded the John Templeton Foundation Fellowship in Religion and Science (2005-7), which coincidentally occurred under the leadership of a self-declared Evangelical Christian in 2006.[57] Nanda has supported Protestantism as being scientific, while describing Hinduism as the exact opposite. Even when she criticizes pseudo-science by westerners, Nanda likes to blame their questionable ideas on Hinduism. For example, Rupert Sheldrake likes to trace his pseudo-scientific theories to Christianity and mentions Father Bede Griffiths as his mentor.[58] But Nanda prefers to link Sheldrake to J.C. Bose, a pioneer in Indian science, and then attack him for Hindu links.[59]

The *India Today* review of her latest book (*The God Market: How Globalization is Making India More Hindu*, Random House, 2009) summarized succinctly her attitude towards India and Hinduism thus: 'Meera Nanda doesn't like India. And she hates popular Hinduism with even greater passion'.[60]

Nanda is representative of a pattern: The Templeton Foundation brings together science with Judeo-Christianity, and uses willing Indians like Nanda to attack Indian spiritual traditions.

Vijay Prashad

Vijay Prashad, a prominent left-wing firebrand academician, is Director of International Studies at Trinity College, Hartford. It is ironic that while his career and public profile are based on fighting capitalism, he occupies a prestigious chair funded by and named after the head of a wealthy derivatives trading company on Wall Street.[61] He runs organizations that recruit Indian American students on American campuses to teach them about the horrors of Indian civilization.

Prashad endorses the Afro-Dalit movement, including the racist theories of V.T. Rajshekar. Apart from endorsing the Lemurian thesis that 'India and Africa was one land mass', which leads him to conclude that 'both the Africans and the Indian Untouchables and tribals had common ancestors', Prashad also points out that Dalits 'resemble Africans in physical features'.[62] Though he is aware of the shortcomings and fallacies of Aryan-Dravidian ethnographic projects undertaken by colonial anthropologists,[63] his writings are designed to provoke suspicion against anything to do with Hinduism and India's legitimacy as a nation-state.

A Canadian blogger named Plawiuk provides an example of how such crackpot ideas can become influential in the Internet age. He credits the writings of Vijay Prashad and V.T. Rajshekar, which he picked up at the Culture and the State conference held at University of Alberta in 2003, for his ideas about Indian civilization as follows:

> Modern Hinduism is fascism and racism. It is the origin of what we would call modern fascism. Based on a religious caste system that is Aryan in origin, it divides up the world into three castes, warriors, priests, merchants, and in a slave class, the Dalits or Untouchables.[64]

A link he provides leads to the web page of an English professor at the University of California supporting the idea that caste equals race.[65]

Angana P. Chatterji

Angana Chatterji is associate professor of Social and Cultural Anthropology at California Institute of Integral Studies (CIIS), an institution that was established specifically to bring the spiritual teachings of Sri Aurobindo to the West. Ironically, she has used this position to do exactly the opposite, namely, to try to demolish the legitimacy of Indian spirituality and the Indian nation. She cites her interests as 'identity politics, nationalisms, self-determination'.[66] Prior to joining CIIS, she worked in policy and advocacy research at the

Indian Social Institute, which is run by Jesuits in Delhi, for the explicit purpose of propagating 'Christian inspiration and following the social teaching of the Catholic Church'.[67]

Chatterji provided 'critical assistance' to a highly libelous and unsubstantiated report that damned a US-based Indian charity organization, India Development Relief Fund (IDRF), alleging that they were funding hatred and atrocities against Indian minorities.[68] The driving force behind this was that IDRF's schools in Indian rural and tribal areas were providing a successful alternative to Christian missionary schools involved in conversion, and Chatterji was brought in to defame the non-Christian competition that IDRF provided.

While she finds US intervention in Iraq and Afghanistan to be a violation of those countries' rights and calls George Bush 'a man who himself should be charged with crimes against humanity',[69] she still wants US intervention in India's affairs, for example, through the US Commission on International Religious Freedom. Chatterji provided testimony before the United States Congressional Task Force on International Religious Freedom on violence in Orissa,[70] chaired by Congressmen Trent Franks and Joseph R. Pitts, both with strong right-wing evangelical connections.[71]

She also sent an unsolicited testimony on Orissa violence to the government of India, in which all her data came directly from the report by the All India Christian Council, which was discussed earlier. Her input was so one-sided that she completely ignored some well-established facts about the aggressive evangelism involved [72] and the nexus between Christian evangelists and Maoists in the state.[73] The violence was precipitated by the murder of a Hindu sage, who she dismisses as 'a male Hindu proselytizer'. She describes the social services done by Hindu organizations, as 'conscription into Hindu activism', even as she praises the same kind of social work in 'health care, education and employment offered by Christian missionaries'.[74]

Chatterji is also a standard and predictable face at major events supporting Kashmir separatists, having declared herself to be working on 'self-determination in Indian-administered Kashmir'.[75] At one such conference on Kashmir, organized by the Pakistani Students

Association at George Washington University, the Embassy of Pakistan, and Pakistan's Minister of Kashmir Affairs, she spoke of the 'growing concern among civil society groups about human rights crises in Indian-occupied Kashmir in the areas of social, political, cultural, religious, and economic rights'. She accused India of 'continued occupation of [certain areas of] Kashmir'.[76] Muhammed Sadiq, who maintains a Kashmiri news and analysis portal, explains how Angana Chatterjee uses human rights concerns in a lopsided way to play in the hands of Islamic terrorists:

> [Angana Chatterji] announced the formation of the 'International Peoples' Tribunal on Human Rights and Justice in Indian Administered Kashmir' on 5 April in Srinagar. Interestingly, this organisation too insists that the focus of HR investigations should be on the Indian side of Kashmir and not in PoK too. Moreover, this is a fault-finding mission. Its only aim is to slam the Indian security forces, further highlight HR issues and vitiate the situation. There is no attempt at reconciliation, offering succour to HR victims or working with the government to ensure that HR violations do not take place. Dr Chatterji, like many before her, are, intent on primarily demonising the Indian security forces and thereby fanning hatred.[77]

By depicting India as an undemocratic state filled with horrors of Hindu savagery, such left-wing academics have blurred the distinctions between Islamic terrorism and what they portray as equally bad violations by Indians against Muslims, Christians and Dalits. This seems to justify terrorist attacks on India as well-deserved. In the aftermath of the 2008 Mumbai terror attacks, this view was reflected by Julian Duin, the religion editor of *Washington Times*:

> The terrorist assault—this time by Muslims—on Mumbai later in the year, highlighted the powderkeg India has become and how often in this Hindu-majority country, the oppressed don't get a lot of justice. The perpetrators in Orissa have gone unpunished.[78]

Another public event at the New York Public Library also featured the same view, namely, that Indians deserved the blame for the Mumbai attacks because they were illegally occupying Kashmir and oppressing Muslims in general. One of the prominent panelists with this view was Columbia University professor of philosophy, Akil Bilgrami, an Indian-American with staunch views against Indian civilization. The meeting was declared closed once a few Indians in the audience, led by Narain Kataria, started to point out the radical one-sidedness of the discussion.

Islamic Tint in the Secular Lens

Our survey of US-based South Asian Studies has revealed a very strong pro-Islamic bias. Hindus and the Indian government are blamed in all sorts of issues concerning Indian Muslims and issues of terrorism in India. Various Islamic advocacy groups in the United States nurture such scholars, and provide forums and mechanisms to bring them together with affiliates in India.[79] An example of a prominent lobbyist influencing the US academy is the Indian Muslim Council.

The Indian Muslim Council (IMC) is a US-based advocacy group for Indian Muslims. One of its most local leaders, Kaleem Kawaja, has been openly sympathetic to the Taliban, even after 9/11.[80] Yet, IMC is successful in influencing US government policies on India.[81] It takes up anti-India stands on issues like Kashmir, and Kawaja writes in Pakistani magazines comparing Kashmir to Kosovo and East Timur.[82] IMC's keynote speakers[83] at its high profile conferences have included Lise McKean (described earlier in this chapter), and Congressman John Conyers, an important liberal Democrat who joined right-wing Republicans to pass a resolution condemning India for 'violations of religious freedom'.[84]

At IMC's 2008 annual conference in the US, Tarun Tejpal, founder and head of *Tehelka* magazine, delivered the keynote, highlighting the oppression of many minority groups in India, including the Muslims, Dalits, tribals and Christians.[85] At the conference, Angana Chatterji was awarded the 'Tipu Sultan' award. PIFRAS, a radical Christian right-wing group (discussed in Chapter Thirteen), participated to show solidarity against their common enemy.[86]

In 2008, IMC arranged an American lecture tour for the activist Teesta Setalvad, whose international fame was based on supplying atrocity literature about claims of Hindu rioters ripping open a pregnant Muslim woman and throwing her fetus into the fire. However, the Special Investigation Team appointed by the Supreme Court of India to probe those communal riots refuted the veracity of this account. Many riot victims said that Setalvad had made them sign the affidavits written in English (which they did not understand) to exaggerate the violence.[87]

In the wake of the Mumbai terror attacks of 2008, IMC's press release related the episode to 'ethnic cleansing and targeting of minorities, police harassment and scapegoating of innocent civilians and fake encounter killings' in India.[88]

Western transnational groups and their India-based associates regularly come together to share intelligence. For example, in 2008 a study on 'Hindu Nationalist Organisations in Social and Political Context' was conducted under the Special Assistance Programme of University Grants Commission (a Government of India body) in collaboration with the Indian Council of Social Science Research, New Delhi. Some of the scholars and institutions (including foreign institutions) had a very clear evangelical bias. This illustrates how several liberal-left postcolonial scholars, who claim to be against US intervention, have been effectively co-opted. There are several causes, which include the lure of academic prestige, underlying Eurocentric bias in the social sciences, and a benign perception of multinational religious institutions operating in India.

15

The US Government's Direct Involvement

Besides the indirect role of government played by various US senators and congressmen in their official capacities, and the indirect role of the helping non-government think-tanks and activists, the US government has been directly active in foreign evangelism as a part of its foreign policy. The present chapter illustrates this by examining the US Commission on International Religious Freedom, created during Bill Clinton's presidency, the USAID programs, as well as how the Obama administration has in some ways played into the hands of the Christian Right.

International Religious Freedom Act

The International Religious Freedom Act (IRFA) was passed into law in the US in 1998 during the Clinton presidency, under heavy lobbying from the Christian Right. Clinton supported this in exchange for Christian support on various legislations that he wanted. Such give-and-take between the right-wing and left-wing politics is one of the reasons for their opportunistic cooperation on certain matters.[1]

The act set up three bodies:

- An ambassador-at-large for International Religious Freedom within the US State Department.
- US Commission of International Religious Freedom (USCIRF) to advise the Congress, the US State Department, and the White House.
- A special advisor on international religious freedom within the President's National Security Council.

The Act originated as a bill introduced by Republican representative Frank Wolf on behalf of conservative Christian groups. The goal was to facilitate mechanisms to bind the Christian populations in the developing nations to the right-wing Christian organizations in the United States. As Allen D. Hertzke would note later:

> What were the conditions underlying the legislative initiative? The first condition is the globalization of Christianity. *The tectonic shift of the Christian population to the developing world of Asia, Africa and Latin America created a constituency around the world that communicates with an American constituency here at home.*[2]

The act was originally designed to impose mandatory sanctions against countries blocking Christian proselytizing, by accusing them of engaging in a 'pattern of religious persecution'. It was quickly modified to allow a presidential waiver if the president felt that imposing sanctions would be counterproductive to US interests. As amended, the act is a flexible tool in the hands of the US president.

The 'religious freedom' programs under IRFA are vigorously supported by right-wing Christian conservatives in the United States, who are vehement critics of the UN as the mechanism for similar issues, because the UN does not give them similar clout as US domestic politics does.

IRFA has been criticized as an interventionist tool rather than a genuine program of human rights, and also because it lacks the jurisdiction to study religious freedom within the US itself. One academic scholar has criticized it as follows: 'Though IRFA's mandate extends to every other country in the world (194 countries), neither the State Department nor the Commission can do a self-assessment of the status of religious freedom within US borders'.[3] Robert A. Seiple, the first ambassador-at-large for International Religious Freedom, also criticized its hypocrisy: 'At the very least, this presents the potential for hubris, arrogance, and hypocrisy. It suggests an inclination to report only on others, refraining from any sort of self-criticism'. A special rapporteur to the UN quoted an unnamed academic: 'US Congress thinks we do just fine on religious liberty issues, and the rest of the world should not be telling us how to get it right'.[4] The rapporteur highlighted the plight of Native Americans who, historically, were subjected to genocide and forced religious conversion.

Another problem with IRFA's implementation that critics have pointed out is that it is under the control of evangelical Christian institutions. The US ambassador-at-large for International Religious Freedom, Robert A. Seiple, was president of World Vision for eleven years and served for four years as president of Eastern College and Eastern Baptist Theological Seminary.[5] In an interview given to a Florida newspaper, Seiple proudly claimed that his Christian faith sustained him during three-hundred combat missions as a marine officer in the Vietnam war.[6]

The second ambassador-at-large for International Religious Freedom was John V. Hanford III, who was a staffer in the office of Senator Richard Lugar, where he led the group that wrote the Act.[7] He holds a Master of Divinity degree from the Gordon-Conwell Theological Seminary, whose mission is defined by its president as follows: 'Our Lord has given Gordon-Conwell Theological Seminary a mission: to train men and women who have commitment, vision, and scholarly competence to reach the world for Jesus . . . where they can become great preachers and teachers, evangelists and missionaries . . .'[8] The Seminary's statement of faith reveals a fundamentalist brand of Christianity[9] and lists among its prominent supporters the preacher Dr Billy Graham, whose son Rev Franklin Graham is famous for his anti-Muslim and anti-Hindu views.[10] Hanford has also served in the pastoral ministry of the Presbyterian Church, and his wife is a supporter of the fundamentalist evangelical organization 'Campus Crusade for Christ'.[11]

US Commission on International Religious Freedom

The US Commission on International Religious Freedom (USCIRF) filters and synthesizes data on India's internal religious affairs for the purpose of strategic policymaking by the US government. Its past commissioners have included John R. Bolton and Eliot Abrams, two prominent members of the foreign policy establishment under several Republican presidents. Bolton often criticized the United Nations and worked against arms control treaties, though he served as the US representative to the UN in 2005-2006. Bolton once commented, 'There is no such thing as the United Nations. There is only the international community, which can only be led by the only remaining superpower, which is the United States'.[12] Eliot Abrams was undersecretary of state for President Reagan, and for his role in the Iran-Contra Affair, a special prosecutor prepared several felony counts against him, but he was eventually pardoned by the first President Bush.[13] Later, the second President Bush appointed him as a USCIRF commissioner and he served as its chairman for a year.

Another key commissioner of USCIRF is Richard Land, who was named by *TIME* magazine as one of the twenty-five most influential evangelicals in America. He is the president of the Southern Baptist Convention's Ethics and Religious Liberty Commission.

Another commissioner is Nina Shea, author of *In the Lion's Den*, 'about anti-Christian persecution around the world'. She is described on the USCIRF website as:

> . . . one of the activists at the forefront of a movement to make religious freedom abroad a US foreign policy priority. It was a conference that Ms Shea organized in January 1996 that brought 100 top Christian leaders together for the first time to address the issue of worldwide anti-Christian persecution. This marked the beginning of a Church mobilization that has turned into a nationwide movement. Newsweek magazine credited her with 'making Christian persecution Washington's hottest cause.'[14]

Shea is also associated with Freedom House, a fiercely anti-Hindu organization, and her work specifically promotes freedom for Christian proselytizing; hence, it is against religious pluralism.

USCIRF hears testimony and produces yearly reports which show its pro-Christian biases and how it provides the US political leverage against India. Its reports are filled with the evangelical spin on events in India.

Initial Indian Protests Ignored

Dr David Gray of Princeton-based Infinity Foundation wrote to the Commission in 2000, expressing his concern over its biases, and offered input on 'Developing Standards for Religious Freedom'. He suggested examining whether the evangelical literature that denigrates another community as 'condemned', 'sinners', 'pagans', or 'heathen', should be deemed as 'hate speech'. He noted that in US freemarket commerce, it is unlawful to trash one's competitor unreasonably or falsely, and hence this standard should also be applied to false portrayals of another's religion. In a section titled 'Consumer Protection', he suggested scrutiny of evangelists who convert by using tangible or non-tangible rewards.[15] His letter was simply ignored by the USCIRF and not even included in its public archive.

Swami Agnivesh, a liberal and brazenly anti-Hindutva monk, turned down the US government's invitation to provide testimony, saying he would not recognize the right of US to act as 'a world policeman'. His press release rejecting the hearings and went on to say: 'The attempt on the part of US to police freedom in other countries . . . amounts to violation of the sovereignty of other nations. While it is understandable that the US would want to undertake exercise of this kind, citizens of other nations cannot aid and abet this process without compromising their national pride and patriotism'.[16]

At first the Indian Catholic Church publicly distanced itself from giving testimony to the commission, with the Catholic Bishops' Conference of India (CBCI) describing as 'unwarranted' the proposed hearing on religious freedom in India being held in Washington. Father D'souza stated that anti-Christian violence at the hands of Hindu extremists has not crossed the 'gross human rights violations situation that calls for interference in internal affairs of the nation'.[17] But to play both sides strategically, the Indian Church allowed John Dayal, the national vice-president of All India Catholic Union, to attend the hearing in the US and present his compilation of allegations of anti-Christian bias against the Indian government. While Father D'souza defended Indian sovereignty, he supported Dayal's testimony in his 'individual capacity and not as a representative of the Church'.[18] Such 'Good Cop / Bad Cop' gamesmanship is a common strategy that Indian Christians have learned from the West. As we shall see later in this section, this Good Cop posture was temporary, and they acquiesced to the Bad Cops subsequently.

2000

The report for 2000 notes the close working relations between the US embassy in India and India-based evangelists to monitor internal religious affairs. It says that embassy officials meet with religious officials on a regular basis:

> US Mission officers traveled to Gujarat and Uttar Pradesh during the period covered by this report to assess the situation of religious minorities in those states. Embassy and consulate officials also engaged with important leaders of all minority communities. The US mission maintains contacts with US residents, including those in the NGO and missionary communities. The NGO community in the country is extremely active with regard to religious freedom, and mission officers meet with local NGOs to keep apprised of developments concerning religious freedom.[19]

The 2000 report is bothered by the re-conversion of Christians back into Hinduism, complaining that, 'In West Bengal, Marxist rulers could not prevent re-conversions of religious minorities by Hindus in some districts'. But conversion into Christianity is championed as a move into greater 'freedom' while any move towards Hinduism is considered entry into 'darkness'. The report failed to mention the financial motives being used by Christians, their hate speech and propaganda materials, and the impact of their work on the peoples' sensibilities in a historically pluralistic society like India. While alleged atrocities against the Christians are presented in specific details, even without any independent verification, the atrocities by anti-national militants such as NLFT linked with the Church are given a very short mention only:

> In Tripura there were several cases of reverse persecution of non-Christians by Christian members of the National Liberation Front of Tripura (NLFT), a militant tribal group that often is evangelical. For example, NLFT tribal insurgents have banned Hindu and Muslim festivals in areas that they control, cautioned women not to wear traditional Hindu tribal attire, and banned indigenous forms of worship.[20]

In fact, during that year, NLFT had performed many violent acts which the USCIRF report ignored. According to one independent report ignored by the Commission:

> On February 2: NLFT terrorists killed 8 people in North Tripura district; September 6: NLFT abducted 16 people from Manu Dhalai district; August 6: NLFT abducted four senior Hindu missionaries; August 12: NLFT terrorists gunned down six persons in Manu, Dhalai district; December 25: three persons are killed and 100 houses burnt down, in Bishramganj, West Tripura district; etc.[21]

2001

The USCIRF report for 2001 again recommended the US government to 'press India to allow official visits from government agencies concerned with human rights, including religious freedom'. It noted:

> India refused to permit an official visit from the US Ambassador-at-Large for International Religious Freedom. As discussed above, although the commission first sought to visit India in the fall of 2000, as of the date of this report it has not received permission from the Indian government to do so. India consistently proclaims itself to be an important member of the international community, and if it wants to be accepted as such, it must act in accordance with international norms of democratic practice, which includes internal—and external—scrutiny. The US government should press for the acceptance of official visits by the Ambassador-at-Large for International Religious Freedom and by the Commission.[22]

With regard to the violence by the Christian separatist group NLFT, the report again employed ambiguous and generalized statements to dilute the horrific acts of terror committed in the name of Christianity. While acknowledging Christian violence, it referred to the Hindus as the 'majority religious community' even though in the northeast Indian states where most such violence occurs, it is Christians who constitute the overwhelming majority not only numerically but also in terms of controlling the government and other civic institutions. The report mentioned the Christian violence as something which others have 'accused', and not as a matter of established fact, despite there being numerous official verdicts and reports in India proving that violence.

It concludes its very brief paragraph on this matter by rationalizing the violence as the fault of the Hindus: 'The group contends that the dominance of Hinduism has resulted in the marginalization of Christians in Tripura'.[23] In other words, Christian violence is caused by their alleged 'marginalization', and is hence justified, even though Hindus have been systematically ethnically cleansed from that region. Unlike its reporting of the alleged atrocities against Christians, where the Hindu side of the story is never given, here the NLFT's reasoning is given prominence.

The specific events of killings of Hindus by NLFT are never discussed. USCIRF simply ignores the numerous reports by South Asian Terrorism Portal (www.satp.org), a terrorism watch group run by professional police and intelligence bureaucrats, that listed twenty-one violent incidents involving NLFT Christians for that year. These included many grave atrocities, as shown in the compilation below:

April 15: NLFT terrorists kill 12 people and injure seven others in West Tripura district; April 20: NLFT terrorists gun down eight people in Laxmipur, North Tripura district; May 18: NLFT terrorists kill four women and three men, besides injuring five others, in South Tripura district; October 27: Five civilians, including a child, killed by suspected NLFT terrorists in Debendra Sarkarpara, West Tripura district; November 19: 14 persons killed by suspected NLFT terrorists and in the subsequent communal violence in Borahaldi in North Tripura district; December 4: NLFT terrorists attack yet another hermitage in Jirania Khola; December 5: Suspected NLFT terrorists ransack a Buddhist temple in Almara village, South Tripura district; December 25: NLFT terrorists kill a Jamatiya leader in Dalak village, South Tripura district, for refusing to embrace Christianity; December 26: NLFT terrorists ransack a Buddhist temple in Almara village, South Tripura district, and escape with scriptures and an idol.[24]

2002

From 2002 onwards, none of the USCIRF reports mention any violence by the Christian secessionist militias operating in Nagaland (NSCN) and Tripura (NLFT). Hindu tribal communities like Reangs, Jamatiya, who are victims of such Christian terrorist violence, were simply ignored as if they did not exist.

All the Indians who testified in 2002 supported the case being built up against their country, with the sole exception of Prof Sumit Ganguly, University of Texas at Austin, who broke ranks with the rest to 'warn the commission that India is a proud and democratic nation, and would not appreciate the US meddling in its internal problems'.

2003

The 2003 report takes a stand against India's Foreigners Act because it regulates the free flow of US evangelists. An investigative report by an Indian journal *Tehelka* said: 'The 2003 US report is a no-nonsense document that conveys the official US policy supporting evangelization. It openly admits that "US officials have continued to engage state officials on the implementation and reversal of anti-conversion laws"'. This US posture echoes John Dayal's testimony before the Commission that, 'It is almost impossible for a foreign Christian church worker, preacher or evangelist to come to India unless it is as a tourist'.[25]

Suddenly, the Catholic Church, which had until then stayed out of such report writing (while allowing its individual activists to participate in their personal capacities), now abruptly changed its stand. The Catholic Bishops' Conference of India explicitly expressed unhappiness with the USA's refusal to designate India as one of the 'Countries of Particular Concern' with regard to religious freedom. It openly called for the US to prosecute India for 'a spate of violence against minority communities'. The Church 'did not share the US administration's decision' that had listed alleged anti-Christian activities but not recommended sanctions against India. The Church wrote to the American Secretary of State, asking that India be placed in the category of 'egregious religious freedom violators' along with five others – Burma, China, Iran, North Korea, and Sudan. Such countries would attract punitive action under the US International Religious Freedom Act.[26] The good cops in the Indian Catholic Church had given way to the hardliners.

The Commission urged US Deputy Secretary of State Richard Armitage to take up the matter with India during his negotiations on Islamic terrorism in the south Asian region. In its report, the Commission said that it had met Armitage to discuss placing India on the list of Countries of Particular Concern. Given the delicate situation in the USA's fight against the Taliban in Pakistan, Armitage told them that USCIRF should not go against India at this time. Expressing unhappiness, All India Christian Council president John Dayal said, 'We are greatly disappointed'.[27] Bishop Sargunam, who was head of the Tamil Nadu Minorities Commission, issued a statement as a press release by the Federation on Indian American Christian Organizations of North America:

> The US government, which stands for justice and freedom around the world, has been complacent in addressing human rights violations continuing to take place in India. Bishop Ezra Sargunam made this point forcefully in his meetings with officials of the State Department in Washington, DC, yesterday and today. On behalf of the Social Justice Movement of India he submitted a Memorandum highlighting the resurgence of attacks against the religious minorities, Dalits and the Tribal people . . . Bishop Sargunam and P.D. John also met officials at the US Commission on International Religious Freedom (USCIRF) and on Capitol Hill . . . Bishop Sargunam expressed his disappointment in the US Administration's reluctance to address these kinds of continuing serious human rights violations with their Indian counterparts.[28]

2004

During the 2004 hearings, a four-member delegation of US Congressmen visited India to investigate on behalf of the USCIRF. Its leader, the Christian fundamentalist Joseph Pitts, said that the delegation would report to Congress about 'the anti-conversion laws, treatment of Dalits and anti-minority violence to be included in the country reports'. Pitts attacked the anti-conversion law calling, it a 'reversal of human rights in the land of the Mahatma Gandhi'.[29] Congressman Steve Chabot compared the situation in Gujarat to that of Rwanda. AICC secretary-general John Dayal said that his delegation of Indian minorities had put concrete demands before the US delegation: 'One of our demands is that there must be reservations for minorities in the foreign companies that collaborate with India'.[30] This mobilized the global Christian lobby to ask for preferences for Indian Christians as employees and in business trade and investment deals at the expense of non-Christians.

What is clear is that Indian Christian leaders collaborate with the US right-wing Christians. The Indians are encouraged to dish out atrocity literature to feed into the US system, so that the Americans can use it as a justification for action. In return, these Indians are built up by their American sponsors and paraded as world-class activists and champions of the oppressed.

When a USCIRF hearing in Chennai led some Indian groups to criticize USCIRF for meddling in India's internal affairs, Ms Joanella Morales, a US official, responded: 'We are not interfering. Your own people have written and spoken to us, asking us to do something about the state of religious freedom in this country'.[31] This is reminiscent of the British colonial rationale for intervention in India on the pretext that certain Indians had invited them. Morales criticized India's own Freedom of Religion Act, which she called an 'anti-conversion law'. A Chennai-based forum, Vigil, pointed out to the US officials that every law has the potential for abuse but that could not be an excuse for meddling in another nation's internal affairs. The Indians presented a hypothetical equivalent scenario, where the Indian Parliament would constitute a commission and office to monitor racism in United States and get Indian embassies and diplomatic missions to gather information by encouraging dissenting groups and anti-Americans in the US and elsewhere.

In another example, Buddhists of Arunachal Pradesh were threatened by Christian Naga terrorists, as reported by Assam Tribune:

> The twin militant outfits NSCN (IM) and NSCN(K) have demanded annexation of land from the Buddhist and other indigenous faith followers of Rima Putak, Thikhak Putak, Motongsa and Longchong villages in Tirap-Changlang district in Arunachal Pradesh, and have issued a decree for their conversion to Christianity. The militant outfits have left the villagers two options – embrace Christianity or face capital punishment. With death staring at their face, most of the adult members have fled the villages to escape torture from both sides, resulting in disruption of agricultural activities.[32]

But the USCIRF report for that year speaks only about the Gujarat riots that had happened two years earlier, and is totally silent about Christian militants threatening Hindus and Buddhists, and about the evangelical dimension of the Hmar-Dimasa conflict.[33]

2005

In 2005, Dalit Freedom Network testified before US lawmakers, urging them to intervene to 'end caste and stop atrocities against low-caste Indians'. A leading Indian columnist observed:

> If Hindu extremists deserve to be slammed (yes, they do) for indulging in hate propaganda against other faiths, can there be a different yardstick for those who equate Hinduism with 'spiritual darkness' . . . ? Doesn't the overtly anti-Hindu—not just anti-Hindutva—propaganda by non-Hindu groups, with a thinly veiled agenda of conversion of Dalits and tribals, harm communal harmony? (Recall last week's violent Muslim-Christian clash in Alexandria, Egypt, on the issue of conversions.) Which community is free of deficiencies within? And whose obligation is it to effect reforms in one's religion – that of its own followers or others? Does religious freedom include freedom to slander or belittle other religions, purportedly in the name of reservations? Let's ponder, honestly.[34]

But in the same year, a Hindu tribe called Dimasas had suffered immensely because of religious strife. This was reported by other prominent human rights watch groups in 2005 but ignored by USCIRF's biased filtering. For example, the US-based Committee for Refugees and Immigrants mentioned that Dimasa tribes were becoming internally displaced refugees. Unfortunately, it failed to provide the religious dimension behind this displacement. It merely acknowledged that 'about two thousand Dimasas, displaced by communal rioting in 2003 between the Dimasa and Hmar tribes over land and governance in the northeast, were still living in camps in southern Assam as well as in Manipur and Mizoram. About three thousand others had likely returned to their homes'.[35] Major Anil Raman, a strategic analyst and commander in the Indian Army in the Northeast, explains the role of Western Christianity in this conflict:

> The Hmars are devout Christians while the Dimasas are mainly Hindus. The Hmar church-bodies and social networks, including those abroad, have been heavily involved in directing political activities. The Dimasas lack this external support and are extremely apprehensive and critical of activities of Hmar religious bodies. The unchecked and widespread proselytism by missionary groups to achieve a 'Christian belt' from Meghalaya to Nagaland has brought them into direct conflict with the Dimasas, who are staunch Hindus.[36]

None of the reports by US-based groups mentioned this religious dimension, and instead chose to report it strictly as a secular issue. The USCIRF report for the same period managed to overlook this aspect completely.

2006

The four-page report on India in 2006 commented on the formation of the government by the Congress-led UPA, and removed India from the list of countries of particular concern (CPC).[37] Evangelical media reported that this was greeted with disappointment by Indian Christians.[38] The report mentioned the Indian state of Rajasthan as a place of 'particularly serious attacks on Christian individuals and institutions'. The incident reported was described entirely from the Christian missionary point of view:

> In March, the head of a Christian organization that runs a number of educational and charitable institutions was arrested on charges of 'hurting religious sentiments' and 'insulting the religious beliefs of a community' because of a book that was on sale in one of his establishments.[39]

By placing the offense done by the evangelicals within quotes (i.e., placing it in doubt) and by providing only the missionary point of view, the USCIRF report once again gives a biased view of the conflict as persecution. The statement of the police official who took action and who belongs to the minority Jain community, reveals the distortion of the report:

> The Rajasthan police say they have seized 719 copies of the book, which 'deliberately denigrates' Hindu and Jain deities, from the Foundation's library. 'The book is highly inflammatory . . .' said AK Jain, Additional Director General of Police (Crime), Rajasthan.[40]

Moorthy Muthuswamy, a US-based nuclear physicist and author, brought to the notice of USCIRF the 'data on the origin of religious conflicts in India' and also 'verifiable data to the attention of USCIRF that points to Christian institutions in India practicing religious apartheid on majority that are in violation of Article 23 and Article 26 of Universal Declaration of Human rights'.[41] He found that the 2006 report ignored the data provided by him. Studying the 2006 report, he concluded:

> When the data and events point to the Hindus being at the receiving hands of Christians/Muslims, USCIRF filters out relevant details to portray the events in a way it likes.[42]

2007

The 2007 Religious Freedom report goes to great lengths in describing political ideologies of Hindu nationalist groups, and mentions the 'glorification of Hitler' in Indian textbooks as though it were a hard fact. It states that 'Hitler is a respected figure among some extreme Hindu nationalists', and that social science books published in Gujarat contained language 'minimizing Hitler's role in the Holocaust' and 'belittling religious minorities'.[43] USCIRF blindly accepted this allegation by a segment of Indian media without any attempt to verify it, and this claim was later proven false. Yet the USCIRF report relied on it.[44] Furthermore, if one compares the Tenth-standard textbooks on social studies in Gujarat and Tamil Nadu, it is the latter that are filled with racist histories and allegations. However, this is not on the USCIRF's radar since such textbooks boost Dravidian chauvinism and help bring about Christian conversions.

2008

USCIRF also becomes a mechanism for certain Indians to settle score with Indian political opponents. In support of their own vested interests, they compromise India's sovereignty by asking the US to intervene and pressure India to change the constitutional provisions which safeguard the weaker sections of society from the onslaught of heavy-handed evangelists. For example, in 2008, Professor Angana Chatterji appeared before the United States Commission in the wake of Orissa Hindu-Christian violence, to request the US government to monitor Hindu groups in the US, and also to force the Indian government to change the law and facilitate evangelism among the tribal populations. She recommended as follows:

> Undertake a systematic, routine, and detailed investigation into the actions of diasporic Hindu nationalist groups to identify and investigate their status, actions, finances, and the actions and affiliations of their membership in the United States, as well as their affiliates and cadre. These groups must be investigated and monitored, and, as appropriate, requisite action must be taken and sanctions must be imposed on their activities . . . The Orissa Freedom of Religion Act, 1967, must be reviewed and repealed. The Orissa Prevention of Cow Slaughter Act, 1960, must be reviewed and repealed.[45]

Ironically, such left-wing firebrands make their careers shouting against American imperialism, but contradict themselves by advocating American interventions in India's democracy to force a change in Indian laws.

2009

In February 2009, Joseph D'souza, the president of All India Christian Council (discussed earlier), briefed USCIRF staff during a visit to Washington and offered to facilitate meetings during their proposed visit to India. However, in June 2009, the newly elected Indian government deferred a USCIRF proposal to visit India.[46] The India-based supporters of US intervention sprang into rapid action. Catholic Secular Forum, an activist forum that facilitates Christian campaigns, questioned the Indian government's move in an email sent to its members:

> India fears accountability, loss of international reputation and they are callous enough to accept the consequences of minorities and other vulnerable communities dragged to the butchers for political capital. If China, Myanmar, Saudi Arabia and Israel can allow USCIRF, why can't we?

It also provided its members' contact details to the USCIRF, asking them to send it their atrocity literature.[47]

In 2009, India joined Afghanistan on the USCIRF watch list of Countries of Particular Concern.[48] In October 2009 USCIRF sent a letter to Orissa's then chief minister, Naveen Pattnaik, and the US ambassador handed over a copy to the prime minister of India, expressing concern over the minorities in Orissa becasue 'even though the episode of violence in Kandhamal is over . . . Christian leadership outside India was still uncertain about the security of the minorities living in India'.[49]

Pew Trust Repackages and Spreads: 'India is Next Only to Iraq'

How the atrocity literature about a country can evolve and gain momentum over time is demonstrated by Pew Research Centre's 2009 international report on social hostility and religious discrimination. The Pew website claimed that its researchers had 'combed through 16 widely cited, publicly available sources of information'.[50]

The report relies solely on secondary Christian sources, without verification and not on any primary research. This means that it serves to legitimize certain secondary sources over others by selecting some and ignoring others. The sixteen sources enlisted are all West-based, mainly the reports of USCIRF, the US State Department and right-wing Christian institutes such as the Hudson Institute.[51] The UN Special Rapporteur on Freedom of Religion or Belief report, which the institute used, was the one published by Asma Jahangir, whose visit to India in 2008 was coordinated by All India Christian Council and Christian Solidarity Worldwide.[52] No local news source has been taken into consideration, and all the remaining sources are based in the West, with strong Christian biases.[53]

Paul Marshall, who participated in the Pew Forum discussion of the report, published a paper titled 'The Rise of Hindu Extremism'.[54] The discussion of the report also involved Timothy Shaw, another high-profile person with an evangelical point of view highly critical of India.[55] The Pew report itself was sensationalized in the media, with titles like 'India next only to Iraq on religious discrimination'.[56] While the report blames the Hindu and Muslim groups for religious strife, it is completely silent on the Christian evangelical provocations and propaganda which stir religious conflicts.

Under the heading 'Incidents of Government Force toward Religious Groups Resulting in Individuals Being Imprisoned or Detained', six incidents are given. All the incidents are based on the US State Department report on religious freedom for 2007. One incident is the arrest of two missionaries for making slanderous remarks on Hindu deities in a provocative manner.[57] Under the heading 'Incidents of Physical Abuse Motivated by Religious Hatred or Bias in Society', the US State Department and USCIRF reports are used to narrate incidents where Hindus are shown as attacking Christians. But these are not based on independent sources or verified. The USCIRF merely cites the sources as 'religious media', which refers to Christian groups' own allegations. The Pew Center report merely regurgitates this without any attempt to verify.

The report claims that 'two independent pastors were arrested by police in Chenapur, Khargone district, after local residents complained that the pastors were hurting their religious feelings'. It gives a clean chit to the pastors, saying, 'The pastors were distributing religious literature'. However, what is 'religious literature' to Christian evangelists can be hate speech when Christian publications classify Hindu image worship as demonic, sinful and in need of being destroyed.[58]

US Government Agency for International Development (USAID)

The US government has had a deliberate strategy to allow its funding of Indian projects to be increasingly controlled by evangelical organizations. A principle vehicle that is directly from the government is USAID, an independent federal government agency that receives overall foreign policy guidance from the US Secretary of State. In 1961, the Foreign Assistance Act was signed into law and USAID was created by executive order following the success of Marshall Plan's reconstruction of Europe after the Second World War. Since that time, USAID has been the principal US agency with the aim of 'furthering America's foreign policy interests', which are done in the guise of 'expanding democracy and free markets while improving the lives of the citizens of the developing world'.[59]

During the Cold War, USAID and transnational evangelical organizations were put to use very effectively by the US to counter the Marxist advances in several areas, including Southeast Asia. *Tehelka* magazine explains that under the then US President Bush, the era of CIA-USAID-Evangelicals partnership came back with a roar, particularly in the Indian context.[60] Actually, using evangelicals in tandem with USAID has been part of US policy even before Bush became president. In 1999, the then president, Clinton appointed Brady Anderson as administrator for the USAID, who explicitly stated that 'in terms of foreign aid the US government has long used Christian organizations . . . big time'.[61]

In 1997, Andrew Natsios, vice president of World Vision, testified before the US Congress Committee on International Relations that World Vision welcomes 'a renewed partnership with the US government in international assistance programming' and he painted an idealistic picture in which faith-based NGOs and the US government would work closely together. There had been reluctance on the part of Christian NGOs concerning partnership with the government because it 'results in loss of religious freedom',[62] meaning that they might have to limit the proselytizing aspects of their work with the poor. To cater to the evangelists, in 2001 George Bush appointed Natsios as the administrator of the USAID.[63] In 2002, Bush removed evangelical fears by assuring them access to government money without changing their mission.[64] USAID website clearly shows that by 'faith' USAID means only Abrahamic faiths.[65]

Brady Anderson, the USAID administrator under President Clinton, is on the World Vision board. Such crisscrossing of career paths between Church multinationals and the US government is not coincidental. Michael Lindsay, assistant director of the Center on Race, Religion, and Urban Life at Rice University, and author of the largest and most comprehensive study of public leaders who are evangelicals, points out:

> This overlap of individuals and social sectors also can be found among other evangelical organizations, like Prison Fellowship Ministries, Christianity Today International, and Fuller Theological Seminary.[66]

Apart from a few secular NGOs, USAID shows preference for Christian faith-based NGOs working in India. The USAID India Mission director, George Deikun, has stated on many occasions that Christian evangelical organizations are USAID's most visible working partners in India: 'USAID India is supporting many organizations such as Catholic Relief Services, SHARAN, YWCA, World Vision, Salvation Army and St Mary's Hospital, to name a few'.[67] For tsunami relief, USAID joined hands with World Vision.[68] In 2006, speaking at the sixtieth anniversary of Catholic Relief Services (CRS) in India, Deikun stated that 'CRS and its broad network have been valued partners for USAID' in several programs that reach out to 'about one million of India's most marginalized tribal and Dalit communities each year'.[69]

In 2008, USAID accepted financing of a joint project by Evangelical Fellowship of India Commission on Relief (EFICOR) and Christian Reformed World Relief Committee (CRWRC) in the tribal state of Jharkhand.[70] CRWRC is a US-based Christian relief organization which claims that it 'strengthens Churches – by working through churches', and ultimately 'resulting in more believers'.[71] The parent body of EFICOR is Evangelical Fellowship of India (EFI), though both are separate legal entities since 1981.[72] EFI's website speaks of 'crossing cultural and geographical boundaries and linking Indian Christians with a worldwide Christian community'.[73]

The funneling of US financial aid to India through mostly Christian NGOs assumes further significance given the fact that by 2007 the US was set to slash thirty-five percent of its aid to India.[74] This meant a dramatic increase in the proportion of US aid being sent through religious NGOs.

The Obama administration has appointed a new head of USAID, an Indian American named Rajiv Shah. Time will tell if this signals a shift away from the foreign support given to Christian evangelism, or if this a new smokescreen by bringing in a Hindu-named person as the head. The Christian Right will continue its pressure and is extremely well organized.

Obama and US Foreign Evangelism

Many Indians believe that the Obama administration will deliver a blow to the Christian Right and hence to US-sponsored evangelism in places like India. Regardless of what might be in President Obama's heart, the pragmatics of Washington politics prevail over such ideological goals. He is a great deal-maker across various boundaries and wants to be non-confrontational where possible. In this give-and-take atmosphere that characterizes any modern democracy, he has to choose his top priorities and be willing to concede on the rest. The fate of India (other than for US interests) is simply not in that top-tier priority list for him or for any other US presidency. Especially the fate of Indian civilization or Hinduism, is hardly worth sacrificing the main legislative agendas and policies.

As stated earlier in this chapter, President Clinton had agreed to the Christian right-wing demands to pass the International Religious Freedom Act (in exchange for wanting their support on other more pressing matters that were on Clinton's agenda). Under the then president, George W. Bush, the right-wing penetrated the government agencies very rapidly. In 2001, Bush created faith-based federally funded programs in each of the following departments of the government: Labor, Health and Human Services, Housing and Urban Development, Education, and Justice. This was expanded in 2002 to install the Judeo-Christian presence officially and explicitly in USAID's foreign operations and in Veterans Administration. In 2004, Agriculture, Commerce, Small Business Administration, and Homeland Security departments also had faith-based programs added to them.

While President Obama is blocking and even reversing this heavy Christian influence in certain areas domestically, the foreign theater is a completely different story. He has allowed the Christian Right to continue to deepen its influence on matters foreign religious interventions by the US government. To understand this, one must appreciate that during Obama's presidential campaign, an enterprising African-American named Joshua DuBois of Chicago successfully mobilized Christian voters on behalf of Obama. This move cut into what had traditionally been the Republican vote-bank. This was a very important segment responsible for Obama's victory. Dubois's brilliant plan was that Christians could be swayed by the liberal ideology of caring for the poor. Dubois successfully projected Obama as a 'lifelong advocate for the poor' in Christian terms.

After entering the White House, President Obama has made Dubois his top advisor on anything concerning religion. Now there is even a strategy to woo Christian evangelists into the Democratic Party. One of the main vehicles to engage religions has been Obama's establishment of the President's Advisory Council on Faith-based and Neighborhood Partnerships. Dubois is its executive director. This Council is the President's eyes and ears into religious affairs both domestic and international, and is his chief advisory body on such matters.

It is telling that despite all the rhetoric from Obama's camp, the Democrats have not yet removed the Christian fundamentalists who control the US Commission on Religious Freedom. But even more revealing is the composition of this new Council mentioned above, where there is no excuse of a hangover of pre-Obama appointees. A brief description of the composition of this twenty-five-member body will set the stage to understand how the right-wing continues to run the show on foreign evangelism, albeit now under the flag of a liberal presidency.[75]

To start with, the president of World Vision, USA, is a member. Another council member is the CEO of an organization called Christian Community Development Association, which officially describes itself as 'currently working with over five-thousand faith-based organizations throughout the world'. Another member's credentials are described by the government as: 'An internationally respected evangelical leader, he serves on the boards of the World Evangelical Alliance (420 million constituents) and the National Association of Evangelicals (30 million members)'. The president emeritus of Southern Baptist Convention, who also runs a powerful evangelical group 'which oversees the work of more than 5,600 missionaries', is a member as well. The president of the National Baptist Convention from 1999–2009 is another active member. A former executive director of the very pro-Protestant Pew Trust's Forum on Religion and Public Life, who was also general counsel of the Baptist Joint Committee on Religious Liberty, is among the heavyweights on this body. The powerful World Council of Churches is represented by one of its Central Committee members.

The Catholic Church is represented by the president and CEO, Catholic Charities (USA), which is the national office of over 1,700 local Catholic Charities agencies and institutions nationwide. It is proudly claimed by the Federal Government that 'Pope Benedict XVI named him to the Pontifical Council Cor Unum, which oversees the Catholic Church's worldwide charitable activities'. He is accompanied by another Catholic member who is the General Counsel, United States Conference of Catholic Bishops. There are another half dozen theologians and lawyers heading various Christian denominations that are also on among the Council members.

Besides this heavily dominated body of Christians, there are three Jewish leaders as well as two Muslims. Each of these comes from a prominent background as a theologian and politically well-connected leader.

The Hindu representation, by contrast, is an outright embarrassment. Lacking cohesiveness as a community or a coherent manifesto of critical issues, the Hindu American representation in such situations is typically a matter of personal lobbying. The woman who was given the 'Hindu slot' simply lacks what it takes to assertively speak for Hinduism on par with the Christian heavyweights surrounding her in the Council. While having the best of intentions, she has been simply out-gunned, out-smarted and out-maneuvered politically. She should have developed a solid consensus among her Hindu constituency to define the top issues and demands, and organized the arguments to counteract what the Christians demand. Instead, she got lured into organizing 'Hindu seva' (social service) in different parts of the US, as her way to establish 'leadership skills'. This depleted her energies without any benefit coming back to the community she was meant to represent. This becomes clearer later in this section as we elaborate what the Christians have managed to push through with little success on her part to prevent this from happening.

The Obama administration started out with the following announcement on the important role of faith-based organizations, which were already empowered by Bush. In practice, such groups amount to Judeo-Christian institutions: 'The White House Office of Faith-Based and the Neighborhood Partnerships has been working with the offices throughout the government to consider how faith-based and community organizations can be involved in the economic recovery'. Obama's well-known economic bailout package, known as the American Recovery and Reinvestment Act (ARRA), is being projected among faith-based groups as 'an unprecedented opportunity' for them to get money. Even the much-touted Obama-Biden comprehensive New Energy for America plan has provisions for faith-based groups to get government funds.

Obama's faith-based initiative says on its website that its international goal includes fighting global poverty, renewing US alliances, talking to 'our foes and friends' and seeking 'new partnerships in Asia', for which US-based religions are being asked to play a role. The US State Department Bureau of Educational and Cultural Affairs has organized several exchanges, speaking tours and training partnerships with faith-based and non-profit organizations. Contrary to the Indian notion of 'secularism', American secularism merely separates church/state at the institutional level, and does not preclude prominent government leaders promoting what Christians advocate as 'Biblical values'. (For instance, Hilary Clinton is among the over one hundred members of the White House and US Congress Christian prayer-group that meets monthly in a high-power informal setting, to set agendas based on shared ideologies.)

The US has also, for the past decade, sponsored the World Bank's program called the Development Dialogue on Values and Ethics, which has 'served as the World Bank's focal point on the intersection of faith and development'. This unit of the World Bank 'maintains partnerships with faith-based organizations', which in practice turns out to be largely Christian organizations.

The Obama policy on religion emphatically supports the role of religious groups in social work, and this is music to the ears of the evangelists, who rub their hands in glee at the prospects of receiving billions in government funding. The White House religion advisors concluded: 'In many areas of the world, religious communities have the best developed, largest, and most enduring social infrastructures. Further, they can be among the most credible and reliable partners'. The report argues:

Religion informs the values and actions of many people around the globe and faith-based institutions make a significant contribution to the delivery of healthcare, education and social services [. . .] Religious communities are potential partners for the delivery of basic services, brokering peace and creating stable societies. US personnel must have a working knowledge of the best means to engage religious communities.

In view of this, it recommends expanding the US government's funding of religious organizations operating in foreign countries, as well 'educating' American officials on religious matters:

The administration should include multi-religious partnerships among the partnerships in which the United States government engages, and equip US agencies related to international affairs for those partnerships. Toward this end, the Advisory Council recommends that the administration request appointment of senior staff for multi-religious engagement in each of the major agencies dealing with international affairs. It also urges President Obama to direct each agency to establish portfolios related to multi-religious engagements and to call for the creation of both intra- and inter-agency working groups on multi-religious engagement.

The government explains that there are already such religion-based programs in five-hundred US college campuses in forty cities with local leaders, and at twenty-five US embassies in foreign countries. The Obama-appointed religion council advocated 'reviving capacity-building support for US development NGOs', thereby helping these foreign faith-based groups not just carry out programs, but also get funds to expand their infrastructures in those countries. In all fairness, the 'theory' behind this Obama policy is pluralistic and the right words are used to prevent abuses: 'President Obama is committed to fostering inter-religious dialogue, cooperation and understanding'. One of the priorities will be 'to seek out and create opportunities for inter-religious cooperation'. This statement has great potential, provided it gets applied. As explained below, this is not what has happened in practice.

While the lone Hindu member on the President's religion council spent her year mobilizing Hindu seva, the wily and experienced Christian members were busy creating sub-committees and drafting policy recommendations. At the last moment, with barely a month left before the deadline to enact these recommendations, Rajiv Malhotra of the Infinity foundation (co-author of this book) suddenly got phone calls and emails from a worried Anju Bhargava (the Hindu member on the council), telling him that there were many recommendations about to pass which could be a problem for Hindus. He decided to spend a couple of days on this issue, and asked her to send him the drafts. Below is an analysis of what was being recommended, what Mr Malhotra tried to change, and how the Christians on the council skillfully blocked these attempts.

One recommendation in their draft was that the government assistance should be 'awarded through partnerships with civil society organizations that have demonstrated commitment to work with poor communities'. Mr Malhotra suggested that while working with the poor was critical, there had to be more requirements added in the spirit of Obama's stated policy of inter-religious harmony and pluralism. He suggested that a sentence should be added with the following intent: 'It is imperative that pluralism in other countries must be encouraged by respecting their native religions'. Bhargava told Malhotra that this was rejected by her colleagues on the council.

Another council recommendation was that the US government should establish a goal that one-third of its development assistance across all departments of the government should be channeled through such faith-based groups. This was clearly meant to open the floodgates of government money ending up in the hands of evangelists. Malhotra sent Bhargava an email with the following point to be added, which was instantly and emphatically rejected by the council: 'Too often, some US-related NGOs have had an aggressive evangelical agenda disguised as social service, leading to inter-religious tensions rather than harmony and pluralism. To prevent this, the US government funding should go to only those organizations that undertake a pledge not to engage in activities that are known to trigger communal disharmony, such as slandering or undermining other faiths' philosophies, deities, rituals, symbols, history, leaders, or practices'.

Another policy they were recommending went as follows: 'USAID should appoint a religion and civil society engagement staff liaison at every AID mission to reach out to and partner with organizations on the ground. This staff position would report directly to chief of mission for that country, would work across US government agencies working in country, would create opportunities for ongoing dialogue between in-country civil society and NGOs and would facilitate the creation of joint programs between the US government and NGOs based on locally identified needs'. Malhotra suggested that the following be added as a safeguard: 'All such hiring should have the intention to avoid staffing that would bring religious prejudices against the predominant faiths in the given foreign country. The standards of religion-based bias that apply under the law within the US should serve as the guideline for avoiding biases overseas by any US government-linked program. Great care should be taken that such capacity-building does not privilege a particular religious group over others or topple the prevailing balance among the religions in the given country'. This also was rejected by the presidential council.

Frustrated that Anju Bhargava was becoming like a rubber-stamp for whatever had been drafted by the council dominated by Christian evangelists, Malhotra wrote to her as follows:

Anju, this is the Christian Right's agenda being taken even further. For example, Recommendation 5 is meant to plant folks representing World Vision type of evangelists inside USAID offices in order to give direction. We are already fighting their invasion on the ground in places like Tamil Nadu, Andhra Pradesh, Northeast India, etc. Obama has been hijacked by the Christian Right in this matter. I wish you had brought in Hindu voices much earlier in this process. Is there a way to insert some language concerning sensitivity towards native religious traditions, saying that US will NOT get involved with any religious NGO that is engaged in proselytizing/conversions? If we don't do this or at least go on the record having asked for it, it will seem like we rubber-stamped the evangelists' agenda. I am available for a conference call in case you want some folks to discuss this right away.

Bhargava replied, 'I had talked about it many times', but that 'They said that is out of scope. They have been resisting getting any other faith included. My recommendations in faith-based were getting squashed . . .'

She concluded: 'I am unable to touch this'.

So Malhotra wrote back to her with the draft of a formal letter that should be sent from her to the council, saying: 'I suggest you put this on file with them officially, with copy for your records.' The draft is reproduced below:

Dear council members,

As the representative of the Hindu American community, I feel it is important for me to go on record with the position of my faith community concerning aggressive proselytizing by certain US-based NGOs in India. There needs to be a statement of policy inserted in this document to the following effect:

'The US government shall not include in its various overseas initiatives any NGO that is engaged in aggressive proselytizing, because such programs cause social tensions and are disrespectful of other faiths. In the event of any complaints, the government shall hear the evidence before making a conclusion as to the merits of the case.'

Furthermore, Recommendation 5 opens the opportunity for one-sided representations favoring proselytizing. Hence, it should be amended to give equal representation to the majority native faith of the given country in question. For instance, if it is an Islamic or Hindu or Buddhist majority, the US appointment under Recommendation 5 shall either be of that faith or else that faith will be represented at least on par with Judeo-Christians in every committee or other body.

Given that the purpose of this council is interfaith harmony, it makes sense for it to not support any programs that end up causing hostilities among faiths. I therefore, wish to place my proposed amendments on the official record of the council.

Malhotra concluded his email to Bhargava: 'I feel this will be an act of courage on your part. You have nothing to lose. It will show that we are not to be taken lightly and pushed around. Otherwise, they will say that the Hindu representative on the Council went along with their proposals. Having this statement in the written record as a dissenting voice is critical. If they pressure you, hold your ground and tell them that dissent is a key part of American democracy and what President Obama stands for. Tell them you want to respect the sentiments of your constituency, hence you are doing this. Also, take good notes on what the Christian Right is saying – names, what he/she said, date. This diary will be useful'.

Bhargava replied: 'Rajiv, I brought this up again at the full council and it is in the records. They said they will look at the language for increasing sensitivity of people who are assigned to the task-force. I have brought it up many, many times. But this draft was developed by World Vision, who has a lot of power'. Bhargava went to tell Malhotra how the drafts were done by World Vision representatives, and that she was clearly told by them that it is 'all about numbers and maximizing one's market share', and that her suggestions were not welcome, but that she was being tolerated and largely ignored.

As a consolation prize, a subsequent draft acknowledged this controversy: 'Some of us believe the Government must or should refrain from directing cash aid (including social service aid) to certain kinds of religious entities, whereas others of us believe that, although the constitution limits the use of direct government aid for religious *activities*, it allows such aid for secular *activities*, regardless of the character of the *provider*.' In other words, Bhargava was acknowledged but overruled very diplomatically.

This saga provides some other important insights as well. NRIs (Non-resident Indians) are jockeying for position to get their names into high-profile posts, whether they qualify or not. It gives them stature. One prominent person serving in such a capacity in Washington told me pointblank that her main goal was to use it as an avenue to get herself a paid job in Washington. The Hindus, unlike other major religions in the US, lack a formal manifesto with concrete positions on important issues and specific action-items they want. Too often, the Indian media overrates the importance of NRIs who get appointed to US government posts, presuming that this is always in India's interests. But in many cases the exact opposite is true: The individuals use their Indian identity to boost their personal careers, and are not willing to stick their necks out and spend personal political capital for India's cause. Many of them lack a clear grasp of what any such cause might be, beyond generic superficialities, Bollywood parties and Indian pop culture.

16

British Intervention in Present-day India

'The empires of the future are the empires of the mind.' (Winston Churchill, speaking at Harvard University)[1]

While we have focused mainly on American Christian interventionism, Europe has its own complex relationship with India, laden with colonial history and missionary accounts. There are new forces which revive this residual imagery to build a case for Christianizing India by taking over its disenfranchised segments of society. We begin with an overview of the most prominent European organizations and examine their activities. While American groups take their complaints about India to the US Commission on International Religious Freedom, European groups are more likely to criticize India in large multinational forums such as the Durban anti-racism conference of 2001, the Geneva conference of 2009, and the European parliament. This chapter focuses on the UK, and the following chapter on the rest of Europe.

Fig 16.1 shows an overview of this chapter, and the major players to be discussed are summarized as follows.

Christian Solidarity Worldwide (CSW)

Christian Solidarity Worldwide is an international Christian activist group based in the United Kingdom. Headed by extreme right-wing elements, it runs European organizations with a Dalit front, which collaborate with similar Dalit-faced evangelical groups in the US. CSW uses Dalit issues as a pretext to carry out rabidly anti-India advocacy in international bodies and with European politicians.

Dalit Solidarity Network-UK

Affiliated with CSW, Dalit Solidarity Network-UK cultivates radical politicians from both the extreme left and right, powerful civil servants, and administrators of financial aid and investments in India. It collaborates with UK-based groups such as London Institute of South Asia (LISA), which openly calls for the balkanization of India. It supports Afro-Dalit forces in India, like *Dalit Voice*. It commissions controversial studies in the UK which profile UK Indians using the stereotypes of caste.

International Dalit Solidarity Network

International Dalit Solidarity Network works across continental Europe collaborating with NGOs and politicians, as well as with academics in South Asian Studies. It brings church-affiliated Dalit activists and academicians from India for lecture tours of Europe and for providing testimonies before European parliamentary bodies. It has strong ties with numerous Indian evangelical organizations.

India-based Dalit Institutions and Individuals with Church Links

Over the years, Christian institutions have created pseudo-secular organizations and nurtured scholars who specialize in blaming Indian culture as incurably anti-Dalit, due to the Aryan race theory. The European Christian groups advocate European intervention by championing these Indian Dalit fronts, such as National Dalit Human Rights Commission and National Dalit Women's Forum, along with individual scholars, as the only true voice of Dalit emancipation.

Fig 16.1 Europe-Controlled Dalit Activism for Re-Colonization of India

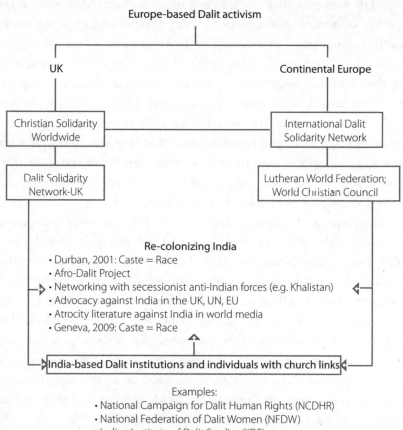

Anti-India Axis in the UK

Although postcolonial studies have criticized the savage images of Indian civilization, Christian right-wing institutions have worked tirelessly in recent years to revive them through propaganda. They work closely with affiliates in the US, Europe and India. Their considerable success is evidenced by caste becoming equated with race in European policy-making institutions, including the European parliament. Academic Dalit Studies have become associated with transnational NGOs.

The subconscious memories of the former British empire inspire some UK elements that want to see India balkanized. Sporadic voices near the centers of power seem to want to push India towards violence and fragmentation. For example in 1991, within a week of the brutal assassination of Rajiv Gandhi by LTTE, the *Times of London*, a voice for the British Foreign Office, wrote an editorial stating that India faced 'the same bloody strains and ignored solutions' that had resulted in the breaking up of the Soviet Union. It compared India with the former Soviet Union and recommended that 'the way forward' without 'murders and riots' was to 'allow States and sub-States their own economic policies, and bring in as much foreign investment and as many free-market principles as they like'.[2]

This separatist message disguised as the economic independence of 'states and sub-states' was further developed and articulated into full-blown balkanization by Max Madden, a member of the British parliament. Speaking in Denmark at a conference on Kashmir, Madden demanded India's self-annihilation. Remembering the disintegration of the Soviet and British empires, he wondered: 'Why should the Union of India and its present boundaries continue forever?' He questioned India's status as the world's largest democracy: 'We all hear from Indians that they have the largest democracy in the world; many of us question that very fundamentally'. Madden suggested that the United Nations should oversee Kashmir's independence, a role that could be extended beyond Kashmir: 'And it may involve the whole region. So be it'.[3] Such suggestions are kept alive to this day. For example, in the website www.countercurrents.org, a decade old *Times of London* article was extensively quoted to conclude that India's best course from the beginning would have been to split into a hundred Hong Kongs.[4]

Christian Solidarity Worldwide

Many Westerners have thus taken up the banner of social justice to attack India. For example, Christian Solidarity Worldwide (CSW) began in 1979 as the UK branch of the Swiss-based Christian Solidarity International. It is an international lobbying organization for evangelicals working in Christian minority nations but presents itself a 'human rights organization'.[5] Its president is Baroness Caroline Cox, a right-wing British politician who was expelled from the Tory party for openly supporting the hardline racist stance of the UK Independence Party.[6]

Since 1998, CSW has had a strategic collaboration with All India Christian Council (AICC). Subsequently, Dalit Freedom Network (DFN) was brought in to forge a powerful triangular nexus: CSW in Europe, DFN in the USA, and AICC in India are tightly coordinated in encouraging European and American government intervention in India. For its international campaign against India, CSW is willing to team up with hardcore Christian organizations such as Intercessors Network, Compass Direct, Liberty World Evangelical Fellowship, Alliance Religious Liberty Commission, and the Seventh Day Adventist Church.[7]

In 2001, CSW worked through British MPs to introduce four Parliamentary Questions on India, while in parallel, the AICC raised the same questions against India in the UN. In 2006, CSW used Labor MP Andy Reed, who used to sit on its board,[8] to lead a campaign against Indian laws that prohibit abusive religious conversions. Reed traveled to India accompanied by a Christian Conservative MP;[9] he carried a letter to the president of India signed by sixteen MPs, which he personally handed to the Indian government.[10]

In 2007, CSW launched a documentary called *India's Hidden Slavery*, which it co-produced with DFN.[11] CSW's annual report notes that its 'briefings on anti-conversion legislation and anti-Christian violence were widely disseminated and quoted, including, at a Congressional hearing in the US'.[12] In the same year, Stephen Crabb, an MP who chairs the Conservative Party Human Rights Commission, started a debate in the British Parliament on Dalit issues, and revealed that he was taken on his fact-finding trip to India by a leader of CSW.[13] Crabb employs research interns from a fundamentalist lobbying body called Christian Action, which the British press confirms, 'has links to the powerful Christian Right in America'.[14]

In 2008, CSW and DFN persuaded the powerful group Human Rights Watch to send joint letters to the UK foreign secretary, the

US secretary of state, the French foreign minister, and the European commissioner for external relations, calling for international statements in favor of Christians in the widespread Hindu-Christian riots in Orissa that resulted from the murder of a Hindu monk.[15] They gave a predictably one-sided view, condemning Hinduism for everything and playing the age-old Christian victimhood card.

CSW's lobbying activities with bodies like the UN Human Rights Councils have been used to undermine India's unity. The 2008 report of the UN Working Group of Human Rights Commission quotes CSW's reports on Dalits and caste conflicts in India,[16] in which CSW asserts that caste-based discrimination should be used as 'an interpretative tool for all major human rights abuses in India'.[17] The same report further reinforces this view by relying upon the allegations made by a Christian militant organization, Tripura People's Democratic Front, 'which has set up a parallel government in some remote areas of the State'.[18]

Dalit Solidarity Network-UK

Dalit Solidarity Network-UK (DSN-UK) was set up in 1998 to raise the issue of caste conflicts before the UK government, parliament, aid agencies, trade unions, and business houses. Its founder is a Methodist minister named David Haslam. In 2000, DSN-UK expanded into International Dalit Solidarity Network (IDSN), headquartered in Denmark.

Initially, DSN-UK was funded 'primarily from Christian Aid, with additional support from the Methodist Relief and Development Fund and the Anglican USPG'.[19] Christian Aid, an evangelical group notorious for its predatory practices among the poor, had sponsored DSN-UK to lobby against the Indian government on caste issues at the 2001 Durban conference. Christian Aid and DSN have an explicit alliance.[20]

DSN-UK is also funded by several other major evangelical Christian organizations,[21] including Anglican USPG. The USPG website is careful not to reveal what 'USPG' stands for. Its original name was Society for the Propagation of the Gospels, which had its roots as a slave-owning group in America where it operated slave plantations.[22] In 1820 it sent missionaries to India, where they played a major role in formulating Dravidian racist theories and using these to encourage a separatist movement.[23]

In 2004, DSN-UK got the International Development Committee of the UK parliament to raise India's caste problem with the Indian government when the committee visited India. In the same year, DSN-UK held a meeting on this issue at the Labor Party Conference. One of its trustees is the former general secretary of the largest trade union in Scotland, which has close connections with the Catholic Church, and such links helped it to spread its anti-India campaign into the private sector.[24]

DSN-UK successfully lobbied to start a UK parliamentary debate on caste conflicts in India, and targeted the Indian diaspora within the UK, alleging rampant caste-based discrimination within the Indian immigrant community. A research proposal framed by DSN-UK and related groups led to a report titled *No Escape: Caste Discrimination in the UK*, which contained many statements that stereotyped Hindus and the Indian Diaspora.[25] British Hindus challenged the report, and in 2008 a survey conducted by the British Hindu Council produced results contradicting the DSN-UK report.[26]

In 2007, DSN-UK, along with Christian Solidarity Worldwide, conducted a meeting on Dalits, featuring speakers associated with the US-based Dalit Freedom Network. Moses Parmer of DFN stated that only Christianity offered freedom for Dalits and Rev David Haslam, Chair of the Network of DSN Trustees, stated that Dalit problems should be internationalized.[27]

Jeremy Corbyn, the labor MP who is also the chair of the DSN-UK, stated, 'We have a real responsibility to continue the struggle, inside the UK Parliament and outside, to raise the consciousness of people in the UK'.[28] Corbyn also supported the banned LTTE terrorist group and lobbied for lifting the ban on LTTE in the European Union.[29] He is also the chairperson of Liberation, a UK-based human rights organization[30] which has brought Indian insurgents to the UN under false names.[31]

Rob Morris, another trustee of DSN-UK, who is also a member of parliament, opposes India's case to become a permanent member of the UN Security Council, alleging caste-based human rights violations.[32] He is also a supporter of Khalistan as a religious state to be carved out of India by Sikh fundamentalists.[33] Corbyn and Morris are both on the powerful parliamentary committee dealing with foreign investments,[34] and hence in a good position to use the UK government's clout to pressure India on behalf of evangelical groups with a Dalit face.

LISA

While organizations like DSN-UK present themselves with the aura of respectability, some organization with which they associate in the UK are openly supportive of violence and racism. One such active organization is the London Institute for South Asia (LISA), a rabidly anti-India institution whose website supports violent separatist movements in three regions within India, claiming that India is responsible for 'perpetual instability and economic misery in the entire region of South Asia'. Its allegations are serious, such as the following:

> The Indian armed forces are brutally suppressing at least seventeen freedom / reform movements, killing hundreds of thousands in Jammu and Kashmir, the Punjab (Sikhs) and the states of Assam. Yet it has been able to maintain its image as a pacifist society – the birthplace of Lord Buddha and followers of Gandhian non-violence.[35]

Brandishing the image of Khalistani terrorist Bhindharanwalle on its website home page, LISA also alleges a Hindu-Zionist conspiracy to suppress the majority of people in India:

> Even today when the non-Hindu majority in India is gaining self-confidence under the leadership of regional and caste-based political parties, the Hindu minority is still able to impose its anti-Islam and pro-Zionists agenda on India.[36]

Both directors of this organization are Pakistanis, one of them being Usman Khalid, a retired brigadier of the Pakistani army. The website also uses the pre-1971 name for Bangladesh – East Pakistan.

Writings of Usman Khalid are also featured in Counter Currents.org, a news portal run by Kerala Christian journalist Binu Mathews, which projects itself as 'alternative news site' with sympathies for 'all those who are engaged in struggles for economic, political, social, cultural, gender, environmental justice'.[37]

LISA champions the 'peoples held captive within India', and for this it presented its International Award to V.T. Rajshekar, Editor of *Dalit Voice*, for his book, *Caste – A Nation within the Nation*.[38] The award was presented by David Haslam, the founder-trustee of DSN-UK. Rajshekar takes a stridently racist and anti-Hindu view, which draws on anti-Semitic literature that praises Hitler, minimizes or denies the Jewish Holocaust, and claims that Brahmins are 'the Jews of India'.[39]

In 2009, LISA presented the international award to Eva-Maria Hardtmann, coordinator of Stockholm Anthropological Research on India (SARI),[40] whose work in promoting a Dalit identity in tension with Hinduism is analysed in the next chapter. The award ceremony also included a seminar on 'exercise of right of self-determination in south Asia'. The speakers included representatives of England-based Council of Khalistan, whose violent terrorist movement for a separate Sikh nation has lost steam in India.[41]

Thus, LISA is working as an important node in the UK in bringing together European Dalit academics, Indian Dalit activists, anti-Indian secessionists and pan-Islamic forces in Pakistan.

The Oxford Centre for Religion and Public Life (OCRPL)

The Oxford Centre for Religion and Public Life has the stated aim to promote 'a better understanding of the role of religion in public life'. But in practice it lends support for US evangelical groups and its website acknowledges that it was built on twenty-five years of research and education by INFEMIT (The International Fellowship of Evangelical Mission Theologians).

INFEMIT is active in pushing for global Christian expansionism, for example, as co-sponsor of a seminar on Religious Militancy in South

Asia, held at Ethics and Public Policy Center (described in Chapter 13). Focusing on Hindu militancy, the discussion was aimed to 'weigh possible US policy responses'.[42] In 2003, INFEMIT received funds from Chicago-based Crowell Trust, which colludes with creationist fundamentalist organizations.

All of the directors of OCRPL come from Christian theological and evangelical organizations.[43] The only American among its fellows belongs to the right-wing Hudson Institute.[44] OCRPL publishes atrocity literature on India by bringing together a select group of activists, journalists and evangelicals. In 2007, it organized a conference titled 'Reporting Religious Controversies', which was sponsored by the Catholic Bishop's Conference of India's Commission for Social Communications.[45]

17

Continental European Interventions

Although Marxists and Christian fundamentalists attack each other in the West, they find common cause against Indian civilization. India has been attacked by this alliance in the European parliament, various international bodies and academic conferences at European institutions. Looking at continental Europe, especially Scandinavia, one finds numerous Marxists who are committed to conflating caste with race. The equation of caste with race owes much to the politics of identity (described in Chapters Five and Six), that was started by colonial missionaries, who identified the Dravidians as a race.

The renewed impetus for conflating caste and race came from the World Conference against Racism, Racial Discrimination, Xenophobia and Related Intolerance, held in Durban, South Africa, in 2001 under the auspices of the UN Commission on Human Rights. The Indian caste-system was on the agenda in spite of these comments by the government of India:

> In the run up to the world conference, there has been propaganda, highly exaggerated and misleading, often based on anecdotal evidence, regarding caste-based discrimination in India. . . . We are firmly of the view that the issue of caste is not an appropriate subject for discussion at this conference. We are here to ensure that there is no state-sponsored, institutionalised discrimination against any individual

citizen or groups of citizens. We are here to ensure that states do not condone or encourage regressive social attitudes. We are not here to engage in social engineering within member states. It is neither legitimate nor feasible nor practical for this World Conference or, for that matter, even the UN to legislate, let alone police, individual behaviour in our societies.[1]

The Durban conference did not, in the end, equate caste with race, but it opened the door, and activists got invigorated to work on this agenda ever since. This chapter will trace some of the groups whose work is leading India toward fragmentation with this idea. Fig 17.1 serves as an outline of the chapter.

Fig 17.1 Continental Europe-Controlled Activist-Academic Networks in India

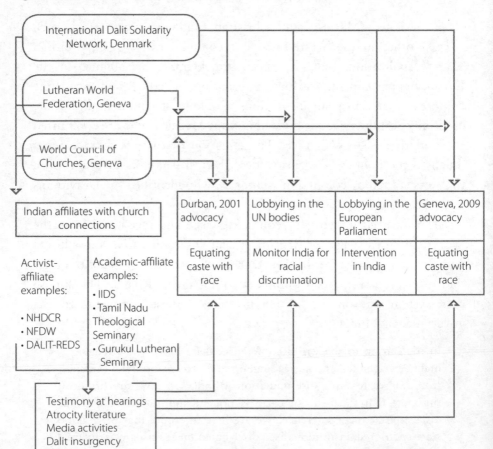

International Dalit Solidarity Network (IDSN)

After the Dalit Solidarity Network had been established in the UK in 1998, the International Dalit Solidarity Network (IDSN) was formed in 2000, headquartered in Copenhagen. Its stated goal is 'facilitating Dalit rights interventions internationally, including before the EU Commission and Parliament, UN human rights mechanisms, the International Labour Organisation (ILO), and other forums'.[2] The financing is almost entirely brought by Christian organizations in the West.[3]

IDSN office-holders also provide consultancy to the National Dalit Task Force based in India, an organization created by the National Council of Churches in India in collaboration with foreign groups such as World Council of Churches, Lutheran World Federation, and Global Mission of the Evangelical Lutheran Church in America. The stated aim is to hold conferences 'outside India on Dalit liberation and activation of the Dalit Task Force'.[4] These organizations, along with IDSN and DSN-UK, provide its strategic direction.[5]

IDSN has branches all over Europe, with most of its office-holders having strong evangelical church links.[6] The approach is to select church officials for top posts, in directing Dalit affairs. For example, the head of its French branch is also project officer for a church group in India.[7] In Germany, IDSN is headed by the Lutheran Church's program officer directing various activities in India.[8] Its Belgium contact is from a Catholic aid organization.[9] In Sweden and the Netherlands, IDSN activism is directed by people well-known for their attacks against India in international forums.[10] One of the co-conveners of IDSN, Paul Divakar, has a strong church background[11] and is also the convener of the National Campaign for Dalit Human Rights, another India-based Christian organization with a Dalit face.

Advocacy Against India in the UN

The persistent advocacy of IDSN and its Indian affiliates resulted in the UN Commission on Human Rights adopting a resolution in 2005 to appoint two Special Rapporteurs to study caste-based discrimination.[12] To achieve this goal, the Lutheran World Federation had submitted a written petition to most member states of the UN, while in parallel IDSN had lobbied Geneva-based government missions.[13] Both the rapporteurs appointed were fundamentalist Christians, one being a graduate from International Christian University at Tokyo,[14] and the other a South Korean sociologist and activist working for church organizations.[15] IDSN worked very closely with both these throughout the project, and provided them working drafts which shaped much of the UN report.[16] IDSN facilitated selective NGO inputs to them, with no opposing inputs by anyone else. It brought in international organizations against racism, along with Lutheran World Federation to host discussions, and its top officials presented its pro-Christian positions very assertively, including submission of a report to the UN High Commissioner for Human Rights.[17] The four-day visit of a UN rapporteur to India was even funded by IDSN.[18]

IDSN believes that equating caste with race will open the floodgates to international interventions in India's internal affairs that would help Christian conversions, and it makes the false claim that Indian Christianity does not suffer from caste biases. When the Government of India provided its own reports to the UN Committee on the Elimination of Racial Discrimination, IDSN proudly reported how it was working to undermine the Indian government:

> Shadow reports were prepared and submitted to the committee by IDSN members and associates: the National Campaign on Dalit Human Rights, India; the Center for Human Rights and Global Justice / Human Rights Watch; the Dalit Network of the Netherlands in association with IDSN; and the Asian Human Rights Commission all submitted substantive reports with full sets of recommendations.[19]

In 2007, pressured by the sustained anti-India campaigning, the UN selected India as the *first* country to be reviewed for human rights violations. IDSN submitted its own report on India in association with the National Campaign on Dalit Human Rights, the Lutheran World Federation, and the International Movement Against all forms of Discrimination and Racism, and called this report 'additional credible and reliable information' received from 'other relevant stakeholders'.[20]

Advocacy Against India in the European Union

In 2005, IDSN arranged for the testimony of the top official of the National Campaign on Dalit Human Rights, at the European Commission. The goal was to establish the 'inaction and unwillingness of government officials in India to take up the issue of violations against Dalits, and its failure to prevent discrimination against Dalits in the relief and rehabilitation efforts following the tsunami.'[21] They petitioned the European Commission to intervene in India's economic development programs. IDSN has become a power center in influencing how development funds from countries of the EU are channeled into India, and organizes top-level meetings where its church officials bring Dalit representatives before the European Commission in Delhi.[22]

In 2006, the Danish Ministry of Foreign Affairs gave a large grant towards IDSN's core mission. IDSN worked with a Dutch government official, who is also a member of Oxfam International, to raise questions on the EU's policy on Dalit human rights.[23] The same year, the EU Commissioner wrote to IDSN that the UN's Special Rapporteur on Discrimination (whose visit to India had been funded by IDSN) was welcome to visit the EU. The EU made a commitment to give political and financial support to the UN study, and criticized the Indian government for not confessing its racist practices.[24] The top EU official who served as the nexus for all this belongs to OVP, the conservative right-wing Austrian People's Party. Interestingly this party is notorious for wanting a Catholic and anti-socialist regime which opposes affirmative action in its own country.[25]

'Not sanctions against India, but at least . . .'

In 2006, the European parliament convened a hearing by its Committee on Development, in which the Dalit issue was discussed. The Indian government did not send its delegates, stating that 'the problem of the Dalits is strictly internal, a private matter'. However, two Indian Dalit NGOs attended. Paul Divakar, representing the India-based affiliate of IDSN, gave testimonies before the European parliament. He was accompanied by another India-based activist, Ruth Manorama of National Federation of Dalit Women, who has also been nurtured by foreign nexuses.[26] Their European lobbying tour was sponsored by IDSN.[27] Paul Divakar stopped short of asking for outright sanctions against India, but he called for Europeans to play the Dalit card 'in all the political dialogues with India'.[28]

The testimonies by Divakar and Manorama and the discussions resulting in the European Parliamentary Committee were reported by an NGO as follows:

> Chair of the committee, Louisa Morgantini of the Socialist group, reacted to the testimonies by Divakar and Manorama, saying that caste discrimination in India is a well-kept secret. Max van den Berg, vice chair of the committee and also of the socialist group, said that thus far the EU has not been able to address this serious issue openly. He felt that the issue cannot be tackled without much more public knowledge and pressure. Jurgen Schroder of the European People's Party asked how India can be called a democracy, when caste discrimination is perpetuated on this scale.[29]

In the same year, the Committee on Development of the European Union initiated a resolution demanding the Indian government to confess that 'caste equals race' and demanded to bring India under the control of international supervision to end racism.[30] IDSN shaped that draft resolution.[31]

This was followed in 2007 by a European parliament resolution condemning India's programs against caste bias as 'grossly inadequate'. The resolution called on the Indian government to engage with the Commission for the Eradication of Racial Discrimination of the United Nations.[32] This essentially means the negation of the Indian government's stand that caste is not equal to race. The process by which the resolution was pushed through the European parliament raised many questions. According to Neena Gill, member of the

European parliament for the Labour party, the report was 'riddled with inaccuracies and does a clear disservice to the Human Rights cause! The value of this report is seriously drawn into question by the whole lack of scrutiny applied to it'.[33] Noting how it was rushed through in a sneaky manner with less than 30 of the 785 European parliament members voting, Gill exclaimed:

> It is a highly sensitive report on a very important issue and the way it has been rushed through parliament without consultation of either the SAARC delegation, the Sub-Committee on Human Rights, nor the Foreign Affairs Committee, is outrageous![34]

The Indian mission in Brussels also criticized this report, saying it showed a negative mindset based on using statistics selectively.[35] But the objective of IDSN was to have something with official credibility that would be broadcast throughout the world by their vast network of influential media and would fuel Christian activism.

In 2008, Denmark's branch of IDSN organized a hearing before the Danish Parliament for selected Indian activists, academicians, and the UN rapporteur. One of the activists flown in was the director of a Tamil Nadu NGO who had earlier been charged by Tamil Nadu police for 'indulging in forceful religious conversions', according to a report submitted to the National Human Rights Commission in 2004.[36] When the question was raised in the Danish parliament on the importance of conversion to Christianity, he responded that Dalits got better access to education by converting to Christianity, and complained about the loss of reservation benefits.[37]

Lutheran World Federation and World Council of Churches Combine Left-wing and Right-wing[38]

IDSN also networks with powerful International church bodies, among which the Lutheran World Federation (LWF) and the World Council of Churches (WCC) are especially notable. The initiatives of IDSN to supplement its advocacy for European intervention into India are often backed institutionally by LWF and WCC, such as a photo-exhibition purportedly showing discrimination against Dalits in India.[39] This traveling photo-exhibition was displayed widely in Europe, and at the hearing on untouchability in the European parliament.[40]

The LWF is a global communion of Christian churches in the Lutheran tradition, established in 1947. Its stated goal is to 'resolve to serve Christian unity throughout the world'.[41] Until the first half of the twentieth century, Lutheran churches were mostly concentrated in Germany, Scandinavia, Baltic countries, and the USA. After the collapse of colonialism, the center of gravity for Lutheran activism shifted to the developing countries, with sizeable number of churches in Africa, Latin America and Asia.[42] LWF is powerful through its political control in developing countries. It has emerged in recent years as an influential international organization that is spearheading the campaign to equate caste with race and to depict India as a society sanctioning apartheid.

Founded in 1948, the World Council of Churches (WCC) claims to be the broadest and most inclusive Christian ecumenical movement in the world. Its goal is 'Christian unity', by which it means 'unity in one faith and one Eucharistic fellowship'. That 'one faith' is naturally, Christianity. It claims to include 349 churches, denominations and church fellowships in more than 110 countries.[43]

WCC also aligns itself with the left-wing, including Marxists, in the developing nations. This left-wing Christian radicalism is a device to undermine local spiritual traditions and cultures, thereby paving the way for Christian conversion once the ground has been cleared by the Marxists. In the case of India, WCC has been supporting and funding the Maoist-Christian insurgency in the strategic Northeast.[44] Thus the right-wing strategy utilizes the left-wing for tactical support.

LWF and WCC organized a Global Ecumenical Conference on 'Justice for Dalits' in 2009 in Bangkok.[45] It is a laudable endeavor to fight for the impoverished sections of Indian populations as well as to oppose social evils that deny basic human dignity to considerable sections of the society. However, as explained elsewhere in this book, the social reformers who have fought against the caste system in the most uncompromised manner and who have won the most significant rights for the subalterns have come from India's indigenous spiritual traditions. The problem with events like the Bangkok conference is that they create religious stereotypes and internal divisiveness. For example, the concept paper of the conference claimed that Indian religious traditions deny the Christian concept of the image of God in every human being.[46] Thus, the LWF and WCC have transformed what is a legitimate struggle for human rights and human dignity into a Christian crusade.

The concept note for the conference explained that WCC and LWF are networking with many Dalit organizations from India 'to bring the Dalit issue to the notice of the international community – especially through the UN human rights bodies and other international forums'.[47] It points out that the Bangkok Conference itself was a preparation for the Durban Review Conference that was scheduled to take place in Geneva in 2009.

In the Geneva conference, a bishop of the Church of South India narrated various atrocities against Dalits and held 'Hindu doctrine' responsible for all their problems. The stories were meant to give 'theological and missiological basis' upon which transnational churches and organizations worldwide could affirm their solidarity with the Dalits. The bishop further stated that the Indian government had failed 'to render justice for the Dalits through the police, the executive and the judiciary'.[48]

Yet the efforts to equate caste with race once again met with failure in the Geneva conference of 2009. *The Times of India* reported: 'It was a major blow to some Scandinavian countries and groups like Human Rights Watch, which have been demanding that India's caste-based discrimination is racism by another name'. The report further pointed out that Dalit activist and writer Chandrabhan Prasad blamed 'stupid NGOs' for the outcome in Geneva, saying it was a mistake to equate caste with race.[49]

The conference projected organizations which support a racist theory of Dalit separatism and insurgency as being the genuine representatives of Dalit movement in India. This is discussed next.

Affiliates of Dalit Dissent in India

The Dalit movement, which intends to oppose racism, at times ends up promoting racist theories of its own. Some of its ideas support a stye of separatist politics that easily turns violent. As we have seen before, a complex network of mostly well-meaning academics, churches, and government institutions end up legitimizing violent insurgency. The following section traces some of these links.

National Campaign for Dalit Human Rights (NCDHR)

Paul Divakar, the Convener of National Campaign for Dalit Human Rights (NCDHR) in Delhi, is also the co-convener of IDSN.[50] Another co-convener of NCDHR is Martin Macwan, an activist trained in a Jesuit seminary, who runs organizations in Gujarat claiming to speak for Dalits, but which the local Dalits accuse of politicizing issues for his own selfish interests.[51] In 2003, Martin Macwan was featured in a National Geographic story on India's untouchables, and projected as 'one of the most visible untouchable organizers since Ambedkar'. The article concluded that in order to solve caste problems, Hinduism should 'cease playing a central role in politics and law enforcement'.[52] In other words, Christianity should take over the civic society.

In 2009, Macwan conducted a survey of the Dalit situation in Gujarat and reported widespread discrimination against them. This report was publicized in the media, directly positioning it against the economic prosperity of Gujarat.[53] Macwan's organization was backed by the Kroc Institute for International Peace Studies at the University of Notre Dame, Indiana. Kroc Institute is a centre conducting research on 'war, genocide, terrorism, ethnic and religious conflict, and violation of human rights' and whose mission is integral to Notre Dame, an international Catholic research university. The center bases itself on the 'rich tradition' that Church has 'of teaching on war, peace, justice, and human rights'.[54]

NCDHR is very aggressive internationally in urging all nations to exert pressure on India. Its 'Dalit caucus' lobbied against India at

Durban in 2001.[55] In an interview with Radio National of Australia, Paul Divakar stated:

> I feel that all this will necessitate a greater campaign across the globe, and specifically focusing on the UN mechanisms—multilateral and bilateral bodies like European Union and World Bank, you know—all these bodies are going to be focused to ensure whether it is human rights, or whether it is development corporation, or trade, that we take a responsibility to address the issue of this heinous crime that is being committed against humankind.[56]

The anchor of the program explained why India is not willing to eradicate the caste system: 'India has laws banning caste discrimination, of course, but with an economy resting on the enslavement of 180 million people, those laws have not been a practical reality'.[57]

An NDTV reporter disagreed:

> But can caste-based discrimination be equated with racism? 'The constitution makes a difference between race and caste. Equating the two for reservations is not correct,' said Ashok Kumar Panda, Senior Counsel and Constitutional Expert. Although the debate does not seem to have many takers, it flies in the face of India's affirmative action in place for the last fifty years. And to say the least, it has far-reaching consequences and can directly affect India's economy march.[58]

Divakar is closely associated with the Evangelical Lutheran Church, and pushes the official church policies dispatched from European headquarters. There are many contradictions in his policies. He rejects B.R. Ambedkar's position as expressed in the Indian Constitution, projecting instead the Christian agenda to convert Dalits to Christianity. At the same time, he demands the Indian government to give caste-based quota benefits even after someone is converted to Christianity, even though the massive foreign funds from the church remain allocated strictly to Christians only.[59]

Another human rights group analyzed the situation and concluded that NCDHR's media coverage and hype had backfired and not helped the Dalit cause. The reasons for this failure were explained as follows:

Other victims of caste discrimination such as the Buraku were completely sidelined. The prominence of the Dalits over other underprivileged communities suffering caste discrimination gave rise to the perception that caste discrimination is an India-specific issue. . . . Moreover, NCDHR's sectarian approach to the campaigning on Dalit rights did not go down well within the broader NGO community. The approach of the delegation of the Holy See to the Indian governmental delegation in Durban on the caste issue only confirmed the Government of India's worst fears about the caste issue being an 'evangelical Christian agenda'. This, and the overwhelming visible presence of one religious persuasion in the NCDHR delegation, did not help the Dalit cause.[60]

In 2006, NCDHR once again went against the official stand of the Indian government, and played a major role in developing a report on India's caste problems for the Commission for the Eradication of Racial Discrimination (CERD).[61] CERD is the body that administers an international convention on race discrimination that dates back to 1965, with India as a signatory.[62] This was followed by another shadow report submitted to CERD in 2007. In 2008, based on these shadow reports, Lutheran World Federation, NCDHR and IDSN submitted a report titled 'Caste Based Discrimination in India', to Universal Periodic Review committee set up by UN.[63] Their march against India gains momentum year after year in one international forum after another.

National Federation of Dalit Women (NFDW)

The National Federation of Dalit Women was set up in 1995 under the leadership of Ruth Manorama. Prior to this, she had participated in a study comparing African Americans in the US and Dalits in India, by examining the lives of Black women and Dalit women. She also represented the issues facing Dalit women at the Fourth UN World Conference on Women in Beijing in 1995. She has been granted an honorary doctorate by the Academy of Ecumenical Indian Theology and Church Administration 'for the distinguished contribution made to church and society.'[64]

Her alleged proximity to Sri Lankan Tamil separatist groups caused a controversy in 2000.[65] At the 2001 Durban conference, she became a prominent voice against the Indian government delegates and was part of the Dalit caucus created by IDSN.[66] In spite of all this controversy, her advocacy earned her a place among the group of one thousand women nominated for a Nobel Peace Prize in 2005, and she was awarded a 'Right Livelihood Award', sometimes called 'the alternate Nobel prize'. She is a member of the Dalit Task Force of the National Council of Churches in India.[67] She personally petitioned the European parliament for to use economic and political leverage against India 'in matters of trade, developmental programmes or political dialogue'.[68]

NFDW also provides regular input to the periodic reports that IDSN submits to various UN bodies and European governmental agencies.[69]

Dalit Panchayat + Dalitology + Dalit Theology → Dalitstan

Among the representatives attending the 2009 Bangkok conference, was an Indian Dalit activist, Dr Jyothi Raj, who along with her husband runs a Dalit organization called Rural Education for Development Society (REDS). Dr Raj spoke at the conference about the Dalit Panchayat Movement. This movement was based on what she described as 'Dalitology', which, Christians feel is complementary to Christian Dalit theology.[70] It will be useful here to see in some detail what Dalitology is and why Christian Dalit theology finds a complement in it.

Dalitology was developed by Jyothi Raj and her husband. It uses the same fabrications as Dravidian race theories, which we examined in Chapters Six and Seven. Dalitology traces the origin of the caste system to 'Aryan conquerors' who 'were divided by differences of blood and racial ancestry from the conquered tribes of India,'[71] and it expounds an elaborate conspiracy theory along with Afro-Dalit kinship:

The Black people of Africa, the *adivasis* of Asia and the Dalit people were not organized on caste basis. Why then did the Aryans bring caste system into India? It is because they found that this system was one of the best tools for them to keep the society in eternal division and through that division to perpetuate their hegemony in the larger society.[72]

Mahatma Gandhi's use of the word Harijan is seen as a cunning ploy to degrade Dalits:

Harijan means the people of God. It is a high-sounding word. But the real meaning is different from what it sounds like. Its meaning is that the Dalit children are born out of temple prostitution, the Devadasi system. They do not know the name of their fathers. Nor will the mothers be able to remember the name of the true father as many Brahmins, Kshatriyas, Vaishyas and others prostitute the Dalit women in the temple. Since the Dalit children are born out of the sexual act that takes place in the temple and since they do not know to which caste they belong and since they do not have a caste they must be called the children of God, Hari Jan, Harijan. It was in this highly derisive meaning that this name was given to the Dalit people.[73]

After giving such a perverted twist to Gandhi's term 'Harijan', Dalitology's own vision for the emancipation of Dalits is 'Dalitstan', which is a plan to break India into several parts, including a separate Dalit nation-state. In the establishment of Dalitstan, they explained to the Bangkok conference that the Dalit Panchayat 'will decide the beneficiaries of government development programmes and that it will form, train and support the Black Army'.[74]

The vision for Dalitstan combines a fascist hatred for the Hindus, with a blueprint to destroy Indian democracy, balkanize it along caste lines, and set up a Maoist government. It explains its vision clearly:

The Brahmin community and all those who have oppressed the Dalits by subscribing to Brahminism will be made to tender a public apology. They will have to surrender all the resources that they have misappropriated from the indigenous people to the Supreme Council of Dalitstan, which will redistribute these resources to communities. . . . Each community in Dalitstan will have the freedom to govern itself internally without interference from the Supreme Council of Dalitstan provided they eschew all mechanisms and instruments of dominance on other communities. Dalitstan will be governed by communitarian democracy. There will be no elections in Dalitstan. . . .[75]

In its blueprint for totalitarianism, Dalitstan will declare the labor of Dalits as a 'national resource', no longer owned by the individual Dalits, but subject to 'appropriate protective and promotional measures' by the state.[76]

All ancient Hindu temples would be converted in Dalitstan 'into universities, hospitals or monuments' and no longer serve as 'symbols of pride and arrogance'.[77]

It is not a coincidence that organizations which promote such totalitarian anti-democratic ideologies and take an anti-India stand in the name of Dalit liberation, are precisely the ones selected by WCC and LWF and projected internationally as the bearers of India's Dalit movement.

Network of Academic Dalit Studies

IDSN sponsors and coordinates Dalit studies across a network of foreign and Indian institutions and uses this to supply academic work that backs up its political activism.

Indian Institute of Dalit Studies

The Indian Institute of Dalit Studies (IIDS)[78] was created in New Delhi using an initial grant of USD 300,000 from the Ford Foundation.[79] The India head, who runs three of the nine institutes comprising the network, is a Jesuit, Martin Macwan of NCDHR. The Indian affiliates of IIDS are mainly Christian organizations, often with Hindu names but controlled by Christians. The foreign affiliates are mainly Christian transnational organizations,[80] as well as the Danish Foreign Ministry.

Trustees of IIDS provide input to DSN-UK for lobbying with labor MPs in the UK.[81] IIDS has prepared a report on atrocities against Dalits in India and presented it to the UN Special Rapporteur when she was on her IDSN-funded visit to India.[82] Encouraged by this international role, IIDS took up an ambitious research project 'to generate new knowledge and documentation on caste-based discrimination in countries where research and documentation on the subject had been limited'.[83] This involved expansion of IIDS into Nepal, Pakistan, Bangladesh and Sri Lanka, funded by the Danish government. The reports are already producing new activism in those countries as a way to further fracture the entire subcontinent.

IIDS has turned itself into a think-tank producing sponsored research for international clients. For example, it has a project to produce a training manual for Christian Aid to empower the poor against the rest of India and to Christianize them.[84] Another project is to provide the German Lutheran church with plans to target specific groups in India.[85]

It has also succeeded in attracting secular clients by disguising its Christian foundations. One such example is its socio-economic work for International Food Policy Research Institute in Washington. Some affiliates do not want to know the Christian fundamentalism at IIDS, because it fits their own image before the public as being left-wing. For instance, Smita Narula, a faculty director of the Center for Human Rights and Global Justice at New York University's School of Law, is one of the foreign associates of IIDS.[86] She collaborates with Martin Macwan in presenting a dismal picture of India's human rights at international conferences.[87] She also participated in the DFN briefing before the US Congress, under a resolution introduced by right-wing Trent Franks (who is on the DFN board), asking the US government to pressure India on caste discrimination.[88] Yet, it is important for her to be seen as a left-winger who hates the right-wing.

IIDS organized a three-day workshop in collaboration with the Princeton University to provide its research methodology for studying discrimination in urban labor markets in India.[89] Other western universities which are among its clients include department of religion, Denmark University; department of social anthropology, University of Stockholm; City University of New York; and the Institute of African American Research, University of North Carolina.[90]

Swedish South Asian Studies Network (SASNet)

The Swedish South Asian Studies Network (SASNet) has been effectively turned into IDSN's organ. Stockholm Anthropological Research on India (SARI) is part of SASNet's program to construct divisive frameworks for exploiting conflicts within India. One of the researchers at this well-funded program, Eva-Maria Hardtmann, is also listed as an academician of IIDS.[91] Among her research topics, is 'Our Fury is Burning – Local Practice and Global Connections in the Dalit Movement'. According to its abstract:

> This study focuses on the cultural discourses as well as the organizational aspects within the contemporary Dalit movement, so as to examine processes related to identity formation. . . . It will also be shown how the Dalit activists have come to share a tacit knowledge regarding their common main conflict with 'Hindus' and 'Hindu values'.[92]

The 'processes related to identity formation' refer to Hartdmann's intervention, as she makes clear that she wants to channel Dalit identity toward Christianity in subtle ways. For example, she privileges V.T. Rajshekar's derogatory view of Gandhi because Gandhi rejected conversion to Christianity as a solution.[93] Hardtmann also participated in a 2006 academic discussion hosted by SASNet.[94] Its balkanization agenda was masked as championing 'divergent images of today's India'. The Dalit Solidarity Network of Sweden opened the discussion and there was a report, 'No Escape – Caste Discrimination in the UK', which was used to stereotype the UK Indian population as casteist.[95]

Peter B. Andersen, from the Department of Cross-Cultural and Regional Studies, University of Copenhagen, is a research associate at IIDS who works on Christian mission studies.[96] In 2007, he spoke on 'TELC (Tamil Evangelical Lutheran Church) among Catholics, Pentecostals and Hindus'. In the same meeting, the main speaker was Professor Robert Eric Frykenberg from the University of Wisconsin, Madison, who presented papers on 'Mission and mission archive related research in India', and 'Hindutva as a political religion'.[97]

The whole exercise looks more like scouting for information from the enemy territory before launching an attack, rather than an academic exercise aimed at genuinely understanding another culture and society.

IDSN also organized seminars in Sweden, in which its trustee, Aloysius Irudayam, lectured on topics such as 'Dalit women, the most oppressed'. Another Stockholm University seminar was organized in collaboration with Sten Widmalm, assistant professor of political science at Uppsala University, who studies village governance in India.[98] In 2007, students from a Catholic institution in India, called Nirmala Niketan, collaborated with IDSN to organize a rally on the birth anniversary of Dr Ambedkar,[99] disguising the fact that IDSN has allied itself against the Indian constitution written by Ambedkar.

Thus IDSN has become a powerful nexus forging alliances between South Asian Studies scholars and its own Indian affiliates. Apart from IDSN, there are also other evangelical institutions with Dalit banners, acting as intelligence-gathering operations for western clients whose interests combine academic, evangelical and political motives.

Tamil Nadu Theological Seminary

Hugo Gorringe, a sociologist from the University of Edinburgh, works in South India on 'the socio-political mobilization of Dalits'. He thanks Tamil Nadu Theological Seminary for helping him forge intimate bonds with Dalits. 'Apart from treating me like royalty, they introduced me to Dalit movements and activists in the northern parts of the state that I would have otherwise neglected'.[100] The Dalit Resource Centre, which hosted him at the seminary, has as its main objective to compile information about the activities of various Dalit movements in India.[101]

Tamil Nadu Theological Seminary serves as a nodal agency to coordinate various transnational evangelical organizations and uses its impressive database to map Dalit issues on to a Christian framework. For example, it conducts workshops for training youth leaders; these workshops are are organized by Student Christian Movement and sponsored by the World Council of Churches. The goal of such 'empowerment workshops' is to stir up passion among young students and thereby channel them into various groups working for spreading Christianity in India.[102] The 'empowered youth' are expected to dance to the tune of the transnational forces which control the purse strings, foreign travel opportunities, prestigious appointments, and, of course, the theological interpretation of social and political life. The welfare of the downtrodden is a convenient headline to underwrite all this.

Gurukul Lutheran Theological College and Research Institute, Chennai

Founded in 1931 and upgraded in 1953, this institute is affiliated to the notorious Serampore College, which was once used to facilitate British colonial rule.[103] It has a department of Dalit Theology, whose head, M. Azariah, was the first person to represent Dalit concerns in the General Assembly of the World Council of Churches in 1983. Azariah was one of the earliest Indian Christians to raise the issue of Dalits in an international Christian forum like WCC and was initially criticized by fellow Indian Christian delegates for raising 'internal Indian matters' in a foreign assembly.[104] He has also participated in the Durban conference.[105]

Azariah supplied much of the data to Adrian Bird's PhD thesis on Dalit Theology at University of Edinburgh, which concludes that the Dalit 'exodus from Hinduism' is 'a liberating experience'.[106] Azariah, a contributor to *Dalit Voice,* argues that Hindu doctrines imprison the Dalits. M.M. Thomas is another admirer of *Dalit Voice* and supplies theology to support it. It is this kind of academic study of Hinduism that is frequently being carried out by Indians, with funding by foreign institutions. The output is geared to supply the lobbying networks in the West.

The Gurukul College also provides the locus from which foreign evangelical educational institutes study various targeted Indian communities. An example is the thesis by Ginda P. Harahap, submitted for the Doctor of Ministry degree in Congregational Mission and

Leadership at Luther Seminary in the USA. The thesis examines the strategic role of Gurukul College as an example of 'how the Indian Lutheran churches have responded to the challenges of religious plurality and Hindu fundamentalism', by taking advantage of its 'mission work among the poor and marginalized Dalits and Tribals'.[107] Thus, Gurukul also acts as a center for gathering intelligence for evangelical programs against Indian traditions.

In 2006, the German ambassador to India presided at the 300th anniversary of the arrival of the Lutheran missionaries in India, and the German consul-general was the guest of honor in 2008. The German connection got a further boost with a Memorandum of Understanding between Gurukul and the Goorg-August University, Gottingen.[108] Such links propagate the 'Dalit theology' as expressed in the pages of the *Dalit Voice*, sharing common ground with Hitler admirers, Holocaust deniers, and assorted conspiracy theorists.[109]

The institution also has a social development dimension.[110] The Centre For Research on New International Economic Order (CReNIEO) was established in 1979 at Gurukul College as a secular-sounding developmental NGO. From the academic year of 1998 onwards, there has been a student and staff exchange program between Gurukul, CReNIEO and the Finnish Lutheran church. CReNIEO also participates in programs with Finnish and Canadian Lutheran churches.[111]

Gurukul is an important partner in the post-graduate degree program in Contextual and Cross Cultural Theology, developed by the Faculty of Theology, Free University, Amsterdam, whose benign-sounding purpose is 'to harvest the richness of cross-cultural theological encounter'.[112] As a part of this, it sends a master's degree-level student to Amsterdam each year for advanced studies. Such links are not coincidental. Dr Maarten Bavinck of University of Amsterdam did his PhD dissertation on 'One sea, three contenders: Legal pluralism in the inshore fisheries of the Coromandel Coast, India'.[113] An active member of Dominicus Church, he has become positioned as an international authority on south Asian fisheries communities, and leads studies in folk law and rights of Indian coastal communities. In 2009, Bavinck got appointed as president of

Commission on Legal Pluralism, an International committee affiliated with the International Association of Legal Science (IALS). It acts as a powerful middleman between various western institutions and local NGOs, like the movement for the recognition of indigenous people's rights.[114] This helps not only the Church to position the proselytizing activities on the coastline of Tamil Nadu, but also allows the West to control the development activites as well as the local communities at the strategically important coastline of India. The Catholic Church has a powerful political grip among the Christian fishermen in South India. It is very active in politics, using Latin American liberation theology models, which European clergymen stationed in India have taught to the Indian Christian leaders.[115] All this is done in the guise of 'development'.

But a different reality is reported by one investigator who writes, 'The Catholic Church's role at the center of coastal social organizations is setting the fishing villages apart from both agrarian and urban communities in the district where competing institutional forces circumscribe the power of religious institutions'.[116] This has made the fishermen community, strategically placed along the long sea border of India, vulnerable to the pulls of foreign forces.

Individual Scholars Propagating Dalit Separatism

Many individual scholars who are strategically placed in policy-making institutes of European states or Indian academic institutions also facilitate this divisive knowledge development and deployment. They provide a view of India as a nation that is embracing fascism and racism. They project all Indian social reformers, including Mahatma Gandhi, as supporters of an oppressive social system. Racist ideologies or motives are attributed to every Indian who is patriotic, while enlightened humanism is attributed to those who interpret Indian society racially or who promoted secessionism. Christophe Jaffrelot and Gail Omvedt are examples of scholars whose work shows this pattern. This process has been depicted in Fig 17.2.

Fig 17.2 Convergence of the Worldviews of Two Scholars in Deconstrcution of India

Worldview of **Christophe Jaffrelot**	Worldview of **Gail Omvedt**
Director, Center for International Studies and Research (CERI), France	Collaborates in projects of Christian Dalit activists like Martin Macwan of IIDS
Hindu reform movements deficient in eradicating caste	Symbols of independence struggle as 'high-caste symbols'
Mahatma Gandhi compromised to orthodoxy	Mahatma Gandhi's *Ram Rajya* as racial theory
Dravidian movement and Phule's racial interpretation projected as positive	Dravidian movement should be expanded all over India
Hindu nationalist policy as racist	Caste should be equivalent to race; advocacy during Durban 2001

Conclusion: Indian culture and spirituality have innate racist elements and are deficient to empower Dalits

Christophe Jaffrelot

Christophe Jaffrelot, the director of Center for International Studies and Research (CERI), is a French scholar studying the political issues of South Asia. He sees British colonialism as an emancipating force for the depressed sections of India, stating that, 'the emancipation of the lower castes was promoted through a system of positive discrimination that the British had devised'.[117]

Jaffrelot consistently portrays Hinduism and Hindu social leaders, including Mahatma Gandhi, as caste-biased. Gandhi is portrayed as someone who compromised himself in his fight against untouchability and backtracked to an orthodox Hindu identity. Jaffrelot writes:

> In 1924 the Dalits of Vaikham in the state of Travancore launched a satyagraha to gain access to a local temple, or at least to use the road adjacent to the temple. Gandhi supported this mobilisation and went to Vaikham, but his dialogue with the local priests did not bear fruit. The latter rejected all his compromise proposals and their arguments prompted him to re-examine his position about Untouchability . . . He lost interest in the Vaikham movement and in various public meetings later declared himself to be a sanatanist, that is a follower of the Sanatana Dharma, the 'eternal religion' according to the orthodox Hindus.[118]

This account is totally fabricated, because in actuality Gandhi had declared himself a 'Sanatani Hindu' *before* the commencement of Vaikham Satyagraha.[119] Gandhi was trying (with considerable success) to appropriate the terms *sanatana dharma* and *varnashrama* from the orthodoxy and turn these into a more egalitarian idea. Also, Jafferlot's depiction of Vaikhom Satyagraha as a failure and a dampener of the spirit of the social equality movement is an erroneous account. S.N. Sadasivan, the noted historian of Kerala, writes:

> The satyagraha was a triumph of the progressive forces, a spontaneous humanistic upsurge, a great wave of social resurgence and a whirlwind that sounded the final warning to the perverse and obstinate orthodoxy all over India to voluntarily put an end to its age-long repression. . . . Vaikhom was the biggest and longest mass movement ever organized in India for social freedom and members of all communities promptly responded to the appeal . . . to participate in it. [120]

He further points out that, contrary to Jaffrelot's allegations, instead of waning, the movement actually spread to other temple towns in Kerala and Dalit Hindus walked the temple roads in different holy places. In 1927, Gandhi also returned to Kerala and reminded the government of its promises. Ultimately the government relented and recognized the right of every individual to freely use the roads in the vicinity of the temples, irrespective of any consideration of birth.[121]

Jaffrelot measures the positive qualities of any social reformer by how much he distanced himself from Hindu society. Thus, Jotiba Govindrao Phule (1827–90) is praised for avoiding 'the traps of Sanskritisation by endowing the low castes with an alternative value system. For the first time, they were presented as ethnic groups which had inherited the legacy of an antiquarian golden age and whose culture was therefore distinct from that of the wider Hindu society'.[122] In other words, Phule's divisive interpretation of Indian society earns him a special place in Jaffrelot's scheme. Jaffrelot also praises Phule's fascination with Christianity and Jesus:

> For Phule, Jesus Christ epitomises equality and fraternity. He also regards him as the spokesman for the poor. . . . Through the vernacularisation of Christian values and symbols, Phule endowed people with a new, positive identity.[123]

While Jaffrelot resorts to convoluted ways to invent racism in the Hindu polity, he develops a blind eye to the racism prevalent in the forging of Dravidian identity. He eulogizes E.V. Ramasami as an 'egalitarian in a western individualist vein'.[124] Jaffrelot completely glosses over the fact that *Kudi Arasu*, the official journal of Ramasami's movement, praises Hitler explicitly and draws parallels between Jews and Brahmins. *Kudi Arasu* quotes at length Hitler's reasons for despising Jews, as found in *Mein Kampf* and how he vowed to purge alleged Jewish dominance in the German society. It admiringly describes how Hitler accomplished his avowed promise of ending Jewish dominance in Germany, and it warns that the Brahmins of South India pose the same danger as the Jews of pre-Nazi Germany.[125] He praises the racist Afro-Dravidianism of Periyar as 'an explicitly ethnic conception of the low castes' identity'. He compares their situation to that of the blacks in South Africa.

Jaffrelot is considered by Western institutions as an authority on the Hindu nationalist movement. His work *The Hindu Nationalist Movement in India* was published by Columbia University Press in 1996. He consistently portrays Hindu nationalism as ethnic nationalism,[126] and calls it a 'special kind of racism'.[127] His work was extensively quoted in the atrocity literature that flooded the western media in the aftermath of Gujarat 'as the authoritative study of [Hindu] groups'.[128] Jaffrelot also has strong influence in the foreign policy of France with regard to India. CERI, where he works, is a think-tank which works closely with CAP, the policy planning unit of the French foreign ministry.[129]

Gail Omvedt: Bringing Dravidian and Dalit Together

Among the academicians manipulatively shaping Dalit Studies, Gail Omvedt occupies a very important place. She is a sociologist from the University of California at Berkeley, and became an Indian citizen in 1983. She combines nineteenth-century colonial categories with Marxist subaltern constructions, seeing Indian culture as a creation by the upper castes to subjugate the lower castes for thousands of years. Anything that united Indians in their fight against colonialism is merely 'high-caste symbols'.[130] She attributes the attitudes of Aryan supremacy to even Mahatma Gandhi, saying that he 'saw Aryans as his ancestors. As against what he saw as the evils of industrialism, he wanted to go back to an idealised, harmonious village society in which tradition ruled. This he called Ram Rajya'.[131]

Omvedt chastises middle-class Dalits when they successfully integrate themselves with the rest of Indian society, and speculates that they are ashamed of their roots.[132] Thus, Omvedt is resurrecting the British colonial project of Lord Risley of 'detaching considerable masses of non-Aryans from the general body of Hindus'.[133] Additionally, she tries to link Hinduism with racism by claiming that 'people are seen as somehow biologically inferior and socially dangerous'.[134]

She tries to bring ideological coherence to the contradictory streams of the Dalit and Dravidian movements.[135] Omvedt sees the Dravidian movement's confinement to Tamil identity as a failure. Instead, she wants to identify a Dravidian substratum throughout India. She states as 'a fact' that 'the Dravidian (or Tamil)-speaking Indus civilisation was based in Northwest India' and she sees 'evidence everywhere of the non-Aryan (usually Dravidian, sometimes Austro-Asiatic or other) origin of popular religious cults and cultural practices throughout India'.[136] Based on these 'facts', she is trying to start movements that would negate what she calls 'the Vedic-Aryan heritage'. Her academic work has the explicit purpose to demonize Indian culture and legitimize fragmentation and insurgencies throughout India.

In 2001 at Durban, she joined Christian advocates in the campaign for equating caste with race. The prominent Indian sociologist Andre Béteille called these efforts 'politically mischievous' and 'worse, scientifically nonsense'.[137] Gail Omvedt responded by writing a two-part article titled 'Caste, Race and Sociologists', where she relied exclusively on the Aryan race theory used by colonial Indologists to interpret the caste system.[138] Despite her much flaunted admiration for Ambedkar and use of Ambedkar as a popular brand, there is not a single quotation cited from him, even though he had written voluminously on this specific subject. This is so beacuse citing Ambedkar would contradict her own position, as Ambedkar rejected the Aryan invasion theory categorically.

Omvedt also devalues works of contemporary scholars like McKim Marriott, Ronald Inden and Nicholas Dirks, who show the role of British colonialism in making the caste hierarchy rigid; she sees these ideas as 'pleasing to the most ardent advocate of Hindutva'.[139]

While she argues against the Indian state and criticizes Indian industrialists, she favors globalization of the Indian economy in ways that would make India subservient to the West. Her former leftist colleagues analyzing her stand on globalization, find a striking continuity in her writings. They point out how she puts into the mouths of Dalits words of appreciation for British rule. According to these critics:

> Such a position authorizes Omvedt's recent pro-liberalization stance: neo-colonialism and economic dependency are abstract, academic concepts irrelevant to the lives of the peasant masses.[140]

Omvedt works with evangelical activists using Dalit fronts. While DFN in the United States and IDSN in Europe are trying to control international funding to India using the Dalit card, she, along with Christian activist Martin Macwan and his IIDS colleague Sukhadeo Thorat, have published in 2009 a book titled *Social Justice Philanthropy: Approaches and Strategies of Funding Organizations*. This book aims to give advice to funding agencies worldwide to give their money in support of her ideology of caste divisiveness.[141]

The Culmination

Besides the few organizations and individuals profiled in this chapter, there are numerous others. For instance, in 2008, Vishal Arora, a member of BosNewsLife, a central European Christian news network, presented a paper at the Center on Religion and Politics in Washington.[142] This paper portrayed Hinduism as being opposed to Dalit rights, and Christian political groups as fighting for them. The laws in various Indian states to curtail fraudulent religious conversions were depicted by Arora as 'anti-conversion' laws. His paper provided atrocity statistics and described the martyrdom of St Thomas (at the hands of Hindus) as the beginning of Christianity in India.[143] He described a number of evangelical and missionary organizations as 'actively involved in the area of religious freedom'.[144]

> All these institutions and individuals are part of a finely choreographed international movement that supports European agencies to internationalize the caste problem through every available means. According to a 2009 story in *The Times of India*, Indian officials have discovered that India is fighting back a renewed onslaught from 'European countries who want to nail India on the charge that the caste system is a form of racism' and that the 'Scandinavian countries have resurrected their stand on the caste system.' Indian officials have explained the inherent dangers this brings to the stability of the region, as 'every caste in India would be a different race.'[145]

18

India's Christian Umma

'The advent of Christian broadcasting in India, transnational as well as local channels, offers the space for identification with a "Christian Umma" far beyond the boundaries of the territorialized nation-state.'
— Pradip Ninan Thomas, Indian Christian scholar[1]

We have seen how foreign scholarship has been used to manipulate Indian identities for almost two centuries, and how recent international interventions strengthen various separatist groups. The inflow of very large sums of foreign money through Christian evangelical channels into the impoverished regions of India has enabled churches and related missions to mushroom. Often, the new churches get into combat against the local cultures and traditions, which are depicted as evil in the minds of the new converts. For example, in the Kanyakumari district of Tamil Nadu, such intense tactics have already created a Christian majority and now Hindus are being pressured against the public celebration or display of their traditions and symbols. New converts are being recruited through propaganda that would be considered hate literature in other pluralistic societies. Hindu shrines are often violently destroyed and local village names are changed to Christian names. Tribal spiritual and healing systems are being made extinct, and replaced with foreign substitutes or else renamed and assimilated into Christianity.

This aggressive conversion often provokes violent reactions from the local populations who try to protect their culture and traditions from the onslaught. Angry natives often turn to Hindu nationalist organizations for support, because the secular groups prefer to stay out or to even help the Christian side. This alignment then gets portrayed by the media as Hindu nationalism fighting Christianity, even though many of the fights erupt when the natives want to protect their historical identities and cultures. The foreign funding of aggressive evangelism has induced this cycle of violence.

The international media backed by evangelical organizations report such episodes widely, but ignore the initial provocations from the evangelists. Such media attention results in the production of atrocity literature. A cottage industry of atrocity literature proliferates among media, academics, and policymakers in the West. The region of conflict is depicted as an area of darkness waiting for the civilized world to intervene. This stimulates more funding from the West for the evangelical cause, and the cycle perpetuates.

Fig 18.1 offers an overview of these processes, which will be described in greater detail.

Fig 18.1 Creating a Spiral of Violence

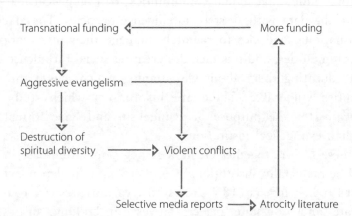

Financing and Building Institutions

This chapter will show that transnational evangelical organizations have devised ambitious plans for evangelizing in India, using secular concepts like development. Organizations such as World Vision, which have partnered with Western intelligence agencies, have invested an enormous amount of financial capital to create huge infrastructure networks across India. Government assistance from the West, such as USAID funding, is also being channeled through these evangelical institutions.

Media

Evangelical satellite TV channels have mushroomed in India to spread a fundamentalist version of Christianity that emotionally binds the masses to the US Christian Right. We will show that apart from such blatantly evangelical channels, Christian journalists have systematically infiltrated India's secular media, from where they are deployed by transnational Christian media networks (like Gegrapha and Boslife) to provide atrocity literature on India to the world.

Intelligence

Elaborate anthropological studies of Indian communities are being conducted by large-scale projects, like Project Joshua based in Denver. They profile individual Indian communities for evangelical marketing and share the data with Western intelligence agencies. They facilitate the transnational agencies to remotely manage their interventions in Indian communities, and this includes creating social turbulence in the guise of educating them about Christianity, which makes the target communities vulnerable. There are institutions which study India academically for the purpose of evangelism and have formal links with Indian evangelical institutions.

All these factors together create a strong population-base in India that will be financially, institutionally and emotionally dependent upon the West's right-wing. Fig 18.2 shows how various western agencies—both state and non-state players—invest in building institutional infrastructural logistics in India, for effective control at social and political levels.

Fig 18.2 Institution Building in India for Transnational Control and Intervention

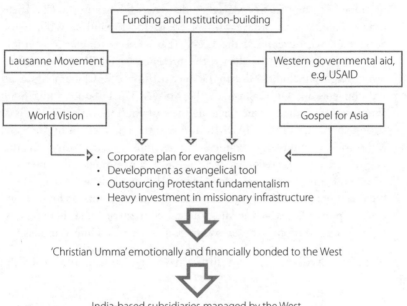

'Christian Umma' emotionally and financially bonded to the West

India-based subsidiaries managed by the West

US-based Expansion of Indian Christianity

A base for Western domination is being effectively constructed within India through evangelical organizations. The goal is to spread a fundamentalist kind of Christianity and create a population of believers with strong emotional bonding and dependence on the West. The Christian Right in the United States is particularly active and ambitious in this regard.

The founding fathers of India's constitution created laws to protect the faith of indigenous communities against evangelical onslaught. But evangelical forces within and outside India coordinate their efforts to try to remove the laws prohibiting abusive proselytization in sensitive border-states like Arunachal Pradesh and Himachal Pradesh, and elsewhere in India.

Pradip Ninan Thomas, a journalism and communication professor from the University of Queensland in Australia, explains how the US nexus has infiltrated deeply into Tamil Nadu politics:

> While Pat Robertson, Paul Crouch and others are not involved directly in influencing politics in India, they do act as lobbies in the US. Their Indian counterparts are very involved in local politics. While Ezra Sarguman, who organized the Every Tribe, Every Tongue convention is associated with DMK (hence the presence of DMK and Congress heavyweights including Indian Finance Minister P. Chidambaram at the convention), Dr Prakash of the SISWA Trust (South India Soul Winners Association) which acts as the distribution arm of TBN, is a strong supporter of the AIADMK and was the chairperson of the State Minorities Commission. Political connections are necessary for the permission to stage religious crusades and conventions by evangelists such as Benny Hinn, who is opposed by sections in India. These organizations in turn act as a conduit for vast amounts of funds from USA in particular, which in the political context of India, is necessary for the organization of mega-events such as Benny Hinn crusades.[2]

Next, we will feature an illustrative list of the major US-based players.[3]

Vishal Mangalwadi: India's Pat Robertson

Vishal Mangalwadi is an Indian American evangelist with a strikingly Eurocentric message of Christianity. He claims that colonialism under the British was very good for India, and has written a book specifically praising one of the nastiest evangelists of the British colonial era, William Carey.[4] His thesis is that India's suffering has been caused by its heathenism. India is one of the societies which has 'looked to many local and regional gods', or have 'postulated that life's goal is to achieve oneness with the absolute nothingness that constitutes ultimate reality', or have somehow got lost in 'esoteric philosophic and religious mysteries'. On the other hand, 'the only civilization that has looked largely to the Bible for its inspiration, the West, has been able to conquer human cruelty, hopelessness and degradation', and this should become the role model for all Indians. He laments that the West has become complacent in its success, forgetting that the Bible was 'the book that catapulted the West to the forefront of world economics, politics, and culture'.[5]

Mangalwadi claims to prove colonial evangelism as a noble 'conspiracy to reform colonial rule and to bless India'. His interpretation of history is that, while India's independence resulted from Mahatma Gandhi's struggle, India's freedom is actually the fruit produced by the Gospel of Jesus Christ. The transformation of India into a free and modern nation was a grand experiment that was envisioned and carried on by leaders who were driven by a Biblical worldview. These great leaders, according to him, were the British evangelists! In other words, the British evangelists should be considered the true founding fathers of India.

He also considers the fame of Gandhian non-violence as something false which has been 'fictionalized in the film'.[6] He equates all Hinduism with Hindutva, all Hindutva with 'cultural nationalism' and 'cultural fascism'. *Indian democracy has failed*, he charges, and the reason is that it did not use the Bible as its moral compass. He attacks yoga in a seemingly objective and intellectual way, giving what most Westerners would regard as a very thoughtful and balanced analysis of various schools of yoga and Hinduism.[7] But his conclusions are biased and outrageous. For instance, he asserts that Tantra is unapologetic about using insanity to reach Reality. It considers that creation itself is divine insanity; therefore, sanity has to be left outside the temple of God.

Since he starts from the premise that Hinduism is a delusion, his analysis of the various gurus and paths leads him to these two possibilities: 'The question is, are they deluded because of the drugs, or because they began their spiritual journey with a mistaken map of reality, a false worldview?' The foundational problem with Hinduism is moral, which only the Bible can solve, he insists. It is not solvable by philosophy or yogic effort. The first paragraph in the excerpt below summarizes his diagnosis that Indian culture suffers due to Hinduism, and the next one summarizes his solution according to the Bible:

> The Indian philosophical tradition, in spite of all its brilliance, could not produce a culture that recognized human rights and the intrinsic worth of the individual. Nor could yogic monism give to Indian

society a framework for moral absolutes, a strong sense of right and wrong, fair and unfair. Yogic exercises indeed gave flexibility to our bodies but unfortunately the yogic philosophy gave too much flexibility to our morals – making us [i.e. Indians] one of the most corrupt nations in the world.

. . .

The Bible teaches that the human problem is *moral*, rather than biological or metaphysical. God created human beings good. (Would you expect anything different from an almighty Creator?) Our first parents [Adam and Eve] chose to disobey God and thereby became sinners. That trait has been transmitted to us all . . . From childhood our tendency is towards evil . . . Our central problem, according to the Bible is that we are sinners. We need a divine Savior who will forgive our sins and transform our hearts – the core of our being.[8]

Mangalwadi further claims that Indian religion was originally barbaric before the civilizing influence of Christianity through the British Empire. He insists that the removal of the British Empire made India slip back into barbarism:

But now that the Christian influence has diminished in India, the old tantric cult is coming back openly on the surface. There are around fifty-two known centers in India where tantra is taught and practiced. In its crudest forms, it includes worship of sex organs, sex orgies which include drinking of blood and human semen, black magic, human sacrifice and contact with evil spirits through dead and rotting bodies in cremation grounds, etc.[9]

His lectures and papers are presented in major theological centers throughout the world. He is also very active in religious politics in India using US evangelical and academic support.[10] Earlier, he had also dabbled with secular politics and reached positions of power. In the mid 1990s, he was put in charge overseeing agricultural reform in the national headquarters of Janata Dal, then India's ruling party.[11] Then he started a 'rural development' Christian organization in Madhya Pradesh, founded a theological research institute in Delhi, and participated in various minority political parties in India over several decades. Now he brings all this expertise to develop 'educational resources for South Asia' on American campuses, as well as 'Hindu Studies' expertise for American seminaries.[12]

Mangalwadi is widely quoted by Christian theologians across the denominations as the authority to 'prove' that Hinduism is inferior to Christianity. For example, one website cites his authority to claim that Hindus have 'genuine difficulty in understanding Christian charity because Hinduism does not have a similar tradition'.[13]

His writings extensively discuss communal civil wars and caste wars in India. In the wake of recent communal violence in Orissa after Maoist-Christian assailants killed an eighty year old Hindu monk, Mangalwadi wrote a long article in a French Christian magazine *Journal Chretien*. He explained how Christians and Maoists coming together could create a new power structure in the mineral-rich eastern state of Orissa:

> Pro-Christian Maoists in Orissa have already warned a number of specific Hindu leaders responsible for anti-Christian violence, that they are next on their hit list. A few hundred 'Christian-Maoist' guerillas will change the power-equation in Orissa.[14]

He informs his readers with obvious delight that 'at least one good American Christian (presumably, unaware of the Christian-Maoist nexus) has asked his Congressman if he should help Christians in Orissa buy guns.' Blaming India's ills on 'Hinduism's gods that require appeasement', he mourns that Hindus have corrupted the 'clean institutions built up by British Christians'. A staunch opponent of secularism, he states:

> Secular democracy has failed but there is no forum in India that teaches biblical economic and political thought. The Church should be training its youth to reform and run the institutions of justice that Hindu secularism has corrupted. Christ and Mao have come together in Orissa because people oppressed for thousands of years have decided to stand up against the Hindu socio-economic system.[15]

Ravi Zacharias International Ministries

A powerful Christian network across North America, the Ravi Zacharias International Ministries is tightly coupled with Indian groups to provide both political ideology and funding. Some of them aggressively solicit institutional grants, while others rely on personal charitable donations. Some mention their evangelical connections, while others downplay their religious roots. Yet all rely to some extent on white guilt to help them save the downtrodden of India.

One of the examples of such close collaborators of Mangalwadi is Ravi Zacharias.[16] In 1984 he founded the Ravi Zacharias International Ministries, based in the US, with a mission of 'Christian evangelism, apologetics and training'.[17] Zacharias migrated as a young man to North America, where he was nurtured by Billy Graham, among others. He has become one of the most effective churchmen advising theologians, government policymakers and students, with influence worldwide.

He has been positioned as one 'who grew up steeped in Hinduism',[18] though in reality he comes from a family which has been Christian for a few generations.[19] Tracing the origin of Hinduism to an amalgamation of religious beliefs of 'dark-skinned Dravidians in the South, India's original inhabitants' and 'the lighter skinned Aryans with their own mixture of paganism',[20] he promotes Dravidian Christianity by slipping St Thomas in the lineage of south Indian savants from Adi Shankara to Dr Radhakrishnan.[21] Like Mangalwadi, he also blames Eastern religions for all social problems that the developing nations face, while completely disregarding the impact of colonialism. His linking of the high rate of prostitution in Thailand to Buddhism generated resentment and strong criticism from sections of the US.[22]

Zacharias, along with other Indians like right-wing political writer Dinesh D'souza and politician Bobby Jindal, governor of Louisiana, has become important within American Christianity. Although D'souza and Jindal are Catholics, like Zacharias they have also joined forces with politically right-wing Protestant fundamentalists.[23] For example, in 2008, Bobby Jindal ignored protests from scientists and allowed a bill (the Louisiana Science Education Act) which is widely considered 'as opening the door for creationism in the state'.[24]

International Institute of Church Management

One of the most aggressive solicitations of grants for spreading Indian Christianity is illustrated by the India-based International Institute of Church Management,[25] which sends out solicitation letters to American organizations. One of their letters starts out by saying: 'We would like to apply for a grant of US $1 Million for the following projects'. The activities it asks to be funded are listed as follows:

- Buy a church or build a church in India.
- Scholarship for poor students who can't pay theological college fees.
- Conduct Christian leadership seminars in India and abroad; 'leadership' is a common euphemism for spreading negative ideas about Hinduism, as 'freedom' is a euphemism for Christian conversion.
- Orphanage, widows, old aged, disabled and other needy people due to disasters.
- Help for children.
- Library books.
- Counseling to the depressed.
- Expansion of Christian ministerial work in the form of day college, evening college and residential college on Theological studies.
- Translations of Christian books into different Indian languages and dialects.
- Spread of Gospel through online internet, TV, VDC, DVD, radio, books and magazines.
- Reach the unreached people in remote areas.

The solicitation letter mentions a track-record of twenty-five years of ministries catering to hundreds of Christian religious, charitable and social work projects. Such solicitation is a perfectly legitimate enterprise in both India and the US. The Indian evangelical group mentions its affiliations at the top of its letter, and these include: International Institute of Church Management of New York; American Accrediting Association of Theological Institutions, North

Carolina; Apostolic Council of Educational Accountability, Colorado; and National Association for Theological Accredition, Bengaluru. Seemingly innocuous, these institutions actually spread Christian fundamentalism among the Indian masses, including the pseudo-science of creationism.[26]

World Vision

World Vision is one of the largest Christian multinationals and has a very aggressive appetite to convert. Its notoreity is evident from the following description by a Western scholar:

> World Vision has, on a number of occasions, functioned as an intelligence-gathering arm of the US government. In the 1970s World Vision was charged with having collected field data for the CIA in Vietnam. After US troops left the region, World Vision played a major role in the administration of refugee camps. . . . World Vision also became a crucial player in the 'yellow rain' campaign to discredit the Soviet Union. . . . World Vision was drawn into the plot when the US embassy in Bangkok requested that the relief agency send medical samples taken from among refugees who claimed to have been poisoned by 'yellow rain'. According to a missionary working with the refugees in Thailand, World Vision's dependence on US grant money obliged it to comply with requests that refugee blood samples be sent to the US embassy rather than to more impartial investigators.[27]

Its Indian website projects a humanitarian image, describing itself as 'a Christian humanitarian organization working to create lasting change in the lives of children, families and communities living in poverty and injustice'.[28] Its US website (from where most of its money is raised) is more forthright about its mission:

> All applicants for staff positions with World Vision United States will be screened for Christian commitment. The screening process will include: Discussion with the applicant of his/her spiritual journey and relationship with Jesus Christ; Understanding of Christian principles; Understanding and acceptance of World Vision's Statement of Faith and/or The Apostles Creed.[29]

The clout World Vision enjoys today in the US government and as an international charity organization, can be explained by its active participation in intelligence-gathering as well as involvement in destabilizing activities in nations which US perceives as enemies. The *Cambridge History of Latin America* quotes an account of how World Vision operates, which suggests a general pattern:

> World Vision and similar missionary groups operate as external factors, which do not work for the local community respecting its organizational identity and its religiosity. . . . Its ideological mechanism constitutes a powerful tool which tends not only to accompany the process of real subsumption of peasant economies to capitalism, but also provokes a sudden atomization of the community, hastening a massive implantation of capitalist relations of productions in circumstances in which the development of the capitalist system in the country will never be able to absorb the de-peasantized labor force.[30]

Another study on development strategies in south American countries reveals how World Vision had induced social disharmony:

> Between 1979 and 1985, World Vision provided more than $4.7 million in aid to Ecuador. . . . World Vision was also granted Ecuadorian government contracts during the 1980s for reforestation, water, rural electrification and small production projects in Ecuador's Indian highlands. . . . State officials complained that World Vision outbid their programs, conditioned community aid on a monopoly of presence, and even induced villagers to destroy competing projects. . . . Funds were generally given to Indian evangelical congregations or emerging Protestant political associations to distribute. In several cases World Vision employees held simultaneous posts in municipal administration. This led to conflicts between traditional and evangelical sectors of Indian communities, including destruction of project property and even violence along with widespread maladministration of funds.[31]

Even more serious was the conduct of World Vision with relation to Salvadoran refugees:

> World Vision played a role in the deaths of three Salvadoran refugees. The World Vision camp-coordinator took them to the local Honduran

army post, where they were immediately arrested. After a short time, Honduran soldiers entered the camp and arrested two other refugees. World Vision administrators did not report the incident to the other relief agencies. Next day, one of the refugees was released, but three days later the bodies of the three others were found, [who were] shot to death on the Salvadoran side of the border. Aside from these 'bad apples', World Vision—as a policy—maintained records on all Salvadoran aid recipients and filed daily reports by telephone and telex with the World Vision office in Costa Rica. World Vision's extensive information-gathering procedures bolstered charges that the group was collaborating with the CIA.[32]

In Sri Lanka, the activities of World Vision raised a strong alarm. Lt Col A.S. Amarasekera of Sri Lanka writes:

After George Bush Jr became the president of the United States, he made a speech in which he said that he would no longer support the developing third-world countries through their respective governments but would channel American aid through the American Christian Relief Organizations in these countries. World Vision is one such organization. Based on the evidence led at the Presidential Commission of inquiry on Non Governmental Organizations, it was proved beyond reasonable doubt that World Vision was an American funded manipulative Christian evangelical organization, which was surreptitiously trying to convert Sinhalese Buddhists to Christianity through a program of work that was identified as 'The Mustard Seed Project'. After they were thus exposed, they wound up the project and remained dormant for several years but have now recommenced their activities with renewed vigor. [33]

World Vision has a strong presence in India both financially and operationally. Every natural disaster in India provides an occasion for it to deepen its infiltration into the grass roots. Even Indian cricket events have been pressed to raise funds for World Vision.[34] Its record in the past illustrates how a so-called relief organization can act as an intelligence-gathering agency for Western governments, as well as an active agent of geopolitics.

An investigate report published by *Tehelka* revealed the deception and financial clout wielded by World Vision in India. The report begins by contrasting World Vision's public relations face with its actual purpose:

> In India, World Vision (WV) projects itself as a 'Christian relief and development agency with more than foroty years' experience in working with the poorest of the poor in India without respect to race, region, religion, gender or caste.' However, *Tehelka* has in its possession US-based WV Inc.'s financial statement filed before the Internal Revenue Service, wherein, it is classified as a Church ministry. . . .

It gives the following assessment of WV's 'development' reach within India:

> The Confederate of Indian Industries (CII) in its 2003 financial report states that 'the Rural Development Department of the Government of Assam recognized WV India as a leading development agency in the state and has recommended that WV be the choice for receiving bilateral funds. The government has also sought WV's assistance in creating a proposal for US$ 80 million for development work in the state.' The income and expenditure account for the year ended 30 September 2002 shows that its total income was Rs 95.5 crores, which included foreign contribution of Rs 87.8 crores. For an organisation that claims to be only involved in development and relief work, it is quite stealthy about its positioning and exact nature of activities.[35]

Although WV is a major player in the economies of several Indian states, it is very careful to keep its proselytizing disguised. The *Tehelka* report mentions how this is done:

> Though none of the literature published by WV India even mentions its evangelization missions, foreign publications of WV India proudly proclaim its 'spiritual' component. . . . In Mayurbhanj, again in Orissa, World Vision (WV) regularly organises spiritual development programmes as part of its ADP package. The WV report says: 'Opposition to Christian workers and organisations flares up occasionally in this area, generally from those with vested interests in tribal people remaining illiterate and powerless. WV supports local churches by organising leadership courses for pastors and church leaders.' World Vision India is active in Bhil tribal areas and openly

admits its evangelical intentions: 'The Bhil people worship ancestral spirits but also celebrate all the Hindu festivals. Their superstitions about evil spirits make them suspicious of change, which hinders community development. ADP staff live among the Bhil people they work with, gaining the villagers' trust and showing their Christian love for the people by their actions and commitment.'[36]

Many of its donors are well-meaning but naïve about the World Vision activities beyond the social work visible on the surface. For example, Rajdeep Sardesai, editor-in-chief of CNN-IBN, sponsored a child through World Vision with the following words: 'As a family, we sponsor a child. Being able to change a life gives us great satisfaction. We hope others will be inspired to do the same. Nothing gives more joy than empowering those who need it most'.[37]

World Vision's infiltration has given it access to top governmental officials. A typical example in Orissa is Radhakant Nayak, a member of the Indian parliament who has been honored for his 'significant contribution towards uplifting of the Dalits and Tribes'.[38] Recently, Nayak was being suspected in the killing of an eighty year old Hindu monk and a woman monk in Orissa (an incident explained in Chapter Twenty, 'Maoist Red Corridor Through India'). The two had been working among the Dalit tribes to establish educational and medical service without, and they were targeted because they were seen as competitors by the Christian evangelists. *India Today* magazine reports that 'political circles in Bhubaneswar believe that police might lay its hands either on R.K. Nayak or his men'. The magazine revealed that Nayak served India's federal government as secretary, and was short-listed for the post of union cabinet secretary during 1996, but was not given the post because of 'adverse Intelligence Bureau reports'.[39] Despite all these disturbing facts about World Vision, the rural development department of the sensitive border-state of Assam has not only recognized WV-India as a leading development agency in the State and recommended that WV be the prime choice for receiving bilateral funds, but also the government has sought WV's assistance in creating a US $80 million proposal for development works in the

State. J.P. Rajkhowa, a former chief secretary to the government of Assam, finds this 'most disturbing'.[40]

Indian watchdog organizations are quick to raise the specter of CIA involvement. It is alleged that the 'foreign agents' that worry the Indian intelligence services come from institutions like World Vision and some such projects are alleged to have affiliations between World Vision and the CIA.

Gospel for Asia

Gospel for Asia (GFA) is a well-funded Texas-based Christian missionary organization with a vast infrastructural network in India. It serves as a case study of an evangelical organization being used as an effective tool in the hands of transnational forces seeking India's subservience. It was founded by K.P. Yohannan, a man who got his training as a teenager while working for the fundamentalist Christian group, Operation Mobilization.[41] GFA owes its existence to fundamentalist preacher W.A. Criswell, notorious for his racist views in 1950s. Backed by oil billionaire H.L. Hunt, Criswell became one of the most visible defenders of segregation, demanding the separation of races as well as religions. He invoked images of filth and dirt associated with African Americans and Mexican Americans, and considered the idea of universal brotherhood of man and fatherhood of God as a spurious idea.[42] Yohannan studied evangelical theology in Criswell's Bible College. Criswell is acknowledged as the spiritual father of GFA.[43]

The same kind of hatred and horrible stereotyping of others is found in the pages of Yohannan's book, *Revolutions in World Missions*, where the target of hatred is shifted to India's native culture and religion:

> Our battle is not against . . . symptoms of sins such as poverty and disease. It is directed against Lucifer and innumerable demons which fight day and night in order to drag the human souls into an eternity without Christ.[44]

He identifies 'Lucifer and innumerable demons' with the spiritual traditions of India, and these traditions get blamed for India's social problems. Yohannan writes:

> . . . viewing the effects of pagan religions on India, I realised that the masses of India are starving because they are slaves to sin. The battle against hunger and poverty is really a spiritual battle, not a physical or social one as secularists would have us believe. The only weapon that will ever effectively win the war against disease, hunger, injustice and poverty in Asia is the Gospel of Jesus Christ.[45]

Even India's food problem is blamed on Hinduism:

> The key factor—and the most neglected—in understanding India's hunger problem is the Hindu belief system and its effect on food production. Most people know of the 'sacred cows' that roam free, eating tons of grain while nearby people starve. But a lesser-known and more sinister culprit is another animal protected by religious belief – the rat . . . The devastating effects of the rat in India should make it an object of scorn. Instead, because of the spiritual blindness of the people, the rat is protected.[46]

When Indian Christians decide to return to Hinduism, he sees it as going 'back into the bondage of Satan'.[47] Yohannan declares that the reason why the West is better than the East is because 'the Judeo-Christian heritage of Europe has brought the favor of God, while false religions have brought the curse of Babylon on all the nations of Asia'.[48]

With such a skewed and fundamentalist worldview,[49] one would expect Yohannan to be relegated to the obscure evangelical backwaters of the US Bible Belt. Instead, he became identified as a valuable asset for Western evangelism. Patrick Johnstone, author of *Operation World* and an evangelical strategist, considers GFA to be 'the most significant pioneer missionary agencies'.[50] Luis Bush, CEO of AD2000 and the visionary behind the 10/40 window strategy, is even more specific and sees GFA as having 'what it takes to penetrate the 10/40 window'.[51] The 10/40 window refers to the region of the world that has been selected as the prime target for Christian conversions, with India being the largest supply of heathens in it. This is explained later in this chapter under the Joshua Project.

Yohannan, along with his German wife, founded GFA in 1978 as a financial support program for ten US missionaries working in India. In 1981, he started GFA in his native state of Kerala. In 1983 it became the Indian headquarters of his operation for receiving foreign funds, mainly from United States.[52] In 1986 GFA started its radio broadcasts. Today, it broadcasts evangelical propaganda in 92 Indian languages, including many tribal languages.[53] www.Ministrywatch.com, a website for informing Christian donors about various missions, speaks of GFA's radio broadcasts as having successfully penetrated the 10/40 Window.[54]

At the 1997 Global Consultation on World Evangelization, Luis Bush and Yohannan held strategic sessions in which Yohannan gave briefings on how Gospel For Asia has deployed church-planting teams among one hundred communities of Joshua Project's list of the most 'unreached peoples' in terms of Christianity. Churches with at least thirty evangelists each had already been planted among thirty of those communities.[55] GFA has declared that its 'focus and goal as a ministry is to reach the 2.7 billion people in the 10/40 window who have never heard about the love of God. In India alone, there are over five hundred thousand villages with no Gospel witness'.[56]

Turning a blind eye to the radical anti-secular stance, Western aid organizations promote such proselytizing groups to carry out development assistance to third-world countries. For example, Australia-based Travel with a Cause is an international travel agency which claims to pour its profits into third-world and developing countries and, other 'worthy causes'.[57] Their mission statement speaks of paying for 'feeding the poor, empowering the under-educated, supporting Christian missions, assisting projects designed to break the back of poverty, disaster relief, health services, and funding other humanitarian work around the world.' It supports GFA's proselytizing activity in India.[58]

GFA describes the caste system as being 'established by the Aryans, a tall, fair-skinned people who invaded the Indian subcontinent three thousand years ago . . . to maintain their status – and keep the native population down'.[59] Yohannan states in his book:

> Mature Christians realize the Bible teaches there are only two religions in the world. There is the worship of the one true God, and there is

a false system of demonic alternative invented in ancient Iran. From there, Persian armies and priests spread their faith to India, where it took root. Hindu missionaries, in turn, spread it throughout the rest of Asia. Animism, Buddhism and all other Asian religions have common heritage in this one religious system.[60]

GFA works closely with US-based Dalit Freedom Network (DFN).[61] It has been accused of 'covert' activities by All India Rationalist Organization.[62]

GFA is extremely dependent on foreign funds. An Indian government report for 2004 has observed:

Gospel for Asia, with Rs 98.9 crore, is the second highest recipient . . . according to the data collected from home ministry's annual report . . .The bulk of the funding for Gospel for Asia in India comes from its parent organization in the US, which heads the foreign donors list with Rs 111.2 crore.[63]

During 2005-6, this increased to Rs 137.18 crore.[64] In 2008, the Kerala home minister revealed that GFA has received Rs 1,044 crore in foreign donations in the last fifteen years. The home minister said that the church had bought nearly 2,800 acres of land, including a 2,200-acre rubber estate.[65] When the government of India pondered further tightening the present Foreign Contribution Regulation Act (FCRA), the All India Christian Council (AICC), which is the India affiliate of US-based DFN, started circulating a critique against the proposed monitoring of foreign funds inflow.[66]

GFA views human misery in unscientific terms. For example, it is proud that one of its workers who ministers children suffering from high fever only prays, but does not 'call a doctor or get them medicine or bring them chicken soup'.[67] It saw the 2004 tsunami in India as 'one of the greatest opportunities'. In Tamil Nadu coastal villages, its activities sparked protests. For example, in the village of Akkaraipettai, GFA set up an unauthorized orphanage, taking more than a hundred traumatized children, mainly Hindus, and making them recite Christian prayers six times a day.[68]

GFA is also accused of misappropriating resources using the Indian government's social welfare programs. When a GFA activist was caught and evicted from land he had misappropriated for his proselytizing center, the matter was widely projected by the Christian media as an atrocity against Christians.[69]

GFA has a special wing called 'festival outreach' to target Hindu spiritual festivals like Kumbh Mela. In the 2007 Kumbh Mela in Allahabad, GFA organized a team of staff members, women from local churches, students and staff from Bible colleges, and pastors from Allahabad. Their job was to distribute abusive materials. Pradip Ninan Thomas points out that Gospel for Asia boasted having distributed six million copies of a booklet to Hindu pilgrims at the Kumbha Mela, describing the event as 'zealotry run riot'.[70] This created tension, and the police asked GFA's women team to leave. The women retreated but the rest of GFA's team continued to distribute hate propaganda, leading to their arrest, a day's detention and subsequent release. GFA used its global media reach to project this incident as Christian persecution in India.[71]

GFA also indulges in political propaganda, floating conspiracy theories through its access to the vast missionary media network. After Islamic terrorists attacked Mumbai in November, leaving nearly two hundred dead, Yohannan expressed sorrow and condemned the terrorists.[72] However, in interviews given to Christian media worldwide he expressed doubts as to whether the attackers were Islamists or 'Hindu extremists'. He claimed incorrectly that all the major terrorist attacks in India in 2008 which were initially attributed to Islamic terrorists were later found to be perpetrated by 'Hindu extremists'. He suggested that the Mumbai attack 'could be a plot' by Hindu extremists to scare the foreign investment so that 'the Dalits will remain in poverty'.[73] Yohannan was widely quoted in Christian media, warning the West not to let the Mumbai attacks overshadow the attacks on Christians in India by Hindus.[74]

Teaching Nuance

There is another project that educates foreign missionaries how to evangelize Hindus in a nuanced manner. This training is quite widespread and is often conducted very discreetly behind the veil of cultural studies in secular institutions. It becomes more explicitly evangelical when conducted in seminaries and Christian colleges. For example, 'Peoples of India', a course offered by a Christian college, is described as follows:

> A study of different customs, social structure, religions, arts, and history of one of the world's most interesting and populous nations, India. Special emphasis will be placed upon the Christian response to one of the greatest contemporary mission fields and the largest unreached people groups of the world. [A] few guest speakers will be attending the class during the semester lecturing on their most recent visit to India. [75]

The tone is usually very polite and students are taught to show respect for Indian ethnicity and culture. Often, the professor does not show bias explicitly, but lets the carefully selected 'visitors from India' and missionary films instill the desired passions against 'heathen religions'.

Marxist Smokescreens

Yet beneath all this soft posturing, the export variety of American Christianity is fundamentalist, and this embarrasses the Indian Marxist supporters in the US academy, because they do not wish to be seen as collaborating with evangelists. Their posturing is paradoxical and revealing. On the one hand, such academics must follow their white leftist peers ideologically, and this requires them to attack Christianity as right-wing, irrational and socially backward. But on the other hand, the nexus of Indian radicals, Christians and Muslims has practical value. Many Indian leftists are fed and supported by Christian funding, which they find embarrassing to admit.

The solution to this contradiction was found by blaming George Bush's version of Christianity, while sparing Christianity more broadly. This means that leftists could take the anti-Bush stance to isolate instances of Christian abuse, while remaining tacitly in support of evangelical Christianity in general. Even with the departure of President

Bush, this strategy is still workable, by blaming the more ignorant and culturally backward elements among American fundamentalists. The fact remains, however, that the brand of Christian teachings peddled in India is not what liberal Christians of America espouse, and is precisely the variety they denounce. This has to be kept under wraps in order to protect the reputations of the leftists who are linked with such Christian institutions.

The second component of this strategy is to bring in Hinduism as the culprit, in order to divert attention away from this awkward love-hate relationship between Indian Marxism and Christianity, even when the matter at hand is specifically about Christianity itself. A good example of such a pragmatic (but less than honest) stance by an Indian American is the position of Vijay Prashad, who was discussed earlier. When pushed to condemn Christian evangelism in a Muslim country, he is cautious to confine his target, and writes: 'US evangelicalism *does not* represent Christianity but *does* represent the Bush administration's agenda for global hegemony'.[76] One would hope that the erudite professor would have examined the views of evangelical American churches, almost every one of which is heavily engaged in foreign evangelism and regards it as inseparable from being a responsible Christian.

Immediately after this criticism of 'Bush-Christianity only', Prashad shifts the subject to the standard attack on Hindu fascism, writing: 'Revelations about the agenda of evangelical missionaries in periodicals like *Tehelka* and elsewhere have given fodder to anti-Christian forces in India'. While his article's title makes it seem like a criticism of Christian expansionism, he cleverly shifts the topic to attacking Hinduism, lashing out against 'the legions that provoked and carried out a violent anti-Christian campaign in Gujarat in 1998 and the murder of the Australian missionary Graham Staines in 1999'.

Unfortunately, the Christian evangelical movement exploits Hindu/Muslim violence as an evangelical opportunity. For example, the Accelerating International Mission Strategies prays that 'the strife between Muslims and Hindus would cause disillusionment, leading them to the true Prince of Peace', implying that Jesus (the true Prince of Peace) is who both Hindus and Muslims should seek.[77]

Christian Media

There are multiple US- and India-based Christian media networks operating in India, and these work in unison. Their working has been shown in Fig 18.3. This will be illustrated by the examples that follow.

Fig. 18.3 Christian Media Creating a Christian Umma Attached to the West

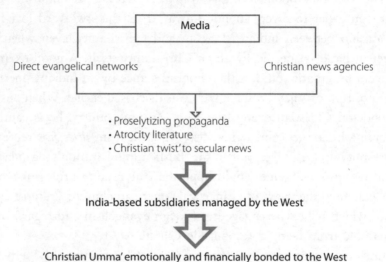

Assist News Service

There are several American pressure groups against India that are extremely well organized, and constantly provide feedback and encouragement to their Indian allies. For instance, Assist News Service, a Christian missionary media service, proclaimed that in 2006 it had succeeded in making India's prime minister start an investigation under international pressure: 'Our letter writing campaign is working', it wrote, quoting the head of one American evangelical group. 'We must continue to write and fax letters of protest this week'. The group was 'asking Christians in the USA to write to their senators and congressmen this week to stop the persecution of Christian humanitarian work in Rajasthan'. They routinely ask for letters and faxes to be sent to the White House, the State Department, the United Nations, and the Indian ambassadors to the US and the UN.

It praises the Federation of Indian American Christian Organizations in the USA (FIOCONA) for having led Christians all over India and around the world to protest the alleged 'persecution of Christian minorities in India'. The media report concludes by explaining how the group's purpose is a benign humanitarian effort to 'end the distress of orphaned and abandoned children, lepers and Dalits, and to provide emergency relief for disaster areas such as the regions affected by last year's tsunami, the Bombay floods, the Gujarat earthquakes . . .'.[78]

Mission Network News

Indian political developments are closely monitored and evaluated by such organizations in terms of the implications for their evangelical activities. When Manmohan Singh was appointed the prime minister of India in 2004, Mission Network News (MNN), an evangelical news broadcasting service, reported that this would be good for evangelism, and that a group called 'Bibles For The World', was planning to start three thousand Christian schools 'around New Delhi' as 'one way of reaching out to the community'.[79]

When Christians face hostilities from Indian Muslims, it is carefully downplayed in order to mask the Islam/Christianity tension and to make it look as if all problems arise from Hindu antagonism against Christianity. For instance, Kashmiri Muslims attacked the Western missionary who was the principle of Burn Hall School and St Joseph's school in Srinagar, and founder of Good Shepherd Mission School in Kashmir. The MNN report merely called them 'unidentified assailants' who threw grenades into the school because of the man's 'evangelistic work in the area', including translating the New Testament and Psalms into Kashmiri. By implication, it was made to look like the work of Hindus, not Muslims. The Global Council of Indian Christians protested, and this was instantly picked up by Gospel for Asia, which passed it for wider publicity to Canada-based The Voice of the Martyrs, whose mission is 'dedicated solely to serving persecuted Christians worldwide'.[80] The Voice of the Martyrs website is appropriately titled, www.persecution.net, and is dedicated to rallying Western Christians, human rights groups and governments to the cause of Christians. It makes no mention of the way some evangelicals provoke encounters in the old Roman tradition of seeking martyrdom by initiating the hostilities.

Western evangelists are rapidly building infrastructure for electronic media network infrastructure as well as content production in India. But the financial control and viability of the apparatus is largely dependent on Western sources. Pradip Ninian Thomas feels that the explosion of evangelical satellite TV channels poses an even greater threat than the direct political interference from overseas.

Local channels give space and breaks to any number of budding tele-evangelists. Any pastor who has the requisite finances can get a broadcast-quality sermon produced by local Christian production houses, such as Good News TV, which have the necessary contact with Raj TV and Tamilan TV to broadcast the program. While this can be seen as an opportunity for a 'citizen clergy' to 'dis-intermediate local hierarchies' (Martelli and Cappello, 2005: 253), it also provides the space for fundamentalist preachers to advocate a separatist identity.[81]

Thomas points out that transnational Christian channels have made Tamil Nadu the epicenter and entry point of Indian infiltration, with heavy investment in both programming and infrastructure. He writes that there are seven transnational Christian channels operating in India and nine local Indian Christian channels, and in addition all the secular channels also provide slots for Christian evangelism.[82] These channels spread Christianity along with overtly political messages. For example, Christian singer Vijay Bernard appears in these channels, singing songs couched in what Thomas calls the 'India for Christ' theme. The visuals involve the appropriation of India's flag and 'its anointing for a Christian nation'. Thomas explains:

> The theme 'Saving the Nation for Christ' is featured at numerous revivals and crusades and includes ritual reclamation of the Indian tricolor for Christ, and by extension, the Indian nation for Christ.[83]

Christian Broadcasting Network

Pat Roberston's Christian Broadcasting Network entered Indian media with a mission to 'reach out to every Indian home'. It started with Dayasagar, a serial on the life of Christ, followed by other evangelical serials including the very radical US right-wing show, the 700 Club, which has been broadcast six days a week on the Home TV satellite channel.[84] Its original US version (which was modified for India) had the following statement by Robertson:

> Hinduism and many of the occult activities that come out of the Orient are inspired by demons and demon worship. . . . There's this concept that all religions are the same and all are good. That is not true. The worship of the Devil is not good.[85]

Pat Robertson's Regent University also trains Indian Christians in mass communication, and many of the graduates go on to demean Indian culture and religion in the international media. For example, Reuben David did his post graduate work at Regent University, specializing in Mass Communication and Christian Worldview. Now he works in the faculty of North Central University. In one article after another written in Western evangelical magazines, he demeans Hinduism by picking up a selection of obscure tribal rituals to ridicule everything Hindu. For example, he highlights an isolated Santhal tribal custom and generalizes it. He conclude: 'Few and fleeting are the [examples of] progress made in shaping India's cultural and human dignity, much of which is dictated by pantheistic Hindu beliefs that settles like a cloud over the rural, real India'.[86]

Another emerging transnational Christian medium in India is BosNewsLife. This is Central Europe's first Christian news agency on the Internet.[87] Among its writers is Vishal Arora, who has worked with various leading Indian national dailies. Arora joined BosNewsLife as its New Delhi Bureau Chief in 2005 and has concentrated on spreading news pertaining to persecution of Christians in India.[88] Apart from providing atrocity literature to the Oxford Centre for Religion and Public Life (which was mentioned in a previous chapter), he also plants stories about what he calls 'Swastika terrorism'. He uses mostly Islamist sources to claim that Hindu terrorism is growing with tactical support from the government. He equates this with Islamic terrorism and declares it as even more dangerous.[89]

'News with a Christian twist'

India's overtly secular media is also heavily influenced by foreign organizations, which helps plant devout Christian journalists to serve their interests. An example of such a journalist is Jennifer Arul, who wields considerable clout as someone with more than thirty years of experience as a broadcast journalist and media executive in Asia.[90] She regularly visits evangelical educational institutions in the West to address students. When she visited Point Loma Nazarene University (USA), which calls itself 'one of the leading Christian universities in the country', the journalism students described the focus of her discussion as 'fighting against violence in the caste system and standing up for the rights of women and mistreated children'. She spoke of her campaign to educate 'her native India to the effects of dowry deaths that, according to her research, took the lives of twenty thousand Indian women' in one year alone. Arul told the students that her solution to dowry deaths was to bring Christianity to India, saying, 'I think that we should use our Christian faith to help people speak out and tell the truth'. It was noted that she always keeps her cross necklace visible when she reports. She explains: 'As a journalist, you can't remain uninvolved. If I can bring this little Christian twist to my story, I'll do it'.[91]

What she avoids mentioning is that dowry deaths are evenly distributed across the Indian religions, including Indian Christianity. In fact, there are especially high levels of this crime in the predominately Christian state of Kerala. When this problem in their own communities was pointed out, Church leaders were hesitant to forthrightly condemn the practice. Instead, the main church denominations in Kerala (the Syro-Malabar, Marthoma and Jacobite churches) asked their followers to merely 'reduce the wedding expenses',[92] but did not condemn the dowry system. On the other hand, the head acharya of Kanchi, considered one of the most orthodox Hindu leaders of India, condemns dowry repeatedly as being against Indian culture and tradition. While dowry abuse and coercion was not a social phenomenon in pre-colonial India, it was practiced until modern times in Christian countries.[93]

Gegrapha and Indian Christian Journalists

Gegrapha is a transnational para-church organization founded by David Aikman, a Christian fundamentalist fighting scientific evolution theory[94] who also declared that Christianity had made George Bush a better president.[95] Gegrapha's official mission statement is a 'call to all journalists who are Christians—Protestants, Catholic and Eastern Orthodox—at all stages of their career . . .'.[96]

Aikman elaborates:

> As journalists all over the world, many of us operate in cultures which either do not acknowledge truth to exist or are hostile to those who claim that it exists and can be known. In this climate, we need to remind ourselves that we serve a King [i.e. Jesus] who embodies both truth and justice, and who indeed is the truth (John 14:6).[97]

In 1997, Aikman produced atrocity literature about India that was outright false.[98] Just before the 1999 General Elections in India, Jennifer Arul was featured prominently at the Gegrapha International Conference in England, and she said:

> The burning of a missionary, the rape of nuns, the destruction of churches, the assault on a priest, are ominous signals to Christians of all denominations. . . . How many perpetrators against the Christian community in India have been brought to book? Commissions of inquiry are appointed but very little comes out of them. Action? Seldom! A true picture or a distorted, engineered report? Against this backdrop we are expected to report objectively and dispassionately, to be correct and impartial. It is no wonder that those who try to do their Christian duty are branded as activists. Talking of activists, three days before I left Chennai I met John Dayal, the editor of the mid-day newspaper, based in Delhi. He has involved himself in the United

Christian Council, which is currently involved in telling Christians about various anti-Christian activities around India, activities which, as a journalist, he obviously is privy to. We are due to have our general elections during the month of September and, the information he gave at that meeting was most valuable. I heard him and I also saw the reaction from the six hundred organisations that were represented. . . . Christian media persons like ourselves have to use the power we have to influence. [99]

At another international meeting of Gegrapha, Arul spoke again about the role of a Christian journalist operating in a non-Christian environment. She referred to non-Christian Indian journalists as those 'who follow different paths', while praising the Christian journalist as someone who has the 'responsibility of telling the truth'. Criticizing the limits placed on evangelism in government media channels, she praised her ability to use private satellite channels to report exclusively on the problems of Hindu society. She advocated that the 'Christian journalist has to bring a perspective to every story', and said that she did not care about being 'accused of inciting violence and not promoting religious tolerance'. Before her applauding Western Christian sponsors, she made it clear that the Christian identity in her takes precedence over the journalist:

Do we believe we are journalists first and foremost and only then does the Christian label get tagged on? It's a tricky question and one that needs thinking about. As for me, I believe that being a Christian journalist puts me in a uniquely privileged position to bring the truth, as I see it, to my 375 million viewers who are of course the Public Square.[100]

Gegrapha is a facilitator of Christian journalists who ground their professional work in personal faith and use their transnational connections. Stephen David is another strategically placed Gegrapha member who is the principal correspondent on political and current affairs for *India Today*, the country's largest news weekly. Such journalists now comprise a rapidly growing group across India's media, where they can act behind the scenes in framing the news. Yet, the impressions that are created internationally by John Dayal, Jennifer Arul and other high-profile Indian Christian journalists, is that the Indian media is anti-Christian, that Hindus terrorize Christians, and hence, foreign intervention is necessary for justice in India. This is music to the ears of their sponsors, who, naturally, reach for the pocket book.

Intelligence-gathering Operations

The West has also established an impressive information-gathering system in India, provided by many of these organizations and their affiliates. The network of institutions, individual scholars, grassroots missions, and media networks collectively comprise an impressive intelligence-gathering system. This enables the remote control of Indian communities and targeted political interventions. The work of Project Joshua and Boston Theological Institute illustrates the process.

Joshua Project: Market Research for Harvesting Souls

By far the most ambitious and far-reaching Christian project in the world to gather propaganda material and marketing data is the Joshua Project, based in Denver, USA. This provides Christian multinationals with the type of market research one would expect from a commercial enterprise such as Coca Cola or IBM. *Tehelka* conducted an in-depth study and reported that the Joshua project grew out of a coordinated effort called AD2000:

> When AD2000 was conceived for India, the plan was based on a military model with the intent to invade, occupy, control, or subjugate its population. It was based on solid intelligence emanating from the ground and well-researched information on various facets of selected people groups. The idea was to send out spying missions to source micro details on religion and culture. The social and economic divisions in the various Indian communities were closely examined.[101]

Tehelka explains that a multinational network is in place to give the US headquarters the ability to direct local actions efficiently in any part of the world in coordination with local units:

A letter written to an agency in the US is re-directed immediately to Bengaluru and the agency in Bengaluru in turn tracks down the nearest evangelist and directs him to take upon the task of ministering the Gospel to the newest seeker. In fact, the mission goal is: 'We need a church within cycling distance, then within walking distance and finally within hearing distance.' The Church growth figures that are with *Tehelka* clearly indicate that this mission mandate is on in full swing.[102]

Joshua Project consolidates evangelical and government databases in India and this can provide evangelicals the leverage to trigger or manage local conflicts, which in turn can get reported internationally. Its mission is to 'identify and highlight the people groups of the world that have the least exposure to the Gospel and the least Christian presence in their midst'. Maintaining a vast database of information, the project 'shares this information to encourage pioneer church-planting movements among every ethnic people group'.[103]

The report by *Tehelka* shows how global evangelism takes advantage of Indian data, such as the People of India Project done by the Anthropological Society of India. The project collected data throughout India by employing five hundred scholars over twenty-six thousand field days. Encouraging Christians to use this database, Luis Bush, Director of Global Consultation on World Evangelization, says:

> Never before has this kind of information on India been so carefully surveyed, prepared, well published and distributed. . . . We do not believe it is accidental. God is allowing us to 'spy out the land' that we might go in and claim both it and its inhabitants for Him.[104]

John Dayal resonates with Luis Bush and wants all Indian proselytizers to study such population databases:

> Dayal suggests that all those seeking consecration or ordination from a Christian institution must be made to read and pass a simple examination based on the contents of at least the first volume, the Preface, of the multi-series book, 'People of India', published on behalf of the Anthropological Survey of India by Seagull Books.[105]

The *Tehelka* report notes how all this impacts India:

Unfortunately, the Bible thumpers are winning and they are being underwritten by the American tax payers. What they are probably not aware [of] is that missionaries in India's back of the beyond villages, like Kerala, have been pulled into Bush's missionary zeal. Sadly, while Pastor Prabhat Nayak is deeply committed to bring the villagers of Kerala to Christ, he is unaware that Christian evangelical theology and money doled out by the White House threatens to rip apart the social fabric of India.[106]

There are approximately 16,300 ethnic groups worldwide, as identified in the Joshua Project database, of which 6,700 are labeled as unreached/least-reached, i.e. they are non-Christians. Of these 'unreached' groups the highest number live in India, making India the largest target market. Fig 18.4 shows the statistics.

Fig 18.4: Countries with the Maximum Least-reached People Groups

Country	Total ethnic groups	Non-evangelized groups
India	2,596	2,283
China	504	415
Pakistan	390	375
Bangladesh	402	355
Nepal	335	312

Source: Status of World Evangelization, 2008: Joshua Project

10/40 Window and Database Marketing

India lies in an area termed by Joshua Project as the '10/40 window', referring to the window between latitudes 10 and 40 degrees north of the equator. This region has been targeted as the biggest market for the business of soul harvesting. Within the 10/40 window, India is the only major non-Christian country which permits evangelism. Islamic countries and China have made tough laws restricting or outright banning this kind of activity, making India the greatest opportunity available. Joshua Project describes the regions within this window as 'the strongholds of Satan'.[107]

Joshua Project's World Evangelical Overview and related materials can be downloaded as a PowerPoint presentation from its website.[108] The strategy is clothed in the marketing language of corporate multinationals. It explicitly draws a parallel between Coca Cola's strategy and evangelism, by profiling different segments based on the market penetration of Christianity. Each market segment is given its own strategic approach, funding, operational management and status reporting.

Fig 18.5 is a sample from such a marketing plan, consisting of hundreds of pages of such details. Careful examination shows how the data correlates with the ground political reality. For example, it shows that the Arunthathiar Dalit community has not responded favorably to evangelism. In a strange coincidence, Tirumavalavan, the Dalit leader with enormous evangelical support, threatened to get them removed from the Scheduled Castes list, which would result in losing all their affirmative action rights under Indian laws. This is despite the fact that this community is among the lowest Dalit groups in socio-economic status and thus the most in need of affirmative action. An attempt to rename Dalits as Adi-Dravidiar (Primitive-Dravidians) by Tamil Nadu government was also supported by Tirumavalavan, while resisted by the Arunthathiyar community, who perceive this as a subtle plot to marginalize them. Tirumavalavan has threatened that the Arunthathiar would be merely 'tolerated' to live in Tamil Nadu but not be allowed to become community leaders.[109] This threat is being issued to those who have not converted to Christianity. Tamil Nadu's Christian leadership has thus hijacked the Dalit emancipation movement to such an extent that the Dalit groups which resist evangelism are made to suffer discrimination even from other Dalits.

Fig. 18.5: Joshua Project data for three major Dalit communities of Tamil Nadu

Community		Progress Scale			Percentage		Spiritual Need
Name	Joshua Project Ethnic	Least-reached status	Evangelicals in the community	Adherents in the community	Hindus	Christians	ranking scale
Arunthathiar	CNN23d	Yes [1.1]	Few, if any believers	< 5 percent	100	0	77
Paraiar	CNN23c	No [3.2]	Evangelicals >5 percent Accelerating growth		75.41	24.56	< 25
Pallar	CNN23d	No [3.2]	Evangelicals >5 percent Accelerating growth		85.30	14.70	< 25

Source: (Joshua Project 2000:2009)

Academic Institutions Example: Boston Theological Institute (BTI)

Information-gathering is also carried out by mainstream academic institutions in the West, under the guise of academic scholarship. Some of these institutions might be quite unaware of how their intellectual efforts play out on the ground in some faraway country.

As an illustrative example of this kind of research, Boston Theological Institute is a consortium of nine institutions based in the United States to 'advance the unity of the Church' and also 'to contribute to the formation of church leaders with strong ecumenical commitment and to strengthen the schools for their respective missions and tasks'.[110]

In 2006, two affiliates of BTI (Andover Newton Theological School (ANTS) and the International Mission and Ecumenism Committee) conducted a consultation for global missions on 'Castes, Tribes and Conversions: Christian Identities in India Today'.[111] The talks positioned the problems of Indian society as evangelical opportunities. There talks were titled 'Negotiating Humanization in India: Caste-founded Identities and Christ-funded Identifications', 'Identity and Tribal Conversion Movements in Northeast India', etc. The meeting was followed by screening of a video, 'Hindu Followers of Christ', presented by Todd Johnson, director, Center for the Study of Global Christianity. According to Johnson, 'India is the statistical center of gravity for the population that has never heard of Jesus Christ'.[112] The only Indian among the five organizers of the conference was Daniel Jeyaraj, a lecturer in Global Christianity at ANTS.[113] His published work highlights how, during the colonial era, Tamil Christians worked as evangelicals among the Tamil diaspora in Tanzania and Myanmar/Burma.[114] He argues that the colonial missionary accounts of India are more trustworthy than secular accounts. He gave the example of a Danish colonial missionary who is, 'for Indian Christians, a living legacy filled with vigor and opportunities for further development'.[115] He is also associated with the Indology and Tamil Studies institute at Cologne University.

In 2006, BTI, ANTS and 'Ecumenical and Evangelical Partners in India' joined hands to conduct a workshop on 'Christian Origins and Witness in India'. Starting with the St Thomas legend, the workshop presented 'the Apostolic origin and witness of Christianity in Kerala and Madras from the first century onwards', and its aim was to discover the forms of global Christianity practiced in India. The workshop wanted to discover how 'processes of globalization and westernization affect Indian society', so as understand what it means 'to be the church in the context of a dominant culture that seeks to identify the modern secular India with a "Hindu" majority'.[116] In other words, the goal was to find ways to decouple secularism from Hinduism and couple it with Christianity.

The workshop brought together Christian evangelical scholars from the US who had travelled to various places in India, visiting Christian evangelical institutions in order to study the cultural and social issues of Christian converts. Their detailed daily travel-logs are posted on the website of BTI. One such travel log informs how Jim Hinds, the missions coordinator of the ANTS, has led a young adult group who are wrestling with the issue of Christian self-identity in India 'that pressures them greatly to conform to the norm'. He showed the Indian Christian youths that 'Jesus asked us to not be conformed'.[117] In other words, this research intends to address the is sues of being Christian within India where they feel pressure to have an Indian identity.

In 1998, BTI organized a lecture by Harvard Indologist Michael Witzel, titled 'Eternal Hinduism? Sanatana Dharma vs Hinduism on the Ground', whose thrust was to show the fragmentation of Hindu society and the opportunities it offers for identity conflicts.[118]

The long-term effect of such investments is to cultivate population sub-groups that will act as receptacles for the intervention of the West. These 'cells' of Western Christian identity will not only welcome Western interference but will proactively help in creating the right situation for intervention at the opportune time. Toward this end, they supply intelligence and atrocity literature. The immediate effect is the rupture of the social harmony, religious tensions and violent conflicts. The next section explores this further.

Effects on the Ground

A less-reported dimension of such activities is the violence unleashed against the native belief systems and cultures. There is a pattern to this violence, which though well-documented, has been ignored by the media. When one examines the violence in such diverse places as Orissa, Assam, Jharkhand and Tamil Nadu, it becomes obvious that the violence is directly proportional to the amount of aggressive evangelism.

Kanyakumari renamed 'Kanni Mary'

1982 marked the beginning of a series of riots between Hindus and Christians in the Kanyakumari district of Tamil Nadu, which resulted in numerous deaths and considerable loss of property. The Tamil Nadu chief minister appointed an inquiry commission under a Supreme Court chief justice who was a Dravidian sympathizer. The commission examined 161 witnesses, perused 323 exhibits filed by various parties, and heard arguments of various Hindu, Christian and Muslim organizations represented by 16 advocates. *It gave a categorical finding that the root cause of the tension and clashes was the aggressive conversion of Hindus to Christianity and the propaganda methods that were adopted for this purpose.* The judge also noted that the Christians demanded that Kanyakumari should be renamed as 'Kanni Mary' (Virgin Mary), stating:

> Article 25 of the Constitution, which confers the fundamental right to propagate one's religion, has degenerated into violent criticism of Hindu religion by Christian missionaries who started the pernicious practice of ridiculing and belittling the Hindu religion and their gods and misinterpreting the Hindu religion. This was reciprocated by equally vile attacks and criticisms of Christian religion by the Hindus. Soon followed open threats and challenges between both the Hindus and Christians when each threatened to desecrate, defile and destroy the place of worship of the opponent. [119]

An example of such Christian provocation is shown in Fig 18.6, which is an image of Lord Krishna with the head cut off. A local evangelical arts center called Jesus Arts sent it in greeting cards to several village priests of Hindu temples, with the words 'Jesus is the head of Purushothama'. In other words, Krishna has no head because Jesus is his head: This is a crude grassroots propaganda of the fulfillment theology, often expressed in sophisticated terms by Christian scholars.

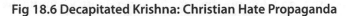

Fig 18.6 Decapitated Krishna: Christian Hate Propaganda

    In 1981, a year prior to the riots, the local church diocese published a highly derogatory book on the Hindu reformer Ayya Vaikundar, in which he was compared to the enemy of man mentioned in the Bible (Mathew 13:25), and a lot of insults were heaped on him and his followers.[120] The district administration declared the book libelous. Despite all this, evangelists in the USA depicted the riots in Kanyakumari as the 'persecution of Christians', and lobbied the US government to interfere. A letter written to the editor of *Christianity Today* said:

Let us highlight also the persecution being heaped on Christians from the Dalits (specially in Kanyakymari and Arunachal) and demand that Washington bring pressure to bear on Delhi to stop all such persecution, church-burning and the like.[121]

Such propaganda is effectively being used for soliciting funding and sympathy, and for pressuring the sovereignty of India using the constant threat of US interference.

Recurring Evangelical Provocations

While most of the time such evangelical attacks on Hindu deities, sacred symbols and literature are ignored by the media, at other times these provocations are advertised by the missionaries with great pride. For example, one prominent evangelical website has the following to say about Varanasi, a holy city of the Hindus:

Varanasi is Hinduism's holiest city, with thousands of temples centering on the worship of Shiva, an idol whose symbol is the phallus. Many consider this city the very seat of Satan. Hindus believe that bathing in the Ganges at Varanasi washes away all sins. A number of Christian workers took up the burden of prayer for this city and in prayer-walks boldly declared before the idols, 'You are not a living god.'[122]

Similarly, evangelical comics for children, like *The Traitor* by Chic publications (USA), demonize Hindu gods and goddesses as bloodthirsty creatures demanding human sacrifices, but powerless before Jesus. Indians are shown as being held in bondage by evil priests in collusion with demonic forces, and with government officials covering up human sacrifices.[123]

In Assam, a church had to apologize and discard an entire set of publications of hymns after the local people opposed the distortions in the translation of *Namghosa*, the most sacred book of the Vaishnavites in Assam. The translations had replaced the names of Rama and Krishna in the original hymns with that of Jesus.[124]

In 2008, the Bible translation in Kurukh (Oraon), an indigenous tribal language, created a major controversy. The tribal community took strong objections to the translation of the Bible's Deuteronomy 12:2. The phrase 'sarna mann', meaning green trees, was distorted into a command of the Christian deity to destroy those who venerate green trees. The protesters accused the church of a conspiracy to destroy their religion. The controversy raged for nearly two months in Jharkhand state before the church apologized and withdrew the translations.[125] However, soon after this incident, Jharkand tribals complained that the textbooks published by Gossner Evangelical Lutheran Church portrayed a prominent freedom fighter from the tribal community in a negative light.[126] The church was forced to withdraw the book.

There have been numerous suicides by those subjected to aggressive evangelism, particularly among young girls in Tamil Nadu and Andhra Pradesh. In one instance, the vice chancellor of a university was removed because he had allowed aggressive evangelism inside the university hostel,[127] while in another case a girl left a suicide note accusing Christianity of ruining her life.[128] A twelve year old girl who alleged religious harassment in a Christian school committed suicide after she was publicly insulted for being unable to read verses from the Bible.[129] From 2007 to 2008, several Hindu temples have been vandalized in districts of Tamil Nadu where Christians are in considerable numbers. In villages where Hindus have become the minority, temples were smashed and Hindus were threatened to leave and make the villages 'Hindu-free'.[130] In 2009, the traditional Tamil harvest festival Pongal has been stopped in a village in Kanyakumari district because of Christian activism against it.[131]

Such attacks and provocations on indigenous spiritual traditions never find their way into international media or the reports about freedom of religion. This is a formidable mechanism of physical violence, demonology and false propaganda to fabricate an ethnic-religious Dravidian Christian identity.

Apart from such evangelical attacks on Hindu society, the Catholic Church in particular and evangelical organizations in general, have built up a vast network and the institutional empire. This has made a developing country like India particularly vulnerable to rampant abuse by the clergy through their power on vulnerable sections of Indian society.

In 2010, Western media revealed that a Catholic clergy absconding from US law had been working in a diocese in Tamil Nadu. Despite numerous entreaties, and efforts by a Minnesota prosecutor to have him extradited on charges of child rape, the accused priest remained in his position as a secretary of the Diocese of Ootacamund's Education Commission. According to the lawyer representing one of the priest's victims the only ones who knew about him being a rapist were the bishop and the Vatican, and this was kept a secret.[132] When the news broke out internationally the bishop of the Indian diocese in which the priest was working reacted calmly, as though it were not a major charge.[133] The Indian media gave a lukewarm reporting to this case and at least one mainstream media person claimed an anti-Indian/anti-Catholic bias as the reason for such allegations.[134]

But what the media—both Indian and International—did not report, is that charges of such child abuses have surfaced in the vernacular media in South India concerning Christian institutions. In March 2010, at a Catholic institution in Kerala a teenage girl died – declared as suicide due to rat poison. However, under pressure from her parents the police investigated the case and two priests were arrested, charged with sexual harassment of the deceased girl.[135] In February 2010, a boy was abused by a Catholic priest and investigations revealed that the priest had been previously accused of misbehavior, but when reported his accusors were fined by the church and he was promoted to a position where he could abuse even more students.[136] In 2008, a Catholic priest was found murdered in the hostel room of a famous Catholic pilgrim center in Tamil Nadu. Subsequent investigations by a news magazine revealed that he was part of a network which abused girls in Catholic orphanages.[137] In 2007, a girl was found hanging to death inside a Catholic convent in Pondicherry. The public suspected sexual abuse and murder.[138] In 2006, a Tamil Nadu Dalit girl was found dead under mysterious circumstances inside a Catholic educational institution. Condoms and liquor bottles were found inside the premises.[139] Subsequent medical reports proved that the girl had been sexually abused.[140]

The contrast in the way the Church has approached the abuses in two countries is painfully obvious. In the case of US accusation, the Indian Catholic Bishop has meekly accepted for the extradition of the accused priest to US. But in the case of the abuse and murder of a Dalit girl, even when the Tamil Nadu education minister requested to the Catholic diocese to merely transfer the school staff in order to pacify public outrage, the Bishop of the concerned diocese bluntly rejected that step. He openly stated that the minister did not have power over the minority educational institution and that not a single person would be transferred. The state minister capitulated.[141]

The covers (see Fig 18.7) of a propaganda booklet released in the state capital of Tamil Nadu in 2008, illustrate that Dravidian separatism

Fig 18.7 Arousing Violence on the Ground

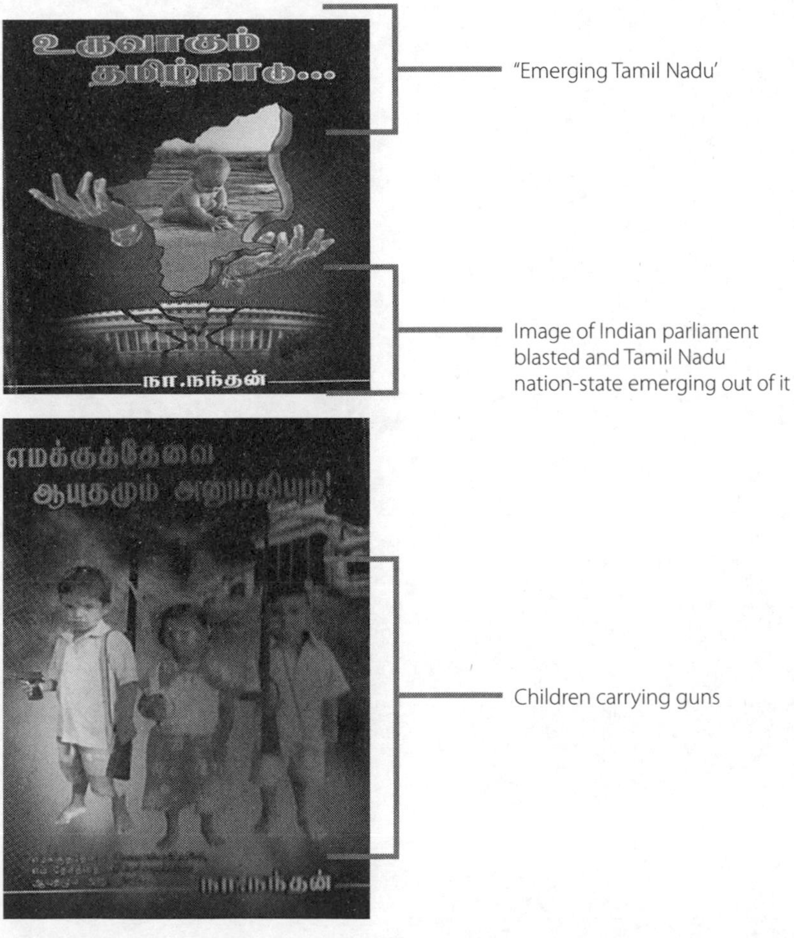

"Emerging Tamil Nadu'

Image of Indian parliament blasted and Tamil Nadu nation-state emerging out of it

Children carrying guns

is not an academic speculation but a call for an insurgency to break up India. The book released in a public function in Tamil Nadu asked people to take weapons and destroy India in order to carve out a sovereign Tamil Nadu. Such ground-level mobilization is not a freak phenomenon but is carefully orchestrated by transnational networks.

19

India in the Clash of Civilizations

It is not that India was never an independent country. The point is that she once lost the independence she had. Will she lose it a second time? It is this thought which makes me most anxious for the future. What perturbs me greatly is the fact that not only India has once before lost her independence, but she lost it by the infidelity and treachery of some of her own people. . . . Will history repeat itself? It is this thought which fills me with anxiety. This anxiety is deepened by the realization of the fact that in addition to our old enemies in the form of castes and creeds we are going to have many political parties with diverse and opposing political creeds. Will Indians place the country above their creed or will they place creed above country? I do not know. But this much is certain that if the parties place creed above country, our independence will be put in jeopardy a second time and probably be lost forever. This eventuality we must all resolutely guard against. We must be determined to defend our independence with the last drop of our blood.

— Dr B.R. Ambedkar's concluding speech at the
Constituent Assembly of India, 25 November 1949[1]

In modern times, three civilization powers are competing for global expansion and each is invested in co-opting and nurturing the divisive forces of India. These are: Maoists/Marxists aligned with China, Christian evangelists aligned with the West, and Jihadis aligned with Islam. Each of them has built a base of Indian supporters and infrastructure that embraces a divisive identity and ideology.

On the one hand there are serious ideological differences and mutual hatred among these three civilizations at the global level, but at the regional level of their vested interests in South Asia, they share common interests implicitly (and perhaps unconsciously) to balkanize India. For example, it seems odd that Indian Maoists collaborate with Western evangelicals, but it makes tactical sense for them because a weakened state opens up more possibilities for them. By undermining the traditional social fabric, they both hope to install their own ideology as the replacement. Both groups, thus, exploit the genuine grievances of the Dalits and manipulate the Dravidian identity and history in order to advance their own agendas. The pragmatic working arrangements at the ground level include Maoist guerrillas hosting American missionaries, and Dravidian politicians remaining complicit about jihadi bombings.

Within India each of these three global nexuses has its distinct presence in politics, finance, media and information-gathering. Each funds, sponsors, champions, trains and remotely manages its own network of individuals and institutions in India. These Indian resources, in turn, see their foreign headquarter as the source of inspiration, funding, political support and authority. Yet such a perspective has not been adequately discussed amongst India's intellectuals, media and policymakers.

The Cover Map

The map shown on this book's cover was posted on a website called www.dalitstan.com,[2] which features writings by many separatist groups claiming mutual solidarity to overthrow India's sovereignty. The author first came across it accidentally when he was having a casual conversation with an African-American scholar at Princeton University, who told him that he had just returned from India, where he had met with some Afro-Dalit scholars. The author probed further in order to learn what that meant, and in that conversation learned of the existence of this map amongst activists. Over the years, the author found it being referenced by activists of various kinds whose only common element is their hatred for Indian civilization as the foundation for a unified nation.

Though the map is from a website of recent years, the idea expressed is older by decades and goes back to the time when British colonialism encouraged sub-national groups to demand separate homelands and thus weaken India's national movement. Muslim demands for the creation of Pakistan were accompanied by similar demands from other groups, for example for a separate Dravidian homeland. These separatist voices are once again intensifying and India is facing a new threshold of danger.

Fig 19.1 depicts these three forces and some of their respective programs. The following three chapters will address these three forces – Christianity, Maoism and Islam.

Fig 19.1 Expansionist Civilizational Forces and Their Take-Over Agents in India

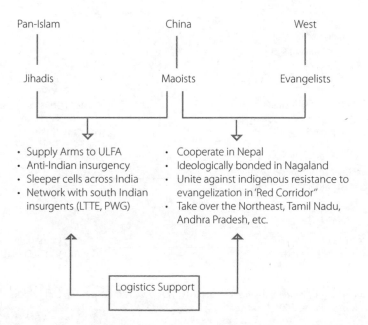

Maoist Red Corridor Through India

'A few hundred "Christian-Maoist" guerillas will change the power-equation in Orissa.' — Vishal Mangalwadi[3]

In India's Nagaland state, there is an insurgency driven by the idea of a Maoist Christian nation-state. The Naga separatist guerillas declared in their manifesto:

The sovereign existence of our country, the salvation of our people in socialism with their spiritual salvation in Christ, are unquestionable. . . . We stand for socialism. . . . We stand for faith in God and the salvation of mankind in Jesus, the Christ, alone, that is, 'Nagaland for Christ'. . . . We rule out the illusion of saving Nagaland through peaceful means. It is arms and arms alone that will save our nation.[4]

Fig 19.2 depicts how the global and local forces collaborate.

Fig 19.2 Executing the Nagaland Model: Nexus between Global and Local Forces

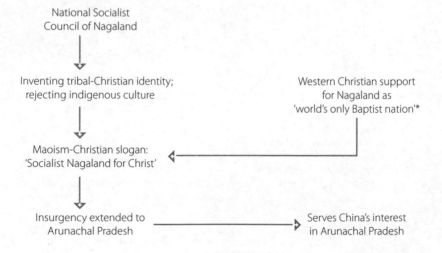

National Socialist Council of Nagaland

Inventing tribal-Christian identity; rejecting indigenous culture

Western Christian support for Nagaland as 'world's only Baptist nation'*

Maoism-Christian slogan: 'Socialist Nagaland for Christ'

Insurgency extended to Arunachal Pradesh

Serves China's interest in Arunachal Pradesh

* Paul Freston, *Evangelicals and Politics in Asia, Africa and Latin America*, Cambridge University Press, 2004, p. 88

In Chapters Six to Nine, we saw how colonial evangelists had first created a separate Dravidian identity, history, and sense of victimhood, with the other Indians being depicted as the villainous oppressors. Later on, this was turned into a Christian-Dravidian identity managed by foreign nexuses. In a similar manner, British colonialists carefully groomed the Naga identity separately from the rest of India, and subsequently the missionaries nurtured this identity within a Biblical framework.[5]

The World Council of Churches (WCC) has actively championed the Nagaland separatism cause in international forums.[6] Today, Naga society is largely controlled by the Baptist Church, which is headquartered in the US. The kind of control that Baptists have in Nagaland can only be compared to the power the Catholic Church wielded in the medieval dark ages of Europe. In 1992, the Indian government appointed a Christian theologian, M.M. Thomas, as the governor of Nagaland for conducting peace talks with the separatists. M.M. Thomas commented that the Naga churches were pursuing 'corruption, violence and mutual revenge'.[7] The government discovered that the church's influence in the state was all-pervasive and that its only option was to negotiate through the church-appointed Peace Council.[8] Today, Naga insurgents have extended their operation into Arunachal Pradesh, a strategically important Indian state on which China is also laying claims.[9]

Nagaland Model in Nepal and India's Red Corridor

Fig 19.3 shows how Maoists and Christian evangelists collaborate in Nepal and India for their shared agenda to undermine traditional cultures that come in their way.

The Maoist insurgency that had been dormant on the Indian mainland for a few decades has suddenly revived vigorously. Until recently, Maoists were confined to very few pockets in the jungles. In 2004, the two major Maoist groups, the Maoists' Communist Centre (in Bihar) and the People's War Group (in South India) joined hands to form the pan-Indian CPI (Maoist). This led to exploding

Fig 19.3 Nepal to Orissa: Missionary Maoist Strategist Nexus

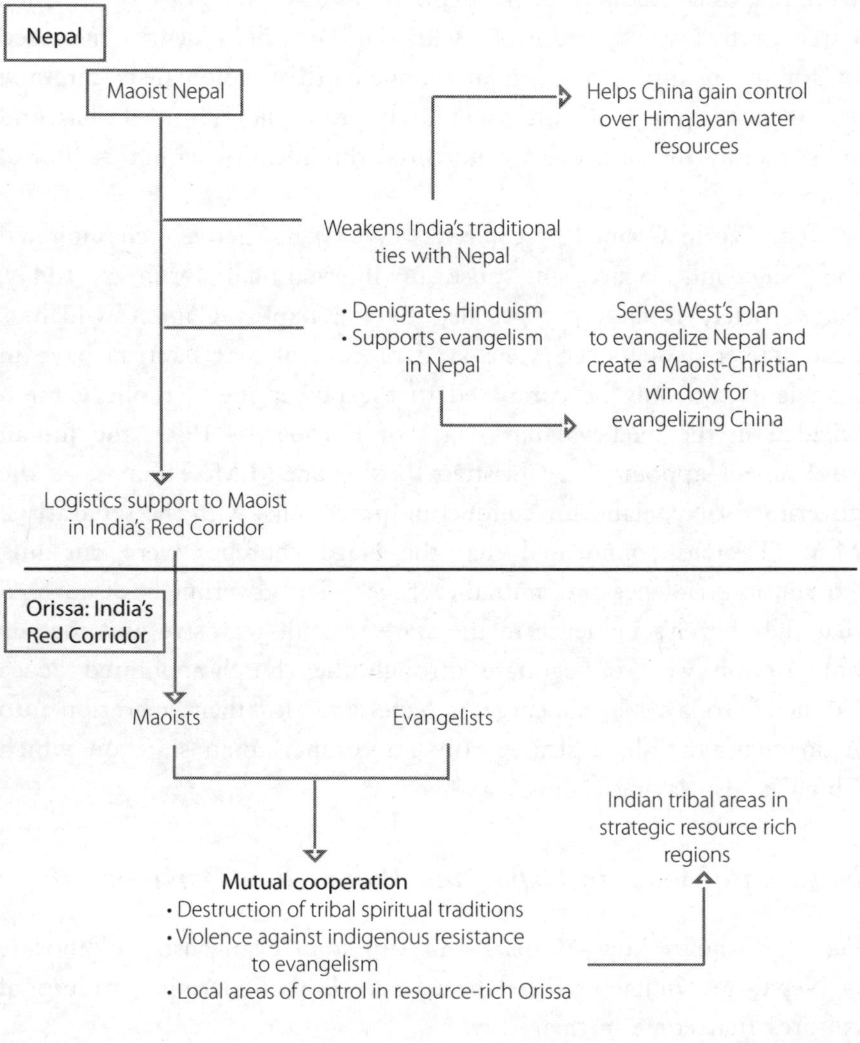

Nepal

Maoist Nepal

Helps China gain control over Himalayan water resources

Weakens India's traditional ties with Nepal

• Denigrates Hinduism
• Supports evangelism in Nepal

Serves West's plan to evangelize Nepal and create a Maoist-Christian window for evangelizing China

Logistics support to Maoist in India's Red Corridor

Orissa: India's Red Corridor

Maoists

Evangelists

Indian tribal areas in strategic resource rich regions

Mutual cooperation
• Destruction of tribal spiritual traditions
• Violence against indigenous resistance to evangelism
• Local areas of control in resource-rich Orissa

landmines, conducting jailbreaks, assassinating politicians in and out of power, and resorting to other extreme forms of lawlessness and violence.

This new activity signaled the emergence of what is known as the Red Corridor – a huge belt of Maoist militancy which stretches all the way from the Nepal border, through India's heartland, to the Indian

Ocean in the South.[10] The strength of the insurgency is far beyond mere sporadic terror attacks; they have established territorial control in select pockets where they administer an underground parallel rule. *India Today* reported in 2007:

> [Maoists] adopt practices like torture, mutilation and killings after trials in kangaroo courts. They are a regular force with squads patterned on army platoons. The 15,000 Maoists in India, with about 10,000 firearms, pose a big internal security challenge. They are active and wield influence in 170 of the 602 districts spread over 16 of the 33 states. . . . With the radicals developing military capabilities like mobile guerrilla warfare, potential investment destinations—particularly for the mineral extraction industry—situated in Maoist-dominated areas in Andhra Pradesh and West Bengal, may become unviable.[11]

Since then, the numbers and intensity of violent incidents have increased dramatically.

It is not a coincidence that the major states in the Red Corridor—Chattisgarh, Orissa, and Jharkhand—are also the major centers for aggressive Christian evangelism. Maoists and Christian evangelists collaborate for the destruction of the tribal spiritual traditions and for breaking up their traditional organic links with mainstream Indian culture. The evangelist leader Mangalwadi reports on a Christian website:

> Besides launching a Jihad against Animism and Hinduism, the Maoists are also active in supporting evangelists. At times, Maoists escort evangelists into remote villages where police officers are afraid to go. They summon everyone to hear the Gospel. The evangelists may show a film such as the 'Jesus Film'. Half-way through the film the Maoists would stop the film and give a lecture on Maoism. Then they would resume the film and ask an evangelist to give Alter Call. Following a fellowship meal the evangelists would be escorted back to their base! I have heard at least one credible report that Christians and some Maoists spent two days together fasting and praying. Christian leaders have not reported these stories to their supporters because (a) many of them can't make sense of what they are hearing, and (b) they are also embarrassed by the fact that their mission is supported by 'terrorists'.[12]

Christian Comrades in Orissa

Orissa is an important part of the Red Corridor because it is endowed with vast mineral deposits like coal, iron-ore, manganese-ore, bauxite, chromite, etc. According to All India Mineral Resources Estimates, the mineral deposits of Orissa in chromite, nickel, cobalt, bauxite, iron-ore were about 98.4%, 95.1%, 77.5%, 52.7% and 33.4% respectively of the total deposits of India.[13]

This state provides an example of how the Maoist-Evangelical network can become a lethal cocktail for triggering violent conflicts. Psychological as well as economic pressures are exerted by aggressive evangelism on economically impoverished communities in the remote districts, and this can explode into communal riots. Even a decade ago, *India Today* had reported this sequence of violence:

> The missionaries, no doubt, are on an overdrive, apparently following the call made at the state pastors' seminar in Cuttack in November 1996 to 'win Orissa for Christ by AD 2000'. Churches of all shapes and sizes have sprung up in most areas of the state in recent years. The state already boasts of ninety Christian missions and over eight-thousand churches. . . . With local Christians referring to Krishnapur as Krishtopur (after Christ) and Hindus maintaining an all-night vigil in Bhubaneswar in January to resist a possible conversion, fanatics are holding centre-stage. . . . As missionaries seek to win over Orissa for Christ, Hindu organisations have begun to strike roots in many places.[14]

As a reaction to the evangelical onslaught, indigenous communities started their own defensive measures. They were often assisted by Hindu nationalists, who saw this as an opportunity to spread their political message to the victims of evangelism. This led to clashes between Hindus and Christians, which have been reported in the international media with an emphatic Christian bias. Subsequently, in 2010 the central and state governments allowed the visit of a European Union delegation to conduct inquiry into the recent Hindu/Christian riots in Orissa, even though local tribal leaders have expressed strong apprehensions that international groups favor one section of the local population over the other.[15]

World Vision is one of the organizations that is blamed by natives as the chief instigator. In 2008, a Hindu monk and four others were gunned down on a Hindu holiday for their work in counteracting the Christian proselytizing. The Maoists issued a statement claiming responsibility for the killing, and stated that there was pressure from Christians to eliminate the eighty-year-old Hindu monk.[16] Prior to the killing of the monk there were provocative speeches made by Christians inciting violence against him. The Evangelical-Maoist connection triggered Hindu-Christian violence. This provided the evangelical machinery with a huge opportunity to generate atrocity literature for use in international forums, and to raise more funds in the West for 'saving innocent Christians' in India.[17]

The Christians also invented a separatist ethnic identity for the natives, claiming this to represent the 'original inhabitants' of the district.[18] A member of National Minorities Commission visiting the violence affected areas of Orissa stated that the Maoists were working with the Christian organizations in the area.[19] Police intelligence also confirmed that evangelists were employing Maoists to attack those tribals who had not converted to Christianity.

Vishal Mangalwadi, the US based evangelist we described earlier in this chapter, appealed to the Christian evangelists in India as well as the Christian Right in the US, to overcome Christianity's bias against Maoists and align with them in the common fight against Hinduism. He saw an opportunity in transforming Marxists who had earlier killed Christians, into tools for Christianity. This alliance with Maoists also offers Christianity another pathway into China. He compared this church strategy of accepting the Maoists, with Gandhi accepting the radical Indian freedom fighters, Bhagat Singh and Subhash Bose.[20]

Such evangelical suggestions are not just wild speculations made in distant US seminaries and think-tanks. In India, these concretize into a dangerous series of insurgencies that are reaching critical mass. In 2009, the Orissa state police discovered arms hidden in a Christian-run rehabilitation center. The news report stated:

> The firearms include one SLR and three AK-47 rifles. The arms were looted from the Nayagarh police armoury during the ghastly Maoist

raid on it in February 2008. . . . Nearly two-hundred converted Christians were staying at the centre. Police sources strongly believe in a possible link between the Maoists and some minority community leaders in the riot-hit Kandhamal district. Police suspect that the deceased was a core member of Vamsadhara division of the banned CPI (Maoist).[21]

Christian Comrades in Nepal

While the Evangelical-Maoist war against Hinduism rages in several states, a decisive battle has already been won by Maoists in Nepal. The Maoists brought an end to Nepal's Hindu monarchy in 2006 and declared it a secular state, abolishing its official status as the only Hindu kingdom in the world. An important consequence was the phasing out of Indo-Nepal long-term special relations. Maoists started calling for the renegotiation of the 1950 Indo-Nepal Treaty. In the Nepali media they started attributing the Indo-Nepal open border as the cause for the lack of economic prosperity in Nepal.[22]

Nepal's new Maoist prime minister, Prachanda (using the assumed 'revolutionary' name of Pushpa Kamal Dahal), became the first Nepalese leader to visit Beijing for his first foreign trip, rather than Delhi.[23] The changes are visibly and uneasily felt by common Nepalis. A columnist in a popular Nepali magazine asked:

> No matter how we present our relations with China, the fact is that cultural differences have mostly prevented us, so far, to have cultural-marital relations established. How can we become culturally close to China while keeping our relations intact with India?[24]

The Maoist regime was bent on destroying the cultural ties between India and Nepal. In an interview to the International Humanist and Ethical Union in August 2008, the chief Maoist ideologue stated that the Maoist aim went beyond 'merely delinking religion and state', and described the popularity of Ramayana and Mahabharatha TV programmes among the Nepalis as 'polluting the minds of the youth'.[25]

Such ideological stands translate into violent disruptions of age-old customs. For example, the Maoist regime tried to end the three-centuries-old tradition of south Indian priests officiating at the Pashupatinath temple in Kathmandu, the country's holiest Hindu temple.[26] Though temporarily thwarted by public complaints, the move was definitely an indicator of the direction in which the Maoist regime aimed to take Nepal. Subsequent developments led to the toppling of the Maoist regime. The new government accepted the traditional appointment of Hindu priests from India, but Maoist militants took the law into their own hands. In September 2009, the newly appointed Hindu priests were brutally attacked. *The Times of India* reported:

> The Pashupatinath temple area turned into an ugly battlefield late afternoon as groups of young men waving the Maoist red flag swarmed the secret room where the two priests had been confined two days ago to fast and undertake holy vows in readiness for the puja ceremony on Saturday. Waving iron rods and batons, the men broke open the lock on the secret door, dragged the two priests out and began thrashing them. Amidst cries of 'filthy Indians, go back home' their clothes were torn and their sacred thread ripped off. The whole incident was also videotaped. . . . Four men, said to belong to the Young Communist League, the Maoist youth wing, were reportedly arrested. [27]

China has been quick to comprehend the opportunities offered by such a change in Nepal. China and Nepal have started building new alliances. In the period 2008-2009, twelve high-level Chinese delegations, including two military teams, visited Nepal.[28] The future of Nepal can be guessed if one sees how China has put a stranglehold on India's water resources from Tibet. One Western scholar notes:

> South Asia's largest rivers flow down from the Tibetan plateau. The headwaters of India's most important rivers and principal sources of groundwater that nourishe the subcontinent, including the Ganges, Brahmaputra, Indua, Chenab, Ravi, Yamuna, Gandak and Saptakosi, to name but a few, rise in Tibet. China, thus, has gained a death-grip over India's main supply of water. India's strategists have long worried that China may at some point dam-divert or interdict its vital water supplies.[29]

China's rapid economic growth, coupled with its dire energy shortage, has driven it into a global hunt for energy. Nepal has one of the world's largest fresh-water supplies from the Himalayan snows and heavy rains, which until now have naturally flowed into India, filling the Ganga river and making North India fertile. But now there are new China-Nepal proposals to harness this water for generating electricity that China will buy as part of its energy imports, and the water once collected for power generation would become available to pump into China as a part of its Three Rivers Gorge infrastructure development strategy. Nepal's politics and media now have active pro-Chinese elements that demand a greater role for China in Nepal and a lesser role for India.[30] At risk may be India's agriculture and water supply from these rivers.[31]

China has the money to fill the appetites of Nepal's politicians and fund some industrialization and job projects, effectively turning Nepal into another Tibet-like colony, except with indirect rather than direct control.

Meanwhile, the evangelical forces are finding a strange partner in the Nepal Maoists. In 1999, the National Council of Churches of Nepal (NCCN) was established, the same year in which the Maoist insurgency started building momentum. Ten years later, when Maoists were struggling to form a government, NCCN became a key ally of the Communist Party of Nepal (Maoist).[32] In return, the NCCN general secretary was made the commissioner of Nepal's National Human Rights Commission.[33]

Subsequently, under Christian pressure Nepal has changed its previous stand with regard to UN monitoring of caste conflicts. The Indian government has opposed the introduction of caste in the UN human rights draft, seeing it as foreign intervention, but surprisingly Nepal's foreign minister welcomed the international initiative to intervene in domestic caste conflicts. This move by Nepal has been welcomed by Dalit Solidarity Network. Udit Raj, an activist with Dalit Freedom Network and All India Christian Council, welcomed Nepal's stand as this would bring 'resources from bodies like the European Union. Aid will flow to India',[34] meaning to Christian NGOs, because the UN has now called on India to follow Nepal's example.

Nepal's Maoists, encouraged by their new political clout, have been helping the Maoist insurgents in India, especially in Orissa where Maoists have joined hands with evangelists to destroy the indigenous resistance.[35] Such reports in Indian media have been initially denied by Nepali Maoists. However, with the Indian Home Ministry deciding to take serious action against the Maoist menace, a senior standing committee member of the Nepalese Maoist party declared that Maoists of Nepal would extend their 'full support and co-operation to the Indian Maoists, who are launching armed revolt'.[36]

Today, Maoists enjoy political legitimacy and clout in Nepal even after they were voted out of power. Now they are trying to integrate the twenty-thousand-strong Maoist combatants within the national Nepal army.[37] The Maoists are making anti-India and pro-China demands as a foundation of their political plank.[38] In such a situation, the mass amalgamation of Maoists into the army would result in a new structure and hierarchy that would tilt the balance of power in favor of the pro-China Maoists.

Thus, the Red Corridor is the battlefield where global nexuses meet in alliances to fight Indian civilization and the Indian state.

Assam: Maoist-ULFA-ISI

The academic legitimacy of the idea that each linguistic group is a sub-nationality has also created an insurgency in Assam. At first this started with the problem of Bangladeshi infiltration, but it has transformed itself into an anti-India secessionist movement. The terrorist group spearheading this separatism, United Liberation Front of Assam, has created very strange alliances. Political analysts Nivedita Menon and Aditya Nigam show the gradual transformation of ULFA ideology, which allowed it to derive support from Maoist as well as pan-Islamic forces:

> ULFA gradually distanced itself from the immigration issue.
> . . . It puts forward the idea of a federal Assam where different
> 'nationalities' would possess maximum autonomy bordering on self-
> rule. . . . ULFA is understood by some to have made a radical shift by

. . . becoming influenced by Maoism, and attempting to give a leftist direction to Assamese nationalism. A new aspect of ULFA's ideology emerged, however when in July 1992, in a publication addressed to 'East Bengal migrants', ULFA identified not only the Indian state, but 'Indians' as the real enemy. . . . This campaign against 'Indians' resulted in a number of targeted killings of poor migrants of UP and Bihar in Assam (for instance, in episodes of 2003 and 2007).[39]

This ideological development brought ULFA access to a larger South Asia network of anti-India subversive activities, including Dravidian separatists. According to Intelligence reports, ISI (Pakistan's military intelligence service) introduced the ULFA to the Liberation Tigers of Tamil Ellam (LTTE) for the purpose of smuggling arms through Myanmar. In April 1996, four Tamils were among those arrested for trying to smuggle more than five-hundred AK-47 rifles, eighty machine guns, fifty rocket-launchers and two-thousand grenades in two ships.[40] The networking capabilities of ULFA with other insurgents, particularly in Tamil Nadu, have increased alarmingly. An ULFA camp was discovered in Tamil Nadu. State intelligence learned that a joint training camp of LTTE and ULFA had been in existence for some years.[41]

From the late 1990s, the Maoists have started creating nexuses with various Jehadhi cells planted throughout India. Lashkar-e-Taiba terrorist Azam Ghouri, for example, was arrested after his meeting with some important Maoist leaders in the Warangal and Nizamabad districts of Andhra Pradesh in September 1999.[42]

Using Intellectual Celebrities

When at last Indian government woke up to the reality of the Maoist threat and launched a nation-wide operation against Maoists, celebrity intellectuals, often groomed by the West, voiced a strong protest against government operations. An example of such support for the Maoists in International media is Arundhati Roy. The Booker prize winner described the Maoist insurgency as one between haves and have-nots, in which the Indian government 'needs an enemy – and it has chosen the Maoists'.[43]

An independent scholar exposed such claims of Roy as blatant falsehoods:

> It is hardly a case of 'an army of the poor against the army of the rich', as Roy suggests. On the contrary, it seems like the Maoists are better armed, better equipped and have better intelligence facilities. . . . Hundreds of policemen and other unarmed people have died in the Maoist attacks while Roy accuses the media of demonising the Maoists and coming up with figures about Maoist violence that are inaccurate and even false.[44]

In fact, the kind of logistics that Maoists are building up at different levels, from media propaganda to gound-level weapons, needs enormous amounts of money. A study of the money trail to Maoists reports:

> Maoists spent over INR 1.75 billion in 2007 for the purchase of weapons, including AK-47s, landmines and rocket launchers. According to the police, an Australian arms dealer had struck a deal with the Maoists to supply a record two-hundred AK-47s by the end of 2008, via the Malaysia-West Bengal drug route. Vehicles, uniforms and medicines are another major component of expenditure. The Maoists have acquired motorcycles with special tyres to make travel easier in dense forests and tough terrain. Publicity and propaganda is another major head on which the Maoists spend considerably. Besides maintaining websites, publishing party magazines *Awam-e-jung* (Hindi) and *CPI-Maoist* (English), they also operate a low-frequency radio in the jungles to campaign against the police and the administration. The Maoists also spent huge sums on communication equipment, and mobile and satellite phones are very common. The Raipur police raided an urban Maoist network centre and seized account books for collection and disbursal of INR 50 million.[45]

Roy says with pride in a propaganda article that the Maoists are having the latest modern weapons: 'serious rifles, INSAS, SLR, two have AK-47s' and that they recruit child soldiers.[46] Maoists get money from foreign-funded NGOs. A Bihar government document lists several NGOs suspected of diverting funds to the Maoists. Most such NGOs are funded by visiting tourists or international donor agencies. The former Bihar Home Secretary, Afzal Amanullah, stated, 'Intelligence agencies did report such things being channelised. Now, we have got to warn foreigners and do a lot of planning to stop this worrisome syndrome from spreading'.[47]

With India intensifying its counter-insurgency operations, Maoist insurgents asked Arundhati Roy to mediate with the state. The use of such celebrities by Maoists to present their case in public is a public relations exercise, far from being an honest attempt for negotiation. One columnist observed that the insurgents adopt celebrities to push their cause in civil society, bypassing the dialogue with the state. The mediating intellectuals help the Maoists to entrench themselves deeper within civil society.[48]

Maoists are 'Gandhians with a Gun' and Gandhi 'a pious humbug'

Arundhati Roy, far from bringing Maoists into the mainstream democracy as some of her supporters have claimed, acts as a spokesperson for violence. In a highly publicized article in *Outlook* just before a major Maoist attack, she exemplified the doublespeak. The article starts with a pious question to the readers to consider Maoists as 'Gandhians with a gun'. But the emotional rhetoric glorifies the founder of India's Maoist violence, Charu Mazumdar, the architect of Maoist terror in India who advocated 'an annihilation campaign', while Gandhian non-violence is called 'pious humbug'. She then goes on to justify every separatist insurgency within India and terms India 'an essentially upper-caste Hindu State' which, from the day of its independence as 'a colonial power, annexing territory', has been 'waging war' against 'Muslims, Christians, Sikhs, Communists, Dalits, Tribals and, most of all, against the poor'.[49] The Indian Home Ministry also observed the misplaced stand of 'India's own intellectuals against the national interests'. It charged the 'role of the foreign-sponsored agencies' for coming in the way of tackling the Maoist insurgency.[50]

Emerging Nexuses

On April 2010, in the deadliest Maoist attack of the recent times, seventy-six Indian soldiers were ambushed to death in Chattisgarh.[51]

Following this macabre incident, a cultural celebration was organized to praise the Maoists at Jawaharlal Nehru University. The massacre led to a nationwide coordinated search by intelligence agencies. In Gujarat, three activists with Maoist links were arrested by the police.[52] This arrest was condemned by Jesuit missionaries.[53] Following the arrest, the link between the Maoists and their Filipino comrades came to light and this was later corroborated by the National Intelligence Coordinating Agency of Philippines.[54] Apart from Gujarat, noted Jesuit activists also provide media support to Maoist insurgency and have enjoyed proximity to Maoists. For example, in a reminiscence of an Australian Jesuit priest who worked in India, another Jesuit recounts how, while they were 'returning from a village in North India where the area had been recently liberated by Maoist rebels' the Australian Jesuit was on friendly terms with the Maoists, who surrounded them and he later called them 'just kids with guns'.[55]

Apart from such grassroots socializing with Maoists, Jesuits also provide sustained propaganda-support for Maoists in mainstream media. Dr Ambrose Pinto S.J., a former director of the Indian Social Institute, New Delhi, and currently the principal of St Joseph's College, Bengaluru, writes passionate eulogies of Maoists in mainstream media which are featured prominently on the website of 'Jesuits for Social Action'(JESA).[56] In the article 'Why we oppose Green Hunt', Pinto reinforces Risley's thesis that tribals are non-Hindus, thereby creating political space for the churchmen to intervene as mediators.[57] Pinto speaks of the 'Dalit or tribal way of life and civilization' as being threatened not by Maoists but by the Indian government.

Another prominent Jesuit voice speaking for Maoists is Xavier Manjooran, who stated that 'to demand one's legal rights and to be a terrorist is the same thing in Gujarat'.[58] Gujarat Adivasi Mahasabha, run by Manjooran, is one of the signatories to a letter against the planned offensive by the government of India, published by Maoist Information Bulletin of the CPI-Maoist in its December 2009 edition. As early as 2003 in an interview to a Pakistani magazine, Manjooran boasted how his organization gives martial training to tribals and alienates them from the mainstream Indian society by indoctrinating them with the Aryan/Dravidian race theory.[59]

Apart from Christian forces, Pakistan also has invested effectively in Maoist insurgency. Ben West, an analyst with STRATFOR, a global team of intelligence professionals, writes:

> STRATFOR sources in India claim that Pakistani intelligence has established business relationships with Naxalites to sell arms and ammunition, and lately has tried to use Naxal bases for anti-Indian activities. There is evidence that the ISI is providing weapons and ammunition to the Naxalites in exchange for money or services, mostly through third parties like the United Liberation Front of Asom (ULFA) or the ostensible Bangladeshi militant leader Shailen Sarkar . . . Naxalite leaders in India deny cooperating with Pakistan but have very publicly pledged their support for separatist movements in India.[60] The analyst further corroborates the central thesis of this book: how civilizational competitors at global level come together in India against their common enemy.

Thus, we see a confluence of forces from different streams, operating at different levels and based in different parts of India, coalescing to transform pluralistic democratic India into a regime of specific totalitarian ideology and/or fundamentalist theology. What is striking in this evolution of new nexuses is how two bitterly opposed ideologies that are clashing globally (i.e. Maoists and Christians) work together within India.

Islamic Slice of Dravidistan

Even prior to Independence, the Dravidian movement had some ideological affinities towards the pan-Islamic movement. Many Muslims justified the demand for a separate Pakistan by claiming that the Aryans were plotting to remove Islamic culture from India, just as they were suppressing the Dravidian culture.[61] Mohamed Ali Jinnah toyed with the idea of encouraging forces that would break up India beyond just the partition to create Pakistan. Soon after the Muslim League had passed its resolution demanding Pakistan in 1940, the Dravidian ideologue E.V. Ramasamy Nayakar (popularly known as EVR) passed a similar resolution demanding a sovereign state, to be called Dravidistan. In 1941, at the twenty-eight Annual session of the Muslim League, Jinnah and EVR shared the dais and Jinnah extended full support to splitting off something called Dravidistan:

> I have every sympathy and shall do all to help, and you establish Dravidistan, where the seven percent Muslim population will stretch its hand of friendship and live with you on lines of security, justice and fair play.[62]

The understanding was that they would support each other's separatism.[63] Jinnah further expanded his vision for the balkanization of India into Pakistan, Dravidistan, and Bengalistan.[64] This gave a common platform for both Dravidian separatists and pan-Islamic voices. EVR supported the Muslim political movement in Tamil Nadu and the movement to create Pakistan. He became a featured speaker at the Muslim League meetings and was invited to speak at Prophet Mohammad's birthday celebrations, where he persistently attacked Hinduism.[65] DMK, the political heir of his Dravidian movement, continued this policy of aligning with political Islam in Tamil Nadu.[66] From the time of Independence in 1947 until 1974, DMK and Muslim League were so closely aligned that one political commentator remarked that 'their organizations become virtually indistinguishable'.[67]

In 1972, DMK split into two parties, one remaining DMK and the new one called AIADMK (All India Anna Dravidian Munntera Kazhakam). Since then, the pan-Islamic political parties have continued to align with one or the other of these Dravidian parties. Between the two, DMK has been more consistent in catering to the appetite of political Islam in Tamil Nadu and has ideologically aligned the Dravidian movement with the pan-Islamic movement.

In parallel with the radicalization of political Islam in Kashmir, Afghanistan, and Palestine, the wave of radicalism has also reached Tamil Nadu. The jihadi networks have been silently building infrastructure in South India, where the political patronage they enjoy shields them. The patronage given to political Islam has often compromised the law-enforcing agencies against jihadi violence. The reason is a combination of ideology and vote-bank pragmatics.

This chapter will trace these recent unpublicized links between Dravidian separatism and political Islam. It will show how the destabilizing forces are nurtured by politicians who are driven by short-term gains, at the expense of national security. While in Tamil Nadu, Dravidianists' ideological affinity with Islamic separatists and their anti-Indian hatred make them turn a blind eye to the growing jihadi forces, there are different factors at work in Kerala. There, the Marxists see Islam as an anti-imperialist force and also as a major vote-bank against political rivals.

Fig 19.4 summarizes how the Islamic forces operate in the three southern states of Tamil Nadu, Kerala, and Karnataka. We will summarize some events for each of them.

Fig 19.4 Islamic Terror Network in South India

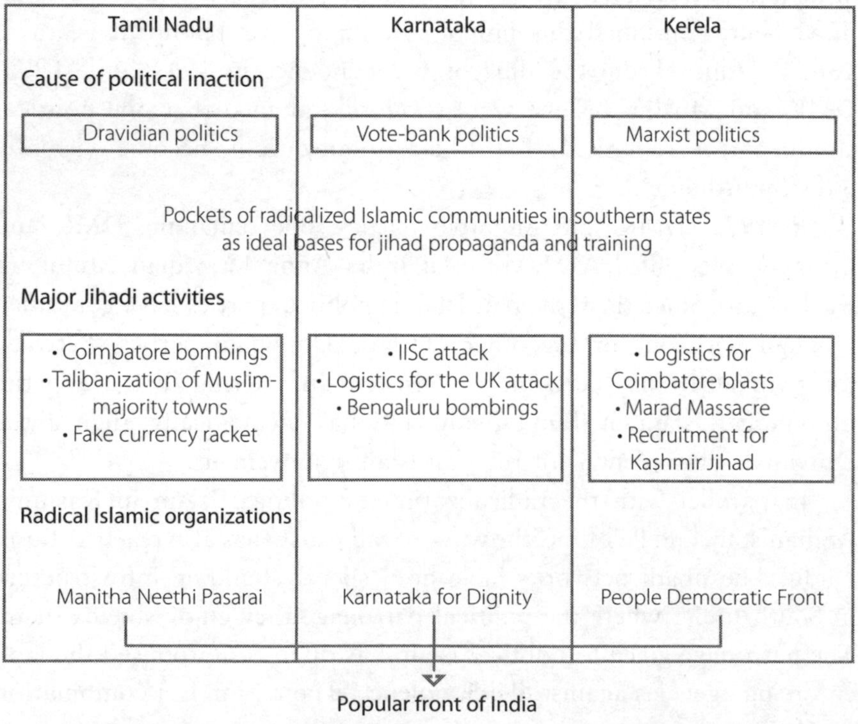

Tamil Nadu	Karnataka	Kerela
Cause of political inaction		
Dravidian politics	Vote-bank politics	Marxist politics
Pockets of radicalized Islamic communities in southern states as ideal bases for jihad propaganda and training		
Major Jihadi activities		
• Coimbatore bombings • Talibanization of Muslim-majority towns • Fake currency racket	• IISc attack • Logistics for the UK attack • Bengaluru bombings	• Logistics for Coimbatore blasts • Marad Massacre • Recruitment for Kashmir Jihad
Radical Islamic organizations		
Manitha Neethi Pasarai	Karnataka for Dignity	People Democratic Front

Popular front of India

Tamil Nadu

All India Jihad Committee (AIJC)

According to police intelligence, Islamic fundamentalist groups started working in Tamil Nadu in 1983.[68] In 1986, All India Jihad Committee (AIJC) was formed by an Islamic fundamentalist preacher named Ahmad Ali, alias Palani Baba, who was known for his radical speeches. Intelligence agencies reported that he was coordinating his activities with the All India Milli Council, which had Saudi-Wahabhi connections.[69]

During the 1980s, various Hindu activists who were accused of insulting Islam were executed by jihadi groups, especially in Coimbatore, the financial capital of Tamil Nadu.[70] Later, in the early 1990s, Israeli intelligence arrested a Palestinian student who had been studying in South India, from where he had been sent to the Israeli-occupied territories to engage in terrorism. His interrogation in Israel revealed the possible presence in South India, particularly in Tamil Nadu, of internationally-linked Islamic cells enjoying local support. The Israeli warnings were rejected as uncorroborated by the local police and intelligence.[71]

1990 saw the unprecedented rise of Palani Baba, who was given tactical support by the Dravidian polity. His activities were centered in a small town which has a famous Sufi shrine visited by people of all creeds. According to the state's director general of police, 'The fact is that the DMK government had taken its own time to reign his tongue. Had it acted earlier the damage could well have been averted'.[72] A report by *The Week* found a strange synergy between Dravidian zealots and jihadis:

> Palani Baba has been stoking fanatical fires for quite some time now, though his organization called Jehad has only a small base in the state. . . . [He] flaunts his close relationship with Chief Minister M. Karunanidhi. He claims to have links with Liberation Tigers of Tamil Eelam and has often boasted that guns are there for his asking. . . . The speeches of Palani Baba, who has been trying to spread the Jehad's influence to Muslim areas all over Tamil Nadu, were

highly volatile ingredients in the communal cauldron. The speeches were replete with vulgar references to the Hindus, their deities and religious leaders like Shankaracharya.[73]

Al Ummah and TMMK

In 1993, Al Ummah was formed as a fraternal group of AIJC that was better structured and more secretive than AIJC. It comprised of eleven modules, each led by a trained Amir (chief).[74] According to a retired senior official in the Intelligence Bureau, Al Ummah became the 'the most active jihadist force, active in Tamil Nadu, Andhra, Kerala, Karnataka. It has connectivity with the Directorate General of Forces Intelligence of Bangladesh (DGFI) and the Inter Services Intelligence (ISI), Lashkar-e-Toiba, HuJI, Jaish-e-Mohammad and SIMI.'[75] Later that year, Al Ummah bombed the headquarters of RSS, a Hindu nationalist group, killing eleven people. The Tamil Nadu police arrested the leader of Al Ummah and fifteen others under the Terrorist and Disruptive Activities (Prevention) Act.[76] Sporadic incidents continued and showed the increased bomb-making capabilities of the Islamic organizations.

In 1995, a parcel bomb killed the wife of a prominent Hindu activist,[77] and pipe-bombs were hurled at the Chennai residence of noted film director Mani Ratnam, for the alleged anti-Muslim bias of his films. In the same year, many members of Al Ummah launched Tamil Muslim Munnetra Kazhagam (TMMK), a socio-political front of charismatic preachers of radical Saudi-style Islam. According to a rival Islamic group, one prominent fundamentalist preacher of TMMK went to Sri Lanka, where he developed contacts with Pakistani Inter Service Intelligence. He desecrated the statues of community leaders, triggering riots between Dalits and Other Backward Castes in Tamil Nadu, and for this he was fined.[78]

To assert their presence in Coimbatore, Al Ummah militants engaged police in a pitched battle at a check-post in a Muslim neighborhood. A local member of parliament promised the militants that the check posts would be removed if he got into power. When his party won the election, Al Ummah activists removed the pickets themselves, leading to further clashes with the police.[79]

In 1997, the Tamil Nadu government released the Al Ummah activists who were being held in connection with the 1993 bombings. From the prison they were taken on a victory procession 'with gun-toting activists in attendance'.[80] Later that year, jihadi groups launched a terror campaign killing five randomly-selected Hindus on a single day.[81] Subsequently that year, explosions destroyed two shops and killed three women,[82] and a traffic constable was publicly executed by Al Ummah. The ensuing riots resulted in police firing and the death of eighteen Muslims.[83] The police arrested two members of a jihadi group for putting up provocative posters,[84] but the government once again released the head of Al Ummah.

In 1998, explosions ripped across different parts of Coimbatore, killing eighty people, just a few hours before a prominent Hindu leader arrived for election campaigning. *The Hindu* reported that the state intelligence organization had issued two specific warnings on the possibility of terror-acts in that city, including one warning recommending preventive steps, such as raiding the militant hideouts and places where explosive were stored, and searching vehicles in sensitive areas.[85] But politics prevailed and there was no crackdown or ban on Al Ummah.[86] There have been numerous militant incidents that received mild responses.[87]

Whatever may have been the security lapses before these bombings, the Tamil Nadu police acted in an exemplary manner after the 1998 Coimbatore blasts. In a swift move, the Crime Branch's Special Investigation Team named 166 people as terrorists. Of them, 145 people were taken into custody and 8 were killed in subsequent clashes with police. Among those accused, 11 were arrested from Kerala, 3 from Andhra Pradesh, 2 from Karnataka and 1 from Kolkata.

Fig 19.5 shows some of the acts of Islamic terrorism in Tamil Nadu in the 1980s and 1990s, most of which received scanty media coverage.

Fig 19.5 Jihadhi Victims in Tamil Nadu

1982-1990	Widespread killing of Hindus by jihadis in Tamil Nadu. Most of the accused are acquitted, and one accused in several murder-attempts later established Al Ummah	
21 January 1993	Chennai bomb-blast	11 killed
14 April 1995	Chennai bomb-blast	2 killed
20 April 1997	Tuticorin – port city	3 killed
14 May 1997	Tuticorin – port city	7 policemen injured
15 May 1997	Blasts inside Madhurai Goddess temple	No casualties
6 June 1997	Thanjavur-Indian national TV station bombed	1 injured
17 June 1997	Tuticorin	2 killed
6 October 1997	Cuddalore	1 killed
1 November 1997	Coimbatore	2 shops damaged
3 December 1997	Coimbatore	1 killed; 5 injured
6 December 1997	Erode – Train explosion	2 killed
6 December 1997	Tiruchi – Train explosion	4 killed
14 February 1998	Coimbatore – serial blast	70 killed
28 March 1998	Public execution of a Gandhian professor in Madurai; warning issued against voting or campaigning for a certain party.	

[Compiled from Tamil newspaper reports)

Kerala

Ironically, pan-Islamic separatism in Kerala was initiated by a Marxist regime which had declared itself avowedly secular. Prominent social observer Nayyar Shamsi explains:

> Communist Party, which loudly swore and still swears by secularism . . . courted Muslim League to grab power in Kerala. It went a step further and created in 1968 the new district of Malappuram,

which has a predominantly Muslim population when the redoubtable E.M.S. Namboodiripad was the chief minister.[88]

Later, Malappuram district would become a hot-bed of jihad activities, as will be explained. Since the 1980s, the jihadi movements have been nurtured in Kerala by the Student Islamic Movement of India (SIMI).[89] They developed a discourse in which they saw themselves as the successors of Zayn-ad-Din, a Kerala resident whose 1580 book, *Tuhfat al-Mujahideen*, called on 'the Faithful to undertake a jihad against the worshippers of the Cross'. This linked jihad in India with the worldwide Salafi-jihadi movement, making it part of an international agenda.[90] After explosives were discovered in Chennai in 1997, Kerala's chief minister told his state assembly that up to eight extremist groups were operating in Kerala who received funds and other support from foreign countries, including Iran and the Arab countries.[91]

Later that year, synchronized with the Tamil Nadu twin express bomb-blasts, there was a blast on an express train in Kerala, killing four and injuring forty-nine. The newly formed Islamic Defense Force (IDF) of Kerala claimed responsibility.[92] In 1998, pamphlets made by IDF were found near a bomb blast. Investigations revealed that IDF was clandestinely functioning within the All India Jihad Committee premises in Chennai, from where the twin blasts in Kerala and Tamil Nadu trains had been planned.[93]

Investigations after the 1998 Coimbatore militant attacks revealed that even before the train bomb blasts, parts of northern Kerala had transformed into a radical Islamic enclave. The news portal www. rediff.com reported that from 1993 onwards, the Kerala jihadis had been gaining strength, which they extended into the neighboring Tamil Nadu jihad.[94]

Abdul Nasser Madhani, Godfather of south Indian Jihad

Among those arrested in connection with the 1998 Coimbatore blasts was Abdul Nasser Madhani, founder of a banned radical group called

Islamic Sevak Sangh (ISS). The group quickly disguised itself by changing into a political party with a secular name, People's Democratic Party (PDP). After the banning of Madhani's ISS, Kerala's Marxist government stopped monitoring its activities. The police discovered that elements within the disbanded ISS had regrouped instantly to avoid attention and had joined various radical organizations with random names to confuse the intelligence agencies.[95] These organizations have overlapping membership.[96] The police soon discovered that the terrorists in Tamil Nadu had been trained by one of these new Kerala groups.[97]

In 1999, on the eve of Indian Independence Day, the Kerala police arrested three members of 'an Islamic fundamentalist organization' which had sent 'human bombs' to assassinate the state chief minister and other prominent leaders, in order to exert pressure for securing the release of Madhani.[98] Even while Madhani was in jail, his party continued to expand among the Kerala Muslim youth, aligning itself during successive elections with both the major political parties in Kerala.[99] PDP (People's Democratic Party) also proposed creating a Dalit-Islamic alliance. Though he was in jail, Madhani's party won two seats in the elections in the state capital, and boosted its legitimacy when the Congress-led United Democratic Front secretly sought its help in the 2001 parliamentary election.[100] Even the state secretary of the Indian Union Muslim League pointed out that political parties had 'promoted groups like PDP that held extreme views' and how this has helped spawn terrorism in the state.[101]

Madhani's political party lobbied for his release during the 2004 parliamentary elections. Both the major parties of Kerala appealed to the Tamil Nadu DMK government for his release. This campaign expanded the Islamist support-base amongst Dravidianists, radical leftists, and human rights activists.[102] The Kerala state assembly passed a resolution for his release.[103] Subsequently, the chief minister of Kerala visited Tamil Nadu to ask his counterpart in that state to provide Madhani with special treatment.[104] *Dalit Voice* brought issues sympathetic to Madhani's condition in jail and alleged a conspiracy to keep him imprisioned.[105]

Marad Massacre

The extent of jihadi entrenchment in Kerala was demonstrated in 2003 in Marad, a sleepy coastal fishing village, where eight Hindu fishermen were hacked to death by a Muslim mob on the beach. The killers then hid inside the nearby Jumma Masjid, where hundreds of local Muslim women converged to prevent the police from entering to catch the attackers. This became known as the Marad Massacre or Second Moplah Massacre.[106] Justice Thomas P. Joseph's commission was set up to investigate the massacre, and it came out with shocking details about the robust infrastructure that the jihadis had built in Kerala. The assistant commissioner of police testified before the commission, stating that National Development Front (NDF) had been receiving very large funds from unspecified foreign countries to carry out its terror training.[107] The commission reported that the Crime Branch had failed to inquire into the source of funds for such a large quantity of weapons and well coordinated attacks.

Another disturbing dimension that the commission brought out was the nexus of politicians, bureaucrats and jihadis. The assistant commissioner was severely criticized for the way he tried to shield one of the prime accused, and for his failure to maintain surveillance on a suspected militant despite intelligence warnings. This police officer tried to remain involved in the massacre area even after he had been transferred in the 'public interest'. The commission pointed out that his appointment was 'shrouded in suspicious circumstances' and that allegations of his links with the terrorists could not be ignored. The commission reported that this official had been appointed without knowledge of the police head and this was done 'to oblige a Muslim leader'.[108]

Such political patronage has made the banned Students Islamic Movement of India very strong in Kerala. SIMI operates behind a dozen front organizations, of which at least two are based in the state capital and others are located in strategic places, like the main seaport. The Kerala government officially declared in 2006 that SIMI's cadres had developed links with the Lashkar-e-Taiba of Pakistan. Police reports indicate that SIMI is operating under the cover of religious study, rural development and research. Some of these organizations are spreading 'extremist religious ideals' among the youth of Kerala, under the guise of 'counseling and guidance centers working for behavioral change'. SIMI is also reported to have established a women's wing. It receives generous funds from Kuwait and Pakistan.[109]

The escalating level of terrorism in Kerala led a retired official, who had served in Jammu and Kashmir, to say that a similar situation had prevailed in Kashmir before terrorism reached unmanageable proportions.[110]

Tamil Nadu–Kerala Jihad Nexus

In Tamil Nadu each of the dominant radical groups that have been spun out of SIMI and their social fronts, has become intimately aligned with one of the two Dravidian parties.[111] Thus, Kerala and Tamil Nadu have been compromised and have become accommodating to jihad. The Tamil Nadu government charged a Muslim senior civil officer with unlawfully attempting to help Madhani, and this official was suspended. But the next government in power revoked the suspension and promoted him as the chief secretary to the chief minister.[112]

An investigation by *The Indian Express* revealed that as soon as the DMK government came to power, it ordered the cases to be dropped against twelve Muslims involved in violence and having Al Ummah contacts. The report said that senior policemen were shocked by the government's 'blatant sympathy' for the radicals.[113]

In 2004, the Tamil Nadu police took action against a new Islamic group which was receiving foreign funds.[114] Founded by the former SIMI president of Tamil Nadu, this group converts disenfranchised Hindus to radical Islam and then deploys them as militants.[115] In 2006, the police arrested youths belonging to this organization with maps and ingredients for bombs. The police officer making the arrest was transferred as a punishment, and the police was harassed by the state officials for making these arrests.[116] Police trying to arrest Al Ummah cadres have been attacked and not allowed to enter the

Muslim area, turning certain areas into 'Muslim-only zones' that are outside government authority.[117]

Radical Islam Terrorizes Liberal Islam

In the 1990s, the All Indian Jihad Committee was involved in the killing of some traditional Muslim imams of Tamil Nadu who would not accept Wahabhi fundamentalism.[118] The soft attitudes of both Tamil Nadu and Kerala governments enabled AIJC to terrorize the Islamic community and destroy the liberal elements within. Women were forced to wear burqas, a practice that had been absent in the south Indian Muslim community. Women were also threatened if they mingled with non-Muslims. Shortly after this fatwa was issued, three women who defied it were ceremoniously executed in broad daylight, which forced the frightened members of the community to fall in line. An officer of TMMK, a supporter of the DMK government, demanded that the Indian government should legalize the stoning of 'immoral' women across India.[119] In neighboring Kerala, the percentage of Muslim women who wore burqa jumped from 10.3 percent in the older generation to 31.6 percent in the younger generation.[120]

Through strategic manipulation of India's vote-bank democracy, radical Islamic groups have edged out the moderate traditional Indian Muslims with a vibrant liberal heritage in South India. The DMK government made a leader of TMMK the chairman of the Tamil Nadu Wakf board, which is a powerful quasi-governmental body managing all the Islamic religious property. He has been accused of demolishing *dargahs,* which are places of syncretic Hindu-Muslim worship associated with Sufi saints, because Sufism is opposed to Wahabhism.[121]

Madhani Released and Jihad Outsourced to Kerala

With the Tamil Nadu government becoming influenced by Islamic fundamentalists, many of the cases against them have been dropped, downgraded, or deferred. It came as no surprise that Madhani was acquitted in 2007. He was paraded in a long victory rally from Coimbatore to Kerala. A reception in his honor was attended by state ministers of Kerala. Meanwhile, jihad has been continuing unabated in Kerala. For example, in 2007 freshly manufactured assault weapons were discovered accidentally in a shipping container from Dubai, destined to an Islamic fundamentalist group in Kerala. Police interrogations led to a base where even more weapons were recovered.[122]

Thus, Madhani's release has infused new blood into the activities of jihadis. However, his release was projected as a victory of human rights in the 2007 Country Reports on Human Rights Practices published by the US Department of State.[123]

Once Kerala's Marxist government changed its position favorably towards Islamic fundamentalists, the state police could not pursue the jihadi activities beyond a point. Police records revealed that it was aware of two SIMI training camps that were held in 2006 and 2007. The police filed cases after each of these camps. After the first camp, the police rounded up SIMI activists, of whom five were named in criminal indictments, but the investigations were shelved and the activists were released. Two of the released then went on to attend the second SIMI camp and were later arrested in the northern state of Rajasthan for their role in subsequent serial blasts in Jaipur. The Kerala home minister conceded that the state government was under 'pressure' to set the SIMI men free, and rationalized it to reporters:

> Terrorists are operating in Kerala. But their main activities are outside the state. When we took police action against some of them, there was a hue and cry from human rights activists saying that minorities were being targeted.[124]

This illustrates that the political atmosphere places heavy burdens and risks on those who try to tackle the issues of security, and when the terrorists based in a given state are operating in another state, the easy thing to do is to ignore them.

As another example of such repercussions in other states, in 2008 there was a bomb blast in the state of Gujarat, and it was revealed by the Gujarat police that the SIMI activists behind the bombings were also trained at the same camp in Kerala.

In 2008, the Indian Army shot dead some jihadis trying to cross into Kashmir from Pakistan, and discovered some youths from Kerala among them. Further investigations revealed that they were part of a group of youths selected from a training camp run by SIMI in Kerala.[125] Upon the surfacing of more Kerala youths in Kashmir, the Kerala police was forced to conduct raids of two recruitment agents who had sent sixty to seventy youths to training camps in Kashmir and Pakistan. The jihadi deployment of new converts to Islam became apparent.[126] Kerala is now exporting jihadis who are well-educated, computer-savvy, and connected with global organizations.

Karnataka

Terror Emerges in Karnataka

In Karnataka also, a jihadi terror infrastructure has been built. Bengaluru's vulnerability to terror was shown in 2005 when militants attacked the prestigious Indian Institute of Science and killed a scientist.[127] Investigations revealed that the mastermind was Maulana Abdul Bari, a Saudi-based cleric and financier of several Tamil Nadu Lashkar-affiliated groups. Investigators detained at least four individuals in Tamil Nadu for their possible role, revealing that jihadi recruitment in Tamil Nadu has revived to the levels of a decade ago.[128]

In 2006, Karnataka police arrested two Pakistani nationals belonging to Al Badr, one of the oldest Pakistani jihadi groups operating in Kashmir.[129] The arrest revealed logistic connections between terror groups in Tamil Nadu, Karnakata and Kashmir. Soon, another organization, called Karnataka for Dignity, was launched as a benign public front for this jihadi network. In 2007, a rally protesting the hanging of Saddam Hussein turned violent and Muslim youth attacked Hindu houses and vandalized a Hindu temple.[130] A month later, three radical movements in Tamil Nadu, Karnataka, and Kerala launched a pan-Islamic movement called Popular Front of India, that held its first conference in Bengaluru. The name was based on the well-known Popular Front of Palestine. *The Indian Express* reported:

> What is worrying the police is the fact that majority of the leaders of this new front belong to the now-banned SIMI. . . . Sources in the Home department said the PFI had been active mainly in coastal Karnataka area and Bengaluru city. Police suspect the outfit's role in the recent violence in Mangalore and Udupi districts.[131]

The Karnataka jihadis' international links were further established when an Islamic engineer from Bengaluru attacked Glasgow airport in 2007. This brought out his connections with a Bengaluru fundamentalist outfit which feeds recruits to Lashkar-e-Taiba.[132] After the 2008 bomb blasts in Bengaluru, anti-terrorism detectives led to the arrests of several persons linked to a Kerala-based unit of Lashkar-e-Taiba, which was sending youths to LeT training camps in Kashmir and Pakistan.[133]

Recent Situation in Tamil Nadu

Tamil Nadu has become a silent haven for jihadi bases with inadequate action being taken by local law enforcement. One of the two Pakistani terrorists arrested in Mysore in 2006 had obtained his driving license in Chennai.[134] In 2007, Delhi police prevented an attempted bombing by two Lashkar terrorists who were planning to flee to Chennai.[135] Investigations revealed that the two were trained in Pakistan and had stayed in Chennai.[136] It was also discovered that Chennai-based Lashkar operatives planned to rendezvous with Sri Lankan Islamists.[137]

The Coimbatore bomb-blast court verdict sentenced the eighty-three jihadis to varying terms of imprisonment, but they were released because their period of detention during trial had equalled the sentence. So they returned for redeployment with two organizations, one of which is Saudi-financed and provided connectivity between the jihadis in prison and their collaborators.[138] The twelve most-wanted terrorists, including three trained in Afghanistan and Pakistan, are on the loose after being involved in bomb attacks in Tamil Nadu.[139]

In 2008, the Tamil Nadu police broke up a plot to plant bombs in Chennai and other districts on the eve of India's Independence Day.

One operative was arrested with explosives and it became known that the plot was masterminded by the leader of Jihad Committee lodged in Chennai jail, where he was imprisoned for eight cases of murder and terrorism.[140] The ambitious plan involved a three-pronged assault: bombs in trains; explosions in seventeen different places, including government offices across the state, the American consulate, and places of Hindu worship; and elimination of Hindu leaders and Muslims who practiced indigenous and liberal forms of Islam. The fallout of this was a shake-up of the prison administration.[141]

In 2008, the Intelligence Bureau alerted the Tamil Nadu director general of police about intercepts by the Indian Army that Lashkar-e-Taiba was planning an attack on Madurai's famous Hindu temple.[142] In a bizarre coincidence on the eve of India's Independence Day, MNP planned parades with the flag of the Islamist Jammu and Kashmir Liberation Front (JKLF) in the temple city of Madurai and painted JKLF flags in various places in Tamil Nadu.

Despite all this, a deceptive calm prevails over Tamil Nadu. Top police officers acknowledge that 'there are deep undercurrents of Muslim extremism'.[143] They also concede that most of the radical Islamist organizations which have been politically legitimized by Dravidian politics never left SIMI and continue to work with the sole objective of establishing Islamic rule in India.[144]

Vote Bank Politics

State agencies investigating Karnataka serial bomb-blasts in 2008 zeroed in on Kerala sources, particularly the wife of Madhani. Meanwhile, Kerala police independently investigating Laskar-e-Taiba activities in the state discovered that even as Madhani was in jail, his wife was emerging as the center of LeT activities in Kerala, where she was arrested by Kerala police.[145] Both the leading political parties in the state were embarrassed by the extent of LeT's and Madhani's People's Democratic Party's involvement. While Congress had sought the support of PDP in the 2001 elections, Marxists had sought the support of PDP in the latest rounds of elections. With both the parties supporting the jihadi outfit for wooing Muslim votes, the PDP has been building logistics to undermine the very democratic environment which helped it grow.[146]

Despite top Marxist politicians publicly regretting their relationship with PDP, the radical Islamic outfit continues to work closely with the Marxist cadre. This came to the foreground when the Marxist cadre joined hands with radical Islamists to operate as the moral police in Kerala. A leading literary figure condemning this as Talibanism was physically assaulted by the Marxist-PDP cadre.[147]

Because of these developments and the near-total compromise of the political apparatus in the state, at the end of 2009, the National Investigating Agency (NIA) took charge of the cases related to terrorism in Kerala. It expressed virtually no confidence in the state authorities, given the local politicians' collusion with terrorists.[148] The Marxist home minister of state has demanded curtailing the investigative scope of NIA in the terror activities.[149]

With mainstream Indian political parties nurturing radicalism, some minority politicians and community leaders started projecting themselves even more radically. For example, in November 2009, the Jamiat-e-Ulema Hind passed a resolution at its national convention in Deoband that Muslims should not sing the patriotic song 'Vande Matram', because it deemed some verses to be against the tenets of Islam.[150] Mainstream politicians capitulated without protest, despite the fact that there are madrasas where the students have been singing the Indian patriotic song for decades with no fear of the fatwas from fundamentalists.[151]

In December 2009, at an international seminar organized by the Indo-Japan Chamber of Commerce, the industry union minister of state for railways, E. Ahmed (of the Muslim League) refused to light a ceremonial lamp, which is a traditional Tamil custom for observing auspicious occasions, stating that it was un-Islamic.[152] A Christian guest, the noted recording star K.J. Yesudas, walked out protesting against the minister's action.[153] These are very recent trends. Until very recently, former president of India, Abdul Kalam a practicing Muslim, routinely lighted ceremonial lamps.

Emboldened, the Popular Front of India (PFI) activists have enacted Taliban edicts. Initially, they terrorized the Islamic community to follow puritan Islam. Now their dictates have started spreading to other communities as well. In one incident, a college professor was dragged out of his car and his hand was chopped off because he had allegedly insulted the prophet in a question-paper he had prepared. Subsequently, Kerala police revealed that the attackers belonged to PFI.[154] Police raids on the PFI offices revealed 'a well-oiled, pan-Islamist network fed by a heady mix of Wahhabism and hawala. Kerala's deep-rooted Gulf links also come in handy for the PFI'.[155] *The Times of India* reported that PFI was running a network of private Taliban courts in the state, and had instructed the Muslim community to shun the government courts.[156] Kerala's home minister admitted that the police had information that religious courts named 'Darul Huda' function in the state, despite earlier denials by the state government.[157]

The chief minister of Kerala had previously sought the help of radical Islamic elements, including the PDP, a constituent of PFI, to get the Muslim votes and had even argued for the release of Madhani, who was at that time jailed in Tamil Nadu for bomb-blasts. However, once the law and order situation went out of hand in July 2010, the same chief minister was forced to confess in a press conference:

> They want to turn Kerala into a Muslim-majority state in twenty years. They are using money and other inducements to convert people to Islam. They even marry women from outside their community in order to increase the Muslim population.[158]

Any punitive action against the kingpin of fundamentalist outfit was opposed by eminent intellectuals like Justice (retd) V.R. Krishna Iyer,[159] and Iyer was awarded 'a prize for human rights and justice' instituted by PDP.[160]

New Developments in 2010

In the aftermath of the death of Sri Lankan LTTE leader Velupillai Prabhakaran, Tamil Nadu separatism got a boost. A Tamil film director suddenly rose into prominence, starting a new movement, 'We, Tamils', using the LTTE emblem as its logo.[161] He was invited by Tamil groups in Canada, where he reportedly said that the war would have ended differently had the rebels bombed a hundred Sinhala schools for every Tamil school bombed by the Sri Lankan forces.[162] He was deported from Canada, and in Tamil Nadu he conducts a series of conferences emphasizing the ethnic and linguistic separatism of the Tamils. His website provides publicity to Maoist and Kashmir separatist causes, such as, for example, a Maoist demonstration to be held in London on the day of Indian Independence, and a Kashmir separatist demonstration in Chennai.[163] Deivanayagam has joined hands with this person to further radicalize the Tamil identity, along with Christianizing it.

Deivanayagam has recently launched an organization named 'Federation of All Self-respecting Tamils', collaborating with separatists. They falsely claimed to be championing the right of everyone to worship in the Kapaleeswarar Temple and to perform puja inside the sanctum sanctorum.[164] He also launched an agitation against the Tamil Nadu chief minister, M. Karunanidhi, accusing him of betraying the Tamil race by including scholars who were brahmins in the Classic Tamil Conference held in 2010.[165]

And simultaneously, in Kanyakumari district, a workshop was conducted for evangelicals on 'how to proclaim that India is a Christian Dravidian Nation' using the St Thomas Myth. In the workshop, Yesuvadiyan (whose book *India is a Christian Nation* has been discussed earlier) asked Christians to seek political power, because Christanity commands them to do so. Many strategies were discussed on confusing the Hindus with issues about their religion, and then answering these issues with Biblical interpretations of Hinduism. One tactic taught was to inform Hindus that Jesus is the real currency, whereas all the Hindu gods are fake photocopies of that currency, with no value.

The street-level provocations of Hindu sensibilities were such that they could easily lead to violence. Amidst such tensions, the Classical Tamil Conference featured anti-Hindu as well as Dravidian Christian voices. A balanced academic tone was used to emphasize a non-Indian Tamil identity, with the full support of and massive funding from the Indian government. For example, a session on the philosophical traditions of Tamils proclaimed:

The idea of Atman and Karma was introduced by Aryans to enslave Dravidians. . . . Karma concept of Dravidians was twisted by evil Aryans to justify Varnashrama Dharma. Thus they became the ruling race of India and they justified their subjugation and humiliation of Dravidians. . . . Anyone who knows Aryan-Dravidian race history will understand that fatalism and idea of soul, etc., were introduced as cunning ploy by Aryans to subjugate Dravidians. Hence, these evil concepts were opposed from Buddha onwards to EVR. In the line of Mao for Tamil social liberation, the three great savants (EVR, Anna and Karunanidhi) are paving the way.[166]

Another scholar recycled the Thomas-Christian claim that Sanskrit and Vedas were created in the second century CE.[167]

Another session titled 'Tamil and Religion' was chaired by Bishop Ezra Sargunam, founder of Evenagelical Church of India. The session demonized Sanskrit, and the chair declared that Sanskrit was created to promote casteism and social inequality. He supported Deivanayagam's claim that Tamil spiritual and ethical literature was Christian influenced, and that the Dravidian movement was started and nurtured by missionaries. He ended his speech with a call for Tamils to convert to either Christianity or Islam, or to embrace 'Dravidian religion' by joining DMK.[168] Thus, the crank theories instrumental in creating a pseudo-scientific Christianized racist identity of Tamils, are being propagated with strong central government assistance.

In the Crosshairs of Three Civilizations

While this book has focused mainly on the Western interventions into the Dravidian movement, one must take a broader look at the global dynamics. The picture that emerges is that far from being isolated phenomena here and there, the move to co-opt the Dravidian identity into a global Christian Dravidian movement is a part of a bigger problem facing India.

There are three major civilizations competing for global domination today: the West (especially the US), China, and Islam. Each has very explicitly stated its determination, if not destiny, to be the dominant world paradigm. Each paradigm competes with the other two, a fact that is less deniable each day. While the US/West leads in wealth, military and intellectual capital, China is set to catch up and supersede within the next few decades. Islam lacks the modern technology, education and freethinking population of the other two, but leads in its ability to mobilize large numbers of people based on a cohesive identity that transcends national and ethnic boundaries. Its deficiency in modernity feeds those elements that thrive on a pre-modern unified idea of Dar-ul-Islam (pan-Islam).

While the US/West is in open war with pan-Islam and in intense competition with China (which could also turn into military tensions), the China/Islam tension is latent and appears nonexistent today. But this could change once China becomes more powerful, and direct confrontations with elements of Islam become unavoidable. The tactical alliances where China supplies capital and buys oil, could turn sour. Ideologically, China's materialism and ethnic nationalism are incompatible in the long-term with Arabic/Iranian-dominated Islamic religiosity.

This clash of civilizations is likely to worsen as the world's growing population seeks better lifestyles, which, in turn, generates greater competition for scarce resources. Collective identities, including religion and nationalism, are likely to become even more important as vehicles through which group interests are pursued.

Indians have tried hard to evade these uncomfortable issues, hoping that by ignoring them they will go away. They hope that the vision of a 'global village' will be a 'flat world' of meritocracy, that is, free from the nuisance of identities. But this postmodern utopia is not the only trend to note. There are two competing trends simultaneously:

1. A postmodern world of consumerism, global brands and freely moving labor and goods. This integrates and creates mutual interdependencies.
2. Global identities that override the individualities and compete as stakeholders in a tough, mean world where demand outstrips the supply of critical resources.

Many modern secular Indians feel secure in the assumption that things will proceed along scenario 1, and that scenario 2 is sensationalist, a product of radical thinking. This book's research concludes that while scenario 1 might prevail on the surface, it would be foolish to ignore the trends towards scenario 2, which are far too conspicuous to be dismissed.

It is important to assess these scenarios in terms of the potential interventions by all three global civilizations, which follows next.

China

As noted in a prior chapter, China has strategic interests in capturing water that presently flows from Nepal into the Ganga river. Additionally, its claims over the Indian state of Arunachal Pradesh are intended to give it the ability to divert much of the Brahamaputra water source toward southeastern China. The third major river of the subcontinent, the Indus, is already in disputed territory, as much of it flows through Kashmir. The strategic implications for India's water supply cannot be overstated.

Additionally, China fears India as the only possible game-spoiler in its drive towards world domination. It has already compromised the West, including the US, given its prominence as the world's banker and ability to invest shrewdly and in unpredictable ways. The US is unwilling to confront China, and this capitulation is likely to worsen over time. On the other hand, India is another vast nation that offers the West many of China's advantages, and this poses a serious threat to China. China has a certain awe of the Indian mind's capabilities, its antiquity that brought much civilization to China through Buddhism, and its large (and younger) labor pool and huge markets.

China has already tied up strategic deals on both sides of India. Myanmar is very much a Chinese satellite, thanks to India's lazy foreign policy and for following the US lead in isolating Myanmar. China has built massive cities on Myanmar's northern border, and has a naval presence in the Bay of Bengal. It has leased a corridor through Myanmar for a road highway, rail and oil pipeline that would connect the Indian Ocean to China through Myanmar. This enables both oil imports and China's manufactured exports to save almost two thousand kilometers by not having to travel through the Straits of Malacca in order to link China with the Indian Ocean.

A parallel situation already exists in Pakistan: China has built a naval base in Baluchistan, and has road, rail and oil highways through Pakistan and Tibet into China. The China-Pakistan collaboration has far worse implications given Pakistan's own designs on India and its state of desperation. China need not take direct military action against India, because Pakistan is ever willing to do so on China's behalf. China is already supplying military hardware to Pakistan, along with financial capital and technology. It is not far-fetched to imagine a scenario where China's actions against India would get unofficially outsourced to Pakistan-based militants. This could also be a sort of 'deal' that China makes with the Islamic militants in exchange for securing peace within its own borders where Muslims comprise a majority. Such deals are well known in world history, wherein enemies collaborate, at least temporarily, to set aside their mutual differences in order to pursue a bigger common enemy. India provides an ideal target to divert China's hostile relations with radical Islam.

Pan-Islam

It is outside the scope of this book to argue that Islamic doctrine requires its followers to spread it worldwide, and that it regards itself as the ultimate social-political system that must rule over all humanity. It is enough to point out that it has had a history of expansion, which Muslims share with pride. Sermons in mosques preach the inevitability of ultimate Islamic victory. While there is enormous diversity across the various Islamic ethnicities—including south Asian, ASEAN, African, Arabic, Iranian, and Western—as well as internal disputes between Sunnis and Shiites, the fact remains that when it comes to external affairs there is tremendous unity of purpose. Whether it was the caliphate movement in the previous century, or whether it is Palestine, Kashmir or Kosovo, Muslims worldwide get mobilized in a united manner. In fact, one might surmise that these extroverted mobilizations serve to divert attention away from the various internal frictions, because a common cause of victimhood and a common program of action gets identified to channel Islamic passion.

We are fully cognizant of the various liberal Islamic attempts around the world that seek to counteract the radical Islam. However, they are far from confident of bringing about the reformation they aspire to. Many of them acknowledge that the Reformation of Christianity in the Middle Ages took a couple of hundred years of violence before the Church agreed to the church/state separation which enabled freethinking and modernity. They fear that their voices are too few and feeble, whereas the radical Islamists have gained momentum and are unlikely to slow down.

Any scenario of India's security simply cannot disregard these realities in the hope that the liberal side will ultimately prevail. Not only is the final outcome uncertain in this internal fight for the future of Islam, the world must be prepared to live amidst this fight for the foreseeable future. It would be naive and foolish to simply wish it away.

Specifically concerning Islam in India, one must start by noting that Indian Muslims are among the most liberal in the world, sharing a great deal of commonality of culture with Hindus over the centuries. They are very patriotic and even nationalistic. Many are secular, well-educated and well-established in various professions and industries.

Yet there are over twenty-nine thousand madrasas in India, many with funding from overseas – mainly Saudi Arabia and Iran. The Kashmir militancy has overflowed in some cases, as noted earlier. Given the poverty, unemployment among youth, lack of secular education in many Muslim communities, and the abundance of foreign Islamic influence, the future of the community is up for grabs by various contenders. Among these contenders has always been Pakistan. For Pakistan, a successfully integrated India, with Hindu-Muslim harmony and prosperity, poses a threat, for that would prove the viability of Gandhi's 'one-nation theory' in which all religions can live together. This would refute the 'two-nation theory' on which Pakistan was founded and on which it survives today.[169]

In short, interference from Pakistan to stir up Indian Muslim youth is likely to continue and must be factored in any security analysis.

Besides its own nuclear capability and its Taliban export capability, Pakistan enjoys a powerful alliance with China.

The American Eagle's Double Vision

In the face of all this, many Indians feel that the US is India's best ally. This may well be true, and yet Indians must understand that all Americans do not have just one point of view. Nor is the American posture towards India stable and constant over time. The American political winds keep shifting, with many competing points of view on every complex issue.

Before we analyze the Indian-American interactions, we should examine the US problems with China and Islamic nations. The United States considers itself as following both a Christian ethos and a very modern enlightened secular ethos. That gives it a divided personality to start with, and now both of these identities are threatened by other civilizations. This is explained below.

The clash with China can be called the clash of modernities. This competition is not based on religion or ideology but on modern materialistic concerns, such as the industrial economy, military strength, political power, and consumerism. The Chinese openly claim that they are going to become more American in various ways than the Americans themselves. With decline in American manufacturing and the outsourcing of many American jobs and industries, this is eating America at the core of its modern industrial complex society. The US is becoming a debtor nation, with China holding much of the debt. The USA sent China the industries, technology and machines, and bought the finished goods. So the US has actually transplanted its entire industrial complex across the Pacific Ocean to China, Japan, and Korea, enabling them to compete effectively with the US economy. This is the first trauma of the United States.

The second trauma is the clash of fundamentalisms. Unlike the China threat, Islamic fundamentalism is not looking for modernity. Islamic countries are not clashing with the US because they have better machines, better factories, or more consumer exports. They are not concerned about that. They are competing against fundamentalist Christianity and its rival claims over historical prophets, with each side claiming to have been given God's final word. Both Christianity and Islam are claiming that they have received God's franchise – in fact, each claims the exclusive franchise and alleges that all other religions are bogus. The franchise claim is global and exclusive. It is interesting that Islam, as an offspring and sequel to Christianity, is now taking on its own Abrahamic parent.

With the Chinese threat on one side and the Islamic threat on the other, America has developed a schizophrenic attitude towards India, which needs to be understood. Essentially, the United States is hedging its bets on India. That is why it is impossible to characterize American attitudes on India one way or the other in any absolute sense.

Fig 19.6 presents the US dilemma. The left-hand side shows the costs and benefits to building up India, while the right-hand side shows the pros and cons of fragmenting India. Both views are embraced by different elements within the US at various times, in a complex and ever-changing political dance.

Fig 19.6 US Dilemma Towards India

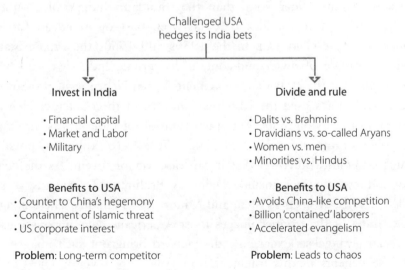

Challenged USA
hedges its India bets

Invest in India

• Financial capital
• Market and Labor
• Military

Benefits to USA
• Counter to China's hegemony
• Containment of Islamic threat
• US corporate interest

Problem: Long-term competitor

Divide and rule

• Dalits vs. Brahmins
• Dravidians vs. so-called Aryans
• Women vs. men
• Minorities vs. Hindus

Benefits to USA
• Avoids China-like competition
• Billion 'contained' laborers
• Accelerated evangelism

Problem: Leads to chaos

The American voices represented on the left-side of the diagram are saying: Let us invest in India's markets, industry and labor; let us have military alliances; let us have regional political alliances. This will counter China's hegemony; it will contain the Islamic threat; it is good for US corporate interests; and India will be a stabilizing force in the third world. The US government has tipped in favor of India and this encouraged US, European, Japanese and Chinese multinationals to also become major investors in India. These stakes would be devastated if India were to fragment because of the disruption in markets, supply chains, and capital flows. There is a new, positive India narrative that is emerging in American business schools, which has begun to balance the earlier discourse on India as a frontier filled with exotic cultures at best and a nightmare of human atrocities at worst. The American business world believes that India's time has come.

But there is also a caution shown at the bottom-left of the diagram: If India becomes too successful, then in the long term the US will have built up another China-like competitor. One China is bad enough; what if another billion people also become successful in competing with the United States? It is good for America to have a strong India, but not too strong.

Moving to the right-hand side of the diagram, the 'Fragment India' voice is a much older voice than the 'Build up India' voice on the left-hand side. It is an idea that has been part of American foreign policy since the Cold War. In the 1950s and 1960s the United States had an attitude of divide-and-contain concerning India. We saw how they supported the Dravidian movement: When Nehru went pro-Soviet, the United States used the Dravidian movement to counteract Nehru's program of unifying India. The fragmentation of India has been a very old policy stratagem for the United States. It seeks to exploit any possible ethnic or political division that it can discover or invent. As the chart shows, these divisions include Dalits vs Brahmins; Dravidians vs so-called Aryans; Women vs Men; and Minorities vs Hindus. These images make India fit the frontier images most Americans have unconsciously. Christian evangelists exaggerate the facts to bring out such images.

The benefits of this fragmentation policy are several: The United States avoids creating another powerful competitor; American companies can still outsource and use the Indian laborers; these cheap laborers will never get out of hand in the absence of an effective state that can stand up to the US on their behalf; and the US can still use Indian workers on its own terms and keep them weak. The policy of division will also accelerate evangelism because when the state is weak, the evangelists can make inroads and there will be less resistance to their aggressive proselytizing. The ensuing conflicts will also create a great market for Western weapons exporters.

Nevertheless, if this fragmentation of India actually causes civil wars, what will ensue will be the worst US nightmare in the form of anarchy and chaos, on a scale that is daunting compared to Iraq or Afghan-Pakistan.

The American bipolar stance on India oscillates between support for the nation as a whole, and support for its various fragments. It wants to meddle in Indian affairs and manipulate Indian internal conflicts to maintain its control. This keeps India under check via 'human rights' sticks and carrots that make it impossible for India to enjoy the kind of runaway economic success as China has achieved, because China is unfettered by these restrictions. Though the Indian economy in a democratic milieu cannot be compared with the centralized Chinese economy with its flagrant and excessive human rights violations, it is noteworthy that it is China and not India that is accorded the 'most favored nation' status with the US.

Even so, American policymakers must know the destabilizing implications that would surely result from breaking India up into fragments. Even though it is clearly not in the American interest to do this, ironically, they have been active in promoting Indian fragmentation as we saw in prior chapters. Indian strategists must accept that the Americans will continue to play both sides in every political game-board.

Appendices

Appendix A

A Short History of Racism from the Nasal Index to the Y-Chromosome

D r Ambedkar (1891–1956), who was a scholar of history as well as the architect of India's constitution, used the European Nasal Index criteria to prove that the whole theory rested on what he called a 'false foundation'. [1] Nevertheless, the ghost of Risley has continued to lurk, and his successors in the academy have tried similar ploys using genetics and biased assumptions of history. The most recent work in genetics, however, disproves the Aryan invasion theory that underlies both the Dravidian and the Dalit claims of separate races.

Caste Chromosomes

In 2001, Michael Bamshad of the Institute of Human Genetics, University of Utah, studied the genetic markers of caste groups from Visakhapatnam district and compared them with various castes and regional groups of India as well as with Africans, Asians, and Europeans. Bamshad announced that the 'genetic distances between upper, middle, and lower castes are significantly correlated with rank; upper castes are more similar to Europeans than to Asians; and upper castes are significantly more similar to Europeans than are lower castes'. [2]

This was reminiscent of Risley's Nasal Index as the 'scientific proof' that Aryans originated caste in India. It triggered an avalanche of enthusiasm among race scientists masquerading as human rights activists keen to prove the racial difference of the downtrodden. Anil Ananthaswamy bought the conclusion wholesale, and wrote a provocatively titled article 'Written in Blood', in the prestigious *New Scientist*, where he repeated Bamshad's conclusions: 'Upper-caste Indians are genetically more like Europeans, while members of India's lower castes are more like other Asians, says an international team of researchers'.[3] Despite being a scientific journal article, the article was mixed up in its categories and cited the pro-missionary scholar, Robert Hardgrave, as an authority:

> Based on such evidence, most historians believe that waves of Indo-European-speaking people from eastern Europe and the Caucasus set up the caste system as they moved into the Indian subcontinent about five thousand years ago. 'When the Aryans came in, they brought with them a social hierarchy,' says Hardgrave. 'We have some historical and archaeological evidence which suggests that as the Aryans came in, they intermarried with indigenous people and also absorbed many of them into their system of ranking.'[4]

In India, *Frontline* framed the results politically, and reported:

> In recent times, with the rise of strident nationalism in the form of 'Hindutva' ideology, which rejects the premise that Aryans were outsiders and views them as part of the continuum from the Indus valley civilisation, an unequivocal answer to this may have political implications. While material evidence of ancient history has not been able to resolve this issue, modern population genetics, based on analyses of the variations in the DNA in population sets, has tools to provide a more authoritative answer.[5]

Presuming the study to be infallible, *Frontline* drew sweeping conclusions:

> The analysis of genetic distances shows that each caste is most closely related to Eastern Europeans. Moreover, the genetic distance between Eastern Europeans and upper castes is half the distance between the middle or lower castes and the Eastern Europeans. The authors

interpret this as the Indian Y-chromosomes, particularly upper-caste Y-chromosomes, being more similar to European than to Asian Y-chromosomes.[6]

Another major study that followed Bamshad was done in 2004 by a team of six scientists, including Richard Cordaux of Max Planck Institute for Evolutionary Anthropology. It was formulated with specific reference to the origin of Hindus:

> The origins of the nearly one billion people inhabiting the Indian subcontinent and following the customs of the Hindu caste system are controversial: are they derived largely from Indian local populations (i.e. tribal groups) or from recent immigrants to India? Archeological and linguistic evidence support the latter hypothesis.[7]

The study claimed to have analyzed 'the most extensive dataset of Indian caste and tribal Y-chromosomes to date'. It concluded unambiguously:

> We conclude that paternal lineages of Indian caste groups are primarily descended from Indo-European speakers who migrated from central Asia 3,500 years ago. Conversely, paternal lineages of tribal groups are predominantly derived from the original Indian gene-pool. We also provide evidence for bidirectional male gene flow between caste and tribal groups. In comparison, caste and tribal groups are homogeneous with respect to mitochondrial DNA variation, which may reflect the sociocultural characteristics of the Indian caste society.[8]

A lone dissenting voice

India Today also reported the study but presented it as 'a controversial genetic study'.[9] The article drew parallels with Risley's 'scientific proof' of the racial foundation of caste, from a century earlier. After providing the accolades heaped on the new study by its supporters, the magazine also gave voice to its critics. *India Today* brought out the observation of Dilip Chakravarti, a Cambridge University archeologist, that 'race itself is not so easily defined when one is speaking of entire continents. Asian, African and European are geographical terms that do not indicate homogeneous populations'.[10] Equally uncomfortable with the study was leading sociologist Andre Beteille, professor emeritus at the University of Delhi, according to whom, 'There's no question of the genetic diversity of the Indian population, but it is quite another thing to be divided into races.'[11] *India Today* also questioned the methodology of the study, showing its serious limitations and errors.[12] The article ended with a caution:

> A hundred years ago, Risley's nose-based theory of the European origin of caste had met its match in B.N. Dutta's nose-based theory of caste. Dutta, Swami Vivekananda's brother, had then disproved the theory that higher castes have 'European' noses merely by making more measurements. Times have changed, and tools too. Now it's genetic tests and it may take many more of these to set to rest the controversy that has returned after a hundred years of quietude.[13]

Y-chromosome exorcised of Risley's ghost

In 2006, a major genetic study of the Indian population was taken up by a team of twelve scientists, among them, Sanghamitra Sahoo of National DNA Analysis Centre, Central Forensic Science Laboratory, India, and V.K. Kashyap of National Institute of Biologicals, Noida, India. The study produced results that contradicted Bamshad's study but did not receive the kind of politicizing and publicity that Bamshad had evoked:

> The Y-chromosome data consistently suggest a largely south Asian origin for Indian caste communities and therefore argue <u>against</u> any major influx, from regions north and west of India, of people associated either with the development of agriculture or the spread of the Indo-Aryan language family.[14]

This was followed by yet another research paper published in *The American Journal of Human Genetics*. Among the fifteen scientists who submitted this paper, were L. Luca Cavalli-Sforza, Department of Genetics, Stanford University, and Partha Mazumdar of Human Genetics Unit, Indian Statistical Institute, India. This study was not charitable towards the much-publicized Bamshad studies and similar works. It refuted the Aryan invasion/immigration model and also exposed as a falsehood the idea that Dravidians were pushed from the Indus Valley by invading Aryans into peninsular India. It concluded: 'Our data are more consistent with a peninsular origin of Dravidian speakers than a source with proximity to the Indus . . .' and that 'the distinctive south Asian Y-chromosome landscape' had not been shaped by Indo-European migrants.[15]

Referring to the Bamshad study of 2001, it confirmed the doubts raised by *India Today* in harsh words atypical of a scientific journal. It said that the Bamshad study had been 'framed in the context of the contemporary social hierarchy and/or linguistic fabric of various groups'. It alleged that the Bamshad study suffered from two major errors: It used 'ethnically ill-defined populations, limited geographic sampling, inadequate molecular resolution', and 'inappropriate statistical methods'.[16] Reflecting on the 2004 study by Richard Cordaux et al., the paper criticized the reliance upon 'specific historical events', and pointed out several alternative ways of explaining the data that were ignored. 'In other words, there is no evidence whatsoever to conclude that Central Asia has been necessarily the recent donor and not the receptor of the R1a lineages'.[17]

Another attempt in 2009

Despite such discarding of the racial basis of jati, modern genetic studies are being twisted to claim just the opposite. In 2009, a paper was published in *Nature*. A team led by scientists at the Centre for Cellular and Molecular Biology (CCMB) in Hyderabad, together with US researchers at Harvard Medical School, the Harvard School of Public Health and the Broad Institute of Harvard and MIT, studied more than 500,000 genetic markers across the genomes of 132 individuals from 25 diverse groups, representing 13 states, all six language families, traditionally 'upper' and 'lower' castes, and tribal groups.[18] A report in *The Times of India* declared that the paper 'has established the antiquity of caste segregations in marriage', and linked it to the 2009 session of the UN Human Rights Council in Geneva, which had suggested declaring 'caste-based discrimination as a human rights violation'.[19]

However, one of the authors of the paper (Thangaraj Kumarasamy, Centre for Cellular and Molecular Biology) categorically rejected this:

> Our paper basically discards Aryan theory. What we have discussed in our paper is pre-historic events. Data included in this study are not sufficient to estimate the time of ANI settlement. However, our earlier studies using mtDNA and Y-chromosome marker, suggests that the ANI are approximately forty-thousand year old. We predicted that the ASI are part of Andamanese migration, therefore they could be about sixty-thousand years old. Our study shows that the Indian populations are genetically structured, suggesting that they practice endogamy for thousands of years. Every population is genetically unique, but we cannot assign genetic information to differentiate whether he/she belongs to higher/lower caste. As one is aware, Jati/caste has been introduced very recently.[20]

Kumarasamy further states that the study 'supports the view that castes grew directly out of tribal-like organizations during the formation of Indian society'.[21] In other words, the jati structures emerged tens of thousands of years prior to any arrival of the so-called Aryans into India. Furthermore, this jati structure was not one of higher/lower status but simply one of marriage within a given community.

Appendix B

Ancient Tamil Religion in Sangam Literature

A common denominator in the ideology of all anti-Indian secessionist forces, ranging from Tamil nationalists to the high-profile activists in Washington, is the emphasis on the distinctiveness of Tamil/tribal/Dalit community and culture from the general mass of Hindu community and culture. However, delineating Tamils as a separate nation culturally unrelated to the rest of India, requires a lot of convoluted reasoning, baseless assumptions, and outdated information. A study of ancient Sangam Tamil literature reveals that the land of Tamils, from its earliest conception, has been predominantly Vedic in its spirituality. Not only is the ancient Tamil literature full of Vedic motifs, but it presents Vedic ideas as nothing alien to the Tamil psyche.

References to the Vedas in Sangam Literature

Sangam is a body of literature in Tamil which flourished from fairly remote antiquity, consisting of 2279 poems written by 473 poets, including women. The age in which this body developed is usually fixed between 500 BCE to 500 CE.[1] Conventionally, Tamil scholars accept two groupings, *Pattupattu* and *Ettutokai*, which in turn consist of ancient ballads.[2]

For example, *Puranannuru* mentions the Vedas as four in number and six-limbed and as the primal scripture that never leaves the lips of the primal God with hair-locks, i.e. Siva.[3] In fact, it mentions four Vedas on several occasions.[4] Apart from praising them with words like 'primal scripture', 'valuable scripture', etc., it also uses the Sanskrit word 'Vedas' itself to refer to them.[5] It uses the term 'Anthanar' as a name for Brahmins, which has relations to Zoroastrian as well as Vedic terms *athravans* and *angiras,* respectively.[6] The Vedas are also described as the 'four scriptures of Brahmins'.[7]

Maduraikanchi, another example of Sangam literature, speaks of Vedas being sung by Brahmins[8] in ancient Tamil cities. According to *Paripatall,* a collection of poems, Brahmins were held in high respect in ancient Tamil society because of their service to the Vedas.[9] It says that in ancient Tamil society orally transmitted Vedas were studied by Brahmins, who never deviated from righteousness.[10] *Perumpannatrupadai,* another Tamil classic of Sangam vintage, speaks of parrots in Brahmin houses, which because of their continuous hearing of Vedic chanting, started chanting Vedas themselves.[11] Centuries later, Adi Sankara from South India and his disciples would witness the same scene of parrots chanting Vedic verses at the house of Mandana Misra at Varanasi in the heartland of North India.[12]

The discipline of Brahmins in their daily lives, including the practice of celibacy, has been described in great detail by Sangam literature.[13] It also mentions that there were some Brahmins whose proximity to kings and chieftains and their role as ambassadors and diplomats made them take to a life of wine and sense-indulgence.[14] Such 'non-practicing Brahmins' in a few generations took to other occupations in ancient Tamil society.[15]

Vedic fire rituals or *yagnas* were very common in the life of ancient Tamils, as portrayed by Sangam literature. Such fire rituals were often conducted by kings, although individual seers conducted the rituals in forests as well. The Vedic fire ritual necessitated that the king perform it with his queens, which was how *Puranannuru* describes a king's fire ritual along with a description of the ritual pillar.[16] According to another poem, ghee was prepared from seventeen cow varieties, some wild and some domesticated, for a Vedic yagna, and this ghee was poured like water into the fire pit, resulting in the ensuing smoke covering the entire city. [17]

Paripatal has an eloquent description of Vishnu emanating as both the structural and functional component of Vedic yagna itself.[18] *Thirumurkaatrrupatai*, another example of Sangam literature attributed to Nakkeran, a legendary Tamil poet who in later narratives assumes the role of a rebel, speaks of one of the faces of the six-faced Murugan guarding the Vedic ritual from deviating from its heritage of sacred chants.[19] In a poetic hyperbole, *Paripatal* declares that the celestials roaming over the ancient Tamil land had their eyes shrouded by the smoke clouds arising from the large number of yagnas conducted there.[20] A Tamil chieftain was identified as 'the ruler of nation of fire sacrifices groomed by Brahmins'. The ritual offerings made in the fire rituals performed by Tamil kings nourished the Devas.[21] *Puranannuru* speaks of the ancestor of a Tamil king as born in the pit of the Vedic fire-altar.[22]

When seers performed sacrifices in the forests, even wild animals helped them. The frame of Vedic yagna can be said to have pervaded the entire spectrum of Tamil life so that providing hospitality itself was termed as 'fire offering to Devas (Havis)',[23] and even war was termed 'battlefield yagna'.[24]

Ahanannuru, another anthology of poems which vividly describe mainly the love life of Tamils, chooses the incomparable greatness of Parasurama's yagna to describe the chaste beauty of the heroine.[25] The holy fire nurtured by Brahmins was tripartite in nature,[26] and was circumambulated.[27]

Pan-Indian Narratives in Sangam Literature

Many of the deities described in the Vedas, as well as their Himalayan home, are named and described in Sangam literature. For example, the imagery of the rainbow as the bow of Indra is a pan-Indian concept. The Hindi term for rainbow itself is Indra-danush. This is found in Sangam literature where the rainbow is described as the 'bow of the

Lord of Vajra'.[28] *Paripatal* speaks of the events leading to the cursing of the god Indra by the seer Gaudhama for desiring the seer's wife. It described that this scene was being painted on ancient temple walls near Madurai and people were enjoying the paintings.[29]

The idea of the Himalayas as the abode of celestials is another pan-Indian conception. Sangam literature speaks of the Himalayas as the abode of gods[30] and also as a place where celestials roam about with their consorts.[31] *Paripatal* speaks of Indra as the guardian of the Himalayas.[32]

Tamil kings were hailed as being in the lineage of Vishnu and sometimes even identified with Vishnu – another pan-Indian phenomenon.[33] Vishnu is described as having a conch shell and a discus as his weapons, and Garuda as his vehicle and flag-mast.[34] Another source describes how folk-dance dramas were enacted by shepherd women in Vishnu's honor.[35]

Several avatars of Vishnu and their missions are mentioned in Sangam literature. These include Boar, who rescued the world;[36] Dwarf, who measured the entire cosmos with his feet;[37] Sri Narasimha, a half-lion and half-human who devoured a demon to protect the freedom of religion of the child of the very same demon;[38] and Parasurama, an ascetic who slew the tyrants.[39]

Tamil Familiarity with *Ramayana* and *Mahabharata*

References to both *Ramayana* and *Mahabharata* episodes reveal the extent to which these two epics became part of Tamil life during the period of Sangam literature. There are two *Ramayana*-related episodes mentioned in Sangam literature. A Tamil poet suffering from poverty, when patronized by a king, speaks of his ignorance to deal with the valuable gifts – comparing his state to the state of monkeys bewildered by the jewels that Sita threw when she was abducted by Ravana.[40] Yet another reference is even more interesting. It discusses that when conducting a meeting to discuss the strategy for invading Lanka at the eastern coast of Tamil Nadu, Rama was disturbed by the noises of birds in the tree under which the meeting was conducted. He ordered the birds to remain silent; hearing his 'words of scriptural quality', the birds obliged and became silent.[41] This is arguably the most ancient reference attesting to the divinity of Rama outside Valmiki in any Indian literature.

The most ancient of the Chera clan of Tamil kings is reputed to have fed the warring armies of both Kauravas and Pandavas.[42] Scholars also opine that the Tamil king did not feed the armies but considering the Kuru dynasty as his ancestors, offered ancestral oblations to both Pandavas and Kauravas killed in the war.[43] The victory of yet another Tamil king was compared to the victory of Pandavas in *Mahabharatha*.[44] The popularity of any event is compared to the popularity of the victory of five princes in the legendary battlefield of Kurukshetra.[45]

Concept of United India in Sangam Literature

Another very important feature revealed in Sangam literature is the conception of the unity of the land-mass stretching from the Himalayas in the north to Kanyakumari in the south. In at least two sources, Tamil kings were praised as having had supremacy amidst all the chieftains who reigned in the land between 'the Himalayan abode of Gods' in the north and Kumari in the south and the lands which have the sea as the frontier.[46] The northern limit of this cultural unity is often referred to as the Himalayas.[47] Ganges in floods, as well as ships travelling on the Ganges, is among the scenes depicted in Sangam literature. Pilgrims from all over India coming to have holy baths at Kanyakumari as well as Rameswaram (Koti) have been mentioned in Sangam literature.[48] Speaking of Himalayas and Kanyakumari in association, is another hallmark of many Sangam poems.[49]

Apart from such spiritual-cultural unity of India depicted in Sangam poems, there is at least one poem that refers to the political unity of India. This poem, from *Puranannuru,* speaks of a time when the whole of India 'from Kanyakumari to Himalayas' was ruled as one nation, unifying the diverse geographical zones of 'plateaus, mountains, forests and human habitations' by kings of the solar dynasty, and identifies Tamil kings as descendants of the solar dynasty.[50]

The use of the term Arya in indigenous Tamil literature from Sangham tradition up to the nineteenth century shows no racial connotations. Thiru Moolar, one of the pioneer Siddhas and author of a Saivite-Tantric treatise *Thirumanthiram*, calls Siva, or supreme guru an 'Arya who burns the inner impurities'.[51] Similarly, Saint Manichavasagar in his *Thiruvasagam* calls Siva an 'Arya who releases (devotees) from bondage and nurtures them'.[52] Vedanta Desika, a great Vaishnavite commentator, praises Thiru Pan Alzhvar—a devotee belonging to what was then considered a defiled caste—as having sung the essence of Vedas in ten verses and calls him 'Vedanta Arya'. Ramalinga Vallalar, a nineteenth-century mystic reformer, uses the term Arya as meaning 'inner noble truth' and Aryans as 'seers who praise the light of grace'.[53]

Despite this voluminous evidence to the contrary, the non-Vedic Tamil identity continues to be reinforced by academicians. For example, the translation of *a* selection titled *The Four Hundred Songs of War and Wisdom: An Anthology of Poems from Classical Tamil: The Purananuru*, by George L. Hart (professor in the Department of South and Southeast Asian Studies, University of California) and Hank Heifetz, has the following description on its book jacket:

> This anthology of four hundred poems composed by more than 150 poets in old Tamil—the literary language of ancient Tamil Nadu—was compiled between the first and third centuries CE before Aryan influence had penetrated the South; it is thus a unique testament to pre-Aryan India. . . . One of the few classical Indian works that confront life without the insulation of a philosophical facade and making no basic assumptions about karma and the afterlife, the Purananuru has universal appeal.[54]

The above quote chooses a date for the literature to be after the time of Jesus, so as to fit into the Christian theory that it was influenced by St Thomas and hence it is a diluted/inferior form of Christianity. The idea of Sangam literature as non-Aryan and pure-Dravidian is propagated in public media as well. For example, Asiff Hussein, writing in a popular magazine, calls Sangam literature:

. . . a veritable goldmine of information, providing us with a glimpse into the romances, marriages, dress, ornamentation, culinary fare and religious life of the early Tamils before they came under Aryan influence.[55]

As explained in this appendix, these descriptions ignore the extensive evidence supporting that the religious life of ancient Tamils was strongly rooted in Vedic traditions.

Appendix C

Parallel Developments in Africa

We have seen how academic studies, mythological identities, evangelical ambitions, and administrative projects have worked together to create strong racial identities and divisions. The same process can lead to genocide, as it already did in Rwanda and Sri Lanka. The parallels are striking, and offer a stark warning. The Rwandan genocide can be traced to a version of the Hamitic myth. Fig A.1 summarizes the flow of this appendix.

Hamitic Myth Shapes Linguistic Ethnography in Africa

The Hamitic myth, which originally marked dark-skinned people as the cursed descendants of Noah's son Ham, was refurbished when Europeans encountered new civilizations that did not fit their own sense of supremacy. As European missionary scholars began to appreciate the culture and civilization of Africa, they wanted an explanation in the form of an outside 'non-Black' factor that could be positioned as superior to the native Africans and yet inferior to the white Europeans. This would help maintain European superiority even after the discoveries of great non-European civilizations.[1]

Such a major challenge came after Napoleon's invasion of Egypt in 1798. Saul Dubow explains that this 'was the catalyst for a new twist to the Hamitic myth: the discovery that Egyptian civilization

Fig A.1 Evolution and Consequence of Hamitic Narrative in Africa

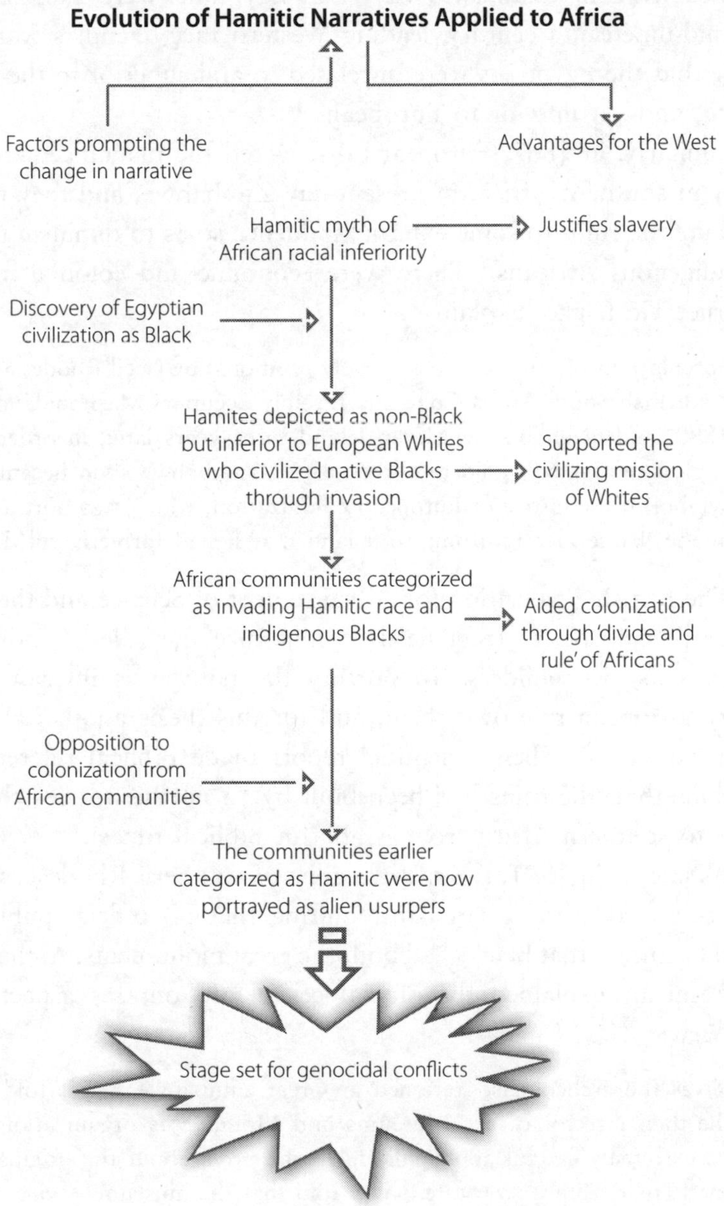

Evolution of Hamitic Narratives Applied to Africa

Factors prompting the change in narrative

Advantages for the West

Hamitic myth of African racial inferiority ──────▷ Justifies slavery

Discovery of Egyptian civilization as Black ──────▷

Hamites depicted as non-Black but inferior to European Whites who civilized native Blacks through invasion ──────▷ Supported the civilizing mission of Whites

African communities categorized as invading Hamitic race and indigenous Blacks ──────▷ Aided colonization through 'divide and rule' of Africans

Opposition to colonization from African communities ──────▷

The communities earlier categorized as Hamitic were now portrayed as alien usurpers

Stage set for genocidal conflicts

predated the classical world of the Greeks and Roman had to be squared with the established view that Egyptians were 'Negroid'.² By the mid-nineteenth century, leading Western race-scientists wanted to prove that the Egyptians were unrelated to and superior to the 'lowly' Negro, and yet inferior to Europeans.³

Similarly, in 1867, Europeans discovered the magnificent ruins of a city in southern Africa, in present-day Zimbabwe, and they tried to attribute the ruins to some external influence so as to diminish the role of indigenous Africans.⁴ There were economic and colonial motives, as Bruce G. Trigger explains:

> Speculations of this sort were actively promoted by Cecil Rhodes after his British South Africa Company forcibly occupied Mashonaland in 1890, and neighbouring Matabeleland three years later, in order to exploit the region's gold resources. Great Zimbabwe soon became a symbol of the justice of European colonization, which was portrayed as the White race returning to a land that it had formerly ruled.⁵

The British Association for Advancement of Science and the Royal Geographical Society tried hard to minimize the role of indigenous Africans as city builders. To portray the natives as inferior would justify European rule over them, and for this thesis another race had to be fabricated. Their 'scientific' report made Biblical references to conclude that 'the ruins had been built by "a northern race" that had come to southern Africa from Arabia in Biblical times'.⁶

As late as in 1971, the racist regime of southern Rhodesia's White settlers issued a secret circular requiring that no official publication should mention that Blacks had built the great monuments. Archeologist Paul Sinclair explained the official censorship on this aspect in an interview:

> I was the archeologist stationed at Great Zimbabwe. I was told by the then director of the Museums and Monuments organization to be extremely careful about talking to the press about the origins of the [Great] Zimbabwe state. I was told that the museum service was in a difficult situation, that the government was pressurizing them to withhold the correct information. Censorship of guidebooks, museum displays, school textbooks, radio programmes, newspapers and films

was a daily occurrence. Once, a member of the Museum Board of Trustees threatened me with losing my job if I said publicly that Blacks had built Zimbabwe. He said it was okay to say that the Yellow people had built it, but I wasn't allowed to mention radio-carbon dates. . . . It was the first time since Germany in the thirties that archeology has been so directly censored.[7]

Degrees of Blackness

Clearly, there was immense pressure to explain non-European civilizations in a manner that would preserve white supremacy, while appearing very scientific. The idea of 'degrees of blackness' thus emerged as a promising solution. In 1880, the German Egyptologist Karl Lepsius suggested that the indigenous peoples of Africa were composed of two major stocks: lighter-skinned Hamitic-Caucasians in the North and darker-skinned Hamitic-Negroes in the South.[8] This allowed explanations in terms of 'degrees of civilization', which was measured by how much European blood was present. Those with lighter skins were labeled as relatively more civilized than their darker-skinned neighbors, on account of having received more Europeanness through intercourse. This division of 'light Blacks' and 'dark Blacks' continues to this day among many peoples of color, including African Americans and south Asians.

Once neighboring groups became defined with separate identities based on physical body-types, the next step was for Europeans to give them different histories according to which one group was shown to be the oppressor of the other.

This academic manipulation eventually led to violent conflicts between the different native communities. Such conflicts could then be blamed as the 'human rights abuse' of a primitive civilization. This provided fresh points for intervention by Western governments and their NGOs in the post-colonial era.

Academicians Set the Stage for Genocide

One such dangerous chain reaction was started when C.G. Seligman (1873–1940), a prominent British ethnographer, proposed that the

Biblical Hamites were the lower strata of white Caucasians, who had entered Africa from Mesopotamia, and gradually intermixed with indigenous Blacks to form different degrees of Blackness. According to him there had been 'waves' of invasions from Europe as well as the Near East, with each fresh wave bringing additional white blood injected by sexual intermixing with indigenous African populations. The result was that some African groups were luckier than others for having multiple European inputs to their stock, making them more civilized.

According to this theory, Hamites could be of any skin color. Regardless of actual skin color, they were all descendants of Ham, and hence inferior to the Europeans who were descendants of Japhet. Earlier, Seligman had done field-work in Sri Lanka (Ceylon) and published a study in 1911.[9] His work was close to the Aryan invasion hypothesis and the British practice of sorting populations into racial categories. Seligman is an important link between race theories supporting colonialism in India and Africa, respectively. He could translate and map from the context of one continent to the other. When Seligman published his famous *Races of Africa* in 1930, it became instantaneously accepted in European academic circles as a great scientific work of anthropology.

Seligman's influence spread through other fields as well, and he was the patron of one of Europe's most famous ethnographers, Bronislaw Malinowski at the London School of Economics, author of *A Scientific Theory of Culture*. Seligman's theory was diffused into the popular psyche of African people through the process of colonial education. This installed European theories of race on top of existing tribal identities, and thereby permanently transformed the relations among indigenous groups.[10]

Given its implications for Africa and its similarity with what is widely believed about Indians, it is important to understand the steps in Seligman's theory by which he explained how civilization came to Africans from the outside. He wrote:

> The mechanism of the origin of the Negro-Hamitic peoples will be understood when it is realized that the incoming Hamites were pastoral 'Europeans'—arriving wave after wave—better armed as well

as quicker-witted than the dark agricultural Negroes, for it must be remembered that there was no Bronze Age in Africa, and we may believe that the Negro, who is now an excellent iron-worker, learnt this art from the Hamite.[11]

Travis Sharp points out the Eurocentrism intended here:

Seligman did not even consider the Hamites to be completely competent members of the White race. In fact, the Hamites were originally forced to migrate out of Mesopotamia and into Africa because they were the dregs of White society.[12]

In the words of another scholar, Ole Bjorn Rekdal, 'Even the cursed among the Euro-Asians were able to completely outshine the original inhabitants of Africa'.[13]

In 1932, C.G. Seligman and Brenda Seligman published their survey of southern Sudanese ethnography, titled *The Pagan Tribes of the Nilotic Sudan*. Using a theory strikingly similar to the Aryan invasion theory of India, they explained how different racial populations came into being in present African society:

At first the Hamites, or at least their aristocracy, would endeavour to marry Hamitic women, but it cannot have been long before a series of people combining Negro and Hamitic blood arose: these superior to the pure Negro, would be regarded as inferior to the next coming wave of Hamites and be pushed further inland to play the part of an incoming aristocracy vis-a-vis the Negroes on whom they impinged.[14]

Peter Rigby explains how this racial depiction of African communities drastically deteriorated the inter-community relations, meanwhile serving the colonial strategy to use one group against its neighbors.[15] Such academic misrepresentations continue to have unfortunate political effects for native peoples throughout Africa even today.

Rigby cites the most widely known anthropological work on Rwanda available in English, and takes its author to task for facilitating genocide. This work is Jacques Maquet's *The Premise of Inequality in Rwanda* (1961). Rigby accuses the scholar of perpetuating:

. . . what he himself calls 'physical or racial stereotypes' by photographing 'tall' Batutsi against the sky, and the 'short' Bahuti ('agricultural negroes') against the ground.' [Maquet] goes on to argue that the colonialist exaggeration of physical differences between Hutu and Tutsi 'into 'racial' categories was a purely a political expedient to divide and rule ('indirectly'!) where different 'tribes' could easily be invented and set against each other.

Rigby goes on to explain:

For colonial administrators, missionaries, and local Christian elites-to-be, the Tutsi were the 'best, most intelligent, most energetic chiefs, best able to understand progress and most acceptable to people.' So they were given privileges all round, special exclusive educational opportunities to 'man the administration at all levels, while Hutu could man the mines and plantations.' . . . Furthermore, when tragic conflict arose between Hutu and Tutsi in the post-colonial states of Rwanda and Burundi, leading to enormous and continuing loss of life and the creation of a major refugee problem in eastern Africa, the strife could be blamed by Western observers upon 'primordial', 'tribal' antagonisms, exculpating entirely the colonial period, politics and government.

The pre-colonial and early colonial history of Rwanda suggests that there were divisions and conflicts, sometimes violent, between pastoralists (eventually called Tuutsi) and agriculturalists (eventually called Hutus). We can see many parallels to Indian history in the way existing divisions were hardened into racial categories. For example, a census undertaken by the Belgians[16] in 1933 led to the issuing of identity cards. All Rwandans were henceforth either Tutsi or Hutu, a practice that continued until such identity cards were abolished in the wake of the genocide. This is reminiscent of how Risley used a census to freeze the Indian castes, which had been more flexible in pre-colonial times.

Revolution, Independence, Division, Conflict

Anti-colonial movements arose in the 1950s, which led to the division of the colony into Rwanda and Burundi, with independence in 1962. Rwanda elected a Hutu-dominated government. During the revolutionary period, there was frequent conflict between the more powerful Tutsis and the more numerous Hutus. This included an important Hutu uprising in 1959, which killed thousands of Tutsis and sent many more into exile. Various waves of exiles—sometimes Hutu, sometimes Tutsi—have fueled several regional conflicts. This includes the Tutsi invasion and subsequent Hutu backlash that killed thousands in 1963, sometimes known as 'The first Rwandan genocide'.

The Church-Academics Axis

The Catholic Church supported the colonial government policy of considering Tutsi and Hutu as distinct races. However, the Church's support to Tutsis waned dramatically with the Rwandan revolution in 1959. The Hamitic myth itself underwent an inversion. René Lemarchand, a political scientist known for his research on ethnic conflict and genocide in Rwanda, points out:

> Filtered through the lens of a rabidly anti-Tutsi, anti-monarchical ideology, the Hamitic hypothesis underwent a striking metamorphosis. What Europeans naively perceived as a superior brand of humanity was better seen as the embodiment of the worst in human nature: cruelty and cunning, conquest and oppression. Where missionaries invoked Semitic origins as a source of racial superiority, Hutu ideologues saw proof of foreignness. . . . What most Europeans perceived as feminine grace was now denounced as yet another ploy designed to subjugate the Hutu.[17]

As nationalist sentiments began to spread in Africa, certain Tutsi intellectuals began to regard the Catholic Church critically as an instrument of colonial power that meddled too much in Rwandan affairs. *The Church, which had been highly instrumental in the depiction of the Tutsi as racially elevated, now switched sides and joined hands with Hutus.* Now missionaries 'began to create opportunities for Hutu in church schools and church employment and cultivated a Hutu counter-elite. White Church Fathers even participated in drafting the 'Bahutu Manifesto' in 1957'.[18] Soon, events drifted towards consolidating racial hatred among Hutus against Tutsis.

In other words, the Church had first supported one native group (Tutsi) as racially superior, and helped to harden these divisive identities, and then switched sides to help the underdog (Hutu) boost its identity and fight against the native 'enemy' group (Tutsi). In a study by a team of academicians, a native Jesuit scholar has recently determined the role of the Church in bringing about genocide, as follows:

> Swiss Bishop Andre Perraudin was the most prominent Church figure in this policy shift. When he was appointed to Kabgayi Diocese he did not question the Church's divisive methods of evangelization. Although he claimed to promote charity among his followers, he continued to pursue the same divisive tactics. In the late 1950s Perraudin and the Belgian colonial administration decided to support the Hutu republican movement, which was an extremist political party led by Catholic trained Hutu intellectuals. With colonial and Church support, this Hutu-republican party called Hutu Emancipation Movement won the elections in 1959 and assumed power. But instead of restoring unity and social justice, the party indiscriminately blamed the colony's ill on the Tutsis, and with the aid of the Belgian colonial administration it initiated the first Rwandan genocide by massacring more than twenty-thousand Tutsis, while another twenty-thousand escaped abroad to neighboring states or were exiled. Those who remained in the country were denied most of their basic human rights. The demonization of Tutsis preceded the 1994 genocide. Even though this was a clear and grave human rights violation, Bishop Perraudin and his senior aides dismissed these events as a social revolution intended to redress social injustices. For thirty years these views were not questioned.[19]

In 1994, the genocide of Tutsis by Hutus exploded in the conscience of global humanity. Niels Kastfelt says that *'although the Church did not always legitimize the genocide explicitly, they formed a close alliance with the Hutu groups that carried it out and thus shared an institutional responsibility for it.'*[20]

Allan Thompson elaborates:

> The Hutu leadership of the Catholics and Anglican churches, with a few notably courageous exceptions, played a conspicuously scandalous role in these months, often directly complicit in aiding

the *genocidaires*, at best remaining silent or explicitly neutral. This stance was easily interpreted by ordinary Christians as endorsement of the killings, as was the close association of church leaders with the leaders of the genocide. Perhaps this helps explain the greatest mystery about the genocide: the terrible success of Hutu power in turning so many ordinary people into accomplices in genocide. In no other way could so many have been killed so swiftly.[21]

More recently, Dominican Fr Emmanuel Ntakarutimana of Burundi pointed out that 'the more Christian an African nation is, the higher the odds of being slaughtered there'.[22] This, he said, suggests that the churches should reconsider their evangelization methods.

In his recent book, *Christianity and Genocide in Rwanda* (Cambridge University Press), Timothy Longman of Boston University shows that several dimensions of Christian theology had become a morphed version of colonialism. He shows how the Church's own organizational structure and inter-denominational competition contributed to and literally accelerated the genocide in Rwanda.[23] The Church projects itself as being free from its colonial baggage, but he shows this to be untrue because of the manner in which it engages in local ethnic politics that lead to genocidal cataclysms. Though the Church is expert at generating atrocity literature blaming other cultures, it has downplayed and censored its own role in various local exterminations and genocides during the 1990s. The Church was content that the Rwanda regime was in full accord with its proselytizing agenda, and even commended the regime for supporting the Church versions of various human rights treaties and 'working as much as possible to, to put them into application'.[24]

Longman points out that during the genocide, the churches played an essential role in facilitating the descent into violence by lending strong support to the regime that was encouraging the exclusion and violence of one ethnic group against the other.[25] In the reactions after the genocide, Christianity once again played predominantly a negative role. Cutting across the various denominations, the Christian churches exhibited a tendency not to hold the Christian state accountable for the genocide.[26] In fact, sermons in Christian churches actually made the general population accept the growing violence as signs of the Second Coming of Jesus.[27]

Parallels with India

In Rwanda, the Biblical myth of Ham was interpreted with evangelical motives, backed by European academicians, used by colonial and post-colonial outside powers, and ended up feeling genocides between communities that had co-existed for millennia without racial hatred. The parallels this process shares with the development of a racial myth in India are striking, and issue a warning we cannot ignore. In India, first the colonial scholars fabricated an Aryan myth and boosted the pride of the so-called Aryans of India, seeing them as their own distant relatives who were now being 'civilized' once again. Then they switched sides to build up the so-called Dravidian identity by claiming them to be separate and victims of the Aryans.

Another disturbing similarity is the parallels in the creation of social hegemony by the Catholic Church on a massive scale among its parishes. In Rwanda, the massive investment of the Church in socio-economic projects helped in creating strong elite sections, which in turn was instrumental in effecting the genocide.[28] Justin Divakar, a Catholic fishermen community leader, in a study of a Catholic diocese in South Tamil Nadu reveals the same pattern of Church stranglehold on the socio-economic infrastructure of the community.[29]

Now the stage is set for the Church-sponsored activists to champion the Dravidian aggression against things depicted as Aryan. In this conflation, Sanskrit and Hinduism are depicted as Aryan-originated, while Tamil and so-called Tamil religion are depicted as Dravidian identity. Now the Dravidian identity and religion are being described to have had Christian origins through St Thomas. Hinduism and Sanskrit are, therefore, shown as impurities and in dire need of being exterminated in order to restore racial and cultural purity.

Appendix D

Thomas Hoax on Native Americans

Long before the myth of St Thomas made its way to India, the myth that he had gone to the Americas had been developed and perfected as a way to dupe the native Americans about their own origins. Historians Wolfgang Hasse and Meyer Reinhold explain how the St Thomas myth was used by missionaries to appropriate and destroy the native American traditions, and to Christianize them:

> At that moment, numerous traces of the presence of St Thomas were discovered especially in South America, where circumstances were favourable for the development of the legend. Under the prodding of the first Jesuit missionaries, a remarkable process of amalgamation began . . . it was easy to see 'Zume' as a deformation of 'Tome' (Thomas) and to transform this native messiah into a Christian apostle. The legend of the journey of St Thomas to the New World was a great success. In the region around Lake Titicaca, it was confused with that of the god Viracocha, which has also left some traces.[1]

Christian missionaries mapped every popular local native American deity to St Thomas, as a way to implant St Thomas into the popular imagination, after which they could replace and eradicate the native deity. To this day, the White Christian accounts of history continue this:

> According to these theories, the apostle St Thomas (associated in Mexico with the Indian deity Quetzalcoatl and in Peru with

Viracocha, among other legendary pre-Inca culture-bearer deities) had appeared among the Indians not long after Christ's crucifixion, and initiated the New World's first age of Christianity. . . . Considerably embellishing sixteenth-century hypotheses, certain clergymen and even devout laymen of the independence-era postulated the splendors of a flourishing native American Christian culture that had been snuffed out at the time of conquest by an Iberian variant of Christianity vitiated by greed, individualism and materialism.[2]

Appendix E

Papers Presented at New York Conference 2005

1. Author: D. Devakala

   Title of the Paper: Early Indian Christianity and Iconography

   Excerpts/Synopsis: Absence of Buddha figures, Tirthankara figures and six-fold religious sculptures in the pre-Christ era clearly indicates that the basic doctrines which are the root cause for the development of these sculptures did not exist at that time. Vedas did not play a role in the origin and development of Saivism and Vaishanvism. The Doctrine of Trinity, Jesus-Avatar, etc., which are the foundational doctrines of Christianity, are the core doctrines of Saivism and Vaishnavism; hence, they are the offshoots of Early Indian Christianity or St Thomas Dravidian Christianity . . . Three-faced Siva can be compared with the concept of 'Homoiousius' and Somaskanda and Mumurthi with the concept of Homoiousis. The term Nataraja and Unitarianism are compared.

2. Author: P. Lazarus Samraj

   Title of the Paper: The influence of Bible on *Thirukural*

   Excerpts/Synopsis: The influence of Bible on *Thirukural* is ascertained by a comparative and critical evaluation of the common principles found in both the works.

3. Author: P. Thiagarajan
   Title of the Paper: Early Christianity and the Tamil Cankam Society
   Excerpts/Synopsis: Long before the advent of Early Christianity on
   the Indian soil, the ancient Tamils had active cultural and commercial
   contact with Babylonian heritage based on the city of 'UR'. The
   relevant references found in the Old Testament of the Bible and
   other related sources bear testimony to the cultural contact between
   Tamil Cankam society and the ancient Christianity, which is a part of
   early Christianity in India . . . St Thomas was the first to plant the
   seeds of early Christianity in India . . . He preached the Gospel and
   stayed in Tamilakam till he faced martyrdom in 72 AD. St Thomas'
   visit turned out to be a catalytic source of development to the early
   Christianity in India, particularly in Tamil Nadu . . . Evidences are
   available to establish the influence of Christian thoughts in Cankam
   Society.

4. Authors: M. Deivanayagam and D. Devakala
   Title of the Paper: Christianity and Saiva Siddhanta
   Excerpts/Synopsis: In the first century AD 'Asian Christian Spiritual
   Movement' was formed on the basis of the life of Jesus Christ (not
   only on the basis of teachings but of His death and resurrection) . . .
   an ancient St Thomas Tamil/Dravidian Christianity paved way for the
   development of 'Saivism' and 'Vaishnavism'. 'Saiva Siddanta (twelfth
   century AD – fourteenth century AD) is the theological exposition of
   St Thomas Dravidian Christianity and is different from the concepts
   of Saiva Siddanthis who embraced Saivism from Jainism. . . .
   Analysis of Sivagnanapotam, the foundational book of fourteen Saiva
   Siddanta sastras, clearly reveals that it is the theological exposition of
   'St Thomas Dravidian Christianity'.

5. Authors: M. Deivanayagam and D. Devakala
   Title of the Paper: Doctrine of Trinity in Sivagnanapotam
   Excerpts/Synopsis: The Christian concepts of consubstantial hypostasis
   Persona and Interpenetration are seen in the concept of God as given
   in Sivagnanapotam. God as Love, God as Guru, God as rescuer,

Siva sattu and Tamiarul Siva sattu becoming Guru through Tamiarul, reflects the Trinitarian concept of Christianity.

6. Authors: M. Deivanayagam and D. Devakala
Title of the Paper: Doctrine of Trinity in *Thirukural*
Excerpts/Synopsis: *Thirukural,* the first ancient St Thomas Tamil/ Dravidian literature that has 133 chapters and 1330 couplets, illuminates Triune God conspicuously. . . . Nittar Perumai: Third chapter can be compared with the affirmation and confession of Irenaeus (AD 115–190), who says, 'what is invisible in the Son is the Father and what is invisible in the Father is the Son. Christological affirmation, Binitarian affirmations and Trinitarian affirmation are noteworthy in Payiram 'Iyalbudaya Muvar' – 'Coeternal', 'Coequal', 'Consubstantial' and 'Physis'.

7. Author: Moses Michael Faraday
Title of the Paper: Siddha literature and Christianity
Excerpts/Synopsis: Tamil Siddhas are well known for their indigenous medicine, alchemy, Yogic skills and their cryptic poems . . . The cryptic connotations ensconced in their poems have to be deciphered with the tools of Christian concepts and teachings, which will also reveal the influence of Christianity on Siddha Literature.

8. Author: Joshua Siromony
Title of the Paper: Christianity and Ithihasa
Excerpts/Synopsis: An objective study of the epic *Ramayana* in the light of Gospel; especially Ramavatara part of *Ramayana,* wherein Kamban describes the possible kingdom of heaven to be realized under the incarnate monarch.

9. *Author:* J.D. Baskara Doss
Title of the Paper: Brahma sutras and Christianity
Excerpts/Synopsis: The Brahma sutras attempt an in-depth analysis of the concepts of God, individual soul, bondage and liberation of the soul. . . . The various epithets that denote Brahman are comparable

to the various names of Jesus; 'Esvar with Jesyus', 'Jypthi with light', 'Aksaram' with word, 'Om' with Amen, 'Sathya' Brahman with truth, and 'Prana' with life. Similarly, the terms connoting the veiling of the soul, such as 'Bandham' and 'Thirokitham' can be likened to the concept of 'original sin' and 'individual sin'. The Vedantic doctrine 'aham eva yagna' is likened to the sacrifice of Jesus too. . . . The problem of caste system is dealt with and how the lower castes were denied access to Brahma Vidya is discussed with further references to Jewish Traditions in this connection.

10. Author: Ramanathan Palaniappan
    Title of the Paper: Christianity and Adi Sankara
    Excerpts/Synopsis: Vedanta differs from Vedas in essence and content. . . . Adi Shankara's Advaita philosophy and its interpretive role in the Vedantic context are analysed. St Thomas Dravidian Christianity is the fundamental principle out of which Vedanta and six darshanas of philosophy have sprung into existence.

11. Author: M.G. Mathew
    Title of the Paper: A short note on Christianity and Vedanta
    Excerpts/Synopsis: The assertion 'Aham Brahmasmi' (I am God) is more sinful than atheism. Vedanta does not seem to show a definite and clear-cut way for salvation of mankind. The teachings of Bible, on the other hand, are unequivocal. It is a history and prophecy regarding the future of this universe and mankind.

12. Author: J.D. Baskara Doss
    Title of the Paper: Six Darshanas and Christianity
    Excerpts/Synopsis: Veda Vyasa the Dravidian saint compiled the Upanishads after second century AD . . . Distinction is made between Vedas and Vedanta on the basis of their tenets such as sacrificial worship and concept of fulfillment of sacrifice . . . The author has attempted to establish that the nature and cause of bondage of the soul is better answered by a comparative study of Bible and Kuran than by the Indian system of philosophy.

13. Author: Mercy Rajadurai

    Title of the Paper: Saktham and Christianity

    Excerpts/Synopsis: The Goddess worship is chiefly attributed to the early Dravidians. . . . As Indian Christian theology uses the variety of symbols available from Indian sources in a creative way, the Indian Christian writers draw the source Shakti, the Mother Goddess, to relate with the Holy Spirit.

14. Authors: Yesupatham Johnson Thagaiya and D. Devakala

    Title of the Paper: Christianity and Kaumaram

    Excerpts/Synopsis: The birth of Kumarakkadavul or Christ as revealed in Bible . . . the history of Abraham the patriarch of Israel, Judaism and Christianity, concepts of Father Son and Holy spirit, State of Guru, Wisdom, Sacrifice, death on the cross, resurrection and redemption are considered . . . The article is based on the beliefs of the Yavana System of beliefs and Saivite System of beliefs, to the exclusion of Aryan system.

15. Authors: M. Deivanayagam and D. Devakala

    Title of the Paper: Christianity and Saivism

    Excerpts/Synopsis: Nature-worship plays an indispensable role in the Vedas. Vedic Rudra is the god of storms and rain, whereas Siva of Saivism is the supreme God in Saivism . . . Basic doctrines of Saivism, viz., Trinity, Avatar, etc., are not found in the Indian worships and religions of pre-Christian era. These doctrines are of Christianity and hence they became apparent in Saivism.

16. Author: M.G. Mathew

    Title of the Paper: Christ versus Krishna – Concept and Mythmaking

    Excerpts/Synopsis: The author compares the virtues of Christ and the not-so-virtuous acts of Krishna. Christ is shown as an ever-merciful, compassionate saviour and guiding light, and Krishna as an ineffective saviour and a self-contradictory being. The self-effacing deeds of Jesus to save mankind outshine the concept of Krishna and Krishna is shown as a myth. Jesus has promised to come again and not Krishna.

17. Author: Jolly Sebastian

    Title of the Paper: Prajapathy and Jesus – A Comparative Study

    Excerpts/Synopsis: There are literacy proto-types for Prajapathy in world literature, namely Prometheus (Greek), Mithra (Persian), Prajapathy (Indian) and Jesus Christ (Hebrew), of which Jesus Christ is the only historical person and the others are mythological. Vedas were compiled by Veda Vyasa only during the Vedantic age. The Prajapathy yagna mentioned in the Vedas point to fulfillment of sacrifice, which was through the Prajapathy yagna of Jesus Christ in AD 30 on mount Calvary. Swami Vivekananda's comment in this context 'Except through Jesus none can see the father' is worth remembering at this juncture.

18. Authors: D. Devakala and D. Devamala Christy

    Title of the Paper: Offshoots of St Thomas Dravidian Christianity

    Excerpts/Synopsis: The Trikayas Dharmakaya, Sambhoga Kaya and Nirmana Kaya of Mahayana Buddhism explain the Trinitarian concept of Christianity, i.e., God the Son, God the father and God the Holy Spirit.

19. Authors: M. Deivanayagam and D. Devakala

    Title of the Paper: Restoration of early Indian Christianity

    Excerpts/Synopsis: *Thirukural*, Bhakti movement, Saivism, Vaishnavism and Mahayana Buddhism are treated as offshoots of St Thomas Dravidian Christianity. Prasthanathrya – consisting of Brahma Sutra, *Bhagavad Gita* and Upanishads were the St Thomas Dravidian Christianity works written in Sanskrit. Saiva Siddhanta too can be categorized as St Thomas Dravidian Christian conception. Due to the influence of Aryan/Brahmin institutions like Varnashrama Dharma and misinterpretation, St Thomas Dravidian Christianity was not given its due recognition.

20. Author: M.S. Venkatachalam

    Title of the Paper: Marriage Metaphor in Bible and Tamil devotional poetry – A comparative study

Excerpts/Synopsis: The generic relationship between the songs of Christian bridal mysticism and devotional Tamil tradition reveals that the Christian tradition exerted deep impact on Tamil devotional poetry.

21. Authors: Raghavan Suppiah and Devakala
Title of the Paper: St Thomas Dravidian Christianity and Varnashrama Dharma
Excerpts/Synopsis: *Thirukural* is seen as a St Thomas Dravidian Christian literature and the Tamil Bhaki movement and its radiants Saivism and Vaishanvism are the offshoots of *Thirukural*. The primary value-systems of Indian culture, such as fraternity and brotherhood, were substituted by the social systems of Varnashrama Dharma brought in by the invading Aryan forces. Varnasrama Dharma was based on color and not on occupation and the caste system is sustained by the principle of work and descent. Fire-worshipping Aryans reigned supreme and the lesser Dravidians were enslaved. The practice was further worsened by the works of Adi Shankara.

22. Author: S. Pannerselvam
Title of the Paper: Early Christian missionaries and martyrs in India
Excerpts/Synopsis: Indian saints like Tiruvalluvar, Veda Vyasa, the sixty three Saivaite Nayanmars, the twelve Vaishanavite Azhwars, Meikandar, Thirumoolar, Nanthanar and Thiruppanazvar were missionaries, as their works reflect the teachings of Christ, and hence they are St Thomas Dravidian Christian Missionaries.

23. Authors: E. James R Daniel and M Sunder Yesuvadiyan
Title of the Paper: Characteristic features of early Christianity in India
Excerpts/Synopsis: Early Christianity was planted directly by St Thomas and St Bartholomew in India. Theistic Saivism and Vaishnavism overtook Jainism and Buddhism, which are atheistic and agnostic. Schisms developed in Jainsim and Buddhism due to influence

of Christian thoughts. *Thirukural*, Saivism and Vaishnavism are offshoots of Early Christianity. Vedas and Vedanta contain concepts of Christianity. All religious literature expresses values of Christianity. A pan Christian picture is thus arrived using internal and external evidences.

24. Author: Joel S Gnanaraj
    Title of the Paper: River Ganges and the doctrine of the forgiveness of sins
    Excerpts/Synopsis: The sanctity ascribed to river Ganges is described in this paper in its historic perspective. . . . the concept of holy water, when equated with to the concept of holy spirit and the concepts of forgiveness of sins, are essentially Christian and hence, it is deduced that the sanctity of Ganges can be assumed to be a later version that shows the influence of Early Indian Christianity or St Thomas Dravidian Christianity upon Hindu religion.

25. Authors: M. Deivanayagam and D. Devakala
    Title of the Paper: Doctrine of Trinity in Hindu religion
    Excerpts/Synopsis: St Thomas Dravidian Christianity is the fountainhead of Hindu Religion, meaning 'Saivism' and 'Vaishnavism', by the very fact they contain certain basic doctrines like the Doctrine of Trinity, Avatar, Forgiveness of Sin, and Salvation by faith. These doctrines are unique to the Hindu religion, which again is an offshoot of Christianity. All ancient Dravidian worship . . . can be read as the concepts of Father, Son and Holy spirit . . . So the family structure of Hindu mythology can be considered as a derivative of Christianity.

Source: Synopsis, Souvenir First International Conference on the history of early Christianity in India, 2005; Institute of Asian Studies, 2005, 145-178

Appendix F

Case of the Disposable Epigraphist

Iravatham Mahadevan, specializing in the Indus script and early Tamil, is an example of a scholar who became co-opted to serve as an academic sepoy for Western manipulations. He is a National Fellow of the Indian Council of Historical Research. His book, *The Indus Script: Texts, Concordance and Tables* (1977) is recognized internationally as a major source-book for research on the Indus script. He has also published *Corpus of the Tamil-Brahmi Inscriptions* (1966), besides numerous papers on aspects of the Tamil-Brahmi script. He has served as the coordinator of the International Association of Tamil Research for twn years, the president of the Annual Congress of the Epigraphical Society of India, and the general president of the Indian History Congress. In 2003, Harvard University Press published his monumental *Early Tamil Epigraphy from the Earliest Times to the Sixth Century AD*.

In 1970, while he was a Jawaharlal Nehru Fellow,[1] Mahadevan came out with a hypothesis that the Harappan script is 'a language which resembles South Dravidian (including Telugu) in general and Old Tamil in particular'. This was music to the ears of those fanning the flames of Dravidian separatism. It supplied social and political theories of India's divided identities by claiming 'amazingly close parallelisms between the hierarchical structure of proto-Indian and the old Tamil polities'. He theorized that the *Mahabharata* was a story of class-war between a priestly oligarchy and common people in Harappan civilization – a gift to Indian Marxists looking for class-conflict wherever possible.[2]

Mahadevan's scholarly interpretation of Indus scripts and symbols with Vedic imagery won international acclaim. He collaborated closely with Michael Witzel of Harvard and the SARVA project, which we earlier identified as a nexus for fragmenting India into ever-smaller tribal identities. He has been an important contributor to Witzel's *Electronic Journal of Vedic Studies* (EJVS).

Mahadevan seemed to practice a double standard, as evidenced by the fact that he was only mildly critical of the Dravidian fantasies of S. Mathivannan, an anti-Sanskrit Dravidianist ideologue, whose theory is based on the lost continent of Kumari Kandam/Lemuria. Mahadevan did question the authenticity of the claims based on photographs of fake paintings, but did not accuse the scholars of a hoax, whereas he harshly condemned a mistake by N.S. Rajaram as an intentional hoax and 'a sad day for Indian scholarship'.[3]

Once he became associated with Dravidian separatism, Mahadevan often applied greater rigor to examine some claims than others. For example, in 2002, in the case of the Gulf of Cambay discovery by Indian scientists of National Institute of Ocean Technology (NIOT), where the scientists suggested that they could have stumbled upon the world's oldest civilization,[4] Mahadevan urged caution and suggested calling in international experts. However, in the case of discoveries that even remotely hinted a Dravidianist hypothesis, Mahadevan took an entirely different approach. In 2006, neolithic tools with some marks on them were discovered in Tamil Nadu. While professional epigraphists were debating whether the marks were deliberate carvings or accidental ones,[5] Mahadevan came out with an incredible explanation. He identified them as 'a text of four signs in the classical Indus script'.[6] Unlike the cautious approach he advocated with the Cambay find, here, even while acknowledging that the findings had not been confirmed by experts, he declared categorically:

> The sequence ensures that the text on the neolithic tool found in Tamil Nadu is not only in the Indus script but also in the Harappan

language. I may add this is the archeological discovery of the century in Tamil Nadu.[7]

He further commented that the discovery provided very strong evidence that the Neolithic people of Tamil Nadu and the Indus Valley people 'shared the same language, which can only be Dravidian and not Indo-Aryan'.[8] Such hyperbole undermined serious scholarship, but was soon echoed by Dravidianist and Afro-Dravidianist scholars. Particularly in Tamil Nadu, the Dravidian political discourse has transformed such statements into political polemics and used to bolster claims of the Lemurian origins of Tamils. The archeologist C.M. Pande cautioned as early as 1971 of the dangers of such politically charged academic work:

This purely academic matter is being exploited for political ends. For instance, these hypotheses regarding the Harappan script (and language) and culture have been accepted as facts by the DMK, which has already incorporated these interpretations in the textbooks used in the schools of Tamil Nadu. The acceptance of these interpretations, some of which are tendentious, is serious and unfortunate, and are indicative of the chauvinistic spirit and linguistic jingoism which is pervading many regions in India.[9]

Despite this warning, the trend has continued. Based on scholarship imported from the West, the idea has taken root that invading/migrating Aryans seized advanced technology, religion and ritual elements of the 'Dravidian Indus valley' and incorporated them into their own religion. This is echoed in Afro-Dravidianist politics that the Aryans were 'barbarian' Whites enslaving the indigenous 'Black' Dravidians through the caste system and stealing their civilization.[10]

However, the American praise for Mahadevan was short-lived. Michael Witzel, the Indologist from Harvard University and his colleague, Steve Farmer, put forward the hypothesis that Harappan civilization was illiterate. When Mahadevan questioned this, he was accused by Farmer as having distorted the Indus signs to look like language alphabets.[11] In 2009, an Indian and American team, with inputs from Mahadevan, made an innovative mathematical analysis of Harappan script and mathematically established that the signs encoded a language. The paper was published in the prestigious journal *Science*.[12] The response from Farmer and Witzel was highly polemical, with comments like 'garbage in, garbage out',[13] applied to Mahadevan's work. In response, Mahadevan accused Farmer of 'a consistently aggressive style'.[14]

Steve Farmer once spoke with the same derision about another Indian archeologist, B.B. Lal, former director-general of the Archaeological Survey of India, calling him a 'right-wing archeologist', and dismissing his monumental life-work by saying that 'absolutely none of Lal's recent work is accepted by any leading Western archeologist.'[15] Similarly, Mahadevan has gone from being the darling of the Dravidianists, to something of a tainted scholar, but only after he had served the Western establishment by discrediting Indian scholarship. This attack on Indian scholarship and the casting of doubts on the integrity of Indian scholars, may indicate an ominous trend, as suggested by veteran Cambridge archeologist Dilip K Chakrabarti:

> If one goes through the archeological literature on Egypt and Mesopotamia, [especially] the areas where Western scholarship has been paramount since the beginning of archeological research in those areas, one notes that the contribution made by the native Egyptian and Iraqi archeologists is completely ignored in that literature. The Bronze Age past of Egypt, Mesopotamia and the intervening region are completely appropriated by the Western scholarship. Also, when Western archeologists write on Pakistani archeology, they seldom mention the contribution made by the Pakistani archeologists themselves. There are exceptions, but they are very rare. After Independence, the Archeological Survey of India pursued a policy of relative isolation, which enabled archeology as a subject to develop in the country and helped Indian archeologists to find their feet. The policy seems to be changing now. . . . There is a great deal of arrogance and sense of superiority in that segment of the first world archeology, which specializes in the third world. Unless this segment of the first world archeology changes its way and attitude, it should be treated with a great deal of caution in the third world.[16]

Appendix G

Monitoring Foreign Funds

India's Foreign Contributions Regulations Act (FCRA), which was formed in 1976, is felt by many concerned officials as outdated in present-day situations. For years, India has known that the foreign-funded organizations have been indulging in subversive activities. Following the Kargil crisis, Government of India appointed a group of ministers to review the national security system. Observing that foreign-funded activities were one of the threats to internal security, the report of the group of ministers, released in 2001, described a proposed revision:

> . . . registration and monitoring of the recipients of foreign contributions would be done at the district level. It is also proposed to involve the banks as an independent channel of data collection and monitoring. The MHA (Ministry for Home Affairs) would continue to lay down policy, control directly the receipt of foreign contribution in border and coastal areas, as well as by religious organisations, and exercise control over the manner in which delegated authority is exercised by the district collectors.[1]

Yet taking action against such organizations has still not been realized because it would be framed as 'religious persecution' by the global nexus of Christianity operating in India. The attempt to revise the outdated 1976 FCRA was resisted by strong Christian bodies,[2] which also lodged protest against the Indian government in international commissions. A BBC report in 2003 precisely explained the dilemma faced by the law-enforcing agencies:

> India's home ministry has blacklisted more than eight-hundred non-governmental organisations (NGOs) in the country's north-east for alleged links with separatist groups. . . . The home ministry official said state governments should take legal action against the blacklisted NGOs under anti- terrorism laws once they had sufficient evidence. . . . But analysts say that since many of these NGOs belong to minority religious groups such as Muslims and Christians, any strong action against them may lead to an outcry. India's north-east has many hot spots where separatists are fighting government rule, including Nagaland, Meghalaya, Tripura and Assam.[3]

However, when the current (2010) UPA government took over power, it was seen as good news by transnational evangelizing agencies which saw the election as a signal to pump in more money for aggressive evangelizing activities.[4] The government yielded to the NGO lobby. According to *The Financial Express*,

> There were stringent screening norms by the government that often restricted NGOs receiving foreign aids. Thanks to constant lobbying from the voluntary organisations and a positive approach of the UPA government, now there will be a change in this age-old system.[5]

The percentage increase in foreign funding rose dramatically in recent years, as revealed by the data from the ministry of home affairs website.[6]

World Vision India topped the recipients with Rs 2,560 million, while Caritas India (a Catholic agency for overseas aid and development) was second with Rs 1,930 million. Church's Auxillary for Social Action received Rs 960 million, and Believers Church India (Kerala) received Rs 770 million. Interestingly, the two top foreign recipients among Indian social service movements were Sri Sathya Sai Central Trust and Mata Amritanandamayi Math, and the combined funds received by both of them were substantially lower than the funds received by each of the two top Christian evangelical institutions.

There is a correlation between foreign funds and the secessionist and/or violent evangelical activities. Thus, Tamil Nadu topped all other states with Rs 16,096.4 million (more than double the amount received in 2003-04: Rs 8,002.2 million) and Orissa with its recent violence happens to be the recipient of highest amount of foreign funding among 'predominantly tribal States and Union Territories' with Rs 1,289.5 million.[7] The government is at last waking up to the to the need to ensure that the more than Rs 70 billion that comes in the name of charity 'is not used for anti-national purposes, including terror funding'.[8]

The aftermath of the tsunami saw much foreign money flow into the evangelical organizations. A tip of this iceberg became visible when US-based Episcopal Relief and Development turned suspicious about misuse of Rs 7.5 crore by some officials in the Church of South India (CSI). Enquiries revealed that a single church in Chennai had received Rs 17.63 crore from the US.[9]

There is growing concern across the political spectrum that the situation has worsened, with 99 organizations receiving contributions above Rs 100 million in 2005-06, as compared to 70 organizations in 2004-05, and 57 in 2003-04. The Administrative Reforms Committee (ARC) headed by veteran Congress leader Veerappa Moily, has suggested monitoring all foreign donations that are over Rs 10 lakh and has proposed amendments in the Foreign Contribution Regulation Act.[10]

The foreigners division of MHA concedes the fact that the accounted foreign funding of Rs 70 billion is 'just the tip of the iceberg. An equal amount of money, if not more, could be going unreported, since half the organizations have failed to submit their records for scrutiny'. An *India Today* report points out that by 2008, nearly 9,000 NGOs had not submitted their account books for the last three years.[11] Finally, the FCRA has blacklisted 44 NGOs. However, any strict action will invite US condemnation in the form of placing India under the list of nations to be monitored in its USCIRF, because the control of foreign funding is being equated with lack of religious freedom.

Trends for 2007-2008:[12]
We see almost the same general trends continue in 2007-2008.

The three largest donors were were World Vision USA; Gospel for Asia Inc., USA; and Fundacion Vicente Ferrer, Spain. Of the top 15 donor organizations 8 are overtly Christian, compared to only 4 in the previous year. Receipts for Tamil Nadu grew by 108 percent over the previous year. Receipts for Delhi grew by 100 percent, Andhra by 70 percent, Karnataka by 68 percent, Kerala by 89 percent and Orissa by 90 percent. Among the top 15 districts that received foreign money, 9 are in South India (with five in Tamil Nadu), including tribal regions.

Appendix H

Lutheran World Federation Targets India

Lutheran World Federation (LWF) has a long history of mixing colonialism and proselytizing.[1] LWF is actively engaged in anti-India activism in Europe and the UN, using caste divides as its principle vehicle. A vast network of Lutheran institutions inside India is funded by LWF to gather data, which it uses in its campaign to designate caste as official racism. This designation would then enable LWF to apply international laws against India in order to gain leverage for evangelism, as shown in Fig A.2.

Besides aggressive evangelism using dubious methods, these Lutheran organizations in India also gather intelligence regarding different vulnerable groups. Biblical frameworks are superimposed in order to reshape their identities in ways that increase internal social conflicts. The conflicts are then reported in a one-sided way to generate atrocity literature, which is used by LWF for its international political campaigns. The India-based Lutheran groups identify prospective candidates, who are groups or individuals with separatist ideologies, and these are recruited for projection in international forums as the only genuine representatives of Dalits.

Historically, Lutheran missions in India engaged in violent proselytizing and accepted discrimination based on caste and social

Fig A.2 Transnational Lutheran Network and its Indian Activities

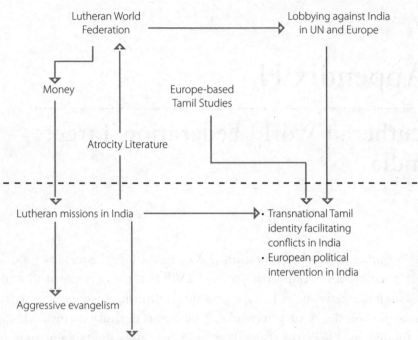

stratifications. But now they have revised their history to make it seem that they always battled against caste, thus positioning caste conflicts as an isolated Hindu phenomenon. They are also building a global Tamil identity using their academic institutions in Europe.

History of the early Lutheran Mission in India

The Lutheran encounter with South India started in the eighteenth century with the arrival of Bartholomäus Ziegenbalg (1682–1719), who answered the call of King Frederick IV of Denmark to spread the Gospel. As the first Protestant missionary in India, he arrived at a small Danish enclave in South India called Tranquebar in 1706, where he learned Tamil from a local scholar. He started out by acknowledging quite candidly that Hindus 'lead a very quiet, honest and virtuous life infinitely outdoing our false Christians and superficial pretenders to a better sort of religion'.[2]

Yet he considered it his duty to destroy idol worship, and wrote how he had destroyed idols in a prominent goddess temple. The Hindus were described as 'being deeply affected with the sight so foppish a set of Gods', and he proudly 'threw some down to the ground, and striking off the heads of others'. He wanted to demonstrate to the 'deluded' Hindus that 'their images were nothing but impotent and still idols, unable to protect themselves and much less their worshippers'. The most remarkable part of this incident was that the Hindus who gathered at the scene of destruction were agitated, but did not allow their agitation to turn violent. One man he described as a 'pagan school teacher (upadhyayan)' calmly entered into a theological debate and proceeded to show the missionary the folly of his actions. He concluded the debate by pointing out to the missionary that from the point of view of absolute being, all forms of matter are constructions of Maya, and that the pottery images the missionary broke were merely symbols.[3]

Refurbishing a Violent Missionary into a Dravidianist-Dalit Hero

Today Ziegenbalg is projected by Dravidianist scholars as a heroic missionary who served the Tamil language. His legacy has been reinvented as the one who introduced the printing press in South India and published the first tracts in Tamil; this account hides the fact that non-missionary materials were prevented from getting published.[4] But modern missionary translators of his writings prefer to depict him as an 'intelligent, honest and fascinating witness to the religious and cultural interactions'.[5] Ziegenbalg's use of the words 'heathen' and 'heathenism' are now reinterpreted to refer to the South Indian way of life in a non-abusive sense:

> Ziegenbalg's word Heyde (heathen) relates to a person who was a non-Christian and also a South Indian. . . . It denoted anyone who did not become a Christian. It did not mean a irreligious or uncivilized person. . . . As a missionary, Ziegenbalg believed that

the south Indian understanding of the Ultimate Reality did not correspond to the concept of the God revealed in the Bible. Hence, he also used this word to designate both the South Indians and their society. Similarly, Ziegenbalg's use of the word Heydenthum refers more to a society rather than to heathenism because his description of this word includes not only belief systems but also the lifestyle of the South Indians. Hence this word is translated as the south Indian society.[6]

But many Western scholars are more forthright about the real intent behind these words:

> For the last category of religions, Ziegenbalg used the word 'heathen' as equivalent to 'pagan' or 'gentile'. It denoted non-monotheistic people and connoted 'ignorant' and 'uncivilized'. All heathens, Ziegenbalg said, are under the rule of the devil, whom they worship as a god. He leads them into idolatry and superstitious rites. The devil is the father of them all, but they have divided into many sects and in Africa, America, and East India, they differ in their gods and teachings.[7]

The modern missionary propaganda projects Ziegenbalg as a crusader against Indian social evils. For example, a publication from Gurukul Lutheran Seminary, a Chennai evangelical center, writes:

> Ziegenbalg's greatest contribution, however, is his interaction with socially and religiously marginalized people in and around Tranquebar. His commitment to serve the poor people and willingness to collaborate with them resulted in a new Tamil Christian community, which still continues. He taught them that they need not labour under the unjust social customs such as untouchability and caste hierarchy.[8]

However, there is nothing in the recorded history of Ziegenbalg to show any such egalitarianism. The New Jerusalem Church built by Ziegenbalg segregated the castes, and on top of that it also brought in racism. Dennis Hudson, a historian of Christian missions, quotes Ziegenbalg, writing that in the church he built, 'those men and women who wear European clothes sit on the benches and stools but those men and women who wear Indian clothes sit on mats and on the paved floor'. Hudson adds that 'the high-caste members sat on the mats while the low caste members sat directly on the paved floor', concluding that evangelists, right from the beginning, recognized caste distinctions.[9] The Lutheran Tranquebar missionaries ordained only those Tamils in the eighteenth century who belonged to land-owning elite caste.[10]

The modern glorification shows Ziegenbalg as the pioneer of creating a transnational Tamil identity through 'his catalytic role in the promotion of Tamil people and their culture both within India and outside India'.[11]

Lutheran Conceptions During India's Freedom Struggle

In 1919, the Tamil Lutheran Evangelical Church (TLEC) was formed. In 1946, Johannes Sandegren, Bishop of TLEC, met Mahatma Gandhi. Gandhi told him that he would stop all conversion activities if he had the power to legislate.[12] Sandegren criticized Gandhi for his social reforms within Hindu society and his position against Christian evangelism in India.[13] He feared the alliance between orthodox and secular Hindus, and saw Dr Ambedkar's integration of untouchable castes into the social order as a problem for his mission. Sandegren wrote that a caste-system is as Christian as an individualistic or communistic form of society. He hoped in 1946 that Ambedkar would choose Protestant Christianity, but Ambedkar rejected Christianity because he was conscious of the caste conflicts within Christian churches, as well as the general position of the Lutheran mission accepting the caste system.

Lutheran conceptions of India were derived from Biblical categories and later these became the fault lines for conflict and evangelization. Cederlof explains that Sandegren's writings:

> . . . draw their meanings from different and intercommunicating contexts of north European nationalism and ideas of a folk church. It is particularly interesting to note how these Swedish missionaries experienced being foreigners in British India. . . . Their 'pro-German sympathies' were more than family ties to a British-enemy nation. . . . It is from this context that the notion of the folk and the nation—also

Tamil folk-church in India—may be understood, where the church was the soul that brought nations together into a higher union. To that extent, the 'Tamil Christian nation' was often seen as being in conflict with the 'Indian secular nation'.[14]

The Lutheran mission saw the independent Indian nation 'as both a threatening competitor as well as Lutheran Christianity's salvation', and in the 1940s Lutheran missionaries were undecided what line they would take.

Lutheran Churches in India after Independence

Several Lutheran organizations are active in India today. In 1975, the United Evangelical Lutheran Church (UELC) was established. Its important constituents include TELC, Andhra Evangelical Lutheran Church, Gossner Evangelical Lutheran Church, Jeypore Evangelical Lutheran Church, Northern Evangelical Lutheran Church, India Evangelical Lutheran Church, Arcot Evangelical Lutheran Church, South Andhra Evangelical Lutheran Church, and Evangelical Lutheran Church of Madhya Pradesh.[15]

Among the Lutheran organizations working in South India, the most active is the Gurukul Lutheran Theological College and Research Institute, Chennai.[16] It defines itself officially as 'an ecumenical theological community for communicating the liberative Gospel of Jesus Christ'.[17] This role includes shaping the Dravidian identity. Its director is a member in the executive committee of Dravidian University established by the government of Andhra Pradesh.[18]

Gurukul Lutheran also works with Dalits to reshape their identities to fit the Biblical myths. One of their theologians identifies Dalits with the Biblical Abel, who was murdered, calling him 'the first Dalit martyr'. This, he explains, is because Abel was associated with cattle, all of which are, according to the theologian, viewed as polluted or polluting in the Indian caste-system.[19] Thus Dalit heritage, which is varied and rich with its own multiplicity of myths and deities is erased and replaced by an Abrahamic identity, which is historically divisive.

Gurukul Lutheran also works to bridge the Dravidianist-Dalit divide to form a united front against Hinduism. Toward this end, it encourages the Dalit leader named Thirumaavalavan, who combines Dalit racism with Dravidianism and puts forward secessionism clothed in the garb of social justice. For example, he proposes that the Viduthalai Chirthaigal (Liberation Panthers) have 'no way other than to take up the weapon of Tamil nationalism'.[20] In 2009, Gurukul Lutheran awarded Thirumaavalavan the 'Doctor of Divinity',[21] even as posters appeared in the same year across the state showing him with Prabhakaran, the late LTTE leader.

Western LWF officials visit their Indian subsidiaries to receive information on issues like 'Dalit liberation, women empowerment, human rights, tribal development and unemployment among Dalit youths'.[22] The Indian branches function like intelligence-gathering agencies for their European headquarters. UELC works to polarize Indian society into Dalit and non-Dalit. In the guise of education, it initiates Dalit youths into the politics of conflict. For example, the Lutherans brag that the computer center run by UELC in a village:

> . . . is not going to be just a technical training centre but will serve as a resource centre for the Dalit and Adivasi youth, where they are conscientized to Dalit realities and involve them in Dalit struggles in order to realize the larger goal of Dalit liberation.[23]

In 2008, UELC hosted the Anglican-Lutheran International Commission, a joint operation by the LWF and the Anglican Consultative Council in Chennai. The faculty of Gurukul presented 'the witness of Christian churches in the face of the injustices which Dalits continue to face'.[24]

UELC masks its activities by giving Hindu names to evangelical organizations, such as Seva Bharat. The Lutheran newsletter informs that the 'Institute of Community Transformation (ICT), Adult Literacy and Children Development Programme are the channels through which Seva Bharat has taken the Gospel to the people in the most remote places'.[25] Many naive parents are unaware that their impressionable children are being subject to Christian propaganda behind such

Over leaf.

Hindu-sounding organizations. For instance, in 2007 the villagers in Coimbatore arranged a building for conducting summer classes by Seva Bharat. But parents became suspicious when their children started abusing Hindu gods and praising Christianity. The villagers demanded to be shown the lessons their children were taught, and were shocked to see that it was entirely Christian propaganda. A complaint was lodged in the local police station by the parents.[26]

UELC also provided input and support for the lobbying that LWF did at the Geneva UN conference in May 2009, and in the preparatory meeting for it in Bangkok that was held in March 2009.[27] The goal of this lobbying was to declare India as a racist state by equating caste with race.

United Theological College in Bengaluru, Karnataka, is another important theological center which has strong Lutheran connections. Following the merger of the Gurukul Lutheran Theological College and Research Institute with the United Theological College, several Lutheran church and mission organizations (Andhra Evangelical Lutheran Church, South Andhra Lutheran Church, Church of Sweden Mission, the Lutheran Church of America, the American Lutheran Church (both presently merged in the Evangelical Church of America), India Evangelical Lutheran Church, and the Leipzig Evangelical Lutheran Mission) have become supporting bodies of the college. In October 2009, United Theological College hosted a conference on 'human rights violation in South Asia', which included talks on Sri Lankan ethnic conflict, 'Human rights violations in north-east states of India', and 'The history of Kashmir and their human rights violation'.

Lutheran churches have also been funding and cultivating factions of Maoists. This came to light as early as the 1980s when feuding Maoist groups accused each other of receiving funds from the Lutheran church. In one such instance, Prakash Karat, head of the CPI(M) party, publicly stated that Maoists in India had 'established contacts with a foreign voluntary agency and a native voluntary agency financed by Western monopoly capital', and that they were 'keeping it secret'. He also pointed out that a group of Maoists themselves had acknowledged this charge: 'It also came to our notice that money was being received by some of our leaders, from the Lutheran Church'.[28]

The India-based Lutheran organizations continue their history of aligning themselves with colonial and evangelical vested interests. Today, they are manipulating the identities and fault lines in India in such a manner that it aggravates the conflicts. They network with their Western governing-bodies to supply intelligence and negative stereotype images of India, which in turn are used by the Western forces to intervene in India. As the above facts also show, Lutheran Missions also do not hesitate to have nexus with secessionist voices which call for India's balkanization.

Endnotes

Chapter 1

1. In his article of 19 October 2006, Suman Guha Mozumder quotes the well-known journalist P. Sainath, who told an audience in New York that while food courts are springing up almost everywhere in India's big city malls, catering to the palates of well-off Indians, 'The average rural family today is eating nearly 100 grams less of food grains than six or seven years ago, and the average per capita availability of food grains has declined sharply. In 1991, when reforms began, availability of food per person was 510 grams; today it has fallen to 437 grams'. He said, 'At a time when people of our class are eating foods like we never had in our lives before, India's agriculture sector is in the midst of a collapse'. He also stated that while India has eight billionaires and hundreds of millionaires, the country ranks 127th in the Human Development Report Index. 'So, on the one hand we have this incredible emerging tiger-economy . . . [on the other hand] it should be remembered that the incredible tiger economy produces a very shameful kind of human development indicators,' Sainath said. 'The life expectancy of an average Indian is lower than people in Mongolia or Tajikistan'. He said that the Vidarbha region in Maharashtra has seen 968 suicides by farmers, including on an average 120, every month in the last three months. In March 2006, the parliament was told by Union Agriculture Minister Sharad Pawar that in the last ten years over, 120,000 farmers have committed suicide in India. 'Suicides by farmers today are actually a symptom of a much wider crisis in India's farm and agricultural sector,' Sainath said, and that this was the result of a systematic and structured move to shift to corporate farming from small family farming-practices as well as mindless deregulation that has ruined the farming community. He further said, 'The claim that India is shining is true. I believe it, although it is happening for just the ten percent of the population'. (See: http://ia.rediff.com/money/2006/oct/19bspec.htm)

2. (Information Warfare Monitor and Shadowserver Foundation 2010, 43)
3. In fact, almost all nation states surrounding India have been listed as among the first 25 of the Failed State Index 2009 released by Carnegie Endowment for International Peace: Afghanistan is ranked 7; Pakistan 10; Burma 13; Bangladesh 19; Sri Lanka 22; Nepal 25.
4. Atrocity literature is a technical term referring to literature generated by Western interests, with the explicit goal to show that the target non-Western culture is committing atrocities on its own people, and hence in need of Western intervention. This will be elaborated in a later chapter.
5. (Oldenburg, 2002)
6. For example, see (Dirks, 2004)
7. (Digby, 1969, 33)
8. (Bagchi, 1984, 81)

Chapter 3

1. (Jones, 1799)
2. (Schwab, 1984, 17)
3. This three-volume work published in London claimed to deal with the 'mythology, cosmogony, fasts and festivals of the Gentoos' (a derogatory term derived from 'gentiles'). It was the main source of Voltaire's ideas on India.
4. In 1781-2, Herder and von Schlozer became the first to apply the term 'Semitic' to a group of languages. The term was named after Shem, son of Noah, as desired in Genesis 5:32.
5. For a detailed presentation of Renan's eulogizing of 'Aryan' virtues along with his preference for Christian monotheism, see (Katz, 1980, 136)
6. In Marxism, God's invisible hand became the dialectical process, an equally mystical notion that was used to justify European colonialism.
7. (Olender, 1992, 7)
8. Ronald Taylor lists various tropes that became Europeanized but were Indian in origin and inspiration, such as: poems with love of flowers and animals, the cult of lotus blossom, the sacred mystery of Ganges, magicians as agents of the supernatural and miraculous, and an overarching influx of moral philosophy.
9. See (A.L. Wilson, 1964)
10. Jones believed that all three linguistic families had descended from the three sons of Noah in the Middle East, from where they dispersed to the corners of the world. (Jones, *The Origin and Families of Nations* 1993).

11. His teacher, possibly the only person in continental Europe who was capable of teaching Sanskrit at that time, was a Scot named Hamilton who had been captured by the French in India and was being held in Paris as a prisoner of war. The development of Schlegel's ideas about India have been traced in (Wichman, 2006, 28).

12. Neo-Classicism refers to certain movements in the decorative and visual arts, literature, theatre, music, and architecture that draw upon Western classical art and culture, usually that of ancient Greece or ancient Rome. These movements were dominant during the mid-eighteenth century to the end of the nineteenth century.

13. (Schlegal, 1860, 514)

14. (Schlegal, 1860, 509-11)

15. Sir H.S. Maine, 'The effects of observation of India on modern European thought', 1875 Rede lecture – quoted in (Trautman, Aryans and British India, 2004, 2)

16. This section on Renan draws heavily on (Olender, 1992, 53-4, 63-71, 73, 76-9)

17. (Olender, 1992, 66)

18. (Olender, 1992, 70)

19. As quoted in (Halbfass, *India and Europe: An Essay in Understanding* 1988, 133)

20. At the end of their lives, they cautioned readers about the dangers of racism brought by their fashionable comparative philology.

21. Max Müller opposed Darwinian theories to explain the origin of languages, which he felt were not of animal origin. He said famously that no process of natural selection will ever distill significant words out of the notes of birds or the cries of beasts. (Max Müller, 1869, 354)

22. (Müller, 1902, 346)

23. Pictet described the Aryan ancestors of European Christians as follows: 'In an epoch predating all historical records, cloaked in the darkness of time, a race destined by Providence one day to dominate the globe, slowly came of age in what was to be the training ground for its brilliant future. Outstripping all others in innate beauty and gifts of intelligence, nurtured by a grand but harsh natural setting that was generous but not lavish with its treasures, this race was destined from the first to conquer. . . . It was therefore quick to develop gifts of the mind, for planning, and energy, for execution. Once initial difficulties were overcome, it enjoyed the tranquil well-being of a patriarchal existence. While thus jubilantly growing in numbers and in prosperity, this fertile race forged itself a powerful tool, a language admirable for its richness, vigor, harmony, and

perfection of form; a language that spontaneously reflected all the race's impressions, its tenderest emotions, its most naive admirations, but also its yearning for a higher world; a language full of images and intuitive ideas, bearing the seeds of future riches, of a magnificent outpouring of the noblest poetry and profoundest thought'. (Olender, 1992, 95-6)

24. Pictet explained the Semite/Aryan division of civilizational assets as follows: 'Faithful guardians of pure monotheism, the Hebrews had a magnificent part in the divine plan, but one wonders where the world would be today if they had remained the sole leaders of mankind. The fact is, while they religiously preserved the principle of truth from which a higher light would one day emanate, Providence had already singled out another race of men to lead the way to further progress. This was the race of Aryas, blessed from the beginning with the very qualities the Hebrews lacked to become the civilizers of the world. . . . The contrast between the two races is as stark as can be. The Hebrews possess the authority that preserves; the Aryas, the freedom that allows for development. The Hebrews display intolerance, which concentrates and isolates; the Aryas, receptivity, which extends and assimilates; the Hebrews direct their energy toward a single goal; the Aryas engage in incessant activity in all directions. On the one hand is a single compact nationality, on the other a vast race divided into a host of diverse peoples. In both we find exactly what was needed to accomplish the providential designs'. (Olender, 1992, 102). But Ferdinand de Saussure (1857–1913) raised serious questions about Pictet's thesis, even though Pictet was his first intellectual guide. Saussure asked: 'Can one really rely on comparative linguistics to draw conclusions about race and the history of the Indo-European people, their homeland and their travels?' He opposed the idea of extrapolating prehistoric anthropology based on reconstructing a lost language.

25. (Olender, 1992, 103-4)

26. (Olender, 1992, 112)

27. (Caine and Slug, 2002, 87)

28. (Halbfass, 1988, 139)

29. (Halbfass, 1988, 139)

30. From Darwin's 1871 book, *The Descent of Man and Selection in Relation to Sex*. Though this line by Darwin could have been used by eugenticists to give scientific credibility to their own movement, Darwin himself used the word 'races' to mean 'varieties' and not human races. (www.talkorigins.org, 2002) While there is no doubt that some of those who supported eugenics cited Darwin's theory of evolution as inspiration or justification, most enthusiastic promoters of the eugenics movement,

which led to policies such as compulsory sterilisation, were evangelical Christians. (Lepage, 2008)

31. The Theosophical Society subsequently published several statements highly critical of the Nazi use of the term 'Aryan'.

32. Teutonic refers to German, Scandivanian and British ancestors, and served as a substitute for what became known as 'White' people.

33. (Steigmann-Gall, 2003, 39)

34. (Redesdale, 2003, xiii)

35. (Chamberlain, 1911; 2003, 292)

36. (Chamberlain, 1911; 2003, 227)

37. (Chamberlain, 1911; 2003, 184) Such depictions of Buddha in Christian literature continue to this day, though in a more theologically nuanced way. A comparison of the depiction of Buddha by Chamberlain and the critique of Buddha made by Pope John Paul in his *Threshold of Faith* will bring this out to the reader.

38. (Redesdale, 2003, xxx)

39. (Chamberlain, 1911; 2003, 174) Chamberlain starts the chapter titled 'The Revelation of Christ' with this quote: 'By the virtue of One all have been truly saved'. The 'One' has been capitalized (which is not in Sanskrit) in order to create an impression that this is a symbolic premonition of Jesus.

40. (Domenico and Hanley, 2006, 108-9)

41. (Chamberlain, 1911; 2003, 266)

42. (Kennedy, 1995, 37)

43. (Levy, 2005, 113)

44. (Bhattacharya, 1999, 194)

45. (Halbfass, 1988, 139)

46. (Cohen, 1997, 202-3)

47. (Gillette, 2002, 63)

48. (Pollock, 1993, 77-8)

49. Pollock will be discussed again in Chapter Fourteen.

50. (Nicholls, 1993, 204-6)

51. (Halbfass, Research and Reflection, *Beyond Orientalism*, 2007, 17)

Chapter 4

1. Genesis 9:22-27

2. (Haynes, 2002)

3. In 1546, Luther wrote *Von den Juden und Ihren Lügen* (*On the Jews and Their Lies*), which stated that Jews are 'full of the devil's feces . . . which they wallow in like swine', and that they should be denied all

rights. Four hundred years later, the Thrid Reich used Luther's anti-Semetic statements as a source of propaganda to validate their racism.

4. (Goldenburg, 2003, 168-9)

5. (Goldenburg, 2003, 169)

6. For tax purposes, slaves were counted as property, along with domestic animals. Since many of the founding fathers of United States were slave owners, the practice of slaverey was written into the original Constitution of the United States, specifying that each Black would be counted as three fifths of a human-being for the purpose of the census of each state.

7. (Haynes, 2002, 66), Some pro-slavery advocates also traced the black race as descending from the cursed Cain, the first murderer in Biblical history.

8. (Goldenburg, 2003, 178)

9. (Priest, 1852, 94)

10. (Haynes, 2002, 247)

11. (Taylor, 1895, 20-1)

12. (Trautman, *Aryans and British India,* 2004, 9) Subsequently, a similar hierarchy was mapped onto 'secularized' notions of progress.

13. Earlier Islamic scholars had concluded that Indians were the Black descendants of Ham, but that they were the first nation to have cultivated the sciences, and hence Allah ranked them above some white and brown peoples. For examples of this, see: (i) The eleventh-century work translated in (*Andalui,* 1991). (ii) Shem is named as the ancestor of Arabs and Persians, Ham as the ancestor of Indians, and Japhet as the ancestor of Turks, Chinese and Russians, in the 1768 work by Firishtah. (iii) A later work places Akbar in the lineage of Japheth, who it regards as the most just of Noah's, while Ham had sons named Hind and Sindh. See (Beveridge 1977, 167).

14. (Trautman, *Aryans and British India* 2004, 42)

15. In his 1728 work, *The Chronology of Ancient Kingdoms,* Isaac Newton also developed a hierarchy of races based on ancient myths. Later, in 1774–6 Bryant evolved this further in his three-volume series titled *Analysis of Ancient Mythology.* The sons of Ham included Egyptians, Greeks, Romans, and Indians. Supposedly, these descendants of Ham had invented the arts but then declined into idolatry.

16. The usually accepted standard English versions of the Bible mention Noah taking his 'family' on board the Ark. Through the centuries, the story has been subjected to multiple embroideries and interpretations.

17. Jones's lectures just two years prior to his death at the Asiatic Society, further reveal what he thought on the subject: '. . . we proceed to the fourth important fact recorded in Mosaic history: I mean the first

propagation and early dispersion of mankind in separate families to separate places of residence. . . . The children of Yafet seem . . . to have spread themselves far and wide and to have produced the races which for want of a correct appellation we call Tartarian; the colonies formed by the sons of Ham and Shem appear to have been nearly simultaneous; and among those of latter branch, we find so many names incontestibly preserved at this hour in Arabia, that we cannot hesitate in pronouncing them the same people, whom hitherto we have denominated Arabs; while the former branch, the most powerful and adventurous of whom were the progeny of Cush, Misr and Rama (names remaining unchanged in Sanskrit and highly revered by the Hindus) were, in all probability the race which I call Indian'. (Jones, Discourses delivered before the Asiatic Society, 1807, 8-9).

18. (Sugirtharajah, 2005, 148, 150)
19. (Trautman, *Aryans and British India*, 2004, 60)
20. (Jones, 1970, 847)
21. Trautmann describes the prominent Hindu images that are on the statue of Sir William Jones in St Paul's Cathedral: 'The scene . . . is presented not under the aspect of a depiction of pagan idolatry but as a benign, independent record of the truth of the Biblical story of the universal flood'. (Trautman, *Aryans and British India*, 2004, 80)
22. For example, Captain Wilford, a capable Sanskritist who followed William Jones, claimed that the *sveta-dvipa* of Puranic geography was England. (Trautman, *Aryans and British India*, 2004, 91)
23. See, for example: (Vallancey, 1786, 506)
24. (Trautmann, 1997, 134)
25. (Errington, 2008)
26. (Errington, 2008, 4)
27. (V. Smith, 1958, 3, 32)
28. While the Catholic Church was also at work with its own agenda in India, the Protestant evangelists and their business partners were more interested in sustained empire-building, with the construction of the Euro-centric grand narratives and the educational institutions to support it.
29. Alexander Hamilton was one of the first Professors of Sanskrit and became the bridge to transfer knowledge picked up in Calcutta to Paris and then on to various colleges in Germany. Paris became the Continental hub for Sanskrit before Germany took over many years later, followed by England.
30. (W. Monier, 1899, ix)
31. (Parsons, 1997, 197)
32. (W. Monier, 1891, 262)

33. See, for example, *Dialogue and History* by Eugene F. Irschick (University of California, Paperback Print on Demand, 1994). Trautmann states that Edward Said was wrong to claim that the colonialists *alone* shaped the knowledge. Natives played a very central role in this construction and distortion, often under influence of personal gain or under naiveté as to the big picture and the strategic implications in the long run.

Chapter 5

1. The caste system was originally a four-fold matrix of social division, based on broad generic classification of social functions: intellectuals, rulers, merchant class and artisans. Not birth-based and more horizontal than vertical, each varna originally formed a social niche where jatis entered and left as per the complex socio-political dynamics of Indian history.
2. (Dubey, 1975, 78)
3. (M.K. Gandhi, 1946)
4. F. Max Müller quoted in (Dirks, 2004, 133)
5. F. Max Müller quoted in (Inden, 2000, 60)
6. F. Max Müller quoted in (Inden, 2000, 61)
7. (Inden, 2000, 60)
8. Among his influential works were: (H.H. Risley, 1891), (H. Risley, *Tribes and Castes of Bengal*. Four Volumes, 1892), (Risley and Crooke, *The People of India,* 1915)
9. (H.H. Risley, 1891, 247)
10. (H.H. Risley, 1891, 259)
11. (H.H. Risley, 1891, 253)
12. (MacDonnell and Keith, 1912. Republished in India as a two-volume set, 1100 pages, 2007)
13. (Trautman, *Aryans and British India,* 2004, 207-8)
14. (Risley and Crooke, *The People of India,* 1915, 9)
15. (van der Veer, 2001, 149)
16. (Risley and Crooke, *The People of India,* 1915, 45)
17. (Risley and Crooke, *The People of India,* 1915, 272-3)
18. (H. Risley, *Tribes and Castes of Bengal*. Four Volumes I, 1892, xxxxviii)
19. (Risley and Crooke, *The people of India,* 1915, 275)
20. (H. Risley, *Tribes and Castes of Bengal,* Four Volumes I, 1892, xxxxviii)
21. Social Darwinism was a popular ideology in the West. It said that the strongest should survive and flourish while the unfit should be allowed to die. Its chief proponent was Herbert Spencer, and though his theory

preceded Darwin, Spencer quickly adapted Darwin's idea of natural selection to boost his own theories. He claimed that the rich and powerful were better adapted socially, and hence it was natural and morally proper for the strong to thrive at the expense of the weak. This theory was later used to justify colonialism.

22. (Inden, 2000, 58).
23. (Risley and Crooke, 1915, 111)
24. (Risley and Crooke, 1915, 109)
25. (Risley and Crooke, 1915, 109-10)
26. (Risley and Crooke, 1915, 275-6)
27. Herbert Risley, quoted in (van der Veer, 2001, 149). Furthermore, Risley gave the following reason for using the Nasal Index: 'No one can have glanced at the literature of the subject and in particular at the Vedic accounts of Aryan advance, without being struck by the frequent references to the noses of the people whom the Aryans found in possession of the plains of India. So impressed were the Aryans with the shortcomings of their enemies' noses that they often spoke of them as "the noseless ones" and their keen perception of the importance of this feature seems almost to anticipate the opinion of Dr Collingnon, that the nasal index ranks higher as a distinctive character than stature or even the cephalic index itself. In taking their nose, then, as the starting point of our present analysis we may claim to be following at once the most ancient and the most modern authorities on the subject of racial physiognomy'. (H. H. Risley, 1891, 249-50) quoted in (Trautman, *Aryans and British India*, 2004, 202). Trautmann responds: 'In doing so, he has of course greatly overstated the Vedic evidence; Risley's frequent references to the aboriginal nose which he says the Aryans often spoke of comes down . . . to a single passage. Both Risley and Max Müller show a tendency to exaggerate the significance of noses in the ancient Indian evidence'. (Trautman, *Aryans and British India*, 2004, 202)
28. (van der Veer, 2001, 149)
29. Clare Anderson provides one such instance: 'Risley's ideas met with some opposition at the time, even from those sympathetic to anthropometric methodology. Crooke wrote that when anthropometry was applied to caste, there were only very slight differences between the high and low castes. This did not show that anthropometry was flawed, but that 'the present races of India are practically one people'. According to Crooke, Risley's Nasal Index table showed no appreciable differences between Brahmins and the so-called lower castes. Indeed, according to Risley's own figures, the latter were more nasally refined than Rajputs in the northwest Provinces. Of course, Crooke linked caste to occupational

differentiation rather than distinct racial origins. There have been hints that Crooke's career suffered as a result of his dispute with Risley'. (Clare Anderson, 2004, 61)

30. Peter van der Veer writes: 'The huge significance of Risley's work was duly noted by the doyen of Indian anthropology S. Ghurye, who severely criticized Risley's correlation between race and caste. In Ghurye's view a long history of racial mingling made this kind of correlation impossible. Ghurye had a fine eye for the politicization of caste that emerged as a consequence of the census operations: "The total result has been, as we have seen, a livening up of caste-spirit". His focus and main concern was the rise of anti-Brahmin movements both in his state Maharashtra and also in Tamil Nadu. These movements, were fed by ideological division between Aryans and non-Aryans, a division scientifically supported by Risley's findings'. (van der Veer, 2001, 150)

31. In the context of American slavery, this involved not only brutality, overwork and lack of freedom, but also the common practice of White men fathering children with their female slaves. Mixed-race children were almost invariably treated as Blacks, thus legally enslaved from birth. Meanwhile, any Black man who took the slightest sexual interest in a White woman was promptly murdered, This is reminiscent of Risely's explanation for how the 'races' mixed in India.

32. (Risley and Crooke, 1915, 275)

33. (Ambedkar, 1948) Chapter Six.

Chapter 6

1. Phillip Wagoner, according to Trautmann, has argued that the Mackenzie project relied on Telugu Brahmins working under the nawab of Arcot, and it was their skills at dealing with multiple languages and scripts that made this colonial breakthrough possible. Furthermore, he asserts that many of the epigraphic practices currently used by the Archaeological Survey of India may be traced backed to that project. (Trautman, 2006, 211)

2. The complexities and contradictions of European Race Science are beyond the scope of this study. However, Caldwell's identification of Dravidian with Scythian is not an offhand speculation. It is a continuation of the colonial ethnographic identification of different Biblical races in the peoples of India. For example, Buddhist images excavated in Western India were considered as of a 'Hamitic' type and Buddha himself was speculated to have belonged to 'Hamitic Scythian' type, and earliest immigrations into India were traced to 'Scythian origin' (Rev Dr Wilson, 1857, 679)

3. Sent by the Scottish Missionary Society, he became a Sanskrit scholar while in India. He was also president of the Royal Asiatic Society, Bombay branch. He later extended the Dravidian hypothesis to also include Marathi.

4. Caldwell questioned ancient Tamil society's exposure to the higher forms of civilization, and doubted the existence of such manifestations as art, science or religion, prior to the arrival of Brahmins (118); Dravidian religion, for instance, prior to the advent of Brahmins, had been a sort of demonolatry or primitive Shamanism (579-97). Nevertheless, Caldwell concluded that even though civilization came with the Brahmins, the beneficial effects of that higher system of knowledge were more than negated by the counter-balancing effect of the the fossilizing caste system (119). Subsequently, Caldwell made the comprehensive case that there were two non-Sanskrit languages families in India: Dravidian; and the languages of Munda and what he called 'the other rude tribes of Central India and Bengal'(42). (Caldwell, 1856; 2009)

5. Trautmann claims that Ellis had made this thesis much earlier, but the work of Caldwell eclipsed it partly because Ellis's papers were lost due to his untimely death in India. (Trautmann, 1997, 150) Another reason not explicitly stated by Trautmann, is that Ellis and Campbell did not share the animosity Protestant missionary scholars had for Brahmins. Trautmann does state that the typical Protestant animosity for Brahmins is missing in Ellis and Campbell (Trautman, 2006, 210). Nevertheless, Ellis too worked within the Mosaic ethnological framework and classified Tamil as connected to Hebrew, which was then called Semitic, in contrast to Sanskrit, which was Hamitic as per the classification of Jones. (Trautmann, 1997, 154)

6. (Caldwell, 1856; 2009, 3-6)

7. Inventing ethnic differences in humanity seems to have been part of the strategy of Society for Propagation of the Gospel (SPG), to which Caldwell attached himself. Earlier, SPG had produced a notorious reputation for being pro-slavery. Additionally, when 'faced with mounting evidence that its work was not producing mass conversions, the Society increasingly misinterpreted its missionary history as evidence of basic difference between human populations'. (Glasson, 2005)

8. In the words of Nicholas Dirks: 'In claiming the independence of the Tamils, [Caldwell] seemed also to claim their souls for Christian conversion'. (1995, 128) quoted in (Pels, 1999, 83)

9. (Brook and Schmid, 2000, 55) The publication of the *Dravidian Etymological Dictionary* by T. Burrow and M. B. Emeneau was another landmark event in Dravidian linguistics.

10. (Mallampalli 2004, 108)

11. (Brook and Schmid 2000, 56)
12. Caldwell quoted in (P. Srinivasan 2006, 231-2)
13. (Brook and Schmid 2000, 57)
14. (Brook and Schmid 2000, 58)
15. Dr G.U. Pope (1820–1908) lived in southern India from the age of nineteen for approximately thirty-five years. He joined the Society for the Propagation of the Gospel in Tirunelveli (following in the footsteps of Robert Caldwell), where he first studied Tamil language and literature. He later returned to Oxford as a chaplain.
16. (Sugavaneswaran 1992, 4334)
17. (Pope 1886:1958, iii)
18. (Pope 1886:1958, iv)
19. Thomas Christianity is a ploy that was developed by missionaries and crack-pot academicians. It sees present day Hinduism as a result of Christian doctrines brought to India by St Thomas. Nestorian Christianity is a Christological heresy that originated in the Church in the fifth century. It reached China in the seventh century, through Persia. In its denial of the divinity of Mary, it resembles evangelical Protestantism. In fact, Catholic critics of Protestants called them 'crypto-Nestorians'. Therefore, in the identification of a Nestorian influence on ancient Tamil culture, the Anglican protestant missionaries were seeking a connecting thread to their own evangelical activities.
20. For example, Christian historian Stephen Neill rejects Pope's fraudulent claim with a tone of empathy: 'The brilliant imagination of Dr Pope has produced a beautiful romance. The sober verdict of historical judgment must be that any such Christian influence on Tamil literature is unlikely. . . Any extensive infiltration of Hindu thought by Christian influences must be ruled out as no more than remote possibility. Here, as elsewhere, what we seem to see is devout minds in different places working on similar problems and arriving independently at comparable results.' (Neill 2004, 62)
21. (Zvelebil, *The Smile of Murugan on Tamil Literature of South India* 1973, 157)
22. (Tambyah T 1985, viii)
23. Caldwell quoted in: (Pels 1999, 83)
24. (Brook and Schmid 2000, 60)
25. (Zvelebil, *The Smile of Murugan on Tamil Literature of South India* 1973, 157)
26. (Pope 1886:1958, xiii)
27. The Jain Encyclopedia explains the injunction against agriculture and ploughing in particular: 'All the tasks connected with the destruction

of living beings or with causing harm to them were considered as prohibited. That is why Jains reject, for example, agriculture, assuming that while ploughing fields, one caused harm to various living beings . . . Evidently, this religious teaching mainly spread . . . even in ancient times.' (N. Jatia 2001, 1491) Even some rare Jain communities which engaged in agriculture ploughing and digging are avoided. See: (Padmakumar n.d.) Against such Jain aversion to agriculture in general and ploughing in particular, *Thirukural* has ten couplets solely in praise of agriculture, under a section titled 'Agriculture' and the very first couplet praises ploughmen in particular. (See: Thirukural, 104. Husbandry 104: 1031 verses 1—10 (1031-1040) praise agriculture: (Bharathiar 1968)

28. Thirukural 55:10(550). (Bharathiar 1968)

29. For example, in the section titled 'The Merit of Ascetics' he states: 'Indra himself has cause to say/ How great the power ascetics' sway.' (3:5 (25)) Also, under the section titled 'Offend Not The Great' he says: 'Before the holy sage's rage / Ev'n Indra's empire meets damage.' (*Thirukural* 90:9 (899)) (Bharathiar 1968)

30. *Thirukural* 61:10 (610), (Bharathiar 1968)

31. *Thirukural* 9:4 (84), (Bharathiar 1968)

32. *Thirukural* 62:7 (617), (Bharathiar 1968)

33. *Thirukural* 56:10 (560), (Bharathiar 1968)

34. *Thirukural* 55:3 (543), (Bharathiar 1968)

35. *Thirukural* 14:4 (134), (Bharathiar 1968)

36. *Thirukural* 69:4 (684), (Bharathiar 1968)

37. (Pope, *The Sacred* Kural *of Thiruvalluvar* 1886) quoted and refuted by (Zvelebil, *The Smile of Murugan on Tamil Literature of South India* 1973, 126)

38. (Zvelebil, *The Smile of Murugan on Tamil Literature of South India* 1973, 125-6)

39. (Basu 2005)

40. (Lochan 2003)

41. (Hudson 1995, 98)

42. (Hudson 1992, 27)

43. (Pope 1900:2002, xxxiii)

44. For example, here is the reaction of a famous Tamil scholar (M.P. Somu) who visited the tomb of G.U. Pope in 1961 (after locating it amidst four thousand other tombs and finding it lying unattended with bush growth): '[We], on behalf of Tamils, paid our homage while circling the tomb in our typical Tamil fashion. The caretaker watching us developed a renewed devotion. He also paid his respects in the Christian tradition. "My friend! Please do not let the bush spread on this tomb. This is the

tomb of one of our forefathers. There are thousands of us, his progenies, living in South India. Future visitors to this site should not go through the same ordeal we have gone through. From time to time smear with oil and keep these letters shining. You will be blessed for your good deed. My fellow countrymen will be grateful." With these words, we also showed him our appreciation.' Quoted in I. Shanmuganathan, *A Tamil Student's Headstone in a Cemetery*, (Nathan) Former Editor, *Thinathanthi* (a Tamil daily), 1999, http://www.tamilnation.org/literature/pope.htm

45. Interestingly, Pope here employs an alternate spelling for Saiva which was used by Dravidianists and missionaries to minimize Sanskrit influence on Tamil.

46. (Pope 1900:2002, viii, xii)

47. (Pope 1900:2002, xxxiii)

48. (Appasamy 1942, 262): Traditional Saiva Siddhanta scholars rebutted such distorted comparisons and showed how Saiva, Siddhanta is in harmony with rest of Indian spiritual traditions and differs with Christianity fundamentally: 'Christianity speaks of one revelation only for all time to come, but in Siddhanta God reveals himself to each and every soul in time. In Christianity, God's grace is for redemption of man's sins, but in the Siddhanta, God's grace is the fulfillment of the soul's destiny. There is no such thing as purgatory or permanent hell or heaven in Saiva Siddanta. . . . Every soul is bound to reach God.' (Mudaliar 1968, 157)

49. (Blackburn 2004, 51)

50. (P.M. Pillai 1904:1994, 76)

51. (P.M. Pillai 1904:1994, 112)

52. (P.M. Pillai 1904:1994, 154-55)

53. (P.M. Pillai 1904:1994, 254-55)

54. There were also numerous literal histories of Tamil written by Vaishnavas, who stressed the 'Tamilness' of Vaishnav literature but were relatively a small population in Tamil areas and tended to be upper-caste. Thus, Vaishnavism, Buddhism, Jainism, and later Islam, even when these were written in Tamil, became classified as 'non-Tamil' or foreign religions. This consolidated the Saivite hegemony in religious literature.

55. (Yesuvadian 2002)

56. (Yesuvadian 2002, 93-4)

Chapter 7

1. Sclater published this theory in an article titled 'The Mammals of Madagascar' published in *The Quarterly Journal of Science*. This was

his explanation of similarities between plants and animals of the two continents.

2. Engels's article was titled 'The Part played by Labour in the Transition from Ape to Man.' See: (Engels 1876)

3. (Blavatsky, Theosophical Gleanings 1890, 502) Interestingly, Blavatsky's theory claimed that the Lemurians were mentally undeveloped and the angry gods sank Lemuria into the ocean. Lemuria was succeeded by Atlantis, which was populated by a superior race. The Dravidian chauvinists ignored all these aspects and used cut-and-paste scholarship to select aspects and fabricate their own myth of superiority.

4. (C. Wilson 1988, 435) Blavatsky first met with Hindu social reformer and founder of Arya Samaj, Swami Dayanand Saraswati, and solicited his support for her budding Theosophical movement. But the Swami dismissed Blavatsky for being naive and for her extreme interests in the occult. She then moved to the South.

5. (Blavatsky 1893, 249)

6. (Blavatsky 1917, 723)

7. In his manual, titled, *The Manual of the Administration of the Madras Presidency*, (1885), Maclean classified people into three race categories of Aryans, Dravidians and Kolarians, and placed them on a civilizational scale from 'savage' to 'civilized.'

8. (Ramaswamy 2005, 101-2)

9. (P.M. Pillai 1904:1994, 4)

10. (Abbas 2000) Incidentally, Abbas considers the erstwhile hate website Dalitstan.org as an authoritative source of Indological data.

11. (Iyengar 1925:2004, 23)

12. (T van yan 1966) in Preface

13. (Ramaswamy 2005, 120)

14. (Nandhivarman 2003) Nandhivarman is the general secretary of Dravida Pervai, a splinter Dravidian movement. This paper was presented by him on 28 September 2003 at the 'National Seminar on The Indus Valley: A Review of Recent Research organized by the Pondicherry Institute of Linguistics and Culture (PILC).' The seminar was inaugurated by the Pondicherry Education Minister K. Lakshminarayanan. The research paper also quoted some dubious scholars. For instance, James Churchward (1851–1936) was actually a tea planter and an occult writer who claimed to have deciphered an ancient dead language in an Indian forest temple and asserted that it provided him knowledge about Mu, which was the birthplace of mankind now sunk in the ocean. He wrote such books as *The Lost Continent of Mu Motherland of Man* (1926), *Cosmic Forces of Mu* (1934), *Second Book of Cosmic Forces of*

Mu (1935). Yet the 'research paper' accepted in the seminar described Churchward's occult speculations as scholarly thesis, in the following words: 'Mr James Churchward, by studying various ancient texts, it is claimed, had discovered the existence of a long-lost continent with an advanced civilization that 60,000 years ago had sunk below the Pacific Ocean after a cataclysmic earthquake. There were 64 million people who died in the sinking, and that is dated back over 50,000 years.'

15. (Aravannan 1980, 4-5).
16. (A.J. Wilson 1988, 27)
17. (Dharmad sa 1992, 55,56) These observations are interesting for various reasons. It shows how fast the racial theories of western academics were internalized by the English-educated natives of Sri Lanka. James D'Alwiss (1823–78), who made these observations, was the product of colonial English education and considered Sinhala language as a 'necessary evil' for an English educated native, 'for the purpose of maintaining intercourse with his countrymen.' (Dharmad sa 1992, 38)
18. (Grant 2009, 59)
19. (A.J. Wilson 1988, 32)
20. (A.J. Wilson 1988, 28)
21. (Obeyesekere 1976, 234)
22. (Bartholomeusz and De Silva 1992, 172)
23. (Tambiah 1992, 131)
24. (Tambiah 1992, 131).
25. (Obeysekere 1992, 152)
26. (Obeysekere 1992, 152)
27. (Blavatsky 1893, 439)
28. (Reuters-India 1 March 2008)
29. (Korn 1999, 28)
30. (Bonner 7 March 1998)
31. (Fund for Peace and Carnegie Endowment for International Peace 2008)
32. (Philp 29 May 2009) Sri Lankan government has rejected this figure, and claims the civilian causality as 6500, though most aid agencies and UN missions are skeptical about the Sri Lankan government's claims.

Chapter 8

1. Thomas is named in the Bible as one of the twelve direct disciples, or apostles, of Jesus. According to Christian belief several of the apostles traveled to other parts of the world to spread his teachings. In the conventional mythic-belief of Thomas reaching India, his arrival is conventionally dated as 52 CE.

2. (Young, 1979, 117-8)
3. (Thakurtha and Raghuraman, 2004, 230)
4. (der Veer, 1996, 119-20)
5. (der Veer, 1996, 119-20)
6. (der Veer, 1996, 119-20)
7. (Deivanayagam. M, *Was Thiruvalluvar a Christian?*, 1969:1970)
8. The titles initially published by Deivanayagam include the following: *Is Thiruvalluvar a Christian?* (1969), *Who is Thiruvalluvar's 'One Who Won the Five Senses'?*(1970), *Who is the Renounced of Thiruvalluvar?* (1971), *Who are 'the noble ones' in Thirukural?*'(1972), *'The Seven Births'* (1972), *Who are the Three whom Thiruvalluvar praises?*(1974), *Thirukural and Bible (1980)* and *Bible, Thirukural and Saiva Siddhanta (PhD disserrtaion, 1983); India in Third Millenium (2000).*
9. (Deivakala. D, 2003, 15)
10. (Rasamanikkam. S.J, 1974, 92-3)
11. (K. Srinivasan, 1979)
12. (Satyam. T.S., 1979, 192-3)
13. Claims made by Deivanayagam in many of his publications. See, for example, at the cover of his commentary on Saiva Siddhanta text 'Siva Gyana Botham', (Deivanayagam. M., 2007)
14. (Mudaliyar, 1991)
15. Of the eleven speakers at the symposium, six were leaders of lower-caste associations, one was his own daughter, another was a Christian missionary, and yet another was a converted Christian and who calls himself the disciple of Deivanayagam: Data from the invitation to 'Rebuttal to the book refuting Deivanayagam and Symposium on 24-1-1992' held at Chennai.
16. (Deivanayagam. M and Devakala. D, 2005, 61)
17. (Sunil. K.P, 1987) The article said: 'Why were the archbishop's suspicions not aroused until he had handed over a whopping Rs 13,49,250 (according to records, though Iyer claims to have received far in excess of that sum) on a spurious research project? Why had the archbishop not bothered to verify the authenticity of the documents produced by Iyer with the museums and other institutions concerned, directly? Why did he not bother to accompany Iyer to the actual site of his research when he had found time to accompany him to Rome, the Vatican, Germany, France, Spain, the United States? . . . What is even more curious is that even as criminal proceedings against Iyer were in progress in the magistrate's court, a civil suit for a compromise had been filed in the Madras high court . . . In other words, Iyer, who had defrauded the archbishop to the tune of about Rs 14 lakhs, was let off without any

further punishment . . . As part of the compromise, Iyer was allowed to retain the large bungalow he had purchased with the archbishop's money.

18. (*Hinduism Today*, 1983)
19. *India Today*, 15 June 1983: quoted in (*Hinduism Today*, 1983)
20. (Mathew. C.P, 1983) [Emphasis added.]
21. (*Hinduism Today*, 1983)
22. (Isaac. C.I., 2006)
23. (Sampth, 2008)
24. (www.stthoma.com, 2002)
25. (Goodman, 2002, 73)
26. Contrary to such claims, in early Christian history the use of the cross as a symbol in Christian art in an unquestionable manner surfaces only from the mid-fifth century. (Metzger. B.M and Coogan. M.D 1993, 57)
27. (Bhaskaran, 2007, 63)
28. (Polo, 2004, 311-2) Whether Marco Polo really visited India and China or was he passing the stories he gathered in his own Christendom as his travelogues is being hotly debated today. See for example: (Lord, 2000) 'The controversy bubbled up in a 1995 book, *Did Marco Polo Go to China?*, by Frances Wood, head of the British Library's Chinese department. Wood notes Polo's omissions and argues that he probably never got beyond Persia.'
29. (Hunter, 2001, 237, 238-9)
30. (Rocher, 1984, 41)
31. H. Heras, quoted in (Neill, 2004, 35)
32. H. Heras, quoted in (Jospeh. T.K, 1955, 28)
33. (Rajasekharan. S, 1989, 287-8, 291)
34. (Tamil Nadu Archeological Survey, 1967, 242)
35. (Tamil Nadu Textbook Society, 1989, 98-9)
36. (Martin. K.A, 2008)
37. (Kumutham Reporter, 2008)
38. (Deivanayagam. M, 2000, 32-3)
39. (Deivanayagam. M, 2000, 34), [Emphasis added.]
40. (Deivanayagam. M, 2000, 45)
41. (Institute of Asian Studies, 2002)
42. (Institute of Asian Studies, 2002)
43. (Zvelebil, 1985, 2)
44. (Zvelebil, 1985, 13-14)
45. (Zvelebil, 1985, 13-14)
46. (Zvelebil, 1985, 13-14)
47. (Zvelebil, 1985, 15)

48. (Chakravarti, 1986, 62)
49. (Sivaramamurti. C, 1976, 169, Fig. 4).
50. (Zvelebil, 1991, Introduction)
51. (Zvelebil, 1991, 9)
52. (Zvelebil, 1991, 11)
53. (Zvelebil, 1991, 89)
54. (Zvelebil, 1991, 89)
55. (Zvelebil, 1991, 89)
56. For example: (Harrigan, Living Heritage 2000:2009) and (Harrigan, Homes 2005:2009)
57. (Harrigan, 2001) Harrigan is viewed as an important authority on Tamil Studies worldwide, as evidenced by the fact that in 1999 he authors a report for IAS, proposing Tamil Virtual University to the government. His report surveyed eight universities in the United States having Tamil studies.
58. He is the Son of Siva and a martial God as well as God of Gnosis. The high popularity this form of worship enjoys in Tamil Nadu has made it specially marked for Christian appropriation. Repeated attempts have been made to appropriate this worship tradition by the Church.
59. (*Hinduism Today*, May-1999). This was modified in (murugan.org, 2001)
60. (Samuel, 2001, 58-60), translated and quoted in (Deivanayagam. M and Devakala. D, 2005, 6-7)
61. (Rocher, 1984, 7)
62. (Rocher, 1984, 13)
63. (Rocher, 1984, 35)
64. (Vasanthakumar. M.S., 2000, 5-20)
65. (Prajapathi.Net, Prajapathi Alleluia Prayer Fellowship, About us, 2007)
66. (Prajapathi.Net, 2007)
67. Testimony – Sadhu Chellappa: http://www.agniministries.org/Testimony.aspx
68. Christian Hoax: Police action http://www.youtube.com/watch?v=eYCCbU1kyB4
69. (IANS 9 October 2008)
70. (Jeyamohan. B., 2009)
71. (Arundale, 2004, 12)
72. Diverse tribal communities across the Indian subcontinent that already had their own sacred dance traditions (much like the Amerindians), readily attached themselves to this refined and codified trunk that was subsequently embodied in Bharata Natyam, giving rise to unique syntheses like the Manipuri, Kathakali, etc., dance traditions. Among

the Newars of the Kathmandu Valley, the Buddhist gardener caste that performed the Bhairava dances annually to renew the Nepali kingdom worshipped Nasa-Dyah (Natarâja) for their patron deity. The point here is that these conscious adaptations served to enrich and even expand the Indic mainstream without aiming to systematically undermine and subvert it to further a religio-political agenda.

73. (Coomaraswamy, 1985, 94-95)

74. (Capra, 2000, 245)

75. (Sagan, 1980, 214)

76. (Arundale, 1954)

77. One of the most vocal champions for the abolition of the system was Dr Muthulakshmi Reddy (1886–1968) the first female doctor of Madras Presidency, an advocate for women's rights, as associate of Mahatma Gandhi, and a member of the legislature who worked for the abolishment of the devadasi system in 1929.

78. Quotes excerpted from (*Hinduism Today* Archives, 1993). It is true that with the loss of royal and other forms of social patronage dating from (in many areas, even before) British times, many of these institutions had sunk to a depraved level indistinguishable from prostitution (with possible elements of coercion, given the patriarchal social structure). However, this was part of a more generalized decadence that could be seen also in the greedy behavior of temple priests at pilgrimage sites due to the same loss of patronage. Just as Bharata Natyam has long since regained its status worldwide, so too well-trained priests have now regained their status in the temples of the Hindu diaspora and in the better maintained temples of India,

79. (*Hinduism Today* Archives 1993).

80. (Rao, Ramamirthammal and Kannabiran, 2003, 210)

81. For example, Western anthropologists (like Frédérique Appfel Marglin) have not just learned Hindu classical dance (the closely-related Odissi form) but have also lived with and given very sympathetic accounts of the daily lives and values of the devadasis. The Tantric inspiration behind these dance traditions, which were earlier the object of so much Christian-inspired censure, has become a badge of honor.

82. Dr Francis Barboza, who later invented Christian Mudras in Bharata Natyam, was instructed in the dance form by two Hindus, Guru Kubernath Tanjorkar and Prof C.V. Chandrasekhar. (Barboza, 2003) Father Saju George, a Jesuit priest, was instructed by Sri K Rajkumar, Khagendra Nath Barman, Padmashri Leela Samson, Nadabrahmam Prof C. V. Chandrasekhar (all from Kalakshetra, Chennai) and Padmabhushan Kalanidhi Narayanan and Kalaimamani Priyadarshini Govind. Of these

Gurus, Leela Samson is a Christian. (Kalai Kaveri 2006) Leela Thompson was instructed by the very founder of Kalakshetra Rukmini Arundale and Sharada teacher, another talented Bharata Natyam gurus of Kalakshetra. Rani David, daughter of an evangelical fundamentalist, was instructed by Shri Shanmugasundaram in the Tanjore style, and later by Smt Mythili Ragahavan, a direct disciple of Smt Rukmini Arundale of Kalekshetra. She later studied Nattuvangam under Shri Seetharama Sharma and Shri 'Adyar' Lakshman. (R. David, 2004:)

83. (Barboza, 2003)
84. (Barboza, 2003)
85. Gesture presented as representative of Bharata Natyam in (Kalai Kaveri 2004) to be compared with 'Christian gesture innovated' in (Barboza, 2002)
86. (Tamil Nadu Govt., 2003-2004)
87. (Kalai Kaveri, 2004:2005)
88. (Stephen. A, 2004)
89. (Stephen. A, 2004)
90. (Kalai Kaveri, 2006)
91. (Arangetram Brochure, 1999)
92. (Arangetram Brochure, 1999)
93. (R. David, 2004:Dead Link)
94. (R. David, 2004:Dead Link)
95. Thus, Sufi-inspired syncretism in India has focused on *rasa* and *dhvani* theory as applied to poetry and music rather than to dance, which had to be 'secularized' into Kathak to enjoy widespread patronage (the trance-inducing *sama* dances have little of the representational or aesthetic dimension of Indian classical dance). However, many among the Muslim audiences and patrons (e.g., in Awadh) could appreciate (at least at the aesthetic level), and despite the apparent contradiction, the backdrop of Hindu mythology with its various deities (esp., the already 'secularized' Krishna). Because of this acknowledged incompatibility, there has been no attempt to Islamize (as opposed to 'secularize') Kathak.
96. (R. David, 2004: Dead Link)
Since the middle of 2009 the website has expired. However, the pseudo-historic narrative attempted by Rani David for Christianizing Bharata Natyam has been approvingly displayed in a prominent Indian dance portal, www.narthaki.com, which is run by a prominent dancer named Anita Ratnam.
97. (www.narthaki.com, 2007)
98. (Arundale, 2004, 20)
99. (Sruthi, (Jan 1996) 2005, 56)

100. (Anantha Vikatan, 20 December 2006)
101. (Deivamuthu. P, 2007)
102. (Prakriti Foundation 2006)
103. (Arundale, 2004, 185)
104. (Arundale, 2004, 148-9)
105. (Deivamuthu. P, 2007)
106. (Samson, 2004)
107. (Arundale, 2004, 186)
108. (Arundale, 2004, 117)
109. (Arundale, 2004, 147)
110. (Lourdu. S.D, 1997, 152)
111. (Lourdu. S.D, 1997, 165) The attempt to equate Jesus and Murugan is not just a stray academic attempt limited to Lourdu. There is a systematic attempt by the Catholic Church to appropriate uniquely Hindu symbols so as to confuse popular Hindu Deities with Jesus. For example, in the altar of San Thome Church at Chennai, Jesus is depicted as standing on a lotus surrounded by two peacocks. Peacocks by the side of a deity in Tamil Hindu iconography is unique to Lord Murugan.
112. (Lourdu. S.D, 1997, 165)
113. (Lourdu. S.D, 1997, 321) The book was published by the folklore department of St Xavier autonomous college, with aid from Ford Foundation for the commemoration of the golden jubilee of Indian independence.

Chapter 9

1. (Tamil.net, 2000)
2. (Deivanayagam. M, and Devakala. D, 2001)
3. (Deivanayagam. M, and Devakala. D, 2001, 23)
4. (Deivanayagam. M, and Devakala. D, 2003, 10-11)
5. (Devakala. D, 2004, 400)
6. (Devakala. D, 2004, 230-1)
7. (Devakala. D, 2004, 255)
8. (John, 2005)
9. (IAS, 2005)
10. Kudumi is one of the ancient hair styles in India. It's a symbol of Hindus in ancient days. It is still popular among south Indian Brahmins.
11. 'St Thomas in discussion with the greatest Tamil sage-poet Thiruvalluvar' and 'Martyrdom of St Thomas', (John, 2005)
12. (Clinton, 2005). [Emphasis added.] Clinton is now Secretary of State, with responsibility for all US foreign policy. It is common practice for

the staff of elected officials to write such messages when asked by constituents. This is American 'politics as usual' and we should not take this to mean that Clinton fully endorses the ideas put forth at the conference. However, this message goes beyond the usual greeting in its mention of the 'political climate of India'. It may signal that Clinton recognizes the usefulness of Christian evangelism as a tool of American policy.

13. (Gnanashikamani. V and Francis, 2005, 59)
14. (Bryant, *Krishna: A Sourcebook*, 2007, 4-7)
15. (Bryant, 2007, 4-7)
16. (Gnanashikamani. V and Francis, 2005, 61)
17. (John, 2005)
18. (John, 2005)
19. (Jesudhas, 2005, 149)
20. (Jeyamohan. B, 2008)
21. For example, see: *Oh Lord Consume our sacrifice, accept the songs of praise we sing, as he who woes accepts his bride* (*Rig Veda,* 3:LII.3)/ *Accept with favor this my song be gracious to the earnest thought, Even as a bridegroom to his bride* (*Rig Veda,* 3.LXII.8)
22. (Venkatachalam, 2001, 82-3)
23. (Venkatachalam, 2001, 84-5)
24. (Venkatachalam, 2001, 89) Among the Tamil poets he names as being influenced by Christianity are: Antal, Kulacekara Alwar, Nammalvar, Thirumankai Alwar, Gyana Sambandar, Manikkavachakar and Ramalinga Adigalar.
25. (Venkatachalam. M.S, 2005, 168)
26. George Iype interviewing Pazha. Nedumaran for Rediff describes him as 'A firebrand separatist, pro-Liberation Tigers of Tamil Elam leader, hardcore Tamil nationalist' (Iype, 2000)
27. (Dravidian Religion July, 2006)
28. (Ninan. M.M, 2004)
29. (Olasky, 2007)
30. (Olasky, 2007)
31. (Olasky, 2007)
32. (NILT, 2004, Friendly Associates)
33. (NILT, 2004, About Us)
34. (Doss, 2004)
35. (Rajan, 2004)
36. (Times News Network, 26 December 2006)
37. (Sargunam, 2007, 31)
38. (Jesudason, 2007, 78)

39. (Doss, 2007, 109)
40. (Farady, 2007, 117)
41. (ICSCI: IAS, 2007, 93,104,119)
42. (ICSCI: IAS, 2007, 368)
43. (Lysebeth, 2002, 229-30)
44. (Griffiths and Fox, 1996, 328)
45. (Consiglio, 2004-2005, 1)
46. (Berry, 1974)
47. (Berry, 1974)
48. (Devakala. M, 2008)
49. (Deivanayagam. M, 2008)
50. Inaugural session address of Varkey Cardinal Vithayathil at First International Conference on the religion of Tamils, Pastoral Center Archdiocese of Madras on 14 August 2008
51. Institute of Asian Studies kept itself away from the conference, but Deivanayagam's participation was prominent.
52. (Victor. Ma. So, 2008, 33-6)
53. (Sekaran, 2008) and the question answer sessions on 15 August 2008: First session
54. (Deivanayagam. M, 2007).
55. (Trautmann, 1997, 124)
56. (Trautmann, 1997, 124)
57. (Trautmann, 2004, 53)
58. (Deivanayagam. M, 2008)
59. M. Deivanayagam, Speech at the concluding function session on 17 August 2008.
60. (Thangaiah and Samson. A, 2008) Morning session of 16 August 2008: First International Conference on the religion of Tamils, Chennai
61. Hitler's Holocaust as a divine punishment to Jews because of their inability to atone for their sins, was mentioned by Deivanayagam in the question-answer session of the morning session on 16 August 2008.
62. (Richard, 1997, 12)
63. (Pagels, 1989, xxi)
64. (S. Pillai, 1896)
65. (S. Mudaliyar, 1920:2001, x)
66. (Irajacekaran. Ira, 2003, 217-8)
67. (Irajacekaran. Ira, 2003, 220)
68. (Variyar, 1973)
69. (Murugan, 2009)
70. (Murugan, 2008)

Chapter 10

1. The connection of Yale University with India begins at the very beginning of the University as the namesake and major benefactor of the University. Elihu Yale (1649–1721) was the President of the Fort of St George at Madras. He was notorious for high taxation and quelling native rebellions with extreme force and for usurping Indians' wealth in his own name. Upon his return to Britain he had become a very wealthy man, and some of the fortune he amassed in India was given as a donation to the American college in exchange for having it named after him. (A. Gandhi, 2005)

2. (Andrew and Hart, 2005)

3. (Emeneau, 1956)

4. (Burrow and Emeneau, 1966, 1968);

5. (www.linguistics.berkeley.edu 2005)

6. Emeaneau (1980) quoted in (Bryant, 2004, 88)

7. Emeaneau (1980) quoted in (Krishnamurti, 2003, 37)

8. (T van yan 1966, Preface). An article titled, 'Dravidian Origin of Sanskrit', posted in 2007 at a website of the Dravidian movement, states that Emeneau and Burrow have found 500 Dravidian words that had been borrowed by Sanskrit, and that the number of Dravidian loans being identified in Indo-Aryan is expected to reach 750. (Nandhivarman. Na 2007)

9. (Southworth, 1979, 204)

10. (T. Burrow, 2001, 31-2)

11. (Sharada. B.A and Chetana. M 2008) From a scholar with a mere 10 citations for his work during the 1950-59, the frequency of citations for Emeneau increased dramatically to 175 in the next decade (1960-69) and reached its peak during 1970-79 at 287 citations.

12. Leopold Sedar Sengkor would later become premier of Senegal, but the concept of 'Negritude' is considered today by African intellectuals themselves as 'reverse racism', (For more on this topic, see, (Nascimento 2007))

13. (Young, 1976, 120)

14. (Annadurai. C.N and Nalankilli, 2005)

15. (Kutty, 1994) quoted in (Kumar, 1997, 448)

16. (*The Telegraph*, 16 October 1994)

17. (Annadurai., C.N, and Janarthanam. A.P, 1970, 63)

18. See: http://news.chennaionline.com/newsitem.aspx?NEWSID=1fa3dfe2-f995-4781-a190-331e10eb55b8&CATEGORYNAME=CHN (Accessed March 2010.)

19. Such a biography may suggest CIA involvement, but of course there is no conclusive evidence.

20. Southworth, along with Michael Witzel, directs the SARVA (South Asia Residual Vocabulary Assemblage) Project. The Project takes the form of a dictionary similar to the etymological dictionary prepared by Burrow and Emeneau.

21. (Bryant, 2001)

22. This ambitious project was conceived in the Fourth Harvard Round Table on the Ethnogenesis of South and Central Asia in May 2002.

23. (Southworth, 2005)

24. Since as early as 1999, Witzel's philological substratum analysis has in a way rehashed Caldwell's thesis to make Dravidians seem as foreign as Aryans: According to these ideas, 'The Dravida entered South Asia from the Iranian highlands. Their oldest vocabulary (Southworth and McAlpin) is that of a semi-nomadic, pastoral group, not of an agricultural community.' (Witzel, 1999, 27). Discussing the Munda tribes in Madhya Pradesh, he has declared that 'the language of the pre-Rigvedic Indus civilisation, at least in the Panjab, was of a (Para-) Austro-Asiatic nature' (Witzel, 1999, 17) and that 'Haryana and Uttar Pradesh once had a Para-Munda population that was acculturated by the Indo-Aryans.' (Witzel, 1999, 46) Though Witzel has strongly singled out Munda as the indigenous Harappan builders, and propagated the hypothesis almost like an established fact, in reality he is careful to add a caveat in his academic papers. For example, he adds this caveat in the academic paper though he seldom refers to this unproven status of his pet hypothesis in his public lectures: 'It must be stressed that neither the commonly found Dravidian nor Munda etymologies are up to the present standard of linguistic analysis where both the root and all affixes are explained. That is why most of the subsequent etymologies have to be regarded preliminary.' (Witzel, 1999) George Cardona, an eminent linguist from University of Pennsylvania, points out that with regard to Witzel's pet theories on Munda substratum in Vedic language 'conclusions and claims made are subject to doubt' and explains that '. . . although Witzel gives a long list of Vedic terms in which he sees Para-Munda prefixes, he does not, as far as I can see, give examples of entire words demonstrably borrowed from Munda and which could have served as a basis for abstracting prefixes. Moreover, while asking rhetorically, "Is the Indus language therefore a kind of Proto-Munda?", Witzel admits, "Against this may speak first of all, as Kupier states, that the RV substrate does not have infixes like Munda."' (Cardona, 2003, 31)

The pattern here is thus very reminiscent of the Yale Indologists:
Lending credence to a ethnic hypothesis which has potential for
creating ethnic tensions in Indian society even as the hypothesis may be
academically weak and dubious.

25. (India Post, 2009)
26. (Joshua Project, 2000:2009)
27. (Witzel, 2008)
28. Richard Sproat was the prime investigator (PI) for the project 'Named
    Entity Recognition and Transliteration for 50 Languages' funded by
    the Central Intelligence Agency with $377,930 (NBCHC040176, 30
    September 2004, 29 September 2006). He was also the PI for the
    project 'Language Adaptation for Colloquial Arabic' with a Supplemental
    NSF grant from the National Security Agency, September 2004–August
    2005.
29. (Farmer, W. Zaumen, et al., 1998:2009)
30. (Farmer, 1998:2009)
31. (Mahadevan, 2009)
32. (Pfaffenberger, 1982, Preface)
33. (www.tamilnation.org, 1991:Dead Link)
34. (www.tamilnation.org, 1991:Dead Link)
35. For example, in his paper George Hart called ancient Tamils the most
    literate people comparable only to ancient Greeks in literacy. Note that
    the history of Tamils has shown them as mixed with other peoples of
    India and did not keep a separate national identity in terms of language
    or culture. Here George Hart shows Tamils to be not only superior to
    rest of India but also as a separate national group like Greeks in ancient
    history.
36. (Hodgin, 1991)
37. (www.tamilnation.org, 2004:Dead Link)
38. (Hart, 1987, 467-492)
39. (Amazon, 1999)
40. (tamil.berkeley.edu, 2000). Also see for more detailed analysis of FeTNA
    and its suspected links to LTTE,
41. (Ilakkuvanar, 2008)
42. (Ilakkuvanar, 2008) Comment in a post titled 'Rice, Wheat and Hindi',
    Here agrees with the writer that Indian government is discriminating
    against its Tamil citizens and unduly favoring North India.
43. (Ilakkuvanar, 2008)
44. (Ilakkuvanar, 2008)
45. (G. Hart, 2000)
46. (University of Chicago Chronicle, 2002)

47. (Hart, 2006)
48. (ls.berkeley.edu, 2005)
49. (Global Telugu Christian Ministries, 2008, 34)
50. (FeNA, 2001)
51. (*Chicago Tribune* 23 August 2006)
52. (CNN, 2006)
53. The Dalit empowerment and Dravidian separatist causes are often in conflict because the Dravidian politics made use of identities that were both anti-Brahminical and anti-Dalit. In recent times there is a big movement to bring together a section of Dalit activists and Dravidianists for the sake of defeating Hinduism.
54. For example, it screened a documentary on ritualistic prostitution and child sex-abuse allegedly prevalent amidst a particular Dalit community in Tamil Nadu. (www.kanavuppattarai.com, 2009) (Downloaded: October 2009. This domain name expired in December 2009). The film was shown across the US, in chapters of the Indian Muslim Council. The authenticity of the documentary has been highly disputed. It is actually a one-sided propaganda with no opposing viewpoints presented. According to Dayalan of Arundathiyar Liberation Front, a Dalit organization, the girl portrayed as Mathamma in the cover of the CDs and website is actually a girl named Amutha who was studying in ninth standard then. The community leaders as well as leading Dalit leaders of Tamil Nadu investigated the place of documentary and contested the authenticity of the documentary. They wrote in the report that while the Dalit communities were suffering from poverty and diseases, certain NGOs are trying to make use of the situation and convert even their deities into sex workers. (Puthia-Kodangi 2004)
55. (*Chicago Tribune,* 23 August 2006)
56. (Associated Press, 24 August 2006)
57. (Kumaran, 2006)
58. (Kumaran, 2006)
59. (Viswanathan.S, 1998)
60. (Malten, 17 March 1998)
61. (Malten, 17 March 1998)
62. (Institute of Asian Studies, 2002)
63. Some samples of his research papers: (Bergunder, 2004), (Bergunder, 2001).
64. (*Dharma Deepika*: Online Journal, 2003)
65. (Schalk, 2002-2003)
66. (Lund University, 2004)
67. (Schalk, 2007)

68. (Schalk, 2007)
69. (*Asian Tribune*, 2008)
70. (Lund University, 2007)
71. (Andersen and Schönbeck, 2008)

Chapter 11

1. Atrocity literature is a technical term referring to literature generated by Western interests with the explicit goal to show that the target non-Western culture is committing atrocities on its own people, and hence in need of Western intervention. This will be elaborated later in this chapter.

2. For example, the product description of the translation of Tamil classic literature by Berkeley-based Tamil Studies scholar George Hart, describes it as being ' composed before Aryan influence had penetrated the South' and that distinguishes it as confronting life 'without the insulation of a philosophical facade' and appreciates it as having universal appeal because 'it makes no basic assumptions about karma and the afterlife.' (Amazon, 1999)

3. Atrocity literature has been used by the American government to justify its interventions in a 'guilt-free' manner. For a historical analysis of atrocity literature and its devastating effect on non-White cultures encountered by White Americans, see: (Malhotra, 2009). For a theoretical framework of cultural violence, see (Gatlung, 1990). He defines cultural violence as 'any aspect of a culture that can be used to legitimize violence in its direct or structural forms.'

4. A very good example of the power of atrocity literature manufactured by colonialism in Indian context is the phenomenon of Thugs. Researcher Martine van Wœrkens, in a detailed analysis of the Thug phenomenon, reveals in the seminal work *The Strangled Traveler* that while it is true that 'many different groups of Thugs actually did exist over the centuries the monsters the British made of them had much more to do with colonial imaginings of India than with the real Thugs.' (Wœrkens and Tihanyi, 2002)

5. Many Americans criticized their government for using such propaganda tactics to build up the public frenzy prior to attacking Iraq in order to frame it as 'savage war'. Human rights scholars compiled the atrocity literature about the plight of Arab women and other citizens, even if the condition of Arab women was far direr in other Arab countries than it was in Iraq. The propagandistic roll of these scholars has not been widely acknowledged. This significant service to propaganda paid by scholars and the media should serve as impetus for further scholarly

introspection into the role of academia and the news media in the creation of atrocity literature that directly influences American foreign policy. This should serve as reason for other scholars to introspect. Importantly, throughout the debates on what to do about the savages, there took place an intellectual game, the purpose of which was to show that a fair and equitable due process was being carried out. Marimba Ani, a Black scholar, calls this 'rhetorical ethics' – a form of ethical hypocrisy that it is not meant to be carried out; it's a mere pretence of carrying out complex procedures.

6. In the American context, these affirmative action policies were designed to combat historic inequalities for African Americans, other minorities, and women in such fields as hiring, university entrance, etc. Developed in the 1970s, these policies have been under continuous attack from the far Right, and are gradually being phased out. For example, right-wing Congressman Trent Franks was cultivated by transnational organizations under the Dalit banner, which supplied him with atrocity literature. He introduced a bill in the US Congress that calls for interventionist measures by the United States in India's caste problems. However, Trent Franks has been given a strong anti-affirmative-action rating by the National Association for the Advancement of Colored People, a major civil rights group in the US; in other words, his concern for racial justice and economic equality do not extend to his own countrymen.

7. The problem is not limited to foreign Christian interventions. There are over twenty-eight thousand madrasas in India that teach the Qur'an as the core curriculum, sometimes with little science or secular education relevant to a modern career. The Saudis are the patrons of many of these madrasas, as sources of funding, teacher training and curriculum development. Contrary to popular belief, a well-entrenched caste system has existed for a long time among Muslims throughout South Asia, the upper castes being called Ashrafs and the lower castes Ajlafs. The Ashraf are those deemed to have come from Arabia or Iran while the Ajlaf are descendants of converted Indians. There is considerable tension between these castes, often the Ajlaf revolts against the Ashraf, who are ceaselessly working to 'upgrade' the 'purity' of the Ajlaf. Therefore, madrasas run by Ashraf upper-caste Muslims teach in the Urdu language and in Arabic, in order to create a pan-Islamic identity that shifts the local community from its ancestral identity. Madrasas run by Ajlaf lower-caste Muslims and other more Indo-centric rooted Indian Muslims tend to use the vernacular language and are less prone to advocate identity separatism. This project to 'Ashrafize' the Indian Muslim enjoys support from very influential places. Ayesha Jalal, one of the co-directors of Harvard's South

Asia Program, ignores this pluralist Indo-centric roots of Indian in local cultural matrix, but champions what she calls 'Muslim identity' across South Asia and 'difference from non-Muslims within India'. This 'well bounded' Muslim identity is being claimed to be inherently separate from all other Indians and to be inseparably linked with Pakistan and Bangladesh. This is a dangerous trend. Furthermore academics like Jalal are developing a theoretical justification and legitimization of Muslim communalism while they delegitimize Indian secularism and paint its Hindu culture as a threat. With a convuluted logic, she finds faults with India's secular nationalism as being incapable to accept Muslim identity She pictures the Indian Muslim community as facing bigotry and organized violence from a determined section of the majority community. Even Indian Muslim scholar Mushirul Hasan, who is not sympathetic to Hindutva type of politics, is accused by her of glossing over 'close imbrications between nationalism and majoritarianism'. (Jalal, 2000, 573) Her approach to the problem of Partition, which has been highly popularized in Indian media recently, has been termed as 'revisionist' by Danish historian Anders Hansen and falsified by the definitve three-volume work on partition by Indian historian Bimal Prasad. (Hansen, 2002, 10,11)

8. Martha Nussbaum is a prominent example of a warrior who is exacerbating the clashes among divese Indian communities.

9. (Thomas, 2008)

Chapter 12

1. (Longman, 2010)
2. (Swann, 1997)
3. (Caldwell, 1856:1998, 101,112)
4. He is known by several other names, including Ramaswami, Thanthai Periyar, or E.V. Ramasamy Naicker – the last term being his caste title. His Dravidianist followers called him Periyar ('great man'), as a counter to Mahatma (great soul) as Gandhi is called in India. The abbreviation to EVR was an attempt to distance himself from his original Hindu name, since he was actively demonizing Hindus. For simplicity, the present volume will refer to him as Ramasamy or EVR.
5. (Ramasamy. E.V. 1940:2007, 6)
6. (Pandian, 1987, 63)
7. (Rudolph, 1979, 413,417)
8. (Devanesan, A., 2004, 8-12)
9. (Parker 1918:1978)

10. (Houston, 1926:2007, 170,171-2) Note that Cushites were descendants of Ham. (Bromiley, 1994, 1059)
11. (Hope, 1968, 34)
12. (ACCES 2002, 1), Published by Chuma promotion, distribution and consultancy service, c/o 23, Glentworth Road, Radford, Notingham NG7 5QN, Tel: 0115 847 7323, Supported by: ACCESS Afrikan Caribbean Cultural Education services (Nottingham) Tel: 0115 8477232
13. (ACCES, 2002, 20)
14. (Arewa, 1997)
15. (ACCES, 2002, 42)
16. (ACCES, 2002, 7,66,72)
17. (ACCES, 2002, 50)
18. It is a colonial research organization which has been reinvented as centre for sponsoring Afro-centric research (Wikipaedia Entry, 2008)
19. (Winters, 1979)
20. (Winters, 1980)
21. (Winters, 1984)
22. (Winters, 1985)
23. (Winters, 1985)
24. (Winters, 1985)
25. For example, in an Internet forum of linguists, Clyde Winters wrote: 'In addition to the anthropological/archeological evidence, other researchers note a genetic relationship between Dravidian and African languages.' He then cited a paper by Aravanan in *Journal of Tamil Studies*. Peter. T. Daniels, a historical linguist from Cornell University, responded: 'The editor's article collects the Tamil legends about a submerged continent and the Tamil Academies that were drowned. The two longest articles are a reprint of a piece by Mlle Homburger, whose crackpottery was exposed in the early 1950s, and an essay on the lost continents of Lemuria and Mu. There is a long introductory essay by the president of Senegal, Leopold Senghor, and several articles on physical anthropology, and only one on languages.' Daniels also examined the nature of the thesis of another two authors, Upadhyaya, P. and Upadhyaya, S.P, who advocate the Afro-Dravidian theory, and are often quoted as authorities by other Afrocentrists: 'U & U compare exactly three African languages—Wolof, Serer, and Fulani—with individual Dravidian languages, pointing out (irrelevant) typological similarities and a host of lexical resemblances that exhibit no systematicity whatsoever. Such lexical resemblances can be discovered between any pair of languages at all' (Daniels, 2005)
26. For example, in 1905 Jospeh Elias Hayne, an Afro-American clergyman, physician, and author, wrote a detailed polemical piece titled 'The

Amonian or Hamitic origin of the ancient Greeks, Cretans, and all the Celtic races'.

27. James Cone quoted in (William R. Jones, 2003, 856)
28. (Kamau, 2004)
29. (Kamau, 2004)
30. (Hindu Press International Archives, 2004)
31. (Yesuvadian, 2002, 78,79,81,82-3)
32. (Yesuvadian, 2002, 82-3)
33. (Yesuvadian, 2002, 115)
34. (*Dalit Voice* Archives, 2006) Donald McGavran was one of the pioneering protestant missionaries in the Dalit Christian movement who supported Rajshekar.
35. For example, the book *African Presence in Early Asia,* speaks of *Dalit Voice* thus: 'The English language fortnightly newspaper *Dalit Voice,* edited by noted activist, author and journalist V.T. Rajshekar, is the best regular publication on the struggling Black untouchables of India.' (Sertima 1988, 245)
36. (*Dalit Voice,* 2007, 25) and (Rajshekar V.T., 2007)
37. (*Dalit Voice,* 2007)
38. (Shariff, 2005)
39. Rajshekar also attacks Mahatma Gandhi. For example, Velu Annamalai, PhD, a native of Tamil Nadu, India, is the president of the International Dalit Support Group and the author of *Sergeant-Major M.K. Gandhi,* published by the Dalit Sahitya Akademy in Bengaluru (V.T. Rajasekhar Group), India in 1995. He currently resides in New Orleans, Louisiana. He writes to 'expose' how Gandhi was against Afro-Dalits and wants blacks to debunk the 'Myth of Mohandas K. Gandhi'.
40. He recommended: 'All the northern governments, non-governmental development aid agencies, multi-and bi-lateral agencies and other groups that give aid to India's poverty-alleviation programme should review their policies and strategies to explicitly reflect the Dalit issues in their papers. We also recommend that at least 50 percent of aid to poverty-alleviation programme should be allocated to programmes that focus on Dalits. This is because out of 345 million poor people in India, 90 percent of Dalits fall under this category and a majority of bonded and child labour are also Dalits. In the North when recruiting staff for the South Asia or India desk, one of the main criteria for person specification is good knowledge of Indian or South Asian development issues for the job. Another general requirement used is gender sensitivity. We recommend that any staff recruited to India or South Asia desks in the North, besides the main person specifications, should also have

a good knowledge and sensitivity to Dalit issues as main criteria for selection. We also recommend that all staff in the North responsible for India aid programme at decision making level should undergo a special training or exposure to Dalit issues.' (Leo Bashyam, 2001)

41. The anti-Indian lobby of IDSN is discussed in detail in the chapter on European interventions in India

42. (*The Hindu*, 4 March 2003).

43. (Prashad, 2000)

44. For example, Simon Charsley, professor of anthropology in the University of Glasgow, gave the inaugural address in a conference in which Rajshekar was a key speaker. In that conference, Rajshekar's target of hatred was Mahatma Gandhi, whom he called a 'cunning Baniah'. The occasion was the two-day national conference on 'Dr Ambedkar's ideologies: Revision and Vision', organized by SPMVV Centre for Ambedkar Studies. (*The Hindu* 2 March 2007). V.T. Rajshekar speech available online: (Rajshekar. V.T., 2007). Interestingly this is an educational institution belonging to Thirupathi Thirumalai Devastanam, an important Hindu pilgrimage centre. It is through the offerings of millions of hardworking Hindus that this educational institution is run. An evangelical Christian, Veena Noble Das, was appointed vice chancellor and she presided over this function where Rajshekar was honored. (*The Hindu*, 2007)

45. For example: In 2007, Alan Hart, who was once prominent at BBC, inaugurated a seminar at the 'Empower India' conference, where Rajshekar spoke: 'Our research has revealed that both the Jews and Brahmins originated from the same geographical area in Middle East and both have the same DNA. Both have the same value-system. The very fact the two are cooperating and collaborating closely in fighting terrorism (read Muslims) proves their close historical affinity and their hate-mongering mental make-up.' (Available online at: (Rajshekar. V.T., 2007))

46. (Carr, 2008)

47. For example: Krishen Kak's message to Dr Karen Carr, dated 22 October 2008 and her reply dated 23 October 2008, as well as subsequent mails.

48. (Grant Duff, 2009, 345)

49. (Hart, 1997)

50. (Ramachandran. S., 2008)

51. (*Hindustan Times*, 23 September 2007)

52. (Weekly journal of Thanthai Periyar Dravidian Kazhagam, July 2005)

Chapter 13

1. Neo-con, or neoconservative, is an imprecise and evolving term. We use it here to designate a nexus between certain American intellectuals, evangelical and/or fundamentalist churches, and the right-wing of the Republican party. After the attacks of 11 September 2001, neo-con foreign policy ideas were widely seen as the philosophy that propelled the US into war with Iraq. This included the idea that the US should promote 'freedom' around the world, for example, by removing Saddam Hussein. This insistence on freedom rarely applies to those dictators who cooperate with American interests.
2. (Lausanne website, 1997:2009)
3. (Lausanne website, 1997:2009)
4. (Thomas, 2008)
5. (Lausanne website, (1980) 1997:2009)
6. (Lausanne website, (1980) 1997:2009)
7. (Lausanne website, (1980) 1997:2009)
8. (Lausanne website, 2000)
9. (Francis, 2003)
10. (Francis, 2000)
11. (Francis, 2000)
12. (Elliston and Burris, 1995, 182)
13. (Elliston and Burris, 1995)
14. (Meyers, 2005)
15. (Longman, 2010, 234-5)
16. (Ferguson, 2004, 22)
17. Quotes of the father-son Robertsons are from (*Hinduism Today* Archives, 1995)
18. (*Hinduism Today* Archives 1995)
19. Dr Pederson quoted in, (*Hinduism Today* Archives, 1995)
20. Dr Pederson quoted in, (*Hinduism Today* Archives, 1995)
21. (*Hinduism Today*, Archives 1995)
22. (International Mission Board, 1999)
23. (DFN, 2003:2010)
24. (Ricks, 2007)
25. The official bio of its international president, Dr Joseph D'Souza, states that he 'lives in India and operates out of London and Denver.' Jospeh D'Souza runs US-based Dalit Freedom Network (DFN). Significantly, he is also featured on the webpage of Gospel of Asia as the executuve director of Operation Mobilization in India. (See (GFA, 1996:2009)) DFN's other directors include: Peter Dance (India Director-OM USA,

Operation Mobilization, Tyrone, GA), Melody Divine, J.D. (Former Judiciary Counsel and Foreign Policy Advisor, Rep. Trent Franks, Rep-AZ Denver), Bob Beltz (advisor to the chairman, The Anschutz Corporation, Denver), Richard Sweeney (chief operating officer, Dalit Freedom Network, Greenwood Village), Gene Kissinger (chairman of the Board Interim President and CEO, DFN Outreach Pastor, Cherry Hills Community Church Highlands Ranch), Cliff Young (lead singer, Caedmon's Call Houston, TX), Ken Heulitt (VP and chief financial officer, Moody Bible Institute, Chicago), Kumar Swamy (South India Regional Director, OM India Bengaluru, Karnataka India).

26. (Fahlbusch, Bromiley and Barrett, 1999, 642)
27. (www.omusa.org 2002)
28. (Cademon's Call, 2004)
29. (DFN, 2003:2010)
30. (www.ccu.edu)
31. (Shashikumar, VK, 2004)
32. (www.maclellan.net) Ironically, Gilman states that 'sometimes the local Hindu priest would even invite them to set up their screen in front of his temple and plug into his electricity,' thereby appreciating the hospitality of the very heathen culture he is determined to destroy.
33. (Mooney 2006, 183)
34. (www.antiochnetwork.org) For a detailed study of Lausanne movement, see the section on transnational evangelical movements.
35. (Gilman, 2006)
36. (Golden, 2006)
37. (DFN, 2003:2010)
38. (Farmer, 2006)
39. (Marsh, 2006)
40. (Farmer, 2006)
41. Later, Farmer withdrew his personal endorsement, but did not remove the damaging material from his discussion board. (Marsh, 2006)
42. Such lobbying has potential to have actual consequences because of a US law known as International Religious Freedom Act, which will be discussed in detail in a later chapter.
43. (indianchristians.in, 2001)
44. (Edamaruku, 2001)
45. (Edamaruku, 2001)
46. http://indianchristians.in/news/content/view/937/48/
47. (Franks, 2007)
48. (Dalit Solidarity, 2007) The confusion is perhaps understandable and perhaps intentional. 'Joint resolutions' include matters of great import,

such as the authorization for the Iraq war. 'Concurrent resolutions' are of interest mainly as public relations.

49. (*The Hindu*, 2004)
50. (Elst, 1999)
51. (*The Indian Express*, 2001)
52. (Ilaiah, 2006) IIT stands for Indian Institute of Technology and IIM stands for Indian Institute of Management. These are considered very prestigious institutions of higher education that produce many of India's leaders in the new economy.
53. (Ilaiah, 2005)
54. (Ilaiah, 2005)
55. (GFA, 1 October 2002)
56. (Ilaiah, 2009)
57. (Ilaiah, 2009, 204-5)
58. (Ilaiah, 2009, 206)
59. (Ilaiah, 2009, 208)
60. (Ilaiah, 2009, 234)
61. (Ilaiah, 2009, 236)
62. (Ilaiah, 2009, 238)
63. (Ilaiah, 2009, xv)
64. (US Commission Global Human Rights, 2005)
65. (asianews.it, 2006)
66. (The AICC Update, 11-Jul-2006)
67. (Christianity Today, 11-Oct-2006)
68. (Le Journal Chretin, 2-May-2007)
69. (www.omccindia.org, 2002:2009)
70. (www.omccindia.org, 2002:2009)
71. (D'souza, 2003:2010)
72. (AICC, 1998:2010)
73. (indianchristians.in, 2001)
74. (CSW, 2001, 14)
75. See the section on US Commission on International Religious Freedom for AICC/John Dayal testimonies against India.
76. *Asia Times,* February 5 2000
77. (*Towns*, 2 August 2001, 18 March 2003)
78. (Assistnews, 11 May 2007)
79. (AICC, December 2007)
80. (AICC, October 2007)
81. (AICC, December 2007)
82. (100, Huntley Street, 2009) Such propaganda hides some of the really worrisome activities of missionary networks in India, For example in

January 2010, Tamil Nadu police exposed a child trafficking network which brought girls from Manipur and Assam, who were bought by evangelists in Tamil Nadu and subjected to abuse. In Manipur, where educational infrastructure has been destroyed by secessionists, the parents are lured by middlemen of evangelists promising good education. Children are sold by middlemen at the rate of Rs 10,000 to 15,000. They in turn, are kept in confinement; abused; compulsorily made to participate in Christian prayers. (*The Telegraph* 10 February 2010); (*Deccan Chronicle* 23 January 2010); (*The Sangai Express* 11 February 2010). While there are good Christian missionaries as well as good Hindu service-organizations that are doing real service to the down-trodden, lure of foreign money and demonization of India through her social problems often result in the emergence of such unchecked abusive networks. Though people like D'souza portray India in black and white, between good liberating Christian forces and savage oppressive native culture in powerful western media, the reality is quite different in the ground.

83. The media group is listed as a resource in the fundamentalist Creationist website for its programs against evolution. (Creation Resource Library, 2005) A talk-show aired by 100, Huntley Street in 1984 accused a Pagan preacher of Satanic abuse. After it was proved to be a fabrication in the court, 100, Huntley Street settled out-of-court for an undisclosed sum. (Cuhulain, 2002)

84. (AICC March, 2008)

85. (AICC and CSW (UK) joint release welcoming UN report)

86. (www.indiancatholic.in, 2008)

87. (*The Earth Times*, 2002)

88. (MNN, 2004)

89. A right-wing think-tank, whose activities are detailed in subsequent pages.

90. (Pitts, 2002)

91. (*The Times of India*, 4 September 2001)

92. (Haniffa, 22 July 2003)

93. (www.votesmart.org)

94. (DFN, 2003:2010)

95. (*Washington Post*, 2005)

96. (EPPC, 2007)

97. (PIFRAS, 2004)

98. (www.ontheissues.org, 2008)

99. (www.rightwingwatch.org, 2008)

100. (DFN, 2003:2010)

101. (www.ccu.edu, 1999:2010)
102. (www.ccu.edu, 1999:2010)
103. (United Methodist News Service, 23 July 2002)
104. (Sharlett, 2008, 260-72). These pages offer a revealing portrait of Senator Brownback.
105. (Towns, 2 Augyst 2001, 18 March 2003)
106. (Towns, Extensions of Remarks 15 February 2005)
107. (Anthony, 2001)
108. (PIFRAS website. 2003 (updated))
109. (Raman.B., 2005)
110. (Raman.B., 2005)
111. (PIFRAS, 2002)
112. This generated complaints from the Indian diaspora in the USA. This happened at the time when Dick Cheney's wife, Lynn Cheney, was the head of the US National Endowment of Humanities, with a strategic committment to spread Judeo-Christian values. For further details, see: http://www.infinityfoundation.com/ECITnehletterframeset.htm
113. (News Media, 23 July 2002)
114. (Shashikumar. VK, 2004)
115. (John. PD, 2002)
116. (Marshall, 2003)
117. (Marshall, *First Freedom* 2007)
118. (*The Times of India* 5 March 2002)
119. (Yajee, 1988, 122)
120. However, Ashutosh Varshney, a professor critical of the Indian government's handling of the Gujarat violence, and author of an important study *Ethnic Conflict and Civic Life: Hindus and Muslims in India,* and Zeyba Rahman, a Muslim woman from Lucknow, disagreed with Dugger and said that the Gujarat riots were an anomaly and India is not on its way to becoming a fascist State. Rahman, chairperson of the World Music Institute, said the Gujarat violence was an 'artificial situation, a blip created by the government to galvanize votes and will ultimately run out of steam.' Indian democracy was alive, she maintained. But Dugger said, '. . . I saw a truck loaded with charred bodies of Muslim children. The Hindus said it compensated for lives of only half the Hindus killed in the train incident.' (*India Abroad*, 4 April 2003)
121. (PTI, 10 August 2005)
122. The conference was held during 7–9 Feb 2002. Later, the proceedings were published by John McGuire (affiliated to Curtin University of Technology). McGuire acknowledged in the journal that the 'Funding support for the conference was generous. Curtin University of Technology, through the

vehicle of the Vice-Chancellory and the Division of Humanities, along with the South Asian Studies Association of Australia, ensured that South Asianists throughout Australia and Singapore could attend. The Ford Foundation, New Delhi, enabled us to bring five distinguished Indian scholars to the conference.' (McGuire, 2002)

123. For example, Teesta Setalvad, an activist who popularized the account of Hindu rioters ripping open a pregnant Muslim woman and throwing the fetus into fire, had visited the United States for lecture tours (MeriNews, 2008) and also has given testimony before US commissions. However, a Special Investigative Team appointed by the Supreme Court of India to investigate the riots in its report has cast doubt on the occurrence of such a nightmarish incident. (Mehta, 2009)

124. (Pitts, 2002)

125. (EPPC, 2003)

126. (Mangalore an Star 2004)

127. (Prakash, 2002)

128. (Shah, 2003)

129. (www.bu.edu, 2009)

130. (www.cfr.org, 2008)

131. (Shah, 2004)

132. (Kurtz, 2003)

Chapter 14

1. (Marsh, 2008)

2. (Marsh, 2008)

3. (Marsh, 2008)

4. (www.borenawards.org, 2007)

5. For example see: (Blank, 2000, 213)

6. (Belief Net, 2000)

7. (Shah, 2003)

8. (Cromwell Trust, 2007)

9. Jonah Blank in (Shah, 2003, 8)

10. (www.sais-jhu.edu)

11. (Nanda, 2000)

12. (Nussbaum, 2001) Regarding the issue of whether the Lutheran Churches of Europe are 'benign', Chapter Seventeen and Appendix H discuss their belligerence towards Indian culture.

13. She worked for Sen at the World Institute for Development Economics Research of the UN, Helsinki.

14. (Nussbaum, 2001)

15. (Nussbaum, 2005-2006)
16. (Nussbaum, 2007)
17. (Nussbaum, 2007, 217)
18. (Nussbaum, 2007, 220)
19. (Leach, 1990, 236-7)
20. (Shaffer and Lichtenstein, 1995, 126)
21. (Nussbaum, 2007, 30)
22. (Nussbaum, 2007, 46)
23. (Nussbaum, 2007, 66) This is a thoroughly exposed falsehood as, as early as 1980s Pakistan's ISI had started working on training Muslim youths to 'liberate' Kashmir as well as create insurgency in other parts of India. (Raman. B., 2002)
24. (Nussbaum and Myers, 2007)
25. (Nussbaum, 2007)
26. (Nussbaum, 2008)
27. (Nussbaum, 2008)
28. Pearson supported apartheid, the manifest destiny of White people over others, racial segregation, and eugenics as a way to 'purify' humanity by making it more white. He became close to Wickliffe Draper (1891–1972), a wealthy American who sponsored the Ku Klux Klan's terroristic activities in Mississippi in the 1960's and a Klan book, *White America*. He founded the Northern League 'to foster the interests, friendship and solidarity of all Teutonic [Germanic] nations.' He recruited Hans F. K. Günther, who received awards under the Nazi regime for his work on race, Ernest Sevier Cox of the Ku Klux Klan who wrote *White America*, and Dr Wilhelm Kesserow, a former SS officer of the Nazis. Pearson joined the Eugenics Society in 1963 and became its fellow in 1977. He was the founding editor of *The Journal of Indo-European Studies* whose benign sounding aim is to serve 'as a medium for the exchange and synthesis of information relating to the anthropology, archaeology, mythology, philology, and general cultural history of the Indo-European-speaking peoples.' He is also the founding editor of *Mankind Quarterly*, a peer-reviewed academic journal dedicated to physical and cultural anthropology, and is currently published by the Council for Social and Economic Studies (CSES) in Washington, DC. This journal became a voice against the US Supreme Court's decision to bring school integration. Yet another neutral-sounding academic journal of which Pearson is general editor is *The Journal for Social, Political, and Economic Studies*, also published by CSES. Much of the funding for these 'research' programs has come from Draper's Pioneer Fund that has been listed as a fascist hate-group by many. Pearson operates through

multiple identities in order to work with a variety of third parties. On one side, he promotes the worst kind of racism, and simultaneously on the other side, he infiltrates mainstream institutions to spread influence. Some of these more mainstream scholars then go on to write what might appear 'liberal'.

29. (McKean, 1996, 308)
30. (McKean, 1996, 313)
31. (McKean, 1996, 272)
32. (McKean, 1996, 287) She suggests that though Nehru meant well, 'Hindu gurus and proponents of Hindu nationalism' appropriated Nehruvian concept of social service, thus implying that any usage of Hindu terms itself is loaded with danger.
33. (PIFRAS, 2002)
34. (McKean, 2002)
35. (History Coalition, 2008)
36. Romila Thapar, in her lecture titled *The Aryan Question Revisited*, delivered at JNU, stated: 'On the Indian nationalist side it could be argued that the upper caste Indian who has always been regarded as "the" Indian, that was the creator of the Indian civilization is Aryan and is related in fact to the coloniser, to the British. And there is one statement which I am very fond of quoting. I quote it in everything that I write, which is Keshab Chandra Sen talking about the coming of the British to India being the coming together of "parted cousins" which, in a sense, gives you an idea of part of the reason why there is the interest in this theory.' This is an academic sleight-of-hand that associates an off-hand remark of a nineteenth-century social reformer with the pioneering stages of Indian nationalism, making it look as if Sen had both racist as well as casteist ideological roots. In spite of this comment, Keshab Chandra Sen was neither a nationalist nor a casteist. A social reformer, he was against caste. Other pioneers of Indian nationalism, including both Sri Aurobindo and Swami Vivekananda, were critical of Aryan race theory. Vivekananda condemned applying the race theory to current Indian society (Vivekananda 1970, 479) while Sri Aurobindo the condemned anti-democratic nature of caste system without compromise. (Ghosh 1907)
37. (Thapar, 2004, 486) Far from being developed as research tools to understand Indian history in a holistic manner, they are seized upon and elaborated by ideologues working for transnational evangelical organizations like Kancha Ilaiah. Under the title 'Subalterns and Christian theology in India' famous Christian theologian Sathianathan Clarke explains how Ilaiah 'polarizes Indian society along the lines of Hindu

caste community versus dalit-bahujan'. While acknowledging that such 'an easy binary notions of Indian society' has 'many problems', Clarke finds that such polarization 'for our purposes' provides 'contextual offering'. (Clarke, 2008, 282)

38. (Barnes(SJ), 2002, 163) In all the references, further he gives Romila Thapar as the reference.
39. (Barnes(SJ), 2002, 163)
40. (Barnes(SJ), 2002, 163)
41. (Frykenberg, 1991, 237)
42. (Thapar, 1989, 229)
43. For example: (Thapar, 1990, 305): She terms Chaitanya's religious experience as 'a strange hysterical trance'.
44. (Thapar, 2004). Here it should be noted that Indian literature, throughout history right from Rig Vedic times (e.g. *Rig Veda* book 10-hymn CXLVI) describes Aranyani, the forest dwelling Goddess, as benign and not demonic. It has regarded spirits of the forest as benign and people of the forest have been held in high esteems as fiercely independent people of nature, sometimes romanticized as more civilized and innocent than country dwelling populations of India (as in twelfth-century Vaishanava literature *Thiruvaranga Kalambagam,* which eulogizes and does not demonize the valour of a tribal chieftain rejecting a marriage proposal from a king). Thapar's speculation thus, stands falsified empirically yet can serve as a powerful propaganda tool by those who want to depict India as historically oppressive of tribal people and culture.
45. (Thapar, 1990, 134-5)
46. (Thapar, 2007). Also, she ignores the archeological finds hinting at a historical core of *Ramayana* events. For example see: (Lal, B.B., 1981, 1990)
47. (Thapar and Witzel, 2006)
48. (Library of Congress, 2003)
49. (Library of Congress, 2008)
50. (*The Times of India* 27 January 2005)
51. Jaroslav Pelikan, as quoted in (Noll, 2004). The Kluge endowment shows a preference for scholars with pro-Christian mindset. For example Mark A. Noll, who *TIME* magazine has called 'one of the twenty-five most distinguished evangelicals in the United States,' was also honored by the John W. Kluge Center at the Library of Congress in 2004. (*TIME,* 2005). Sharing the award was Jaroslav Pelikan, whose accomplishment was that he wrote 'a history of the Christian tradition on a scale no one else has attempted in the twentieth century.' (Noll, 2004) Noll also holds the McManis Chair of Christian Thought at Wheaton College, an

evangelical institution. In 2005 the Kluge Center organized a lecture by Mark Noll on 'The Bible in American Public Life, 1860-2005,' (Library of Congress 2005) His importance at Kluge is further highlighted by the fact that he is the holder of the prestigious chair in American History and Ethics at the Library of Congress's John W. Kluge Center.

52. Thapar is presented in the authoritative *A Dictionary of the Marxist Thought* as a Marxist historian in the dictionary entry for Hinduism. (Bottomore. T.B., 1991, 232)

53. According to Romila Thapar, Indian asceticism 'was motivated . . . by a desire to escape from the insecurity of a changing society . . . admitting the ineffectiveness of a community attempt to reach moments of magic and power.' (Thapar, 2006, 44)

54. (Nanda, 2000)

55. (Nanda, 2004)

56. (Nanda, 2004)

57. In an interview published in the website of Templeton, Jack Templeton declared that as an evangelical Christian, he finds no conflict of interest with the objectives of the Foundation. (Templeton Foundation, 2006) Underscoring the selective silence of Meera Nanda, there is the assertion of another science journalist who found the Templeton Foundation supporting perspectives 'clearly skewed in favor of religion and Christianity.' (Horgan, 2006)

58. (Sheldrake, 1997)

59. (Nanda, 2005)

60. (Mitra, 2009)

61. Prashad occupies the George and Martha Kellner Chair that was funded from Wall Street derivatives trading profits.

62. (Prashad, 2000) Though Prashad critiques what he described as the 'epidermic determinism' of V.T. Rajshekar, Prashad makes a convoluted argument defending it as a tool for social justice.

63. (Prashad, 2000, 97-8)

64. ('Plawiuk', 2006)

65. (George, 2002)

66. (www.ciis.edu, 1999:2009)

67. (www.fides.org, 2004)

68. (www.proxsa.org, 2002)

69. (*Frontline*, 25 March 2005)

70. (AICC, 19 December 2008)

71. (Franks, Cleaver and Pitts, 2008)

72. See, for example, the report (*India Today,* 30 March 1998). According to this report, several Christian provocations such as row over the

desecration of a village temple, Christians spreading rumors that Hindus were 'poisoning the village wells' – incidentally a rumor used in medieval Christendom against Jews, changing the names of villages like referring Krishnapur as Krishtopur and 'the missionaries on an overdrive'.

73. Press Trust of India reported on 5 October 2008 that Maoist leader admitted that they derived support from Christians and that there was pressure from Christians to eliminate the Hindu sage.

74. (indianchristians.in, 2008)

75. (www.ciis.edu, 1999:2009)

76. (Al-Jazeerah, 30 October 2006)

77. (Sadiq, 2008)

78. (Duin, 2008)

79. Infinity Foundation has done an analysis of the biases present in the past thirty-five years of South Asian Studies conferences held annually at University of Wisconsin, Madison. The asymmetries of the treatment of Hindu and Muslim problem areas, is explicit and dramatic. This analysis will be presented in a future volume.

80. (Kawaja, 2002)

81. For example, IMC, as a founding member of the Coalition against Genocide, was successful in its campaign to deny a US visa to Narendra Modi. (*The Milli Gazette*, 2005) It should be noted here that the denial of visa by the United States was seen by Indian Prime Minister Manmohan Singh with 'anguish, concern and regret' even though Singh was stringently opposed to Modi's politics. (PTI, 19 March 2005)

82. (K. Kawaja, 1999)

83. (IMC-USA, 7 October 2005)

84. House Resolution 160, introduced by Representative Joseph Pitts (R-PA) and Representative John Conyers (D-MI) on 16 March 2005

85. After Tarun Tejpal attended this conference, his magazine *Tehelka* ran a series of articles defending Students Islamic Movement of India (SIMI) – a dreaded organization implicated in many deadly bomb attacks in India. In 2001, Indian intelligence officers unearthed links between SIMI and Chicago-based Consultative Committee of Indian Muslims (*The Times of India*, 23 August 2008). In 2002, IMC-USA was formed in Chicago.

86. (NRIInternet.com, 2008)

87. (*The Times of India*, 14 April 2009) and also (*The Times of India*, 16 April 2009)

88. (IMC-USA, 27 November 2008)

Chapter 15

1. Besides political opportunism, there are other reasons for liberals to go along with the positions associated with the Christian Right. For instance, Jimmy Carter, one of the most liberal presidents, was a devout Christian evangelist. He wrote after he left the presidency that his Christian faith had been the guiding principle in his policymaking even when it was politically incorrect for him to admit publicly. The same may also be said of Hilary Clinton's deep faith in Christianity. Secondly, even those who are not privately Christian have a sense of Western civilizational superiority embedded in them. So the spread of Christianity abroad is seen as a way to spread their civilization values to help others. Yet, others may be the Good Cops behaving to be on the non-Western, non-Christian side, but eventually this posture becomes unsustainable in the face of the Bad Cop who is overtly chauvinist and who ends up prevailing.
2. (Hertzke, 2006)
3. (Fore, 2002)
4. (www.unhchr.ch, 1998)
5. Intervarsity Press, Robert A. Seiple, https://www.ivpress.com/title/ata/seiple.pdf, 10 November 2008
6. (Foucherau, 2001)
7. http://www.uscirf.gov/index.php?option=com_content&task=view&id=227&Itemid=1
8. (www.gordonconwell.edu, 2001:2009)
9. (www.gordonconwell.edu, 2001:2009)
10. (www.gordonconwell.edu, 2001:2009)
11. One example of Campus Crusade for Christ activities in India is that it employs American illusionists to dupe impoverished Indians into converting to Christianity. See: (www.ccci.org) See also: (*Christianity Today,* 1999)
12. (Watson, 03 August 2008)
13. (Walsh, 1998).
14. (www.uscirf.gov)
15. (Gray, 2000)
16. (Catholic World News Service, 14 September 2000)
17. (Catholic World News Service, 14 September 2000)
18. (Catholic World News Service, 14 September 2000)
19. (USCIRF 2000, Section III)
20. (USCIRF 2000, Section I)
21. Incidents involving National Liberation Front of Tripura: (www.satp.org 2003)

22. (USCIRF, 2001, 70)
23. (USCIRF, 2001, 52-3)
24. Incidents involving National Liberation Front of Tripura: (www.satp.org, 2003)
25. (Dayal, 1999, 7)
26. (BBC, 17 May 2003)
27. (BBC 17 May 2003)
28. (FIACONA, 8 August 2003). Bishop Sargunam is former chairman of the Minorities Commission, of the State of Tamil Nadu and the presiding bishop of the Evangelical Church of India.
29. (*The Times of India*, 10 January 2004)
30. (*The Times of India*, 10 Jannuary2004)
31. (www.ivarta.com, 2004)
32. (*The Assam Tribune*, 23 August 2004)
33. (USCIRF, 2005, 126-139)
34. (Kulkarni, 2005)
35. (UNHCR, 2005)
36. (Raman, 2004)
37. (USCIRF, 2006, 1)
38. (in.crossmap.com, 2006)
39. (USCIRF, 2006, 3)
40. (*The Indian Express*, 25 March 2006)
41. (Muthuswamy, 2006)
42. (Muthuswamy, 2006)
43. (USCIRF, 2007, 253)
44. As this may make a digression from what is discussed here, how the Gujarat textbooks were misinterpreted to suggest Nazi glorification and how actually they were critical of Nazis, the reader can find a detailed study in (Elst, 2007, 9-17)
45. (Chatterji 10 December 2008)
46. (www.uscirf.gov, 2009)
47. (CSF, 2009)
48. (Rediff News, 2009)
49. (www.uscirf.gov, 2009)
50. (Pew Research Center, 2009)
51. (Pew Research Center, 2009). The only source of information from the countries being reported is taken from their constitutions.
52. (AICC, March 2008, 2-3)
53. (Pew Research Center, 2009)
54. (Marshal, 2004)
55. (pewforum.org, 2009) and (Shah, 2003)

56. (*The Economic Times,* 22 December 2009)
57. All instances of examples from the data-coding have been taken from this document.
58. A typical evangelical rant against Hindu idol-worship which evokes hatred against Hindus is given here: 'It is a well known fact that my country India is full of idols and she promotes idol worship, blood sacrifice and all sorts of wicked activities. India is getting drowned in the ocean of wickedness, which sins against God like scripture tells us in Romans chapter 1; 21 to 32. But God wants to save her from destruction. In this fury God has taken decision to wipe out the land of idol worship.' (http://education.vsnl.com/missionary/) Many Christian tracts distributed at ground zero are often provocative and offensive to Hindus – a factor that is never taken into account by the US-based study groups.
59. (www.usaid.gov)
60. (Shashikumar. VK., 2004)
61. (Lindsay, 2007, 44)
62. (Monsma, 2001, 203-4)
63. (www.usaid.gov, 2001)
64. (www.usaid.gov, 2002)
65. (www.usaid.gov, 2002, slide 9/15)
66. (Lindsay, 2007, 214)
67. (Deikun, 2005)
68. (www.usaid.gov, 2005)
69. (Deikun, 2006)
70. (www.usaid.gov, 2008)
71. (facebook.com, 2010)
72. (www.eficor.org, 2000:2009)
73. (www.eficor.org, 2000:2009)
74. (PTI, 25 July 2007)
75. The members of this council described are those who served the first one-year term beginning in March, 2009. A full copy of its first-year report may be downloaded at: http://www.whitehouse.gov/sites/default/files/microsites/ofbnp-council-final-report.pdf (valid as of April 2010). All quotes in this section are from the government website on faith-based initiatives.

Chapter 16

1. Winston Churchill, speech at Harvard University, 6 September 1943
2. (*Times of London,* 26 May 1991)

3.   (Hoyos, 1995)
4.   (www.countercurrents.org, 2009)
5.   (Wikipedia)
6.   (Pallister, 2007)
7.   (CSW, 2001, 16)
8.   (www.andyreedmp.org.uk, 2006)
9.   (Hindu Forum of Britain, 2007, 29)
10. (CSW, 2006)
11. (CSW, 2007)
12. (CSW, 2006/07, 7)
13. (Assistnews, 11 May 2007)
14. (*The Independent*, 30 Mar 2008)
15. (CSW, 2008)
16. (Human Rights Commission, 2008, 3)
17. (CSW, November 2007, 6)
18. (Sahni, 2004)
19. (DSN-UK, 2003-2004)
20. Christian Aid reported to an external inquiry: 'We proudly supported
     the participation of the Dalit Solidarity Network-UK, to raise issues of
     caste discrimination. . . [For the 2009 conference] We may once again
     provide funding to the International Dalit Solidarity Network or similar
     partners to attend.' (www.ngo-monitor.org, 2008)
21. (DSN-UK)(Apart from the already mentioned three major Christian
     organizations, St Clare and St Francis Trust is the fourth Christian
     organization funding DSN-UK)
22. Its predecessor organization was called SPG, which sent missionaries to
     India in 1820. SPG 'was a slave-owner in Barbados in the eighteenth and
     early nineteenth centuries, with several hundred slaves on the Codrington
     Plantation. The plantation was bequeathed to the Society in 1710 by
     Christopher Codrington and was run by managers on behalf of the
     Church of England, represented by the archbishop of Canterbury and a
     committee of bishops. It relied on a steady new stream of slaves from
     West Africa as, by 1740, thirty years after the Church took over, four out
     of every ten slaves bought by the plantation died within three years. This
     contrasted with some Southern US plantations where the death rate was
     lower, suggesting a deliberate "work to death" policy was in operation,
     as was commonly the case in the West Indies and South America.' See:
     (Wikipedia)
23. (Wikipedia)
24. For example in 2000 Catholic Archdiocese of Glasgow's Social Care
     sector entered into an agreement with the UNISON as it will be the only

one union recognised to represent staff working for the Archdiocese's social care projects. (Unison 2000) Also see (Amoore 2005, 312)

25. (DSN-UK, July 2006, 11)
26. (www.hinducounciluk.org, 2007)
27. (DSN-UK, 23 March 2007)
28. (DSN-UK, 23 March 2007)
29. (www.tamilnet.com)
30. (www.liberationorg.co.uk)
31. *Liberty* was instrumental in sponsoring to the UN meet a leader from Assamese terrorist organization with Delhi Interpol alert against him. *Liberation* had sponsored this ULFA leader with two names: one his native 'Anup Chetia' and another Christian name 'John David Salomar'. (Ghose, 2001, 92)
32. (www.parliament.uk, 2007)
33. (www.khalistan-affairs.org, 2002)
34. (*The Hindu*, 16 September 2006)
35. (LISA, 2005:2010)
36. (LISA, 2005:2010)
37. (Khalid, 2007) and (Khalid, Musharaff, *Beginning to End*, 2007)
38. (Shariff, 2005)
39. Like most conspiracy theories, understanding these connections requires a side trip into very murky territory of Holocaust denial. See, for example, (Sharif, 2006)
40. (*Dalit Voice*, 2009)
41. (LISA, 2009)
42. (EPPC, 2002) In 2005 INFEMIT also worked with EPPC on a study of Islamic states contrasting them with the Chrisian West (EPPC, 2005)
43. (OCRPL, 2008)
44. Dr Paul Marshall a Fellow of the center and the only one from the United States, is from Hudson Institute. (www.hudson.org) For Hudson Institute's right-wing stand, See (Reese, 2006, 169)
45. (OCRPL, 2007)

Chapter 17

1. (Abdullah, 2001)
2. (IDSN, 2009)
3. Examples of major funding sources are: Comité Catholique contre la Faim et Pour le Dévelopment (Catholic Committee against Hunger and for Development - CCFD), DanChurchAid, Cordaid, ICCO and Christian Aid. (IDSN, 2005, 33)

4. (NCCI, 2006)
5. (NCCI, 2006)
6. (IDSN 2009)
7. (www.focnou.com, 2007)
8. (NCCI, 2006)
9. (CIDSE, 1998, 4)
10. For example, Hans Magnusson, as Amnesty's (Swedish section) co-coordinator for India, rejects the Indian government's assertion that the youths in terrorism-infested Kashmir cross over the LOC, as a reason for disappearances. (Kashmir Human Rights website, 2008)

    Gerard Oonk of IDSN also heads the India Committee of the Netherlands (ICN) which was accused of 'cyber crime, acts of racist and xenophobic nature and criminal defamation' and served notice by an Indian court on behalf of an Indian garment factory with which ICN-supported campaigners went for an out of court settlement. (www.indianet.nl, 2007)
11. (Wikipedia, 2008)
12. (Thekaekara, 2005)
13. (IDSN, 2005, 6)
14. This is the fully accredited evangelical university in Japan offering an undergraduate curriculum in theology (Japan Student Services Organization 2006) from which Yozo Yokota graduated (Project Eleanor, 2004)
15. She was the staff, public relations department, Korean National Council of Churches (KNCC), and advisor, policy committee of YWCA: (United States Human Rights, 2007).
16. (IDSN, 2005, 9)
17. (IDSN, 2006, 6)
18. (IDSN, 2006, 8)
19. (IDSN, 2006, 11-12)
20. (IDSN, 2006, 6)
21. (IDSN, 2005, 16)
22. (IDSN, 2005, 16)
23. (Wikipedia)
24. (IDSN 2006, 15)
25. (Wikipedia) and (Wikipedia 2009)
26. (www.europarl.europa.eu, 2006)
27. (IDSN, 2006, 20)
28. (www.europarl.europa.eu, 2006)
29. (One World South Asia, 2006)
30. (IDSN 2006, 48)

31. (IDSN, 2006, 24)
32. (Human Rights News, 2007)
33. (www.nerve.in, 2007)
34. (www.nerve.in, 2007)
35. (*The Times of India*, 3 February2007)
36. (www.ahrchk.net, 2006)
37. (DSN-DK, 24 September 2008, 2)
38. See Appendix H for further details on the Lutheran Church's historical and current role in undermining Indian civilization.
39. (Dalit Network, 2008)
40. (Green: European Free Alliance, 2008) It is interesting to note here that Michael Cashman, an MEP from the UK, who vehemently supported the European intervention for ending the discrimination against the Dalits stating 'this barbarism has to end.' (http://www.neurope.eu/articles/87378.php), also happens to be a vehement opponent of outsourcing of European jobs to developing countries including India. (IANS, 20 February 2004)
41. (Lutheran World Federation 2009)
42. (WCC, 2009)
43. (WCC, 2009)
44. Col Ved Prakash states that Geneva-based World Council of Churches generates awareness of Naga cause internationally. (V. Prakash 2007, 1945) J.P. Rajkhowa, the former chief secretary of Assam, states that NSCN, a Maoist-Christian insurgency movement, gets 'financial support from the World Council of Churches', (Rajkhowa, JP., 2008)
45. (*Christianity Today*, 21 March 2009)
46. (Global Ecumenical Conference, 21-24 March 2009)
47. (www.lutheranworld.org, 2009)
48. (WCC, 2009)
49. (*The Times of India*, 26 April 2009)
50. (IDSN, 2006, 6)
51. (Merrinews.com, 2008)
52. (O'Neill, 2003)
53. For example, *The Times of India* presented the study with the sensational headline (*The Times of India* 8 December 2009)
54. (kroc.nd.edu, 2008) Also supporting were Dartmouth College at the University of Michigan and Robert F Kennedy Centre for Social Justice and Human Rights, Washington. Both these liberal institutions with genuine concern for human rights issues got roped in, alongside church-based institutions which have a vested interest.

55. In an interview after his return from Durban, Kancha Ilaiah conceded in an interview that while the majority of Dalits were 'non-Christian', 'the leadership of the Dalit caucus' consisted of Paul Divakar, Ruth Manorama, Jyoti Raj, Martin Macwan – all Church-affiliated personalities and that they have 'shown an ability to carve out spaces within the UN bodies for dalit NGOs through the NCDHR', (Illaiah, 2001)

56. (P. Divakar, 2002)

57. (P. Divakar, 2002)

58. (NDTV, 12 November 2006)

59. (NDTV, 12 November 2006)

60. (www.hrdc.net, 2001)

61. (NCDHR, 2006)

62. Article One, International Convention on the Elimination of All Forms of Racial Discrimination (ICERD)

63. (IDSN, 2008)

64. http://www.rightlivelihood.org/ruth-manorama.html

65. An allegation that a mysterious woman having connections with Sri Lankan Tamil groups, negotiating with separatist Tamil Nadu Liberation Army brigand Veerappan, was connected with Ruth Manorama, appeared in a prominent English Newspaper (*The Hindu,* 17 November 2000) and it was subsequently denied by Manorama (*The Hindu,* 18 November 2000)

66. (Associated Press, 2001)

67. (NCCI, 2006)

68. (Manorama, 18 December 2006, 2-3)

69. (IDSN 2008, 6)

70. (WCC, 2009)

71. (Raj, M.C, 2001)

72. (Raj, M.C, 2001, 4)

73. (Raj, M.C, 2001, 12, 13)

74. (Raj and Raj, 2008, 9)

75. (Raj and Raj, 2008, 9)

76. (Raj and Raj, 2008, 10)

77. (Raj and Raj, 2008, 10)

78. (IIDS, 2008)

79. (Macwan, 2007, 1)

80. Including Christian Aid, Cordaid (a Netherlands-based Catholic aid organization, see: (Reuters 2008)), Germany-based 'Bread for World', a Lutheran initiative, and IDSN.

81. (DSN-UK, 2004-5, 3)

82. (IDSN, 2006, 9)

83. (IDSN, 2007)
84. (Macwan, 2007, 39)
85. (Macwan, 2007, 53)
86. (IIDS, 2008)
87. (Macwan and Narula, 2001)
88. (Aloys, 2007)
89. (Macwan, 2007, 47)
90. (IIDS, 2008)
91. (IIDS, 2008)
92. (Swedish South Asian Studies Network, 2006)
93. (*Business Standard*, 4 December 2008)
94. (Swedish South Asian Studies Network, 2006)
95. (DSN-UK 2006, 7)
96. (IIDS, 2008)
97. (Swedish South Asian Studies Network, 2007)
98. (Swedish South Asian Studies Network, 2007)
99. (Swedish South Asian Studies Network, 2007)
100. (Gorringe, 2005, Acknowledgement)
101. (DRC, 2009)
102. (Student Christian Movement India, 2006-2007)
103. (www.gltc.edu, 2005)
104 (nativenet.uthscsa.edu, 2008)
105. (www.gltc.edu, 2005)
106. (Adrian Bird, February 2008, 50)
107. (Asian Lutheran News, 2005)
108. (http://www.gltc.edu/, 1998:2008)
109. See for example: (Jamanadas, K, 2006); (Shariff, 2005); (Sharif, 2006) and (Rajshekar. V.T., 2008)
110. (Elliston and Burris, 1995, 182)
111. (www.gltc.edu, 2004)
112. (www.gltc.edu, 2004)
113. (Bavinck, 1998)
114. (University of Amsterdam, 2009)
115. (Subramanian, 2003, 279)
116. (Subramanian, 2003, 280)
117. (Jaffrelot, 2003, 18)
118. (Jaffrelot, 2003, 16-17)
119. (M.K. Gandhi, 1921) Here Gandhi also made an explicit reference to his belief in Varnashrama Dharma, which he stated 'strictly Vedic but not in its presently popular crude sense.'
120. (Sadasivan, N.S., 2000, 522-4)

121. (Sadasivan, N.S., 2000, 522-4)
122. (Jaffrelot, 2003, 155)
123. (Jaffrelot, 2003, 153)
124. (Jaffrelot, 2001)
125. For an example, see: (KudiArasu, 29 August 1937). Despite such open borrowing of Nazi model racism by Dravidian movement under EVR, Jaffrelot finds the Dravidianist movement to be based on the 'notion of human dignity.'
126. (Jaffrelot, 1996, 25)
127. (Jaffrelot, 1996, 55) Here Jaffrelot alleges that Golwalkar claimed influence of Hitler in formulating his early political thought. While this book does not necessarily agree with the politics or modus of operandi of Hindutva movement, the particular allegation has been disproved completely by Belgian Indologist Elst. (Elst, 2001, 2.1-5)
128. (*New York Times,* 13 May 2002)
129. (McGann and Weaver, 2002, 162)
130. (Omvedt, 2006, 63) In this she includes Arya Samaj, Ramakrishna and Vivekananda, although the fact is that Arya Samaj was definitely anti-caste and some of the earliest Dalit emancipators came from that movement and it was the first institution to use the term Dalit for the upliftment of suppressed castes. Vivekananda attacked upper castes harshly for their inhuman treatment of weaker sections of the society, and Ramakrishna, a Brahmin by birth, broke caste barriers by cleaning the night soil of Dalits and renouncing the holy thread – a caste mark of Brahmins.
131. (Omvedt, 2002)
132. (Omvedt, 2001)
133. (H. Risley, 1892)
134. (Omvedt, 2003)
135. Gail Omvedt attributes Dalit-Dravidianist antagonism to the Hindu nature of the then-popular Dalit leader M.C. Rajah: 'The major problem of the Dravidian movement remained the difficulty of winning Dalit support . . . In Tamil Nadu, it was not the radical Ambedkar but the Hindu Mahasabhaite M.C. Rajah who was the most well-known Dalit leader, and his alienation from the Dravidian movement was the other side of the distancing of the movement itself from dalits.' (Omvedt, 2006, 62) This is typical of Omvedt's tactics – attributing negativity to Dalits when they do not fit into her worldview. The reason for Dalit-Dravidianist antagonism was much deeper than M.C. Rajah's alienation from the Dravidian movement. M. Venkatesan, a young Dalit research scholar, enumerates virulent anti-Dalit statements issued by Dravidian

ideologue E.V. Ramasami, and how the Dravidian movement was anti-Dalit from its very inception. In a detailed study (Venkatesan. M, 2004, 138-58), points out that in 1968, when DMK was the ruling party, Communist Party of India organized Dalits against the landlords to raise their daily wages. Subsequently, forty-two Dalits were burned to death by landlords in rural Tamil Nadu. EVR, then the chief ideologue of the Dravidian Movement, condemned the leftists for making Dalits agitate and demanded that the Communist Party should be banned. (Viduthalai, dated 20 January 1969 quoted in (Venkatesan, M., 2004))

136. (Omvedt, 2001)
137. (Béteille, 2001)
138. (Omvedt, 2001)
139. (Omvedt, 2001)
140. (Natrajan, Faoláin and Philip, 1998)
141. (Macwan, Sukhadeo and Omvedt, 2009) (Rawat Publications, 2002:2009)
142. (BosNewsLife, 2006)
143. This is a topic we will discuss more fully in another chapter. Basically, an old myth has been embroidered into a justification for many questionable Christian projects in India.
144. (Arora, 2008)
145. (*The Times of India*, 18 April 2009)

Chapter 18

1. (Thomas, 2008, 125).
2. (Thomas, 2008, 122)
3. Besides the ones featured below, yet another example of aggressive evangelism from USA is Gospel Fellowship Trust India, USA. Based in Georgia, it explains its annual funding of Rs 2.29 billion to India-based activities as follows: To plant another 300 Baptist Churches, start 10 Christian Schools and to establish 3 Bible colleges within the next 10 years. It proudly boasts that it has already planted 156 Grace Baptist churches and converted 20,000 people. 'We focus our Church planting efforts in two groups – the un-reached people group, living in 500,000 un-reached villages and the poor living in city slums. Churches are planted in the home or village, either through the believer's personal witness, through gospel crusades or through adult literary centers as people are taught to read using the Bible as the textbook.' Its website has been removed from the net (http://gospelfellowshipindia.net/flash/gfi.swf). However, the mission statement has been reproduced in many

other websites (*Hinduism Today*, July/August/September 2008). India's Ministry of Home Affairs has listed this mission as one of the largest receivers of foreign funds. (MHA, 2005-2006)

4.   (www.vishalmangalwadi.com, 2000:2009)
5.   (www.vishalmangalwadi.com, 2000:2009)
6.   (Mangalwadi, 1998)
7.   (Mangalwadi, 2001)
8.   (Mangalwadi, 2001)
9.   (Mangalwadi, 1977)
10. He solicits funds for his missionary activity through BOM International, which is based at Pasadena California, (www.vishalmangalwadi.com, 2000:2009). He also networks with academic centers. For example, his links section show the Maclaurin Institute at the University of Minnesota 'provides a forum for integrating the Christian faith into the world of academics.' (www.vishalmangalwadi.com, 2000:2009)
11. (Mangalwadi, 1998)
12. For example: (www.intervarsity.org, 2005)
13. Mangalwadi quoted in (Kuruvachira J., 2002)
14. (Mangalwadi, 2008)
15. (Mangalwadi, 2008)
16. (www.vishalmangalwadi.com, 2000:2009)
17. (www.rzim.org, 1997:2008)
18. (*The Washington Times*, 6 December 2008)
19. (www.cbn.com, 2001)
20. (Zacharias and Sawyer, 2006, 48)
21. (Zacharias and Sawyer, 2006, 33)
22. (Banerjee, 2004)
23. (Time-CNN, 2007)
24. (NCSE, 2010)
25. http://www.geocities.com/iicmonlineindia. The solicitation letter was sent to various US funding agencies in November 2005, and is typical of similar efforts that are very common.
26. For example, one of these organizations 'International Institute of Church Management' has in its course curriculum under the title General Theological/ Bible Courses - 92, a lesson advocating Creationism.
27. (Diamond, 1989, 220-1)
28. http://www.worldvision.in
29. http://worldvision.org/content.nsf/about/hr-requirements
30. (Bethell, 1984)
31. (Brysk, 2004, 38-9) The term 'Indian' in this discussion refers to indigenous native American populations.

32. (Diamond, 1989, 222)
33. Lt Col A.S. Amarasekera, Manipulative Christian evangelism, URL: http://www.lankaweb.com/news/items01/081201-2.html
34. http://cricket.deepthi.com/tsunami-world-asian-XI.html
35. All sections quoted from (Shashikumar, VK, 2004)
36. All sections quoted from this report: (Shashikumar, VK, 2004)
37. http://www.worldvisionindia.org/?185
38. (New England College, 2008)
39. (Ahmed, 17 October 2008)
40. (Rajkhowa, J.P., 2008)
41. (W.C. Smith, 2009, 193)
42. (Phillips, 2006, 134) Criswell changed his stand on segregation later – only after the US Supreme Court ruled out against segregation.
43. (W.C. Smith, 2009)
44. (Yohannan, K.P., 1986:2004, 109)
45. (Yohannan, K.P., 1986:2004, 29)
46. (Yohannan, K.P., 1986:2004, 141) This statement of Yohannan, like many others of his is a palpable falsehood. For example, the architect of India's green revolution, Dr M.S. Swaminathan, states that he chooses to be a Hindu because he considers it to be in harmony with science. (Swaminathan, M.S., 1982, 9)
47. (Yohannan, K.P., 1986:2004, 135)
48. (Yohannan, K.P., 1986:2004, 138)
49. Interestingly, this fundamentalist and hate-filled worldview is being provided an academic clothing by academics sponsored by organizations like Dalit Freedom Network. For example, Kancha Ilaiah, who is in the advisory board of DFN, calls Hinduism 'spiritual fascism' and traces all social problems of India to Hinduism. The connecting thread between theology of GFA and thesis of Kancha Ilaiah is through DFN, which sponsors Ilaiah and as Operation Mobilization endorses GFA.
50. (Eternity, Biz, 2010)
51. (GFA, 1996:2009), Another endorsement comes from Jospeh D'Souza, who runs the US-based Dalit Freedom Network (DFN).
52. (Bergunder, 2008, 54)
53. (Thomas, 2008, 106)
54. (Ministry, Watch 2008)
55. (www.ad2000.org, 1997)
56. (GFA, 1996:2009)
57. (Travel with a cause, 2005:2009)
58. (Travel with a cause, 2005:2009)
59. (GFA, 1996:2009)

60. (Yohannan, K.P., 1986, 99) In subsequent editions mention of Buddhism by name was strategically left out to read 'Animism and all other Asian religions have a common heritage in this one religious system.' (2004 edition)

61. (DFN, 2006). Also see: (GFA, 1996:2009)

62. (Edamaruku, 2001)

63. (*The Economic Times*, 20 January 2004)

64. (MHA, 2005-2006, 4)

65. (*The Telegraph*, 13 July 2008)

66. (The AICC Update February, 2007, 3)

67. (GFA, 1996:2009)

68. (*Chicago Tribune*, 22 January 2005)

69. (www.indianchristians.us, 2007) For a Hindu version of the incident, see: (www.christianaggression.org, 2007)

70. (Thomas, 2008, 144)

71. (www.christianpersecution.info, 2007)

72. (GFA, 2008)

73. (*Christian Telegraph*, 2008)

74. (*Christian Today*, 11 December 2008)

75. This webpage has been since mid-2009 moved Web admin: into the zone forbidden for outsiders by http://people.biola.edu/faculty/georgea/PeoplesofIndia.htm

76. All quotes by (Prashad, 2005)

77. http://www.ad2000.org/uters4.htm

78. (*Ireland*, 20 March 2006)

79. (*Maranatha Christian Journal*, 2004)

80. http://www.persecution.net

81. (Thomas, 2008, 125)

82. (Thomas, 2008, 114)

83. (Thomas, 2008, 126) With regard to Christian appropriation of national symbols, some Catholic institutions in Kerala have gone one step further and have created an alternative anthem addressed to the Pope but set to the tune of India's national anthem, In its 2006 version it was addressed to Pope John Paul II (Prabhan, 2006). In 2009 it addressed Benedict XVI (Prabhan, 2009). Another popular video evangelist from Kerala gives a communal interpretation to India's national flag. The evangelical claims that because the white portion represents Christianity, having the wheel at the center located on white background is a prophecy that the authority of the Indian state would ultimately come to Christians. (J.S. George, 2009)

84. (www.cbn.com, 2008)

85. (Robertson, 1988)
86. (David, 2005)
87. (BosNewsLife, 2006)
88. (BosNewsLife, 2006)
89. (Arora, 2008)
90. Based in Chennai, she is the resident editor and bureau chief in South India for New Delhi Television Ltd. She is also chief operating officer of an Indonesian news and information channel, Astro Awani, honored in its first year for best current affairs programming in Indonesia. (Bio-data of Jennifer Arul as presented in 'Journalism Through the Eyes of Faith' section of Bethel University: URL:http://www.bethel.edu/special-events/ jtef/bios). In 2007, she launched a similar Astro service in Malaysia. According to ChennaiTVNews.com, Jennifer Arul has been made the managing editor of a new channel in association with 'The Hindu' newspaper. (ChennaiTVNews.com 2008)
91. (Ebrahimi and Schweizer, 2007)
92. (NDTV, 28 November 2004)
93. For example, when in sixteenth century, the famous scientist Galileo fell behind on his dowry payments for his sister, his brother-in-law threatened to get him arrested (Discovery, (8) 1987, 117)
94. (Creation, 1997)
95. (Aikman, 2004)
96. (Gegrapha, 1998:2007)
97. (Aikman, 1998:2007)
98. (Elst, 2007, 516)
99. (Arul, 1999)
100. (Arul, 1998)
101. (Shashikumar, VK, 2004)
102. (Shashikumar, VK, 2004)
103. (Joshua Project, 2000:2009)
104. (Joshua Project, 2000:2009)
105. (Arora, 2007)
106. (Shashikumar, VK, 2004)
107. (Joshua Project, 2001)
108. (Joshua Project, 2001:2009)
109. (The New Indian Express, 4 March 2007)
110. (BTI, 1999:2008)
111. (BTI, 2006)
112. (Christian Post, 2007)
113. (BTI 2006, 4)
114. (Daniel, 2002)

115. (Daniel, 2006). See also (Robert, 2007, 8)

116. (BTI, 2006)

117. (BTI, 2002)

118. (BTI, 1998, 3) The word 'mission' here does not necessarily mean missionary work, or evangelism. The institutions described in this section, such as Harvard Divinity School and Andover Theological Sschool, work within an upper-class intellectual/establishment nexus quite different from the right-wing missionary fundamentalism described elsewhere in this chapter. Again, as we have seen elsewhere, Americans who would be barely on speaking terms at home can find common cause in India.

119. (Venugopal, P, 2004)

120. (Jeevaraj, V, 1981)

121. (McGavran, 1983)

122. http://www.ad2000.org/uters4.htm : quoted in (Thomas, 2008, 144)

123. (Chick publications, 1990)

124. (*The Hindu*, 8 January 1999)

125. (IANS, 2008)

126. Sahdeo was a freedom fighter and is revered by the people of Jharkhand. His statues have been installed at several places across the state. The book portrays him as an oppressor.

127. (*The Hindu*, 2007)

128. (Nitharsanam.net, 29 February 2008)

129. (Nagarajan, R, 26 Febuary 2009)

130. (HinduHumanist, 2006)

    The hatred for Hindus and the violent campaign to get Christian majority villages free of Hindus are strikingly similar to the concept of 'Judenfrei' – Christian town or villages free of Jews in pre-Holocaust Germany. (Stackelberg, 2007, 279)

131. From 2007 to 2008, several temple vandalizations have been reported in Kanyakumari district by local editions of *Dinakaran* and *Tamil Murasu* – both pro DMK newspapers.

132. (Oberman, 5 April 2010)

133. (*The Times of India*, 6 April 2010)

134. (Shetty 2010)

135. (Kerala Kaumudi, 2010) In this south Indian state where Church is a key player in politics, many cases of abuses are hushed. The most famous case is that of Abhaya – whose death in 1992 was declared as a suicide by the state police but was later found to be a homicide in 1998 by Central Bureau of Investigations, and such was the power of the Church that it was found that the forensic reports were tampered with. It was only in 2008 that the accused priest and nun were arrested – only after

the Kerala High Court had blamed the state investigating agency over the slow progress in its probe and asked the Kerala unit of the CBI to take over. (Asianet India, 2008)
136. (Junior Vikatan February 2010)
137. (Kumutham Reporter, 2008)
138. (Dinamalar, 23 October 2007)
139. (Dinamalar, 22 November 2006)
140. (Tuglaq, 25 July 2007)
141. (Dinamalar, 22 November 2006)

Chapter 19

1. (Ambedkar and G, 2001)
2. Though the website itself has been now removed, the map and its variants have been making the rounds in various anti-Indian websites since its first appearance in late 1990s.
3. (Mangalwadi, 2008)
4. Quoted in (Freston, 2004, 91)
5. Paul Freston states: '(Christianity) helped to create the very identities used today as rallying cries. . . . Naga nationalism is a classic case of ethnic 'invention' aided by religion – even perhaps as a union of the "tribes" on the Israelite model.' (Freston, 2004, 88-9)
6. According to the former chief secretary of Assam, NSCN – the main Maoist-Christian insurgency movement gets 'financial support from the World Council of Churches', (Rajkhowa, JP, 2008)
7. Quoted in (Freston, 2004, 89)
8. *Frontline*, 19 June 1992, p.50
9. (Arpil 2005, 352)
10. (BBC, 21 June 2006)
11. (*India Today*, 20 December 2007)
12. (Mangalwadi, 2008) Interestingly, with the Indian government declaring that Maoist terrorism is its chief concern in recent times, this link became extinct and subsequently, the new form appeared with references to Maoists removed. However, the article by Vishal Mangalwadhi is available on another evangelical website (Mangalwadi, 2008)
13. (GIS Development, 2008)
    Mining operations in Orissa have often generated protests from activists, with multinational forces aligning themselves on both sides of the battle. Their own agenda has been to turn the local populations into puppets. Thus, when Vedanta, a controversial company, gained mining rights in a tribal area, the issue was taken to forums in Europe by one of the

NGOs, Actionaid. Following this, the Church of England announced that it would sell its stakes in Vedanta, revealing how multinational forces have interests in the Indian resources and how the entire process of decision making has shifted its centre of gravity outside India by both the multinationals and the NGOs. (*The Economic Times*, 8 February 2010)

14. (*India Today*, 30 March 1998)
15. (PTI, 6 February 2010)
16. (PTI, 5 October 2008)
17. For example: (Barnabas Fund ,2009)
18. (Mahapatra, 4 September 2008)
19. (www.nerve.in, 2008)
20. (Mangalwadi, 2008)
21. (*The Economic Times*, 1 October 2009)
22. (A. Bhattacharya, 2008)
23. (*The Times of India*, 24 August 2008)
24. (www.telegraphnepal.com, 2009)
25. (Gumaste, 2009)
26. (Daily News Agency, 4 January 2009)
27. (*The Times of India* 5 September 2009)
28. (Nayak, 2009)
29. (Margolis, 2000, 213)
30. (www.telegraphnepal.com, 2009)
31. (*The Wall Street Journal*, 3 October 2009)
32. (Golder, 2008)
33. (NCCN, 2007)
34. (*Telegraph* (UK), 29 September 2009)
35. (*The Indian Express*, 28 July 2008)
36. (*The Times of India*, 3 November 2009)
37. (*Asia Times*, 6 February 2010)
38. (PTI, 5 February 2010)
39. (Menon and Nigam, 2007, 144)
40. (Capie, 2004, 204-5)
41. (Karim, 1993, 64-5)
42. (Maitra, 2003)
43. (Roy, 2009)
44. (Parashar, 2009)
45. (Singh and Diwan, 2010)
46. (Roy, *Walking With the Comrades*, 2010)
47. (Singh and Diwan, 2010)
48. (Devji, 2010)

49. (Roy, 2010)

50. (*The Hindu,* 20 February 2010)

51. (*Hindustan Times,* 07 April 2010)

52. (PTI, 30 March 2010)

53. (Cath News India, 2010)

54. (*The Times of India,* 2010)

55. (Crotty, 2005)

56. For example, the article Ambrose Pinto wrote denouncing Indian government's offensive against Maoists titled 'Why We Oppose Green Hunt?' was first published in *Mainstream,* a Delhi-based left magazine and was later featured in JESA website (Pinto, 2010)

57. (Pinto, 2010)

58. (Cath News India, 2010)

59. (Manjooran, 2003) Despite the anti-imperialist postures of liberation theology in Asia, it has strong ties with US agencies. For example, when secular-left rebels threatened to overrun the corrupt Marcos rule in Philiphincs, liberation theology was used by the Church to gain entry into and control the left-radical movement. US-funded Radio Veritas served the cause of liberation theologians and CIA played a proactive role in helping the liberation theologian Jesuit Cardinal Jaime Sin in the overthrow of Marcos and election of Aquino. This helped clergy to expand their interventions in the secular polty and prevent the left from take over. (Pomeroy, 1992, 280) Bastan Wielenga an Asian Liberation Theologian explains that this led to 'a political situation in which the Maoist-oriented left lost part of its influence and is now facing a split. This has probably reduced the appeal of the "theology of struggle" as far as support for the armed struggle is concerned' (Wielenga, 2007, 72) Naturally for such theologically motivated radical cadre, countries like India can become an outlet and strategic playgrounds. As Wielenga candidly states, 'the struggle for democratic rights is not enough just as the change of governments through parliamentary elections in India or Sri Lanka is not enough. The question is not only that of the use of violent or non-violent means in the overthrow of a repressive government. The question is how and by whom . . . to initiate a liberating transformation of society.' (Wielenga, 2007, 72) The subtext here is that the secular democracy is not enough for Asian countries and that the social problems the developing countries face should be used as opportunities to initiate 'a liberating transformation of society', which is of course Christianity in non-Christian countries, through the 'use of violent or non-violent means'.

60. (Ben, 2010)

61. (P. More, 1997, 176)
62. Mahomed Ali Jinnah, quoted in (Johari, J.C., 1993, 198)
63. (R. Rao, 2009)
64. (Menon, V.P., 1998, 106)
65. (P. More, 1997, 179)
66. DMK is an abbreviation of Dravida Munnetra Kazhakam, or Dravidian Upliftment Association.
67. (Subramaniam, 1993, 271)
68. (CBCID, 1999)
69. (Shourie, 1994)
70. (Ludra, 2000)
71. (Raman, B, 2002)
72. (*The Week*, 12 August 1990)
73. (*The Week,* 12 August 1990)
74. (CBCID, 1998)
75. (Dhar, 2008)
76. Popularly known as TADA, this was the first and only legislative effort by the Union government of India to define and counter terrorist activities. The act, which was brought in 1987, was criticized by human rights organisations and political parties and was permitted to lapse in May, 1995.
77. (Dinamani, 4 July 1995)
78. (Tmpolitics.blogspot.com, 2007)
79. (*India Today*, 15 December 1997)
80. (*India Today*, 15 December 1997)
81. (*Dinamani*, 19 September 1997)
82. (*Malaimurasu*, 9 December 1997)
83. (PTI, 31 December 1998)
84. (*Dinamani,* 15 December 1997)
85. (*The Hindu*, 19 February 1998)
86. (Subramanian, T.S., 1998)
87. Some examples: There was a bomb blast inside the famous Hindu temple at Madurai, for which a leader of TMMK was arrested. (*Dinamani,* 22 May 1996). Another explosion in the state capital killed one person, and yet another bomb at Madras railway station injured twelve. Even a lodge directly opposite the state High Court was bombed injuring ten persons in Tamil Nadu. (*Malaimurasu,* 28 January 1997). There were seven incidents killing individuals, of which two attacks were on police personnel and a police station. Al Ummah activists hacked to death one prison official in Madurai right in front of the prison. (tnpolice.gov.in, 2008) In one incident, two different express trains were bombed, killing

six persons. (*The Week*, 1998). Earlier the state police, following a tip-off, had seized a huge cache of explosives from a house in Chennai. Two radicals belonging to Al Ummah, including the brother of its leader, were arrested. (Subramanian, T.S., 1998)

88. (Shamsi, 2004, 359)
89. (www.satp.org, 2002)
90. (*The Hindu*, 9 March 2008)
91. (*Frontline*, 20 March 1998)
92. (UNI, 6-Dec-1997).
93. (tnpolice.gov.in, 2008)
94. Rediff reported: 'Fifteen cinema theatres were set ablaze in Malappuram district in 1993 and 1994. Explosive-fitted cigarettes are believed to have been used for the purpose. The police suspect the ISI-aided Al Umma of involvement in the incident . . . Large-scale manufacture of pipe bombs in Malappuram were unearthed in 1995 after a person was killed in an explosion at a manufacturing site. A number of Islamic extremists groups like the Islamic Defence Force are suspects . . . Ninety one pipe bombs were recovered from the Kadalundi river in Malappuram district in 1996. The Islamic Dawa Mission is believed to be behind the incident . . . Four Hindu activists were killed in separate incidents in 1995 and 1996 in Thrissur, Palakkad and Malappuram districts. Suspects: The Al Umma, Jama Iyyathul Ihsania and Sunni Tiger Force. The police arrested P.A. Muhammad Sharief, Abdul Khader, Syed Alavi of the Al Umma and Husain Musaliyar and P Subair of the Sunni Tiger Force.' See: (Rediff News 2000)
95. NDF stands for either National Defense Force or National Democratic Front, The name was changed when the group attracted too much attention.
96. (Frontline 20-Mar-1998)
97. See for example: (tnpolice.gov.in, 2008)
98. (*The Indian Express*, 15 August 1999)
99. This shows how the destabilizing forces use the weakness of vote bank politics. With political parties sacrificing national security concerns before the vote bank politics, the secessionist and destabilizing forces gain strength using the very democracy that they seek to destroy. What is more disheartening in this case is that this pampering of secessionist forces is done in the case of Kerala by national parties, namely CPI(M) and Indian National Congress (INC).
100. (Iype, 2001)
101. (*The Economic Times*, 30 October 2008)
102. (Puthiya Kaatru, 2006)

103. (PTI, 15 March 2006).
104. (*The Hindu*, 11 June 2006) Also, *The Indian Express* revealed that following this, Madhani was provided by the DMK government with a 35-day Ayurvedic massage treatment, costing Rs 50,000, paid by the Tamil Nadu government itself. (*The Indian Express*, 23 July 2006) In a video taped interview, the father of a bomb blast victim who was stationed at the government hospital to serve Madhani alleged that the treatment was only a pretext for the jailed jihadis to meet their colleagues from outside. (Webber, 2007)
105. See (DV Editorial, 2001), (DV Editorial, 2002) and (DV Editorial, 2004).
106. (Wikipedia, 2003)
107. (*The Pioneer*, 27 September 2006)
108. (Krishnakumar, R., 2006)
109. (www.satp.org, 2002)
110. (*The Hindu*, 16 March 2006)
111. For example, it was a former zonal SIMI president who founded the MNP; the leader of TMMK, who enjoys very close intimacy with the present DMK regime, was a state president of SIMI. Another president of a Tamil Nadu SIMI unit is now the general secretary of the Tamil Nadu Thouheed Jamat, which is close to AIADMK. (*Frontline*, 21 December 2007)
112. (*The Indian Express*, 23 July 2006)
113. (*The Indian Express*, 08 August 2006)
114. (*The Hindu*, 29 October 2004)
115. (*The Indian Express*, 27 July 2006)
116. (*Dinamalar*, 4 September 2006)
117. (*Dinakaran*, 20 July 2006)
118. For example, see: (tnpolice.gov.in, 2008)
119. (*The Indian Express*, 26 March 2007)
120. (Aravindan, K.P., 2006, 135)
121. (*Kumutham Reporter* 23 November 2008)
122. (*Dinakaran* 10 January 2007)
123. (www.state.gov, 2007)
124. (*The Economic Times*, 18 August 2008)
125. (*The Hindu*, 10 October 2008)
126. (V. Kumar, 2008)
127. (Rediff News, 2005)
128. (*The Hindu*, 10 January 2006)
129. (Raman, B, 2006)
130. (*Dinathanthi*, 20 January 2007)

131. (*The Indian Express*, 17 February 2007)

132 (*The Hindu*, 08 July 2008)

133. (*The Indian Express*, 7 Feb 2009)

134. (*The Indian Express*, 4 November 2006)

135. (*The Hindu*, 1 January 2007)

136. (*The New Indian Express*, 8 January 2007)

137. (*Dinamalar*, 9 January 2007)

138. (*Frontline*, 21 December 2007) This is further elucidated by the Letter of Samsunisha Ansari of Charitable Trust of Minorities dated 7 June 2006 which is available with the authors.

139. (*The Times of India*, 6 December 2008)

140. (*The New Indian Express*, 28 July 2008)

141. (*Frontline*, 16 August 2008)

142. (Rediff News, 2008)

143. (*Frontline*, 21 December 2007)

144. (*Frontline*, 21 December 2007)

145. (*The Times of India*, 18 December 2009)

146. (*The Pioneer*, 19 December 2009)

147. (*The Peninsula*, 11 January 2010)

148. (*The Economic Times*, 30 December 2009)

149. (*Deccan Herald*, 27 December 2009)

150. (*Headlines Today*, 03 November 2009)

151. (*Deccan Herald*, 12 November 2009)

152. (*Deccan Chronicle*, 13 December 2009)

153. (*Deccan Chronicle*, 13 December 2009)

154. (CNN-IBN, 6 July 2010)

155. (*The Times of India*, 18 July 2010)

156. (*The Times of India*, 18 July 2010)

157. (*The Indian Express*, 28 July 2010)

158. (Radhakrishnan. M.G., 2010)

159. (*The Hindu*, 15 July 2010)

160. (*The Indian Express*, 31 July 2008)

161. (*Naam Tamilar*, 2010)

162. (*The Hindu*, 27 November 2009)

163. (*Naam Tamilar*, 2010) and (*Naam Tamilar*, 2010)

164. (*The New Indian Express*, 3 May 2010)

165. (*Chennai Times*, 13 June 2010)

166. Session on Tamil Philosophy (24 July 2010: World Classical Tamil Confeernce) Paper by Professor V. Siva Prakasam (WCTC10 2010)

167. Session on Tamil Philosophy (24 July 2010: World Classical Tamil Confeernce) Paper by Professor A. Karunandham (WCTC10 2010)

168. Session on Religion and Tamil (24 July 2010: World Classical Tamil Confeernce) Paper by Bishop Ezra Sargunam (WCTC2010 2010)
169. For more details on the One versus Two Nation Theories, see 'The Roots of India-Pakistan Conflicts,' by Rajiv Malhotra, posted at: http://rajivmalhotra.sulekha.com/blog/post/2002/02/the-root-of-india-pakistan-conflicts.htm

Appendices

Appendix A

1.   (Ambedkar, 1948)
2.   (Bamshad, et al, 2001)
3.   (Ananthaswamy, 2001).
4.   (Ananthaswamy, 2001)
5.   (Ramachandran, R., 2001)
6.   (Ramachandran, R., 2001)
7.   (Cordaux, 2004)
8.   (Cordaux, 2004)
9.   (Bezbaruah and Samrat, 2001)
10. (Bezbaruah and Samrat, 2001)
11. (Bezbaruah and Samrat, 2001)
12. (Bezbaruah and Samrat, 2001) The article said, 'All the blood samples for the different castes were from a specific geographic area in Andhra Pradesh, and the sample size in some castes was as small as ten. "If more samples are studied, the results could be different," points out Shrivastava. Caste itself is also highly elastic. B.N. Chattopadhyaya, professor of ancient history at Jawaharlal Nehru University, Delhi, cites the example of the Boya tribe of Andhra Pradesh. They became warriors and claimed the status of Kshatriyas. Those among them who performed religious rituals even became Brahmins. In the 1960s, anthropologists Karve and Malhotra compared four Brahmin sub castes with four peasant sub-castes. They found that the variation within the Brahmin sub-castes was greater than the variations between Brahmin and peasant castes. Caste mobility happens even today, though post-Mandal the traffic is bidirectional.'
13. (Bezbaruah and Samrat, 2001)
14. (Sahoo, et al, 2006)
15. (Sengupta, et al, 2006)
16. (Sengupta, et al, 2006)
17. (Sengupta, et al, 2006)

18. (Reich, et al, 2009)
19. (*The Times of India,* 2009) The report was widely circulated by NGOs campaigning against India in UN, as in: (samatha.in, 2009), (indianchristians.in, 2009) and (dalitnetwork.org, 2009)
20. (Kumarasamy, 2009)
21. (*Science Daily,* 2009)

Appendix B

1. (Sen, 1999, 204)
2. (These groupings within them consisted of such core works of ancient Tamil literature like *Aha nannuru, Pura nannuru, Pattinappalai, Maturaikanci, Paripadal, Thirumurukarruppatai*) (S. Pillai, 1996)
3. *Puranannuru* quoted in (S. Pillai, 1996, verse:166:1)
4. *Puranannuru* quoted in. (S. Pillai, 1996, verse:26:13;93:7;362)
5. *Puranannuru* quoted in (S. Pillai, 1996, verse:2:18; 15:17)
6. (Ramachandran, S., 2007, 94)
7. *Puranannuru* quoted in (S. Pillai, 1996, verse:363:8,9)
8. *Maduraikanchi* quoted in (S. Pillai, 1996, verse:655-6)
9. *Paripatal* quoted in (S. Pillai, 1996, verse:9:12-13)
10. *Paripatal* quoted in (S. Pillai, 1996, verse:2:24-5)
11. *Perumpannatrupadai* quoted in (S. Pillai, 1996, verse:300-1)
12. (Madhava and Tapasyananda, 1996, 81)
13. *Thirumurkattrrupatai:* quoted in (S. Pillai, 1996, verse:179-80); *Perumpannatrupattai* quoted in (S. Pillai, 1996, verse:297, 310)
14. *Puranannuru* quoted in (S. Pillai, 1996, verse:113)
15. *Ahanannuru* quoted in (S. Pillai, 1996, verse: 24:1-3)
16. *Puranannuru* quoted in (S. Pillai, 1996, verse:224:5 9)
17. *Puranannuru* quoted in (S. Pillai, 1996, verse:384:15 18)
18. *Paripatal* quoted in (S. Pillai, 1996, verse:2:60 68)
19. *Thirumurkattrrupatai* quoted in (S. Pillai, 1996, verse:94 98)
20. *Paripatal* quoted in (S. Pillai, 1996, verse:17:28 32)
21. *Puranannuru* quoted in (S. Pillai, 1996, verse:377 : 5 6)
22. *Puranannuru* quoted in (S. Pillai, 1996, verse:201 : 8 12)
23. *Pathirtupathu* quoted in (S. Pillai, 1996, verse:21:13)
24. (S. Pillai, 1996, 11)
25. *Ahanannuru* quoted in (S. Pillai, 1996, verse:220:5 9)
26. *Puranannuru* quoted in (S. Pillai, 1996, verse: 2:22, 367:13)
27. *Kalithogai* quoted in (S. Pillai, 1996, verse:69:5)
28. *Paripatal* quoted in (S. Pillai, 1996, verse:18:38 39)
29. *Paripatal* quoted in (S. Pillai, 1996, verse:19:50 53)

30. *Pathirtupathu* quoted in (S. Pillai, 1996, verse:143:6 8)
31. *Natrtinai* quoted in (S. Pillai, 1996, verse:356:3 4)
32. *Paripatal* quoted in (S. Pillai, 1996, verse:9:1 3)
33. *Perumpannatrupadai* quoted in (S. Pillai, 1996, verse:29 30)
34. *Paripatal* quoted in (S. Pillai, 1996, verse:29 30); (S. Pillai, 1996, verse:3:15 18)
35. *Kalithogai* quoted in (S. Pillai, 1996, verse:103:74 75); (S. Pillai, 1996, verse:104:78)
36. *Paripatal* quoted in (S. Pillai, 1996, verse:2:16 19)
37. *Mullai* quoted in (S. Pillai, 1996, verse:3)
38. *Paripatal* quoted in (S. Pillai, 1996, verse:4:10 21)
39. *Ahanannuru* quoted in (S. Pillai, 1996, verse:220:5 9)
40. *Puranannuru* quoted in (S. Pillai, 1996, verse:378:9 22)
41. *Ahanannuru* quoted in (S. Pillai, 1996, verse:70:13 15)
42. *Puranannuru* quoted in (S. Pillai, 1996, verse:2:13 16)
43. (Ramakrishnan, S., 1971, 210)
44. *Perumpannatrupadai* quoted in (S. Pillai, 1996, verse:415 420)
45. *Kalithogai* quoted in (S. Pillai, 1996, verse:104:57 9).
46. *Maduraikanchi* quoted in (S. Pillai, 1996, verse:70 74); *Pathitrupathu* quoted in (S. Pillai, 1996, verse:43:6 11)
47. *Ahanannuru* quoted in (S. Pillai, 1996, verse:265:1 3) and also *Puranannuru* quoted in (S. Pillai, 1996, verse:2:24)
48. *Ahanannuru* quoted in (S. Pillai, 1996, verse:70:13 14)
49. *Puranannuru* quoted in (S. Pillai, 1996, verse:67:6 7; 380:12); *Pathitrupathu* quoted in (S. Pillai, 1996, verse:11:23 25; 43:6 8)
50. *Puranannuru* (S. Pillai, 1996, verse:17:18)
51. *Thirumanthiram* 1.118
52. *Thiruvasagam: Sivapuranam*
53. (Swamigal, verses 281-2)
54. (Amazon, 1999)
55. (Hussein, 2002).

Appendix C

1. The German missionary Johann Ludwig Krapf (1810–81), was the first to use the term 'Hamitic' to refer to a class of languages, and he classified all African languages spoken by black people to be Hamitic. He made distinctions among African communities combining their languages with different degrees of darkness of skin. (See: (Krapf and Ravenstein, 1860, 144)
2. (Dubow, 1995, 84)

3. (Dubow, 1995, 84)
4. The same process was at work in attempts to explain remnants of a great civilization in the Mississippi Valley region of what is now the United States. 'A lost tribe of Israel' was invented, since the Native Americans surely could not have built such enormous earthworks. For a brief summary see: (Hirst, 2005)
5. (Trigger, 1989, 197)
6. (Trigger, 1989, 131)
7. (Frederikse, 1990, 10-11)
8. (Trigger, 1989, 130)
9. (Seligman and Seligman, 1911) The Veddhas are an indigenous tribal group in Sri Lanka. They include speakers of both Tamil and Sinhala. Their religion is originally animist, with overlays of both Buddhism and Hinduism, but they are now being targeted by Christian evangelicals. They are also disputing among themselves over which group's members are the original inhabitants. See various articles posted at: http://vedda.org/
10. (Rigby, 1996, 68)
11. (Seligman, *Races of Africa*, 1966, 100-1)
12. (Sharp, 2004)
13. (Rekdal, 1998, 20) quoted in (Sharp, 2004)
14. (Seligman and Seligman, 1932, 4) quoted in (Rigby, 1996, 68). The invasion theory went as follows: 'The Negro Hamitic people will be understood when it is realized that the incoming Hamites were pastoral Caucasians, arriving wave after wave, better armed and of sterner character than the agricultural Negroes.'
15. All quotes that follow are from: (Rigby, 1996, 69,70).To simplify the language, we have substituted Hutu and Tutsi as the names rather than the variations used in the original.
16. Belgium took over Rwanda from Germany after the first World War.
17. (Lemarchand, 1999, 10-11)
18. (Longman, 2005, 87)
19. (Elisse, 2006, 176)
20. (Kastfelt, 2005, 16)
21. (Thompson and Annan, 2007, 28)
22. His remarks as summarized by a Catholic journalist, John L. Allen Jr. (Allen Jr, 2009).
23. (Longman, 2010)
24. (Longman, 2010, 151-2)
25. (Longman, 2010, 161)
26. (Longman, 2010, 175)

27. (Longman, 2010, 175-6)
28. (Longman, 2010, 232-7)
29. (Divakar, 2007, 38-42)

Appendix D

1. (Haase and Reinhold, 1994, 217)
2. (McManners, 2001, 425)

Appendix F

1. These fellowships are sponsored by the government of India.
2. (Mahadevan, 1970)
3. (Mahadevan, 2002)
4. (Chengappa, 2002)
5. (Ramachandran, S., 2006)
6. (Mahadevan, 2006)
7. (Mahadevan, 2006)
8. (*The Hindu*, 1 May 2006)
9. (Pande, B.M., 1971, 21)
10. (Rajshekar, V.T., and Rashidi, 1988)
11. (Farmer, Undated)
12. (Rao, P.N., 2009)
13. (Callaway, 2009)
14. (Mahadevan, 2009)
15. (S. Farmer, 2006)
16. (Chakrabarti, 2009)

Appendix G

1. (Ministry of Defense, 2001, 45)
2. (*The Hindu,* 17 November 2001)
3. (BBC, 18 June 2003)
4. (Maranatha Christian Journal, 2004)
5. (*The Financial Express*, 18 October 2006)
6. (MHA, 2005-2006)
7. (MHA, 2005-2006)
8. (Aurora, 2008)
9. (*The Indian Express,* 12 October 2009)
10. (Daily News and Analysis, 5 November 2008)

11. (Aurora, 2008)
12. (MHA, 2007-8)

Appendix H

1. How Lutheran World Federation and the WCC combine the right-wing and left-wing forces of the West in its fight against India is discussed in detail in Chapter 17. However, here we deal with the theological and colonial development of the Lutheran church in India and the destabilizing activities where Lutheran organizations are involved in India.
2. (Hudson, 2000, 17)
3. (Hudson, 2000, 18)
4. Despite a vast network of printing presses established by missionaries, they published only missionary literature and never bothered to publish anything for the secular public welfare. Indian manufacture of paper started in 1760s, but a printing press owned by Hindus and Muslims was never allowed to materialize. However, a fully Indian-owned press brought out a Tamil book first time in 1819 by a Tamil Hindu from Kanchi. A government press took up for the public only at the end of East India Company rule in 1857. This legacy of the early native pioneers is being suppressed to glorify Ziegenbalg. See: (More, 2004, 81)
5. Daniel Jeyaraj in Preface, (Ziegenbalg, 2005)
6. Daniel Jeyaraj in Preface, (Ziegenbalg, 2005)
7. (Hudson, 2000, 54)
8. (www.gltc.edu. 2006)
9. (Hudson, 2000, 50) In his footnote, Hudson also points out that in the 1956 Christian Literature Society translation of Ziegenbalg, the distinction between those sitting on mats and floor was removed and all were depicted as sitting on the mats.
10. (Kent, 2004, 24)
11. (www.gltc.edu, 2006) Chapter 10 (Dravidian Academic-Activist Network Outside India) of this book explains how this missionary aspect has been used in building an academic network to support Tamil identity in Europe,
12. (Cederlof, 2009, 197)
13. (Cederlof, 2009, 197)
14. (Cederlof, 2009, 215)
15. (Fahlbusch and Bromiley, 2003, 357)
16. For a detailed study of Gurukul Lutheran Theological college with respect to its being a part of the network of academic Dalit studies which facilitate continental European intervention in India see, Chapter 17.

17. (www.gltc.edu, 2006)
18. (Dravidian University, 2008-2009, 2)
19. (Devasahayam, S., 1992, 8-12)
20. (Thirumaavalavan, 2004, 171)
21. (Thiruma.net, 2009)
22. (www.uelci.org, 2007, 2)
23. (www.uelci.org, 2007, 2)
24. (www.uelci.org, 2008, 1)
25. (www.uelci.org, 2008, 3)
26. (Junior Vikatan, 2007).
27. (www.uelci.org, 2009, 1) For an account of how militant Dalit insurgency and racial Dalit identities were encouraged in Bangkok conference of LWF, see Chapter 17 (under the sub-title: Dalit Panchayat+ Dalitology+ Dalit Theology > Dalitstan).
28. 'Our differences with Nandy Rana group', PCC CPI(ML), 29. Quoted in (Karat, 1985).

Glossary

Ambedkar: See Baba Saheb Ambedkar.

Arya Samaj: Indian socio-spiritual reform movement founded by Swami Dayananda Saraswati (1824–1883) in 1875. The movement called for the abolition of castes and for radical social reforms. British colonial administration considered it as anti-British and hence closely monitored and restricted its activities.

Aryan: Borrowed from Vedic language into ninetheenth-century English, the word has been used by Western Indologists to denote a language group (now known as Indo-European or alternatively, Eurasian). The term also came to refer to the speakers of the language. Various European nation-states tried to trace an Aryan ancestry. While in India, historically the term never had a racial meaning, in Europe the term acquired a racist meaning and was grossly misused by racists, especially the Nazis.

Ayya Vazhi: An Indic spiritual tradition that originated in the Travancore princely state of British India in the nineteenth-century. It was founded on the teachings of Ayya Vaikundar (1801–1859), who united the depressed sections of the society to fight against both caste oppression and proselytization.

Ayyan Kali: Ayyan Kali (1863–1941) was a leader of the depressed sections of the population in the Travancore princely state of British India. He founded the Sadhujana Paripalana Sangham (Association for the Welfare of the Poor) in 1905. Although faced with stiff opposition from upper castes, he started schools for Dalit children and was elected to the legislative assembly of Travancore. He was supported in his fight for social justice by Sri Narayana Guru, Mahatma Gandhi, Arya Samaj and Hindu Maha Sabha.

Baba Saheb Ambedkar: Dr Bhimrao Ramji Ambedkar (1891–1956), the leader of the depressed sections in India, and today a pan-Indian icon. He fought against the social discrimination the depressed sections faced in India. He was also the architect of free India's constitution. In 1956, Ambedkar, along with his followers, was converted to Buddhism.

Babri demolition: On 6 December 1993, an assembled mob of Hindus gathered by BJP at the temple town of Ayodhya unlawfully brought down the disputed masque. Subsequently, Hindu-Muslim riots broke out throughout India. Media reports often depict this as mosque demolition, though the building unlawfully demolished by the mobs was not a functional mosque but has been a functional temple for more than four decades.

Chilapathikaram: A Tamil epic written by Ilango, a Jain monk who was originally a Tamil prince. The epic revolves around Kannagi, who challenges the unjust capital punishment meted out to her husband, burns the city, and ultimately becomes a Goddess.

Dalit: The word 'Dalit' comes from the Sanskrit language, and means 'ground', 'suppressed', 'crushed', or 'broken to pieces.' Initial use of the word is variously attributed to Maharashtrian social reformer Jotiba Govindrao Phule (1827–1890) and Arya Samaj. The term has been used increasingly in academic and political circles to denote the former untouchable communities, replacing the word coined by Gandhi – Harijan.

Dalitstan: Homeland for Dalits to be made by partitioning India. Many forces interested in the balkanization of Indian state promote the idea of Dalitstan. The now-defunct website www.dalitastan.org used to promote the idea in cyberspace.

Dasyu: Vedic term for the enemies of goodness and virtue. Western Indologists gave a racial meaning to the term. In the racial interpretation of ancient Indian history, the term is said to denote the aborigines who were killed and enslaved by the invading

Aryans. Dr Ambedkar conclusively established that the term is cultural and not racial in nature.

Dharma: Indic spiritual term common to Vedic, Buddhist, Jain and Sikh traditions. Dharma is a highly persistent, dynamic and yet evolving principle of virtuousness operating at different levels in Indian society, from individual to global.

DMK: Dravida Munnetra Kazhagam (Dravidian Progress Federation) was founded in 1949 by Dravidianist ideologue Annadurai (1909–1969) following differences of opinion with his mentor, E.V. Ramasamy. The party initially had a separatist agenda for a separate Dravidistan, which it abandoned officially in 1963. In 1969 it captured power in the state of Tamil Nadu. In 1972 DMK suffered a split and AIADMK (All Indian Anna DMK) was formed by the charismatic actor-politician M.G. Ramachandran. Since then, the two rival Dravidian parties have been ruling Tamil Nadu. DMK is perceived by political observers as more separatist and friendly towards secessionist and de-stabilizing elements under its present leader and Tamil Nadu chief minister, M. Karunanidhi.

Dravidian: Originally, found in Hindu mythology and Jain works, the term refers to the region south of Vindya mountain ranges. Dravidian land is hailed as the birth place of Bhakti (devotion) in Hindu tradition. With colonial Indology, it became the term for the family of languages spoken in South India. British missionary Robert Caldwell championed the term as an ethno-linguistic identity for non-Brahmin communities in Madras Presidency (what is now Tamil Nadu).

Dravidistan: Separate homeland for those who speak Dravdian languages (Tamil, Telugu, Kannada and Malayalam). But the demand was in vogue only within Tamil Nadu, and even there it found few takers. DMK initially advocated separate Dravidistan as its final destiny, but officially dropped it. However, fringe elements in the Dravidianist politics and armed secessionist groups like Tamil Nadu Liberation Army (TNLA) periodically revive the demand for separate Dravdistan.

E.V. Ramasamy (Periyar) (1879–1973): Dravidianist and self-styled rationalist. Popularly known as EVR or Periyar to his followers he added virulent racist dimensions to disputes between non-Brahmins and Brahmins.

Harijan: The term literally means the children of Hari (Vaishnava term for God). It was coined by Mahatma Gandhi to empower the former untouchables. However, the Left and missionary scholarship has been advocating the term Dalit in the place of Harijan. A recent study revealed that the former untouchable communities themselves prefer the term Harijan to Dalit.

Hindutva: Cultural nationalist conception of Hindu polity. It was based on the book with the same title, written by Hindu nationalist Vinayak Damodar Savarkar in 1920s. The conception of Hindutva combines reductionist approach of European nation-states with cultural unity of India. Nevertheless, the conception is remarkable, if only for the insight that the racial categories dividing humans are all artificial, given the period of its genesis (1920s).

Jati: A community based mainly on profession and work roles, also kinship. Often it is termed as caste. A Jati is mostly a localized community which is more like a vast extended family than a guild. In colonial Indology as well as social studies, Jatis are often depicted as fixed, rigid and stratified. However, post-colonial researches have shown that Jatis have dynamic maneuverability within the varna matrix and they are not as stratified as previously depicted.

Jihad: Holy war prescribed in Koran. It is waged against idolaters.

Jotiba Govindrao Phule: Also known as Mahatma Jotiba Phule (1827–1890), he was an anti-Brahmin social reformer. He was one of the earliest Indian social reformers to accept the racial interpretation of Indian society and he called Brahmins devils and aliens. Dr Ambedkar, the leader of Dalits, though having respect for the social reform zeal of Phule, nevertheless rejected the racial interpretation.

Khalistan: Homeland for Sikhs to be made by partitioning India. In 1980s the Khalistan movement was the major source of terrorism in India. Sikh separatist insurgency was nurtured initially by Indira Gandhi, the late prime minister of India, to intimidate the non-Congress Punjab state government, which ultimately resulted in her assassination by Sikh terrorists. It was KPS Gill, an extraordinarily iron-willed Sikh police officer, who brought the militancy under control. Today, Khalistan movement is a spent force which finds no support among the Sikhs though foreign forces bent on destabilizing India use a fringe group of expatriate Sikhs to voice the demand.

Kumari Kandam: A mythical lost continent south of the present Indian mainland. Tamil legends speak of ancient Tsunami-like waves destroying a graet Tamil civilization of hoary past and present Tamils as remnants of that disaster. Dravidianists weave this along with Theosophical Lemuria and claim that Kumari Kandam was the birth place of human civilization and Tamil was the first language of humanity. Evangelical propaganda in Tamil Nadu mixes this narrative with pre-Babel stage of humanity (see also, Lemuria).

Lemuria: A mythical lost continent which was popularized by Theosophists in the nineteenth century in South India. Initially proposed by Philip Sclater, a bio-geographer, to explain certain zoological similarities between continents long separated by ocean, Lemuria became a mystical-theo-historical doctrine in the hands of Theosophists in the late nineteenth century and was later incorporated in the Dravidian narrative identified with Kumari Kandam (see Kumari Kandam).

LTTE: Liberation Tigers of Tamil Eelam or simply 'Tigers' is a Tamil insurgency group formed in Sri Lanka in 1976 following anti-Tamil riots and discrimination. The initial sympathies it won with south Indian Tamils ended with the brutal assassination of previous Indian prime minister Rajiv Gandhi in 1991 by an LTTE suicide bomber. LTTE was routed in recent Sri Lankan military operation in 2009. Its leader Prabhakaran was captured and killed by Sri Lankan army. LTTE also networked with secessionist forces in India, including Tamil as well as Assamese separatists.

A section of Catholic clergy in Tamil Nadu supports the cause of LTTE.

Mahabharata: Ancient Indian epic traditionally ascribed to Vyasa, a sage who came from the lineage of fishermen. It narrates the battle between two branches of an ancient Indian dynasty. It has thousands of branch stories within it. Its geographiy covers all of India and presents it as one indivisible cultural matrix.

Mahavamsa: An ancient Pali text which literally means a chronicle of a great dynasty, narrates the relation between Sri Lankan rulers and Buddhist religious institutions. It was used by colonial administrators to create ethnic identities with a one-to-one mapping between language, race, and religion. According to post-colonial studies of Mahavamsa and other ancient records of Sri Lanka, before the emergence of European mediated Sinhalese nationalism, Singhala identity was not considered a necessary attribute of virtuous rule.

Masjid demolition: See Babri demolition.

Moplahstan: A proposed Islamic state to be carved out of South India by Jehadhi forces in South India. The term Moplah refers to the Moplah rebellion that happened in 1921 in which the anti-British Muslim agitation took an anti-Hindu turn. Widespread killing and conversion of Hindus was followed by declaration of Caliphate in the Malabar region of Kerala.

Murugan: Hindu God for celestial armies and wisdom literally means Beauty. He is considered the son of Siva. He killed demon king Sura and Tharaka. He is called Skanda in Sanskritic tradition. His brides are a tribal girl Valli, and the daughter of Indra. Thus for Tamil people, Murugan is a symbol of confluence of diverse elements harmonized in Divinity.

Narayana Guru: See Sri Narayana Guru

Phule: See Jotiba Govindrao Phule

Ramayana: Ancient Indian epic traditionally ascribed to Valmiki, a hunter-bandit turned saint. The epic describes the odyssey of prince Rama and his epic battle with the demonic Ravana. *Ramayana* has many narratives and local variants. It has been considered for ages as one of the symbols of national unity in India. In the racial interpretation of western Indologists, the epic becomes a narrative of Aryan conquest of the South. However in all traditional Indian narratives, *Ramayana* symbolizes the victory of good over evil.

RSS: Rashtriya Swayamsevak Sangh (national volunteers corps) – a Hindu social movement which is a cross between boy scouts and para-military outfit, founded in 1924 in Maharashtra by Hindu nationalist Dr K.B. Hedgewar. It has been often blamed by its adversaries for attacks on religious minorities and praised by its admirers for its rescue operations during natural calamities.

Saiva Siddhantha: Saiva Siddhantha is a mainly south Indian as well as Sri Lanka-based Siva worshipping (Saivite) spiritual tradition. It has connections with tenth-century Kashmiri Saivism. In South India it has evolved into a huge system of philosophy, devotion, art and sculpture. The core canon of Saiva Siddhantha is the twelve-volume compilation of Saivite mystics and poet-devotees. Saiva Siddhantha has been particularly marked for appropriation by Christian missionaries who, along with Dravidianists, try to project it as indigenous and unrelated to rest of pan-Indian Hindu spirituality.

Sangham or Cankam literature: An anthology of ancient Tamil literature compiled most probably between third century BCE and early centuries of Common Era. The poets came from both genders and varied sections of the society, including Brahmins. This literature has been used by Dravidianists to claim a separate cultural identity for Tamils though the literature speaks of a spiritual life full of Vedic rituals and veneration for Vedic deities as something integral and central to ancient Tamil life.

Sivalinga: A non-anthropomorphic icon representing Siva. It dates back to neolithic period and has had a continous evolution as a spiritual symbol in India. Western Indology has often overplayed it as a phallic symbol, The word Linga itself means only a symbol (etymologically related to lingua and hence language). Most propably it had its origin in symbolic representation of cosmic axis represented in Vedic fire rituals as a pillar.

Smritis: Ancient Indian law books for virtuous living. Smritis are varied and localized. They are not ever-binding laws like Messianic laws in Abrahamic religion. They are subject to critical reviews and amenable to change. The most famous of all Smritis is attributed to Manu. Certain discriminatory and archaic aspects of *Manusmriti* have been used to tar the entire Hinduism as casteist and anti-Dalit and anti-woman, though historical evidence points to the contrary. *Manusmriti* is not the only Smriti. There are many Smritis and Dharma Sastras with regional variations.

Sri Narayana Guru: (1855–1928) Hindu seer who applied Advaitic principles for the upliftment of depressed classes in Kerala. Sri Narayana Guru empowered not only the untouchables but also the sections of humanity despised by upper castes as unapproachables. He installed temples and made them priests and imparted Vedic knowledge to them. He inspired them to launch passive resistance to win entry into temples and public roads and resources.

Swami Vivekananda: (1863–1902) Hindu monk who brought Vedanta to the West and also heralded the national renaissance in India. Vivekananda criticized the racial interpretation of Indian society and urged the masses to empower themselves through education. He warned the upper castes to give up their social hegemony and serve the poor and uplift them. He founded the Ramakrishna mission and also helped Tata establish Indian Institute of Science.

Tamil Eelam: Separate Tamil homeland to be obtained by the vivisection of Sri Lanka – the aim for which LTTE fought the bitter civil war in Sri Lanka. Tamil separatists in India see Tamil Eelam as the first step towards reviving the demand for Dravidistan through armed conflict.

Tamil Tigers: See LTTE

Thirukural: A poetic ethical treatise written by famous Tamil poet Thiruvalluvar in classic Smriti tradition of India. What marks out *Thirukural* is its non-sectarian nature. There are elements which can be claimed as belonging to Vedic, Jain and Buddhist traditions. Tamils have an emotional attachment to the treatise.

Thiruvalluvar is said to have lived two thousand years ago and traditional narratives depict him as a weaver.

Vaikkom Satyagraha: A Satyagraha (passive resistance) movement (1924–25) launched for the opening up of temples as well as roads adjoining the temples to the depressed sections of the society in the state of Travancore in British India. The movement was supported by progressive and humanistic Hindus from across all sections of the society. The movement had the blessing of Sri Narayana Guru, and also Mahatma Gandhi.

Varna: The fourfold system of: intellectuals (Brahmins), rulers (Kashtriyas), merchants (Vaisyas) and laborers (Sudras). Ancient Indian scriptures like *Bhagavad Gita* speak of the fourfold classification of the society as based on innate and manifest abilities of the person and not on birth. According to it, when the questioner speaks of varna as based on hereditary duty (Kula Dharma), Krishna the God-teacher speaks of varna as based on righteousness as applied to an individual (Swa-Dharma). Varna represents a social space, and Jatis have historically moved in and out of these spaces.

Vedas: The most ancient Hindu scriptures, they are four in number. They are hymns written in spiritual ecstasy or inspired by a spiritual insight. The seers who perceived these hymnal insights came from all sections of the society (including women) as well as those sections which were later marginalized during the latter historical developments. Some of the cardinal principles that form the core of Indian civilization can be traced to Vedic lore.

Bibliography

www.ccu.edu. Colorado Christian University: Welcome. 1999:2010. http://www.ccu.edu/welcome/ (accessed 2010).

'Plawiuk'. 'Hinduism is Fascism'. 2006. http://plawiuk.blogspot.com/2006/10/hinduism-is-fascism.html (accessed 10 December 2008).

100, Huntley Street. '3000 Years of Slavery in India – 1,2 and 3: Talk with Joseph D'Souza. 27 March 2009. http://www.youtube.com/watch?v=WD32shDqFXw ; http://www.youtube.com/watch?v=chRCpatrsaM and ; http://www.youtube.com/watch?v=yJckGiQf8t8 (accessed 12 January 2010).

Abbas, Samar. 'Dravidian India'. 2000. http://saxakali.com/southasia/dravidian_india.htm (accessed September 2008).

Abdullah, Omar. 'Statement by H.E. Indian Minister of State for External Affairs, World Conference Against Racism, Racial Discrimination, Xenophobia and Related Intolerance Durban, South Africa'. United Nations Website. 2 September 2001. http://www.un.org/WCAR/statements/indiaE.htm (accessed 19 January 2009).

ACCES. 'Afrikan History Diary 2002 with amazing facts about Afrikan people, culture, history, wise sayings, fables and proverbs'. Afrikan Caribbean Cultural Education Services (ACCES), 2002.

Adrian Bird, M.M. Thomas. *Theological Signposts for the Emergence of Dalit Theology.* PhD thesis, University of Edinburgh, February 2008.

Ahmed, Farzand. 'Cong MP Suspected Behind VHP Leader's Murder'. web report, *India Today,* 17 October 2008.

AICC. 'A Report on Activities of the AICC'. Month Report, All India Christian Council, October 2007.

AICC. 'A Report on Activities of the AICC'. Month Report, All India Christian Council, March 2008.

AICC. 'A Report on the Activities of the AICC'. Month Report, All India Christian Council, December 2007.

— All India Christian Council. 1998:2010. http://www.aiccindia.org/newsite/0804061910/aboutus.asp (accessed 10 January 2009).

AICC. All India Christian Council Press Release. All India Christian Council, 19 December 2008.

AICC. 'Key Role in Visit by UN Special Rapporteur on Religious Freedom'. A report on activities of the AICC, AICC, March 2008.

Aikman, David. 'Christianity Makes George Bush A Better President (Interview)'. *www.beliefnet.com*. October 2004. http://www.beliefnet.com/story/154/story_15405_1.html (accessed 10 January 2009).

— Gegrapha Explained. 1998:2007. http://www.gegrapha.org/AboutUs-GegraphaDefinition.asp.

Al-Jazeerah. 'Kashmir Event at George Washington University'. TV News, 30 October 2006.

Allen Jr, John L. 'Synod for Africa Opens to High Hopes, but Realism'. *National Catholic Reporter*, 2 October 2009.

Aloys, Evina. 'Congressman Trent Franks Introduces Resolution on Untouchability'. 2 May 2007. http://journalchretien.net/spip.php?page=imprimir_articulo&id_article=10306 (accessed 10 August 2009).

Amazon.com. Product Description of translation of Tamil Classic Poetry by George Hart. 1999. http://www.amazon.com/Four-Hundred-Songs-War-Wisdom/dp/product-description/0231115636 (accessed 28 January 2009).

Ambedkar, Bhimrao Ramji, and Bhat, S.G. *Bharata Ratna Dr B.R. Ambedkar and the Indian Constitution*. Pondicherry: Journal Society, Dr Ambedkar Govt. Law College, 2001.

Ambedkar, Dr. *The Untouchables Who Were They And Why They Became Untouchables? Part III,* Chapter VIII. 1948.

Amoore, Louis. *The Global Resistance Reader*. Routledge, 2005.

Anantha Vikatan. 'Bharathanatyam Removed from Hinduism?' News, Chennai, 20 December 2006.

Ananthaswamy, Anil. 'Written in Blood'. *New Scientist*, 19 May 2001.

Andersen, Peter B, and Oluf Schönbeck. 'Conversion and the Rationalities behind Conversion'. *20th European Conference on Modern South Asian Studies: Panel 36 Christians, Cultural Interactions, and South Asia's Religious Traditions.* 8-11 July 2008. http://www.arts.manchester.ac.uk/ecmsas/panels/ecmsaspanel33to41/panelpdfs/Fileuploadmax10Mb,134403,en.pdf (accessed 10 January 2009).

Anderson, Clare. *Legible Bodies: Race, Criminality and Colonialism in South Asia*. Berg Publishers, 2004.

Andrew, Garrett, and George Hart. *In Memoriam: Murray Barnson Emeneau*. 29 August 2005. http://www.universityofcalifornia.edu/

senate/inmemoriam/murraybarnsonemeneau.htm (accessed 12 December 2009).

Annadurai, C.N., and Janarthanam, A.P. *The Anna Commemoration Volume.* Chennai: Periyar Research Library, 1970.

Annadurai.C.N, and Thanjai Nalankilli. *Tamil Tribune*: Speech Delivered at the Dravidar Kazagam State Conference in Tiruchi in the 1940s. (Translated from Tamil to English by Thanjai Nalankilli). May 2005. http://www.tamiltribune.com/05/0501.html (accessed 10 February 2009).

Anthony, Susai. 'Heinous Acts of Hindu Nationalists'. 2001. http://www.fiacona.org/Susai_report.htm (accessed 10 January 2009).

Appasamy, A.J. *The Gospel and India's Heritage.* London: Society for the Promotion of Christian Knowledge, 1942.

Arangetram Brochure. 'About the Guru'. 1999.

Aravannan, KP. *Anthropological Studies on the Dravidian-Africans.* Chennai: Tamil Kootam, 1980.

Aravindan, K.P. *Kerala Padanam.* Kozhikode: Kerala Sastra Sahitya Parishad, 2006.

Arewa, Caroline Shola. 'Yoga: Complete holistic care system'. *Pride Magazine*, July 1997.

Arora, Vishal. *Religion and Politics in India*, Oxford Centre for Religious and Public Life. 1 August 2008. http://www.ocrpl.org/?p=260 (accessed September 2009).

— Review of John Dayal's book *A Matter of Equity: Freedom of faith in Secular India*,' John Dayal's webpage at Sulekha.com. May 2007. http://johndayal.sulekha.com/blog/post/2007/05/john-dayal-s-new-book.htm (accessed August 2008).

— 'Swatika Terrorism' *The Caravan*, 16-31 December 2008.

Arpi, Claude. *India and Her Neighbourhood: a French Observer's Views.* New Delhi: Har-Anand Publications, 2005.

Arul, Jennifer. 'Journalism, Truth, and the Public Square'. *Gegraoha.* 1998. Jennifer Arul, http://www.gegrapha.org/JenniferArulinLondon.asp (accessed 10 January 2009).

— 'The Power and Influence of Journalists'. *Gegrapha.* 1999. http://www.gegrapha.org/JenniferArul1.asp (accessed 10 January 2009).

Arundale, Rukmini Devi. 'Philosophy of Dance'. All India Radio, April 14, 1954.

— *Some Selected Speeches and Writings of Rukmini Devi Arundale –Vol-I.* Chennai: Kalakshetra Foundation, 2004.

Asia Times. 'Nepal Trying to March in Step'. 6 February 2010.

Asian Lutheran News. 'Doctorate Thesis of Dr Ginda P. Harahap'. Newsletter for July/August 2005.

Asian Tribune. 'Integrity of Roberts Evan Questioned'. 9 October 2008. http://www.asiantribune.com/?q=node/13617 (accessed 10 January 2009).

Asianews.it. 'US Congress set to Scrutinize Anti-Dalit Discrimination'. 2006. http://www.asianews.it/index.php?art=4347&l=en (accessed 10 October 2009).

Assistnews. 'British House of Commons Debates Caste Discrimination in India'. News, 11 May 2007.

Associated Press. 'Broken and at the Bottom of Life's Heap'. *wcar.alrc.net.* 31 August 2001. http://wcar.alrc.net/mainfile2.php/News/52/ (accessed 10 January 2009).

Associated Press. *Davis: I've Seen No Evidence Terrorist Group Funded Sri Lanka Trip.* News, Associated Press, 24 August 2006.

Aurora, Bhavana Vij. 'Foreign Funds: Turning Off the Tap'. *India Today,* 3 November 2008.

Bagchi, Amiya. *The Political Economy of Underdevelopment.* Cambridge University Press, 1984.

Bamshad et al., Michael. 'Genetic Evidence on the Origins of Indian Caste Populations'. June 2001: 994-1004.

Banerjee, Aditi. 'Hindu American Foundation Response to Inflammatory Remarks by Evangelist Zacarias in *India Abroad* dated 25 June 2004'. *India Abroad,* 9 July 2004.

Barboza, Francis. *Experiencing Christianity in and through Bharata Natyam.* March 2003. http://www.drbarboza.com/inno.htm (accessed 10 April 2008).

— 'Gesture No. 1: God the Father'. 2002. http://www.drbarboza.com/ges1.htm (accessed 10 April 2008).

— 'Men (purush) in Religious Dance'. March 2003. http://www.drbarboza.com/purush.htm (accessed 15 April 2008).

Barnabas Fund. 'Persecution Continues against Christian Communities in Orissa. Will you help?' December 2009. http://www.barnabasfund.org/UK/News/Archives/Persecution-continues-against-Christian-communities-in-Orissa-Will-you-help.html (accessed 10 January 2010).

Barnes(SJ), Michael. *Theology and the Dialogue of Religions.* Cambridge University Press, 2002.

Bartholomeusz, Tessa J, and Richard Chandra De Silva. 'Buddhist Fundamentalism and Minority Identities in Sri Lanka'. In *Buddhist Burgers and Singala Buddhist Fundamentalism,* by Tessa J Bartholomeusz. University of Chicago Press, 1992.

Basu, Ratan Lal. 'Human Development: Ancient Kingship, Modern Politicians and the Problem of Corruption in India, The Culture Mandala'. *The Bulletin of the Centre for East-West Cultural and Economic Studies* 7, no. 1 (December 2005).

Bavinck, Maarten. 'A Matter of Maintaining Peace: State Accommodation to Subordinate Legal Systems – The Case of Fisheries along the Coromandel Coast of Tamil Nadu, India' *Journal of Legal Pluralism and Unofficial Law*, 1998: 151-70.

BBC. 'India Blacklists 800 NGOs'. News, BBC, 18 June 2003.

BBC. 'India Faces Maoist "Red Salute"'. News, BBC, 21 June 2006.

BBC. 'India: Church unhappy with US for not Acting against India on Religious Issue'. News, BBC Monitoring South Asia, 17 May 2003.

Belief Net. 'Your Questions to Jonah Blank'. July 2000. http://www.beliefnet.com/Faiths/2000/07/Your-Questions-To-Jonah-Blank.aspx (accessed 10 January 2009).

Bennett, Clinton. *In Search of Jesus: Insider and Outsider Images*. Continuum International Publishing Group, 2001.

Bergunder, Michael. 'Contested Past Anti-Brahminical and Hindu Nationalist Reconstructions of Indian Prehistory'. *Historiographia Linguistica* xxxi, no. 1 (2004): 59-104.

Bergunder, Michael. 'Miracle Healing and Exorcism: The South Indian Pentecostal Movement in the Context of Popular Hinduism'. *International Review of Mission*, 2001: 103-112.

— *The South Indian Pentecostal Movement in the Twentieth Century*. Wm. B. Eerdmans Publishing, 2008.

Berry, Thomas. 'Foundations of Indian Culture'. In *Six Pillars: Introduction to the Major Works of Sri Aurobindo*, by Robert A McDermott. Wilson Books, 1974.

Béteille, Andre. 'Race and caste'. *The Hindu*, 10 March 2001.

Bethell, Leslie. *The Cambridge History of Latin America*. Cambridge University Press, 1984.

Beveridge, Henry, trans. *The Akbarnama of Abu-l-Fazl: (History of the reign of Akbar including an account of his predecessors)*. Ess Ess Publications, 1977.

Bezbaruah, Supriya, and Choudhury Samrat. 'White India'. *India Today*, 30 July 2001.

Bharathiar, Shuddhananda. *Thirukkural With English Couplets*. Tinnevelly: SISS Works Publishing Society, 1968.

Bhaskaran, Vijayan P. *The Legacy of St Thomas*. Mumbai: The Bombay St Paul Society, 2007.

Bhattacharya, Abanti. 'China and Maoist Nepal: Challenges for India'. *Institute for Defence Studies and Analyses: IDSA Strategic comments*. 23 May 2008. http://www.idsa.in/publications/stratcomments/AbantiBhattacharya230508.htm (accessed 23 August 2009).

Bhattacharya, Sutapas. *The Oneness/Otherness mystery; The Synthesis of Science and Mysticism*. Motilal Banarsidas, 1999.

Blackburn, Stuart H. *India's Literary History: Essays on the Nineteenth Century.* Orient Blackswan, 2004.

Blank, Jonah. *Arrow of the Blue-skinned God.* Grove Press, 2000.

Blavatsky, Helena Petrovna. *The Secret Doctrine, the Synthesis of Science, Religion and Philosophy.* London: Theosophical Publishing Society, 1893.

— *The Secret Doctrine: The Synthesis of Science, Religion and Philosophy.* California: Aryan Theosophical Press, 1917.

Blavatsky, Helena Petrovna. 'Theosophical Gleanings'. *Lucifer: A Theosophical Magazine*, March-August 1890: 502.

Bonner, Raymond. 'Rebels in Sri Lanka Fight with Aid of Global Market in Light Arms'. News, *New York Times*, 7 March 1998.

BosNewsLife. BosNewsLife Christian News Agency: About Us. 2006. http://www.bosnewslife.com/about-us (accessed 3 March 2009).

— BosNewsLife: Christian News agency: Writers. 2006. http://www.bosnewslife.com/about-us/writers (accessed 30 November 2008).

Bottomore, T.B. *A Dictionary of The Marxist Thought.* Wiley-Blackwel, 1991.

Bromiley, Geffery William. *International Standard Bible Encyclopedia.* Wm. B. Eerdman's Publishing, 1994.

Brook, Timothy, and Andre Schmid. *Nation Work: Asian Elites and National Identities.* University of Michigan Press, 2000.

Bryant, Edwin. *Krishna: A Sourcebook.* Oxford University Press, US, 2007.

— *The Quest for the Origins of Vedic Culture.* Oxford University Press, US, 2004.

— 'When Scholarship Matters: The Indo-Aryan Origins Debate : A panel discussion held at the annual meeting of the American Academy of Religion in Denver'. www.barnard.edu. 17 November 2001. http://www.barnard.edu/religion/defamation/bryant.htm (accessed 30 March 2009).

Brysk, Alison. 'Civil society to collective action in resurgent voices in Latin America'. In *Indigenous Peoples, Political Mobilization, and Religious Change*, by Edward L Cleary and Timothy J Steigenga. New Brunswisk, NJ: Rutgers University Press, 2004.

BTI. Boston Theological Institute: Mission statement. 1999:2008. http://www.bostontheological.org/about_the_bti/mission_statement_and_history.htm (accessed 10 January 2009).

— 'Christian Origins and Witness in India, 2006'. 27 June 2006. http://www.bostontheological.org/programs/india/june27.pdf (accessed 21 January 2009).

— 'Costas Consultation in Global Mission'. March 2006. http://www.bostontheological.org/archive/spring6/costasprog6.pdf (accessed 10 January 2009).

— 'Newsletter'. Vol. XXVIII . no. 6. Boston Theological Institute, October 1998.

— 'Programs India'. Boston Theological Institute. July 2002. www. bostontheological.org/programs/india/july02.pdf (accessed 10 May 2009).

Burrow, Thomas, and Murray Banson Emeneau. *A Dravidian Etymological Dictionary.* Clarendon Press, 1966.

— *A Dravidian Etymological Dictionary: Supplement.* Clarendon Press, 1968.

Burrow, Thomas. *The Sanskrit Language.* New Delhi: Motilal Banarsidass Publications, 2001.

Business Standard. 'Bringing Dalit fury centrestage – at home and abroad'. News, 4 December 2008.

Cademon's Call. 'Lyrics from the Song Mother India'. Album: *Share The Well.* 2004.

Caine, Barbara, and Glenda Slug. 'Gendering European History'. 87. London: Leicester University Press, 2002.

Caldwell, Robert. *A Comparative Grammar of the Dravidian or South Indian Family of Languages.* Charleston: Bibliolife LLC, 1856:2009.

— *A Comparative Grammar of the Dravidian Or South-Indian Family of Languages.* New Delhi: Asian Educational Services, 1856:1998.

Callaway, Ewen. 'Scholars at odds over mysterious Indus script '. *New ScientiSt* April 23, 2009. http://www.newscientiStcom/article/dn17012-scholars-at-odds-over-mysterious-indus-script.html (accessed May 01, 2009).

Capie, David. 'Trading the Tools of Terror: Armed Groups and Light Weapons Proliferation in Southeast Asia'. In *Terrorism and Violence in Southeast Asia: Transnational Challenges to States and Regional Stability*, by Paul J. Smith and Sharpe, M.E., 2004.

Capra, Fritjof. *The Tao of Physics: An Exploration of the Parallels between Modern Physics and Eastern Mysticism.* Shambhala, 2000.

Cardona, George. *The Indo-Aryan Languages.* Routledge, 2003.

Carr, Karen. 'Ramayana Project for Kids'. *History for Kids.* 2008. http://www. historyforkids.org/crafts/india/ramayana.htm (accessed 10 December 2009).

Catholic World News Service. 'Indian Church Opposes US Congressional Hearing On Religious Freedom'. News, 14 September 2000.

CBCID. 'Press Note'. Chennai, (Coimbatore Camp): Office of the Inspector General of Police, Crime (SIT), CBCID, Admiralty House, 5 May 1999.

— 'Press Note'. Chennai, (Coimbatore Camp): Office of the Inspector General of Police, Crime (SIT),CBCID, Admiralty House, 28 September 1998.

Cederlof, Gunnel. 'Anticipating Independent India: The Idea of the Lutheran Christian Nation and Indian Nationalism'. In *India and the Indianness of Christianity: Essays on Understanding Historical,Theological, and Bibliographical in Honor of Robert Eric Frykenberg*, by Robert Fox Young. Wm. B. Eerdman's Publishing, 2009.

Chakrabarti, Dilip K. 'Who Owns the Indian Past: The Case of the Indus Civilization'. 21 July 2009.

Chakravarti, Mahadev. *The Concept of Rudra-iva through the Ages*. Motilal Banarsidass Publications, 1986.

Chamberlain, Houston Stewart. *Foundations of the Nineteenh Century*. 1911. Vol. 1. Elibron Classics Series: Adamant Media Corporation, 1911; 2003.

Chatterji, Angana. 'The Threat Religious Extremism Poses to Democracy and Security in India: Focus on Orissa'. Recommendations for action, 2168 Rayburn in Washington D.C, 10 December 2008.

Chengappa, Raj. 'The Lost Civilization'. *India Today*, 11 February 2002.

ChennaiTVNews.com. 'NDTV and the Hindu soon in TV'. August 2008. http://www.chennaitvnews.com/2008/08/ndtv-and-hindu-soon-in-tv.html (accessed 22 March 2009).

Chicago Tribune. 'Congressman's Trip Tied to Group U.S. Considers Terrorists'. News, Chicago Tribune, 23 August 2006.

Chicago Tribune. 'Critics Say Some Christians Spread Aid and Gospel'. News, 22 January 2005.

Chick publications. 'The Traitor'. Chick publications. 1990. http://www.chick.com/reading/tracts/0070/0070_01.asp (accessed 20 June 2007).

Christian Post. 'Center for World's Unreached in India, Says Global Church Expert'. 16 September 2007. http://www.christianpoStcom/article/20070916/center-for-world-s-unreached-in-india-says-global-church-expert.htm (accessed 10 January 2009).

Christian Telegraph. 'Gospel For Asia Leader Cries out Against Mumbai Terrorist Attacks'. 26 November 2008. http://www.christiantelegraph.com/issue3990.html (accessed 12 January 2009).

Christian Today. 'Mumbai Terrorism Overshadows Anti-Christian Violence'. News, 11 December 2008.

Christianity Today. '100,000 Dalit Christians to Attend "World Religious Freedom Day" Rally in India'. News, 11 October 2006.

Christianity Today. 'Ecumenical Conference to Highlight Plight of Dalits'. News, 21 March 2009.

— 'John [Hanford], a young minister, works in the senate on issues of international religious liberty, and Jody [Hanford] works for campus Ccrusade for Christ' www.christianitytoday.com. May-June 1999. http://

www.christianitytoday.com/tc/1999/mayjun/9r3020.html?start=4 (accessed 10 January 2009).

CIDSE. Newsletter: June. Advocacy, International Alliance of Catholic Development Agencies, 1998.

Clarke, Sathianathan. 'Subalterns and Christian Theology in India'. In *Christian Theology in Asia*, by Sebastian Kim. C.H. Cambridge University Press, 2008.

Clinton, Hillary Rodham in India, 2005. 'Message from United States Senate'. First international conference on the history of early Christianity, New York. New York: Chennai: Institute of Asian Studies, 2005.

CNN. 'US Charges 8 over "Tiger Plot". edition.cnn.com. 21 August 2006. http://edition.cnn.com/2006/US/08/21/srilanka.terror/index.html (accessed 10 August 2009).

Consiglio, Cyprian, Winter. 'Awaken and Surrender'. *The Golden String Bulletin of the Bede Griffiths Trust* 11, no. 2 (2004-2005).

Coomaraswamy, Ananda K. *The Dance of Shiva*. Courier Dover, 1985.

Cordaux, Richard. 'Independent Origins of Indian Caste and Tribal Paternal Lineages'. *Current Biology*, 3 February 2004: 231-235.

Creation. 'Pressing on a Chat with World-renowned Journalist David Aikman'. *Creation*, 19 September 1997.

Creation Resource Library. 'Creationism'. 2005. http://www.creationism.org/library/ (accessed 2010).

Cromwell Trust About Us. 2007. http://www.crowelltrust.org/ (accessed 2009).

CSF. 'Communication through personal email <trinityworld@mtnl.net.in>'. 21 June 2009.

CSW. *A Submission to the United Nations Human Rights Council Universal Periodic Review*. Christian Solidarity Worldwide, Nov-2007.

— 'Annual Report'. *www.csw.org.uk*. 2007. http://www.csw.org.uk/annualreport.htm (accessed January 11, 2009).

CSW. 'Annual Report 2006/07'. Activities, 2006/07.

— 'Anti-conversion Legislation Enhanced in Indian state as New Report Condemns Abuses of the Laws'. 2006.: http://dynamic.csw.org.uk/article.asp?t=press&id=536 (accessed 30 January 2009).

CSW. *India Annual Report 2001*. Activities Report, Christian Solidarity Worldwide, 2001.

CSW. *India Report 2001*. Annual Report, Christian Solidarity Worldwide, 2001.

— 'India: CSW, Dalit Freedom Network, Human Rights Watch Call forWorld Action over Anti-Christian Violence in Orissa'. 29 August 2008. http://dynamic.csw.org.uk/article.asp?t=press&id=769 (accessed 30 January 2009).

Cuhulain, Kerr. 'Raschke Paints Things Black'. *Pagan Protection Center*. 25 November 2002. http://www.witchvox.com/va/dt_va.html?a=cabc&c=whs&id=4805 (accessed 2010).

D'souza, Joseph. Who Told Us that Gandhi Ended the Caste System in India? (Product Description). 2003:2010. http://www.dalitnetwork.org/go?/dfn/resources (accessed 10 January 2009).

Daily News Agency. 'Sacking of Indian priests in Nepal sparks protests'. News, Daily News Agency, 4 January 2009.

Daily News and Analysis. 'Panel Recommends Monitoring of Foreign Donations'. News, Mumbai: *Daily News and Analysis*, 05 November 2008.

Dalit Network. 'We are not Untouchable'. Dalit Network, Nederland. June 2008. http://www.dalits.nl/pdf/wearenotuntouchable.pdf (accessed 10 January 2009).

Dalit Solidarity. *Untouchability Resolution*. 2007. http://www.dalitsolidarity.org/untouchability_legislation.php (accessed 10 January 2009).

Dalit Voice. 'Israel knew of 9/11 WTC attack?' *Dalit Voice*, 1 April 2007.

Dalit Voice Archives. *Dalit Voice Archives*. January 2006. http://www.dalitvoice.org/Templates/jan2006/articles.htm (accessed September 2008).

Dalit Voice. 'China Cautioned Against Falling into Zionist Trap: Dangers of Private Property Rights'. Editorial. 16-30 April 2007. http://www.dalitvoice.org/Templates/april_a2007/editorial.htm (accessed 30 March 2009).

— London book Award function on 29 June. June 2009. http://www.dalitvoice.org/Templates/june2009/articles.htm (accessed 10 January 2010).

dalitnetwork.org. 'UN Set to Treat Caste as Human Rights Violation'. Septemper 2009. http://www.dalitnetwork.org/go?/dfn/news/2009/09/ (accessed December 2009).

Daniel, Jeyaraj. 'Missionary Attempts of the Tamil Protestant Christians in the East [i.e. Tanzania] and in the West [i.e. Myanmar/Burma] During the Nineteenth Century'. In *Transcontinental Links in the History of Non-Western Christianity*, by Klaus Koschorke, 131-144. Wiesbaden: Harrassowitz Verlag, 2002.

— 'Making Missionary Heritage Alive through Archival Research: Experiences of a Researcher-Archivist 26 August 2006. http://www.missionstudies.org/archive/rescue/jeyaraj.htm (accessed 30 January 2009).

Daniels, Peter T. Summation Re: [ANE] 'Why is anyone continuing to flog this dead horse?' University of Chicago. 11 December 2005. https://listhoStuchicago.edu/pipermail/ane/2005-December/021225.html (accessed 5 November 2008).

David, Rani. Rani David: Guru. 2004: Dead Link. http://www.ranidevi.com/18KNSGuruChristian.htm (accessed 10 January 2008).

— 'The Concept of Christianizing. . . .' 2004: Dead Link. http://www.ranidevi.
com/173KNSChristi anizing.htm (accessed 10 January 2008).

David, Reuben. 'When Girls Marry Dogs and Gods Drink Human Blood'.
World Peace Herald, 2005.

Dayal, John. 'Religious Freedom in India'. Prepared Testimony, United States
Commission on International Religious Freedom, 1999.

Deccan Chronicle. '3 More Manipuri Kids Were in Horror House'. News,
23 January 2010.

Deccan Chronicle. 'Ahmed Refuses to Light Lamp'. News, 13 December
2009.

Deccan Herald. 'Defying decrees: A Madrassa Where Students Sing Vande
Mataram'. News, 12 November 2009.

Deccan Herald. 'Kerala Government on Collision Course With NIA'. News,
27 December 2009.

Deikun, George. Remarks at Launch of the Health and HIV/AIDS Policies of
the Catholic Bishop's Conference of India, New Delhi. www.usaid.gov.
31 August 2005. http://www.usaid.gov/in/newsroom/speeches/augS31_5.
htm (accessed 1 October 2009).

— Speech at the sixtieth anniversary of CRS'. www.usaid.gov. 2 April 2006.
http://www.usaid.gov/in/newsroom/speeches/apr02_6.htm.

Deivakala, D. *Hindu Religion is the Offshoot of StThomas Dravidian
Christianity*. Chennai: Meiporul Publishers, 2003.

Deivamuthu, P. 'Anti-Hindu activities at Kalakshetra, Chennai'. *Hindu Voice*,
8 April 2007.

— 'Demolishing a Tradition at Kalakshetra'. *Organiser*, 29 April 2007.

Deivanayagam, M. 'Introductory Note to International Dravidian Religion
Conference'. *Dravidian Religion, (Tamil Magazine)*, May-June 2008.

— *India in Third Millennium*. Chennai: Dravidian Religion Trust, 2000.

— 'Science-Philosophy-Theology – Soullogy, a comparative study'. *Souvenir
of the First International Conference on the Religion of Tamils*. Chennai:
Pastoral Center Archdiocese of Madras, 2008. 5-32.

— *Was Thiruvalluvar a Christian?* Madras: Meporul Publishers, 1969:1970.

— *World's First Language Tamil ... How?* (Tamil Handout). Chennai:
International Tamil Spiritualism Movement, 2007.

Deivanayagam, M, and Devakala, D. *Creeds and Doctrine of Trinity in
St Thomas Dravidian Christianity*. Chennai: Meiporul Publishers, 2005.

— 'International Racism is the Child of India's Casteism'. Chennai: Dravidian
Religion Trust, 2001.

— 'Who are the Indian Dalits?' Dravidian Spiritual Movement, 2003.

Deivanayagam, M. *Siva Gyana Botham – Commentary* (Tamil). Chennai:
Meiporul Publishers, 2007.

der Veer, Peter van. *Conversion to Modernites: The Globalization of Christianity.* Routledge, 1996.

Devakala, D. *India is a Thomas-Dravidian Christian nation ... How? : Manual for Evangelism* (Tamil). Chennai: Meiporrul Publishers, 2004.

— 'Paper on Indian Religious Iconography'. Souvenir of the First International Conference on the Religion of Tamils. Chennai: Pastoral Center Archdiocese of Madras, 2008. 68-73.

Devakala, M. 'Feministic aspect of God in Indian Worships and Religions in Relation to Trinity'. *Dravidian Religion*, July 2008.

Devanesan, A. *History of Tamil Nadu (up to AD 2000).* Marthandam: Renu Publications, 2004.

Devasahayam, S. *Outside the Camp: Bible Studies in Dalit Perspective.* Chennai: Gurukul Lutheran Theological College, 1992.

Devji, Faisal. 'Why the Maoists Want Arundhati Roy'. *The Guardian*, 9 March 2010.

DFN. Dalit Freedom Network. 2003:2010. http://www.dalitnetwork.org/go?/dfn/about/C141/ (accessed 2009).

— Dalit Freedom Network Advisory Board. May 2006. http://www.dalitnetwork.org/go?/dfn/about/C22/ (accessed 2 February 2010).

— Dalit Freedom Network: About Us. 2003:2010. http://www.dalitnetwork.org/go?/dfn/about/c33/ (accessed 12 January 2009).

— Dalit Freedom Network: Opportunities. 2003:2010. http://www.dalitnetwork.org/go?/dfn/opportunities/C169/ (accessed 10 January 2009).

— 'Does the Dalit Freedom Network have a religious affiliation?' 2003:2010. http://www.dalitnetwork.org/go?/dfn/about/C8/ (accessed 30 January 2009).

Dhar, Maloy Krishna. 'South India and the Enemies Within'. sify.com. 27 February 2008. http://sify.com/news/fullstory.php?id=14611728 (accessed 10 March 2009).

Dharma Deepika: Online Journal. 'Consultants: International Consultants'. March 2003. http://www.dharmadeepika.org/dictionary/consultants.html (accessed 10 January 2009).

Dharmadasa, K. En. *Language, Religion, and Ethnic Assertiveness: the Growth of Sinhalese Nationalism in Sri Lanka.* University of Michigan Press, 1992.

Diamond, Sara. *Spiritual Warfare: The Politics of the Christian Right.* South End Press, 1989.

Digby, William. *'Prosperous' India: A Revelation from Official Records.* New Delhi: Sagar, 1969.

Dinakaran. 'Arms Haul in Ship Container' (Tamil). News, 10 January 2007.

Dinakaran. 'Police Attacked by Extremist' (Tamil). News, Thirunelveli, 20 July 2006.

Dinamalar. 'Chennai based Lashkar Operatives Planned Rendezvous with Sri Lankans' (Tamil). News, 9 January 2007.

Dinamalar. 'State Police Feel Harassed' (Tamil). News, 4 September 2006.

Dinamani. 'Bomb Blast in Madurai Temple: TMMK Leader Arrested' (Tamil). News, 22 May 1996.

Dinamani. 'Five Persons Killed' (Tamil). News, 19 September 1997.

Dinamani. 'Two Arrested for Provocative Posters' (Tamil). News, Coimbatore, 15 December 1997.

Dinamani. 'Wife of Hindu Activist Killed in Parcel Bomb Blast' (Tamil). News, 4 July 1995.

Dinathanthi. 'Saddam Rally Violence in Bengaluru' (Tamil). 20 January 2007.

Dirks, Nicholas. *Castes of Mind: Colonialism and the Making of Modern India*. Hyderabad: Orient Blackswan, 2004.

Discovery (8). 'Galileo and The Heavens'. London: Marshal Cavendish, 1987.

Divakar, Justin. 'Social investments of district Catholic Diocese'. In *Valikalil Chikkiyavan (Caught in the net)* [Tamil], by Justin Divakar. Nagerkovil: Cape Education Trust, 2007.

Divakar, Paul. 'Dalits Demand Rights in India, (The Religion Report – Full Transcript)'. National Radio. 2 October 2002. http://www.abc.net.au/rn/talks/8.30/relrpt/stories/s691166.htm (accessed 10 January 2009).

Domenico, Roy Palmer, and Mark Y Hanley. *Encyclopedia of Modern Christian Politics*. Greenwod Publishing Group, 2006.

Doss, Baskara David. *Contribution of St Thomas to the Development of Indian Religion and Philosophy*. 'Research' Paper, NILT publication, 2004.

— 'Purva Mimasa, Uttara Mimamsa and the Bible'. Souvenir of the Second International Conference on The History of Early Christianity in India. Chennai: International Center for the Study of Christianity in India, Institute of Asian Studies, 2007.

Dravidian Religion. 'Announcement' (Tamil). Announcement on the back cover, July 2006.

Dravidian University. Prospectus. 2008-2009.

DRC. Dalit Resource Centre. 2009. http://drctts.com/DRC_htm/Home.htm (accessed 2010).

DSN-DK. Report on the Hearing of the Foreign Affairs Committee on Dalits and Caste Discrimination at Parliament of Denmark, Christiansborg Palace, 24 September 2008. Atrocity, Dalit Solidarity Network-Denmark, 24 September 2008.

DSN-UK. Annual Report. Activity, Dalit Solidarity Network-UK, 2004-2005.

DSN-UK. 'Annual Report of Dalit Solidarity Network (UK) for Annual General Meeting, 2003-2004.

— Dalit Solidarity Network-UK Links. http://www.dsnuk.org/useful_links.htm (accessed 30 January 2009).

DSN-UK. 'No Escape Caste Discrimination'. Survey Report, Dalit Solidarity Network UK, July 2006.

DSN-UK. 'No Escape Caste Discrimination in the UK'. Survey, London, 2006.

DSN-UK. 'Press Release'. 23 March 2007.

Dubey, S.M. *Social Mobility among the Professions*. Popular Prakashan, 1975.

Dubow, Saul. *Scientific Racism in Modern South Africa*. Cambridge University Press, 1995.

Duin, Julian. 'Year's Best Religion Stories'. *Washington Times*. December 2008. http://insider.washingtontimes.com/weblogs/belief-blog/2008/Dec/22/years-best-religion-stories/ (accessed 10 February 2009).

DV Editorial. 'Conspiracy to Keep Madhani in Jail?' *Dalit Voice*, 1 April 2004.

— 'Madhani Rotting in Coimbatore'. *Dalit Voice*, 16 February 2002.

— 'Madhani Rotting in Jail'. *Dalit Voice*, 15 March 2001.

Ebrahimi, Sherene, and Andrew Schweizer. 'Renowned Journalist Shares Heart, Experiences With PLNU'. Point Loma Nazarene University. January 2007. http://www.pointloma.edu/News/Headlines/Renowned_journalist_shares_heart__experiences_with_PLNU.htm (accessed 10 January 2009).

Edamaruku, Sanal. 'God Longs for All Hindus! Covert Operations of the Evangelical Church in India'. *Rationalist International Bulletin*, 29 November 2001.

Elisse, Rutagambwa. 'The Rwandan Church: The Challenge of Reconciliation'. In *The Catholic Church and the Nation State: Comparative Perspectives*, by Paul Christopher Manuel, Lawrence Christopher Reardon and Clyde Wilcox. Washington: Georgetown University Press, 2006.

Elliston, Edgar J, and Stephen E Burris. *Completing the Task: Reaching the World for Christ*, College Press, 1995.

Elst, Koenraad. *Decolonizing the Hindu Mind*. Rupa, 2007.

— *Return of the Swastika: Hate and Hysteria versus Hindu Sanity*. New Delhi: Voice of India, 2007.

— 'The Official Pro-invasionist Argument at Last', *Bharatvani.org*. 1999. http://koenraadelStbharatvani.org/reviews/hock.html (accessed September 2009).

— *The Saffron Swatika*. Voice of India, 2001.

Emeneau, M. 'India as a Linguistic Area'. *Language*, 1956: 3-16.

Engels, Frederick. 'The Part Played by Labour in the Transition from Ape to Man'. Marxists Internet Archive. 1876. http://www.marxists.org/archive/marx/works/1876/part-played-labour/index.htm (accessed September 2008).

EPPC. 'Evangelicals in Civic Life'. 12 August 2003. http://www.eppc.org/programs/ecl/programID.31/default.asp (accessed 10 February 2009).

— 'Governance, Polity, and Civil Society in Islam and Christianity'. Ethics and Public Policy Center. March 2005. http://www.eppc.org/conferences/eventID.96/conf_detail.asp (accessed 10 January 2009).

— 'Rick Santorum Joins Ethics and Public Policy Center, establishes program on America's enemies'. Ethics and Public Policy Center. 9 January 2007. http://www.eppc.org/news/newsid.2818/news_detail.asp (accessed 30 January 2009).

— 'South Asian Studies and Religious Nationalism'. Ethics and Public Police Center. 22 May 2002. http://www.eppc.org/programs/southasian/publications/programID.38/default.asp (accessed 10 January 2009).

Errington, James Joseph. *Linguistics in a Colonial World: A Story of Language, Meaning and Power*. Blackwell Publishing, 2008.

Eternity Biz. *Meet Lakshmi, A Dalit Girl, and the Story of a Indian Church Planter*. 17 January 2010. http://eternity.biz/news/meet_lakshmi_a_dalit_girl_and_the_story_of_a_indian_church_planter/ (accessed 2 February 2010).

facebook.com. 'Christian Reformed World Relief Committee'. 2010. http://apps.facebook.com/causes/beneficiaries/12828?m=370a5b0b (accessed 2010).

— 'Christian Reformed World Relief Committee'. 2010. http://apps.facebook.com/causes/beneficiaries/12828?m=370a5b0b (accessed 2010).

Fahlbusch, Erwin, and Geoffrey William Bromiley. *The Encyclopedia of Christianity*. Vol. 3. Grand Rapids MI: Wm. B. Eerdmans Publishing, 2003.

Fahlbusch, Erwin, Geoffrey William Bromiley, and David B Barrett. *The Encyclopedia of Christianity*. Wm. B. Eerdmans Publishing, 1999.

Farady, Moses Michael. 'Siddha Literature and Christianity'. Souvenir of the second international conference on The history of early Christianity in India. Chennai: International Center for the Study of Christianity in India, Institute of Asian Studies, 2007.

Farmer, Steve. 'Discussion Forum Message'. *www.hallofmaat.com*. 16 January 2006. http://www.hallofmaat.com/read.php?4,376713,378370#msg-378370 (accessed 17 January 2006).

— Hearing Transcript (HAF Lies Worse Than We Thought!), Message #374'. Indo_Eurasian_Research group, 28 April 2006.

— Moderator Note to Message Number #3147 of Benjamin Marc'. Indo_ Eurasian_Research Yahoo group, March 2, 2006.

— Steve Farmer's website. 1998:2009. http://www.safarmer.com/.

— 'The problem of "reconstructed" Indus inscriptions'. Undated. http://www. safarmer.com/indus/reconstructions/axehead.html (accessed 13 February 2010).

Farmer, Steve, W. Zaumen, Richard Sproat, and Michael Witzel. 'Project Description: Simulating the Evolution of Political-Religious Extremism: Implication for International Policy Decisions'. www.safarmer.com. 1998:2009. http://www.safarmer.com/simulations.version.3.0.pdf (accessed 12 December 2009).

Ferguson, Niall. *Colossus: the Price of America's Empire*. Penguin, 2004.

FetNA. About FetNA. 22 May 2001. http://www.fetna.org/index. php?option=com_content&view=article&id=47&Itemid=59 (accessed 18 February 2010).

FIACONA. Bishop Ezra Sargunam Briefs US Officials. Press Release, Federation of Indian American Christian Organizations of North America, 8 August 2003.

Fore, Matthew L. 'Shall Weigh Your God and You: Assessing the Imperialistic Implications of the International Religious Freedom Act in Muslim Countries'. *Duke Law Journal*, November 2002.

Foucherau, Bruno. 'Secular Society at Stake'. *Le Monde Diplomatique*, June 2001.

Francis, Ezekia.V. About Berachah. March 2003 . http://www.ezekiahfrancis. org/about/berachah.php (accessed 10 January 2009).

— 'Spiritual Conflict in the Indian Context'. 2000. http://www.lausanne.org/ nairobi-2000/indian-case-study.html (accessed September 2008).

Franks, Trent. Dalit Resolution. 2007. http://www.house.gov/list/press/az02_ franks/dalit_resolution.html (accessed 10 January 2009).

Franks, Trent, Emmanuel Cleaver, and Joseph R Pitts. 'Threat Religious Extremism Poses to Democracy and Security in India: Focus on Orissa'. Federation of Indian American Christian Organizations of North America. 2008. http://www.fiacona.org/newsdetail.php?catid=100&newsid=755 (accessed 31 January 2009).

Frederikse, Julie. 'Before the war:Interview (1982)'. In *None But Ourselves*, by Biddy Partridge. Harare: Oral Traditions Association of Zimbabwe with Anvil Press, 1990.

Freston, Paul. *Evangelicals and Politics in Asia, Africa and Latin America*. Cambridge University Press, 2004.

Frontline. 'Building New Bases'. News, 21 December 2007.

Frontline. 'Concern in Kerala'. News, 20 March 1998.

Frontline. 'No Entry for Modi'. News, 25 March 2005.

Frontline. 'Plot Unraveled'. News, 16 August 2008.

Frontline. 'Terror links'. News, 21 December 2007.

Frykenberg, Robert Eric. 'Hindu Fundamentalism and the Structural Stability of India'. In *Fundamentalisms and the State: Remaking Polities, Economies, and Militance*, by Martin E Marty, Scott. F Appleby and Scott. R Appleby. University of Chicago Press, 1991.

Fund for Peace and Carnegie Endowment for International Peace. 'The Failed States Index 2008'. Foreign Policy. Fund for Peace and Carnegie Endowment for International Peace, July/August 2008.

Gandhi, Ajay. 'Yale, India, and the Failure of the "Global University"'. *The Hindu*, May 4, 2005.

Gandhi, Mohandas K. 'Harijan'. 28 July 1946.

Gandhi, Mohandas Karamchand. *Young India*, 10 June 1921.

Gatlung, Johan. 'Cultural Violence'. *Journal of Peace Research* 27, no. 3 (August 1990): 291-305.

Gegrapha. Gegrpha Mission Statement. 1998:2007. http://www.gegrapha.org/AboutUs.asp.

George, Jithin Sam. 'Pastors spreading Communalism (Malayalam)'. *Jithin Sam George's Channel*. 26 March 2009. http://www.youtube.com/watch?v=85nMEtbHFxE (accessed 10 February 2010).

George, Nirmala. 'Indian Caste System Discriminates'. University of California, Santa Barbara. 2002. http://aad.english.ucsb.edu/docs/georgesept62001.html (accessed 10 October 2009).

GFA. 'Indian Social Reformer to Visit Dallas/Fort Worth'. Press Release, 1 October 2002.

— 'Dalits: From Fatalism to Hope'. 1996:2009. http://www.gfa.org/dalit/reaching-the-dalits/ (accessed 30 January 2010).

— 'Distinctives'. 1996:2009. www.gfa.org/distinctives (accessed 30 January 2010).

— Gospel for Asia Endorsement page. 1996:2009. http://www.gfa.org/about/endorsements/ (accessed 30 January 2010).

— K.P. Yohannan Cries out against Mumbai Terrorist Attacks, Questions Cause. 2008. http://www.gfa.org/news/articles/mumbai-terrorist-attacks-cause/ (accessed 30 January 2009).

— 'Reaching the Dalits'. 1996:2009. http://www.gfa.org/dalit/reaching-the-dalits/ (accessed 2 February 2010).

— 'She has a gift to share'. 1996:2009. http://www.gfa.org/news/articles/she-has-gift-share (accessed 30 January 2010).

Ghose, Arundati. 'Terrorists, Human Rights and the United Nations'. In *Terror and Containment: Perspectives of India's Internal Security*, by Ajai Sahni Kanwar Pal Singh Gill. Gyan Books, 2001.

Ghosh, Aurobindo. 'The Unhindu Spirit of Caste Rigidity'. *Bande Mataram*, 20 September 1907.

Gilman, John. 'Dayasagar and the Life of Christ in India'. Lausanne World Pulse. September 2006. http://www.lausanneworldpulse.com/perspectives.php/470/09-2006?pg=all (accessed 10 January 2009).

GIS Development. 'A Study on Industrial Growth along Coast Line of Orissa and its Undesirable Effect on environment using GIS – an olive ridley (sea turtle) Perspective'. *GIS Development*. 2008. http://www.gisdevelopment.net/application/environment/wildlife/mi08_250.htm (accessed 10 January 2010).

Glasson, Travis F. *Missionaries, slavery, and race: The Society for the Propagation of the Gospel in Foreign Parts in the eighteenth-century British Atlantic world*. Columbia University Press, 2005.

Global Ecumenical Conference. 'Justice for Dalits – A Call for Solidarity from the Global Church'. Concept paper, 21-24 March 2009.

Global Telugu Christian Ministries. 'Christian Family Conference'. Souvenir, 2008.

Gnanashikamani.V, and Dayanandan Francis. 'History of Early Christianity in India – A Survey'. First International Conference on the history of early Christianity in India, New York. New York: Chennai: Institute of Asian Studies, 2005.

Golden, Daniel. ' New Battleground In Textbook Wars: Religion in History'. *Wall Street Journal*, 25 January 2006.

Goldenburg, David M. *The Curse of Ham: Race and Slavery in Early Judaism, Christianity, and Islam*. Princeton University Press, 2003.

Golder, Evan W. 'Maoists and the church: Strange Bedfellows in an Emerging New Nepal'. 10 May 2008. http://www.globalministries.org/news/sasia/maoists-and-the-church.html (accessed 11 December 2009).

Goodman, Martin. *On Sacred Mountains*. Heart of Albion, 2002.

Gorringe, Hugo. *Untouchable Citizens: Dalit Movements and Democratization in Tamil Nadu*. SAGE, 2005.

Grant Duff, Mountstuart Elphinstone. *Notes from a Diary, Kept Chiefly in Southern India, 1881-1886*. BiblioBazaar, LLC, 2009.

Grant, Patrick. *Buddhism and Ethnic Conflict in Sri Lanka*. SUNY Press, 2009.

Gray, David. 'Letter to the The US Commission on International Religious Freedom'. Infinity Foundation, 11 September 2000.

Green: European Free Alliance. 'We are not untouchable: Photo exhibition and public hearing'. www.greens-efa.org. June 2008. http://www.greens-efa.org/cms/default/dok/236/236455.we_are_not_untouchable@en.htm (accessed 10 January 2010).

Griffiths, Bede, and Matthew Fox. *The Other Half of My Soul: Bede Griffiths and the Hindu-Christian Dialogue*. Quest Books, 1996.

Gumaste, Vivek. 'Are Nepal's Maoists a threat to India?' Rediff News. 15 September 2009. http://news.rediff.com/column/2009/sep/15/guest-are-nepal-maoists-a-threat-to-india.htm (accessed 2 October 2009).

Haase, Wolfgang, and Meyer Reinhold. *The Classical Tradition and the Americas: Myths and Expansionism on American Continent*. Berlin: Walter de Gruyter, 1994.

Halbfass, Wilhelm. *India and Europe: An Essay in Understanding*. New York: State University of New York Press, 1988.

Halbfass, Wilhelm. 'Research and Reflection; Beyond Orientalism'. In *Beyond Orientalism: The Work of Wilhelm Halbfass and Its Impact on Indian Cross-cultural Studies*, by Wilhelm Halbfass, edited by Karin Preisendanz Eli Franco. New Delhi: Motilal Banarsidass Publishers, 2007.

Haniffa, Aziz. 'Indian officials to boycott "Kashmir Conference" in US, 22 July 2003'. News, 22 July 2003.

Hansen, Anders Bjorn. *Partition and Genocide: Manifestation of Violence in Punjab: 1937-1947*. New Delhi: India Research Press, 2002.

Harrigan, Patrick. Curriculum Vitae of Patrick Harrigan. 2001. http://murugan.org/PatrickHarriganResume.htm (accessed 10 January 2009).

— 'Homes'. 2005:2009. http://www.anathi.org/homes.html (accessed 10 January 2009).

— 'Living Heritage'. 2000:2009. http://livingheritage.org/index.html (accessed 10 January 2009).

Hart, George. 'Early Evidence of Caste in South India'. In *Dimensions of Social Life: Essays in honor of David G. Mandelbaum*, by Paul Hockings. Mouton de Gruyter, 1987.

— 'Grantha and Kampan'. Tamil Discussion archive message, 3 October 1997.

— 'Sangam Ambivalence in the Kamparamayanam: Papers Submitted at Second Annual Tamil Conference'. University of California at Berkely Department of South and South East Asian Studies, Center for South Asian Studies and Berkeley Tamil Chair. 22 April 2006. http://tamil.berkeley.edu/Tamil%20Conference%202006%207.0%20Site/Program%20and%20Abstracts.html (accessed 10 February 2009).

— 'Statement on the Status of Tamil as a Classical Language'. Berkeley Tamil Chair. 11 April 2000. http://tamil.berkeley.edu/Tamil%20Chair/TamilClassicalLanguage/TamilClassicalLgeLtr.html (accessed 28 September 2008).

Haynes, Stephen R. *Noah's Curse: the Biblical Justification of Slavery.* Oxford University Press, 2002.

Headlines Today. 'Jamiat Issues Fatwa Against Singing Vande Mataram'. News, 03 November 2009.

Hertzke, Allen D. 'Legislating International Religious Freedom'. Pew Forum on Religion & Public Life, 20 November 2006.

Hindu Forum of Britain. *Caste in the UK*, 'A Summary of the Consultation with the Hindu Community in Britain'. Survey, 2007.

Hindu Press International Archives. 'Denver Post Column Draws Criticism'. Hindu Press International, 1 May 2004.

Hindu Humanist 'Agony of Tamil Hindus in Kanyakumari district'. Youtube. com. 26 March 2006. http://www.youtube.com/watch?v=i0gkD16-_GY (accessed 27 March 2006).

Hinduism Today Archives. 'Archives'. *Hinduism Today.* July 1995. http://www.hinduismtoday.com/archives/1995/7/1995-7-04.shtml   (accessed 6 August 2006).

— 'Devadasis Outlawed as Harlots'. *Hinduism Today*, December 1993.

Hinduism Today. 'Avalanche of Christian "Aid" Falls on India'. News, July/August/September 2008.

— 'Stone Cross Unearthed in India Ignites Christian-Hindu Dispute'. *Hinduism Today*, October 1983.

Hinduism Today. 'Symposium Om Muruga!' News, May 1999.

Hindustan Times. 'Ravana is a hero for Sinhala nationalists'. *Hindustan Times*, 23 September 2007.

Hirst, Kris K. 'Lost Race Myth'. 2005. http://archaeology.about.com/od/lterms/g/lostraces.htm (accessed 21 October 2009).

History Coalition. Historians Peter Brown and Romila Thapar Named 2008 Kluge Prize Recipients. 2008. http://historycoalition.org/2008/12/03/historians-peter-brown-and-romila-thapar-named-2008-kluge-prize-recipients/ (accessed 27 March 2009).

Hodgin, Deanne. 'On the Use of Governmental Aggression to Suppress a Minority's Quest for Self-determination'. International Tamil Eelam Research Conference. 1991.

Hope, Guy Ashley. *America and Swaraj: The US Role in Indian Independence.* Public Affairs Press, 1968.

Horgan, John. 'The Templeton Foundation : A Skeptic's Take'. *The Chronicle of Higher Education*, 7 April 2006.

Houston, Drusilla Dunjee. *Wonderful Ethiopians of the Ancient Cushite Empire.* Forgotten Books, 1926:2007.

Hoyos, Linda de. 'Terrorism in South Asia: London's Assault on the Nation-State'. Executive Intelligence Review, 13 October 1995.

http://www.gltc.edu/. Gurukul Lutheran Theological College and Research Institute. 1998:2008. http://www.gltc.edu/ (accessed 2009).

Hudson, Dennis D. 'Arumuga Navalar and the Hindu Renaissance Among the Tamils'. In *Religious Controversy in British India: Dialogues in South Asian Languages*, by Kenneth W Jones. Sunny Press, 1992.

— *Protestant Origins in India: Tamil Evangelical Christians, 1706-1835*. Grand Rapids MI: Wm. B. Eerdmans Publishing, 2000.

Hudson, Dennis D. 'Tamil Hindu Responses to Protestants: Nineteenth-century Literati in Jaffna and Tinnavelly'. In *Indigenous Responses to Western Christianity*, by Steven Kaplan. New York: New York University Press, 1995.

Human Rights Commission. 'Human Rights Council –Working Group on the Universal Periodic Review, A/HRC/WG.6/1/IND/3'. 2008.

Human Rights News. 'India: 'Hidden Apartheid' of Discrimination Against Dalits'. 13 February 2007. http://www.hrw.org/english/docs/2007/02/13/india15303.htm (accessed 12 January 2009).

Hunter, W.W. *The Indian Empire: Its History, People and Products*. Routledge, 2001.

Hussein, Asiff. 'Ancient Tamil Society as Reflected in Sangam Literature'. *Sunday Observer*, 22 September 2002.

IANS. 'Children in Kerala Initiated into The World of Letters'. News, 9 October 2008.

IANS. 'Stop British Firms from Moving Jobs to India: MP'. News, London: Indo-Asian News Service, 20 February 2004.

— 'Tribals Call Meeting after Bible Translation Attacks Their Beliefs'. 13 October 2008. http://www.samachaar.in/Jharkhand/Tribals_call_meeting_after_Bible_translation_attacks_their_beliefs_62021/ (accessed 18 October 2008).

IAS. 'First International Conference / Seminar On The History Of Early Christianity In India'. Institute of Asian Studies. 2005. http://www.xlweb.com/heritage/asian/christianity-conference.htm (accessed 20 August 2008).

ICSCI: IAS. Souvenir of the Second International Conference on The History of Early Christianity in India. International Center for the Study of Christianity in India, Institute of Asian Studies, 2007.

IDSN. 2005 Report. Annual Activities Report, International Dalit Solidarity Network, 2005.

IDSN. Annual Report. Annual Activities Report, International Dalit Solidarity Network, 2006.

IDSN. Annual Report. Activity, International Dalit Solidarity Network, 2007.

— IDSN statutes. 2009. http://idsn.org/about-idsn/idsn-statutes/ (accessed 12 January 2010).

IDSN. Joint NGO submission Related to India for the first session. Periodic Review, International Dalit Solidarity Network, 2008.

— *Networks in Europe*. 2009. http://www.idsn.org/about-idsn/who-we-are/networks-in-europe/ (accessed 12 January 2010).

IIDS. 'Academicians Abroad: Indian Institute of Dalit Studies'. 2008. http://www.dalitstudies.org.in/associates.php?link=Associates&Mlink=4 (accessed 2009).

— Indian Institute of Dalit Studies. 2008. http://www.dalitstudies.org.in/ (accessed 2009).

— International Organizations. 2008. http://www.dalitstudies.org.in/associates. php?link=Associates&Mlink=2 (accessed 2009).

Ilaiah, Kancha, interview by *Christianity Today*. 'Interview with Dr Kancha Ilaiah – Leading Dalit Rights Campaigner in India' (12 November 2005).

— *Post-Hindu India*. New Delhi: Sage Publications, 2009.

Ilakkuvanar. Comment in a post titled Rice, Wheat and Hindi. 2008. http://forums.sulekha.com/forums/food/Rice-Wheat-and-Hindi-3560.htm (accessed 10 January 2009).

— 'I love you America – Part-I'. Illakkuvanar Sulekha Blog. August 2008. http://ilakkuvanar.sulekha.com/blog/post/2008/08/i-love-you-america-parti.htm (accessed 4 January 2009).

— 'I Love You America – Part-IV'. Ilakkuvanar Blog Sulekha. October 2008. http://ilakkuvanar.sulckha.com/blog/post/2008/10/i-love-you-america-part-iv.htm (accessed 4 January 2009).

— 'Sexual Assault on Christian Nun'. Ilakkuvanar Blog in Sulekha. October 2008. http://ilakkuvanar.sulekha.com/blog/post/2008/10/the-sexual-assault-on-a-christian-nun.htm (accessed 4 January 2009).

Illaiah, Kancha, interview by Daipayan Halder. 'Institutes like IITs and IIMs should be closed down'. Daily News and Analysis, 9 April 2006.

— 'Towards a Constructive 'Globalization'. Seminar (Web). 2001. http://www.india-seminar.com/2001/508/508%20interview.htm (accessed 10 January 2009).

IMC-USA. 'IMC-USA Convention A Huge Success'. Press Release, 7 October 2005.

IMC-USA. 'US based Indian American group denounces terrorist attacks in Mumbai'. Press Release, 27 November 2008.

in.crossmap.com. 'Christians disappointed with USCIRF's failure to recommend India as CPC'. *in.crossmap.com*. 2006. http://in.crossmap.com/cmboard/view.php?&bbs_id=news&page=&doc_num=204 (accessed 10 January 2010).

Inden, Ronald. B. *Imagining India*. C. Hurst & Co. Publishers, 2000.

India Abroad. 'Asia Society Holds Debate on India's Pluralist Future'. News, India Abroad, 4 April 2003.

India Post. 'Maoists resent Hinduism among tribals'. 2009. http://indiapostcom/article/perspective/4299/ (accessed December 2009).

India Today. 'Counting the dead'. News, 15 December 1997.

India Today. 'Desparate Acts of Faith'. News, 30-Mar-1998.

India Today. Red Corridor. News, *India Today*, 20-Dec-2007.

indianchristians.in. 'Angana Chatterji Memo to Orissa Judicial Commission of Inquiry'. Indian Christians. 2008. http://indianchristians.in/news/content/view/2133/45/ (accessed 10 February 2009).

— 'Historical Milestones of the All India Christian Council'. 2001. http://indianchristians.in/news/content/view/1810/120/ (accessed 10 January 2009).

— 'UN Set to Treat Caste as Human Rights Violation'. September 2009. indianchristians.in/news/content/view/3473/48/ (accessed December 2009).

Institute of Asian Studies. Institute of Asian Studies, Chennai: Pongal-2000 Project and the Online Tamil Lexicon. 2002. http://xlweb.com/heritage/asian/main.htm (accessed 12 February 2010).

Institute of Asian Studies. *Institute of Asian Studies*. 2002. http://www.xlweb.com/heritage/asian/ (accessed August 23, 2009).

International Mission Board. *Prayer for Hindus*. Southern Baptist Convention, 1999.

Irajacekaran, Ira. *Caivap peruveliyil kalam* (Tamil). Chennai: Narmata Patippakam, 2003.

Ireland, Michael. 'India's Prime Minister Launches Investigation into Arrest and Persecution of Indian Christians: Global Protest Increasing Against Jailing of Christians in Rajasthan'. News, ASSIST News Service, 20 March 2006.

Isaac, C.I. 'Kerala, the Gateway to Indian Christianity'. Vivekananda Kendra Patrika (Vivekananda Kendra Prakashan) 35, no. 1 (2006).

Iyengar, Sesha T.R. *Dravidian India*. New Delhi: Asian Educational Services, 1925:2004.

Iype, George. 'He is the Ultimate Leader of the Muslims'. Rediff News portal. 3 May 2001. http://www.rediff.com/news/2001/may/03spec.htm (accessed 10 March 2005).

— 'Interview with Pazhanedumaran'. Rediff News. October 2000. http://www.rediff.com/news/2000/oct/16veer2.htm (accessed 20 August 2008).

Jaffrelot, Christophe. *India's Silent Revolution the Rise of the Lower Castes in North India*. Orient Blackswan, 2003.

— 'India: Caste Stronger than Religion?' IIAS Newsletter, November 2003.
— 'Positive Discrimination and the Transformation of Caste in India'. CERI. April 2001. http://www.ceri-sciencespo.com/archive/april01/artcj.pdf (accessed 10 January 2008).
— *The Hindu Nationalist Movement and Indian Politics: 1925 to the 1990s: Strategies of Identity-Building, Implantation and Mobilisation (with Special Reference to Central India)*. C. Hurst & Co. Publishers, 1996.
Jalal, Ayesha. *Self and Sovereignty: Individual and Community in South Asian Islam Since 1850*. Routledge, 2000.
Jamanadas, K. 'Is it possible to destroy Hindutva without harming Hinduism?' *Dalit Voice*, January 2006.
Japan Student Services Organization. *Tokyo Christian University*. 2006. http://www.jasso.go.jp/cgi-bin/user/univ_search_result.cgi?&univid=1104&prefecturename=Chiba (accessed 10 January 2010).
Jeevaraj, V. *Muthukutti Narayana Swami*. Nagerkovil: Diocese Press, 1981.
Jesudason, Hephzibah. 'Christianity and the Ramayana'. Souvenir of the Second International Conference on The History of Early Christianity in India. Chennai: International Center for the Study of Christianity in India; Institute of Asian Studies, 2007.
Jesudhason, Hephzibah. 'Synopsis of the paper'. The First International Conference of Early Christianity (held at New York). New York: Chennai: Institute of Asian Studies, 2005.
Jeyamohan, B. *Malayala Manorama* (Malayalam) report September 2009 translated to Tamil as "Christian Vijayadasami"'. 18 September 2009. http://jeyamohan.in/?p=4434 (accessed 10 October 2009).
— 'Thomas who Taught Tamils to Think (Tamil)'. Jeyamohan Website. 12 August 2008. http://jeyamohan.in/?p=600 (accessed 16 August 2008).
Johari, J.C. *Voices of Indian Freedom Movement*. New Delhi: Anmol Publications, 1993.
John, Samuel G. 'On the history of early Christianity in India Genesis and Growth'. Souvenir: First International Conference on the History of Early Christianity in India, Institute of Asian Studies, 2005.
John, PD. 'Press Release: Human Trafficking and the Spread of HIV in South Asia'. Policy Institute for Religion and State. 18 July 2002. http://www.pifras.org/Press_Releases/PR_Human_Trafic/pr_human_trafic.html (accessed 17 September 2008).
Jones, William. *Discourses delivered before the Asiatic Society*. Vol. 2. 1807.
Jones, William. 'On the Hindus: The Third Discourse'. Asiatic Researches 1 (1799): 422-423.

— *The Letters of William Jones*. Edited by Garland Cannon. Oxford: Clarendon Press, 1970.

Jones, William. 'The Origin and Families of Nations'. *The Collected Works of William Jones* (New York University Press) iii (1993): 193-203.

Joshua Project. Great Commission Resources and Downloads. 2001:2009. http://www.joshuaproject.net/download.php# (accessed 30 January 2009).

— Joshua Project Overview. 2000:2009. http://joshuaproject.net/overview.php (accessed 11 August 2009).

— 'People-in-Country Profile Joshua Project'. *Joshua Project Net*. 2000:2009. http://www.joshuaproject.net/peopctry.php?rog3=IN&rop3=106893 (accessed 10 January 2009).

— 'The 10/40 Window'. 2001. http://www.joshuaproject.net/10-40-window.php (accessed 30 January 2009).

Jospeh, T.K. *Six St Thomases of South India: A Muslim Non-Martyr (Thawwama) Made Martyr After 1517 A.D.* Bharatha Deepam Press, 1955.

Junior Vikatan. 'Something in the summer camp'. (Tamil) 23 May 2007.

Kalai Kaveri. 'Kalai Kaveri – Movement into Wholeness'. 2004:2005. http://www.kalaikaviri.org.uk/index.htm (accessed 10 August 2009).

— Kalaikaviri Off Campus University. 2004. http://www.kalaikaviri-offcamp.com/university.htm (accessed 10 April 2008).

— *Saju*. 2006. http://www.kalaikaviri.org.uk/saju.htm (accessed 10 April 2008).

Kamau, Pius. 'A history of racial tension'. *Denver Post*, 28 April 2004.

Karat, Prakash. 'Naxalism Today: At an Ideological Deadend'. *The Marxist* 3, no. 1 (January-March 1985).

Karim, Afsir (Maj. Gen.) *Transnational Terrorism, the Danger in the South*. Lancer Publications, 1993.

Kashmir human rights site. Kashmir Human Rights News. 20 February 2008. http://kashmir.ahrchk.net/mainfile.php/news200208/193/ (accessed 12 January 2009).

Kastfelt, Niels. *Religion and African Civil Wars*. London: C. Hurst & Co. Publishers, 2005.

Katz, Jacob. *From Prejudice to Destruction: Anti-Semitism, 1700-1933*. Cambridge: Harvard University Press, 1980.

Kawaja, Kaleem. 'Kashmir, Kosovo, and East Timur'. *Pakistan Link*, 1 October 1999.

Kawaja, Kaleen. 'Brother, Can You Spare a Tear for Taliban'. *Milli Gazette*, 1 March 2002.

Kennedy, Kenneth A.R. 'Have Aryans been identified in the prehistoric skeletal record from South Asia?' Vol. 1, in *The Indo-Aryans of ancient South*

Asia: Language, material culture and ethnicity Vol 1 of Indian philology and South Asian studies, by Kenneth A.R. Kennedy. Walter de Gruyter, 1995.

Kenoyer, Jonathan M. *Ancient Cities of the Indus Valley Civilization.* Oxford University Press, 1998.

Kent, Eliza F. *Converting Women: Gender and Protestant Christianity in Colonial South India.* New York: Oxford University Press, 2004.

Khalid, Usman. 'Musharaff Beginning to End'. 10 March 2007. http://www.countercurrents.org/pak-khalid190307.htm (accessed 10 January 2009).

— 'Time for Musharaff to Go'. March 2007, 2007. http://www.countercurrents.org/pak-khalid270307.htm (accessed 30 January 2009).

Korn, David A. *Exodus Within Borders: An Introduction to the Crisis of Internal Displacement.* Brookings Institution Press, 1999.

Kramrisch, Stella. *Presence of Siva.* Princeton University Press, 1994.

Krapf, Johann Ludwig, and Ernest George Ravenstein. *Travels, Researches and Missionary Labours during an Eighteen Years Residence in Eastern Africa.* London: Trubner, 1860.

Krishnakumar, R. 'Inquiry commission: Marad shocks'. *Frontline,* 7-20 October 2006.

Krishnamurti, Bhadriraju. *The Dravidian Languages.* Cambridge University Press, 2003.

kroc.nd.edu. Kroc Institute for International Peace Studies: About us. 2008. http://kroc.nd.edu/aboutus (accessed 2010).

KudiArasu. 29 August 1937.

Kulkarni, Sudheendra. ' "Social Justice" Through US Intervention'. *The Indian Express,* 30 October 2005.

Kumar, Girja. *The Book on Trial.* Har-Anand Publications, 1997.

Kumar, Vinod A. 'Kerala's Emergence as a Terror Hub: Repeated Warnings Ignored'. Institute for Defense Studies and Analyses. 11 November 2008. http://www.idsa.in/publications/stratcomments/VinodKumar111108.htm (accessed December 2, 2008).

Kumaran, Thillai. 'FeTNA letter to the California State Board of Education'. FeTNA, 19 February 2006.

Kumarasamy, Thangaraj. Email respons'. 19 October 2009.

Kumutham Reporter. 'Hyder Ali demolishing Darghas?'. News, 23 November 2008.

Kumutham Reporter. 'Super Star as Thiruvalluvar: Film Planned (Tamil)'. *Kumutham Reporter,* 17 July 2008.

Kurtz, Stanley. 'The Job Ahead, Bringing Democracy to Iraq will Take More than Election'. *Wall Street Journal.* 21 April 2003. http://www.opinionjournal.com/extra/?id=110003378 (accessed 21 December 2006).

Kuruvachira, J. 'Madhav Sadashiv Golwalkar on Hindu Rashtra, Indian Muslims and Christians'. www.donboscoindia.com. 2002. http://www. donboscoindia.com/english/resourcedownload.php?pno=1&secid=247 (accessed 13 September 2008).

Kutty, Govindan K. *Seshan, an Intimate Biography*. New Delhi: Konark, 1994.

Lal, B.B. 'Archaeology of the Ramayana Sites Project: Its Genesis and a Summary of the Results'. *Manthan:* Journal of Deendayal Research Institute, October 1990.

Lal, B.B. 'Thermo Luminescence Dating of Pottery from Sringaverapura – A Ramayana Site'. Proc. Indian Acad. Sciences (Earth Planet Sci.) 90 , no. 2 (July 1981): 161-172.

Lausanne Website. 'Christian Witness to Hindus, Report of the Consultation on World Evangelization, Lausanne Occasional Paper 14'. *Lausanne.* (1980) 1997:2009. http://www.lausanne.org/all-documents/lop-14.html (accessed 10 January 2009).

— *'Deliver us from Evil Consultation', Nairobi, Kenya.* August 2000. http:// www.lausanne.org/nairobi-2000/overview.html (accessed 30 January 2009).

— 'History and Heritage of the Lausanne Movement'. 1997:2009. http://www. lausanne.org/about.html (accessed 10 January 2009).

— 'The Lausanne Occasional Papers (LOPs)'. 1997:2009. http://www. lausanne.org/documents.html (accessed 30 January 2009).

Le Journal Chretin. 'Congressman Trent Franks Introduces Resolution on Untouchability'. News, 2 May 2007.

Leach, Edmund. 'Aryan Invasions over Four Millennia'. In *Culture Through Time: Anthropological Approaches*, by Emiko Ohnuki-Tierney. Stanford University Press, 1990.

Lemarchand, René. 'Ethnicity as Myth: The View from the Central Africa'. Copenhagen: University of Copenhagen: Centre of African Studies, 1999.

Leo Bashyam. 'International Development Aid: Addressing Dalit Issues'. *www. ambedkar.org.* February 2001. http://www.ambedkar.org/Worldwide_ Dalits/intl_aid_addressing_dalit_issues.htm (accessed 10 March 2009).

Lepage, Michael. 'Evolution: 24 Myths and Misconceptions'. *New Scientist*, April 2008.

Levy, Richard S. 'Antisemitism: A Historical Encyclopedia of Prejudice and Persecution'. ABC-CLIO, 2005.

Library of Congress. *'Historians Peter Brown, Romila Thapar Named Recipients of $1 Million 2008 Kluge Prize for Study of Humanity'.* 2008. http://www.loc.gov/today/pr/2008/08-225.html (accessed 30 March 2009).

— *Mark Noll to Discuss 'The Bible in American Public Life, 1860-2005':* News from Library of Congress. May 2005. http://www.loc.gov/today/pr/2005/05-055.html (accessed 10 February 2009).

— *'Romila Thapar Named as First Holder of the Kluge Chair in Countries and Cultures of the South at Library of Congress'.* 2003. http://www.loc.gov/today/pr/2003/03-068.html (accessed 30 March 2009).

Lindsay, Michael D. *Faith in the Halls of Power: How Evangelicals Joined the American Elite.* Oxford University Press US, 2007.

LISA. 'Book Award Flyer '. 2009.

— London Institute of South Asia. 2005:2010. http://www.lisauk.com/default.asp (accessed 10 January 2009).

Lochan, Pramila. 'The Eternal Values of Manu Smrithi-Lecture by Rama Jois'. IGNCA Newsletter, January-February 2003.

Longman, Timothy. *Christianity and Genocide in Rwanda.* Cambridge University Press, 2010.

Longman, Timothy. 'Churches and Social Upheaval in Rwanda and Burundi Explaining Failures to Oppose Ethnic Violence'. In *Religion and African Civil Wars,* by Niels Kastfelt. London: C. Hurst & Co. Publishers, 2005.

Lord, Lewis. 'The Fabulous Fabulist: Did Marco Polo Really Make it to China'. US News online. 24 July 2000.

Lourdu, S.D. *Nattar Vazhakatriyal Sila Adipadaikal' (Folklore Studies Some Funadamentals)* [Tamil]. Pallyamkottai: Folklore Research Center, St Xavier Autonomus College, 1997.

ls.berkeley.edu. People: Department of South and Southeast Asian Studies. 2005. http://ls.berkeley.edu/dept/sseas/people/faculty.html (accessed 10 February 2009).

Ludra, Thakur Kuldip S. 'Inter Services Intelligence Directorate's Fourth Leg in India – The Al Ummah cited in (P. G. Rajamohan) Tamil Nadu: The Rise of Islamist Fundamentalism'. South Asia Terrorism Portal. 2000. http://www.satp.org/satporgtp/publication/faultlines/volume16/Article5.htm (accessed 10 March 2009).

Lund University. 'Newsletter 77'. *Swedish South Asian Studies Network, Lund.* 14 September 2007. http://www.sasnet.lu.se/newsletter77.html (accessed 10 January 2009).

— 'Tamil Panel: Panel 38'. Swedish South Asian Studies Network/Lund University. July 2004. http://www.sasnet.lu.se/panelabstracts/38.html (accessed 10 January 2009).

Lutheran World Federation. 'Who We Are'. 2009. http://www.lutheranworld.org/Who_We_Are/LWF-Welcome.html (accessed 2010).

Lysebeth, Andre Van. *Tantra: The Cult of Feminine.* Motilal Banarsidass Publications, 2002.

MacDonnell, A.A., and A.B. Keith. *Vedic Index of Names and Subjects*. 1912. Republished in India as a two-volumne set, 1100 pages, in 2007.

Macwan, Martin C. *IIDS: 'Five Year Journey, November 2003 – October 2007'*. Activities Report, Indian Institute of Dalit Studies, 2007.

Macwan, Martin, and Smita Narula. ' "Untouchability"; The Economic Exclusion of the Dalits in India'. The International Council on human rights policy. Geneva: 2001.

Macwan, Martin, Thorat Sukhadeo, and Gail Omvedt. *Social Justice Philanthropy: Approaches and Strategies of Funding Organizations*. Rawat Books, 2009.

Madhava, and Tapasyananda. *Sankara dig vijaya: The Traditional Life of Sri Sankaracharya*. Chennai: Sri Ramakrishna Math, 1996.

Mahadevan, Iravatham. 'Aryan or Dravidian or Neither? A Study of Recent Attempts to Decipher the Indus Script (1995 2000)'. Edited by Michael Witzel. Electronic Journal of Vedic Studies (EJVS) 8, no. 1 (March 2002): 3-19.

— Communication to his colleagues working on the celt. 30 April 2006.

Mahadevan, Iravatham. 'Dravidian parallels in Proto Indian script'. Journal of Tamil Studies 2 (1970).

— 'Significance of Mayiladuthurai Find'. *The Hindu*, 1 May 2006.

— 'The Indus 'non-script' is a Non-issue'. *The Hindu*, 3 May 2009.

Mahapatra, Sampad. *Kandhmal: Mystery Surrounds Swami's Death*. News, NDTV, 4 September 2008.

Maitra, Ramtanu. 'India's Maoists on a Growth Spurt'. *Asia Times*, 23 August 2003.

Malaimurasu. 'Badshah and Others Released'. (Tamil) News, 28 January 1997.

Malaimurasu. 'Women Killed in Bomb Blast'. (Tamil) News, Coimbatore Edition, 9 December 1997.

Malhotra, Rajiv. 'American Exceptionalism and the Myth of the Frontiers'. In *The Challenge of Eurocentrism*, by Rajani Kannepalli Kanth, 171-216. New York: Palgrave Macmillan, 2009.

Mallampalli, Chandra. *Christians and Public Life in Colonial South India, 1863-1937: Contending With Marginality*. Roultedge, 2004.

Malten, Thomas. 'Tamil Studies in Germany'. Lecture at Max Mueller Bhavan, Chennai, 17 March 1998.

Mangalorean Star. Rev Fr Cedric Prakash. July 2004. http://mangalorean. com/browsearticles.php?arttype=mom&momid=21 (accessed 10 February 2009).

Mangalwadi, Vishal. 'A Radical Proposal for a Very Difficult Situation in Orissa'. www.vishalmangalwadi.com. 2008. http://www.vishalmangalwadi.com/vkmWebSite/orissa_proposal.pdf (accessed 10 January 2009).

— 'Conversations: Vishal Mangalwadi'. *Christianity Today,* 12 January 1998.

— 'Christmas May Become (Bloody) Good Friday in India'. 8 December 2008. http://masihivandana.com/blog/2008/12/08/christmas-may-become-bloody-good-friday-in-india-vishal-mangalwadi/ (accessed 17 February 2010).

Mangalwadi, Vishal. 'Five Ways to Salvation in Contemporary Guruism'. *Themelios* 2, no. 3 (May 1977): 72-77.

Mangalwadi, Vishal. 'Hinduism in Double Trouble: Mao and Christi Come Together in Orissa'. *Journal Chretien*, November 2008.

— Why Do the Maoists Support Christians? 8 December 2008. http://www.sakshitimes.com/index.php?option=com_content&task=view&id=352&Itemid=43 (accessed 10 January 2009).

— 'Yoga: Five Ways of Salvation in Hinduism'. *Website of Vishal Mangalwadi.* 2001. http://www.vishalmangalwadi.com/files/yoga.pdf (accessed 10 January 2009).

Manorama, Ruth. 'The Situation of Dalit women – Formerly Known as Untouchables/Scheduled Castes'. Presented before the Committee on Development of the European Parliament, 18 December 2006.

Maranatha Christian Journal. 'Thousands of Christian Schools Planned in India, URL: MCJ Online. 1 June 2004. http://www.mcjonline.com/news/04a/20040601e.shtml (accessed 21 February 2006).

Maranatha Christian Journal. 'Thousands of Christian Schools Planned in India'. June 2004. http://www.mcjonline.com/news/04a/20040601e.shtml (accessed 10 March 2005).

Margolis, Eric S. *War at the Top of the World: The Struggle for Afghanistan, Kashmir, and Tibet.* Routledge, 2000.

Marsh, Benjamin. Message number #3147. Indo_Eurasian_Research Yahoo Group, 2006.

— 'Dalit Freedom Network Petition on Anti-Conversion Laws, Message #4511'. Indo-Eurasian_research Yahoo Groups, 17 July 2006.

— 'Free the Dalit: Benjamin Mash Blog'. 10 November 2008. http://freethedalit.blogspot.com/2008/11/more-on-obama-advisor-sonal-shah.html (accessed 1 December 2008).

— 'Free the Dalit: Blog of Benjamin Mash'. 6 August 2008. http://freethedalit.blogspot.com/2008/08/book-arrow-of-blue-skinned-god.html (accessed 1 December 2008).

Marshal, Paul. 'First Things: Hinduism and Terror'. *Hudson Institute*. 1 June 2004. http://www.hudson.org/index.cfm?fuseaction=publication_details&id=4575 (accessed 10 January 2010).

Marshall, Paul. 'First Freedom'. *National Review Online*, 9 July 2007.

Marshall, Paul. 'The Rise of Hindu Extremism'. Summary Report, Center for Religious Freedom, Freedomhouse, 2003.

Martin, K.A. 'Film on St Thomas planned'. *The Hindu*, 11 June 2008.

Mathew, C.P. 'Letters to the Editor'. *The Hindu*, 4 June 1983.

Max Müller, Frederich. *Lectures on the Science of Language*. New York: Charles Scriber and Company, 1869.

McGann, James G., and Kent, R Weaver. *Think Tanks and Civil Societies*. Transaction Publishers, 2002.

McGavran, Donald. 'Letter to the Editor'. *Christianity Today*, 12 October 1983.

McGuire, John. 'The BJP and Governance in India: An Overview'. *South Asia: Journal of South Asian Studies* (Routledge) 25, no. 3 (December 2002): 1-15.

McKean, Lisa. 'The Militant Hindu Movement'. *PIFRAS*. 2002. http://www.pifras.org/Programs/Past_Programs/Sumposium_report/Symposium_speeches/Lise_Mckeon/lise_mckeon.htm (accessed 30 March 2009).

McKean, Lise. 'Bharat Mata Mother India and Her Militant Matriots'. In *Dev: Goddesses of India*, by John Stratton Hawley and Donna Marie Wulff. University of California Press, 1996.

— *Divine Enterprise: Gurus and the Hindu Nationalist Movement*. University of Chicago Press, 1996.

McManners, John. *The Oxford Illustrated History of Christianity*. Oxford University Press, 2001.

Mehta, Pratap Bhanu. 'An Unconscionable Act'. *The Indian Express*, 15 April 2009.

Menon, Nivedita, and Aditya Nigam. *Power and Contestation: India Since 1989*. Zed Books, 2007.

Menon, V.P. *Transfer of Power in India*. Hyderabad: Orient Longman, 1998.

MeriNews. *Setalvad and R.B. Sreekumar on Lecture Tour to US*. 7 July 2008. http://www.merinews.com/catFull.jsp?articleID=137155 (accessed 5 January 2009).

Merrinews.com. 'Traumatised gang rape victim seeks justice'. 29 June 2008. http://indianchristians.in/news/content/view/2196/52/.

Metzger, B.M, and Coogan, M.D. *The Oxford Companion to the Bible*. Oxford University Press, 1993.

Meyers, Bryant. 'Theological Reflections on the Christian Humanitarian Response'. Lausanne World Pulse. 2005. http://www.lausanneworldpulse. com/themedarticles.php/62/10-2005 (accessed 10 October 2009).

MHA. *Receipt of Foreign Contribution by Voluntary Associations, Annual Report.* Ministry for home affairs, government of India, 2005-2006.

Ministry of defense. *Reforming the National Security System: Recommendations of the Group of Ministers, Government of India.* Security Report, government of India, 2001.

Ministry Watch. *'Ministry Watch Profile for GFA'.* 2008. http://ministrywatch. org/profile/gospel-for-asia.aspx (accessed 30 January 2010).

Mitra, Chandan. 'Divine Comedy: Review of Meera Nanda's book Divine Market'. *India Today*, 15 October 2009.

MNN. *Open Doors Seminars Helping Persecuted Pastors in India.* 11 February 2004. http://mobile.mnnonline.org/article.php?id=5665 (accessed 10 January 2009).

Monier, Williams. *Sanskrit-English Dictionary.* 1899.

Monier, Williams. *Modern India and the Indians.* London, 1891.

Monsma, Stephen V. 'Faith-Based NGOs and the Government Embrace'. In *The Influence of Faith: Religious Groups and US Foreign Policy*, by Elliott Abrams. Rowman & Littlefield, 2001.

Mooney, Chris. *The Republican War on Science.* Perseus Books Group, 2006.

More, Prashant J.B. *Muslim Identity, Print Culture, and the Dravidian Factor in Tamil Nadu.* Hyderabad: Orient Blackswan, 2004.

More, Prashant J.B. *Political Evolution of Muslims in Tamilnadu and Madras 1930–1947.* Hyderabad: Orient Blackswan, 1997.

Mudaliar, Murugesa N. *The Relevance of Saiva Siddhanta Philosophy.* Annamalai University, 1968.

Mudaliyar, Arunai Vadivel. *A Rebuttal to the Comparative Study of Bible-Thirukural-Saiva Siddhanta (Tamil).* Dharmapuram: International Saivasiddhanta Research Institute, 1991.

Mudaliyar, S. Sabaratna. *Life of Thiru Gnana Sambanthar.* Colombo: Young Men Hindu Association: Kumaran Press, 1920:2001.

Muller, Friedrich Max. *The Life and Letters of the Right Honourable Friedrich Max Muller.* Georgina Adelaide Grenfall Muller. Vol. 1. Longmans, Green, and Co, 1902.

Murugan, Sathiyavel M.P. 'Dravidian Religions and Social Harmony' (Paper presented at Dravidian University Kuppam). 6 March 2009. http://www. dheivathamizh.org/sorpozhivugal.htm#kuppam (accessed 12 January 2010).

— 'Tamil Thirumurai Thirumanam (Marriage)'. www.dheivathamizh.org. 14 May 2009. http://www.dheivathamizh.org/thirumurai_thirumanam. html (accessed 21 January 2010).

— 'Web page of dheivathamizh.org praising Chief Minister'. www. dheivathamizh.org. 2008. http://www.dheivathamizh.org/pazhanthai1.htm (accessed 21 January 2010).

murugan.org. Meet on Murugan: *Hinduism Today*, May 1999. 'Murugan Bhakthi: Skanda Kumara Super Site'. 1 February 2001. http://www. murugan.org/evnts/ht_may99_article.htm (accessed 10 January 2009).

Muthuswamy, Moorthy. 'USCIRF's Disregard for Truth'. Letter written to Speaker Dennis Hastert. 8 May 2006.

N. Jatia. 'Development of Jains Outside Bihar'. In *Encyclopaedia of Jainism*, by Narendra Singh. Anmol Publications Pvt. Ltd., 2001.

Nagarajan, R. 'Girl Suicide: Religious Conversion Torture in School?' (Tamil). Investigative Report, Chennai: *Tamilan Express*, 26 February 2009.

Nanda, Meera. 'Postmodernism, Hindu Nationalism and "Vedic science"'. *Frontline*, 03-16 January 2004.

— 'Making Science Sacred'. Seminar Web Edition. 2005. http://www. india-seminar.com/2005/545/545%20meera%20nanda1.htm (accessed 30 March 2009).

Nanda, Meera. *Prophets Facing Backward: Postmodern Critiques of Science and New Social Movements in India*. PhD Thesis, New York: Science and Technology Studies: Rensselaer Polytechnic Institute, 2000.

— 'Calling India's Freethinkers'. *The Hindu*, 22 May 2004.

Nandhivarman, Na. 'Is Indus Valley the Cradle or Catacomb of the Dravidian Civilization'. 28 September 2003. http://www.dravidaperavai.org.in/page. php?art=8 (accessed 13 February 2010).

Nandhivarman, Na. *Dravidian Origin of Sanskrit*. 11 November 2007. http:// nandhivarman.wordpress.com/2007/11/06/dravidian-origins-of-sanskrit/ (accessed 13 December 2009).

Nascimento, Elisa Larkin. *The Sorcery of Color: Identity, Race, and Gender in Brazil*. Temple University Press, 2007.

nativenet.uthscsa.edu. 'World Council of Churches Dalit Solidarity Programme'. 2008. http://nativenet.uthscsa.edu/archive/nl/9208/0074.html (accessed 2008).

Natrajan, Balmurli, Ciarán ó Faoláin, and Kavita Philip. 'SAPs, Dust, and Hot Air: Gail Omvedt and Liberalization'. *Ghadar*, November 1998.

Nayak, Nihar. 'Nepal: New 'Strategic Partner' of China?' *Institute for Defense Studies and Analyses: IDSA Strategic comments*. 30 March 2009. http://www.idsa.in/publications/stratcomments/NiharNayak300309.html (accessed 15 May 2009).

NCCI. Dalit Task Force: About. 2006. http://nccidalittaskforce.com/dalit-task-force/about.html (accessed 10 August 2008).

— Dalit Task Force: Church. 2006. http://nccidalittaskforce.com/dalit-task-force/church.html (accessed 10 August 2008).

— Dalit Task Force: About. 2006. http://www.nccidalittaskforce.com/dalit-task-force/about.html (accessed 10 August 2008).

— Members: Dalit Task Force. 2006. http://nccidalittaskforce.com/dalit-task-force/members.html (accessed 2008).

NCCN. 'National Council of Churches of Nepal: Activities'. May 2007. http://nccnepal.org/activities/ (accessed 10 January 2010).

NCDHR. 'Alternate report for the Republic of India to the Committee on the Elimination of Racial Discrimination'. Atrocities, National Council for Dalit Human Rights, 2006.

NCSE. 'NCSE advises Louisiana'. January 2010. http://ncse.com/news/2010/01/ncse-advises-louisiana-005271 (accessed February 12, 2010).

NDTV. 'Dowry Practice Plagues Christian Community'. TV News, 28 November 2004.

NDTV. 'India's Reservation Policy Unfair: NCDHR'. TV News Report, 12 November 2006.

Neill, Stephen. *History of Christianity in India: The Beginning to AD 1707*. 2004: Cambridge University Press, 2004.

New England College. 'NEC Announces Commencement Speakers'. 2008. http://www.nec.edu/news/nec-announces-commencement-speakers (accessed 30 December, 2009).

New York Times. 'Hindu Nationalists Are Enrolling and Enlisting, India's Poor'. News, 13 May 2002.

News Media. 'Extremism Threatens Peace in South Asia, World, Speakers Say'. News, News Media, 23 July 2002.

NILT. 'National Institute of Leadership Training'. 2004. http://niltindia.org/home.htm (accessed 25 August 2008).

Ninan, M.M. *Hinduism: What Really Happened in India (Hinduism A Christian Heresy?)* Global Publishers, 2004.

Nitharsanam.net. 'Young Woman Committed Suicide due to Conversion Trauma'. (Tamil) News, http://nitharsanam.net/?p=13680, 29 February 2008.

Noll, Mark. 'The Doctrine Doctor'. *Christianity Today*, December (Web-only), 2004. December 2004. http://www.christianitytoday.com/ct/2004/decemberweb-only/12-27-42.0.html (accessed 12 February 2009).

NRIInternet.com. 'IMC-USA 2008 Convention'. NRI Internet. 2008. http://www.nriinternet.com/Associations/USA/A_Z/I/IMC-USA/2008_May31/index.htm (accessed 10 October 2009).

Nussbaum, Martha. 'Fears for Democracy in India'. *Chronicle Review*, 18 May 2007.

— 'Against Academic Boycott'. *Dissent*, Spring Issue 2007.

— 'Terrorism in India has Many Faces: A Cloud Over India's Muslims'. *Los Angels Times*, 30 November 2008.

— *The Clash Within: Democracy Religious Violence and India's Future*. Harvard University Press, 2007.

— To the participants in the Yale Seminar on Antisemitism. Yale university. 2005-2006. http://www.yale.edu/isps/seminars/antisemitism/2005-06/nussbaum.pdf (accessed 10 January 2009).

— 'Transcript of Online Discussion with Martha Nussbaum'. *The Chronicle of Higher Education*. October 2001. http://chronicle.com/colloquylive/2001/10/nussbaum/ (accessed August 2008).

Nussbaum, Martha, and J. Jonanne Myers. 'The Clash Within: Democarcy, Religious Violence and India's Failure'. *Carnegie Council*. 3 May 2007. http://www.cceia.org/resources/transcripts/5433.html (accessed 2009).

O'Neill, Tom. 'India's Untouchables'. National Geographic, June 2003.

Obeyesekere, Gananath. 'Personal Identity and Cultural Crisis: The case of Anagārika Dharmapala of Sri Lanka'. In *The Biographical Process: Studies in the History and Psychology of Religion*, by Frank Reynolds and Donald Capps. Walter de Gruyter, 1976.

Obeysekere, Gananath. 'Dutthagamani and the Buddhist Conscience'. In *Religion and Political Conflict in South Asia: India, Pakistan, and Sri Lanka* , by Douglas Allen. Greenwood, 1992.

OCRPL. 'Conference: Reporting Religious Controversies'. Oxford Centre for Religion and Public Life. September 2007. http://www.ocrpl.org/?page_id=89 (accessed 12 January 2009).

— 'Oxford Centre for Religion and Public Life: About'. *www.ocrpl.org*. 2008. http://www.ocrpl.org/?page_id=3 (accessed 10 January 2009).

Olasky, Marvin. 'How did Jesus Change Hinduism?' 2007. http://www.sakshitimes.com/index.php?option=com_content&task=view&id=158&Itemid=43 (accessed 20 August 2009).

Oldenburg, Veena Talwar. *Dowry Murders: The Imperial Origins of a Cultural Crime*. New York: Oxford University Press, 2002.

Olender, Maurice. *The Languages of Paradise: Race, Religion, and Philology in the Nineteenth Century*. Harvard University Press, 1992.

Omvedt, Gail. *Dalit Visions: The Anti-caste Movement and the Construction of an Indian Identity*. Oriental Blackswan, 2006.

— 'The Dravidian Movement'. 2001. http://www.ambedkar.org/gail/Dravidianmovement.htm (accessed 20 January 2009).

— 'Caste, Race and Sociologists I & II'. *The Hindu*, 18 & 19 October 2001.

— 'Hindutva and Ethnicity'. *The Hindu*, 25 February 2003.

— 'What went Wrong-II'. *The Hindu*, 9 April 2002.

— 'The Dalits: Dynamic Upsurge'. *The Week*, 30 December 2001.

One World South Asia. 'India Must Get Rid of Caste Discrimination: European Parliament'. 19 December 2006. http://socialjustice.ekduniya.net/Infocus/document.2006-12-21.7136296971 (accessed 12 January 2009).

Pagels, Elaine H. *The Gnostic Gospels*. Vintage Books, 1989.

Pallister, David. 'The Numbers Game'. *The Guardian*, 21 March 2007.

Pande.B.M. 'Decipherment of the Harappan script'. *Conflux*, May 1971.

Pandian, Jacob. *Caste, Nationalism, and Ethnicity: An Interpretation of Tamil Cultural History and Social Order*. Popular Prakashan, 1987.

Parashar, Swati. 'A Response to Arundhati Roy: The heart of India is under attack'. South Asian Analysis Group. 5 November 2009. http://www.southasiaanalysis.org//papers35/paper3489.html (accessed 20 March 2010).

Parker, George Wells. *Children of the Sun*. Baltimore: Black Classic Press, 1918:1978.

Parsons, Gerald. *Religion in Victorian Britian: Culture and Empire*. Manchester University Press, 1997.

Pels, Peter. 'From Texts to Bodies – Brian Houghton Hodson and The Emergence of Ethnology in India'. In *Anthropology and Colonialism in Asia and Oceania*, by Jan van Breman and Akitoshi Shimizu. Routledge, 1999.

Pew Research Center. 'International Report on Social Hostility and Religious Discrimination'. *Pew Forum*. 2009. http://pewforum.org/docs/?DocID=491 (accessed 6 January 2010).

— 'Sources of Data for the Report'. 2009. http://pewforum.org/docs/?DocID=500#Sources (accessed 5 January 2010).

pewforum.org. 'Transcript: Global Restrictions on Religion'. Pew Forum. 2009. http://pewforum.org/events/?EventID=223 (accessed 2010).

Pfaffenberger, Bryan. *Caste in Tamil Culture: The Religious Foundations of Sudra Domination in Tamil Sri Lanka*. Syracuse University, 1982.

Phillips, Michael. *White Metropolis: Race, Ethnicity, and Religion in Dallas, 1841-2001*. University of Texas Press, 2006.

Philp, Catherine. *The Hidden Massacre: Sri Lanka's Final Offensive Against Tamil Tigers*. News, *The Times* (UK), 29 May 2009.

Pictet. *95-96*. Olender, 1992.

Pictet. *103-104*. Olender, 1992.

PIFRAS. 'Symposium on South Asia'. 2002. http://www.pifras.org/Programs/Past_Programs/Sumposium_report/Symposium_speeches/Bruce_Robertson/bruce_robertson.html (accessed 12 February 2009).

— 'Trent Franks: Remarks at the Seminar on India'. www.pifras.org. 2004. http://www.pifras.org/Programs/Past_Programs/March3104/Trent_Franks/trent_franks.html (accessed 30 March 2009).

PIFRAS website. Policy Institute for Religion and State. 2003 (updated). http://www.pifras.org/.

Pillai, Nallaswami. *Studies in Saiva-Siddhanta*. BiblioBazaar, LLC, 1911:2009.

Pillai, Purnalingam M.S. *A Primer of Tamil Literature*. New Delhi: Asian Educational Services, 1904:1994.

Pillai, Shanmukham M. *Cankattamilarin Valipatum Catankukalum (Worship and Rituals of Tamils in Sangham age)* [Tamil]. Chennai: International Institute of Tamil Studies, 1996.

Pillai, Sundaram. 'Age of Thirugnanasambanthar'. *Indian Antiquary*, June 1896.

Pitts, Jospeh. 'Address at the Seminar on India'. 31 March 2002. www.pifras.org/Programs/Past_Programs/March3104/Joseph_Pitts/joseph_pitts.html (accessed 10 January 2009).

— 'Congressional Record'. frwebgate.access.gpo.gov. 18 June 2002. http://frwebgate.access.gpo.gov/cgi-bin/getpage.cgi?dbname=2002_record&page=H3612&position=all (accessed 4 May 2009).

Pollock, Sheldon. 'Deep Orientalism? Notes on Sanskrit and Power Beyond the Raj'. In *Orientalism and the Postcolonial Predicament: Perspectives on South Asia*, by Sheldon Pollock, edited by Peter van der Sheldon Carol A Beckenridge, 77-78. Philadelphia: University of Pennsylvania Press, 1993.

Polo, Marco. *Travels of Marco Polo*. Translated by Aldo Ricci. Routledge, 2004.

Pope, George Uglow. *The Sacred Kural of Thiruvalluvar*. 2. Madras: The SISS Works Publishing Society, 1886:1958.

— *Tiruvacagam: Sacred Utterances of the Tamil Poet, Saint and Sage Manikka-Vacagar*. New Delhi: Asian Educational Services, 1900:2002.

Prabhan, Sajith. 'Parody of Janaganamana by Christians'. *Sajith Prabhan's Channel*. 2006. http://www.youtube.com/watch?v=zDpIn03gEi8 (accessed 10 February 2010).

— 'Parody of Janaganamana by Christians'. *Sajith Prabhan's Channel*. 2009. http://www.youtube.com/watch?v=5bO21MQ1LtI (accessed 10 February 2010).

Prajapathi.Net. Prajapathi Alleluia Prayer Fellowship About us. 2007. http://prajapathi.net/Aboutus.html (accessed September 2009).

— Prajapathi Alleluia Prayer Fellowship Testimonial. 2007. http://prajapathi.net/testimonial.html (accessed September 2009).

Prakash, Cedric(SJ). 'A Written Testimony to the US Commission on International Religious Freedom: USCIRF Hearing on Communal Violence in Gujarat and the US Response'. US Commission on International Religious Freedom. 10 June 2002. http://uscirf.gov/hearings/10jun02/prakash.php3?mode=print (accessed 21 December 2006).

Prakash, Ved. *Encyclopaedia of North-East India*. Vol. 5. Atlantic Publishers and Distributors, 2007.

Prakriti Foundation. *Prakriti Foundation Invitation*. 8 December 2006. http://www.prakritifoundation.com/inv/kf.html (accessed 10 August 2009).

Prasad, Vijay. *The Karma of Brown Folk*. University of Minnesota Press, 2000.

Prashad, Vijay. 'An Afro-Dalit Story: Badges of Color'. March 2000. www.zmag.com (accessed 29 March 2009).

— 'Eastward, Evangelical Soldiers!' *Frontline*, 25 February 2005.

Priest, Josiah. *Bible Defense of Slavery: And Origin, Fortunes, and History of the Negro Race*. Fifth. Glasgow, 1852.

Project Eleanor. 'Brief biographies of members of the Sub-Commission'. 2004. http://www.projecteleanor.com/2004/bios.html (accessed 10 August 2009).

PTI. '9 Charge Sheeted for Incident that led to Coimbatore Riots'. News, Press Trust of India, 31 December 1998.

PTI. 'Kerala Assembly Passes Resolution on Madhani'. News, Press Trust of India, 15 March 2006.

PTI. 'Manmohan Concerned Over Visa Denial to Modi'. News, Press Trust of India, 19 March 2005.

PTI. 'Nepal's 3 Maoist Parties Join for Anti-India Campaign'. News, Press Trust of India, 5 February 2010.

PTI. 'Tribals doubts EU teams Kandhamal visit, seek reply from state'. News, Press Trust of India, 6 February 2010.

PTI. 'US Group Says RSS is Like al-Qaeda'. News, Press Trust of India, 10 August 2005.

PTI. 'US Slashes Aid to India by 35%'. News, Press Trust of India, 25 July 2007.

PTI. 'Why Swami Laxmanananda was Killed?' News, Press Trust of India, 5 October 2008.

Puthia-Kodangi. 'Mathamma'. (Tamil) *Puthia-Kodangi*, 2004.

Puthiya Kaatru. 'Joint declaration of writers and human rights activists'. (Tamil) *Keetru*. September 2006. http://www.keetru.com/puthiyakaatru/sep06/writers.php (accessed 10 March 2009).

Raj, and Raj. 'Speech_Dalitology.pdf (a condenation of principles set forth in 830 pages book Dalitology'. *www.dalitreds.org*. 2008. : http://www.

dalitreds.org/articles/Speech_Dalitology.pdf) (accessed 29 December 2009).

Raj, M.C. 'Strategies-Practices: Context of casteism: Paper presented on behalf of REDS at world social forum'. *www.dalitreds.org*. 29 January 2001. http://www.dalitreds.org/articles/World_Social_Forum_Papers.pdf.

Rajan, Soundara. R. *Vyasa School of Thought and Christianity*. 'Research' Paper, NILT Publication, 2004.

Rajasekharan, S. 'Mylapore pilgrimage center – a historical and literary stud'. 1989.

Rajkhowa, J.P. 'Christian Conversions and North East India'. *The Sentinel*, 12 May 2008.

Rajshekar, V.T. 'DV Report on Israeli Hand in 9/11 Finally Proves Right'. *Dalit Voice*, 1 February 2007: 19.

— '"Jews of India" Get Closer to Jews'. *Dalit Voice*, February 2008.

— DV Editor Speech. *Dalit Voice*. April 2007. http://www.dalitvoice.org/Templates/april2007/articles.htm (accessed 25 March, 2009).

Rajshekar, V.T. and Runoko Rashidi. 'Daits the Black Untouchables of India'. In *African Presence in Early Asia*, by Runoko Rashidi and Ivan Van Sertima, 233-249. Transaction Publishers, 1988.

Ramachandran, R. 'The Genetics of Caste'. *Frontline*, 09-22 June 2001.

Ramachandran, S. *Maraiyum Maraiyavarkal (The Disappearing Brahmins and Other Essays* [Tamil]). Chennai: AnyIndian Publication, 2007.

— 'On recent archeological discoveries'. (Tamil) *Thinnai*. 11 May 2006. http://www.thinnai.com/?module=displaystory&story_id=60605128&format=html (accessed 12 May 2006).

Ramachandran, S. *Kshatriya Rama and Brahmin Ravana, South Indian Social History Research Institute* (Tamil). 2008. http://www.sishri.org/ramar.html (accessed September 2009).

Ramakrishnan, S. *Inthiya Panpaadum Tamizharum (Indian Culture and Tamils* [Tamil]). Chennai: Meenakshi Puthaka Nilayam, 1971.

Raman, Anil (Major). 'The Dimasa-Hmar Conflict: Another Ember in the Fire'. www.usiofindia.org. 8 September 2004. http://www.usiofindia.org/article_Jul_Sep04_8.htm (accessed 10 June 2007).

Raman, B. 'Arrest of Al Badr Terrorists in Mysore: International Terrorism Monitor'. *South Asia Analysis Group*. 28 October 2006. http://www.southasiaanalysis.org/%5Cpapers21%5Cpaper2007.html (accessed 4 December 2008).

Raman, B. *Islamic Terrorism in India: Hydra Headed Monster*. Paper No. 526, 03 October 2002, South Asia Analysis Group, 2002.

— 'I Stand by My Assessment'. *Outlook*, 11 April 2005.

Ramasamy, E.V. *Dravidar-Aryar* (Tamil). Periyar Dravida Kazhagam, 1940:2007.

Ramaswamy, Sumathi. *Fabulous Geographies, Catastroophic Histories: The Lost Land of Lemuria.* Orient Longman, 2005.

Rao, Anupama, Muvalar Ramamirthammal, and Kalpana Kannabir n. *Muvalur Ramamirthammal's Web of Deceit.* Kali for Women (Organization), 2003.

Rao, Ramakrishna K.V. 'EVR, Ambedkar and Jinnah: A Historically Important Meeting'. (Tamil) *Thinnai.* 15 January 2009. http://www.thinnai. com/?module=displaystory&story_id=20901159&format=html&edition_ id=20090115 (accessed 20 January 2009).

Rao, P.N. 'Entropic evidence for linguistic structure in the Indus script'. *Science.* 23 April 2009. http://www.sciencemag.org/cgi/content/abstract/1170391 (accessed 1 November 2009).

Rasamanikkam, S.J. 'Christianity in Thirukural'. (Tamil) In *Thirukural Karutharangu Malar*, by Subbu, N. Dr Reddiyar. 1974.

Rawat Publications. *Social Justice Philanthropy.* 2002:2009. http://www. rawatbooks.com/ShowDetails.ASP?BookID=1921 (accessed 20 February 2010).

Redesdale. *Foundations of the Nineteenth Century.* 1911. Elibron Classics Series: Adamant Media Corporation, 2003.

Rediff News. *For US Body, India is Same as Somalia and Afghanistan,* . 13 August 2009. http://news.rediff.com/report/2009/aug/13/us-body-places-india-on-watch-liSthtm (accessed 20 August 2009).

— 'ISI Activities in Malapuram'. *Rediff.* 28 July 2000. http://www.rediff.com/ news/2000/jul/28isia.htm (accessed 30 November 2008).

— *Lashkar Could Target Madurai's Meenakshi Temple: IB.* 28 July 2008. http://www.rediff.com/news/2008/jul/26terror.htm (accessed 30 July 2008).

— *Terror Attack at IISc, Bengaluru; 1 Killed, 4 Injured.* 28 December 2005. http://www.rediff.com/news/2005/dec/28bang.htm (accessed 4 December 2008).

Reese, Ellen. 'The Influence of Right-wing Think tanks and the Christian Right on Welfare Reform'. In *The Promise of Welfare Reform: Political Rhetoric and the Reality of Poverty in the Twenty-first Century* , by Keith Michae Kilty and Elizabeth A Segal. Haworth Press, 2006.

Reich, David, Kumarasamy Thangaraj, Nick Patterson, Alkes L Price, and Lalji Singh. 'Reconstructing Indian population history'. *Nature*, 24 September 2009: 489-494.

Rekdal, Ole Bjorn. 'When hypothesis becomes myth: the Iraqi origin of the Iraq'. *Ethnology*, 1998: 17-32.

Reuters. *Humanitarian Organizations*. 2008. http://www.alertnet.org/db/whowhatwhere/cordaidnl_AF_REC.htm (accessed 2009).

Reuters-India. *Sri Lanka Military, Rebels Trade Death Toll Claims*. News, Reuters, 1 March 2008.

Rev Dr Wilson. 'Communication on the Description of Caves and Cave Temples by Arthur A. West' *Journal of the Asiatic Society of Bombay* (Bombay Educational Society's Press) 5 (July 1857).

Richard, Valantasis. *The Gospel of Thomas*. London; New York: Routledge, 1997.

Ricks, Nancy. *World Vision: Dalit Story*. 2007. http://www.worldvision.org/worldvision/radio.nsf/stable/wvradiostory_090207_dalitfreedom (accessed 10 January 2009).

Rigby, Peter. *African Images: Racism and the End of Anthropology*. Oxford: Berg Publishers, 1996.

Risley, H.H. 'The Study of Ethnology in India'. *Journal of the Anthropological Institute of Great Britain and Ireland* 20 (1891): 247.

Risley, H.H. *Tribes and Castes of Bengal*. Four Volumes, Bengal Secretariat Press, 1892.

Risley, H.H. and William Crooke. *The People of India*. 1915.

Robert, Dana L. *Converting Colonialism: Vision and Realities in Mission History, 1706-1914*. Wm. B. Eerdmans Publishing, 2007.

Robertson, Pat. *On Hinduism (700 Club)*. 26 July 1988.

Rocher, Ludo. *Ezour Vedam: A French Veda of the Eighteenth Century*. John Benjamins Publishing Company, 1984.

Roy, Arundhati. *The Heart of India is Under Attack*. 30 October 2009. http://www.guardian.co.uk/commentisfree/2009/oct/30/ (accessed March 2010).

Rudolph, Lloyd I. 'Urban Life and Populist Radicalism: Dravidian Politics in Madras'. In *Urban Sociology in India*, by Rao, M.S.A. Orient Longman, 1979.

Sadasivan, N.S. *A Social History of India*. APH Publishing, 2000.

Sadiq, Muhammed. 'The Indian Establishment Responds to Human Rights Issues in Kashmir'. www.JammuKashmir.com. 28 May 2008. http://jammukashmir.com/insights/insight20080428.html.

Sagan, Carl. 'Cosmos'. Ballantine, 1980.

Sahni, Ajay. 'Survey of Conflicts and Resolution in India's Northeast'. South Asia Terrorism Portal. 2 August 2004. http://www.satp.org (accessed 12 October 2009).

Sahoo et al, Sanghamitra. 'A prehistory of Indian Y chromosomes: Evaluating demic diffusion scenarios'. *PNAS*, 24 January 2006: 843-848.

samatha.in. 'UN set to treat caste as human rights violation'. September 2009. http://samatha.in/2009/10/08/un-set-to-treat-caste-as-human-rights-violation/ (accessed December 2009).

Sampth, Arjun. 'Do not lie for in thy heart you know the truth'. (Tamil). *Dinamani*, 15 July 2008.

Samson, Leela. 'History And Myths of Indian Classical Dances'. August 2004. http://www.4to40.com/discoverindia/index.asp?article=discoverindia_historyandmyth (accessed 10 April 2008).

Samuel, John G. *St Thomas Who Came to Tamil Nadu* (Tamil). 2001.

Sanghamitra, and Sengupta. 'Polarity and Temporality of High Resolution Y Chromosome Distributions in India Identify Both Indigenous and Exogenous Expansions and Reveal Minor Genetic Influence of Central Asian Pastoralists'. *The American Journal of Human Gene*, 2006:202-221.

Sargunam, Ezra. 'Impact of Christianity on the belief systems, cultural heritage of India with special reference to Early Indian Christianity'. Souvenir of the Second International Conference on The History of Early Christianity in India. Chennai: International Center for the study of Christianity in India: Institute of Asian Studies, 2007.

Satyam, T.S. *The Developments in Thirukural Research in the Twentieth Century*. Madras University, 1979.

Schalk, Peter. 'Caivam – a Religion Among Tamil Speaking Refugees from Sri Lanka'. *Refugee Survey Quarterly* 26, no. 2 (2007): 91-107.

Schalk, Peter. 'From "Do and Die" to "Do or Die": Semantic Transformations of a Lethal Command on the Battlefield in Eelam/Lanka'. *Orientalia Suecana* 51-52 (2002-03): 391-398.

— 'What is wrong with the EU's evaluation of the conflict in Sri Lanka?' 9 April 2007. http://www.negotiatedpeace.com/doc_en/news/eu_what_is_wrong_schalk.html (accessed 12 December 2008).

Schlegal, Friedrich. 'On the Language and the Wisom of the Indians, Translated by E.J Millington'. In *The Aesthetic and Miscellaneous Works of Frederick von Schlegal*, 514. London: Henry G Bohn, 1860.

Schwab, Raymond. *Oriental Renaissance: Europe's Discovery of India and the East, 1680-1880*. New York: Gene Patterson-Black and Victor Reinking, 1984.

Science Daily. 'Ancestral Populations of India and Relationships to Modern Groups Revealed'. *Science Daily*. 24 September 2009.

Sekaran, Sathur. 'Tamils who Went West of Indus valley and Those Who Stayed in India'. *Souvenir of the First International Conference on the Religion of Tamils*. Chennai: Pastoral Center Archdiocese of Madras, 2008. 37-39.

Seligman, Charles G. *Races of Africa*. Oxford University Press, 1966.

Seligman, Charles G. and B.Z. Seligman. *Pagan Tribes of the Nilotic Sudan.* Routledge & Sons, 1932.

— *The Veddhas.* Cambridge University Press, 1911.

Sen, Sailendra Nath. *Ancient Indian History and Civilization.* New Age International, 1999.

Sengupta, Sanghamitra, et al. 'Polarity and Temporality of High-Resolution Y-Chromosome Distributions in India Identify Both Indigenous and Exogenous Expansions and Reveal Minor Genetic Influence of Central Asian Pastoralists'. *The American Journal of Human Genetics*, February 2006: 202-21.

Sertima, Ivan Van. *African Presence in Early Asia.* Transaction publishers, 1988.

Shaffer, Jim G, and Diane A Lichtenstein. *The Concepts of 'Cultural Tradition' and 'Palaeoethnicity' in South Asian Archaeology.* Vols. Indian Philology and South Asian Studies Vol-1, in *The Indo-Aryans of Ancient South Asia: Language, Material Culture and Ethnicity*, by George Erdösy. Walter de Gruyter, 1995.

Shah, Timothy Samuel. 'Hindu Nationalism vs. Islamic Jihad: Religious Militancy in South Asia A Conversation with Cedric Prakash, Teesta Setalvad, Kamal Chenoy, Sumit Ganguly, Sunil Khilnani, and Jonah Blank'. Ethics and Public Policy Center. 3 February 2003. http://www.eppc.org/programs/southasian/publications/pubID.1533,programID.38/pub_detail.asp (accessed 12 February 2009).

Shah, Timothy Samuel. 'The Bible and the Ballot Box: Evangelicals and Democracy in the "Global South"'. *SAIS Review* 24, no. 2 (2004): 117-132.

Sharada, B.A, and Chetana, M. 'Web Page Creation for Eminent Scholar's Contributions and Their Citations: M B Emeneau – A Case Study'. *Indian Science* 44, no. 15 (August 2008).

Sharif, Iqbal Ahmed. 'Jews and "Jews" of India'. *Dalit Voice.* January 2006. http://www.dalitvoice.org/Templates/jan2006/articles.htm (accessed 12 January 2009).

Shariff, Iqbal Ahmed. 'Brighter Side of Hitler: DV to Reveal Facts Suppressed by History'. *Dalit Voice.* June 2005. http://www.dalitvoice.org/Templates/june2005/ articles.htm (accessed 30 March 2009).

Sharlett, Jeff. *The Family: The Secret Fundamentalism at the Heart of American Power.* New York: Harper Perennial, 2008.

Sharp, Travis. 'The Hamitic Hypothesis: A Pseudo Historical Justification for White Superiority'. *Writing for a Real World* 2004–2005: University of San Francisco. 2004. http://www.usfca.edu/rhetcomp/journal/wrwtoc04 05.html (accessed 8 July 2008).

Shashikumar, V.K. 'Bush's Conversion Agenda for India: Preparing for the Harvest'. *Tehelka*, February 2004.

Sheldrake, Rupert. *Biography of Rupert Sheldrake PhD – Part II.* 1997. http://www.sheldrake.org/About/biography/biography2.html (accessed 30 March 2009).

Shourie, Arun. 'Muslims ... were looking to Pakistan for help ...'. *The Observer*, 16 December 1994.

Singh, Upinder. *A History of Ancient and Early Medieval India: From the Stone Age to the 12th Century.* Pearson Education India, 2009.

Sivaramamurti, C. *Nataraja in Art, Thought and Literature.* New Delhi: National Museum, 1976.

Sivaratnam, C. *Origin and Development of the Hindu Religion and People.* Colombo: Ranco, 1978.

Smith, Vincent. Clarendon Press, 1958.

Smith, Warren Cole. *A Lover's Quarrel with the Evangelical Church.* Biblica, 2009.

Solomon, Richard. *Indian Epigraphy: A Guide to the Study of Inscriptions in Sanskrit, Prakrit, and the Other Indo-Aryan Languages.* Oxford University Press US, 1998.

Southworth, Franklin. 'Lexical Evidence for Early Contacts Between Indo-Aryan and Dravidian'. In *Aryan and Non-Aryan in India*, by Madhav Deshpande and Peter Vook, 191-233. Ann Arbon: University of Michigan Press, 1979.

— 'The SARVA (South Asia Residual Vocabulary Assemblage) Project'. ccat. sas.upenn.edu. 21 September 2005. http://ccat.sas.upenn.edu/~fsouth/ SARVAProject2005.pdf (accessed 20 March 2008).

Srinivasan, Kamachi. *Religion of Kural* (Tamil). Madurai Kamaraj University, 1979.

Srinivasan, Perundevi. 'Can We Cross the Chasm? Agency and Orientalist Discourse in Colonial Tamil Context'. In *Reorienting Orientalism*, by Chandreyee Niyogi. Sage, 2006.

Sruthi (Jan 1996). 'Advice from a Veteran': Interview with Sarada. In *Nirmalam–The Genius of S Sarda*, by Anita Ratnam. Arangam Trust, 2005.

Stackelberg, Roderick. *The Routledge Companion to Nazi Germany.* Routledge, 2007.

Steigmann-Gall, Richard. *The Holy Reich: Nazi Conceptions of Christianity 1919-1945.* Cambridge University Press, 2003.

Stephen, A. 'Indian Dance and Music'. 2004. http://www.kalaikaviri.org.uk/ article1.htm (accessed 10 August 2009).

Student Christian Movement India. 'Challenging Dalit Women's Status Amidst Economic Globalization'. 2006-2007. http://www.scmindia.org/eventdetail.php?AID=113 (accessed 10 January 2009).

Subramaniam, Narendra. 'Ethnicity, Populism and Pluralist Democracy: Mobilization and Representation in South India'. PhD dissertation, Massachusetts Institute of Technology, 1993.

Subramanian, Ajantha. 'Mukkuvar Modernity: Development as a Cultural Identity'. In *Regional Modernities: The Cultural Politics of Development in India*, by Sivaramakrishnan, K. and Arun Agrawal. Stanford University Press, 2003.

Subramanian, T.S. 'A Time of Troubles'. *Frontline*, March 7-20, 1998.

Sugavaneswaran. 'Thirukkural'. In *Encyclopedia of Indian Literature*, by Mohan Lal. New Delhi: Sakitya Academy, 1992.

Sugirtharajah, Rasiah S. *The Bible and Empire: Postcolonial Explorations*. Cambridge University Press, 2005.

Sunil, K.P. 'Hoax!' *Illustrated Weekly of India*, 26 April to 2 May 1987.

Swamigal, Ramalinga. *Thiruvarutpa*. Annamalai University, 1989.

Swaminathan, M.S. *Dr M.S. Swaminathan, Economic Ecologists of India*. Indian Environment Society, 1982.

Swann, de Bram. 'On the Psycho and Sociogenesis of the Hatred of Distant Strangers: Reflections on Rwanda'. *Theory, Culture & Society* (SAGE) 14, no. 2 (1997): 105-122.

Swedish South Asian Studies Network. Department of Social Work, Stockholm University. 2007. http://www.sasnet.lu.se/socworksth.html (accessed 2008).

— Newsletter. 14 September 2007. 14 September 2007. http://www.sasnet.lu.se/newsletter77.html (accessed 2009).

— Newsletter. 9 October 2007. http://www.sasnet.lu.se/newsletter78.html (accessed 10 January 2010).

— Newsletter-66. 17 October 2006. www.sasnet.lu.se/newsletter66.html (accessed 19 January 2010).

— Stockholm Anthropological Research on India. 2006. http://www.sasnet.lu.se/antrosthlm.html (accessed 19 January 2009).

Tambiah, Jeyaraja Stanley. *Buddhism Betrayed? Religion, Politics and Violence in Sri Lanka*. University of Chicago Press, 1992.

Tambyah T., Isaac. *Psalms of a Saiva Saint*. New Delhi: Asian Educational Services, 1985.

Tamil Nadu Archeological Survey. 'Tamil Nadu Archeological Survey Report'. Tamil Nadu Archeological Survey, 1967.

Tamil Nadu Govt. 'Development Cullture and Religious Endowments: Policy

Note, Directorate of Culture'. 2003-2004. http://www.tn.gov.in/policynotes/archives/policy2003-04/tdc2003-04-3-8.htm (accessed 30 August 2009).

Tamil Nadu Textbook Society. 'Social Science: Sixth Standard'. Chennai: Tamil Nadu Textbook Society, 1989.

tamil.berkeley.edu. 'Background'. *Tamil Chair Berkeley*. 2000. http://tamil.berkeley.edu/Tamil%20Chair/Background.html (accessed 10 September 2008).

Tamil.Net. 'Dravidian Religion'. May 2000. http://tamil.net/list/2000-05/msg00387.html (accessed 21 August, 2008).

Tamil Webber. 'Jihadi Victims of Coimbatore, Tamilnadu – 3'. Youtube.com. 16 May 2007. http://www.youtube.com/watch?v=2WFqxnvBvk0 (accessed 10 March 2009).

Taylor, Troup. *The Prophetic Families, Or The Negro: His Origin, Destiny and Status*. Atlanta, 1895.

Telegraph (UK). 'UN Says Caste System is a Human Rights Abuse'. News, 29 September 2009.

Templeton Foundation. 'Interview with John M. Templeton, Jr., M.D'. www.templeton.org. 2006. http://templeton.org/capabilities_2006/jt_interview_2.html (accessed 17 February 2010).

Tevaneyan, Ñanamuttan. *The Primary Classical Language of the World*. Nesamani Publishing House, 1966.

Thakurtha, Paranjoy Guha, and Shankar Raghuraman. *A Time of Coalitions: Divided We Stand*. New Delhi: Sage Publications, 2004.

Thangaiah, Johnson A, and Samson, A. 'Ancient Tamil Society and Casteism: Before and After 7th Century AD'. *Souvenir of First International Conference on the Religion of Tamils*. Chennai: Pastoral Center Archdiocese of Madras, 2008.

Thapar, Romila. *A History of India Vol-I*. Penguin, 1990.

— *Ancient Indian Social History: Some Interpretations*. Orient Blackswan, 2006.

— *Early India: From the Origins to AD 1300*. University of California Press, 2004.

Thapar, Romila. Interview by Champakalakshmi, R. Environmental History: Interview with Romila Thapar Chennai: *The Hindu*, (19 December 2004).

Thapar, Romila. 'Imagined Religious Communities? Ancient History and Modern Search for Hindu identity'. *Modern Asian Studies* 23, no. 2 (1989).

— 'Where Fusion Cannot Work – Faith and History'. *The Hindu*, 28 September 2007.

Thapar, Romila, and Michael Witzel. 'Creationism by Any Other Name …'. *Outlook*, 28 February 2006.

Thapar, B.K., and Shaffer, J.G. *Pre-Indus and Early Indus Cultures of Pakistan and India*. Vol. 1, in *History of Civilizations of Central Asia*, by Ahmad Hasan Dani and Ahmad Hasan Masson. Motilal Banarsidass Publications, 1999.

The AICC Update. 'A Report on Activities of the AICC'. Activities Report, All India Christian Council, February 2007.

The AICC Update. *D'Souza Speaks at Historic Washington D.C. Religious Freedom Event*. News, AICC, 11 July 2006.

The Assam Tribune. 'Arunachal Buddhists Allege Militants Harassment'. News, 23 August 2004.

The Earth Times. 'Young Girl's Longing for Equal Rights'. Earth Times Website. 16 May 2002. http://www.earthtimes.org/may/younggirlslongingmay3_02. htm (accessed 10 January 2009).

The Economic Times. 'Arms Found from Rehab Centre in Kandhamal'. News, *The Economic Times*, 1 October 2009.

The Economic Times. 'From Kashmir to Kerala, How did Terrorism Spread?' News, 30 October 2008.

The Economic Times. 'India Next Only to Iraq on Religious Discrimination: US Think-tank'. News, 22 December 2009.

The Economic Times. 'Kerala Cries Foul as NIA Takes Charge'. News, 30 December 2009.

The Economic Times. 'Kerala Goes Soft on SIMI, Country Pays'. News, 18 August 2008.

The Economic Times. 'NGOs Hit Pay Dirt on Dollar Trial'. News, 20 January 2004.

The Economic Times. 'Vedanta Hurt by Church of England Decision to Sell Stake'. News, 8 February 2010.

The Financial Express. 'NGO Lobbying Spurs Centre to Review Foreign Contributions Act'. News, *The Financial Express*, 18 October 2006.

The Hindu. 'Proselytisation' Angle to Student's Suicide?' 19 May 2007. http://www.hindu.com/2007/03/19/stories/2007031910180500.htm (accessed 25 May 2007).

The Hindu. 'A Smart Operation by the Doctor'. News, 17 November 2000.

The Hindu. 'Achuthanandan Seeks Treatment for Maudhany'. News, 11 June 2006.

The Hindu. 'Behind Bengaluru: The Long Jihad Today'. News, 10 January 2006.

The Hindu. 'Church Apologises for Distortions in Translation'. News, 8 January 1999.

The Hindu. "Dalit in-fighting cause for concern". News, 2 March 2007.

The Hindu. 'Discovery of a century in Tamil Nadu'. News, 1 May 2006.

The Hindu. 'FCRA Bill, Anti Poor, Sys Christian Council'. News, 17 November 2001.

The Hindu. 'Fundamentalist outfit busted at Nellikuppam'. News, 29 October 2004.

The Hindu. 'India Can be Put on the Mat for Discrimination: Dalit lobbyist' News, 4 March 2003.

The Hindu. 'Intellectual Support Stands in the Way of Tackling Maoists: Chidambaram'. News, 20 February 2010.

The Hindu. 'Prior Warning Not Taken Seriously'. News, 19 February 1998.

The Hindu. 'Provide Quota, Dalit Leader Urges British Investors'. News, 16 September 2006.

The Hindu. 'Ruth Manorama's Denial'. News, 18 November 2000.

The Hindu. 'Terror Trail Links Kerala With Kashmir'. News, 10 October 2008.

The Hindu. 'Terrorists Enjoy Political Backing in North Kerala?' News, 16 March 2006.

— 'Kancha Illaiah gets US Dalit network fellowship'. *The Hindu*, 1 October 2004.

The Hindu. 'The Jihad in God's Own Country'. News, *The Hindu*, 9 March 2008.

The Hindu. 'Two Lashkar Conduits Held'. News, 1 January 2007.

The Hindu. 'Was Car Bomb Designed in Bengaluru?' News, 8 July 2008.

The Independent. 'Right-wing Christian Group Pays for Commons Researchers'. Exclusive News report, 30 March 2008.

The Indian Express. 'Dalits Want to Kill Sanskrit: Kancha Illaiah'. 3 December 2001.

The Indian Express. '2500 Hindus Converted to Islam in 5 Years in TN'. News, 27 July 2006.

The Indian Express. 'Bengaluru Serial Blasts Case Cracked'. News, 07 February 2009.

The Indian Express. 'DMK govt ordered Six Cases Dropped Against Muslim Hardliners in TN'. News, 8 August 2006.

The Indian Express. 'DMK Turns Jail into Spa for Coimbatore Terror Accused'. News, 23 July 2006.

The Indian Express. 'In Tamil Nadu Town, Fundamentalists Play Moral Cops, Even Kill to Have Way'. News, 26 Mar 2007.

The Indian Express. 'Mysore Terrorist Got Driving License from Chennai'. News, 04 November 2006.

The Indian Express. 'Nepali Maoists Infiltrate into India, Spotted in Orissa'. News, *Indian Express*, 28 July 2008.

The Indian Express. 'New Islamic Outfit Has Cops on Alert'. News, 17 February 2007.

The Indian Express. 'Plot to Kill Kerala CM, Other Leaders Bared; ISI Men Held'. News, 15 August 1999.

The Indian Express. 'Rajasthan Cops Launch Hunt for Emmanuel Foundation Chief'. News, 25 March 2006.

The Indian Express. 'Two Arrested for Swindling Tsunami Fund'. News, Chennai, 12 October 2009.

The Milli Gazette. 'Indian Muslim Council – USA'. *The Milli Gazette*, 18 March 2005.

The New Indian Express. 'Chennai Next Terror Target? Bomb Maker Held in Nellai'. News, 28 July 2008.

The New Indian Express. 'Delhi STF Comes Calling to Chennai to Probe Terror Links'. News, 8 January 2007.

The New Indian Express. 'GO on "Adi Dravidars" Seen as a Bid to Divide Dalits'. News, 4 March 2007.

The Peninsula. 'Police Yet to Nab Attackers of Kerala Writer'. News, 11 January 2010.

The Pioneer. 'After Sufiya Arrest, Madani a Liability for Cong, CPM'. News, 19 December 2009.

The Pioneer. 'Kerala Stunned by Revelations on Marad Massacre'. News, 27 September 2006.

The Sangai Express. '74 Girls Brought to TN from Manipur, Assam Missing'. News, 11 February 2010.

The Telegraph. 'God's Own Country'. News, Calcutta, 13 July 2008.

The Telegraph. 'Manipuri Children Narrate "Horror Home" Tales'. News, 10 February 2010.

The Telegraph. 'Seshan Biography Angers Dravidian Parties'. News, 16 October 1994.

The Wall Street Journal. 'With Increasing Water Needs, Will China Dehydrate India?'. Online News, 3 October 2009.

The Washington Times. 'Christian Worldview – an Interview with Ravi Zacharias'. Interview, 6 December 2008.

The Week. 'Fervour of the Fanatics'. Investigative Report, 12 August 1990.

— 'Statistics of Bomb Blasts in Tamil Nadu from "Coimbatore Bomb City"'. *The Week*, 1 March 1998.

Thekaekara, Mari Marcel. 'Discrimination against Dalits'. *The Hindu*, 2 May 2005.

Thiruma.net. *Thirumaavalavan Awarded Doctorate by Gurukul Lutheran*. 2009. http://thiruma.net/node/1128 and http://thiruma.net/node/1123 (accessed 20 December 2009).

Thirumaavalavan. *Uproot Hindutva: The Fiery Voice of the Liberation Panthers*. Translated by Meena Kandasamy. Popular Prakashan, 2004.

Thomas, Pradip Ninan. *Strong Religion, Zealous Media: Christian Fundamentalism and Communication in India*. New Delhi: Sage Publications India, 2008.

Thompson, Allan, and Koffi Annan. *The Media and the Rwanda Genocide*. London: Pluto Press, 2007.

Time Magazine. 'The 25 Most Influential Evangelicals in America'. *Time Magazine*, 7 February 2005.

Time-CNN. 'The Second Coming of Bobby Jindal'. 4 October 2007. http://www.time.com/time/politics/article/0,8599,1668433,00.html (accessed 2 February 2010).

Times News Network. 'Thomas's Visit Under Doubt'. News, 26 December 2006.

The Times of India. 'Cops had SIMI Email Intercepts in 2001'. News, 23 August 2008.

The Times of India. 'Caste Bias Can't be Equated With Racism: India'. News, 18 April 2009.

The Times of India. *Caste: Racism in All But Name?* News, Times of India, 26 April 2009.

The Times of India. 'India slams European ruling on Dalits'. News, 3 February 2007.

The Times of India. 'Indian Priests Stripped, Thrashed in Nepal: India Lodges Protest'. News, *The Times of India*, 5 September 2009.

The Times of India. 'Nepal Maoists Admit Link with Indian Naxals'. News, *The Times of India*, 3 November 2009.

The Times of India. *Nepal PM Prachanda Chooses China Over India*. News, *The Times of India*, 24 August 2008.

The Times of India. 'NGOs, Teesta Spiced up Gujarat Riot Incidents: SIT'. News, 14 April 2009 .

The Times of India. 'PDP leader Madani's Wife Held on Terror Charges'. News, 18 December 2009.

The Times of India. 'Report Based on SIT Findings'. News, 16 April 2009.

The Times of India. 'Romila Rejects Padma Award'. News, 27 January 2005.

— 'UN Set to Treat Caste as Human Rights Violation'. *Times of India*, 28 September 2009.

The Times of India. 'TN's Most Dangerous Ultras Still at Large'. News, 06 December 2008.

The Times of India. 'US Congress Wants Justice For Riot Victims'. News, 10 January 2004.

The Times of India. *US Human Rights Report Invites Scorn*. News, *The Times of India*, 5 March 2002.

The Times of India. *US Lawmakers Want Curbs on Pak to Go*. News, *The Times of India*, 4 September 2001.

The Times of India. 'Vibrant Gujarat? 98% Dalits Have to Drink Tea in Separate Cups'. News, 8 December 2009.

Times of London. 'Home Truths'. News, 26 May 1991.

Tmpolitics.blogspot.com. 'P. Jainulabdeen: A Special report'. (Tamil) *Tamil Muslim Political Platform*. 11 June 2007. http://tmpolitics.wordpress.com/2007/06/special-report.html (accessed 14 March 2009).

tnpolice.gov.in (a). 'Official website of Tamil Nadu state police: webpage announcing wanted terrorists'. Tamil Nadu Police website: Extremists/Terrorists. 22 November 2008. http://tnpolice.gov.in/Wanted/Want8.html (accessed 10 March 2009).

tnpolice.gov.in (b). 'Official website of Tamil Nadu state police: webpage announcing wanted terrorists'. Tamil Nadu Government Police website. 2008. http://tnpolice.gov.in/Wanted/Want3.html (accessed 10 January 2009).

tnpolice.gov.in (c). 'Wanted Terrorists/Extremists'. Tamil Nadu Government Police website. 2008. http://tnpolice.gov.in/Wanted/Want4.html; http://tnpolice.gov.in/Wanted/Want10.html (accessed 10 January 2009).

Towns, Edolphus. 'Extensions of Remarks'. *Congressional Record*. 2 August 2001, 18 March 2003.

— 'Extensions of Remarks'. *Congressional Record*. 15 February 2005.

Trautman, Thomas R. *Aryans and British India*. New Delhi: Yoda Press, 2004.

— *Languages and Nations: The Dravidian Proof in Colonial Madras*. New Delhi: Yoda Press, 2006.

Trautmann, Thomas R. *Aryans and British India*. University of California, 1997.

Trautmann, Thomas R. 'Discovering Aryan and Dravidian in British India'. *Historiographia Linguistica* xxxi, no. 1, 2004.

Travel with a cause. India. 2005:2009. http://www.travelwithacause.org/india.php (accessed 2 February 2010).

— Travel with a cause. 2005:2009. http://www.travelwithacause.org/home. php (accessed 2 February 2010).

Trigger, Bruce G. *A History of Archaeological Thought.* Cambridge University Press, 1989.

UNHCR. 'US Committee for Refugees and Immigrants World Refugee Survey 2005'. *United States Committee for Refugees and Immigrants.* 20 June 2005. http://www.unhcr.org/refworld/docid/42c928902.html (accessed 21 February 2008).

UNI. '10 Killed 64 Hurt in 3 Train Blasts'. News, UNI, 6 December 1997.

Unison. Scotland Unison News. 2000. http://www.unison-scotland.org.uk/ news/2000/archive.html (accessed 30 January 2009).

United Methodist News Service. 'Extremism Threatens Peace in South Asia, World, Speakers Say: Reporting on a South Asia Conference on July 18, 2002'. News, 23 July 2002.

United States Human Rights. 'Human Rights Council Documents'. www2. ohchr.org. 2007. http://www2.ohchr.org/english/bodies/hrcouncil/ docs/7session/A.HRC.7.64_fr.doc (accessed 10 August 2009).

University of Amsterdam. 'Maarten Bavinck appointed president of Commission on Legal Pluralism'. 10 December 2009. http://www.fmg. uva.nl/gsss_news/news.cfm/779D8494-1321-B0BE-A469A55284BE8C26 (accessed 20 February 2010).

University of Chicago Chronicle. 'Norman Cutler, 1949-2002'. University of Chicago Chronicle. 28 March 2002. http://chronicle.uchicago.edu/020328/ obit-cutler.shtm (accessed 11 February 2008).

US Commission Global Human Rights. 'Equality and Justice for 200 Million Victims of Caste System'. 2005. http://commdocs.house.gov/committees/ intlrel/hfa23825.000/hfa23825_0f.htm (accessed 10 October 2009).

USCIRF. 'India Religious Freedom Report '. Annual Report, 2000.

USCIRF. 'Report of the United States Commission on International Religious Freedom'. Annual Report, 2005.

USCIRF. 'Report of the United States Commission on International Religious Freedom (India)'. Annual Report, 2006.

USCIRF. 'Report of the United States Commission on International Religious Freedom'. Annual Report, 2007.

USCIRF. 'Report of the United States Commission on International Religious Freedom'. Annual Report, 2001.

Vallancey, Charles. *A Vindication of the Ancient History of Ireland.* 1786.

van der Veer, Peter. *Imperial Encounters: Religion and Modernity in India and Britain.* Princeton University Press, 2001.

Variyar, Thirumuruga Kirupanantha. 'Variyar Amutham'. *Kumutham* [Tamil magazine], 8 February 1973.

Vasanthakumar, M.S. 'Expound Christ from Non-Christian Texts'. *Dharma Deepika*, July-December 2000.

Venkatachalam, M.S. 'Bridal Mysticism'. *Journal of the Institute of Asian Studies* XIX , no. 1, September 2001.

Venkatachalam, M.S. 'Marriage Metaphor in Bible and Tamil Devotional Poetry, a Comparative Study'. *The first international conference of early Christianity*. New York:Chennai: Institute of Asian Studies, 2005.

Venkatesan, M. *The Other Side of EVR* (Tamil). Indian Forward Block, 2004.

Venugopal, P. 'Necessity and Validity of an Act Banning Conversion'. *Organiser*, 7 November 2004.

Victor, Ma. So. 'Origin of continents (Tamil)'. 'Souvenir of the First International Conference on the Religion of Tamils'. Chennai: Pastoral Center Archdiocese of Madras, 2008.

Viswanathan, S. 'Tamilology and a German Quest' *Frontline*, 25 April- 8 May 1998.

Vivekananda, Swami. *Complete works*. Vol. IV. Mayavati: Advaita Ashrama, 1970.

Walsh, Lawrence E. 'Chapter 25 United States. v. Elliott Abrams'. Final Report of the Independent Counsel For Iran/Contra Matters Volume I: Investigations and Prosecutions. United States Court of Appeal For the District of Columbia'. www.fas.org. 8 April 1998. http://www.fas.org/irp/offdocs/walsh/chap_25.htm (accessed 3 October 2007).

Washington Post. 'Battle on Teaching Evolution Sharpens'. 13 March 2005. http://www.washingtonpoStcom/wp-dyn/articles/A32444-2005Mar13.html (accessed 10 Janaury 2009).

Watson, Roland. *Bush Deploys Hawk as New UN Envoy*. News, *The Times*, 3 August 2008.

WCC. 'Dalits' Inner Strength Defeats Caste-based Discrimination'. 15 April 2009. http://www.oikoumene.org/ru/news/news-management/a/rus/article/1634/dalits-inner-strength-de.html?tx_ttnews[cat]=89&cHash=f4db884ddf 15.04.09 (accessed 12 January 2010).

— Lutheran World Federation. 2009. http://www.oikoumene.org/en/member-churches/church-families/lutheran-churches/lwf.html (accessed 2009).

— Who are we. 2009. http://www.oikoumene.org/en/who-are-we.html (accessed 2009).

— World's Churches Wrestle With the Ancient System of Caste-based Discrimination. 25 March 2009. http://www.oikoumene.org/en/news/news-management/eng/a/browse/3/article/1634/worlds-churches-wrestle.html (accessed 10 May 2009).

Weekly Journal of Thanthai Periyar Dravidian Kazhagam. 'Ramayana is against Tamil culture – exposition by Prabhakaran (Tamil)'. July 2005.

Wichman, Stefan Arvidsson and Sonia. *Aryan Idols: Indo-European Mythology as Ideology and Science.* Chicago: University of Chicago Press, 2006.

Wikipaedia entry. 'Institut Fondamental d'Afrique Noire'. *Wikipaedia.* 17 March 2008. http://en.wikipedia.org/wiki/Institut_Fondamental_d'Afrique_Noire (accessed 10 January 2009).

Wikipedia. Entry on Universal Society for the Propagation of Gospel. http://en.wikipedia.org/wiki/USPG (accessed 30 January 2009).

Wikipedia. Austrian People's Party. 2009. http://en.wikipedia.org/wiki/Austrian_People's_Party (accessed 10 January 2010).

— Entry for Christian Solidarity Worldwide. http://en.wikipedia.org/wiki/Christian_Solidarity_Worldwide (accessed 10 January 2009).

— Entry on Benita Ferrero Waldner. http://en.wikipedia.org/wiki/Benita_Ferrero-Waldner (accessed 30 January 2009).

— Entry on Max van den Berg. http://en.wikipedia.org/wiki/Max_van_den_Berg (accessed 10 January 2009).

— 'Marad Massacre Page in Wikipedia'. 2003. http://en.wikipedia.org/wiki/Marad_massacre (accessed 10 January 2009).

— Paul Diwakar. 2008. http://en.wikipedia.org/wiki/Paul_Diwakar (accessed 10 August 2009).

— 'Society of Propagation of the Gospel in American Slavery'. http://en.wikipedia.org/wiki/Society_for_the_Propagation_of_the_Gospel_in_America#Slave_owning_by_the_SPG (accessed 10 January 2009).

William R Jones, 'Divine Racism: The Unacknowledged Threshold Issue for Black Theology'. In *African American Religious Thought: An Anthology,* by Cornel West and Eddie Glaube. Westminster: John Knox Press, 2003.

Wilson, A Jeyaratnam, *The Break-up of Sri Lanka: The Sinhalese-Tamil Conflict.* C. Hurst & Co, 1988.

Wilson, A Leslie. *A Mythical Image: The Idea of India in German Romanticism.* Durham: Duke University Press, 1964.

Wilson, Colin. *The Occult.* London: Graffton, 1988.

Winters, Clyde Ahmad. 'Are Dravidians of African Origin?' *P. Second ISAS.* Hong Kong: Asian Research Service, 1980. 789-807.

Winters, Clyde Ahmad. 'The Far Eastern Origin of the Tamils'. *Journal of Tamil Studies,* 1985: 65-92.

— 'The Genetic Unity of Dravidian and African Languages and Culture'. *Proceedings of the First International Symposium on Asian Studies (PIISAS).* Hong Kong: Asian Research Service, 1979.

Winters, Clyde Ahmad. 'The Harappan Writing of the Copper Tablets'. *Journal of Indian History* LXll, no. 13 (1984): 1-5.

Winters, Clyde Ahmad. 'The Indus Valley Writing and Related Scripts of the 3rd Millennium BC'. *India Past and Present* 2, no. 1 (1985): 13-19.

Winters, Clyde Ahmad. 'The Proto-Culture of the Dravidians, Manding and Sumerians'. *Tamil Civilization* 3, no. 1 (1985): 1-9.

Witzel, Michael. 'Interesting Perspective on Harappa etc. From Pakistan'. *Indo-Eurasian Research Yahoo Groups (Message#10159)*. Indo-Eurasian Research Yahoo Groups, 25 May 2008.

— 'Early Sources for South Asian Substrate Languages'. *Mother Tongue Special Issue*, October 1999.

Witzel, Michael. 'Substrate languages in Old Indo-Aryan (Rgvedic, middle and late Vedic)'. *Electronic Journal of Vedic Studies* 5, no. 1 (1999).

Wœrkens, Martine van, and Catherine Tihanyi. *The Strangled Traveler: Colonial Imaginings and the Thugs of India*. University of Chicago Press, 2002.

Woolley, Leonard. *History Unearthed: A Survey of Eighteen Archaeological Sites Throughout the World*. E. Benn, 1958.

www.ad2000.org. 'Mission Executives Challenged to Cooperate in Reaching the Unreached Peoples'. 1997. http://www.ad2000.org/gcowe97/upd703ml.htm (accessed 12 January 2009).

www.ahrchk.net. 'Asian Human Rights'. 2006. http://www.ahrchk.net/ua/mainfile.php/2006/1489/ (accessed 10 September 2008).

www.andyreedmp.org.uk. 'A Brief History'. 2006. http://www.andyreedmp.org.uk/personalbiography-abriefhistory.html (accessed 5 January 2009).

www.antiochnetwork.org. 'Antioch Network: Journey'. http://www.antiochnetwork.org/journey.htm (accessed 10 January 2009).

www.borenawards.org. 'Boren Fellowships for International Study'. 5 November 2007. http://www.borenawards.org/boren_fellowship (accessed 10 January 2009).

www.bu.edu. 'Timothy Shah at Boston University CURA Institute of Culture, Religion and World Affairs'. 30 October 2009. www.bu.edu/cura/faculty-staff/research-associates/shah/shahcv/ (accessed 16 February 2010).

www.cbn.com. 'India'. CBN. 2008. http://www.cbn.com/worldreach/worldreach_region_asia_india.aspx (accessed 10 March 2009).

— 'What Makes the Christian Message Unique?' Discussion with Gordon Robertson and Ravi Zacharias. February 2001. http://www.cbn.com/spirituallife/ChurchAndMinistry/Evangelism/What_Makes_the_Christian_Message_Unique.aspx (accessed 10 February 2010).

www.ccci.org. 'Campus Crusade for Christ India: Illusionists Carry the Gospel to 500 Thousand'. http://www.ccci.org/locations/asia/india/illusionists-carry-the-gospel-to-500-thousand.aspx (accessed 10 January 2009).

www.ccu.edu. 'CCU to the World'. 1999: 2010. http://www.ccu.edu/ccu2theworld/default.asp (accessed 20 February 2010).

— 'Colorado Christian University Alumni Heal a Himalayan Community'. http://www.ccu.edu/admissions/news/news_story.asp?iNewsID=738&strBack=%2Fadmissions%2Fnews%2Fnews_archive.asp (accessed 10 January 2009).

www.cfr.org. 'Timothy Shah'. May 2008. www.cfr.org/content/bios/Shah_CV_May08.pdf (accessed 10 February 2009).

www.christianaggression.org. 2007. http://www.christianaggression.org/item_display.php?type=NEWS&id=1138636306.

www.christianpersecution.info. 'Gospel for Asia Missionaries Beaten and Arrested at Indian Festival'. 2007. http://www.christianpersecution.info/news/gospel-for-asia-missionaries-beaten-arrested-at-indian-festival (accessed 12 January 2009).

www.ciis.edu. 'Angana Chatterji'. 'California Institute of Integral Studies'. 1999:2009. http://www.ciis.edu/faculty/chatterji.html (accessed 10 January 2010).

www.countercurrents.org. 25 March 2009. http://www.countercurrents.org/maitra250309.htm (accessed 5 January 2010).

www.eficor.org. 'Evangelical Fellowship of India Commission on Relief: About'. 2000:2009. http://www.eficor.org/about_eficor.htm (accessed 30 January 2009).

www.europarl.europa.eu. 'Committee on Development, The Dalits Rights in India Summary report'. *European Parliament: European Union.* 18 December 2006. http://www.europarl.europa.eu/comparl/deve/meetings_hr/20061218/summary.pdf (accessed 12 January 2009).

www.europarl.europa.eu/. 'Committee on Development, The Dalits Rights in India Meeting'. 2006. http://www.europarl.europa.eu/comparl/deve/meetings_hr/default_en.htm (accessed 10 August 2009).

www.fides.org. 'Indian Social Institute: Now NGO accredited to United Nations'. Agenzia Fides. 2004. http://www.fides.org/eng/news/2004/0405/25_2441.html (accessed 5 October 2009).

www.focnou.com. 'Pax Romana'. 'International Catholic Movement for Intellectual and Cultural Affairs'. 2007. www.focnou.com/blog/200705/ProgramRome2007.pdf (accessed 10 August 2008).

www.gltc.edu. 'Department of Dalit Theology: Faculty Profile'. 2005. http://www.gltc.edu/gurukul/03-academic/academic/faculty/dalit.htm (accessed 10 January 2009).

— Gurukul Lutheran Theological College & Research Institute. 2006. http://www.gltc.edu/ (accessed 10 January 2009).

— 'Gurukul-CReNIEO-Finland and Canadian Lutheran Church Extension Programs'. August 2004. http://www.gltc.edu/gurukul/05-projects/index. htm (accessed 10 January 2009).

— History. 2005. http://www.gltc.edu/gurukul/01-overview/overview/history. htm (accessed 2009).

— 'Tercentenary Celebration, 300 years of Protestant Mission/Church in India'. 2006. http://www.gltc.edu/tercentenary/ziegenbalg.htm (accessed 11 November 2009).

www.gordonconwell.edu. 'Gordon-Conwell Theological Seminary: About'. 2001:2009. http://www.gordonconwell.edu/about/index.html (accessed 3 April 2009).

— 'Gordon-Conwell Theological Seminary: Basis of Faith'. 2001:2009. http:// www.gordonconwell.edu/about/basis_faith.html (accessed 3 April 2009).

— 'Gordon-Conwell Theological Seminary: History'. 2001:2009. http://www. gordonconwell.edu/about/history.html (accessed 3 April 2009).

www.hinducounciluk.org. 'The Caste System: Report'. *UK Hindu Council*. 2007. http://www.hinducounciluk.org/newsite/report/hcuk_thecastsystemreport. pdf (accessed 30 January 2009).

www.hrdc.net. 'Caste Away Or How the Dalit Cause Was Lost in Durban'. Human Rights Features. September 2001, 2001. http://www.hrdc.net/ sahrdc/hrfeatures/HRF44.htm (accessed 20 March 2005).

www.hudson.org. *Bio of Paul Marshall*. http://www.hudson.org/learn/index. cfm?fuseaction=staff_bio&eid=MarsPaul (accessed 10 January 2009).

www.indiancatholic.in. 'Christians Want to Join the Congress as Candidates for the Elections in Maharashtra'. 2008. http://www.indiancatholic.in/ news/storydetails.php/13416-1-6-Christians-want-to-join-the-Congress-as-candidates-for-the-elections-in-Maharashtra (accessed 10 January 2009).

www.indianchristians.us. 'Pator Evicted in Himachal Prades'. 2007. http:// www.indianchristians.us/newsdetail.php?id=5 (accessed 2010).

www.indianet.nl. 'http://www.indianet.nl/a070815.html'. web-report, 2007.

www.intervarsity.org. 'Hindus: International Student Ministry'. 2005. http:// www.intervarsity.org/ism/cat/33 (accessed 10 January 2009).

www.ivarta.com. 'Plainspeaking the US State Department '. http://www.ivarta. com/columns/OL_041114.htm, Chennai, 2004.

www.kanavuppattarai.com. 'Mathamma'. 2009. http://www.kanavuppattarai. com/mathamma.htm (accessed 2010).

www.khalistan-affairs.org. Khalistan Calling Newsletter. 25 September 2002. http://www.khalistan-affairs.org/Main/K_Calling/kc09252002.htm (accessed 30 January 2009).

www.liberationorg.co.uk. 'Liberty: Who we are'. http://www.liberationorg. co.uk/about%20us%20whoweare.html (accessed 10 January 2009).

www.linguistics.berkeley.edu. Murray Barnson Emeneau (1904-2005). 2005. http://www.linguistics.berkeley.edu/people/emeneau/obit.html (accessed 12 September 2008).

www.lutheranworld.org. 'What We do?' *Lutheran World*. March 2009. http://www.lutheranworld.org/What_We_Do/OIahr/Issues_Events/OIAHR-DalitConf0309_concept.pdf (accessed 10 September 2009).

www.maclellan.net. *Maclellan Foundation*. http://www.maclellan.net/about/newtemplate3.asp (accessed January 2009).

www.narthaki.com. *Review of Maryland Dance Festival*. 2007. http://www.narthaki.com/info/rev07/rev479.html (accessed 19 September 2009).

www.nerve.in. 'India Slams European Parliament Resolution on Dalits'. February 2007. http://www.nerve.in/news:25350032769 (accessed 10 January 2009).

— 'Maoists Working with Christian Organizations in Orissa'. 17 January 2008. http://www.nerve.in/news:253500124058 (accessed 10 January 2009).

www.ngo-monitor.org. 'NGO Monitor Correspondence with Director of Christian Aid on Durban II Funding'. *30* June 2008. http://www.ngo-monitor.org/article/ngo_monitor_correspondence_with_director_of_christian_aid_on_durban_ii_funding (accessed 30 January 2010).

www.omccindia.org. 'Dalit Schools Ground Breaking Features'. 2002:2009. http://www.omccindia.org/ourschools.htm (accessed 10 January 2009).

— 'Operation Mercy Charitable Company India: About Us'. 2002:2009. http://www.omccindia.org/about.htm (accessed 10 January 2009).

www.omusa.org. 'Operation Mobilization USA: About Us'. 2002. http://omusa.org/about-us/ (accessed 10 January 2009).

www.ontheissues.org. "On the Issues: Trent Franks'. 2008. http://www.ontheissues.org/House/Trent_Franks.htm.

www.parliament.uk. 'Parliamentary Business'. United Kingdom Parliament. 8 May 2007. http://www.publications.parliament.uk/pa/cm200607/cmhansrd/cm070508/halltext/70508h0006.htm (accessed 30 January 2009).

www.proxsa.org. 'Foreign Exchange of Hate. 2002'. http://www.proxsa.org/newsflash/index.html (accessed 2010).

www.right-wingwatch.org. 'Right-wing Watch on Trent Franks'. 2008. http://www.right-wingwatch.org/category/individuals/trent-franks (accessed 10 January 2009).

www.rzim.org. Ravi Zacharias International Ministry. 1997:2008. http://www.rzim.org (accessed 2 February 2010).

www.sais-jhu.edu. John Hopkins University South Asian Studies Faculty. http://www.sais-jhu.edu/academics/regional-studies/southasia/faculty/jonah-blank.htm (accessed 10 January 2009).

www.satp.org. 'National Liberation Front of Tripura'. South Asia Terrorism Portal. 2003. South Asian Terrorism Portal: http://www.satp.org/satporgtp/countries/india/states/tripura/terrorist_outfits/NLFT_tl.htm (accessed 10 January 2009).

— 'Student Islamic Movement of India'. *South Asian Terrorism portal* . 2002. http://www.satp.org/satporgtp/countries/india/terroristoutfits/simi. htm (accessed 21 August 2009).

www.state.gov. '2007 Country Reports on Human Rights Practices – South and Central Asia – India'. U.S. Department of State. 2007. http://www. state.gov/g/drl/rls/hrrpt/2007/100614.htm (accessed 10 March 2009).

www.stthoma.com. Sculptures and carvings: Museum. 2002. http://www. stthoma.com/museum/Sculptures/sculptures_carvings.php (accessed 20 August 2009).

www.talkorigins.org. 'Claim CA005'. The TalkOrigins Archive. 2002. http://www.talkorigins.org/indexcc/CA/CA005_2.html (accessed 2010).

www.tamilnation.org. *1991* International Tamil Eelam Research Conference. 1991: Dead Link. http://www.tamilnation.org/conferences/US91/index. htm (accessed 10 January 2008).

— Tamil Nation Without a State. 2004: Dead Link. http://www.tamilnation. org/diaspora/tamilnadu.htm (accessed 23 August 2008).

www.tamilnet.com. Call on UK to lift ban on LTTE. http://www.tamilnet.com/ art.html?catid=13&artid=20755 (accessed 30 January 2009).

www.telegraphnepal.com. India-Nepal-China: Roti-Beti Vs Latta-Kapada. 8 April 2009. http://www.telegraphnepal.com/news_det.php?news_ id=5169 (accessed 10 May 2009).

— 'Nepal: We need more support from China'. 2009. http://www.telegraphnepal. com/news_det.php?news_id=4859 (accessed 2009).

www.uelci.org. The Indian Lutheran E News . Vol. 3: Issue 1. 1 January to 31(sic) February 2008.

www.uelci.org. The Indian Lutheran E News. Vol. 2: Issue 1. February-March 2007.

www.uelci.org. The Indian Lutheran E News. Vol. 2: Issue 3. July-August 2007.

www.uelci.org. The Indian Lutheran E News. Vol. 3 Issue.3. May-June 2008.

www.uelci.org. The Indian Lutheran E News. Vol. 4: Issue 2. March-April 2009.

www.unhchr.ch. 'Report submitted by Mr. Abdelfattah Amor, Special Rapporteur'. UN High Commission on Human Rights. 1998. http:// www.unhchr.ch/Huridocda/Huridoca.nsf/0811fcbd0b9f6bd58025667300 306dea (accessed 2010).

www.usaid.gov. Bio of Andrew Natsios. 2001. http://www.usaid.gov/about_usaid/bios/bio_asn.html (accessed 30 January 2009).

— 'Faith Based and Community Initiative 2001-2002'. 2002. http://www.usaid.gov/our_work/cross-cutting_programs/private_voluntary_cooperation/pvoconf03_faithbasedslides.pd (accessed 30 January 2009).

— 'US AID, India: Child Survival Health Grants Project'. 23 April 2008. http://www.usaid.gov/in/our_work/activities/Health/health_child.htm (accessed 30 January 2009).

— US AID, India, Activities. January-April 2005. http://www.usaid.gov/in/our_work/activities/DM/tsunami_wv.htm (accessed 30 January 2009).

— US AID: About. http://www.usaid.gov/about_usaid/ (accessed 30 January 2009).

www.uscirf.gov. Bio of Nina Shea. http://www.uscirf.gov/cirfPages/bio_Shea.php3 (accessed Janaury 10, 2009).

— 'USCIRF sends letter to Orissa CM'. October 2009. http://www.uscirf.gov/index.php?option=com_content&task=view&id=2781 (accessed 5 January 2010).

— 'Visa Denied to USCIRF'. 2009. http://www.uscirf.gov/index.php?option=com_content&task=view&id=2520&Itemid=58 (accessed 17 December 2009).

www.vishalmangalwadi.com. Contact. 2000:2009. http://www.vishalmangalwadi.com/vkmWebSite/contact.php (accessed 10 January 2009).

— Links. 2000:2009. http://www.vishalmangalwadi.com/vkmWebSite/links.php (accessed 10 January 2009).

— The Legacy of William Carey (1993). 2000:2009. http://www.vishalmangalwadi.com/vkmWebSite/works_carey.php (accessed 30 January 2009).

— Vishal Mangalwadi: Works. 2000:2009. http://www.vishalmangalwadi.com/vkmWebSite/works.php (accessed 10 January 2009).

www.votesmart.org. Page on Jospeh Pitts. http://www.votesmart.org/issue_rating_category.php?can_id=BC031572&type=category&category=Conservative (accessed 10 January 2009).

Yajee, Sheel Bhadra. *CIA, Manipulating Arm of the US Foreign Policy: 40 Years of CIA*. Criterion Publications, 1988.

Yesuvadian, Sunder M (a) Mankad M.S. *India is a Christian Nation*. Nagerkovil: Anaryan Publication, 2002.

Yohannan, K.P. *Revolution in World Missions*. Texas: GFA Books, 1986:2004.

— *Revolution in World Missions*. Creation House, 1986.

Young, Crawford. *The Politics of Cultural Pluralism*. University of Wisconsin Press, 1976.

— *The Politics of Pluralism*. University of Wisconsin Press, 1979.

Zacharias, Ravi K, and Scott Sawyer. *Walking from East to West: God in the Shadows*. Zondervan, 2006.

Ziegenbalg, Bartholomaeus. *Genealogy of the South Indian deities: an English Translation of Bartholomäeus Ziegenbalg's Original German Manuscript With a Textual Analysis and Glossary*. Translated by Daniel Jeyaraj. London: Routledge, 2005.

Zvelebil, Kamil. *Ananda-Tandava of Siva-Sadanrttamurti*. Chennai: Institute of Asian Studies, 1985.

— *Tamil traditions on Subrahmanya – Murugan*. Chennai: Institute of Asian Studies, 1991.

— *The Smile of Murugan on Tamil Literature of South India*. BRILL, 1973.

Index of Schematic Diagrams and Figures

Acknowledgments

Numerous persons deserve our sincerest thanks for going through the entire manuscript, and giving us important feedback and advice at various stages.

These include: Kamala Kanti Vijai, Veera Pandian, Dhiru Shah, Subash Razdan, Thukaram Gopalrao, Ravishankar, Ram Sidhaye and Kamlesh Kapur, among others.

We also express our appreciation for the hard work by Edna Perkins, who copy edited an earlier draft. The entire team at Amaryllis, our publisher, as well as our cover-designer Radhika, deserve the highest praise. Badri Seshadri has played a very important role as the publisher of the Tamil edition, giving us the benefits of his knowledge and insights into the subject matter. Many other friends and well-wishers, such as Shefali Chandan and others, deserve thanks for their critiques and advice in a variety of ways. Dr Manohar Shinde has been a tireless ambassador of our efforts for many years, and his efforts to bring this work to the attention of others is commendable.

Finally, we thank Raghu Rao and Sashi Kejriwal, both NRIs based in the US, for their financial support in the completion and production of this book.

Index